Writing the Woman Artist

Writing
the Woman Artist
Essays on Poetics, Politics, and Portraiture

Edited by
SUZANNE W. JONES

UNIVERSITY OF PENNSYLVANIA PRESS   Philadelphia

Permission is acknowledged to reprint material from published sources. These sources are listed at the end of the Acknowledgments section in this book.

Library of Congress Cataloging-in-Publication Data
Writing the woman artist : essays on poetics, politics, and
    portraiture / edited by Suzanne W. Jones.
        p.   cm.
    Includes bibliographical references and index.
    ISBN 0–8122–3089–2. — ISBN 0–8122–1343–2 (pbk.)
    1. Feminist literary criticism.   2. Feminism and literature.
    3. Women artists in literature.   I. Jones, Suzanne Whitmore.
    PN98.W64W7   1991
    809'.89287—dc20   91-426
                                                                        CIP

Contents

Acknowledgments

When Pam Caughie and I put together a panel on the woman artist figure for the South Atlantic Modern Language Association Conference in 1986, we had a difficult time choosing four papers from the many I had received. The idea for this collection was born out of the overwhelming response to that conference panel and to my subsequent call for essays, and the book came into being in part because of a faculty research grant from the University of Richmond. Some of the theoretical and political issues developed in the collection were first discussed in the feminist theory reading group at the University of Virginia.

Many people have helped to make this book possible. I am grateful to Pam Caughie and Ann Ardis for their emotional and intellectual support throughout this project, to Holly Laird for her shrewd advice on the structure of the collection, to Estella Lauter and Susan Friedman for suggestions about theoretical matters, to Margaret Stetz and Mark Lasner for their aesthetic opinions, to Tom Bonfiglio for editorial help, to Mary Massey for assistance with the index, and to Solange Crenshaw for graphics. Thanks go also to my husband, Frank Papovich, for his patience and encouragement. I am indebted to the many readers who very generously gave their time to advise me about the contents of the collection, to Wendy Thompson and Kathy Zacher, the untiring secretaries in the English Department at the University of Richmond, and to the hardworking staff at the University of Pennsylvania Press, particularly my editor, Patricia Smith. My largest debt, however, is to the contributors for their fine essays and their help in weaving this collection together.

Permission is acknowledged to reprint material from published sources as follows:

From "Margaret Drabble's *The Waterfall*: New System, New Morality" by Gayle Green. *NOVEL: A Forum on Fiction,* vol. 22, no. 1, Fall 1988. Copyright © 1989 NOVEL Corp. Reprinted by permission of the publisher.

From " 'Sisters in Arms': The Warrior Construct in Writings by Contemporary U.S. Women of Color" by Mary DeShazer. *NWSA Journal,* vol. 2, no. 3, Summer 1990. Copyright © 1990 Ablex Publishing Corporation. Reprinted with permission of the publisher.

From *HERmione* by H.D. Copyright © 1981 by the Estate of Hilda Doolittle. Copyright © 1981 by Perdita Schaffner. Reprinted by permission of New Directions Publishing Corporation.

From letters of Hilda Doolittle. Reprinted by permission of the Collection of American Literature, Beinecke Rare Book and Manuscript Library, Yale University.

From the manuscripts of Hilda Doolittle. Reprinted by permission of the Houghton Library, Harvard University.

From *End to Torment: A Memoir of Ezra Pound by H.D. with the poems from "Hilda's Book" by Ezra Pound,* edited by Norman Holmes Pearson and Michael King. Copyright © 1979 by New Directions Publishing Corporation. Copyright © 1979 by the Trustees of the Ezra Pound Library Property. Copyright © 1979 by Michael King. Reprinted by permission of New Directions Publishing Corporation.

From *The Cantos (1–95)* by Ezra Pound. Copyright 1934, 1937, 1940, 1948 by Ezra Pound; reprinted 1956 by New Directions. Reprinted by permission of New Directions Publishing Corporation.

From *Personae, The Collected Shorter Poems of Ezra Pound* by Ezra Pound. Copyright 1926 by Ezra Pound. Reprinted by permission of New Directions Publishing Corporation.

From *The Collected Poems 1927–1979* by Elizabeth Bishop. Copyright © 1979, 1983 by Alice Helen Methfessel. Reprinted by permission of Farrar, Sraus and Giroux, Inc.

From *Oral History* by Lee Smith. Copyright © 1983 by Lee Smith. Reprinted by permission of the author and The Putnam Publishing Group.

From *The Quest for Christa T.* by Christa Wolf. Translation copyright © 1970 by Farrar, Straus and Giroux, Inc. Reprinted by permission of Farrar, Straus, and Giroux, Inc.

From *The Woman Warrior* by Maxine Hong Kingston. Copyright © 1975, 1976 by Maxine Hong Kingston. Permission granted courtesy of the author, Schaffner Agency, Inc., and Random House, Inc.

From *Les Guerrillères* by Monique Wittig. Copyright © 1969 by Les Editions de Minuit. English translation copyright © 1971 by Peter Owen.

From *Civil Wars* by June Jordan. Copyright © 1981 by June Jordan. Reprinted by permission of the author.

From *Living Room: New Poems* by June Jordan. Copyright © 1985 by June Jordan. Reprinted by permission of the author and Thunder's Mouth Press.

From *On Call: Political Essays* by June Jordan. Copyright © 1985 by June Jordan. Reprinted by permission of the author.

From *Passion: New Poems, 1977–1980* by June Jordan. Copyright © 1980 by June Jordan. Reprinted by permission of the author.

From *Things That I Do in the Dark: Selected Poetry* by June Jordan. Copyright © 1967, 1968, 1969, 1970, 1971, 1972, 1973, 1974, 1975, 1977 by June Jordan. Reprinted by permission of the author.

Excerpts from "Towards a New Consciousness," "How to Tame a Wild Tongue," "To Live in the Borderlands Means You," and the preface, all in *Borderlands/La Frontera: The New Mestiza* by Gloria Anzaldúa. Copyright © 1987 by Gloria Anzaldúa. Reprinted by permission of Aunt Lute Books.

From *The House of the Spirits* by Isabel Allende, trans. by M. Bogin. Translation copyright © 1985 by Alfred A. Knopf, Inc. Reprinted by permission of Alfred A. Knopf, Inc. and the author.

From *O Taste and See, New Poems* by Denise Levertov. Copyright © 1962, 1963, 1964 by Denise Levertov Goodman. Reprinted by permission of New Directions Publishing Corporation.

Cover art, "A Gaslight Study" by H. H. La Thangue, is reproduced by kind permission of the Metropolitan Borough of Serfton Libraries and Arts Services Department.

Introduction

Suzanne W. Jones

> I mean, what is a woman? I assure you, I do not know. I do
> not believe that you know. I do not believe that anybody can
> know until she has expressed herself in all the arts and profes-
> sions open to human skill.
> —Virginia Woolf, "Professions for Women"

> These places of possibility within ourselves are dark be-
> cause they are ancient and hidden; they have survived and
> grown strong through that darkness. Within these deep places,
> each one of us holds an incredible reserve of creativity and
> power, of unexamined and unrecorded emotion and feeling.
> —Audre Lorde, "Poetry Is Not a Luxury"[1]

The essays in this collection explore the many ways in which women
writers have seen and dreamed the woman artist as a character in their
works. In describing this character, her struggles and her visions, we as
feminist critics run the risk of prescribing her, and yet failing to name
her means failing to know her. We confront this difficulty not by
defining the woman artist figure but by identifying many. Recognizing
as Teresa de Lauretis has suggested that the social construction of
gender is "a common denominator"[2] among women, we examine the
different representations of the woman artist figure as gender is mediated by race, class, nationality, ethnicity, motherhood, sexual orientation, and historical era as well as literary movements and theories of
language. Although a concern with so many positions may seem to
suggest a paradoxical passive creator determined by external elements
alone, Linda Alcoff argues that "the concept of positionality includes
two points: first . . . that the concept of woman is a relational term
identifiable only within a (constantly moving) context; but, second, that
the position that women find themselves in can be actively utilized
(rather than transcended) as a location for the contruction of meaning."[3] The title of the collection, *Writing the Woman Artist,* suggests both
the social construction of women artists and their own imaginative
construction of the artist figure; it registers the tension between the
fictional and the empirical figure, the problematic relationship between language and reality.

The collection builds on a number of earlier works about the artist figure. One important and influential study of the *Künstlerroman* in western literature is *Ivory Towers and Sacred Founts* (1964) by Maurice Beebe. His thesis is that the artist hero is a divided self—a human being of sensual longings, who is drawn to life, the "Sacred Fount," and a detached creative spirit living apart in an "Ivory Tower," who transcends life through art.[4] Beebe argues that writers have tipped the scales toward art or life depending on their visions of the artist's role in society and their views of the nature and function of art. Beebe traces the beginning of the artist archetype in literature to Johann Wolfgang von Goethe and Jean-Jacques Rousseau. Goethe popularized the portrait of the artist genre and delineated the main conflict as one between art and life. In Goethe's *The Sorrows of Young Werther* (1774), Werther fails because he cannot accept life; in Goethe's *Wilhelm Meister's Apprenticeship* (1795–96), Wilhelm fails because he becomes too immersed in life. Thus, Beebe deduces that for Goethe, "the true artist stands midway between the Ivory Tower and the Sacred Fount,"[5] a position Beebe champions as that of the very best novelists in the genre. At the same time Beebe views Rousseau's *Confessions* (1781–88) as a model for literary self-portraits. Rousseau not only made the confessional novel popular but also described, though he did not praise, the sensitive and introspective traits that we have come to associate with the "artistic temperament." Beebe locates the origins of the "Sacred Fount" tradition, which assumes that the artist must be immersed in life in order to create, in the Romantic movement, and he locates the origins of the "Ivory Tower" tradition, which assumes that the artist must be aloof and solitary in order to create, in the aesthetic movement.[6]

Although Beebe does discuss a few *Künstlerromane* by women, particularly George Sand's work, he was unaware of the considerations of gender for the form. For the most part, Beebe's artists are men, and his muses are women. Not until 1979 was any attention paid to the effect of gender on the representation of the artist figure. Grace Stewart in *A New Mythos, The Novel of the Artist as Heroine, 1877–1977* (1979) and then Linda Huf in *A Portrait of the Artist as a Young Woman: The Writer as Heroine in American Literature* (1983) sought to define the characteristics of *Künstlerromane* by women and to differentiate them from works by men. Both Stewart and Huf see the conventional conflict of the artist figure as doubly frustrating for women. According to Stewart, "whereas the man feels split between personal and social being, the woman experiences that split and the separation of sexual and personal identity."[7] Similarly, Huf argues that unlike the artist hero, the artist heroine "is torn not only between life and art but, more, specifically between her role as a woman, demanding selfless devotion to others, and her aspirations as an artist, requiring exclusive commitment to work."[8]

In *A New Mythos* Stewart argues that neither of Beebe's definitions of the artist as seeking personal fulfillment through experience or as experiencing transcendence through aloof, solitary reflection fits woman's traditional role of selfless nurturer of others. Thus, Stewart reasons that the woman artist figure must "defy the cultural definition of artist or of woman if she is to remain artist and woman."[9] Noting that male artists have often identified themselves with the myths of Prometheus, Daedalus, Icarus, and Faust, Stewart argues that twentieth-century women writers have reworked these myths "to focus on the meaninglessness of incessant striving."[10] Stewart suggests that a more appropriate narrative for *Künstlerromane* by women may be the Demeter-Persephone myth because artist heroines "must always wrestle with mothers, with daughters, or with their own identity in either role."[11]

While Stewart delineates structural differences between *Künstlerromane* by men and women, Linda Huf in *A Portrait of the Artist as a Young Woman* examines differences in characterization. She describes the artist hero as having conventional "feminine" traits—passivity, sensitivity, shyness—and the artist heroine as having conventional "masculine" traits—liveliness, strength, fearlessness. She argues that women writers of the artist novel pit their female protagonists against sexually conventional foils and that they do not create male muses because they do not idealize men.[12]

Although too categorical at times, these two studies were valuable for emphasizing gender as a factor in discussing the representation of the artist. They laid the foundation for subsequent work, including the essays in this collection. Stewart concludes *A New Mythos* with a call for a historical approach to the genre that "notes variations, details the effect of time or events on these patterns, and shows trends."[13] In 1981 Susan Gubar took up this task with "The Birth of the Artist as Heroine: (Re)production, the *Künstlerroman* Tradition, and the Fiction of Katherine Mansfield," a historical approach to the conflict between role and vocation in *Künstlerromane* by women. Gubar notes that whereas nineteenth-century artist figures gave up their art for motherhood, turn-of-the-century new women artists renounced motherhood for their careers. Finally in the 1920s and 1930s, Gubar argues, women writers reshaped the *Künstlerroman* with domestic images of creativity, thereby freeing their artist figures from the either/or imperative. Gubar believes that declining infant and maternity mortality rates and new birth control technology and awareness, which freed women from compulsory maternity, resulted in a valorization of domesticity and motherhood. Gubar points out, however, that after World War II when it became clear "that a feminine mystique was replacing female self-definition, women's *Künstlerromane* suffered a critical disillusionment."[14] She concludes that only with the contemporary feminist movement does resolution of the dilemma between role and vocation once more return to the optimism of the modernist period. Contributors in Part III of this collection chart the same literary history that Gubar outlined, but often their conclusions differ because they complicate Gubar's historical analysis with other factors such as race, class, age, motherhood, or childlessness.

The essays in this collection broaden the study of the woman artist figure beyond the novel as a genre, beyond literature written in English, beyond conflicts emerging from the dilemma of role and vocation, and beyond fictional characters and poetic personae who are white, middle-class heterosexual women. The first two sections of the book concern women writers and their artist figures who struggle with the conventions bequeathed to them by male and female literary ancestors. Although the section on the fathers is concerned with revising men's traditions and the section on mothers with revaluing women's, essays throughout the collection focus on what is helpful and what is harmful for women artists in each tradition, rather than valorizing one heritage at the expense of what is useful in the other.[15] The third section examines artist figures who deal differently with the conflict between women's domestic roles and their artistic desires depending on the way gender relations are mediated by other social relations and by language itself. The fourth section analyzes the politics of art and the potential for social change, and the fifth section treats the aesthetic theories of women artist figures who try to break down old oppositions and create new possibilities.

The divisions of the collection, which I decided upon after several readings of the essays, are neither mutually exclusive nor exhaustive. The section titles should be seen not as an attempt to compartmentalize but as a guide to the multiple related issues encountered in writing the woman artist. Indeed, it is difficult to maintain categories since many of the essays touch on most of the issues. One concern treated in several sections, but without a heading of its own, is the relationship between women artist figures and their muses. Essays by Susan Stanford Friedman, Josephine Donovan, Margaret Stetz, Linda Hunt, Ann Ardis, and Mary DeShazer all examine this relationship. Although Linda Huf concludes in *A Portrait of the Artist as a Young Woman* that *Künstlerromane* by women do not have muses, contributors to this collection discover muses in literature by women when they look for ways in which women writers have redefined the relationship between artist and muse. If viewed as nurturing as well as inspiring, as mutually desirous rather than productive of desire, the muse of the woman artist can be female friend, male friend, female lover, mother, or a community of women.

Part I: Deconstructing the Fathers' Tradition

Essays in Part I analyze how three American poets, H.D., Adrienne Rich, and Elizabeth Bishop, redefine the terms *artist* and *muse* and revise literary conventions that depict women as powerless, passive objects in male artists' lives rather than powerful, creative subjects in their own. In *Sexual/Textual Politics* (1985), Toril Moi argues that "women's relationship to power is not exclusively one of victimization. Feminism is not simply about rejecting power, but about transforming the existing power structures—and, in the process transforming the very *concept* of power itself."[16] The women writers discussed in this section of the collection do not believe that creative power is necessarily synonymous with autonomy and authority. In rewriting these relationships between artist, subject, audience, and muse, Elizabeth Bishop, Adrienne Rich, and H.D. transform the concept of power, envisioning it as connection rather than control, as reciprocity rather than dominance. Contributors in this section use an American feminist-revisionist form of deconstructive analysis to examine these transformations. As Susan Stanford Friedman and Mary Poovey have noted, while Derrida shows how a *text* deconstructs, feminist critics in the United States will often show how the *author* deconstructs cultural binary oppositions thus integrating concepts of "self," "agency," and "intention" with theories of deconstruction.[17]

In "Portrait of the Artist as a Young Woman: H.D.'s Rescriptions of Joyce, Lawrence, and Pound," Susan Stanford Friedman analyzes H.D.'s rewriting of the relationship between women and art, artist and muse in her autobiographical work *HER* (1927). Friedman points out that the use of the objective pronoun Her as the artist's name cleverly transforms the woman from muse to artist, from object in Pound's text to subject in H.D.'s. Friedman shows that H.D. self-consciously comments on Joyce's, Lawrence's, and Pound's representations of the artist figure by refusing "to be split into body or soul," refusing "to choose between love and writing." Whereas Friedman sees the relationship between artist and muse in *Portrait of the Artist* and *Sons and Lovers* as fundamentally Oedipal, she identifies this relationship in *HER* as pre-Oedipal: "the daughter, rejecting Oedipal love, returns to the fusion of the pre-Oedipal in her love for Fayne, to the merged identities of two women." Friedman argues that H.D. transforms the relationship between artist and muse into a "mutually desirous and creative" one.

Adrienne Rich continues H.D.'s deconstruction of the fathers' tradition by transforming the poet's persona and her relationship to her subject and her readers. For Adrienne Rich, writing is "re-vision" and re-vision is "survival," equations set forth in her influential essay, "When We Dead Awaken: Writing as Re-vision" (1971).[18] In "Power and Poetic Vocation in Adrienne Rich's *The Dream of a Common Language*," Lynda K. Bundtzen argues that Rich revises masculine concepts of godlike power and individual heroism by exploring mutual strength in collectivity. Bundtzen believes that while Rich "assuredly re-invokes the Romantic aspiration to mythmaking power," she "re-shapes the Romantic poet's chosen role as prophet and oracle," creating a poetic persona that "invites community with her reader" and challenging an aesthetics that privileges poetics over politics.

Elizabeth Bishop also revises the way Romantic lyricists assumed authorial power by choosing a lyric voice that is unobtrusive, marginally positioned, sexually ambiguous, and often plural. Adrienne Rich, searching for a "clear female tradition," wished for a central female voice in Bishop's work and later decided that, in her peripheral poetic stance, Bishop had written woman's position as outsider. In "Lyric Voice and Sexual Difference in Elizabeth Bishop," Kathleen Brogan sees Bishop's poetic voice as more subversive, as blurring the distinctions between inside and outside—a feminist attempt to underscore the dangers of hierarchy and to avoid a narrow, dualistic conception of sexual identity. Brogan, like Mary DeShazer in Part IV, suggests that behaviors, such as tenderness or aggression, are not gender specific.

Part II: Thinking Back Through Our Mothers

With *A Room of One's Own* (1929) Virginia Woolf focused attention on women's literary history by writing "we think back through our mothers if we are women."[19] Essays in Part II examine how women writers and the artist figures they create have perceived their relationship with their literary foremothers and biological mothers. While Willa Cather sees this exercise as transforming, Anita Brookner views it as a painful but necessary step in the creative process. The essays on Cather and Brookner both discuss "the gift of sympathy" that can be learned from the maternal world. The essay on George Eliot and Virginia Woolf in this section and the one on Margaret Drabble in Part IV, however, argue that thinking "back through our mothers" can be dangerous because their lives and their work can offer their female inheritors what Margaret Homans calls "a debilitating training" in conventional roles and techniques.[20]

In *No Man's Land, The Place of the Woman Writer in the Twentieth*

Century, Sandra Gilbert and Susan Gubar continue Virginia Woolf's interest in women's literary history by defining a twentieth-century "female affiliation complex," in which women writers oscillate "between their matrilineage and their patrilineage in an arduous process of self-definition."[21] Willa Cather is an example of such problems of affiliation. Early in her career, Cather rebelled against nineteenth-century women writers, whom she judged sentimental scribblers, and allied herself with her literary forefathers. Josephine Donovan's "The Pattern of Birds and Beasts: Willa Cather and Women's Art" documents Cather's gradual move away from a masculine identification in her early years toward an artistic practice rooted in traditional women's household practices. Whereas Cather had first viewed the artist as appropriating material and imposing his or her ego upon it, Donovan argues that with Sarah Orne Jewett's influence Cather saw the value for the artist in abandoning her ego and embracing her subject through a "gift of sympathy." Analyzing *The Song of the Lark* (1915), *One of Ours* (1922), and *The Professor's House* (1925) from a Marxist perspective, Donovan demonstrates how Cather's artist protagonists, both women and men, discover a traditional women's aesthetic, become inspired by it, and subsequently begin to value the emotional integration with their subjects that they gain from it.

Similarly, in "Anita Brookner: Woman Artist as Reluctant Feminist," Margaret Diane Stetz argues that not until Anita Brookner's artist protagonist Frances accepts her mother in herself is she able to write the fatalistic but sympathetic narratives of which *Look at Me* (1983) is an example. However, Stetz raises the question of whether a woman writer might not exhibit feminist aesthetics even though she does not subscribe to feminist politics. Acknowledging Brookner's own pronouncement that "You'd have to be crouching in your burrow to see my novels in a feminist way,"[22] Stetz looks from just that angle and terms Brookner's writing "reluctant feminism." She argues that if Brookner is not politically feminist, she is aesthetically feminist, in part because her women artist figures look back through biological mothers and literary foremothers, in part because Brookner herself champions literature written by and for women and values aesthetic and/or emotional bonds between women writers and their women mentors and audiences.

Alison Booth views George Eliot's influence on Virginia Woolf as enabling but also troubling. In "Incomplete Stories: Womanhood and Artistic Ambition in *Daniel Deronda* and *Between the Acts*," Booth suggests that George Eliot haunted Virginia Woolf's efforts "to reconceive women's creativity beyond motherhood and self-sacrifice." While Woolf saw herself as a more outspoken feminist and sought to demonstrate that gender roles were socially conditioned, she remained subject to what Booth considers "an ideal of essential feminine selflessness as an antidote to masculine forms of power," an ideal apparent not only in Woolf's portrait of Eliot but also in the fictional portraits of female dramatic artists in Eliot's and Woolf's last novels.

Part III: Confronting the Dilemma of Role and Vocation

Essays in Part III analyze women artists' conflicts between the social roles inherited from their mothers and their own artistic desires, at the same time that they explore differences among women by considering how gender is mediated by other social constructions—the complex "positionality" to which Linda Alcoff refers. In *Writing Beyond the Ending: Narrative Strategies of Twentieth-Century Women Writers* (1985), Rachel Blau DuPlessis argues that whereas nineteenth-century women found traditional roles a barrier to their artistic achievement, twentieth-century women writers have solved the "dilemma of role and vocation" for their artist characters "by having the fictional art work function as a labor of love, a continuation of the artisal impulse of a thwarted parent, an emotional gift for family, child, self, or others."[23] The first three essays in this section, by Linda Dittmar, Jane Rose, and Katherine Kearns, bear out but complicate her argument as they examine more specifically the complex social positions of nineteenth- and twentieth-century women writers and their artist figures. The next two essays, by Mara Witzling and Linda Hunt, question the universality of DuPlessis's twentieth-century narrative resolution, and the last, by Renate Voris, locates meaning, not in the relation between text and world, but in the relation between text and text, arguing that the use of language itself may reinscribe structures oppressive to women. This last argument questions all forms of empiricism, including feminists' dreams of autonomy and liberation and critics' notions of feminine subjectivity and feminine *écriture*. All of the essays in this section reveal textual tensions where women writers struggle to negotiate conflicts between social roles and artistic expression.

The first essay in Part III concerns creative female characters who do not produce art but who make themselves into art objects. Linda Dittmar's "When Privilege Is No Protection: The Woman Artist in *Quicksand* and *The House of Mirth*" explores both the difficulty women face in resisting the social constructions that prevent them from perceiving or expressing their creativity and women's collaboration in these very constructions that serve patriarchal interests. In contrast to Susan Gubar, who in her essay " 'The Blank Page' and the Issues of Female Creativity" depicts women as the victims of cultural inscription,[24] Dittmar views them as playing a "more active, more participatory, and even productive" part in determining their roles. Dittmar's argument, like Brogan's about Bishop, subverts the conventional dichotomy between "we" and "they," outside and inside. She pairs works by black and white American writers to highlight the ways that considerations of race and class affect gender relations. Dittmar uses these two works by Larsen and Wharton to illustrate that only when women fully understand the complexity of their social positions will they be able to transcend them.

In "The Artist Manqué in the Fiction of Rebecca Harding Davis," Jane Atteridge Rose adds another element to the equation—age. Unlike Larsen's and Wharton's protagonists, Davis's are productive artists, but they are caught in the double bind of many nineteenth-century women artist figures: the pursuit of art seems to suggest failure as a woman, and the pursuit of domesticity seems to mean failure as an artist. Rose plots Davis's fiction alongside her life to suggest that the forms of failure her artist figures experience reflect Davis's own changing attitudes toward the dilemma of the woman artist as she grew older and experienced different stages of marriage and motherhood.

Similarly in "From Shadow to Substance: The Empowerment of the Artist Figure in Lee Smith's Fiction," Katherine Kearns argues that only as Lee Smith reconciles herself to her own vocation as an artist, do her fictional artist figures resolve the conflict between role and vocation. Kearns delineates three stages in the women's growth as artists in Smith's work. In the first stage the artist character, though sensitive and perceptive, creates herself as she crafts an acceptable social persona. In the second stage, she discovers matriarchal power, which she uses to create consumable artistries, which nourish family and friends. In the third stage the artist figure in *Fair and Tender Ladies* (1988) creates and nourishes others, but mostly herself, through the permanence of the written word. Kearns deals with two important and not totally resolved issues in Lee Smith's work: her wariness of the very term "artist" applied to herself or to her characters, who are often poor Appalachian women, and her need to reconcile the writer's vocation to the demands of family and community life.

While sculptor and painter Judy Chicago never shied away from defining herself as an artist, she did feel repressed by the limitations placed on the content of her art by the men who were her teachers. In *"Through the Flower*: Judy Chicago's Conflict Between a Woman-Centered Vision and the Male Artist Hero," Mara Witzling argues that even though Chicago eventually found "a visual language that merged her identity as an artist with her identity as a woman," her autobiography *Through the Flower* communicates a contradictory message in relating her development as an artist. Witzling finds the "feminine" content of Chicago's work, which celebrates female sexuality and reproduction, at odds with her "masculine" mode of production, which subordinates relationships to artistic creativity and which defines the artist as autonomous and obsessed.

Twentieth-century Norwegian writer Cora Sandel creates an artist figure in her *Alberta Trilogy* (1926–39), who redefines what it means to be an artist. In *"The Alberta Trilogy*: Cora Sandel's Norwegian *Künstlerroman* and American Feminist Literary Discourse," Linda Hunt argues that Alberta is able to pursue her career only by extricating herself from the binary oppositions of gender; when Alberta no longer sees "men and women as opposites, she no longer sees 'artist' and 'woman' as contradictions." Hunt emphasizes that an important step in breaking down gendered oppositions comes when Alberta reconceptualizes artistic productivity as work and begins to think of her writing as a way to support herself and her son. Then the artist becomes for her not a selfish person, an exalted being, isolated from the world, but an ordinary worker, involved in routine activities and social responsibilities. Hunt compares Cora Sandel's rather negative representations of traditional domesticity and motherhood to the more positive ones of her British contemporaries Woolf, Richardson, and Mansfield[25] and speculates that perhaps these writers overly valorize motherhood because, unlike Sandel, they were not mothers.

In "The Hysteric and the Mimic: Reading Christa Wolf's *The Quest for Christa T.*," Renate Voris argues that Wolf's paradoxical novel enacts "what Julia Kristeva has called the two fates of woman in Western culture: that of the classic hysteric who is denied her place in language, yet represents in that negativity a sort of disturbance of the symbolic order, of power and domination, *and* that of the mimic who takes her place in language and represents in that positivity a submission to the symbolic order, to masculine power and authority." In the novel a female narrator tells the story of a female writer and mother, Christa T.—a repetition, Voris contends, of the familiar paradigm of the female subject who does not speak for herself. Voris sees the narrator as the mimic who lets Christa T., the hysteric, speak "only in order to subordinate her speech to the (sexist) narrative of procreation."

Part IV: Rethinking the Politics of Art

When Krista Brewer asked Alice Walker why she writes, Brewer informed her of James Baldwin's answer to the same question: "writers write to change the world." Alice Walker replied, "I have written to stay alive. I've written to survive. That was from the time I was eight years old until I was 30. Then from the time I was 30 until now at 36 maybe

I'm ready to change the world."[26] Such a comment indicates that artists' motivations for writing differ as their position in the world changes. In *Writing Beyond the Ending* (1985), Rachel Blau DuPlessis argues that twentieth-century women writers have created a tradition that "counters the modernist tradition of exile, alienation, and refusal of social roles—the *non serviam* of the classic artist hero, Stephen Dedalus. The woman writer creates the ethical role of the artist by making her imaginatively depict and try to change the life in which she is also immersed."[27] Mary DeShazer and Z. Nelly Martínez support DuPlessis's theory about the social roles of women artists and the political function of their art, even though the artist figures they describe define their roles differently, from the warrior poets of U.S. women of color to Allende's artist healers. Elsewhere in this collection, however, Katherine Kearns and Margaret Diane Stetz suggest that contemporary writers Lee Smith and Anita Brookner envision a more personal function of art for some women artists, art as a means of survival, as a means of defining and nurturing the self. The nature and function of art discussed in this section, indeed in this collection, is as varied as the needs and desires of the artist figures represented, a topic Pamela Caughie returns to in Part V with her essay on Virginia Woolf's diverse portraits of women artists and their works. In the last two essays in Part IV, Gayle Greene and Ann Ardis debate the revolutionary possibilities of art.

In "'Sisters in Arms': The Warrior Construct in Writings by Contemporary U.S. Women of Color," Mary DeShazer uses Chicana feminist theorist Aída Hurtado's assessment that women of color are more effective than white feminists in using their anger to promote social change because middle-class white women are protected by their class and race from acquiring a political consciousness until later in their lives.[28] Acknowledging the problem many feminists have with the term *warrior*, DeShazer delineates three ways in which U.S. women of color use the warrior figure: identifying themselves as warrior poets, naming themselves war correspondents, and invoking warrior muses. Writing about such authors as Audre Lorde, Gloria Anzaldúa, Ntozake Shange, June Jordan, and Maxine Hong Kingston, DeShazer argues that U.S. women of color use the warrior figure "both to articulate an impassioned feminist politics and to inspire them to undertake its attendant sociocultural transformations."

Similarly, for both contemporary South American writer Isabel Allende and her protagonist Alba, writing is a political act. The novel Alba writes not only denounces the cruelties of patriarchy and the brutalities of totalitarian government, but also calls on women to change the world. In "The Politics of the Woman Artist in Isabel Allende's *The*

House of the Spirits," Z. Nelly Martínez emphasizes that Allende's devaluation of the patriarchal god and her elevation of the goddess figure
is especially empowering for women in Latin America, "where military
rulers assume a truly godlike role." Asserting that Allende links wom-
en's creative power with the erotic, Martínez develops a point that
Estella Lauter explores further in Part V. Martínez sees Allende's
women artists as healers, celebrating life in their fight against male
violence and patriarchal dictatorships, and she views their art as spiritual, healing the split between women and men, peasants and over-
lords. Martínez argues that the writing of Alba's novel, as well as its
many potential readings, is subversive because it expresses the energies
that patriarchal cultures have repressed as feminine.

With Doris Lessing as her revolutionary guide, Margaret Drabble
rewrites George Eliot's *The Mill on the Floss* (1860) in writing *The Waterfall* (1969). In "Margaret Drabble's *The Waterfall*: New System, New
Morality," Gayle Greene suggests that Drabble's revisionary work about
heterosexual love goes beyond Lessing's because she investigates language as well as narrative. Greene shows how writer-protagonist Jane
Gray's alternating first- and third-person narratives test the relationship of language to reality and how her refusal to close her novel conventionally suggests a resistance to positing a single truth and erasing
interesting contradictions. Jane's linguistic play is equally subversive,
an example in Greene's mind of French feminists' *l'écriture féminine*.
Greene emphasizes how Jane's word play "liberates words such as 'do,'
'make,' and 'have' from syntax and word order in which they denote
possession and product, something one person does to another, and
makes them not only describe but also reflect processes of reciprocity
and mutuality." Greene concludes that such revision of narrative and
linguistic conventions creates revolutionary possibilities for both writers and readers by releasing them from the old ideologies and the
traditional subject-object relations, reenacted in such conventions.

In contrast, Ann Ardis speculates that feminist theorists such as
Hélène Cixous and Catherine Clément may be too optimistic in con-
tending that writing is revolutionary because it changes the symbolic
order.[29] In "'Retreat with Honour': Mary Cholmondeley's Presentation of the New Woman Artist in *Red Pottage*," Ardis shows how the
critical paradigms of the conservative readers within Cholmondeley's
novel cause them to misread her protagonist's fiction and to devalue
her narrative technique. Ardis also demonstrates that even today feminist critics, burdened by narrow definitions of woman and of modernism, have not credited such "New Woman" novels as Cholmondeley's
with the literary experimentation they evidence.

Part V: Reconceiving Feminist Aesthetics

In the last few years feminist critics, with much debate, have worked to codify what they have variously called *l'écriture féminine*, "a female aesthetic," "a women's poetics," and "a feminist aesthetics." More recently, such efforts have been labeled both potentially essentialist and politically dangerous. In Part V Holly A. Laird, Pamela L. Caughie, and Estella Lauter take up this debate by analyzing the work of three women writers, who theorized about aesthetics in their poetry and their prose.

In the mid-1970s French feminists Hélène Cixous and Luce Irigaray formulated a poetics based on the female body. In "Le Rire de la Méduse" (1975) Cixous linked a female language, "*l'écriture féminine*" with the mother's voice and body, arguing that women must "write their bodies" with "white ink" or mother's milk, thereby producing a discourse very different from "phallic" discourse with its emphasis on linearity, authority, homogeneity, mastery, and unity. With a similar focus on the female body, Luce Irigaray, in *Ce Sexe qui n'en est pas un* (1977), theorized that because women's sexual organs are multiple, female eroticism, if not repressed, would express itself in a use of language different from "phallic" discourse. Both theorists suggest that a "*féminine*" writing style would exhibit reciprocity, multiplicity, and fluidity and that it would disrupt traditional logic, syntax, and diction.[30] Although both Cixous and Irigaray have at various times insisted on the possibility of bisexuality in writing, viewing certain works by men as examples of *l'écriture féminine*, they have at other times focused exclusively on women writers. Because of their focus on the female body, a number of critics have judged their theories essentialist and exclusionary, even as they find their discussions of language provocative.[31]

In 1979 Rachel Blau DuPlessis and the members of Workshop 9 formulated "a female aesthetic," which DuPlessis defined as determined "by women's psychosocial experiences of gender asymmetry and by women's historical status in an (ambiguously) nonhegemonic group."[32] DuPlessis argues that art produced by this experience has a nonhierarchic structure, a both/and (as opposed to an either/or) vision, and a social function. DuPlessis concludes that this "female" aesthetic, which is essentially a poetics of critique, is "not exclusively female" but rather an "aesthetic position that could be articulated by any nonhegemonic group."[33]

Similarly, Gisela Ecker in the introduction to *Feminist Aesthetics* (1985) argues for a poetics of critique, which she terms a "feminist aesthetics."[34] However, Ecker does not define any formal or thematic characteristics of this aesthetic, and she objects to DuPlessis characterizing the following as features of women's writing: "Any list of the characteristics of postmodernism would at the same time be a list of the traits of women's writing: inwardness, illumination in the here and now (Levertov); use of the continuous present (Stein); the foregrounding of material (Woolf); the muted, multiple, or absent telos; a fascination with process; a horizontal world; a decentered universe where 'man' (indeed) is no longer privileged."[35] Although DuPlessis qualifies her definition by saying that "women reject this position as soon as it becomes politically quietistic,"[36] Ecker claims that such a list is exclusionary, ahistorical, and prescriptive. Like Ecker, Rita Felski in *Beyond Feminist Aesthetics: Feminist Literature and Social Change* (1989) contends that one cannot develop an abstract theory of "feminine" writing or "feminist aesthetics" apart from the particular social and historical conditions of a text's production and reception.[37]

In the mid-1980s Lawrence Lipking and Josephine Donovan looked to women's traditional experiences to formulate women's poetics. In 1983 Lipking wrote "a woman's poetics" entitled "Aristotle's Sister: A Poetics of Abandonment," based on plot patterns involving the seduction and betrayal of innocent young women.[38] He argues that abandonment may be the archetypal female experience and therefore may provide an understanding of female creativity and its literary expression, which he defined as advocating expression over imitation, the personal over the impersonal, and affiliation over authority. A year later in "Toward a Women's Poetics," Josephine Donovan, arguing that Lipking's theory was derived in part from texts written by men, defined a women's poetics based on works by women and deriving from traditional women's household practices. Noting the diversity of women's histories and cultures and not wishing to define a tradition common to all women writers, Donovan, however, identifies "six structural conditions that appear to have shaped traditional women's experience in the past and in nearly all cultures":[39] (1) a psychology of oppression or otherness, (2) confinement to the domestic sphere where labor is nonprogressive, repetitive, and static, (3) creation of objects for use rather than exchange, (4) shared physiological experiences such as menstruation and sometimes childbirth and breastfeeding, (5) childrearing or caretaking, what Sara Ruddick calls "maternal thinking," which involves "keeping" rather than "acquiring," "holding" rather than "questing,"[40] and (6) a gender personality that values relationships, as Nancy Chodorow explains in her theory of the reproduction of mothering. While Donovan focuses on traditional women's household practices to formulate her aesthetic, she does not suggest that all women make this kind of art or that it is reflective of all women's experience, or that any one woman consistently engages in producing "women's art."

Heide Göttner-Abendroth also looks to women's experiences, but to art produced in matriarchal societies, in order to develop her "Nine Principles of a Matriarchal Aesthetic" (1985). According to Gottner-Abendroth, matriarchal art has the following features: (1) it involves magic, used in ancient art to influence nature and in modern art to change society; (2) its structure is determined by matriarchal mythology, which differs according to regional, individual, and social conditions; (3) it is not a product, but a process in which artist and audience participate collectively; (4) it joins artist and audience and unites feeling, thinking, and doing; (5) because "it is a process which takes place between the participants, matriarchal art cannot be evaluated and interpreted by outsiders nor sold as a commodity on the art market and later stored away in a dusty archive or exhibited in a museum"; (6) it cannot be subdivided into genres nor can art be separated from craft; (7) it arises out of a different value system than that of the patriarchy; thus, it is based on the erotic rather than on work, discipline, and renunciation; on the continuation of life rather than on war; and on a sense of community rather than on authority, dominance, and egoism; (8) it overrides the divisions between elitist and popular art, emerging "as the most important social activity and bringing about the aestheticisation of the whole of society"; and (9) it is not divorced from life, but matriarchal art is itself "energy, life."[41]

The essays in this section of the collection continue to try to come to terms with the aesthetics of women writers. They caution against establishing the defining, and thereby confining, traits of a female or women's aesthetic. They examine the works of women writers who do not so much define such an aesthetic as seek to break down gendered oppositions. Just as other contributors to this volume have sought to change our way of thinking about "woman" and "artist," they seek to change our way of thinking about "women's art," from how it is defined to how it is used in a particular context. The aesthetics these essays argue for are feminist in being informed by gender rather than wholly determined by it.

Holly Laird summarizes the aims of this section in this way: "In previous discussions of female and feminist aesthetics, critics have found themselves either arguing for an author who expresses her experience in her writing, or dissolving the author into her work, usually by arguing for a pre-determinant structure of language that writes the female body or is disrupted by a 'feminine' excess, and they have thus produced theories in which the author stands up against her art or else may be deconstructed. The essays in this collection, however, all postulate the woman artist as an operative factor within women's writings which, by implication, should be included in the formulation of any feminist aesthetics."[42]

In "*Aurora Leigh*: An Epical *Ars Poetica*," Holly Laird emphasizes the danger of a prescriptive women's poetics, arguing that the effect of Lipking's "alternative poetics" for women is "to recolonize women, to allow them personal expression rather than heroic authority, to hear them speaking as agonized sufferers but not as proud suffragists." Laird contends that when Lawrence Lipking went looking for Aristotle's sister, he should have widened his search. If he had included Elizabeth Barrett Browning's *Aurora Leigh* (1857) in his study, he would have found a heroic figure, an artist who spoke for and to her age, not "an abandoned woman speaking of her private woes to a small community." Laird argues that in her novel-poem Browning does not restrict her artist figure to Lipking's either/or vision, but champions with her key terms, "twofold" and "double-faced," "a poetics that gives equal weight to action and character, to mimesis and expressive form, to the double aim to teach and to delight." Laird emphasizes that "In contrast to New Critical irony and structuralist binarism, whose self-cancellations enable the critic to achieve a transcendent detachment, and in contrast to Derridean *différance* with its endlessly radicalizing erosions, Browning's terminology enacts embrasure, enfolding possibilities, multiplying choices, permitting alternatives."

Similarly, in "'I must not settle into a figure': The Woman Artist in Virginia Woolf's Writings," Pamela Caughie sees in Virginia Woolf's many different portraits of women artists and their varying art forms a caution against defining *a* "female aesthetic." Caughie argues that it is precisely because feminist critics have exposed literary conventions employed by men "as arbitrary constructs, as a universalizing of provisional and provincial concepts of art," that we cannot now offer an alternative set of conventions; for "we have made the concept of *any* appropriate form suspect." Caughie suggests that an alternative, then, to discussing Woolf's novels in terms of the *nature* of art is to discuss them "in terms of the various *functions* of the artworks themselves." While Caughie agrees that for Woolf, "sexual differences have everything to do with art," she argues that this alternative approach enables us to understand as well that for Woolf, "sexual differences in writing are provisional, variable, and contingent." Emphasizing Woolf's changing artistic practices, Caughie concludes that Woolf was "less concerned with how to write authentically as a woman than with how to adapt and survive as a woman artist."

Feminist critics' current concern with differences among women in a world that has often made women feel uncertain of their power to create and their authority to make choices sends Estella Lauter searching for "the power to be gained from shared visions." She finds such a vision in Audre Lorde's figure of "the Black mother within." In "Re-visioning Creativity: Audre Lorde's Refiguration of Eros as the Black Mother Within," Lauter argues that Lorde has moved beyond her sources, both Western and African, to a vision of creativity that challenges binary oppositions between women and men, black and white, chaos and order, life and art, almost ad infinitum. In her definition of the erotic as the "drive toward completion, satisfaction, and excellence which informs our physical, emotional, psychic and intellectual experience as we become responsible to ourselves," and in her personification of this drive in female form, Lorde displaces centuries of thinking about creativity as male genius. She challenges Western culture at its roots in its conception of Eros. Lorde spiritualizes, politicizes and re-sexualizes the erotic desire to create as a communal act of recovering the energies and materials repressed by patriarchal cultures. Thus "Poetry Is Not a Luxury"; it is a necessity for social change. Lauter considers Lorde's view of creativity especially valuable for women, not only because it validates women's authority, removing "the necessity for certification of one's ideas by the dominant group," but also because it refuses to restrict women's creativity to one sphere, one aesthetic norm (whether formalist or feminist), one function. Because Lorde's vision encourages radical rethinking of the premises on which our relationships are built, it can create new bridges between people who are otherwise threatened by their differences from each other.

As all of the essays in this collection show, writing the woman artist is complicated by numerous variables. Many different portraits of the woman artist have been written. But the women writers who create these portraits share in making problematic old oppositions between procreativity and creativity, romantic passion and artistic desire, process and product, theory and practice, women and men, woman and artist.

Notes

1. Virginia Woolf, "Professions for Women," in *Women and Writing,* ed. Michèle Barrett (New York: Harcourt Brace Jovanovich, 1979), p. 60; Audre Lorde, "Poetry Is Not a Luxury," in *Sister Outsider: Essays and Speeches by Audre Lorde* (Trumansburg, N.Y.: Crossing Press, 1984), pp. 36–37.

2. See Teresa de Lauretis, who argues in *Feminist Studies, Critical Studies* (Bloomington: Indiana University Press, 1986) that "the differences among women may be better understood as differences within women. For if it is the case that the female subject is en-gendered across multiple representations of

class, race, language, and social relations, it is also the case . . . that gender is a common denominator: the female subject is always constructed and defined in gender, starting from gender" (14).

3. Linda Alcoff, "Cultural Feminism Versus Poststructuralism: The Identity Crisis in Feminist Theory," *Signs: Journal of Women in Culture and Society* 13.3 (1988), 434. In "Postmodernism and Gender Relations in Feminist Theory," *Signs* 12.4 (spring 1987), Jane Flax makes a similar point, "the experience of gender relations for any person and the structure of gender as a social category are shaped by the interactions of gender relations and other social relations such as class and race. Gender relations thus have no fixed essence; they vary both within and over time" (624). A difference between Alcoff and Flax is that whereas Flax places feminist theory within two categories, the analysis of social relations and postmodern philosophy, Alcoff situates positionality as a third option to cultural feminism and poststructuralism.

4. Maurice Beebe, *Ivory Towers and Sacred Founts: The Artist as Hero in Fiction from Goethe to Joyce* (New York: New York University Press, 1964), p. 6.

5. Beebe, p. 38.

6. Beebe, p. vi.

7. Grace Stewart, *A New Mythos: The Novel of the Artist as Heroine, 1877–1977* (St. Albans, Vt.: Eden Press, 1979), p. 175.

8. Linda Huf, *A Portrait of the Artist as a Young Woman: The Writer as Heroine in American Literature* (New York: Frederick Ungar, 1983), p. 5.

9. Stewart, p. 14.

10. Stewart, p. 39.

11. Stewart, p. 47.

12. Huf summarizes her assessment of the differences between artist novels by women and men in Chapter 1 of *A Portrait of the Artist as a Young Woman,* pp. 1–14.

13. Stewart, p. 181.

14. Susan Gubar, "The Birth of the Artist as Heroine: (Re)production, the *Künstlerroman* Tradition, and the Fiction of Katherine Mansfield," in *The Representation of Women in Fiction,* ed. Carolyn G. Heilbrun and Margaret R. Higonnet (Baltimore: Johns Hopkins University Press, 1983), p. 50.

15. Susan Suleiman argues that rereadings and rewritings accomplish two complementary objectives: "They appropriate positive but male-oriented symbols like the golden fleece or the holy grail by feminizing them, and they reverse negative, female-associated symbols like the head of the Medusa by endowing them with a positive value." "(Re)writing the Body: the Politics and Poetics of Female Eroticism," in *The Female Body in Western Culture: Contemporary Perspectives* ed. Susan Rubin Suleiman (Cambridge, Mass.: Harvard University Press, 1986), p. 20.

16. Toril Moi, *Sexual/Textual Politics: Feminist Literary Theory* (New York: Methuen, 1985), p. 148.

17. Susan Friedman's arguments about the Americanization of many concepts of European critical theory appears in "Weavings: Intertextuality and the (Re)Birth of the Author," in *Influence and Intertextuality,* ed. Jay Clayton and Eric Rothstein (Madison: University of Wisconsin Press, 1991) and "Post/Post-Structuralist Feminist Criticism: The Politics of Recuperation and Negotiation" (paper presented at the 1989 MLA Convention, Washington, D.C.). See also Mary Poovey, "Feminism and Deconstruction," *Feminist Studies* 14.1 (1988), 51–65.

18. Adrienne Rich, "When We Dead Awaken: Writing as Re-vision," in *On Lies, Secrets, and Silence: Selected Prose 1966–1978* (New York: Norton, 1979), p. 35.

19. Virginia Woolf, *A Room of One's Own* (New York: Harcourt Brace Jovanovich, 1929, rpt. 1989), p. 79.

20. Margaret Homans, *Bearing the Word: Language and Female Experience in Nineteenth-Century Women's Writing* (Chicago: University of Chicago Press, 1986), p. 278.

21. Sandra M. Gilbert and Susan Gubar, *No Man's Land: The Place of the Woman Writer in the Twentieth Century*, Vol. 1, *The War of the Words* (New Haven, Conn.: Yale University Press, 1988), p. 169.

22. John Haffenden, "Anita Brookner," in *Novelists in Interview* (London: Methuen, 1985), p. 70.

23. Rachel Blau DuPlessis, *Writing Beyond the Ending: Narrative Strategies of Twentieth-Century Women Writers* (Bloomington: Indiana University Press, 1985), p. 104.

24. Susan Gubar, "The Blank Page and the Issues of Female Creativity," in *The New Feminist Criticism: Essays on Women, Literature, and Theory*, ed. Elaine Showalter (New York: Pantheon Books, 1985), pp. 292–313.

25. See Gubar's "The Birth of the Artist as Heroine."

26. Krista Brewer, "Writing to Survive, An Interview with Alice Walker," *Southern Exposure* 9.2 (1981), 13.

27. DuPlessis, *Writing Beyond the Ending,* p. 101.

28. Aída Hurtado, "Relating to Privilege: Seduction and Rejection in the Subordination of White Women and Women of Color," *Signs: A Journal of Women in Culture and Society* 14.4 (1989), 849–54.

29. Hélène Cixous and Catherine Clément, *The Newly Born Woman*, trans. Betsy Wing (Minneapolis: University of Minnesota Press, 1986), pp. 147–60.

30. For English translations of Cixous and Irigaray, see *New French Feminisms: An Anthology*, ed. Elaine Marks and Isabelle de Courtivron (New York: Schocken Books, 1981), and *This Sex Which Is Not One* (Ithaca, N.Y.: Cornell University Press, 1985).

31. For helpful summaries and evaluations of these theories, see Ann Rosalind Jones, "Writing the Body: Toward an Understanding of *l'écriture féminine*," in *The New Feminist Criticism*, ed. Showalter, pp. 361–77; Silvia Bovenschen, "Is There a Feminine Aesthetic?" in *Feminist Aesthetics*, ed. Gisela Ecker, trans. Harriet Anderson (Boston: Beacon Press, 1985), pp. 23–50; Toril Moi, *Sexual/Textual Politics;* and Susan Rubin Suleiman, "(Re)Writing the Body: The Politics and Poetics of Female Eroticism."

32. Rachel Blau DuPlessis and Members of Workshop 9, "For the Etruscans: Sexual Difference and Artistic Production—The Debate over a Female Aesthetic" in *The Future of Difference*, ed. Hester Eisenstein and Alice Jardine (Boston: G. K. Hall, 1980), pp. 139–40.

33. DuPlessis, "For the Etruscans," p. 149.

34. See Gisela Ecker's Introduction to *Feminist Aesthetics*, pp. 15–22.

35. DuPlessis, "For the Etruscans," p. 151.

36. DuPlessis, "For the Etruscans," p. 151.

37. Rita Felski, *Beyond Feminist Aesthetics: Feminist Literature and Social Change* (Cambridge, Mass.: Harvard University Press, 1989).

38. See Lawrence Lipking's "Aristotle's Sister: A Poetics of Abandonment," *Critical Inquiry* 10 (September 1983), 61–81.

39. Josephine Donovan, "Toward a Women's Poetics," in *Feminist Issues in Literary Scholarship,* ed. Shari Benstock (Bloomington: Indiana University Press, 1987), p. 100.

40. Sara Ruddick, "Maternal Thinking," *Feminist Studies* 6 (summer 1980), 342–67.

41. See Heide Göttner-Abendroth's "Nine Principles of a Matriarchal Aesthetic," in *Feminist Aesthetics,* ed. Ecker, pp. 81–95.

42. Letter from Holly Laird to Suzanne Jones, June 11, 1990.

Part I
Deconstructing the
Fathers' Tradition

Chapter 1
Portrait of the Artist as a Young Woman: H.D.'s Rescriptions of Joyce, Lawrence, and Pound

Susan Stanford Friedman

> Women, who for centuries had been the *objects* of male theorizing, male desires, male fears and male representations, had to discover and reappropriate themselves as *subjects:* the obvious place to begin was the silent place to which they had been assigned again and again, that dark continent which had ever provoked assault and puzzlement.
> —Susan Rubin Suleiman

> Writing. Love is writing.[1]
> —H.D.

"Love is writing." This impossible equation startles off the page of H.D.'s *HER,* her autobiographical *Künstlerroman,* her portrait of the artist as a young woman, her exploration of poetic origin that she wrote in 1926–27, but left in the silent speech of manuscript until she handed it, carefully corrected, for safekeeping to her literary executor, Norman Holmes Pearson.[2] *HER* is full of such impossible formulae. Yoking two abstract and grammatically unbalanced nouns, the linking verb "is" oscillates between the metaphoric and the literal. Since "love" is not literally "writing," the "is" suggests metaphoric comparison. But when the metaphoric structure produces no meaningful analogy, the "is" ultimately reasserts without clarification its literal meaning—Love *is* writing. The novel is a self-reflexive poetic narrative that explores the meanings and conflicts embedded in this difficult formula for living and creating. Like a microcosm of the novel itself, "Love is writing" embodies H.D.'s superposition and intermingling of poetics and erotics in the story of a young woman's maturation into the adult world of sexuality and artistic vocation.

This equation of erotics and poetics is a radical renunciation of the culturally imposed choice many women artists felt compelled to make, a choice that often fuels narrative movement in women's *Künstler-*

romane—the choice to be an artist or a woman, categories culturally constituted as mutually exclusive.[3] H.D.'s negation of that binary opposition stands significantly at odds with Virginia Woolf's autobiographical *Künstlerroman* published in the same year H.D. finished her own—that is, of course, *To the Lighthouse,* in which Lily Briscoe confronts the specter of Victorian femininity, redefines it as a source of maternal empowerment for the daughter-artist who nonetheless must repudiate it as a model, and ultimately pours her erotic fountain of energy solely into her creativity.[4] Lily resolves the double bind of the woman artist by channeling eros into art, by ecstatically painting her vision of the relation between masses, by renouncing the exploration of erotic relation in the realm beyond the boundaries of the canvas.

While Woolf's *Künstlerroman* focuses on the threat and potential empowerment the procreative mother poses for the woman artist, H.D.'s emphasizes the story of the lover, of the woman artist who would renounce neither writing nor adult sexuality. *HER*'s narrative invokes in order to revoke the male economy of desire, specifically the muse tradition in which the male artist's desire for woman is inscribed in a text that becomes the sign, symptom, and scene of his possession. Possessed by desire, the male artist comes to possess the object of his desire through the act of representation, especially in the love lyric.[5] This loop of desire circulating through the male subject and text presumes a silent muse, a woman who inspires, but does not speak, who is called into being by his act of naming, never by her own. "The traditional muse," writes Rachel Blau DuPlessis, "is a contact with a pure force, yet, at the same time, is a voiceless, wordless figure who needs you (a male poet) to interpret and articulate what it is she represents."[6] Woman is, as Sandra M. Gilbert and Susan Gubar have punned, "penned in" by man's "sentence."[7] "Woman is," as Teresa de Lauretis writes, "the very ground of representation," "both telos and origin" of the representation in which she is "both absent and captive." Male "desire provides the impulse, the drive to represent" which is "bound up with power and creativity, is the moving force of culture and history."[8] Within this closed system of male desire, "love *is* writing."

H.D.'s project in *HER* is to find what she called in another *Künstler-roman* a "loophole" for the woman artist.[9] She seeks to maintain the equation she evokes—"love is writing"—by redefining its terms and consequences for the woman writer. Claiming subject status for the muse, H.D. reconstitutes woman as desirous, not simply the object of desire; as namer, not the thing named. To accomplish this re-vision, H.D. engages in a particularly self-reflexive, combative intertextuality. *HER* resonates with a number of specific texts epitomizing the muse tradition—from the mythic figures of Pygmalion and Galatea, Orpheus and Eurydice, and the folk legend of the mermaid Ondine (who gave up her voice for love), down through the conventions established by the troubadours, Petrarch, Dante, and Shakespeare, and into the contemporary period in which Joyce's *Portrait of the Artist as a Young Man* and D. H. Lawrence's *Sons and Lovers* stand as literary beacons, while the unpublished poems Pound wrote for H.D. during their engagement (about 1906–1907) constitute a potent personal gift affirming the muse tradition. However, H.D. activates these vibrations of male convention only to transform this initial resonance into dissonance. Present in the textual grid of *HER,* they are ultimately rescripted into a gynocentric version of the equation, "love is writing." A gynopoetic, a lesbian erotic, displaces the male loop of textual desire.

I will focus particularly on H.D.'s rescriptions of Joyce, Lawrence, and Pound, all of whom contributed particularly striking texts to the muse tradition and played a special role in H.D.'s life as her contemporary masters. Joyce was not a personal friend, but H.D. admired his work greatly.[10] From her intimate friends, Sylvia Beach and Adrienne Monnier, H.D. must have heard a great deal about Joyce. Certainly her own prose experiments with interior monologue, begun in 1921 (and possibly earlier), demonstrate why novels like *Portrait of the Artist* and *Ulysses* would have interested her. It was *The Egoist,* after all, that published *Portrait of the Artist:* first serially in 1914–15 while Richard Aldington, H.D's husband, was literary editor and then as a volume in 1917 while H.D. was herself literary editor.[11] Oscillating between the heroic and the ironic, *Portrait* brought the Romantic image of the artist into the twentieth century, showing in its variation on the muse convention a particular interest in exploring the connection between erotic and aesthetic desire. Sexuality is central to Stephen's *Bildung* as an artist in the making (on the make)—from the infant sexuality of the novel's opening page to the early morning production of his villanelle in a scene whose aesthetic reveries emerge out of erotic ones. From mother to imagined lover, from virgin to whore, from Mary to the bird-girl, woman serves as the elusive matrix of body and soul, the longing for which leads Stephen into the theory and practice of representation. Reflecting its Jesuit context, Stephen's muse is split into spirit and flesh, purity and sexuality, grace and guilt. The Virgin Mary, Mercedes, and E. C. form one untouchable pole, while the prostitute represents the other. Swerving from one to the other, Stephen seeks to reunite the two, to recover the prelapsarian bliss evoked on the novel's first page, when his mother's smell and music merged with the smells of his own body, when his mother's flesh had not yet become taboo.[12]

The bird-girl, the novel's major muse who initiates Stephen's vocation into the secular religion of art, appears to unite the sexual and the spiritual. Strands of the novel's virginal and erotic imagery weave together as Stephen gazes at the silent girl standing in the water (171). Called to his destiny as Daedalus by his desire for the image of woman who possesses him, Stephen becomes the artist in chapter 5 who discourses on a theory of aesthetics and produces a love poem for E. C. that gives him linguistic possession of the image he desires. While the novel's pervasive irony suggests that Stephen may be Icarus rather than Daedalus, the muse figure of *Portrait* remains a figment of Stephen's desire, the silent object of his longing, a presence without autonomous voice, a creature fixed in his gaze and by his pen.[13]

As potent as Joyce's text must have been for the woman whose first volume of poems, *Sea Garden*, had already won her the reputation of being the "perfect imagist," Lawrence's *Künstlerroman* and Pound's poems must have been even weightier because H.D. was erotically as well as poetically entangled with these men. Pound was her first love and first poet, her first "initiator," as she called him, into both love and writing. They were engaged for a period of time after she left Bryn Mawr College in 1906, in a courtship that was complicated by the scandal of Pound's dismissal from Wabash College, the disapproval of her parents, his departure for Europe in 1908, and the rumors of his engagement to Mary Moore of Trenton. After Pound's return, their relationship resumed ambiguously, further entangled by H.D.'s intense friendship with Frances Josepha Gregg, an aspiring artist and writer. As H.D. gradually withdrew from Pound and became more involved with Gregg, Pound and Gregg secretly engaged in a liaison that ended when he once again left for Europe. In 1911, the two women traveled together with Gregg's mother to France and England, where Pound gained them access to London's literary society. Much to H.D.'s distress, Gregg returned to the States and abruptly married Louis Wilkinson in 1912. H.D.'s growing intimacy with the British poet Richard Aldington replaced this earlier triangulated story of desire. But Pound continued to remain important to H.D. In an incident that has achieved legendary status, Pound launched her poetic career in 1912 from the British Museum tearoom, where he pronounced about the three poems she showed him," 'But, Dryad, . . . this is poetry!' ", then slashed out words, shaped her lines, named her "H.D., Imagiste," and finally sent them to Harriet Monroe of *Poetry*. Some forty years later, their importance to each other was still evident in the correspondence they resumed, in selected cantos in which Pound evoked H.D., and in H.D.'s *End to Torment: A Memoir of Ezra Pound*. Their fifty-year association began, however, in the meadows and forests of Upper Darby where the two wandered together when Pound was still a student at the University of Pennsylvania.[14]

The volume of poems the young Pound wrote and handbound for her during their courtship invokes the tall, beautiful Hilda as his lady love and muse. Although Pound published some of the poems in his early collections, the volume remained unknown until its publication under the title *Hilda's Book* in H.D.'s *End to Torment*. Adapting the pastoral idylls of Theocritus and Troubadour lyrics, Pound self-consciously explored the connections between making poetry and making love about and to a woman brought to full being by his words. The setting is the woodlands, meadows, and streams of the pastorale, the world of "nature" imaginatively reconstituted as temporarily outside culture. Like Stephen's bird-girl, Pound's Lady says not a word but rather stands impassive and elusive as the gentle winds of poetic imagination circulate about her and through the poems. The scene of desire is the male poet's text; his gaze and speech repeatedly fix her as his creation—like Pygmalion and his statue Galatea, like Stephen and the E.C. of his villanelle. Like Stephen as well, the poet loves his Lady with eyes and words, not touch. As an image of his desire, she is untouched and untouchable, a perpetual lure whose eroticism is displaced onto the poet's page.[15]

Lawrence, whom H.D. met in 1914 just as the war started, was nearly as important to H.D. as Pound, though for a much briefer period. Lawrence quickly filled the vacuum Aldington left when the pressure of the war led him to abandon their special poet-lover relationship. H.D. and Lawrence exchanged manuscripts—including his draft of *Women in Love* and her poem "Eurydice"—in what she described as an intensely cerebral, vibrant meeting of twin souls. An erotic charge permeated their relationship, fueled in part by Frieda's apparent desire for them to have an affair. But Lawrence recoiled from H.D.'s touch, and then recoiled again when she went off with Cecil Gray in 1919. While they never saw each other after the birth of H.D.'s daughter in 1919, they both fictionalized the other into subsequent novels: Lawrence's *Aaron's Rod, Kangaroo,* and *The Man Who Died* and H.D.'s unpublished novel *Pilate's Wife* and *Bid Me to Live (A Madrigal).* H.D.'s various memoirs return repeatedly back to Lawrence as another of her key "initiators."[16]

For the most part, H.D. felt more akin to Lawrence as poet than Lawrence as novelist or essayist. In particular, she did not like *Women in Love* and *Lady Chatterley's Lover.* But she did say that she found *The Rainbow* "magnificent" and that she liked the "pre-Rainbow paperbacks," both of which she "preferred" to his later novels.[17] Like *Portrait, Sons and Lovers* locates the making of the artist in the matrix of desire, where the image of woman serves as catalyst for and consequence of the act of representation. Even more than Joyce, however, Lawrence regarded the psychosexual dynamics of the family as central to the artist's *Bildung*. Paul Morel's youthful loves for Miriam and Clara reenact in split form his forbidden desire for his mother and his deeply repressed desire for his father. But like *Portrait, Sons and Lovers* explores the young artist's conflicted sexuality in terms of binary opposition: spirit and flesh, body and soul. The dissolution of the Morel marriage leads the young Paul to see his parents in dualistic terms—his mother representing the spirit and the mind while his father represents the mute body.

In his struggle to pass into sexual and vocational adulthood, Paul replicates that dualism in the two women he loves—Miriam representing purity, whose eroticism is displaced into a passion for flowers, just like his mother; and Clara representing passion and consummated sexuality, allied therefore with his father, but also with the maternal body.[18] With delicate irony, Lawrence shows that Paul repudiates Miriam's sexual advances by insisting that she fulfill his need for her as an asexual, purely spiritual image of woman. To touch Miriam is to touch his mother, what he both fears and desires. With her open sexuality, Clara seems to free Paul from his mother, but he is unable to establish a full relationship with her because he is compelled to see her only in terms of sexual desire and satiation, compelled as well to return wordlessly to her breast like a child to his mother. Paul has split the mother-muse he desires into two muses, both of whom are essential to his art. With Miriam, he discusses his work, listening to her criticism, desiring her praise, drawing vitality from her spiritual apprehension of his art. With Clara, he never talks about his work. Instead, Clara is the image he draws and redraws, the sight that leads him into the act of representation. With his two muses, Paul enacts the two sides of his desire for his mother. For Paul, love is painting.[19]

In H.D.'s novel, the muse speaks. She refuses to be the object of the male gaze, refuses to be caught in the male loop of desire, refuses to be split into body or soul, refuses to choose between love and writing. These negations are self-conscious commentaries on *Portrait of the Artist, Sons and Lovers,* and *Hilda's Book.* In this *roman à clef* for which she provides the biographical key on the manuscript, H.D. tells the story of Hermione, nicknamed Her, the young woman who has just flunked out of college, who feels like a total failure because she is neither a married woman nor an independent "modern" woman with a profession. The arrival of two letters sets the narrative in motion by propelling Hermione out of the stasis of psychic paralysis into the kinesis of love, first for the disreputable poet George (the Pound figure), then for the visionary Fayne (the Frances Gregg figure).

Engaged to George, Hermione hopes that marriage will free her

from the conventionality of her family and initiate her into his bohemian world of art. But as the relationship unfolds, she recognizes her
entrapment as a muse for his poems, an object of his sexual desire.
Disengaging from George, whose kisses "suffocate" her, she falls in
love with Fayne, whose gaze frees Her to create. Fayne's betrayal of this
love in her affair with George leads Hermione into an underworld of
madness. But this psychic death becomes the chrysalis of rebirth, the
emergence of a healed Hermione. At the beginning of the novel,
Hermione is only a nascent writer, to whom it had scarcely occurred "to
put the thing in writing" (13). Nine months later, her body itself has
become the artist's pen, walking across the virginal text of fresh snow:
"Her feet were pencils tracing a path. . . . Now the creator was Her's
feet, narrow black crayon across the winter whiteness" (223). A matrix
of desire, Fayne's image accompanies her as she pencils her path into
the future: "When she said Fayne a white hand took Her. . . . Her saw
Her as a star shining white against winter daylight" (225). Image
merges with reality in the last line of the novel, when Hermione
returns home to find Fayne waiting for her. Lesbian love ultimately
replaces heterosexual love as a form of desire compatible with women's
creativity. "Love is writing."

The avant-garde self-reflexivity of *HER,* a major mark of its modernism, is central to H.D.'s transpositions of her inter-texts. She experiments with the conventional split subject of autobiography—the "I"
("eye") who regards the past self and the "I" who enacts the present
story being regarded.[20] From a position of distance and authority, the
narrator, who may or may not be the older Hermione, inserts authoritative commentary into her narrative. "She could not know that the
reason for failure," the narrator wisely tells us near the story's beginning, "was possibly due to subterranean causes. She had not then
dipped dust-draggled, intellectual plumes into the more modern science that posts signs over emotional bog and intellectual lagoon ('failure complex,' 'compensation reflex'). . . . Hermione Gart could not
know that her precise reflection, her entire failure to conform to expectations was perhaps some subtle form of courage" (4). From the very
beginning, the narrator "knows" what Hermione "could not know,"
what Hermione painfully learns in the course of the story the narrator
teleologically unfolds.

A source and sign of the narrator's privileged knowledge and
authority is her self-conscious transposition of male texts into a female
(con)text. The narrator is present in the text as the *reader* who "eyes"
male texts that she deconstructs and reconstructs in the act of telling
her story. This reading is more than the creative "mis-reading" Harold
Bloom identifies as essential for the "strong" writer who must displace

his literary fathers.[21] It is also more than the essentially and necessarily intertextual process of writing Julia Kristeva describes, whereby "the one who writes is the same as the one who reads."[22] Initiated by the objectification of woman in male texts, H.D.'s reading is a deadly accurate deconstruction, a re-reading of convention from a feminist slant, analogous perhaps to the Hegelian slave whose survival depends on "reading" the master more accurately than the master "reads" himself. As DuPlessis asks, "What does it mean to claim Otherness? In H.D.'s terms, it is to claim 'Her' . . . the subject claims its dominated, object case for scrutiny."[23] The narrator's intertextual transposition of contemporary male masters in *HER* forms a kind of metanarrative, a "story" of inter-textual action (or textual interaction) that sits on top of (or underneath) the story of Hermione.

This metanarrative as commentary on male texts is generally evident in the way Hermione's passage into adulthood parallels and then diverges from the narratives of *Portrait* and *Sons and Lovers*. In psychodynamic terms, H.D.'s *HER* both echoes and alters the complex triangulations of desire in the novels of Joyce and Lawrence. The *Künstler* narratives of both *Portrait* and *Sons and Lovers* are fundamentally Oedipal: the son, desiring the forbidden mother, displaces onto the women he loves his feelings for his mother. Mothered by these muses, the youth passes into adulthood, erotically charged and alone, ready to spill his seed onto the blank page and canvas of his art. The *Künstler* narrative of *HER*, on the other hand, is fundamentally pre-Oedipal: the daughter, rejecting Oedipal love, returns to the fusion of the pre-Oedipal in her love for Fayne, to the merged identities of two women evident in the formula "She is Her. I am Her. Her is Fayne. Fayne is Her" (181–82).

As a further intertextual commentary, H.D.'s novel has a double ending, the first of which echoes Lawrence and Joyce, the second of which sharply revises them. The final chapter of *HER* features Hermione alone, much like Paul and Stephen. Neither of her relationships has worked out, but out of the chrysalis of failure, she emerges as an artist. Her determination on the novel's final page to use her inheritance for travel to Europe evokes both Paul's decision to go to London and Stephen's flight for Paris in the final pages of the earlier novels. But the very last line of *HER* breaks across that resonance by suddenly, unexpectedly, and without explanation reintroducing Fayne. Fayne, we learn, is waiting for Hermione in her room, an open ending that suggests the reconstitution of the lesbian lovers, a reaffirmation that "Love is writing."

The underlying psychodynamic structure of all three novels can be imaged in a progression of triangles that capture the beginnings, middles, and endings of the *Künstler* narrative. The intertextual resonance and dissonance between *HER* and the prior two novels is starkly evident in the schematic chart of triangulated desires.

H.D.'s rescription of Pound's poems is fittingly lyric rather than structural. As I have argued at greater length elsewhere, H.D. literally appropriates lines and images from *Hilda's Book,* deconstructs these *words* as textual sources of her own objectification, and finally reconstitutes them as lyric expressions of a forbidden female identity as speaking subject—not the object of desire, but desirous; not a cultural product in man's text, but a cultural producer through the agency of the poetic word.[24] In short, Pound's love poems for her are transposed into lyric celebrations of Her's love for Fayne. In their new context, the images do not reproduce the male economy of desire, but rather create a scene in which the two women are mutually desirous and creative, neither fixed in the text of the other.

In a number of the poems in *Hilda's Book,* for example, Pound's nickname for H.D.—Dryad—is fleshed out into full-scale poems about his tall, willowy lady love as a tree nymph. "Domina" begins: "My Lady is tall and fair to see / She swayeth as a poplar tree / . . . / Her lips part, tho no words come / When the wind bloweth merrily" (73–74). In "Rendez-Vous," Pound writes: "She hath some tree-born spirit of the wood / About her . . . / The moss-grown kindly trees, meseems, she could / As kindred claim" (84). In "The Tree," Pound allows the silent tree-spirit to speak, but significantly in a voice like Daphne's, the woman who became a tree to avoid the poet Apollo's attempted rape: "I stood still and was a tree amid the wood / Knowing the truth of things unseen before / Of Daphne . . ." (81).

In *HER,* H.D. wittily inserts Pound's lyric identification of her as a tree-nymph and muse into her own lyric characterizations of Hermione. At first, Hermione feels freed from feminine conventionality by being George's tree-spirit. But as the relationship begins to smother her identity, Pound's tree images appear in H.D.'s text to signify entrapment: "Trees barricaded her into herself, Her into Her" (64). Transposing the evocation of rape in Pound's "The Tree" and the swaying motion of "Domina," H.D. has George back Hermione into a tree from which she draws strength: "George turned facing Her, rubbed cheek against a tree trunk. 'Don't talk,' he now said. . . . She now braced herself decisively against her own tree. She rubbed her shoulder blades against that small tree. Small hard tree trunk . . . swayed a little, upright swaying little tree swayed. She was stronger than the upright little tree" (68). Gradually, trees become the motif of Hermione's autonomous inner self. Trapped as a "tree" in Pound's lyrics, H.D. frees herself by reclaiming "treeness" for Hermione in her

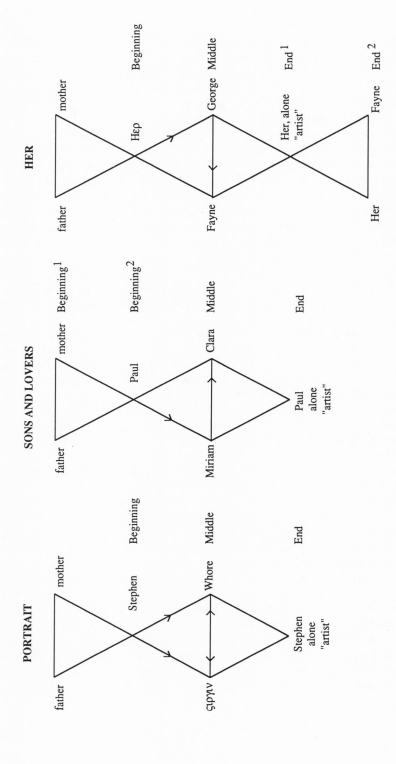

own text: "Tree on tree on tree. TREE. I am the Tree of Life. Tree. I am a tree planted by the river of water. I am...I am...HER exactly. . . . I am in the word TREE, I am TREE" (70, 73). By the end of the novel, Hermione thinks: "I am Tree exactly. George never would love a tree, she had known from the beginning. . . . I knew George could never love a tree properly" (197).

H.D.'s lyric transformation of Pound's words records not only Hermione's disengagement from George, but also her engagement with Fayne. The complicated wordplay and syntactic disruptions surrounding Hermione's nickname "Her" is key to these lyric inter-texts. The awkward "Her" is an intertextual play on Pound's poem "Shadow." In this poem, the poet four times recalls gazing at his Lady in a refrain that structures the poem. As the object of the poet's speech, woman is trapped in the word, just as she is fixed by man's gaze.

> I saw her yesterday.
> And lo, there is no time
> Each second being eternity.
> . . . .
> I saw HER yesterday.
> . . . .
> I saw her yester e'en.
> . . . .
> I saw her yesterday
> Since when there is no sun.   (76)

In *HER*, H.D. picks up on Pound's repetition and capitalization of "HER" to establish the same pattern of textual entrapment and liberation evident in the evolution of the tree motif. In the novel, Hermione is literally the "HER" of Pound's text. The opening lines of the novel suggest this intertextual reference and her related distress: "Her Gart went round in circles. 'I am Her,' she said to herself; she repeated, 'Her, Her, Her'" (3). Hermione is the "HER" of Pound's poem, an object in his text and of his gaze. The disturbing disruption of grammar ostensibly justified by Hermione's nickname points to her object status. "I am Her" is correct from the standpoint of naming but incorrect in relationship to pronouns. This ambiguity emphasizes that linguistic objectification embodies a corresponding cultural objectification of which Hermione gradually becomes aware: "There was that about George, he wanted to incarnate Her, knew enough to know that this was not Her. There was just a chance that George might manage to draw her out half-drowned, a coal scuttle, or push HER back, drowned, a goddess" (64). "Suffocating" and "smudged out" by his desire, she later realizes that "He wanted Her, but he wanted a her that he called decorative. George wanted a Her out of the volumes on the floor" (73, 83, 172). "You are a poem, though your poem's nought," George tells her; "Your melic chorosos aren't half so bad as simply rather rotten" (212, 167). As George's Lady, she is his text. HER *is* text, that is, a word without its own voice, the object of its male speaker.

Having deconstructed Pound's "I saw HER," H.D. reconstructs Hermione's identity through a forbidden love of doubled "Hers," which changes the scene of desire from heterosexual to lesbian. When Hermione tells George that she can never marry him, she says: "Anyhow I love—I love Her, only Her, Her, Her" (170). "Her" is simultaneously Hermione and Fayne, a point linguistically made in several of the intense, lyric moments of complete communion between the women when narrative space and time are suspended. The linguistic ambiguity of "I love her/Her" emphasizes reciprocity instead of hierarchy, as when the two women sit *mutually* gazing into each other's eyes: "Eyes met eyes and the storm held, storm of ice, some storm in an ice crater" (161). This narcissistic love transforms the object status of "I am Her, Her, Her" in the opening lines of the novel into an image of birth: "I know her, I know her. Her. I am Her. She is Her. Knowing her, I know Her. She is some amplification of myself like amoeba giving birth, by breaking off, to amoeba" (158).[25]

This birth of twin selves is expressed in the radical alteration of syntax, when the object "her" appears in both subject and object position as Hermione watches the sleeping Fayne: "I will not have her hurt. I will not have Her hurt. She is Her. I am Her. Her is Fayne. Fayne is Her. I will not let them hurt Her. . . . Her is asleep. Her must stay there sleeping" (181–82). This passage transposes Pound's poem "Sancta Patrona Domina Caelae," in which he writes: "Saint Hilda pray for me. / Lay on my forehead / Cool hands of thy blessing Out of thy purity / Lay on my forehead / White hands of thy blessing" (83–84). In the novel, Hermione lays cool hands not on George's forehead, but on Fayne's. "'Your hands are healing,'" Fayne tells Hermione. "'They have dynamic white power. . . . Your hands are white stars. Your hands are snowdrops" (180). Hilda's virginal innocence in Pound's poem becomes the "indecent" innocence of lesbian love in *HER*. "'Isn't Swinburne decadent?'" Fayne asks Hermione. "'In what sense exactly decadent, Fayne?' 'O innocence, holy and untouched and most immoral. Innocence like thine is totally indecent'" (164). In the reversals that characterize the novel, what is conventionally moral—such as her engagement to George—becomes immoral. What is conventionally indecent—such as lesbian love—becomes the sacred center of innocence. The poems of Swinburne that Pound brought to H.D. in their courtship become in the novel the code for the lesbian love through which Hermione creates both her self and her sense of artistic vocation.[26]

The novel's transposition of the erotic from heterosexual passion to lesbian love is connected with Hermione's development as an artist.[27] Hermione shows her poems to Fayne, as she did to George. Instead of his scorn, based partially in jealousy, Fayne tells Her that she is not threatened by her writing: "Your writing is the thin flute holding you to eternity. Take away your flute and you remain, lost in a world of unreality" (162). Even though the love between Fayne and Hermione is broken by deceptions, the image of the love that created a matrix of desire and creativity remains to inspire Her in the final pages of the novel. Walking across the white snow, with her body as the poet's pen, Hermione repeats Fayne's name: "When she said Fayne a white hand took Her. Her was held like a star invisible in daylight that suddenly by some shift adjustment of phosphorescent values comes quite clear. Her saw Her as a star shining white against winter daylight" (225). Hermione has found her muse and like the runner Pheidippides, she will "run, run, run" with her "message" (220).

The birth of Hermione's identity, desire, and poetic calling in *HER* rewrites Pound's own poem about the origins of the poet "H.D." Cyrena Pondrom has suggested that Pound's poem "Ortus" might describe not only the creation of a poem, but more specifically his transformation of Hilda Doolittle into "H.D., Imagiste." As Pondrom notes, Pound originally published "Ortus" in April of 1913, in the same issue of *Poetry* in which he and Flint laid out imagist doctrine for the first time and just one issue after H.D.'s first three imagist poems had appeared.[28] In both readings of "Ortus," the text is female, while the creator is male. The labor reproduces the creation of the universe by the potent Word. "In the beginning was the Word, and the Word was with God, and the Word was God," the Gospel of John reads. The linguistic authority of the poet to name a thing into existence resonates with a corresponding religious and sexual authority as well:

> How have I laboured?
> How have I not laboured
> To bring her soul to birth,
> To give these elements a name and a centre!
> She is beautiful as the sunlight, and as fluid.
> She has no name, and no place.
> How have I laboured to bring her soul into separation;
> To give her a name and her being!

Surely you are bound and entwined,
You are mingled with the elements unborn;
I have loved a stream and a shadow.

I beseech you enter your life.
I beseech you learn to say "I,"
When I question you;
For you are no part, but a whole,
No portion, but a being.[29]

For H.D., the poem may have represented the problematic nature of the artistic, sexual, and religious authority Pound and later men repeatedly assumed in relationship to her. The significance of words and naming in *HER* can be read as H.D.'s rewrite of Pound's poem celebrating his role in the origins of her identity. The butterfly and birth imagery pervasive throughout *Her* may well be an intertextual echo of the birth imagery of "Ortus." Just as likely, the refrains in the novel about identity—names, places, and things—may answer Pound's lament: "she has no name, and no place." The repetitious web of Hermione's thoughts return over and over to such observations as "Names are in people, people are in names" (5); "she could put no name to the things she apprehended" (13); "Things make people, people make things" (25); "People were in things, things were in people. Names were in things, things were in names" (74); "I don't know what her name is. . . . she was nameless" (81); "I am Hermione Gart and will be Hermione Lowndes...it wasn't right. People are in things, things are in people. I can't be called Lowndes" (112); "People are in names, names are in people" (131); "Things are in people, people are in things" (134); "People are in things. Things are in people and people should think before they call a place Sylvania" (198). *HER* is all about how Hermione finds her own center, place, and name. But the agent of creation is not the potent male poet who brings her into existence. Instead, her self-creation emerges out of her disengagement from George and engagement with Fayne. This redefinition of the role of desire in the making of identity coexists with Hermione's reclamation of the word, the power to name which she appropriates in acts of self-conscious blasphemy: "God is in a word. God is in a word. God is in HER. She said, 'HER, HER, HER. I am Her. . . . I am the word...the word was with God...I am the word...HER'" (32). Through opposition to George rather than obedience to his command, Hermione transforms her very body into the poet's pen; she writes herself into the role of Creator as she walks across the virginal text of snow at the end of the novel.

"Words are my plague and my redemption," Hermione realizes (62). Trapped as a muse in a male text of desire, she reuses the phallo-centric word to reconstitute desire in a gynopoetic (con)text. George tells her, "Love doesn't make good art, Hermione." But Her discovers, "Writing. Love is writing." H.D.'s answer to Pound through Hermione's odd equation of "Love" and "writing" also makes a response to Law-rence and Joyce. Rescripting their narrative structures in *Sons and Lov-ers* and *Portrait of the Artist as a Young Man,* transposing Pound's lyric images in *Hilda's Book,* H.D. connects sexuality and textuality with herself in the position of the subject. She attempts in *HER,* as in her other *Künstlerromane,* to confront what Woolf writes in "Professions for Women" that she was unable to do: "telling the truth about my own experiences as a body." Women writers, Woolf theorizes, are like the young girl who fishes in the streams of the unconscious, only to come up against some thoughts she did not dare to express: "she had thought of something, something about the body, about the passions which it was unfitting for her as a woman to say. Men, her reason told her, would be shocked. The consciousness of what men will say of a woman who speaks the truth about her passions had roused her from her artist's state of unconsciousness. She could write no more."[30] In *HER,* H.D. fished in those streams, challenged what "men will say of a woman" through her rescriptions of their texts, and reconfigured the matrices of language and desire. But the price of her speech was public silence. *HER* accomplishes what Susan Rubin Suleiman identifies as the task of women writers: "to discover and reappropriate themselves as *subjects*" (7). But unlike the narratives of Joyce, Lawrence, and Pound, *HER* remained absent from the domain of letters until 1981, its publication record itself a witness to the liminality of H.D.'s subjectivity.

Notes

1. Portions of the argument in this essay first appeared in "Palimpsest of Origins in H.D.'s Career," *Poesis* 6 (1985), 56–73; an expanded version is in *Penelope's Web: Gender, Modernity, H.D.'s Fiction* (New York: Cambridge University Press, 1990). The epigraphs are from Susan Rubin Suleiman, "(Re)Writing the Body: The Politics and Poetics of Female Eroticism," in *The Female Body in Western Culture: Contemporary Perspectives,* ed. Susan Rubin Suleiman (Cambridge, Mass.: Harvard University Press, 1986), p. 7, and H.D., *HERmione* (New York: New Directions, 1981), p. 149.

2. H.D.'s original title, which I will follow throughout, is *HER,* changed by New Directions to *HERmione.* The typescript for *HER,* with H.D.'s penciled revisions, is at Beinecke Rare Book and Manuscript Library, Yale University. The name "Helga Doorn," the pseudonym H.D. used for her three films from 1927 through 1930, appears on the title page, along with a handwritten key that identifies the characters in the novel with the actual people who were her

38   Susan Stanford Friedman

models. In " 'I had two loves separate': The Sexualities of H.D.'s *HER*," Rachel
Blau DuPlessis and I argued that H.D. chose not to publish the novel in her
lifetime because of its lesbian content (*Montemora* 8 [1981], 7–30). I am indebted to DuPlessis for the ideas about this novel that we worked out jointly for
this collaborative essay and for her essay "Family, Sexes, Psyche: An Essay on
H.D. and the Muse of the Woman Writer," first published in 1979 and reprinted in *H.D.: Woman and Poet*, ed. Michael King (Orono, Maine: National
Poetry Foundation, 1986), pp. 69–90. All quotations from *HER* are taken from
the New Directions edition and are cited parenthetically in the text.

3. For discussions of the woman artist's double bind in the *Künstlerroman*,
see Rachel Blau DuPlessis, *Writing Beyond the Ending: Narrative Strategies of
Twentieth-Century Women Writers* (Bloomington: Indiana University Press,
1985), pp. 84–104; Linda Huf, *A Portrait of the Artist as a Young Woman: The
Writer as Heroine in American Literature* (New York: Frederick Ungar, 1983);
Grace Stewart, *A New Mythos: The Novel of the Artist as Heroine, 1877–1977*
(Montreal: Eden Press, 1981); Sandra M. Gilbert and Susan Gubar, *The Mad-
woman in the Attic: The Woman Writer and the Nineteenth-Century Literary Imagina-
tion* (New Haven, Conn.: Yale University Press, 1979), pp. 3–104; Susan
Gubar, "The Birth of the Artist as Heroine: (Re)production, the *Künstlerroman*
Tradition, and the Fiction of Katherine Mansfield," in *The Representation of
Women in Fiction*, ed. Carolyn G. Heilbrun and Margaret R. Higonnet (Bal-
timore: Johns Hopkins University Press, 1983), pp. 19–59; and Mary K.
DeShazer, *Inspiring Women: Reimagining the Muse* (New York: Pergamon Press,
1986), pp. 1–44.

4. For the erotic fountain imagery associated with both Lily's painting and
Mrs. Ramsay's creative power, see *To the Lighthouse* (1927; rpt. New York:
Harcourt Brace & World, 1955), pp. 238 and 58. See also my discussion of this
connection in "Lyric Subversion of Narrative in Women's Writing: Virginia
Woolf and the Tyranny of Plot," in *Reading Narrative: Form, Ethics, Ideology*
(Columbus: Ohio State University Press, 1989), pp. 162–85. In " 'Retreat with
Honour': Mary Chomondeley's Presentation of the New Woman Artist in *Red
Pottage*" (in this volume), Ann L. Ardis argues that Lily Briscoe's reconfigura-
tion of the relation between life and art had its precursors in nineteenth-
century "new woman" novels for which the maternal figure was central. This
mother-daughter plot exists as a subtext in H.D.'s *HER*, as Deborah Kelly
Kloepfer demonstrates in "Flesh Made Word: Maternal Inscription in H.D.,"
Sagetrieb 3 (spring 1984), 27–48.

5. For a related analysis of the woman poet's heretical relation to the lyric
tradition, see Lynda K. Bundtzen's "Power and Poetic Vocation in Adrienne
Rich's *The Dream of a Common Language*," in this volume. For a discussion of the
place of woman as specular object in the love lyric, see Margaret Homans,
" 'Syllables of Velvet': Dickinson, Rossetti, and the Rhetorics of Sexuality,"
Feminist Studies 11 (fall 1985), 569–93. See also DuPlessis, "Family," and De-
Shazer, *Inspiring Women*.

6. DuPlessis, "Family," p. 74.

7. Gilbert and Gubar, *Madwoman*, p. 13.

8. Teresa de Lauretis, *Alice Doesn't: Feminism, Semiotics, Cinema* (Bloomington: Indiana University Press, 1984), pp. 13–14.

9. In *Bid Me to Live (A Madrigal)* (1960; rpt. Redding Ridge, Conn.: Black
Swan, 1983, p. 136), H.D. used the term "loophole" for the woman artist's
androgynous identity of "woman-man," which is posed as the solution to the

double bind of the woman artist and as a direct contradiction of Lawrence's "man-is-man" and "woman-is-woman" in *Women in Love* (1920; rpt. New York: Penguin, 1976). The "loophole" in *HER* is an androgynous lesbian identity, in contrast to the heterosexual narrative of *Bid Me to Live*. For discussion of H.D.'s resolutions of the double bind in her later poetry, see Raffaella Baccolini's dissertation, "Tradition, Identity, Desire: H.D.'s Revisionist Strategies in *By Avon River, Winter Love,* and *Hermetic Definition*" (University of Wisconsin-Madison, 1989).

10. See H.D., *Palimpsest* (1926; rpt. Carbondale: Southern Illinois University Press, 1968), and L. S. Dembo, "Norman Holmes Pearson: An Interview," *Contemporary Literature* 10 (autumn 1969), 435–46.

11. *Portrait*'s publication history is a tortuous one, confounded by many rejections by British publishers and censorship by printers. After Harriet Shaw Weaver committed *The Egoist* to publication of the volume, the American publisher B. W. Huebsch brought out the first edition in the United States on December 29, 1916; *The Egoist* edition appeared in England on February 12, 1917. The edition from which I will quote, with parenthetical identification, is a reprint of the 1916 edition (New York: Viking, 1964). For extended discussion of H.D.'s experimental fiction, see *Penelope's Web*.

12. See Joyce, *Portrait* (7, 14); Stephen's socialization into the "tribe" of boys at school centers on his being taught that his acceptance depends on his denial that he kisses his mother before he goes to bed. For a discussion of Joyce's representation of the maternal figure in *Portrait, Stephen Hero,* and *Ulysses,* see my "The Return of the Repressed in Joyce: (Self)Censorship and the Making of a Modernist," in *The Languages of Joyce,* ed. Christine van Boheemen, Rosa Bosinelli, and Carla Marengo (Philadelphia: John Benjamins, 1991).

13. The silence of Stephen's muse is highlighted by a comparison between Emma Cleary in *Stephen Hero* (a portion of an earlier version of *Portrait,* ed. John J. Slocum and Herbert Cahoon [New York: New Directions, 1963]) and E. C. in *Portrait*. In the earlier version, Joyce fleshed out the character of Stephen's first love into what Bonnie Kime Scott describes as "a central, sustained, individualized portrait of a modern, urban, intelligent young woman who is permitted to some extent to speak her mind and direct her affairs" (*Joyce and Feminism* [Bloomington: Indiana University Press, 1984], p. 133); in the later version, however, E. C. exists merely as an ethereal presence in Stephen's life, signaled by her silence and the barrenness of her initials. See also Suzette Henke, "Stephen Dedalus and Women: A Portrait of the Artist as Young Misogynist," in *Women in Joyce,* ed. Suzette Henke and Elaine Unkeless (Urbana: University of Illinois Press, 1982), pp. 82–107.

14. For information on her relationship with Pound, see for example, H.D., *End to Torment: A Memoir of Ezra Pound, with the Poems from 'Hilda's Book' by Ezra Pound,* ed. Norman Holmes Pearson and Michael King (New York: New Directions, 1979); Friedman and DuPlessis, "'I had two loves separate'"; Barbara Guest, *Herself Defined: The Poet H.D. and Her World* (New York: Doubleday, 1984); Emily Mitchell Wallace, "Athene's Owl," *Poesis* 6 (1985), 98–123; and Baccolini. See particularly Canto LXXXIII (p. 108) of *The Cantos (1–95)* (New York: New Directions, 1956) for Pound's address to "Dryad." H.D.'s long sequence poem *Winter Love* printed in *Hermetic Definition* (New York: New Directions, 1972) also transmutes aspects of their relationship (*Hermetic Definition,* 85–117). H.D. describes the scene in the tearoom in *End to Torment,* p. 18.

For an account of H.D.'s relationship with Gregg and Gregg's association with Pound, see Guest, pp. 22–28; Penny Smith, "Hilda Doolittle and Frances Gregg," *The Powys Review* 6 (1988), 46–51; and *Penelope's Web*.

15. For feminist discussions of "the male gaze" in film, applicable as well, I believe, to the male love lyric, see E. Ann Kaplan, *Women and Film: Both Sides of the Camera* (New York: Methuen, 1983), especially pp. 23–35; Laura Mulvey, "Visual Pleasure and Narrative Cinema," *Screen* 16 (autumn 1975), 6–18; and Homans. See also Luce Irigaray, who in *This Sex Which Is Not One* associates touch with feminine eroticism and specularity with masculine desire (trans. Catherine Porter with Carolyn Burke [Ithaca, N.Y.: Cornell University Press, 1985]).

16. See H.D., *Tribute to Freud* (1956; rev. ed. Boston: David R. Godine, 1974), pp. 116, 128, 131–35, 140–42, 144–45, 149–50; her unpublished memoir *Compassionate Friendship* (1955) at Beinecke Library; her account of their relationship in her *Bid Me to Live*. The manuscript for *Pilate's Wife*, written in 1924, 1929, and 1934, is at Beinecke. See Lawrence, *Aaron's Rod* (London: Heinemann, 1922), *Kangaroo* (London: Heinemann, 1923), and *The Man Who Died* (New York: Knopf, 1931). Janice Robinson's suggestion in *H.D.: The Life and Work of an American Poet* (Boston: Houghton Mifflin, 1982) that H.D. and Lawrence were lovers and that Lawrence was the father of H.D.'s daughter Perdita has no support in the vast collection of H.D.'s papers at Beinecke Library. H.D. wrote Bryher, for example, "how grateful I am . . . that I never slept with D. H. L." (16 January 1935); H.D.'s letters to Bryher during November of 1934 relate how happy she is that Bryher is showing Perdita her father's house in Cornwall. See also Schaffner's moving account of meeting her father, Cecil Gray, for the first time, in "A Profound Animal," in *Bid Me to Live*, pp. 185–94.

17. See *Tribute* (133–34). To Amy Lowell, she wrote "Did you read 'Rainbow'? Magnificent—And he has had such stupid reviews" (Letter, October 4, 1916, at Houghton Library, Harvard University). She wrote Aldington: "I am reading *Rainbow* carefully, from quite a different angle. It is better than lots that came after. . . . Have you the pre-Rainbow in paperbacks? I prefer them" (Letter, February 27, 195[6?], at the University of Southern Illinois.)

18. *Sons and Lovers* (1913; rpt. New York: Penguin, 1976). In a reversal typical of Lawrence, the colors red and black associated with Miriam's appearance link her to Paul's father, who is also described with imagery of red and black. Conversely, the colors yellow, gold, and white appear in the descriptions of both Gertrude and Clara. In essential spirit, however, Miriam is allied with Paul's mother, while Clara's physicality connects her with Paul's father. Lawrence suggests that behind Paul's desire for both Miriam and Clara lies his tabooed desire for his mother and his even more forbidden homoerotic desire for his father.

19. See Maurice Beebe's discussion of the male artist's relationship to female muse figures in *Ivory Towers and Sacred Founts: The Artist as Hero in Fiction from Goethe to Joyce* (New York: New York University Press, 1964); his basic point is that in the tradition of the *Künstlerroman*, the artist either withdraws from life into an "ivory tower" or plunges headlong into experience of life's "sacred fount." The muse for the first type is idealized, untouchable; for the second, a woman with whom the artist consummates his desire. In both Joyce and Lawrence, we might add, these traditions intertwine, with the contradictions between them fueling the narrative's kinetic movement. Beebe's pathbreaking

book is still to my mind the best synthetic study of the *Künstlerroman* in Western literature. Unusual for 1964, he even discussed a few women writers, especially George Sand, but he was unaware of how gender considerations fundamentally alter the economies of desire in male and female texts. An integrative literary history of the *Künstlerroman* that takes into account the mediating factors of gender, race, ethnicity, historical era, sexual preference, class, and so forth, has yet to be written.

20. I am adapting Elizabeth Bruss's argument in "Eye for I: Making and Unmaking Autobiography in Film" that in autobiographical film the split subject of the narrating "I" becomes the filmic "Eye" (in *Autobiography: Essays Theoretical and Critical*, ed. James Olney [Princeton, N.J.: Princeton University Press, 1980], pp. 296–320). H.D.'s *HER*, written as her involvement in avant-garde cinema was initiated, seems especially suited to Bruss's formulation. For other discussions of the split subject in autobiography, see for example Louis A. Renza, "The Veto of the Imagination: A Theory of Autobiography," in Olney, pp. 268–95, and Sidone Smith, *A Poetics of Women's Autobiography: Marginality and the Fictions of Self-Representation* (Bloomington: Indiana University Press, 1987), especially pp. 44–62. Kathleen Brogan's "Lyric Voice and Sexual Difference in Elizabeth Bishop," in this volume, suggests that Bishop's lyric "I" revises the Emersonian centrism of the unitary self. The decentered and communal speakers of H.D.'s late poetry were first developed through the split subjects of her autobiographical prose.

21. See Harold Bloom, *The Anxiety of Influence* (New York: Oxford University Press, 1973) and *A Map of Misreading* (New York: Oxford University Press, 1975).

22. Julia Kristeva, *Desire in Language: A Semiotic Approach to Literature and Art*, ed. Leon S. Roudiez (New York: Columbia University Press, 1980), p. 63.

23. DuPlessis, *H.D.: The Career of That Struggle* (Brighton: Harvester Press, 1986), p. 34.

24. Quotations from Pound's *Hilda's Book* are identified within the text and taken from H.D.'s *End to Torment*, pp. 67–84. For extended discussion of H.D.'s transpositions of Pound's poems as well as her own famous imagist poems into *HER*, see *Palimpsest* and *Penelope's Web*. For an Irigarayan analysis of the fetishization of H.D. as Image within Pound's theory of the Image, see Elizabeth A. Hirsh, "Imaginary Images: 'H.D.,' Modernism and the Psychoanalysis of Seeing," in *Discontented Discourses: Feminism, Textual Intervention/Psychoanalysis*, ed. Marlene Barr and Richard Feldstein (Urbana: University of Illinois Press, 1989), pp. 141–59.

25. For a different reading of this passage, see S. Travis, "A Crack in the Ice: Subjectivity and the Mirror in H.D.'s *Her*," *Sagetrieb* 6 (fall 1987), 123–40. Using Irigaray's punning images of *glace* (ice/mirror), Travis suggests that Her's periods of amoebic union with Fayne represent a stage (based in the Imaginary) through which Her must pass beyond (by cracking the *glace* in her walk through the words near the end of the novel) in order to become an artist. I would suggest instead that even as Her cracks the ice with her foot and marks the snow with the sign of her presence, she is still thinking back on those epiphanic moments of fusion with Fayne, memories which foreshadow Fayne's reappearance in her room on the final page of the novel. Rather than a stage to be moved beyond, these moments function (I would argue) more like Woolfian moments and as revelations of an ideal that is at odds with what is possible in historical time.

26. See also Cassandra Laity's discussion of how H.D. revises Romanticism and Swinburne in particular, in "H.D. and A. C. Swinburne: Decadence and Modernist Women's Writing," *Feminist Studies* 15 (1989), 461–84. Bundtzen's discussion in this volume of how Romanticism haunts Rich's *The Dream of a Common Language,* which subjects the prior tradition to re-vision, is analogous to H.D.'s project in *HER.*

27. See *Penelope's Web* for an extended discussion of the mother-daughter subplot in relation to Her's reclamation of the Word.

28. Conversation with the author; see also her groundbreaking discussion of the influence H.D.'s first imagist poems had on Pound when she showed them to him in September of 1912, before he wrote "In the Station of the Metro" ("H.D. and the Origins of Modernism," *Sagetrieb* 4 [spring 1985], 73–100).

29. Ezra Pound, "Ortus," in *Personae: Collected Shorter Poems* (New York: New Directions, 1926), p. 84.

30. Virginia Woolf, "Professions for Women," in *The Death of the Moth and Other Essays* (New York: Harcourt Brace Jovanovich, 1970), pp. 235–42.

Chapter 2
Power and Poetic Vocation in Adrienne Rich's *The Dream of a Common Language*

Lynda K. Bundtzen

> . . . and the poem reproached her because she had refused to become a luxury for the poet.
>
> The choice still seemed to be between "love"—womanly, maternal love, altruistic love—a love defined and ruled by the weight of an entire culture, and egotism—a force directed by men into creation, achievement, ambition, often at the expense of others, but justifiably so. For weren't they men, and wasn't that their destiny as womanly, selfless love was ours? We know now that the alternatives are false ones—that the word "love" is itself in need of re-vision.
>
> —Adrienne Rich[1]

Although my essay belongs to a section of this book titled "Deconstructing the Fathers' Tradition," I wish to remind my readers of Adrienne Rich's strategic term for confronting her literary fathers. Instead of deconstruction, she proposes "re-vision—the act of looking back, of seeing with fresh eyes, of entering an old text from a new critical direction" (*OLSS* 35). I cannot think of a more influential essay in the past twenty years than Rich's "When We Dead Awaken: Writing as Re-vision," for persuading women writers and readers to recognize and to reflect critically on the way our imaginations have been ideologically shaped to accept, unquestioningly, male definitions of the artist, his special powers and gifts, his egotistical need to create, and his difference from ordinary mortals, especially women. For Rich, precisely those words we feel most certain of—those words charged with a priori cultural meaning and literary signification—like love and power, hero and creation, are "in need of re-vision," re-construction from a woman-identified perspective.[2]

Susan Stanford Friedman, in her chapter on H.D., forcibly demonstrates where woman is located in the male artist's text. She is the object of his desire, the muse who "inspires but does not speak, who is called into being by his act of naming." She does nothing, she says nothing, but the male artist's desire for her favor energizes both narrative movement toward artistic maturity in the *Künstlerroman*, as it is delineated by Friedman, and the impulse toward spiritual transcendence in the lyric poem. Whether she is Stephen Dedalus's "dark plumaged dove" who returns "his gaze, without shame or wantonness,"[3] Wordsworth's sister Dorothy, recompensing his loss of youthful at-one-ness with nature by dedicating her own youth to his re-presence (and poetic representation) at Tintern Abbey,[4] or Yeats's cruel lady, Maud Gonne, aesthetically transformed into a "Ledaean body" that inspires meditation and aspiration,[5] she, woman, is no more than a prop for the male artist, who in Friedman's words, "comes to possess the object of his desire through the act of representation." She is a trope for erotic power, trans-figured by the male creative genius into aesthetic power, affirming his genius and his gifts.

For the youthful Rich, with her own poetic aspirations, the effect of noticing "that men wrote poems and women frequently inhabited them" (*OLSS* 39) was one of self-division—a "split between the girl who wrote poems, who defined herself in writing poems, and the girl who was to define herself by her relationships with men" (*OLSS* 40). Her response was also ambivalent: two mutually exclusive identities, one as a daughter to an exacting father, and later wife and mother to three sons, and separately as a poet who believed "poetry was where I lived as no one's mother, where I existed as myself."[6] This split, as Rich describes it, generates a moment-by-moment choice, culturally imposed, between womanly labors of selfless love dedicated to family, and "egotistical" desires for solitude, for time and energy devoted to "the energy of creation" (*OLSS* 44): "I always felt the conflict as a failure of love in myself" (*OLSS* 43–44).

In Rich's poetry, re-vision of the male lyric tradition becomes an "act of survival" (*OLSS* 35) as a woman and a poet, leading to the dissolution of differences between acts of love and acts of power, woman's heroism of self-sacrifice and man's heroism of quest and self-assertion. Inevitably, too, Rich's practice of re-vision is also an act of deconstruction, an effort to create a new voice for the lyric poet that does not empower his 'I', his subjectivity, his self-possession, at the expense of an 'other' dispossessed of independent voice, agency, and meaning except as endowed by the male artist's creative faculties. While Rich begins this process of re-vision in earlier volumes, I will be examining its implications for understanding her poetics in *The Dream*

of a Common Language, especially as she "re-scripts," to borrow Friedman's term, the mythopoeia of the Romantic lyric.

   Adrienne Rich's *The Dream of a Common Language* (1978) is generally regarded as a revolutionary volume in its effort to fuse literary
heroism with feminist activism. Feminist critics particularly praise its
"gentle poetics:"[7] Rich's openly expressed desire for earnest and intimate exchange with ordinary women; a poetic language that strives to
be free of literary egotism—indeed, a language aspiring to "common"
speech, without rhetorical designs or pretensions to "mastery" of its
audience; and the hoped-for effect in her audience of immediate,
intuitive understanding based on women's shared experience, emotions, and knowledge of the world. Despite the proclaimed newness of
Rich's "gentle poetics," I think it is noteworthy that her "common
language" is similar to Wordsworth's in his "Preface" to *Lyrical Ballads.*
As Wordsworth portrays the ideal poet, he is merely "a man speaking to
men," with heart-to-heart sincerity and sweetness, and without flourish
or embellishment.[8] So Rich identifies herself as a woman speaking to
and for women, extolling "the universe of humble things"[9] in the
common woman's life. Unlike Wordsworth, who goes on in his "Preface" to make uncommon claims for the special sensitivity and sensibility of the poet,[10] Rich does not . . . or tries not to. But is it possible
for Adrienne Rich, an uncommon woman of extraordinary powers,
sincerely to "cast [her] lot" with ordinary women?

> . . . with those
> who age after age, perversely,
>
> with no extraordinary power,
> reconstitute the world.   (*DCL* 66)

The overt gesture is one of allegiance to a hypothetical "everywoman."
Yet Rich cannot avoid echoes of her poetic precursors who claim
poetry's, not the ordinary woman's, extraordinary power for reconstituting the world. Further, Rich's own critical pause, "perversely,"
implies a rift between her and the common woman reader: somewhere
in Rich's consciousness is a sense of dogged perversity in woman's lot.
   The first section of *The Dream,* entitled "Power," is especially important, I believe, in preventing this potential rift from growing into a
major cleavage between the poet who knows herself to be "uncommon"
because of her power over language, her poetic vocation, and the ordinary woman who feels both inarticulate and disempowered by her lot—

what Rich elsewhere terms "the sustenance and repair of daily life" ("Conditions for Work," *OLSS* 214). Rich's first two poems, "Power" and "Phantasia for Elvira Shatayev," immediately ask readers to rethink cultural fantasies about fame and power, especially those we may have about women singled out by history books as heroines. Simultaneously, Rich claims a poetic identity that invites community with her reader in the effort to envision a new type of female heroism.

From a literary perspective, what is so striking about this overture to *The Dream* is that Rich does not adopt a conversational, easy, woman-to-woman tone as her strategy for a "common language." Instead she immediately confronts the difference in "verbal privilege"[11] between herself and her readers, acknowledging the temptation of "Power" in her meditation on the career of Marie Curie, and then, in the visionary "Phantasia for Elvira Shatayev," creating a myth for female power that places uncommon demands both on her own eloquence and her readers' imaginations. Rich is neither plainspeaking nor folksy in these first poems delineating a "common language." In fact, as I will argue, both of these opening poems, but especially "Phantasia," address issues that might be deemed exclusively literary. Primary here is the question of identity and vocation: Who is the poet? A self-absorbed creator and craftsman who produces her most sublime and universal work in eccentric solitude? Or a politically engaged sister, immersed in a common struggle?[12] Rich challenges what she regards as an elitist "aesthetic ideology" which asserts, "The song is higher than the struggle, and the artist must choose between politics—here defined as earthbound factionalism, corrupt power struggles—and art, which exists on some transcendent plane."[13] For Rich, I believe, poetics and politics—"the song" and "the struggle"—must merge in a passionate alliance that sacrifices neither.

"Power," written in 1974, is a hesitant, ambivalent poem in its handling of Marie Curie. Rich glances with surprised pity and wonder at a woman so dedicated to her scientific work that

> It seems she denied to the end
> the source of the cataracts on her eyes
> the cracked and suppurating skin   of her finger-ends
> till she could no longer hold   a test-tube or a pencil   (*DCL* 3)

Not until 1977, in "Power and Danger: The Works of a Common Woman," does Rich express an absolutely negative judgment of the so-called "great" women of history: "For us, to be 'extraordinary' or 'uncommon' is to fail. History has been embellished with 'extraordinary,' 'exemplary,' 'uncommon,' and of course 'token' women whose lives have left the rest unchanged" (*OLSS* 255). "Power" is much less certain in its motives, although Rich does seem to be groping toward a similar revelation—that Curie's fame and achievement, her "power," are based on repression, denial of a strength she shares with other women.

Rich's gentle treatment of Curie rests, I believe, on a veiled recognition of their kinship. The scientist and poet share a compulsion to realize one's self in original work, to give one's self over completely to individual quest and discovery.[14] Rich defines this compulsion as an ultimately self-damaging mode of self-exploration—self-aggrandizing and available only to a privileged minority. It is a type of power, a temptation she resists, choosing something that the opening of her poem presents as older, pre-literate:

> living in the earth-deposits of   our history
>
> Today a backhoe divulged   out of a crumbling flank of earth
> One bottle   amber   perfect   a hundred-year-old
> cure for fever   or melancholy   a tonic
> for living on this earth   in the winters of this climate   (*DCL* 3)

Rich appeals here to unrecorded history, to magic over science, to secrets "divulged" from mother earth ("a crumbling flank"), and finds in this a "cure" for what strike me as literary ailments—the "fever" and "melancholy" endemic to the lyric poet's famed seclusion from the world.

Indeed, in Rich's image of Curie, no longer able to hold "a test-tube or a pencil," Sandra Gilbert and Susan Gubar might note the classical symptomatology of the woman-writer—her dis-ease with the power of the pen. Rich, however, sees a greater disease literalized in Curie's physical ailments, in appropriating power for herself alone, with an eye to literary fame, or in Curie's example, the history of science. Rich prefers a humble "tonic" over Curie's discovery of radium, the genie in the bottle that once opened, unloosed the atom bomb and the destructive forces of man. "Power" is, then, self-chastening, a warning Rich delivers to herself and to her readers about female heroism as it is tokenized in cultural history. Curie "died   a famous woman   denying / her wounds" (*DCL* 3). Fame is inextricably linked to denial by Rich's long caesuras, as if she ponders the vainglory of worldly "success."

"Power" implicitly raises the question of what is possible for women. Is power to be given up altogether? Are heroic fame and glory inherently corrupt and therefore easy, even fortunate deprivations for women? "Phantasia for Elvira Shatayev," Rich's second poem, answers these questions with a re-vision of our concepts of power, fame, glory, heroism, making them accessible achievements for both her women readers and for Rich herself as a woman poet. In terms of lyric tradition, "Phantasia" is an especially bold digression from Rich's poetic "fathers"—especially Wordsworth in *The Prelude*—who are, I believe, haunting presences at this scene of writing: Rich vigorously contends with their depiction of the poet-hero as a solitary creator, as meditatively disengaged from "mortal woe" by virtue of his "higher" calling. While re-figuring the heroic in a "common" and feminine form, Rich also invents a new type of woman-poet-as-hero, an essentially heretical voice who is, to borrow Rich's term, "disloyal to civilization" (*OLSS* 275). "Phantasia" is, I will argue, an exemplary poem for Rich's poetics and politics in *The Dream*, giving sensuous form to her conviction that "Poetry is . . . a criticism of language" and "above all a concentration of the *power* of language, which is the power of our ultimate relationship to everything in the universe" (*OLSS* 248; Rich's italics). In this assertion, Rich assuredly reinvokes the Romantic aspiration to mythmaking power, and as I will demonstrate in the performance of "Phantasia," re-shapes the Romantic poet's chosen role as prophet and oracle for a feminine audience.

"Phantasia" is based on Christopher Wren's front-page *New York Times* articles, "8 Soviet Women Climbers Killed by Storm in Lenin Peak Ascent," "Burial on Soviet Peak: A Husband's Tribute," and a brief paragraph in the Sunday *Times* "Week in Review," "Mountain Man." This last title illustrates forcefully what happens to a woman's story as it is subverted, expropriated for a masculine civilization. Wren's story is one of unmotivated, unintended endings, arbitrary storms, high winds, avalanches, earthquakes, and Lenin Peak, a "majestic snow bulwark" unconquered by Elvira Shatayev's all-woman mountaineering team: "The frozen, snow-dusted bodies of seven of the women were discovered Thursday where they had died just a few hundred feet below the summit of Lenin Peak."[15] The "tragedy" for Wren seems to be both the women's deaths and their poignant failure to reach Lenin Peak's summit before dying. Wren reports their final radio message, "Good-by, we will die" ("8 Soviet Women" 6), but unlike Rich, he sees no special significance in their bond.

Instead of Wren's "tragedy," "accident," "disaster," Rich's version of this event is about beginnings, about potential relationships formed by love, and about a heroism figured in mountain climbing, but hardly limited to the individual male achievement of getting to the top, conquering the mountain's physical height. The women's desire exceeds the cliché, " 'Why did you climb that mountain?' 'Because it was there.' " Eros does not press toward such closure in Rich's version. Speaking in Shatayev's voice, who, in turn, speaks for the women as a group, Rich proposes her alternative narrative:

When you have buried us   told your story
ours does not end   we stream
into the unfinished   the unbegun
the possible   (*DCL* 5)

From a newspaper account of eight women's deaths, we move into the
realm of mythopoeia with Rich's poem. Apotheosized, made eternal by
Rich's art, the women assume the unending form of archetype, or to
use Northrop Frye's definition, they "convey the sense of unlimited
power in a humanized form."[16] Where for Frye this power is centered
in an image of "the god, whether traditional deity, glorified hero,
or apotheosized poet" (*Anatomy* 120), Rich's archetype is ardently communal.

Rich erases her own identity, as a sibylline voice blends with Shatayev's in utterance that claims identity for word, world, and body:

Every cell's core of heat   pulsed out of us
into the thin air   of the universe
the armature of rock beneath these snows
this mountain   which has taken   the imprint of our minds
through changes elemental and minute
as those we underwent
to bring each other here   (*DCL* 5)

As the mountain is imprinted with the women's minds, especially their
love for one another and a desire that exceeds individual aspiration, so
Rich's poem, to quote Frye once again, is no longer an alternative
"commentary on life or reality, but contain[s] life and reality in a system
of verbal relationships" (*Anatomy* 122). Like other myths, then, Rich's
story "is somewhere   still enacted   and continuing" (*DCL* 5), always
bodying forth new representations of eros, socially and comically conceived as playing itself out within a community of women. Instead of
natural catastrophe and arbitrary death, Rich's narrative emphasizes
strife overcome and epiphany achieved. Strife is re-visioned as "down
there" in the society from which the women have removed themselves
and epiphany is not a panoramic and solitary vision attained by reaching a pinnacle but a revelation of what women can be for one another:
"*A cable of blue fire ropes our bodies / burning together in the snow*" (*DCL* 6;
Rich's italics). As Northrop Frye defines epiphany, it is a "point at which
the undisplaced apocalyptic world and the cyclical world of nature
come into alignment" (*Anatomy* 203). Similarly in Rich, the mountain is
no longer a natural place, but for the women, a site of communal
vision: it "has taken   the imprint of our minds / through changes

elemental and minute" (*DCL* 5); its "armature" is transmuted, sculpted, and molded to protect and support a female body of imagination.

Wren's second piece is a compelling story about Shatayev's husband Vladimir, who, "against the advice of friends" and driven by a compulsion to learn how "one of the worst tragedies in Soviet mountaineering had taken place," ascended Lenin Peak to "recover his wife's body and bury her and seven companions there."[17] Wren firmly displaces the focus of the narrative to Shatayev's husband, who emerges as a romance hero, in quest of answers to the mystery of the women's deaths, which he hopes to find in his wife's diary: "'she was in very good spirits and felt like writing. I hoped I could find it so that I could know what happened, but I couldn't find her blue rucksack anywhere'" ("Burial" 12). Vladimir appears driven to perform a final rite of recovery and burial, putting his wife to rest both physically and in his own mind.

It would be foolish to deny that Wren creates a very moving story about the husband's tragedy. Embedded, however, in his vivid account of "tents torn apart and the equipment blown away" ("Burial" 12), of Vladimir's paralysis before Elvira's body ("'I couldn't approach her for a long time,' he remembered. 'It was such a contrasting picture and she was just lying there.'" ["Burial" 12]), are statements that Rich may view as professional and male bewilderment over what the expedition was all about for the women: "'It is very difficult to imagine how the girls behaved when we were not there. I kept thinking what I could have done if I had been there'" ("Burial" 12). Wren envisions "a free spirit, a temperamental, artistic woman" and the husband, though "opposed to women's ascents," relents "'because I saw the results. . . . They took it very seriously'" ("Burial" 1), implying, of course, an original belief that women are not serious enough for such ventures. The husband also cites a general attitude in the Soviet Union that "'mountain climbing is not for women because it will make them coarse. . . . But people cited Elvira as an example of femininity. They cited her as proof that mountains do not hurt women, because she never lost her femininity. Some of my journalist friends called her the fairy of the mountains'" ("Burial" 12). Vladimir also reports that Elvira Shatayev "'believed that women should feel equal in [not equal to] the mountains. She said that, in joint teams with men, women were never allowed to go first'" ("Burial" 1).

Rich takes this male condescension and homage for the exceptional woman, the woman who can do what a man does without "betraying" her femininity, and turns it upside down. She also boldly presumes access to the "mystery" of the women's deaths by quoting from Elvira's diary—the diary her husband could not find—but transmutes this mystery into a mythic account that literalizes Wren's and Vladimir's hyperbolic compliments. Hence, the apotheosized Elvira truly is a fairy of the mountains, a genius of the place. Similarly, mountains are so far from hurting women that the merging of the women's bodies with the wind, snow, and sky is a consummation and affirmation of women's unity: "that *yes*   gathered / its forces   fused itself   and only just in time / to meet a *No* of no degrees" (*DCL* 4; Rich's italics). As Frye might describe this meeting of female community and nature, it is a conventional movement in comedy, which shifts our perspective to a place where "we see the action . . . from the point of view of a higher and better ordered world" (*Anatomy* 84). So in the poem, the women *"know now we have always been in danger / down in our separateness"* (*DCL* 6; Rich's italics). "The black hole" of nonentity, of individual death and dissolution, is met and overcome in a transgressive movement out of a social order dependent on women's isolation from one another to a mythic order where women and mountain fuse: "our frozen eyes unribboned   through the storm / we could have stitched that blueness   together   like a quilt" (*DCL* 5) suggests festivity, quilting bees, where each woman contributes a square to the quilt as an artful whole, but here transferred to a winter wasteland transformed by women's play—"the women I love   lightly flung   against the mountain" (*DCL* 5), as if resting from a dance with the wind their consort. The blue sky is itself the unribboned eyes of the women, hence, a visionary omnipresence to the scene. Rich carries this surreal image one step further, though, to undercut its implications of transcendence or removal: they "could have stitched that blueness / together" because such is their newly arrived-at power, but they do not, in no need of shelter or protective warmth from a natural scene so thoroughly imprinted with their presence.

In terms of literary form, "Phantasia for Elvira Shatayev" is a surprise, I believe, because we expect elegy, not comedy. The poem shares certain conventions with, for example, "Lycidas," "Adonais," or "When Lilacs Last in Dooryard Bloom'd." Like their literary antecedents, the women are resurrected as quasi-divine mountain nymphs. Yet Rich's setting is novel, evoking neither classical nor Christian myth nor even the imagery of spring's renewal. The women's eternal return does not depend on the seasonal cycle but belongs to an unchanging frozen landscape that utters power and danger. There is, quite simply, no pathos in the pathetic fallacy of "Phantasia," no mourning phase in the poem's structure or development. This motive belongs to the husband and, as such, is explicitly set off as narcissistic:

You come (I know this)   with your love   your loss
strapped to your body   with your tape-recorder   camera
ice-pick   against advisement
to give us burial in the snow   and in your mind
While my body lies out here
flashing like a prism   into your eyes
how could you sleep   You climbed here for yourself
we climbed for ourselves   (*DCL* 5)

Elegy consoles the living, and active celebration, not consolation, is Rich's intention. Even more, as a literary form elegy tends to focus on the bereaved voice of the poet and his fears over the limits of mortality on his genius.[18] Rich, in contrast, effaces her own identity to articulate the women's, willing the poet's disappearance from the scene. In this, she shares the women's meaning, generously giving her own voice to Shatayev and her team:

If in this sleep I speak
it's with a voice no longer personal
(I want to say   *with voices*)   (*DCL* 4; Rich's italics)

For elegy, one must turn to Christopher Wren's second newspaper piece and its shift of narrative focus to the husband. At the end of Wren's account, he writes, "Had the tragedy affected his own love of the mountains to which he had brought his wife, Mr. Shatayev was asked. 'No', he replied" ("Burial" 12). Wren's ending is rhetorically effective, and it triumphantly affirms the husband's mourning. The event has been, to borrow Hélène Cixous's terms, subjected—and I mean this both as subdued and integrated with the male writing subject—to "masculine incorporation":

Man cannot live without resigning himself to loss. He has to mourn. It's his way of withstanding castration. He goes through castration, that is, and by sublimation incorporates the lost object. Mourning, resigning oneself to loss, means not losing. When you've lost something and the loss is a dangerous one, you refuse to admit that something of your self might be lost in the lost object. So you "mourn," you make haste to recover the investment made in the lost object.[19]

Opposed to this masculine economy of incorporation is a feminine expenditure of self, a "not withholding":

Woman, though, does not mourn, does not resign herself to loss. She basically *takes up the challenge of loss* in order to go on living: she lives it, gives it life, is capable of unsparing loss. She does not hold onto loss, she loses without

holding onto loss. This makes her writing a body that overflows . . . as opposed
to masculine incorporation. . . . She loses, and doubtless it would be to the
death were it not for the intervention of those basic movements of a feminine
unconscious (this is how I would define *feminine sublimation*) which provide the
capacity of passing above it all by means of a form of oblivion which is not the
oblivion of burial or interment but the oblivion of *acceptance*. This is taking loss,
seizing it, living it. Leaping. This goes with not withholding, she does not
withhold. She does not withhold, hence the impression of constant return
evoked by this lack of withholding. It's like a kind of open memory that
ceaselessly makes way. And in the end, she will write this not-withholding, this
not-writing; she writes of not-writing, not-happening. . . . She crosses limits:
she is neither outside nor in, whereas the masculine would try to "bring the
outside in," if possible.[20] (Cixous's italics)

Although Cixous attempts to define rather than to enact a feminine expenditure of self, as she is seized by the "oblivion" she describes,
the incantatory and celebratory rhythms of her prose begin to resemble the sibylline voice in "Phantasia." In the opening of "Phantasia,"
Rich also invokes a form of oblivion, a "not-withholding" of personal
consciousness to give the women's voices agency: "If in this sleep I
speak / it's with a voice no longer personal" are lines that completely
erase, negate the lyric 'I'. "If" suggests the hypothetical and imaginary
realm where the words on the page exist; they are not written so much
as spoken, and in a sleep that immerses self and self-consciousness in
the unconscious and multiple selves. Like Cixous, Rich proposes a
"kind of open memory that ceaselessly makes way" where the poet is
"neither outside nor in" the experience she offers to her reader. Further, this entry of a "voice no longer personal" onto the scene of writing
is a "not-writing" both in its declaration of presence and immediacy of
"voices" and in the repeated assertion of being situated outside the
subject's enclosure of desire in language: "we had no need of words";
"What we were to learn   was simply   what we had / up here   as out
of all words" (*DCL* 4).

The title of Rich's poem is "out of all words" in a way similar to the
poem's repudiation of elegy and mourning. A *fantasia* is Italian in
derivation, originally applied to a musical piece in which several forms
are combined. Transposed to literature, the dictionary offers "a work
(as a poem or play) in which the author's fancy roves unrestricted by set
form or verisimilitude" and further, "something strange or foreign by
reason of grotesque, bizarre, or seemingly unreal qualities."[21] Rich's
title, then, suggests her awareness of defying convention, originating a
new form that in some of its metaphors (e.g., "frozen eyes unribboned") approaches the bizarre or grotesque. The Greek root, *phan-
tazein,* is closer to Rich's spelling, more generic in its meaning—appearance, image, imagination[22]—and for Rich, may well apply to the

poem's conjuring power, as if the poet-as-sibyl has raised the women's phantasmal forms in her words.

Yet the closest word to Rich's is *phantasiast.* Is Rich a phantasiast in the sense of one who writes a phantasia? The dictionary defines a phantasiast as a heretic, "one who believes that Christ's body was only a phantom."[23] The heresy denies incarnation in the body, a descent into flesh, asserting the primacy of Christ's spirit even in his earthly form. Aside from the connotations of heresy, departing from and defying doctrinaire belief, which are essential to Rich's poetic project, this definition is highly suggestive of the poetic guise Rich assumes in "Phantasia"—not re-presentation in literary form of what Shatayev thought and felt, not the ventriloquism of dramatic monologue where the speaker is a persona, a poetic device wrought for a series of artificed effects. Instead Rich seeks actual, unmediated presence in the form of Elvira Shatayev's spiritual phantom and the phantoms of the other climbers haunting the poem's words, imprinting them as surely as they do the mountain. As the phantom Christ comes to dispel the illusory reality of earthly existence in favor of an imagined, substantial spiritual love, so the women's recognition is one of rejecting an earthly life characterized only by waiting, routine tasks, and especially separateness in favor of a dream that refigures survival and love in unbounded communal form. The dream's limitlessness is symbolized in the natural forms of mountain, sky, sun, and snow and in the cultural form of "unfinished," "unbegun" potential for narrative:

> choosing ourselves   each other   and this life
> whose every breath   and grasp   and further foothold
> is somewhere   still enacted   and continuing   (*DCL* 5)

Endowing mountains with female presence is no mean feat in literature or myth, and in this, Rich's bold heroism as a poet, her special role in relation to female community, emerges forcefully. Like "the poet of earlier times" Rich imagines in *Of Woman Born,* she wants "to call up before women a different condition than the one we have known, to prime the imagination of women living today to conceive of other modes of existence."[24] Rich's "Phantasia for Elvira Shatayev" renames mountains as female and thereby argues with a long and powerful tradition in poetry that asserts not only the maleness of mountains but their divine and patriarchal signature, imprinted with the Father-God's mind.

Rich's "heresy" against an "old language" becomes apparent when we situate her myth of "unfinished" and "unbegun" potential for narrative against previous poets' renderings of the mountain epiphany. While I cannot argue confidently that Rich specifically intends to address the Romantic poets on Mont Blanc, I share Margaret Homans's belief that Rich is acutely aware of Lenin Peak as a familiar scene of writing. Mont Blanc is a virtual palimpsest of Romantic mythopoeia, a blank page overwritten with, in Homans's words, "the major Romantic project[s] of having the mind transcend its boundaries to imprint nature with its power . . . [and] to transcend the limits of death and find beyond it power and sublimity." Unlike Homans, who argues that Rich achieves the transcendence the Romantics sought but could not achieve "under the conditions of Romantic egotism,"[25] I regard "Phantasia" as repudiating transcendence in favor of immediate presence.

To illustrate Rich's heretical relation to lyric tradition, I will briefly examine Wordsworth's famous epiphany in *The Prelude* as he leaves Mont Blanc and the Alps. His moment of imaginative revelation unveils the world as incarnate word:

> The unfettered clouds and region of the Heavens,
> Tumult and peace, the darkness and the light—
> Were all like workings of one mind, the features
> Of the same face, blossoms upon one tree;
> The types and symbols of Eternity,
> Of first, and last, and midst, and without end.[26]

Editors frequently note Wordsworth's echo of both Revelation 1.8—"I am Alpha and Omega, the beginning and the ending, saith the Lord"—and Milton's declaration in *Paradise Lost* V.153–65 that the creation reflects its Creator, calling on all to extol "Him first, Him last, Him midst, and without end."[27] For Wordsworth the Alps are a "type" and "symbol" for originary creative power and a place where he perceives his own limitless imagination. Initially Wordsworth is subdued by the "unveiled . . . summit of Mont Blanc" (*NA* 272, 525), depicting himself in puny contention with a grandeur of design and/or destructive potential that mocks his own ability to generate images. He "grieved"

> To have a soulless image on the eye
> That had usurped upon a living thought
> That never more could be. (*NA* 272, 525–28)

The confused syntax itself reflects the dissolution of Wordsworth's ego before Mont Blanc's puissance. The mountain in a strange way imprints itself, usurping human consciousness ("a living thought"), and thereby threatening the poet's power. This is Wordsworth's overture to the famous ascent of the Alps. Only in retrospective vision does he turn his defeat and disappointment at not knowing "that we had crossed the Alps" into imagination's victory:

> Imagination—here the Power so called
> Through sad incompetence of human speech,
> That awful Power rose from the mind's abyss
> Like an unfathered vapour that enwraps,
> At once, some lonely traveller. I was lost;
> Halted without an effort to break through;
> But to my conscious soul I now can say—
> 'I recognise thy glory': in such strength
> Of usurpation, when the light of sense
> Goes out, but with a flash that has revealed
> The invisible world, doth greatness make abode.
> There harbours, whether we be young or old,
> Our destiny, our being's heart and home,
> Is with infinitude, and only there;
> With hope it is, hope that can never die,
> Effort, and expectation, and desire,
> And something evermore about to be.   (*NA* 274, 592–608)

As Geoffrey Hartman argues, Wordsworth's "adventurous spirit," questing for a nature commensurate "to deep childhood impressions, finds instead *itself,* and has to acknowledge that nature is no longer its proper subject or home."[28] Even more, "an unfathered vapour" and "such strength / Of usurpation" suggest Wordsworth's independence and defiance of a father-creator who seems peculiarly absent from His creation—Mont Blanc is a "soulless image," a white blank page that threatens human consciousness with erasure of all but its own sensory imprint on the eye. Only after a struggle in which Wordsworth achieves mastery of the mountain's meaning as a sign, moving from the feared "never more could be" of Mont Blanc to his own imaginative "infini-tude"—"And something evermore about to be"—can Wordsworth make peace with a father-God, re-cognizing and re-figuring his cre-ation as "first, and last, and midst, and without end." The resurgence of Wordsworth's famed "egotistical sublime" is suspended between "blankness and revelation" (*WP* 40), the abyss of usurpation by a "soulless image" and apocalyptic unveiling of the eternal "workings of one mind" and depends precariously yet effectively on Wordsworth's absence from the scene. As the Norton editor notes, the visionary experience of "Imagination" "occurred not in the Alps but at the time of writing"—"Before the eye and progress of my Song."[29] Wordsworth achieves an "independence of imagination from nature" (*WP* 41) that imitates a father-God's transcendence of his own creation. The poet's ego masters nature and experience in the act of writing.

The essential feature of Rich's poem, in contrast to Wordsworth, is its effort to be "out of all words," or to reiterate Cixous, "she writes of not-writing," "she is neither outside nor in, whereas the masculine would try to 'bring the outside in'. . . ." Hence, Rich easily permits her own ego to dissolve into the mountain-mind of Shatayev's team, perceiving no threat to her own poetic powers—no originary father-creator—but instead a new strength in collectivity. Her images embody that usurpation of a "living thought" which "grieved" Wordsworth. Instead of, in Hartman's words, "a curious melancholy related to the 'presence' of imagination and the 'absence' of nature" (*WP* 43)—a mourning phase that seems inherent in the Romantic poet's realization of his own power—Rich joyously suffuses nature with human consciousness. The blinding light that obliterates the husband's sleep—"While my body lies out here / flashing like a prism into your eyes" (*DCL* 5)—and the "cable of blue fire" that binds the women are oxymorons celebrating a heightened consciousness, not transcendence, of the body as a medium for a new relation between women and nature. Lenin Peak is at once a mountain-mind and mountain-body, the spiritual and physical incarnation of female power and archetype for Rich's phantasiast heresy against transcendence. The phantasiast heresy does not sustain a mind-body dualism; there is no "descent into the flesh" by Christ's spirit, hence, no higher/lower valuation placed on soul over body. As such, Rich's new myth for power may well exemplify in practice the "feminine sublimation" Cixous theorizes. Finally, beside Wordsworth's myth of transcendence, which depends on temporal discontinuity between experience and its writing, on compensatory mourning for original loss, and on the superior power, the mastery, of the poet's imagination, Rich places a myth that promises unity, not mastery, of the poet's imagination with experience, of mind and nature, of woman's body and soul. These claims are neither "gentle" in their demands upon women readers nor part of our "common language" for power and heroism. But then Rich dreams of a feminism and a poetry that will radically alter our perception of the world: "the necessity of poetry has to be stated over and over, but only to those who have reason to fear its power, or those who believe that language is 'only words' and that an old language is good enough for our descriptions of the world we are trying to transform" (*OLSS* 181).

Notes

1. From "When We Dead Awaken: Writing as Re-vision" (1971), in *On Lies, Secrets, and Silence: Selected Prose (1966–1978)* (New York: Norton, 1979), pp. 39, 46–47. Subsequent quotations from this volume will be indicated in parentheses as *OLSS* with page number.

2. Rich shares Audre Lorde's desire to challenge "patriarchal symbolic codes," as described in Estella Lauter's essay in this volume. Lorde's poem "Recreation," *The Black Unicorn* (New York: Norton, 1978), pp. 78–79, demonstrates both her own and Rich's desire to re-vision the symbolic codes in which "creation" is inscribed. Instead of the Father's Word creating World, Lorde "re-creates" the world in terms of two female bodies—"sexts"—in pleasurable erotic play.

3. James Joyce, *A Portrait of the Artist as a Young Man* (New York: The Viking Press, 1964), p. 171.

4. In his "Lines Composed a Few Miles Above Tintern Abbey on Revisiting the Banks of the Wye During a Tour, July 13, 1798" in *The Norton Anthology of English Literature,* ed. M. H. Abrams et al., 5th ed. (New York: Norton, 1986), vol. 2, 155–58, Wordsworth introduces Dorothy in the final section of his poem, as one who bears witness to what he has lost, and as text for what Wordsworth once was:

> . . . in thy *voice* I catch
> The *language* of my former heart, and *read*
> My former pleasures in the shooting lights
> Of thy wild eyes. Oh! yet a little while
> May I behold in thee what I was once.
> My dear, dear Sister!   (ll. 116–21; italics added)

5. In "Among School Children" ("I dream of a Ledaean body"), in *Selected Poems and Two Plays of William Butler Yeats,* ed. M. L. Rosenthal (New York: Collier Books, 1962), p. 115.

6. *Of Woman Born: Motherhood as Experience and Institution* (New York: Norton, 1976), p. 31.

7. This is Joanne Feit Diehl's term in " 'Cartographies of Silence': Rich's *Common Language* and the Woman Poet," in *Reading Adrienne Rich: Reviews and Re-Visions, 1951–81,* ed. Jane Roberta Cooper (Ann Arbor: University of Michigan Press, 1984), p. 104.

8. "Wordsworth's Preface of 1800, with a collation of the Enlarged Preface of 1802," in *Lyrical Ballads 1798,* ed. W. J. B. Owen (London: Oxford University Press, 1969), p. 165.

9. "Natural Resources" (1977), in *The Dream of a Common Language: Poems 1974–1977* (New York: Norton, 1978), p. 66. Subsequent quotations from this volume will be cited parenthetically as *DCL* with page numbers.

10. "What is a poet? To whom does he address himself? And what language is to be expected from him? He is a man speaking to men; a man, it is true, endued with more lively sensibility, more enthusiasm and tenderness, who has a greater knowledge of human nature, and a more comprehensive soul." "Wordsworth's Preface of 1800," p. 165.

11. "North American Time" (1983), in *Your Native Land, Your Life: Poems* (New York: Norton, 1986), pp. 33, 34.

12. There are strong similarities between Rich's efforts to develop a new poetics in this volume and what Holly Laird describes in her essay on *Aurora Leigh* as Elizabeth Barrett Browning's attempt to reconcile "ethical discussion and ecstatic inspiration," the didactic agenda of Carlyle with the expressive aesthetic of Wordsworth, in her own ars poetica.

13. "Blood, Bread, and Poetry: The Location of the Poet" (1984), in *Blood, Bread, and Poetry: Selected Prose (1979–1985)* (New York: Norton, 1986), pp. 170, 178.

14. See, for example, Rich's chapter, "Anger and Tenderness," in *Of Woman Born* (pp. 21–40), where she quotes extensively from her diaries in the 1960s concerning her "selfish" need for a life apart from her children in her poetry. In this period, she clearly regarded her poetry-writing as a mode of self-realization: "For me, poetry was where I lived as no one's mother, where I existed as myself" (31). Since then, it is equally clear that Rich has come to repudiate a poetry of elitist self-absorption as politically irresponsible.

15. "8 Soviet Women Climbers Killed by Storm in Lenin Peak Ascent," *New York Times*, August 13, 1974, sec. A, pp. 1, 6. Subsequent quotations from this article will be indicated in parentheses as "8 Soviet Women" with page number.

16. *Anatomy of Criticism: Four Essays* (New York: Atheneum, 1965), p. 120. Subsequent quotations from this text will be indicated in parentheses as *Anatomy* with page number.

17. "Burial on Soviet Peak: A Husband's Tribute," *New York Times*, September 25, 1974, sec. A, pp. 1, 12. Subsequent quotations from this article will be indicated in parentheses as "Burial" with page number.

18. Edward King, for example, is forgotten in Milton's *tour de force*. As Robert Graves ironically comments, "Milton was obsessed by thoughts of his own fame. His strongest reaction to the news of Lycidas's drowning was: 'Heavens, it might have been myself! Cut down before my prime, cheated of immortal fame!'" Quoted in *Milton's 'Lycidas'*, ed. Scott Elledge (New York: Harper & Row, 1966), p. 240.

19. "Castration or Decapitation?" trans. Annette Kuhn, *Signs* 7 (1981), 54.

20. *Ibid.*

21. *Webster's Third New International Dictionary,* unabridged ed. (Springfield, Mass.: G. C. Merriam Co. 1971), pp. 822–23.

22. *Third International*, under "fancy," p. 821.

23. *Third International*, p. 1693.

24. Pages 107–8.

25. *Women Writers and Poetic Identity* (Princeton, N.J.: Princeton University Press, 1980), p. 233.

26. From Book 6, ll. 635–41, in *The Norton Anthology*, vol. 2, p. 275. All citations from Book 6 of *The Prelude* are taken from this abridged version and will subsequently be indicated as *NA* with page and line numbers.

27. *Norton Anthology*, n. 4.

28. *Wordsworth's Poetry 1787–1814* (New Haven, Conn.: Yale University Press, 1971), p. 39. Subsequent quotations from this text are cited parenthetically as *WP* with page number.

29. See n. 8, p. 284.

Chapter 3
Lyric Voice and Sexual Difference in Elizabeth Bishop

Kathleen Brogan

In her 1983 review of Elizabeth Bishop's posthumously published *Complete Poems,* Adrienne Rich calls for new readings of Bishop, sensitive to her understanding of "outsiderhood" and "difference."[1] Rich acknowledges that her view of Bishop as an outsider who "was critically and consciously trying to explore marginality, power and powerlessness" (*BBP* 135) came late, after years of difficulty with Bishop's poetry. As a young poet "looking for a female genealogy," she failed to find in Bishop's polished, reserved work a model for the boldly personal, politically engaged feminine aesthetics Rich herself would later define. Rich ascribes her earlier short-sightedness to her own urgent need for an unequivocally "clear female tradition," a need that could not accommodate that tradition's veiled, "often cryptic" expression in Bishop's work (*BBP* 125).

It is hardly surprising that a poet like Rich would find Bishop's cooler, more guarded poetry difficult to claim for a "clear female tradition." What is more striking is the realization that Bishop's handling of "marginality"—which Rich now identifies as Bishop's engagement of the defining concerns of a women's tradition—is largely responsible for the neglect of her work by some younger poets—and, until very recently, feminist critics—committed to defining a distinctly female voice. Bishop's feminist readers have been troubled by the lack of a direct, explicit presentation of gender issues and by the absence of a strong, central, explicitly female voice in her poetry, a voice like that of Rich's when, toward the end of a cycle of love poems, she acknowledges, "I am Adrienne alone" (*DCL* 34).[2] Bishop carefully hides the

gender of her speakers, creating an unobtrusive, reticent poetic persona, quite unlike Rich's own experiment with the androgynous voice,
which still retains a boldly central stance in the poem: "I am here"; "I
am she: I am he"; "I am the androgyne" (*DW* 24, 19). Diving into the
wreck of history to cut away obfuscating myth, Rich's androgyne,
usurping the masculine role of quester, draws the poem about himself/
herself. In "When We Dead Awaken: Writing as Re-vision," Rich associates her movement into the self-proclaiming "I" (from the oblique
"she" of "Snapshots of a Daughter-in-Law") with a literary coming into
one's own (*OLSS* 44–45). Her poetic persona arrogates the traditional
lyric voice, now radicalized by its definition as female: "I am an American woman" (*PSN* 238), "I am a woman in the prime of life" (*WC* 19),
and daringly invoking the stance of poet as divine creator, "I am I"
(*PSN* 225).[3]

Bishop's speakers, by contrast, hover at the edges of a scene, often
physically peripheral to the center of interest. Compounding her lyric
reticence is the frequent choice of the plural voice, which mutes the
focus on self. Less than a quarter of the poems Bishop published from
1936 to 1976 refer to an "I." When the "I" does appear, it is typically
elusive, receding quickly from view. In "At the Fishhouses," for example, we are suddenly alerted to the poet's presence thirty-two lines into
the poem when another figure "accepts a Lucky Strike."[4] When, almost
twenty lines later, the speaker's first-person pronoun finally appears, it
is an "I" scantily elaborated, who observes the sea from the shore and,
unlike Rich's questing poet-diver, *imagines* immersion. "In the Waiting
Room" is the only poem in which Bishop names herself ("you are an
Elizabeth"), but the second-person address takes an outsider's stance in
relation to the self—a self-presentation strikingly different from Rich's
"I am Adrienne alone."

Focusing on Bishop's definition of an unobtrusive, ambiguously
gendered, peripherally positioned lyric voice, I would like to pursue
Rich's suggestion that Bishop's work explores issues of outsiderhood
and difference. Bishop's mapping of lyric voice offers, I will argue, a
critique of the way literary authority is often constituted through the
construction of a gendered hierarchy, and through the marginalization
or appropriation of otherness.[5] The question of lyric positioning is, in
Bishop's work, inextricably linked to her self-positioning in relation to
literary tradition. Bishop's famed elusiveness, the marginal stance she
assumes within the space of the poem, relates to her resistance to the
centrism integral to the Transcendentalist tradition she claimed for
herself.[6] While she recognized herself as an essentially Romantic poet,
an inheritor of the Emersonian sublime, Bishop rejects the strong,
central, implicitly masculine voice that marks the Romantic lyric, a

voice that tends to objectify, dominate, or internalize its subjects. Her alternative to the masculine, centrally positioned lyric self is a voice that is socially or geographically marginal, often plural, and sexually ambiguous. In looking at Bishop's choice of a marginal lyric stance and her resistance to sexual specificity, I will also briefly touch on how her lyric positioning relates to a thematics of outsiderhood. Bishop's choice of the outsider's stance, as well as her rejection of a strong, central female voice, suggests that we need to remain open to forms of revisionism in women's writing that resist easy location in Rich's "clear female tradition." The portrait of the female poet that emerges in Bishop's poems invites us to consider a revisionism more radical than the simple transposition of female for male, the valorization of the opposite side of a hierarchical gender dualism. To read Bishop's decentered, sexually ambiguous voice as an evasion of female identity is to miss the deeply subversive implications of her project.

Early in her career, Bishop linked the insistence on centrality of voice with masculinity and aggression. In "Roosters" (1941), from her first volume, *North and South*, "we" are awoken by the "horrible insistence" of cock cries. "Combative" roosters commandeer subject hens with their militaristic parading and insistence on ownership:

> At four o'clock
> in the gun-metal blue dark
> we hear the first crow of the first cock
>
> . . . .
> Cries galore
> come from the water-closet door,
> from the dropping-plastered henhouse floor,
>
> where in the blue blur
> their rustling wives admire,
> the roosters brace their cruel feet and glare
>
> with stupid eyes
> while from their beaks there rise
> the uncontrolled, traditional cries.
>
> Deep from protruding chests
> in green-gold medals dressed,
> planned to command and terrorize the rest,
>
> the many wives
> who lead hens' lives
> of being courted and despised . . . (35)

As the poem progresses, the aggression implicit in the roosters' possessiveness and vanity breaks into open warfare. The roosters begin to fight in midair, their metallic feathers that fall in flames invoking the image of warplanes. Bishop sent a draft of "Roosters" to Marianne Moore who, disapproving of the jingly rhythm, repetitions, and indecorous details, revised and retyped the poem, giving it the new title, "The Cock." Bishop wrote back: "I cherish my 'water-closet' and other sordidities because I want to emphasize the essential baseness of militarism. . . . That's why, although I see what *you* mean . . . I want to keep as the title the rather contemptuous word ROOSTERS rather than the more classical COCK; and I want to repeat the 'gun-metal'. (I also had in mind the violent roosters Picasso did in connection with his GUERNICA picture.) . . . I can't bring myself to sacrifice what (I think) is a very important 'violence' of tone. . . ."[7] The violence that Bishop locates in the territoriality of the roosters is founded on a gendered structure of oppression at home, in which the females are "terrorize[d]"—subjected first to submission, finally to death (they must fall with their "husbands"). The repetition of the word "first" ("the first crow of the first cock") underscores the roosters' insistence on their own precedence. In attempting to establish themselves as prior they relegate all others to a position of secondariness.

The cries of the males, Bishop takes care to point out, are "traditional," implicating both societal and literary convention. The poem suggests that in becoming authorized as traditional, one voice gains monopoly over other voices, establishing itself as the dominant, central voice through the suppression or marginalization of other (here, female) voices. "Roosters" reveals the basis of Bishop's antipathy for the self-aggrandizement of a centrist (identified as masculine) poetic stance. Each rooster maniacally insists on the focal position of his own existence; each cry of "'Here!' and 'Here!'" pulls the world around it, a self-locating that gives the cock the right to "tell us how to live":

> each one an active
> displacement in perspective;
> each screaming, "This is where I live!"   (36)

The stance of the roosters may be read as a brutally comic version of the Emersonian "central man." Emerson envisions the process of symbolization as a remapping, an energetic, willful reorganization of a silent (silenced, feminized) landscape in which the (male) seer/sayer arrogates a central position: the poet "unfixes the land and the sea, makes them revolve around the axis of his primary thought, and disposes them anew. Possessed himself by a heroic passion, he uses matter as symbols of it."[8] The roosters' voice, which accompanies grotesquely "heroic" combat, similarly remaps the landscape; each cock's solitary, self-announced "I" becomes one of many "glass-headed pins" "marking out maps like Rand McNally's," the mapping of "war-projects," as Bishop explained to Moore. The angry question, "Roosters, what are you projecting?" suggests the image of a projection map, the planning of war, as well as the externalization of an internal, eroticized violence ("deep from raw throats / a senseless order floats / all over town"). The roosters' projection, their insistence on defining a perspective determined by an aggressively central self, dramatizes the potential oppressiveness of an Emersonian poetic topography. Each cock's cry of "This is where I live!" parodically invokes Emerson's metaphoric connection in "Nature" between the establishment of a home and the achievement of centrality and dominion over nature ("Every spirit builds itself a house; and beyond its house, a world. . . . Know then, that the world exists for you").[9]

In "Roosters" Bishop identifies the self-assertive cry, which in usurping a central position attempts to displace all other "perspective," as the "traditional" masculine voice. The ultimate rejection of the roosters' cry—"and what he sung / no matter"—at once identifies the cock song as a poetic voice and undermines the validity of such a stance. The self-centering "Here!" is linked to both aggression and the silencing of peripheral voices (the hens "admire," but they have no voice of their own).

Bishop, it should be emphasized, questions both terms of the Emersonian definition of the poet as "central man," understanding the dangers of any system of exclusivity and hierarchy, whether based on gender or on positioning. The claim to centrality traces a hierarchical map that effectively marginalizes that which lies beyond the defined center. Because one's centrality both creates and depends on the peripheral positioning of others, the threat of the excluded must be suppressed through subordination and silence (the condition of the hens who revolve around the roosters). "Roosters" exposes the flaw in an Emersonian model of poetic representation. In expanding the self to incorporate the "Not-Me" into the "Me," the Emersonian poet eradicates the very otherness he claims to speak for, his representation a narcissistic magnification of his own self. By multiplying the roosters so that each comically cancels the central stance of the other's "I," Bishop suggests that a central poetic position exists only as imposition, and is ultimately untenable.

In contrast to the rooster's aggressive self-definition, the narrative voice of the poem remains vaguely defined, marginal to the central action of the roosters: the "we" referred to directly only once at the beginning of the poem recede, surfacing briefly for an angry direct address to the roosters ("Roosters, what are you projecting? / . . . what right have you to give / commands and tell us how to live"), to return through the indirect suggestion of personal sorrow at the poem's end, when the "cocks are now almost inaudible." The gender as well as the relationship of the "we" is unclear, although the plot of sad awakening casts the poem as an alba, suggesting two lovers—possibly, given Bishop's own affectional choices and the strong male/female polarization of the poem's opening, both women. The oblique presence of the lovers distinguishes them positively from the uncontrollable egotism of the cocks. Yet any simple opposition between male aggression and female pacifism is overturned by a blurring of outside and inside. The put-upon "we" violently awoken in the "gun-metal blue dark" of what is presumably a bedroom are clearly linked to the dominated, more submissive hens in the "blue blur" outside. Less obvious but more ominous is the resemblance between the lovers and the roosters themselves. The cocks' cries of " 'Here!' and 'Here!' " remind the speaker of her own morally compromised location: "*here* where are / unwanted love, conceit and war" (emphasis added). The line between enemy and self breaks down, as the speaker acknowledges the potential for a rooster-like violence that is not gender-specific. The plot of (male) friendship and betrayal that unfolds in the relationship of Christ and Peter described in the poem's second half may also have poisoned the intimacy of the poem's (female?) lovers: "how could the night have come to grief?" As Susan Schweik has argued in her reading of "Roosters," the "latent private strain" between the lovers "implicates the woman speaker in psychic structures of conflict, violence, and betrayal formerly reserved for specifically male or vaguely generalized others.[10]

In resisting a clearly gendered voice, Bishop accomplishes two things: she undoes the male/female dichotomy that characterizes the hierarchical world of the roosters and suggests that character traits (such as propensities for violence or forgiveness) transcend gender. The very implication that "we" share with the roosters an impulse toward aggression breaks down the singularity and exclusiveness that each rooster's voice attempts to legislate. In recognizing difference while also overturning clear boundary distinctions between, in the poem's final words, "enemy, or friend," the poem's "we" make their most positive turn away from the violence the roosters represent. The plurality of the speaking voice aligns with this rejection of a self-dramatizing, singular "I," which maintains its superiority by imperialistically remapping the terrain with itself as center. Evident in *North and South* and continuing throughout her career, the tendency toward plural voice resists lyric self-aggrandizement as well as evades the reductive, dangerously oppositional structure of a gendered dualism.

"The End of March" (1975), a late poem in which the narrative voice modulates between "we" and "I," provides a particularly interesting case of Bishop's use of the plural voice because of the connection it establishes between plurality, marginality, and outsiderhood. The poem, which reflects back on the many images of temporary, vulnerable enclosures that abound in Bishop's work, is important to an understanding of her handling of positioning or placement. Throughout Bishop's career we find a tension between nostalgia for the securities of home and the sense of enclosure as dangerously static or narcissistically self-validating (as in "Roosters," where the aggressive possession of one's own place ("This is where I live!") links to the assumption of a single, central perspective and dominion over others). Bishop moves, however, toward an acceptance of her position as that of the outsider; the inside or central position, though temptingly protected, becomes seen as increasingly threatening to her authorial voice.

An icy offshore wind creates a barrier between the beach-walkers and the sea, the traditional source of inspiration in the genre to which "The End of March" belongs, the American shore ode.[11] The desired but unattained end of a cold beach walk, a "proto-dream-house, / my crypto-dream-house" (179) appears as a coffinlike "crooked box." While the dream-house lures with the promise of a shell-like enclosure, the retirement it offers veers dangerously close to a cessation of all work (she would "retire there and do *nothing*"), and possibly of life. The poem hints that the sanctuary provides a security that will prove nullifying. Turning away from the house, turning back to the beach, the speaker is rewarded with a landscape suddenly illuminated:

> The sun came out for just a minute.
> For just a minute, set in their bezels of sand,
> the drab, damp, scattered stones
> were multi-colored,
> and all those high enough threw out long shadows,
> individual shadows, then pulled them in again.
> They could have been teasing the lion sun,
> except that now he was behind them
> —a sun who'd walked the beach the last low tide,
> making those big, majestic paw-prints . . .   (180)

Harold Bloom has suggested that the "lion sun" refers us to Wallace Stevens in "An Ordinary Evening in New Haven," in which his "incessant use of the same figure" "culminates": "The great cat must stand potent in the sun." Bloom observes that Stevens's "lion tends to represent poetry as a destructive force, as the imposition of the poet's will-to-power over reality," while Bishop's lion sun has "something better to do than stand potent in itself. The path away from poetry as a destructive force can only be through play, the play of trope."[12] Play enters the poem through the "long shadows" that tease the lion sun, a vision only possible when "we" turn away from the dream house and, so to speak, turn the other cheek to the harsh landscape ("On the way back our faces froze on the other side"). The gesture of self-exposure (very different, as Bloom notes, from violent self-imposition) and acceptance of the outsider's position are rewarded by the momentary opening out (the rocks "threw out" their shadows) of a previously ungenerous, "indrawn" landscape.

In walking the beach, Bishop's figures re-enact the earlier movement of the

> . . . sun who'd walked the beach the last low tide,
> making those big, majestic paw-prints,
> who perhaps had batted a kite out of the sky to play with.

Following the lion sun's steps, the beach-walkers retrace a literary tradition (the American shore ode) that includes Whitman and Stevens (whose "paw-prints" or self-inscriptions may loom "big" and "majestic" to poets engaging this tradition). In representing "the poet's will-to-power over reality," the lion sun figures Stevens's "central man," his version of the "sovereign" Emersonian poet who "stands on the centre."[13] The playfulness of the lion sun, however, differs from the gentler teasing of the "long shadows" because of its implicit violence: the poem's speakers have already encountered a man-sized, sodden ghost, a "thick white snarl" of kite string awash at the edge of the water. By turning away from the dream house, the beach-walkers position the lion sun, representative of masculine power, the dominion over nature or otherness, and a centrist or Emersonian stance, "behind" the more delicate lights of the "multi-colored" stones.[14]

The move away from the singular sun of masculine tradition to the many, variously colored lights of a more oblique sublime finds a parallel in the modulation of voice: the poem's "we" turns into an "I" when the "crypto-dream-house" is considered, but reverts back to the plural when that isolating retirement is rejected. Recent work by feminist critics has identified the choice of the plural voice as a characteristic revisionist technique of women writers. Margaret Homans, for example, argues that Dickinson's poetic technique of splitting into two selves (as in "Abdication— / Me—of Me" or "Ourself behind Ourself") constitutes an effort to dismantle the "unitary self" and the self-other dualism inherent in the Emersonian tradition. Homans sees the same criticism of Romantic egotism underlying the move toward a collective voice in contemporary poetry by women.[15]

Bishop's use of the plural speaker engages this subversive tactic of self-multiplicity, defeating the expectations of a genre that traditionally emphasizes the singularity of the poet-speaker. "Exchanging Hats" (1956), written in the middle of her career, supports the view that the resistance to sexual specificity in Bishop's poetry is motivated by a desire to subvert conventionally restrictive understandings of gender division. The poem, as many critics have noticed, forwards Bishop's most direct attack on a reductive sexual dualism:

> Unfunny uncles who insist
> in trying on a lady's hat,
> —oh, even if the joke falls flat,
> we share your slight transvestite twist
>
> in spite of our embarrassment.
> Costume and custom are complex.
> The headgear of the other sex
> inspires us to experiment.
>
> . . . .
>
> Unfunny uncle, you who wore a
> hat too big, or one too many,
> tell us, can't you, are there any
> stars inside your black fedora?
>
> Aunt exemplary and slim,
> with avernal eyes, we wonder
> what slow changes they see under
> their vast, shady, turned-down brim.   (200–201)

Sexual identities, represented by gender-specific dress, are manipulable, inconstant, and fluctuating with "the tides of fashion," conventional, as the jingling of "costume" and "custom" suggests. Bishop hints, in references to the outmoded "crown" and "miter," that political hierarchies are similarly unnatural, existing as cultural impositions validated through false claims to universality. One's "true" identity remains indeterminate: we never discover what lies in the uncle's magic black fedora. Affirming that mysterious "slow changes" rather than a fixed identity shape the self, the poem comically uncovers a knowledge confronted only in darkness and secrecy: the fictive nature of an unambiguous, unitary sexual identity.

The experimental "transvestite twist" of the aunts and uncles relates to the "fantasies of transvestism" that Sandra Gilbert finds in modernist literature. Gilbert argues that male and female modernists handle in markedly different ways the imagery of clothing and its relation to sexual identity. Finding in the work of male writers a dichotomy between a sexually fixed true self and the possible falsification of costume, Gilbert observes that "feminist modernist costume imagery . . . implies that no one, male or female, can or should be confined to a uni-form, a single form or self." Women writers have attempted 'to define a gender-free reality behind or beneath myth, an ontological essence so pure, so free that 'it' can 'inhabit' any self, any costume."[16] Bishop's resistance to a strongly defined feminine voice, which has troubled women writers who prefer to center their work in specifically female experience, can be seen as an expression of this implicitly feminist effort to discover an identity that moves beyond a rigid gender dichotomy and notions of a naturally gendered identity. The "we" who speak in "Exchanging Hats" escape through their multiplicity the conventional gender definition that the aunt and uncle, each repressed by a "straight"-jacketing sexual code, receive. Through a sexually indefinite plurality they elude confinement in what Hélène Cixous calls "a two-term system, related to 'the' couple man/woman."[17]

Significantly, in the most explicitly autobiographical of Bishop's poems (the only one in which she names herself: "you are an *Elizabeth*"), the move from the singular to the communal protagonist provides the central drama of the poem. "In the Waiting Room" (1971), the opening poem of Bishop's last volume, dramatizes the discovery of a gendered self and the shaping of a poetic subjectivity by circling back to the poet's childhood to re-envision that moment when the child first finds her voice.

The occasion of the poem is a trip to the dentist's office with "Aunt Consuelo," taken three days before the speaker's seventh birthday. While the aunt is inside the office, the child, in the outer waiting room, reads the recent *National Geographic* with a mixture of curiosity and fear. The images come to the child as violently unsettling: dark, ashy volcanoes that suddenly erupt; explorers in militaristic garb; black women and babies with distorted bodies; a dead man, the prey of cannibals. The series of photographs prepares for the central action of the poem, when the child loses a sense of clear ego boundaries, and inner and outer space become confused:

Suddenly, from inside,
came an *oh!* of pain
—Aunt Consuelo's voice—
not very loud or long.
I wasn't at all surprised;
even then I knew she was
a foolish, timid woman.
I might have been embarrassed,
but wasn't. What took me
completely by surprise
was that it was *me*:
my voice, in my mouth.
Without thinking at all
I was my foolish aunt,
I—we—were falling, falling,
our eyes glued to the cover
of the *National Geographic*,
February, 1918.   (160)

Images of inner and outer space—the interior space of the poem and
the external world, the division of the interior setting into inner and
outer rooms, the inside and outside shots of the volcano—mirror the
speaker's confusion about the boundaries of the self. The merging of
self with other is experienced as a frightening loss of consciousness, an
engulfment by a "big black wave." The child attempts to recover herself
by reminding herself of her age and coming birthday, but finds that her
personal specificity only circles back to an identity with others: "I felt:
you are an *I*, / you are an *Elizabeth*, / you are one of *them*" (160).

Fifteen years before the appearance of "In the Waiting Room," Bishop published a prose account of the trip to the dentist's office, part of a
memoir of her childhood years in Worcester. An important difference
from that earlier, perhaps more strictly factual, account is the inclusion
of the magazine's photographs. In the earlier version, the young Elizabeth never opens the magazine but stares at the cover and reads the
date, February 1918. The series of photographs that Bishop describes
both anticipates the child's disorienting shift in identity (the erupting
volcano figuring the child's erupting self-realization) and introduces
the issue of intercultural violence. Photographed in Africa, the white
explorers Osa and Martin Johnson are outfitted "in riding breeches, /
laced boots, and pith helmets," an almost military garb that underlines
the implicit aggression of their project to investigate a "primitive"
culture. Their powerful position is reflected, as Lee Edelman has observed, in the stance of the child herself, whose reading of the *National*

Geographic grants her the ethnographer's illusion of "mastery."[18] Imaging the objectification of the human (a dead man becomes an object to be consumed) and, more specifically, the circumscription of women and children, whose bodies are distorted by cultural convention, the photographs work to undermine the child's initial sense of mastery and induce the vertigo that leads to the cry of pain. Particularly fascinating to the reading child are the naked bodies of the women, whose "awful hanging breasts" are mentioned again later in the poem, breasts that remind her of the mature female body she will acquire. Thus, the child's confrontation with her own self ("what it was I was") foregrounds her simultaneous discovery of her undeniably female identity and the cultural objectification of the female, an objectification that ironically she enacts herself in reading the *National Geographic*. Elizabeth thus finds herself, as inheritor of both her own culture's imperialism and the transcultural history of female objectification, both privileged voyeur and, distressingly, object held up to vision.

The child's splitting of the self, through this double identification, into multiple selves is forecasted in the phrasing of the earlier prose account:

> I felt . . . *myself*. In a few days it would be my seventh birthday. I felt *I, I, I,* and looked at the three strangers in panic. I was *one* of them too, inside my scabby body and wheezing lungs. "You're in for it now," something said. How had I got tricked into such a false position? I would be like that woman opposite who smiled at me so falsely every once in a while.[19]

The recognition of a newly found and inescapable identity ("*I, I, I,*") introduces a frightening multiplicity of self; the "three strangers" the young Elizabeth views with panic are both the "two men and a plump middle-aged lady" and the strange triple *I* that composes her self—a self so strange that it is experienced as an alien place in which one dwells ("How strange you are, inside looking out"). The child vaguely understands that she's "in for it": inside her own body, as well as inside a larger human community (the values of which define how she experiences her own body as well as the bodies of others).

The condescension with which she views the prospect of shared identity (how awful to be like "that woman opposite") translates in the poetic version as a distaste for her aunt, whose description as "a foolish, timid woman" recalls common, derogatory caricatures of women. The child's attempt to distance herself from the aunt may reflect, given her new, subliminal awareness of the cultural construction of gender, a repugnance for a stereotypic, misogynistically framed female identity. Unlike the prose account, however, the poem valorizes the recognition of connectedness by associating interpersonal merging, however terrifyingly disorienting, with the valuable acquisition of voice (the cry, "the family voice / I felt in my throat" is not heard in the memoir). The child's finding of voice marks a discovery of a poetic self. She inherits her voice when she loses a sense of herself as rigidly defined, individual, unrelated to others: the identification with her aunt (whose name is changed from Jenny to "Consuelo" to introduce cultural difference as well as the idea of consolation or sympathy) extends to the photographed black women, and finally to an empathy with humankind: we are, strangely, "all just one."

The experience of merging attaches to the vicarious sharing of pain, and specifically to the sharing of a woman's pain. The two voices become one with a cry that, as many critics have noticed, recalls the scream of the poet's mother in the autobiographical short story, "In the Village." The mother's scream, which heralds her final slipping into insanity, erases the identity of the child: "She screamed. The child vanishes" (253). In the poetic recasting of this scene, the aunt replaces the lost mother, and at the sound of their shared cry, the child loses herself only to find, through the "mother"-daughter merging, a larger sense of self that extends beyond rigid individuation. In commenting on Bishop's poem, Alicia Ostriker has noted the applicability of Nancy Chodorow's argument that a girl's unbroken pre-oedipal identification with her mother forms the basis for a disposition toward empathetic bonding and community in general.[20] While the child Elizabeth moves from her moment of shared identity to a realization of interhuman connectedness, however, it must be emphasized that Bishop's poem does not represent interpersonal merging as particularly easy or natural for the emergent female poet. Chodorow tends to locate ambivalent struggle for girls less in bonding than in the process of individuation: difficulty arises in separating from, rather than in identifying with, the m/other. Consonant with her rejection of a revisionism that simply valorizes the opposite term of a hierarchical gender dualism, Bishop resists the comforts of any notion of an authentic female identity defined by a tendency toward empathy. In viewing the photographs Elizabeth comes to a recognition of her own female sexuality at the same time that she confronts both the cultural construction of the feminine and her complicity in the objectification of what is other. As in "Roosters," the speaker of "In the Waiting Room" does not completely escape implication in the very violence the poem condemns.

Elizabeth's similarity to both victims and aggressors, the "unlikely" connection that both induces the child's vertigo and gives her voice, holds out a possible alternative to an aggression rooted in the belief in absolute difference. The return to individual separateness at the end of the poem marks a return to war:

Then I was back in it.
The War was on. Outside,
in Worcester, Massachusetts,
were night and slush and cold,
and it was still the fifth
of February, 1918.   (161)

In Bishop's original account of her experience in the waiting room, no mention of war is made, although the memoir discusses the war earlier (using the same sentence, "The War was on"). By directly referring to the war only indirectly introduced earlier in the poem by the 1918 date, Bishop underscores the intercultural aggression that informs the *National Geographic*'s photographs, which emphasize cultural opposition: Osa and Martin Johnson's heavy, almost armored, dress preserves their absolute separateness from the naked Africans they encounter, a separateness the child cannot maintain.

Many critics have noted that the poem's photographs do not in fact appear in the February 1918 issue of the *National Geographic*, a situation made more puzzling by Bishop's assertion in an interview that she had actually read the March issue and had mistaken the date; the photographs, however, do not appear in either issue. The February issue, however, becomes more interesting when we consider not what it lacks but what it does contain: articles on war and photographs of uniformed soldiers. (The entire year of *National Geographic* issues features heavy coverage of wartime activities, along with numerous photographs of troops and weapons.) In transposing the ethnographic photographs for war scenes, Bishop exposes the violence of an identity authorized by the myth of absolute otherness. The link between the impulse toward aggression and the divisiveness of rigid self-definition that Bishop establishes here echoes the similar tactic in "Roosters," in which the "we" woken by cock cries are set against the self-centeredness of the "very combative" roosters.

"In the Waiting Room" conflates the eruption of a self-consciously female self with the discovery of cultural and sexual objectification. Female identity is defined here less as outsiderhood than as the blurring of inside and outside, which is mapped as the marginal zone of the waiting room, positioned between the outside world and the inner office. While the figure of Elizabeth occupies, in contrast to the voices of "Roosters" and "The End of March," a poetically central position, the poem works to undermine any clear opposition between what is positioned as central (Elizabeth, her own culture) and as marginal (the aunt, the strangers, other cultures).

This blurring of boundaries finds reflection in "Santarém," published in 1978, seven years after the appearance of "In the Waiting Room." In "Santarém" Bishop comments on her rejection of a restrictively gender-coded self:

> Of course I may be remembering it all wrong
> after, after—how many years?
>
> That golden evening I really wanted to go no farther;
> more than anything else I wanted to stay awhile
> in that conflux of two great rivers, Tapajós, Amazon,
> grandly, silently flowing, flowing east.
> ·
> I liked the place; I liked the idea of the place.
> Two rivers. Hadn't two rivers sprung
> from the Garden of Eden? No, that was four
> and they'd diverged. Here only two
> and coming together. Even if one were tempted
> to literary interpretations
> such as: life/death, right/wrong, male/female
> —such notions would have resolved, dissolved, straight off
> in that watery, dazzling dialectic.   (185)

"[T]wo / . . . coming together" rather than "diverg[ing]" recalls Bishop's favored plural, sexually ambiguous voice. "Santarém," although spoken by a singular voice, sets a more fluid self against the rigid gender division that the poem locates in patriarchal biblical tradition (appropriately, a church appears later in the poem divided by a "crack all the way down" its tower). As Joanne Feit Diehl, who notes the significance of Eden as the original site of "sexual differentiation," points out, Bishop's rejection of sexual dualism revises both the Judaeo-Christian tradition and the "hieratic distinctions of self-other" central to Emersonianism.[21]

The poem's speaker, as traveler, maintains a peripheral, outsider's relation to the scene described, a position strongly contrasting that of the Portuguese conquistadors in the earlier "Brazil, January 1, 1502," who install themselves as the rightful possessors of a New World they attempt to refashion in Edenic terms. Bishop's career-long predilection for the outsider's perspective leads me to qualify Diehl's view that in her work Bishop "recovers herself as center of a self-made world."[22] Rarely do Bishop's poems, even those most strongly revisionist, reposition her centrally; more characteristically, they emphasize the degree to which "self-made" worlds tend to be, as both "Brazil, January 1" and "Roosters" illustrate, worlds made narcissistically and oppressively in the image of the self. Her resistance to a central poetic stance, which celebrates the poet's will-to-power and ascendancy over what becomes defined as marginal, may constitute Bishop's strongest critique of her Emersonian inheritance. "In the Waiting Room" illustrates how deeply perspective and identity are culturally constructed rather than self-made, a recognition that gives the poem its subversive edge. Similarly, "Roosters," in acknowledging how one may participate in the very mechanisms of violence one abhors, avoids the simple opposition of a female or sexually neutral utopia to a male world of aggression. "Santarém" approaches an alternative, ideal vision, yet the poem stubbornly resists a utopian casting: some of Santarém's endearing oddities—the blue eyes and oars—are the legacy of cultural imperialism and slavery, the violent impositions of earlier travelers.

As a memory, "Santarém" marks a form of return that questions the very possibility of return ("Of course I may be remembering it all wrong"); the speaker's acknowledgment of uncertainty suggests that meaning, like identity, is continually renegotiated. In invoking (only to disavow) an Edenic analogy, the poem reflexively considers the nature of nostalgia: the desire for return to the original home and the yearning for the unambiguous, "true" self that a point of origin would authorize. As Janice Doane and Devon Hodges have argued in *Nostalgia and Sexual Difference*, the impulse to recover a lost " 'natural' grounding principle" reflects the need to establish a "stable referent" for sexual identity, a referent that Bishop's poetry consistently rejects.[23] "Santarém" collapses clear identic distinctions ("male/female"), however, even as it washes away a reductive and falsely absolute moral vision ("right/wrong"). The poem defines, in Diehl's words, an "alternative Eden" only in the sense that it carefully evades, in foregrounding fluidity and change, the terra firma that the concept of an original home offers. Water, whose "dazzling dialectic" undoes the either/or of the Edenic home, dampens the soil of Santarém ("The street was deep in dark-gold river sand"), erodes the foundations of buildings, and ultimately carries the poet away ("Then—my ship's whistle blew. I couldn't stay").

The traveler departs bearing a "small, exquisite," "empty wasps' nest" that, being made of paper, represents the beautiful, if always provisional and transient, house of Bishop's own writing.[24] The speaker carries with her the appropriately "empty" nest, symbol of the enclosure always left behind, as she leaves the golden Santarém. As "The End of March" suggests, outsiderhood has its sublime rewards, not the least of which is the avoidance of a roosterlike insistence on a self-aggrandizing possessiveness: "This is where I live!" Not in the secure possession of a homeground but in the condition of outsiderhood,

Bishop locates the fluid, sexually indeterminate voice with which she undermines a dualistic, hierarchical conception of gender, and the central, masculine self of the Romantic tradition.

Notes

1. "The Eye of the Outsider: The Poetry of Elizabeth Bishop," in *Blood, Bread, and Poetry: Selected Prose 1979–1985* (New York: W. W. Norton, 1986), p. 125. When referring to Rich's volumes I use the following abbreviations: *BBP* (*Blood, Bread, and Poetry*); *DCL* (*The Dream of a Common Language* [New York: Norton, 1978]); *DW* (*Diving into the Wreck* [New York: Norton, 1973]); *OLSS* (*On Lies, Secrets, and Silences: Selected Prose 1966–1978*) [New York: W. W. Norton, 1979]); *PSN* (*Poems: Selected and New* [New York: Norton, 1975]); *WC* (*The Will to Change* [New York: Norton, 1971]).

2. For example, Alicia Ostriker, arguing that "the muting of the female throughout our literature requires a poetry able to assert the female self," regrets Bishop's lack of a clearly gendered voice as an inhibition that her successors need to overcome (*Stealing the Language: The Emergence of Women's Poetry in America* [Boston: Beacon Press, 1986], pp. 54–55). Joanne Feit Diehl clears ground in arguing that we can read Bishop's lack of a clear female poetic identity as a revisionist tactic ("At Home With Loss: Elizabeth Bishop and the American Sublime," in *Coming to Light: American Women Poets in the Twentieth Century*, ed. Diane Middlebrook and Marilyn Yalom [Ann Arbor: University of Michigan Press, 1985], pp. 123–37). I share Diehl's view that sexual ambiguity in Bishop subverts the hierarchical male/female dualism central to Western and in particular to Emersonian tradition. Our readings diverge on the issue of Bishop's investment in the centrism of American Romanticism. I argue that Bishop's critique of sexual dualism extends to a critique of the Emersonian vision of the central poet (whether defined as male, female, or transsexual) as a conception of poetic authority that rests upon priority and exclusion.

3. Rich has more recently moved away from this celebration of the singular female "I," which she has come to see as a mirroring of the solitary male poetic self, toward a collective female voice (that nevertheless maintains a dominant, central stance within the poem). For a discussion of the turn to female community as a form of Romantic revisionism in Rich's work, see Lynda K. Bundtzen's chapter in this collection.

4. Bishop, *The Complete Poems: 1927–1979* (New York: Farrar, Straus, and Giroux, 1983), p. 64. All further citations from Bishop's poems refer to this edition; page numbers will be given in parentheses.

5. Bishop's redefinition of poetic authority shares the resistance to binary oppositions and to the appropriation of otherness that Susan Stanford Friedman, in this collection, traces in H.D.'s revisionist *Künstlerroman, HER*.

6. In a letter to Anne Stevenson, Bishop writes that she and Robert Lowell "in very different ways are both descendants from the Transcendentalists" (Stevenson, "Letters from Elizabeth Bishop," *Times Literary Supplement*, March 7, 1980, p. 261).

7. Letter from Bishop to Moore, October 17, 1940. Quoted by Candace W. MacMahon in *Elizabeth Bishop: A Bibliography 1927–1979* (Charlottesville: University Press of Virginia, 1980), p. 149.

8. *The Collected Works of Ralph Waldo Emerson*, ed. Robert Spiller, Alfred R.

Ferguson, et al. (Cambridge, Mass.: Belknap Press, Harvard University Press, 1971), vol. 1, 31. For an important discussion of the implications for women writers of a Romantic poetic model, in which the male poet stands over and against a female silent landscape, see Margaret Homans's *Women Writers and Poetic Identity: Dorothy Wordsworth, Emily Brontë, and Emily Dickinson* (Princeton, N.J.: Princeton University Press, 1980).

9. Emerson, *Collected Works,* vol. 1, p. 44.

10. See Schweik, "An Oblique Place: Elizabeth Bishop and the Language of War" in her forthcoming book, *A Gulf So Deeply Cut: American Women Poets and the Second World War* (Madison: University of Wisconsin Press). The implicit connection between the speaker and the roosters has also been noted by Alfred Corn, who observes that the poem "begins to hint that the 'we' . . . might have participated in a form of violence comparable to the roosters' " ("Elizabeth Bishop's Nativities," *Shenandoah* 36.3 [1986], 145).

11. Harold Bloom has noted that "The End of March" represents "another great poem of the American shoreline to go with Emerson's 'Seashore,' Whitman's 'Out of the Cradle . . .' and 'As I Ebb'd. . . ,' Stevens's 'The Idea of Order at Key West,' and Crane's *Voyages I*" (" 'Geography III' by Elizabeth Bishop," *New Republic,* February 5, 1977, p. 29).

12. Bloom, "Foreword," in *Elizabeth Bishop and Her Art,* eds. Lloyd Schwartz and Sybil P. Estess (Ann Arbor: University of Michigan Press, 1983), p. xi.

13. Emerson, *Collected Works,* vol. 3, p. 5.

14. I am grateful to Langdon Hammer for the suggestion that Bishop's "long shadows" echo Dickinson's poem 764 (*The Complete Poems of Emily Dickinson,* ed. Thomas H. Johnson [Boston: Little Brown, 1960]). If we read the "long shadows" that the transformed rocks throw out as a reference to Dickinson ("Presentiment—is that long Shadow—on the Lawn— / Indicative that Suns go down—"), then the poet's exilic vision aligns not with authorial centrality, but with the subversive eccentricity of a feminine tradition, shaped by writers who have stood outside the legitimated descent of authority through a line of literary sons. The descending of "Suns" in Dickinson may seem foreboding, indicating as it does "That Darkness—is about to pass—" but Dickinson often associates the sun with male power and the night with female creativity: her "Presentiment" can be read as referring to the opening into possibility rather than to the coming of death; see, for example, Dickinson's poem 106. In creating her dream-house, which is also a house of solitary writing, Bishop may have had Dickinson's own "retirement" in mind, a self-enclosing that nevertheless represents a radical literary unhousing, a critical turn away from the Emersonian tradition that Bishop accomplishes as well.

15. Homans, *Women Writers,* pp. 209–12, 232–34. For other discussions of plurality in women's writing, see Rachel Blau DuPlessis (*Writing Beyond the Ending: Narrative Strategies of Twentieth-Century Woman Writers* [Bloomington: Indiana University Press, 1985]) and Alicia Ostriker, *Stealing the Language.* Both Nancy Chodorow's theory of female development and Luce Irigaray's substitution of a subversive female multiplicity for phallic singularity have been influential to critics who argue for the revisionist force of the plural voice in women's writing. See Chodorow, *The Reproduction of Mothering: Psychoanalysis and the Sociology of Gender* (Berkeley: University of California Press, 1978) and Irigaray, *This Sex Which Is Not One,* trans. Catherine Porter with Carolyn Burke (Ithaca, N.Y.: Cornell University Press, 1985).

16. Gilbert, "Costumes of the Mind: Transvestism as Metaphor in Modern Literature," in *Writing and Sexual Difference,* ed. Elizabeth Abel (Chicago: University of Chicago Press, 1982), pp. 195–96.

17. Cixous, "Sorties," trans. Ann Liddle, in *New French Feminisms: An Anthology,* ed. Elaine Marks and Isabelle de Courtivron (New York: Schocken Books, 1981), p. 91.

18. Edelman, "The Geography of Gender: Elizabeth Bishop's 'In the Waiting Room,'" *Contemporary Literature* (summer 1985), 187.

19. Bishop, *The Collected Prose,* ed. Robert Giroux (New York: Farrar, Straus, and Giroux, 1984), p. 33.

20. Ostriker, *Stealing the Language,* p. 70.

21. Diehl, *Coming to Light,* p. 131.

22. Diehl, *Coming to Light,* p. 135. In Diehl's view, the recovery of a central position is necessary for "a woman poet who would face the Romantic imagination's insistence upon the poet as central man" (p. 135). I would argue that Bishop subverts her Romantic inheritance not only by positing a self that moves beyond sexual dualism, but also by deconstructing hierarchies based on center/margin, inside/outside oppositions.

23. *Nostalgia and Sexual Difference: The Resistance to Contemporary Feminism* (New York: Methuen, 1987), p. 8.

24. Bishop makes the connection between the wasps' nest and writing paper explicit in the earlier "Jerónimo's House," in which the delicate clapboard house is compared to a "gray wasps' nest" marked with "writing-paper / lines of light" (34).

Part II
Thinking Back Through
Our Mothers

Chapter 4
The Pattern of Birds and Beasts: Willa Cather and Women's Art

Josephine Donovan

> When Queen Mathilde was doing the long tapestry now shown
> at Bayeux,—working her chronicles of the deeds of knights and
> heroes,—alongside the big pattern of dramatic action she and
> her women carried the little playful pattern of birds and beasts
> that are a story in themselves . . .
> —Willa Cather, *The Professor's House* (1925)

It is well known that in her youth Willa Cather emphatically rejected femininity and all its trappings, particularly what she perceived as sentimentalist emotionalism. She affected a masculine style in dress and hairstyle, preferred to be called "William," and endorsed liberal, masculinist notions of scientific progress.[1]

Her 1890 high school graduation address is characteristic; it defends the use of scientific experimentation on animals, in particular vivisection, a practice that was the subject of heated controversy in the late nineteenth century.[2] The antivivisectionists were largely women, characterized by their opponents as sentimentalist and reactionary.[3] That Cather had herself engaged in vivisection and that she pridefully defended that position in her graduation speech is a clear sign of her masculinist identification and her rejection of feminine cultural attitudes and traditions. It also connects to her early identification of the artist with the vivisector and her perception of the practice of art as a form of sadism, as indicated in a series of statements assembled in Sharon O'Brien's excellent, recent biography. "In the 1890s, Cather considered technology's victory over nature analogous to the 'virile' writer's praiseworthy triumph over recalcitrant subject matter in the creative process."[4]

Ironically, in view of the fact that she later endorsed the story as one of her favorites, Cather's provivisection position implies a negative critique of Sarah Orne Jewett's celebrated story, "A White Heron" (1886), published just four years previously. In that story, which concerns the confrontation between a young rural girl and an urban male ornithologist over a heron, the traditional feminine ethic—that of the sanctity of natural life—is upheld. The girl refuses in the end to reveal the bird's whereabouts to the scientist who wishes to kill it and stuff it for his collection. In preserving the life of the bird, the girl "identifies" with nature and makes a holistic statement rejecting the claims of science and affirming the value of all life forms.

In her early reviews and articles, Cather reveals that her rejection of the feminine included a repudiation of women's literary traditions as well, especially the sentimentalist. Her unfair critique of Kate Chopin's novel *The Awakening* (1899) is characteristic. She castigates the heroine for being hyperemotional and for having wrongly allowed her rational faculties to atrophy.[5] In another review Cather stated:

I have not much faith in women in fiction. They have a sort of sex consciousness that is abominable. . . . They are so few, the ones who did anything worth
while; there were the great Georges, George Eliot and George Sand, and they
were anything but women, and there was Miss Brontë who kept her sentimentality under control, and there was Jane Austen who certainly had more
common sense than any of them and was in some respects the greatest of them
all. Women are so horribly subjective.[6]

Cather was joined in her rejection of women's sentimentalist literature by the other great American women realists of the early twentieth
century, especially Edith Wharton and Ellen Glasgow. Wharton, for
example, once stated that she had written her stark novel *Ethan Frome*
(1911) in order to counter the "rose-coloured" vision of New England
presented by her "predecessors" Mary E. Wilkins Freeman and Sarah
Orne Jewett.[7] The women of Cather, Wharton, and Glasgow's generation were, as "new women," in conscious rebellion against the women's
cultural traditions bequeathed to them by their literary mothers. This
rebellion produced a complex of problems, the most serious of which
was a profound ambiguity about gender identity that is manifest in
their literature. The temptation to adopt a masculine self-identification
when rejecting the feminine, to see themselves as serious and therefore
masculine authors, in contrast to the silly "scribbling" women of the
nineteenth century, proved compelling for the women writers of Cather's generation. Wharton, for example, nearly always used a masculine
Jamesian narrative persona in her fiction; and more often than not
Cather similarly used male personae as narrators and sometimes as
protagonists.[8]

But Cather's attitude toward her literary foremothers was different from Wharton's in one important respect. Unlike Wharton,
Cather did not reject the nineteenth-century New England local color
women writers, Jewett and Freeman, as sentimentalist. On the con-

trary, she turned to Jewett as a literary mentor, and the Jewett influence was decisive in moving Cather away from the masculinist identification manifest in her early years, toward a re-vision of women's artistic traditions and toward a more feminine conception of artistic practice. Indeed, especially in her novels of the early twenties, Cather's thematics point in the direction of a "women's art."

In order to explore more fully this shift in Cather's aesthetic values, it is necessary to discuss the term *women's art*. As Rachel Blau DuPlessis notes in *Writing Beyond the Ending*, the "fusion of artisanal and high art" has long been a dream of radicals.[9] It has recently been implicitly identified by a number of feminist critics as the defining characteristic of "women's art."[10] That is, many have recognized that women's traditional art—pottery, quilts, gardening, cooking—is rooted in the world of "everyday use" (the title of an Alice Walker story that explores this very issue). The theoretical approaches by which critics reach their definition of women's art vary, however.

One avenue is through neo-Freudian theory about the female psyche, especially that developed by Nancy Chodorow (*The Reproduction of Mothering*) and amplified by Carol Gilligan (*In a Different Voice*). A second is that pioneered by Margaret Homans (*Bearing the Word*); also dependent upon neo-Freudian theory, especially that developed by French theorist Jacques Lacan, it sees women's art as positioned with the literal as opposed to the metaphoric. A third path (much less traveled than the Freudian, however) is that which utilizes Marxist theories about the genders' relations to use and exchange value production and which urges that the historical material practices of a cultural group conditions its art. Here I would like to explore each of these theoretical approaches in order to lay the groundwork for a discussion of women's art in Cather's later fiction.

Those who rely on the Chodorow-Gilligan model stress the artist's relationship with the maternal or pre-oedipal realm and urge that women's psychic development tends them more toward emotional identification with the maternal and toward aesthetic forms that are reflective of this continuity of relationship.

Various studies of Jewett, for example, have proposed that her art is reflective of "a mode of thinking that is contextual and inductive rather than formal and abstract" or that the structure of Jewett's *Country of the Pointed Firs* is weblike rather than linear, again following Gilligan's model of female relationship.[11]

An interesting spin-off of this approach is the idea that "professional" women artists may take their mothers, who are nonprofessional craftswomen-artists, as models or muses. DuPlessis suggests that in the nineteenth-century *Künstlerromane* by women "the daughter becomes an artist to extend, reveal, and elaborate her mother's often thwarted talents." Mothers and daughters thus become "collaborators" in creating an art that expresses "a poetics of domestic values—nurturance, community building, inclusiveness, empathic care."[12] In an article entitled "I Sign My Mother's Name," Mary Helen Washington argues that black women writers have been concerned to transcribe the oral histories, the stories of their mothers. Paule Marshall, for example, said her mother "laid the foundation of [her] aesthetic," and Dorothy West observed, *"All my mother's blood came out in me. I was my mother talking."*[13]

In her biography O'Brien takes this tack, arguing that in both *O Pioneers!* and Jewett's *Pointed Firs* "daughter/artists receive a creative inheritance from mothers whose arts are domestic" (441). Similarly, O'Brien sees Cather's reconnection with a female literary tradition through Jewett as "strongly replay[ing] the preoedipal issues characterizing the early mother-daughter bond" (165, n. 2). In a striking reinterpretation of Jewett's story "Martha's Lady," O'Brien sees the country servantwoman Martha as an apprentice artist learning the craft of flower arranging and other domestic graces from Helena, thus, interpreting the story as another that collapses domestic and professional art (348–49).

A more complex Lacanian approach to the question of women's art is taken by Margaret Homans. She argues that language is a symbolic sign system that depends upon "the absence of the [literal] referent," "a chain of signifiers that refer, not to things, but always to other signifiers." Citing Terry Eagleton in *Literary Theory,* she notes, "Human language works by . . . the absence of real objects which signs designate. . . . We are severed from the mother's body. . . . We spend all of our lives looking for it."[14]

Because they are identified with the maternal and because they so identify (according to Chodorow), women are linked with the absent referent, or with the literal, with nature. However, "the literal is ambiguous for women writers because women's potentially more positive view of it collides with its devaluation by our culture" (5). Thus, Homans suggests that women writers may express (often covertly) a partiality for the literal, for presence, for nature as opposed to favoring the use of figurative language, which is built upon a distancing from (and, I might add, perhaps a subdual of) the (absent) referent.[15]

O'Brien (independently of Homans, whose work came out more or less at the same time as the biography) similarly observes that in "The Enchanted Bluff," a story written under Jewett's influence, Cather "fuses the descriptive and the metaphoric." Like Jewett's and other works in the women's tradition, the description is literal and realistic, but like works in the male tradition, the "Edenic landscape" is

infused with "spiritual and imaginative meaning" (*Willa Cather* 372)—
thus suggesting that Cather is moving toward a kind of androgynous
style.

But it is Homans's discussion of Heathcliff in Emily Brontë's
Wuthering Heights that seems particularly relevant to Cather's aesthetic
shift. Noting an instance of Heathcliff's sadism—he separates lapwing
birds from their parents thus allowing them to starve to death—
Homans observes, Heathcliff, "not only victimizes nature but does so
specifically through his actions as symbol maker" (that is, he is reenacting symbolically his own orphanage through the birds). Cathy, by
contrast, hopes to "protect nature from figurative and literal killing at
the hand of androcentric law" (78).

Cather's early identification with the vivisector, then, is not irrelevant. Indeed, as noted, O'Brien catalogues numerous early statements
by Cather in which she equates writing with a kind of sadistic dominance. For the early Cather "the links between [the] sword, the dissec-
tor's knife, the surgeon's scalpel, and the writer's pen are literal as well
as metaphoric" (*Willa Cather* 148; see also 149–54). However, O'Brien
argues, by the time she wrote the preface to Jewett's *Pointed Firs* (in
1925), Cather had come to reject the idea of the sadist-artist who
imposes upon the subject matter "by using his 'imagination' upon it
and twisting it to suit his purpose" (388). As opposed to this "masculine
aesthetic," Cather comes (again through the influence of Jewett) to see
a female aesthetic as one animated by the "'gift of sympathy,' [the]
ability to abandon the ego rather than to impose it upon her subject"
(388). Jewett indeed had herself developed a similar theory of the artist
as one who does not "tell a story" (that is, create a figurative artifice) but
who merely "*tell[s] the thing*" (that is, who transmits the literal without
imposing upon it one's own design). In her own criticism Jewett faulted
Hawthorne's use of a pretentiously arty style in his *American Notebooks*,
preferring instead a literal travelogue that was not dressed up in artificial tropes.[16]

Thus, unlike the artist-scientist (proposed, for example, in Zola's
Roman expérimental), who is a vivisector distanced from the subject
matter and who tortures it to behave in accordance with his own
designs, Cather is by the early twenties developing a theory that sees
the artist as integrated with her material. The model for such integration is provided by the mother-craftswoman-artist.

The Marxist approach to the question of women's art is based on
the assumption that a group's historical material practices help to
shape its epistemology and ultimately its aesthetic.[17] Marx and Engels
contrasted two modes of production: one for "use," the other for
"exchange." Production for use takes place primarily in the household

and is work done primarily by women. It creates objects for immediate consumption/use: food, clothes, and so forth. Production for exchange involves creation of material that is valued as a commodity for its monetary or exchange worth.

The person who creates objects for use is thus related in a personal, "sacred" way (following Mircea Eliade's use of the term in *The Sacred and the Profane*)[18] to the material created, and it in turn remains in the context of "everyday use." Production for exchange involves a distancing between producer and produced, a valuing of the object for its abstract, "profane" properties and a removal of the product from the everyday context.

Nancy Hartsock has argued convincingly that the division of labor has meant that men and women have engaged in very different production practices and that these in turn have created different epistemologies in the genders.[19] My extension of this idea is that these practices have also shaped different aesthetics, that women's historical household practices are the material base for women's everyday art.[20] This approach therefore differs from the Freudian in that it stresses the social and historical context and does not rely on Freudian categories (pre-Oedipal, sadist, etc.) to make its case.

A recognition that the life-experience of the domestic woman is based upon a production practice that is relatively unalienated, is repetitive or cyclical, and is integrated into sacred space can help us to recognize correlative aesthetic patterns. Jewett, for example, wrote many stories that are "plotless" (in the sense of the quest plot), "static," and cyclical in structure.[21] These patterns may be reflective of the traditional woman's household labor.

In 1927 Cather commented, "The German housewife who sits before her family on Thanksgiving Day a perfectly roasted goose, is an artist."[22] This radical idea that women's art is to be found in the everyday practices of the domestic woman—a notion amplified in Alice Walker's classic article, "In Search of Our Mothers' Gardens" (1974), in which gardens are seen as a form of art—shows the distance Cather has moved from the traditional view of art as discrete objects divorced from the everyday world and created by world-renowned individuals for the consumption of a wealthy elite—profane objects valued as exchange commodities.

The impetus that led Cather to valorize women's domestic art came from the influence of Sarah Orne Jewett. In order to further refine the nature of this influence, which I and O'Brien have discussed at length elsewhere, I would like to focus once again on a celebrated piece of advice Jewett gave her young protégé in 1908. In a letter dated November 17, Jewett criticized Cather's story "On the Gulls' Road," published in *McClure's* the following month, for its use of a male persona.

> The lover is as well done as he could be when a woman writes in the man's character—it must always, I believe, be something of a masquerade. I think it is safer to write about him as you did about the others, and not try to be he: And you could almost have done it as yourself—.[23]

While this advice seems primarily to reflect Jewett's rejection of the need to disguise a romantic friendship between two women as a heterosexual affair, and therefore to connect to the complex shift in attitudes toward female friendship that had occurred around the turn of the century,[24] the comments also open up the difficult issue of Cather's use of masculine personae as narrators and as protagonists.

While a number of reasons have been proposed to explain Cather's continuing use of male personae,[25] despite Jewett's advice, a look at Cather's great novel *My Ántonia* (1918) suggests that the male narrator Jim Burden comes to represent the *logos*, the autonomous rational ego, where the subject of the novel, Ántonia, comes to symbolize the integrative powers of the nonrational, of the collective side of the psyche, in touch with other people as well as with animals and nature. Jim Burden represents the autonomous daughter artist, while Ántonia signifies the integrative powers of the maternal.

As Evelyn Helmick suggested over a decade ago, the novel follows the ritual pattern of the Eleusinian mysteries—the ancient religious rite based on the Demeter-Persephone myth.[26] By the novel's end the narrator Jim becomes a kind of profane initiate into the sacred mysteries of Ántonia-Demeter, the mother welcoming the daughter home.

While Cather refused to follow Jewett's specific advice to use a female narrative persona, she did attend to the issue implied in Jewett's counsel, how to write authentically as a woman. In 1913 Cather explained that she had dedicated her first major novel, *O Pioneers!* (1913), to Jewett because "I had talked over some of the characters in it with her one day . . . and in this book I tried to tell the story of the people as truthfully and as simply as if I were telling it to her by word of mouth."[27] Cather was thus wrestling with the problem of how as a woman to "tell" fiction without resorting to such forms as a male narrator. Here she proposes to "tell" *O Pioneers!* as if she were relating it directly to another woman (Jewett), engaging thus in a feminine-maternal narrative style, that of informal "kitchen table" conversation. (O'Brien indeed proposes that this mode is a characteristic Jewett format [*Willa Cather* 340, 365].) That the daughter figure (here Cather) wants to tell her vision to the mother (Jewett) suggests a desire to integrate her world with that of the mother.

Cather's quest for feminine-maternal artistic forms—for a feminine-maternal aesthetic—is reflected in the novels she wrote between *O Pioneers!* and 1927, when she made the comment about the German housewife's roast. In particular, *The Song of the Lark* (1915), *One of Ours* (1922), and *The Professor's House* (1925) concern protagonists' connection with a maternal realm and its art objects, reflecting Cather's own desire as autonomous daughter-artist to connect with feminine artistic traditions, seen in her relationship with Jewett. Significantly, two of these novels have a masculine protagonist and the other a careerist woman—in other words, they are "logos" figures distanced from the maternal realm.

The Song of the Lark concerns a woman artist, Thea Kronberg, an opera singer. It is in some respects a typical *Künstlerroman* in that it deals with the artist's struggle to realize herself. Thea, like any ambitious artist—male or female—must in order to succeed pander to the existing artistic production system. She must leave her home, move to the city, make the right contacts. In short, she must manipulate her life according to a rational scheme; she must operate within the existing operatic institutions. Such a modus operandi means that she must repress the domestic, emotional, collective side of her self. She must become an autonomous actor in a prescripted reified system; she must engage in alienated labor, commodifying her gift in order to succeed.

But Thea finds that something is missing in her life and her enthusiasm for her career begins to wane. Seeking reinspiration she visits the Southwest of the United States where she spends time in Panther Canyon, the site of ancient cliff-dwelling peoples. Ellen Moers notes that the features of this canyon present "the most thoroughly elaborated female landscape in literature."[28]

Here Thea undergoes a ritual similar to that experienced by Jim Burden in *My Ántonia;* it involves the dissolution of the ego, the logos side of the personality. As Thea approaches the canyon, we learn indeed that "the personality of which she was so tired seemed to let go of her."[29]

Deep within this feminine landscape described as a "v-shaped inner gorge," a "hollow (like a great fold in the rock)" (297), Thea establishes herself in a "rock-room," a cave—always a feminine symbol—surrounded by flowers that are "sickeningly sweet after a shower" (299). Here she meditates in solitude, loses herself in the sounds of nature, reconnects with the ancient Indian women who once lived there, and takes ritual baths.

On the first day Thea climbed the water trail she began to have intuitions about the women who had worn the path, and who had spent so great a part of their lives going up and down it. She found herself trying to walk as they must have walked, with a feeling in her feet and knees and loins which she had never known before. . . . She could feel the weight of an Indian baby hanging on her back as she climbed. (302)

Thus, Thea absorbs the maternal powers of the traditional women whose lives she imagines. She regularly bathes in a stream that expresses "a continuity of life that reached back into the old time." "Thea's bath came to have a ceremonial gravity. The atmosphere of the canyon was ritualistic" (304).

In an epiphanic moment she reflects upon the Indian women's pottery—like the German housewife's goose, an example of women's anonymous everyday art. It was, she reflected, "their most direct appeal to water, the envelope and sheath of the precious element itself" (303). "What was any art," she thought, "but an effort to make a sheath, a mould in which to imprison for a moment the shining, elusive element which is life itself. . . . The Indian women had held it in their jars" (304). In other words, the Indian women's art is integrated with nature, with the everyday, with the literal in a way that commodity masterpiece art is not.[30] Thea applies this realization to her own art; thus occurs the desired reinspiration.

As Sharon O'Brien has suggested, this moment provides Thea "with a connection to feminine creativity outside the patriarchal artistic tradition" ("Mothers, Daughters" 284). This feminine rebirth, accomplished through reconnection with the ancient mothers enables Thea to return to her career, which she pursues thenceforth successfully. In this she resembles her creator, Willa Cather, who had similarly despaired of creating authentic art until she connected with her literary mother Jewett.[31] (Of course, both Thea and Cather remain professional artists, engaged in commodity production, but they lean toward and find inspiration from the unalienated art of the mothers.)

Although it earned Cather the Pulitzer Prize, the novel *One of Ours* (published in 1922) has not been judged one of her great novels; indeed, it is sometimes dismissed (by Hemingway for one) as an unsuccessful attempt at a war novel. But this is to miss the very important thematic concerns that are at work. For, once again, it is a matter of an autonomous daughter figure, disguised behind a male persona (Claude Wheeler), in ambivalent relationship to her mother and her mother's art. The novel is indeed dedicated to Cather's own mother.

Two episodes illustrate these thematic concerns. One revolves around the Wheelers' old servantwoman, Mahailey. Mahailey is the Hestia of the novel: together with Claude's mother she helps to constitute its feminine-domestic cosmos; she keeps the feminine-maternal spirits alive. Mahailey assists in child-rearing and nurtures Claude and his mother; she cooks and in one symbolic episode refuses to bequeath her own mother's quilts to Claude's brother Ralph, who is a ruthless entrepreneurial type, found throughout Cather's fiction, and representative of capitalist patriarchy.[32]

Mahailey's gesture of preserving her mother's quilts, her mother's art, refusing to capitulate to patriarchal authority, illustrates Cather's continuing interest in women's art forms. For the quilts represent the emotional integration of the home, just as the Indian women's pottery signified a similar experience to Thea. They are items produced for use rather than exchange and therefore share in the sacred character of the domestic realm sanctified by feminine ritual, rather than the profane, alienated character of the public realm of industrial capitalism where art objects are valued as commodities for exchange. For Ralph would have sold the quilts.

Another episode in the novel also emphasizes women's traditional cultural relations. Claude like many "new women" in the early twentieth century (and like his author) leaves home to attend the university. There he learns that scholarship is an exercise of the logos; one must purge it of personal feelings. In working on a paper on Joan of Arc Claude prides himself "that he had kept all personal feelings out."[33]

Claude finds, however, "that after all his conscientious study he really knew little more about the Maid of Orleans than when he first heard of her from his mother, one day when he was a boy" (62). He found "a picture of her in armour, in an old book," and had taken it "down to the kitchen where his mother was making apple pies . . . and while she went on rolling out the dough and fitting it to the pans, she told him the story" (62). Thus, it is not patriarchal knowledge derived from the objective modes of university learning that Claude finds most powerful; rather it is the tradition of oral feminine literature (analogous to Cather's desire to "tell" *O Pioneers!* to Jewett) that has remained persuasive in his memory.

The Professor's House (published in 1925) deals, allegorically, with the attempt by the daughter to connect her art with maternal sources, and with the increasingly tenuous nature of that connection. The protagonist is a Professor Godfrey St. Peter, another Cather persona. His financial success has allowed him to build a new house, but when the time comes to move, he finds he cannot leave his old study, which is located in an attic.

Also in the attic are dressmaker forms used by Augusta, his wife's seamstress. The attic, the female forms, and Augusta constitute the maternal/pre-oedipal/matriarchal realm to which the professor seems attached, some critics say infantilely.[34] The subtextual reason for the professor's attachment, however, is that the attic is the site of the maternal muse, which the professor (the artist) fears losing if he moves (disconnects) from it. If, as French feminist Hélène Cixous has suggested in Freudian terms, women's ink is white because it comes from the mother's milk[35]—that is, that the inspiring source or muse for the woman writer is the mother—the concern of the professor, who represents Cather, is understandable. Significantly, when he and Augusta start to pack up for the move, he notices that their papers are all mixed together. He says, "I see we shall have some difficulty in separating our life work, Augusta. We've kept our papers together a long while now."[36] This integration suggests the desired union Cather is coming to wish between the art of the mothers, as seen in the German housewife's cooking, the Indian women's pottery, and Mahailey's quilt, and the autonomous art learned by the wayward daughters, the "new women" of the early twentieth century.

Later, in another significant episode, the professor is elated when he learns from Augusta that the Blessed Virgin had "composed the Magnificat" "just as soon as the angel had announced to her that she would be the mother of our Lord" (100). He repeats the information to himself and feels that it has "brightened" his study: "(Surely she had said that the Blessed Virgin sat down and composed the Magnificat!)" (100).

The reason the professor (Cather) is elated is that the image is one of a mother creating art, indeed that her maternity is the source of her inspiration. This idea is reinforced as the professor recollects how in the past, while he worked in the attic study, the sounds from the domestic world below had filtered up, helping him to feel in touch with it.

Just as, when Queen Mathilde was doing the long tapestry now shown at Bayeux,—working her chronicles of the deeds of knights and heroes,—alongside the big pattern of dramatic action she and her women carried the little playful pattern of birds and beasts that are a story in themselves: so, to him, the most important chapters of his story were interwoven with personal memories. (101)

This wonderful epic simile is a paradigmatic description of the dynamic in women's art between the marginal "literal" greenworld of the mothers, on the one hand—"the little playful pattern of birds and beasts that are a story in themselves"—and on the other, the central masculine scripts—"the deeds of knights and heroes"—that have traditionally been considered the stuff of great (patriarchal) art. The image of Queen Mathilde surreptitiously slipping in marginal feminine matter is poignant. Like Claude Wheeler's study of Joan of Arc, the professor finds that his own work, "his most important chapters," are those informed with the personal, which derives from feminine-maternal tradition.

The second part of the novel is a first-person narration told by Tom Outland, a precocious student, to the professor (recalling that Cather said she wrote *O Pioneers!* as if she were telling it directly to Jewett). His story is a repetition of the cliff-dwellers narrative seen in *The Song of the Lark* and other Cather works. For Tom, as for Thea Kronberg, the discovery of this ancient feminine utopia is epiphanal.

In his exploration of the ruins of their deserted cave city, Tom discovers a female mummy—another symbol of the feminine-maternal on the order of the dressmaker forms. He and his companion nickname her "Mother Eve" (214). Tom keeps a journal (his art) of his days in the Southwest and when he leaves the area, he secretes it in a niche near Mother Eve, another gesture that suggests an attempt to integrate daughter-art with the maternal source. Later he and St. Peter retrieve it.

Before he returns East for good, Tom spends a summer alone on the mesa. His experience is similar to Thea's; it provides a kind of spiritual rebirth, a reconnection with the sacred: one moonlit night (the moon, of course, a symbol of the feminine),

It all came together in my understanding, as a series of experiments do when you begin to see where they are leading. Something had happened in me that made it possible for me to co-ordinate and simplify, and that process . . . brought with it great happiness. . . . It was my high tide. . . . I had found everything. (251)

The experience of integration suggests a dissolution of the masculine logos—and a discovery of intellectual holism—the feminine way.

In book 3 the professor works on editing Tom's journals. (Tom is now dead.) In that process and in his own experience of dying, St. Peter too moves toward an experience of integration; it involves a shedding of his surface, civilized, autonomous, oedipal self, and a return to his "primitive" pre-oedipal or maternal core, a return to the "literal," to nature.

He was a primitive. He was interested in earth and woods and water. Wherever sun sunned and rain rained, and snow snowed, wherever life sprouted and decayed, places were alike to him. . . . He was earth and would return to earth. (265)

It is an image of triumphant Demeter.

These works document, I propose, Cather's own quest for an art that was not disconnected from its natural everyday sources. Unlike the art produced by daughter-artists, "new women" under the sway of patriarchal stylistics, in a world of commodity production, the art of ordinary women achieves that integration. The work produced by the German wife, the Indian women, and Mahailey's mother is integrated with its environment in a way that the art of the sophisticated daughter is not; in the latter there is always a disconnection, an alienation, the intervention of the logos, the male persona Jewett counseled Cather to remove. While Cather never fully resolved this artistic problem, these novels reveal her inclination toward a different kind of art than that bequeathed to her in the patriarchal tradition, toward a women's art.

Notes

1. Much of this material is presented in more detail in Sharon O'Brien, *Willa Cather: The Emerging Voice* (New York: Oxford University Press, 1987).

2. E. K. Brown, *Willa Cather: A Critical Biography* (New York: Knopf, 1953), pp. 44–45.

3. See Coral Lansbury, *The Old Brown Dog: Women, Workers, and Vivisection in Edwardian England* (Madison: University of Wisconsin Press, 1985).

4. O'Brien, *Willa Cather,* p. 389; see also pp. 148–51. Further references are cited parenthetically in the text with page numbers.

5. Willa Cather, "Four Women Writers" (1899), in *The World and the Parish: Willa Cather's Articles and Reviews, 1892–1902,* ed. William M. Curtin (Lincoln: University of Nebraska Press, 1970), vol. 2, 697–99.

6. Willa Cather, "The Literary Situation in 1895," in *The World and the Parish,* vol. 1, 277.

7. Edith Wharton, *A Backward Glance* (1933; rpt. New York: Scribner's, 1962), p. 293.

8. For a further discussion of these matters, see Josephine Donovan, *After the Fall: The Demeter-Persephone Myth in Wharton, Cather, and Glasgow* (University Park: Pennsylvania State University Press, 1989).

9. Rachel Blau DuPlessis, *Writing Beyond the Ending: Narrative Strategies of Twentieth-Century Women Writers* (Bloomington: Indiana University Press, 1985), p. 104. DuPlessis notes that Marxist Theodor Adorno saw the separation of "mental and physical work" as the "original sin" (104); see also Hilary Rose, "Hand, Brain, and Heart: A Feminist Epistemology for the Natural Sciences," *Signs* 9. 1 (autumn 1983), 73–90.

I use the term *women's art* in this chapter specifically to mean art that is rooted in traditional women's household or domestic practices, which are artisanal in nature. I do not mean that all women make this kind of art nor that it is reflective of all women's experience, nor even that any one woman consistently engages in producing "women's art." Nor am I implying that this is necessarily the "right kind" of art for women. Rather I am simply using the term to refer to a particular kind of art—to which some women writers (Cather for one) have felt an attraction.

An article that complements my approach here is Ann Romines, "After the Christmas Tree: Willa Cather and Domestic Ritual," *American Literature* 60. 1 (March 1988), 61–82. I would also like to acknowledge Suzanne Jones's suggestions and criticisms which helped me get this chapter in shape.

10. In addition to DuPlessis, *Writing Beyond the Ending*, see O'Brien, *Willa Cather;* Alice Walker, "In Search of Our Mothers' Gardens," *Ms.* 2.11 (May 1974); reprinted in *In Search of Our Mothers' Gardens* (New York: Harcourt Brace Jovanovich, 1983); Elaine Showalter, "Piecing and Writing," in *The Poetics of Gender,* ed. Nancy K. Miller (New York: Columbia University Press, 1986); and Josephine Donovan, "Toward a Women's Poetics," *Tulsa Studies in Women's Literature* 3.3 (winter 1984), 99–110.

11. Carol Gilligan, "Women's Place in Man's Life-Cycle," *Harvard Educational Review* 49.4 (1979), 442; Josephine Donovan, "Sarah Orne Jewett's Critical Theory: Notes Toward a Feminine Literary Mode," in *Critical Essays on Sarah Orne Jewett,* ed. Gwen L. Nagel (Boston: G. K. Hall, 1984), p. 214; Elizabeth Ammons, "Going in Circles: The Female Geography of Jewett's *Country of the Pointed Firs,*" *Studies in the Literary Imagination* 16 (fall 1983), 83–92. O'Brien also identifies Jewett's aesthetic theory as essentially feminine: "collaborative and domestic." She claims Jewett saw "the creativity [country women] expressed in daily tasks like cooking, gardening, and herb-gathering" as connected to "the artist's imagination" (*Willa Cather,* 340). O'Brien adduces the evidence for this largely from Jewett's fiction, however, not from any theoretical statements.

12. DuPlessis, *Writing Beyond the Ending,* pp. 93–94, 103.

13. Mary Helen Washington, "I Sign My Mother's Name," in *Mothering the Mind: Twelve Studies of Writers and Their Silent Partners*, ed. Ruth Perry and Martine Watson Brownley (New York: Holmes & Meier, 1984), p. 151. For a further elaboration of women writers' connection to their mothers, see Jane Marcus, "Thinking Back through Our Mothers," in *New Feminist Essays on Virginia Woolf,* ed. Marcus (Lincoln: University of Nebraska Press, 1981), pp. 1–30, and the chapter by Margaret Stetz in this volume.

14. Margaret Homans, *Bearing the Word: Language and Female Experience in Nineteenth-Century Women's Writing* (Chicago: University of Chicago Press, 1986), pp. 7–8. Further references are cited parenthetically in the text with page numbers.

15. I noted a similar resistance to Ciceronian rhetoric in a number of seventeenth- and eighteenth-century British women writers in "The Silence Is Broken," in *Women and Language in Literature and Society,* ed. Ruth Borker, Nelly Furman, and Sally McConnell-Ginet (New York: Praeger, 1980). See also the chapter by Ann L. Ardis in this volume.

16. Donovan, "Sarah Orne Jewett's Critical Theory," pp. 212–13; see also Marcia Folsom, "'Tact is a Kind of Mind-Reading': Empathic Style in Sarah Orne Jewett's *Country of the Pointed Firs,*" *Colby Library Quarterly* 18.1 (March 1982).

17. For a brief introduction see Josephine Donovan, *Feminist Theory: The Intellectual Traditions of American Feminism* (New York: Continuum, 1985), chapter 3. See also Donovan, "Women's Poetics," p. 103. Of course, there has been much debate over how deterministic material conditions are; it is not necessary to review it here. My position is that while other factors undoubtedly impinge, material conditions are a major factor in shaping a group's aesthetics.

18. Mircea Eliade, *The Sacred and the Profane* (1957; rpt. New York: Harper's, 1961); see also Kathryn Allen Rabuzzi, *The Sacred and the Feminine: Toward a Theology of Housework* (New York: Seabury Press, 1982).

19. Nancy C. M. Hartsock, "The Feminist Standpoint: Developing the Ground for a Specifically Feminist Historical Materialism," in *Discovering Real-*

ity, ed. Sandra Harding and Merrill B. Hintikka (Dordrecht: Reidel, 1983), and *Money, Sex, and Power: Toward a Feminist Historical Materialism* (New York: Longman, 1983).

20. Of course, these practices have varied in different historical periods and cultures and among classes, but for the purposes of analyzing Willa Cather's aesthetic it is the household practices of nineteenth- and twentieth-century middle-class whites in the United States that are relevant.

21. See n. 11 above.

22. Cited in Sharon O'Brien, "Mothers, Daughters, and the 'Art Necessity': Willa Cather and the Creative Process," in *American Novelists Revisited: Essays in Feminist Criticism,* ed. Fritz Fleischmann (Boston: G. K. Hall, 1982), p. 268. Further references follow in the text.

23. Annie Fields, ed., *Letters of Sarah Orne Jewett* (Boston: Houghton Mifflin, 1911), pp. 246–47.

24. See Donovan, *After the Fall,* chapters 1 and 2.

25. See Deborah Lambert, "The Defeat of a Hero: Autonomy and Sexuality in *My Ántonia,*" *American Literature* 53. 4 (January 1982), 476–90; Brown, *Willa Cather;* James Woodress, *Willa Cather: Her Life and Art* (New York: Pegasus, 1970); and O'Brien, *Willa Cather,* pp. 217, 369.

26. Evelyn Helmick, "The Mysteries of Ántonia," *Midwest Quarterly* 17. 2(January 1976), 173–85.

27. Willa Cather, "Willa Cather Talks of Work" (August 9, 1913), in *The Kingdom of Art: Willa Cather's First Principles and Critical Statements, 1893–1896,* ed. Bernice Slote (Lincoln: University of Nebraska Press, 1966), p. 449.

28. Ellen Moers, *Literary Women* (Garden City, N.Y.: Doubleday, 1977), p. 391.

29. Willa Cather, *The Song of the Lark* (1915; rpt. Lincoln: University of Nebraska Press, 1978), p. 296. Further references are cited parenthetically in the text with page numbers.

30. See also Katherine Kearns's essay in this volume.

31. Cather, "Willa Cather Talks of Work," p. 449.

32. Other notable examples include Krajiek and Wick Cutter in *My Ántonia* and Ivy Peters in *A Lost Lady.*

33. Willa Cather, *One of Ours* (New York: Knopf, 1922), p. 61. Further references are cited parenthetically in the text with page numbers.

34. Leon Edel, "A Cave of One's Own" (1959), in *Critical Essays on Willa Cather,* ed. John J. Murphy (Boston: G. K. Hall, 1984), p. 207, and Blanche Gelfant, "The Forgotten Reaping Hook: Sex in *My Ántonia*" (1971), in *Critical Essays on Willa Cather,* p. 151.

35. Hélène Cixous, "The Laugh of the Medusa" (1976), in *New French Feminisms: An Anthology,* ed. Elaine Marks and Isabelle de Courtivron (1980; rpt. New York: Schocken Books, 1981), p. 252.

36. Willa Cather, *The Professor's House* (New York: Knopf, 1925), p. 23. Further references are cited parenthetically in the text with page numbers.

Chapter 5
Anita Brookner: Woman Writer as Reluctant Feminist

Margaret Diane Stetz

In Anita Brookner's *Hotel du Lac* (1984), the protagonist, herself a professional novelist, brings lunch with a literary agent to a halt with an impassioned defense both of her female readers and of the sort of fiction she gives them, a speech so vehement that it causes the nervous agent "to make a discreet sign to the waiter for the bill."[1] Their quarrel starts when the agent, a man, characterizes the typical bookbuyer as a "girl with the executive briefcase" who "wants something to flatter her ego when she's spending a lonely night in a hotel" in Brussels and who, therefore, requires more "sex" in novels than Edith Hope provides.[2] Edith's first response, as the better writer of the two, is to correct his portrait of this imaginary figure—the woman executive would be packing novels for a business trip to Glasgow, not to Brussels; her version emphasizes the banality, rather than the glamor, of the working woman's lot. Her second response is to challenge his claim to understand either the female psyche or the moral life of women: it is not the reality of sex that her readers want but "myths" of love, in which "unassuming" heroines receive their rewards for honest and scrupulous conduct. "'You see, Harold,'" she insists to the skeptical agent, "'my readers are essentially virtuous.'"[3] By "virtuous," she does not mean sexually inactive, rather, she views the audience for so-called women's fiction as composed of believers in impracticable, yet nonetheless admirable, codes of behavior based on fair play, integrity, and openness—a group that rejects contemporary notions of worldly success at all costs and embraces an older set of Judeo-Christian ethics it wishes to see dramatized. Hers is an extraordinary plea on behalf of the much maligned and despised "woman's market" of publishing, an account that invests the average bookbuyer with a high degree of dignity and moral awareness. In Edith's opinion, women—especially those raised on the traditions of romance literature—are the only segment of the public today that can be relied on to appreciate heroines who use patience and merit, not shrewdness and violence, to earn their prizes of love or social position. And behind Edith Hope's public gesture of support for her female audience stands the very private figure of Anita Brookner, reaching out to make seemingly sincere contact with her own readers as she attributes to them the same values, including belief in the need for good will toward others and for good behavior, that she herself endorses throughout her fiction.

Individual women characters do constitute the villains in Brookner's oeuvre—Helen Weiss of *A Start in Life* (1981), Miss Fairchild of *Providence* (1982), Alix Fraser of *Look at Me* (1983), Jennifer Pusey of *Hotel du Lac* (1984), Betty of *Family and Friends* (1985), and "Mousie" of *A Misalliance* (1986)—a procession of sisters, mothers, students, and acquaintances, all of them tirelessly manipulative and demanding, who rob the heroines of their opportunities for love or security. Nevertheless, women as a class come off well in these novels. If it is true that the Brookner protagonist is always pursued by a female nemesis, it is also true that she is usually buoyed up by a circle of comforting, well-meaning figures who, like Mrs. Duff of *A Misalliance,* appear at times of crisis with "that deep compassionate look, that succouring arm" of support.[4] For such services, Brookner's heroines offer, albeit sometimes belatedly, the tribute of gratitude to womankind. Indeed, Edith Hope does a sort of penance on behalf of all these characters as she thinks

with shame of her small injustices, of her unworthy thoughts toward those excellent women who had befriended her, and to whom she had revealed nothing. I have been too harsh on women, she thought, because I understand them better than I understand men. . . . I know . . . because I am one of them. I am harsh because I remember Mother and her unkindnesses, and because I am continually on the alert for more. But women are not all like Mother, and it is really stupid of me to imagine that they are.[5]

Brookner herself extends the same concession to her female audience, allowing for the kindliness of its intentions, as she displays to it one nakedly vulnerable heroine after another and trusts in it to embrace these sufferers. Though her plots may turn on female betrayal, the implied relationships in her novels between the characters and the readers are close and respectful ones, involving a mutual "befriending." Even in a work such as *A Friend from England* (1987), which questions the possibility of friendship between women in general while tracing the deterioration of one particular acquaintanceship from shared respect to shared contempt, Brookner's readiness to place her female narrator in the reader's power, as she lays bare Rachel's fears and neuroses for inspection, remains undiminished.

But while Brookner shows confidence in her audience as a whole, she repeatedly excludes one category of woman reader from her good will. "Feminists," she appears to believe, must be hostile to her work and she must be hostile in return, throwing down the gauntlet to them both in her published remarks to journalists and in her fiction. "'I think I can take on the feminists,'" she has told one interviewer,[6] even though she has claimed on other occasions to "'*hate* . . . adversative positions.'"[7] Her characterizations of feminism have been broad and dismissive: "'I do not believe in the all-men-are-swine programme,'" she has said in defining her opposition to feminist thought.[8] Through her fictional spokeswomen and spokesmen, she has gone further, allowing Frances Hinton of *Look at Me* to refer slightingly to the "women's guerilla movement"[9] and Mr. Neville of *Hotel du Lac* nearly to persuade Edith Hope into a marriage of convenience, by threatening her with the prospect of watching herself sink into feminism if she carries on alone:

"And then you would discover that you had a lot in common with all the other discontented women, and you'd start to see a lot of sense in the feminist position. . . . Do you really want to spend the rest of your life talking to aggrieved women about your womb?" he went on, inexorably.[10]

Again writing in her own voice, Brookner has tried to head off any critical inquiry into similarities between her works and those of the proponents of this antagonistic philosophy by assuring an interviewer that "'You'd have to be crouching in your burrow to see my novels in a feminist way.'"[11]

＊　　＊　　＊

Why do both Brookner and her fictional spokespeople feel so estranged from feminism? In some ways, the alienation is surprising. One might expect the author to sympathize with a movement that shares her dislike of a common enemy, the type that in an earlier era was called the "womanly woman"—one who gets what she can at the expense of other women while masking her intentions behind a charade of "ultrafeminine" helplessness. Feminist theorists, who find this behavior abhorrent, see it nonetheless as culturally determined, something to be altered through education. But Anita Brookner and her fictional mouthpieces break with feminism in their repeated assertions that such a type is no mere product of a culture, subject to change or eradication, but an ineluctable phenomenon of nature. As Rachel, narrator of *A Friend from England,* explains ruefully, "These are the women who say, 'I'm afraid I was a little bit naughty,' after committing some gross misdemeanour, or 'I'm afraid I got rather cross,' after screaming their way to victory. Women like this have always existed: they still do, in spite of all the changes that have taken place."[12] Brookner has stated often in print that she believes competition between women, especially for men, to be inescapable, and that such battles must always be won by the underhanded, "feminine" manipulator, who represents, in Darwinian terms, the "fittest." Both Brookner and her fictional protagonists position themselves squarely within the philosophical framework identified as "nonfeminist" by Evelyn Fox Keller and Helene Moglen in their article "Competition and Feminism: Conflicts for Academic Women":

In the prevailing, nonfeminist view of human nature and the world that dominates organizational, economic, and evolutionary thought, individuals are assumed to be essentially autonomous units and the world a finite reservoir of inexpandable and accordingly scarce resources. In the struggle for survival that inevitably ensues, in which each individual is primarily motivated by self-interest, competition (either tacit or overt) is obligatory.[13]

Feminists, according to Keller and Moglen, "have quite rightly taken exception to this formulation,"[14] but Brookner and her characters choose to take exception to feminism instead. Brookner sees feminists as naïve, if not dishonest, so long as they refuse to acknowledge the degree to which most women are locked in a competition with one another for love and recognition, a competition that she has described as "inborn,"[15] a biological given. In a conversation recorded in John Haffenden's collection, *Novelists in Interview,* she has reiterated her belief that feminism cannot affect women's conduct as a whole in any positive way: "'What women want is the clean part of the programme; how they get it is the dirty part.'"[16] Indeed, she appears to feel that feminist literature—unlike her own novels or the stories of love and morality composed by her author-heroines—actually has done its readers a disservice by denying that the struggle between women exists and by not preparing them to recognize or to defend themselves against the tactics of what she calls the "ultrafeminine" sorts.

Brookner splits off from feminists, moreover, in her willingness to concede that the spoiled and grasping "womanly" types have, despite their essential amorality, a very real charm. In Brookner's novels, such characters are always given credit for their energy and magnetism. They draw the affections not only of every man in sight, but of the narrator-heroines as well, who often confess to wishing that they could exercise the same power that these women do. Brookner calls them the "fortunate" ones or, in *A Friend from England,* the "privileged," as Rachel says, contemplating a representative of the type,

I felt the old sickening sense of loss that privileged people always visit on me. It is a peculiar sort of love affair that I have with them. I want to be like them, yet at the same time I want to be taken under their wing, into their protection. And this can never be. For such people know, even before I do, that I am not like them.[17]

In her 1985 interview with John Haffenden, Brookner has admitted to sharing the ambivalence expressed through her fictional protagonists. "'I would love to be extremely plausible and flattering and dishonest: there are useful dishonesties,'"[18] she has said wistfully; "'I'm very envious of careless people,'"[19] meaning those who are "careless" of the needs of others as they pursue their own.

By depicting and by fleshing out such characters through fiction, of course, Brookner is able, however briefly, to enter into their personalities, to "be like them." The same liberty is open to those of her protagonists, such as Frances Hinton of *Look at Me,* who are also novelists, writing about the "privileged" characters of their own acquaintance. The pampered, hedonistic life of the "ultrafeminine" woman dazzles, just as much as it repels, both Brookner and her writer-heroines.

In contrast, the life that the feminist movement, according to Brookner, has made possible or even inevitable for most women seems grim and unappetizing. Over and over in the novels, the "liberated" alternative is seen as producing loneliness, absence of love and family, compulsive careerism, and the Pyrrhic gain of independence for its own sake with no increase of pleasure. As Rachel of *A Friend from England* observes, "Among my women friends I have noticed one or two wilting under the strain, however brave and resolute they are in pursuit of their own form of fulfillment, the kind we are told to value these days."[20] She goes on to paint an explicit and depressing picture of women who "secretly would have been happier sitting at home listening to Woman's Hour [the BBC daytime radio program], but instead are to be found on the city streets early in the morning, tapping their way along the pavement in the sort of high-heeled shoes that are supposed to go with attainment, on their way to another day with the computer, or the Stock Exchange prices, or an important presentation, or a client to be exhaustively entertained."[21] Her own remedy for "such women" is to "decree a dear little house, in some established suburb, and a leisurely walk to the shops with a basket over one arm, and an afternoon with one's feet up on the sofa, reading a magazine."[22] The tone of these remarks should not mislead the reader into thinking that the suggestion is offered wholly facetiously, either by Rachel or by Brookner herself. Later, Rachel states quite seriously, "It will be a pity if women in the more conventional mould are to be phased out, for there will never be anyone to go home to,"[23] and insists that a traditional housewife can be " 'like the virtuous woman in the Bible, anxious to see others happy, and all prospering around her.' "[24] As for Brookner, she herself has responded to an interviewer's reminder that she is "successful on two counts: as an academic and as a novelist"—two roles which, in the eyes of feminist intellectuals, would certainly carry high status—by replying, " 'Those two activities that you've mentioned are outside the natural order. I only ever wanted children, six sons. . . . instead of being this grown-up orphan with what you call success.' "[25]

Yet such a belligerently philistine statement represents only one facet of Brookner's thought. The other, more dominant side is her intense and almost exaggerated respect for art, accompanied by her eagerness to locate in works of art the quality of "radiance, a power beyond the image: vision"[26] which she encounters nowhere else. Compared to literature, life has, in her view, "no selection"—it is merely "piecemeal."[27] " 'Novels are about selection and just desserts; life is about accumulation and opportunities and the winner takes all,' " Brookner has said, weighing the satisfactions of fictional experience against those of lived experience.[28] Brookner is a kind of moral aesthete, valuing art over life because of the superior moral order of the former. What she finds in the roles of artist and academic writer—roles which, in large part, have been opened to her because of the feminist movement—and what she gives in turn to her author-heroines are opportunities both to exercise "vision" and to make the "just" prevail, achievements that do seem to go beyond anything offered by more stereotypically "feminine" pursuits, however attractive these may occasionally appear. In the end, the ability to assume authorial "privilege" makes one the most "privileged" person of all.

We can review, then, in a different spirit the pronouncement that "You'd have to be crouching in your burrow to see my novels in a feminist way."[29] Though Brookner makes this statement in a tone designed to cut off discussion, I think it may be possible to treat it instead as a challenge, to turn it into an opportunity and a starting point. "To see . . . [her] novels in a feminist way" is the task of this essay—maybe not so hard a task as Brookner suggests. Certainly, many feminist readers have been enjoying Brookner's fiction all along and have not felt forced to abandon their own principles in order to do so. Perhaps what they have been responding to, apart from the sheer pleasure of encountering Brookner's meticulously beautiful prose style, is a sort of unconscious feminism—the "reluctant" feminism, as I will call it, of a writer who values the creation of art above all other activities and who depicts relations with other women as the wellspring of that endeavor for the woman artist. In continually emphasizing the importance of social and emotional ties between women as the primary influences upon and stimuli to women's writing, Brookner shapes a philosophy of creativity quite compatible with that of the group she disowns. Thus, she becomes an author who, if not politically feminist, is nonetheless aesthetically feminist. She stands in the long line of twentieth-century novelists and critics who echo and interpret literally Virginia Woolf's pronouncement in *A Room of One's Own* that "we think back through our mothers if we are women."[30] What is more, she demonstrates repeatedly in her fiction that "if we are women" and writers, "we" depend upon the examples and imaginations of other female artists to provide us with inspiration and material.

*   *   *

"My mother's fantasies," explains Edith Hope in *Hotel du Lac*, "taught me about reality":

She bequeathed to me her own cloud of unknowing. She comforted herself, that harsh disappointed woman, by reading love stories, simple romances with happy endings. Perhaps that is why I write them.[31]

For Brookner's heroines to acknowledge a bond between themselves and their biological mothers and then to "think back through" them in a creative way is an excruciatingly painful business, given the unappealing personalities of these maternal figures. Some of them, such as Sofka of *Family and Friends*, are well-meaning monsters, who destroy their daughters' happiness by accident; others, like Helen Weiss of *A Start in Life*, are shameless vampires, draining the energy out of everyone in their domestic circle; even the best of them, such as Frances Hinton's mother in *Look at Me*, possess merely the negative virtues of being passive and undemanding; and almost all of them, like Yvette Hartmann of *Latecomers* (1988), believe that "the only success for a woman was an early marriage,"[32] insisting stubbornly upon traditional destinies for their daughters and rejecting other possibilities out of hand. Yet despite their many flaws that make them unacceptable as guides to ordinary conduct, they do prove crucial agents in the creative process. It is by coming to terms with these mothers that Brookner's artists also discover their own literary destinies, what and how they will write.

We can see this principle illustrated most clearly in *Look at Me*, a novel that charts two interconnected movements: the heroine's disillusionment with life, and her gradual triumph over despair and suicidal impulses through the act of writing. It is a novel that places Brookner in the tradition of George Eliot and Virginia Woolf, as outlined by Alison Booth, by demonstrating that "women cannot hope for perfection both of the art and the life."[33] In the course of the plot, Frances Hinton is cheated of her hope of marriage through the duplicity of a woman who claims to be her friend, as well as the complicity of a man who appears, at first, to love her. After a humiliatingly public betrayal, she experiences her dark night of the soul, played out emblematically in a nightmarish walk into "the blackest night I had ever seen" (171). But she does not die. She returns "like a pilgrim who at last reaches the place of his pilgrimage" (171) to her late mother's bedroom, "not knowing how to recover, but working at it, with my pen and my notebook" (181).

If art is what helps Frances Hinton to carry on, then she owes much to her mother for having first uncovered her talent and guided her toward the "pen" and "notebook" which will be the tools for survival. Frances's literary career grows directly out of the storytelling in which she engages to divert her ill parent:

> I used to make my mother laugh when I went home in the evenings and described the characters who came into the Library. "My darling Fan," she used to say, her eyes widening, "I think you have a gift." She knew all their habits, and where they lived; it was like a serial story to her. She encouraged me to write it all down, and so I bought the usual large exercise book and kept a sort of diary. (16)

With the death of her mother, Frances loses not only a beloved parent, but an appreciative and responsive audience: "Since my mother died, I have had no one to talk to about these things, no one who is so interested, who knows the characters, who wants to find out what happens next" (16), she realizes mournfully. Her writing, which first blossomed out of a gesture of love, changes character after the object of love vanishes. Unwilling to confront directly either the trauma of her grief or her own fears of reenacting her mother's fate—that is, to suffer a life of frustrated hopes and an early end—Frances attempts, for much of *Look at Me,* to use literature as a defense against memory, sympathy, and identification. She begins making notes toward a satirical novel—"one of those droll and piquant chronicles enjoyed by dons at Oxford and Cambridge colleges" (16)—because she associates such comedy with hardness, with people who succeed at living without pain. She invokes the spirit of satire both to anaesthetize herself and to express her anger at fate, which has forced her to act as her mother's nurse and then cruelly deprived her of a responsibility at once dear and depressing:

I think I longed to use my sharp tongue and to be restless and critical and amusing, even if it was at other people's expense. To me in those days it seemed like freedom not to have to care for anybody's feelings if I didn't want to. I hated every reminder that the world was old and shaky, that human beings were vulnerable, that everyone was, more or less, dying. I had lived with all this for far too long. (43)

"Hate" comes to be the undertone in her relations with a great many of the people who surround her: "I do hate low-spirited people. I would even say I hate unfortunate people" (16), she confesses to the reader. And hate begins to infect her writing. Late in the action, she discovers in herself "the anger of the underdog, plotting bloody revolution, plotting revenge" (163). Her choice of verb in this case is a revealing one, for as she encounters new disappointments, she turns increasingly for relief to the invention of stories about those who have hurt her, to strategies of exploiting such people in "a satirical novel": "If they were to meet their fate at my hands, and all unknowing, would this not be a very logical development?" she asks, convinced of the "logic," though not of the morality, of such a course (184). Throughout *Look at Me,* Frances is in danger of misusing the tools of "pen" and "notebook" which her mother had placed in her hands, and she nearly succumbs to the temptation of wielding them immorally, with the same callousness and malice that others have shown in brandishing their own weapons of charm and sexual magnetism. At the point of greatest peril, Frances herself is aware of having "performed some sort of surgery on myself and eliminated all feelings save those of mockery and judgment," while also recognizing "somewhere, but far away in my mind, that this was a terrible and decisive moment, and that I might never again recover my wholeness" (135). Both her psychological health and the "wholeness" of her writing are in jeopardy.

It is the spirit of her dead mother that saves her from error, or more specifically, it is Frances's own willingness, in the end, to accept the identification between her mother and herself that does the job. Throughout her narrative, Frances has repeatedly intoned the elusive and allusive sentences, "Once a thing is known it can never be unknown. It can only be forgotten. And, in a way that bends time, so long as it is remembered, it will indicate the future" (see, for example, 5, 84, 191). The chief "thing" that Frances has attempted to deny, for much of the novel, is the likeness between her mother's personality and values—"that simple childish cheerfulness, that delicacy of intention, that sigh immediately suppressed, that welcoming of routine attentions, that reliance on old patterns, that fidelity, that constancy, and the terror behind all of these things" (30–31)—and her own. To accept this resemblance is to acknowledge herself as one of those "unfortunates," whose company she has rejected at the library where she works, and to give up expecting future success and satisfaction in life. But if that is the painful consequence, the reward, nevertheless, is self-knowledge— a quality essential to the artist. Near the conclusion of *Look at Me*, Frances dresses herself in a "white nightgown with long sleeves that I did not immediately recognize. . . . Then it came to me. It was one of the nightgowns I had bought for my mother" (175); she moves out of her own bedroom into the one formerly used by her mother, because "It felt quite natural for me to be there" (190). And in this new setting, Frances arrives at the moment of epiphany that will make her writing possible, that will allow her to advance from the stage of note-taking to the creation of art.

Fearing to see in herself her own mother and her mother's fate, Frances has remained, up until this point in the narrative, unable to "see" herself at all. The image confronting her now and again in mirrors has been the face of a stranger, detached from the self—on some occasions, "a slight and almost childish person, with fixed and fearful eyes" (175) or "some beady Victorian child" (155); on others, an unfamiliar woman whose "expression [is] lively with anticipation" (87). Her recourse has always been to seek the attention of others, hoping that they will affirm her existence. Indeed, her aborted romance with James Anstey had been just such a quest for recognition: "Look at me, I wanted to say. Look at me. . . . [On one occasion] I edged round him so that I was facing him . . . I looked at him, but he would not meet my eye" (126–27). Not until Frances takes up residence in her mother's bedroom and, emblematically, accepts the presence of her mother in herself does she achieve a sense of identity. What, moreover, the male protagonist of Willa Cather's *The Professor's House* (1925) discovers by entering an attic containing the "female forms" of dressmaking, Brookner's protagonist locates by entering the dead mother's bed— that is, "the site," as Josephine Donovan calls such realms, "of the maternal muse."[34] On the final page of the novel, Frances describes to the reader how the darkened window of her mother's room becomes the true mirror she has needed all along, as well as a "window" into her own literary imagination:

I moved to the bed and switched on the bedside lamp. . . . The window, black with night, shuts me in, and I see in its reflection Dr Constantine, crouched over the telephone, his brown eye vacant and without resource. I see Dr Simek braced against the back of his chair, his amber cigarette holder clenched in his teeth. I see Mrs Halloran, becalmed on her bed in South Kensington, a bottle beside her. I see Miss Morpeth, writing to her niece. I see myself. (191–92)

The choice of persons here is significant. These are the figures whom she has tried to exclude from her life and exile from her writing, except to treat them as the butts of jokes. They belong to the cautious, scrupulously moral sphere that Frances calls "my mother's world" of "sad and patient virtues" (30–31); thus, they are also part of Frances. In these lines, Frances not only restores them to their rightful place in her memory, as she recalls their roles in scenes she has witnessed, and locates herself in their company, but she begins to fictionalize them. (Indeed, Frances has never visited Mrs Halloran in her lodgings or "seen" Miss Morpeth in the act of composing a letter.) Her new mental images, however, have nothing of either "mockery" or "judgment" about them. They signal a change in Frances, away from the mode of harsh satire and toward the sort of narrative exemplified by *Look at Me* itself—fatalistic, yet sympathetic. Frances has grown into the writer of the kind of novel which the reader has just read and admired. As the author of such works about "unfortunates," Frances has at last defined and "seen" herself.

Look at Me, like many a woman's *Bildungsroman*, ends with what is in fact a beginning. Immediately after the words "I see myself," Frances tells the reader,

> Nancy [the maid] shuffles down the passage, and I hear her locking the front door. It is very quiet now. A voice says, 'My darling Fan.' I pick up my pen. I start writing. (192)

One expects Anita Brookner to leave the heroine in such a position; indeed, this is the only "happy" resolution possible to a novel that presents life as tragic and endorses the solitude and seclusion of a writing career as the best way of coping with misery. But what is unique and extraordinary in this conclusion is the presence of the unidentified "voice," which functions as the woman author's muse. Its words brand it, unambiguously, as the spirit of Frances's mother, to whom Frances was always "'My darling Fan.'" The dead mother has been internalized, becoming part of Frances's consciousness and also her inspiration. Thinking "back through" her turns Brookner's heroine into an artist before the reader's eyes.

*   *   *

Although, in Brookner's fiction, the heroines' own mothers may be the chief influences upon female creativity, they are certainly not the only influences. When Woolf offered her feminist maxim, "For we think back through our mothers if we are women," the context of her statement suggested that she had more than just biological mothers in mind; Woolf meant literary forbears, the women writers who have preceded us. Brookner, too—like the suspect "feminists" from whom she distances herself—acknowledges the importance of paying tribute to female precursors, doing so both in her own voice and through statements made in the voices of her protagonists.

In interviews, Brookner has spoken of the debt of "gratitude" she owes to other authors, " 'who have provided me with so much *information,* information of a kind I could never possibly have found elsewhere,' "[35] by which she appears to mean not factual "information," but interpretations of experience, what Matthew Arnold might have called guides to beauty and to the conduct of life. Male writers do turn up frequently on her lists of the figures who have taught her: Proust, James, Dickens, Diderot, and Stendhal; male painters turn up even more plentifully and often (Brookner, an art historian by profession, has published studies of Greuze, Watteau, and David); but it is with women authors of the earlier twentieth century that she seems to have the closest and most fruitful relations. " 'The women novelists I really admire in the English tradition are Rosamond Lehmann and Elizabeth Taylor,' " she has said,[36] paying her compliments to authors whose literary concerns were—as are her own—women's interior lives and domestic circumstances, and "the question of what behaviour most becomes a woman."[37] *Hotel du Lac* is, in fact, dedicated to Rosamond Lehmann. To Colette, she has made a bow on several occasions, calling the French storyteller "marvellous"[38] and placing her in the ranks of the earlier writers on whom literary daughters can depend for wisdom and support. At low moments in her own creative process, Edith Hope of *Hotel du Lac* goes to Colette:

Embroiled in her fictional plot . . . she felt a weariness that seemed to preclude any enthusiasm, any initiative, any relaxation. Fiction, the time-honoured resource of the ill-at-ease, would have to come to her aid, but the choice of a book presented some difficulties, since when she was writing she could only read something she had read before. . . . She . . . regretfully, disqualified Henry James. Nothing too big would do, nothing too small would suffice. . . . In the end she picked up a volume of short stories, the beautifully named *Ces plaisirs, qu'on nomme, à la légère, physiques.* Colette, that sly old fox, would she trusted, see her through. (66–67)

And she does not trust in vain. Colette not only sees Edith through the composition of her own novel, but sees Brookner through to the end of *Hotel du Lac,* reappearing in a submerged reference on the final page. As Edith faces the tremendous question of whether to accept a mere marriage of convenience to Mr. Neville, she makes a decision based, in part, on her determination not to sacrifice what she speaks of as "those pleasures which are lightly called physical" (184). Brookner's public assertion that literature is "the source of everything I know"[39] is as true for her fictional protagonists as for their creator; both she and her characters demonstrate, again and again, that women's literature in particular has taught them indispensable lessons, pointed them toward proper values, given them the best advice upon how to survive.

Brookner has also demonstrated how, on some occasions, thinking back through literary "mothers" can save women artists from those self-destructive impulses which are their true enemies (much more potent enemies than the greedy, scheming, but ultimately pathetic, antagonists who surround the heroines). When Edith Hope, who has complained about the Hotel du Lac because it is filled with "women, women, only women, and I do so love the conversation of men" (21), comes near to making "a false equation" and to cutting herself off from female companionship, the memory of another woman rescues her from this mistake: "She bent her head, overcome by a sense of unworthiness. I have taken the name of Virginia Woolf in vain, she thought" (88). The phrasing here is, of course, intentionally comic, playing with religious language and alluding to the exaggerated reverence in which Woolf is often held by her readers. The sentiment behind it, however, is quite serious—merely the other side of Brookner's own unironical pronouncement, in an interview, that "'Great writers are the saints of the godless.'"[40]

Throughout *Hotel du Lac*, Edith invokes the specter of her predecessor, claiming for herself a "physical resemblance to Virginia Woolf" (8; see also 63, 75, and 158). Beyond the external similarity, however, is a more important temperamental affinity; for much of the narrative, Edith hovers on the brink of dissolution, contemplating a fate like Woolf's own. Indeed, the opening lines of the novel appear to be pointing her toward a reenactment of Woolf's suicide by drowning:

From the window all that could be seen was a receding area of grey. It was to be supposed that beyond the grey garden, which seemed to sprout nothing but the stiffish leaves of some unfamiliar plant, lay the vast lake, spreading like an anaesthetic towards the invisible further shore. (7)

And while Edith describes herself as haunted by the image of Woolf, she also bears an unspoken resemblance to Woolf's heroines. Like Rachel Vinrace of *The Voyage Out* (1915), Edith leaves England and home for a journey to a foreign hotel that is also a journey into the perilous areas of the self; like Rachel too, she arrives at the boundaries that separate the rational mind from the unconscious, and the will to live from the urge to give up consciousness—an impulse expressed through metaphors involving water:

And at this very late hour, she felt her heart beat, and her reason, that controlling element, to fragment, as hidden areas, dangerous shoals, erupted into her consciousness. . . . Perhaps the champagne, the cake, the celebration, had eroded the barriers of her mind. . . . She had thought that by consenting to this tiny exile [to the Hotel du Lac] she was clearing the decks . . . and that she would be allowed to return . . . in due course, to resume her life. . . . [But] maybe I shall not go home, she thought, her heart breaking with sorrow. And beneath the sorrow she felt vividly unsafe, as she did when she saw that the plot of a novel would finally resolve itself, and how this might be brought about. (117)

Edith, however, unlike Woolf's heroine, is a novelist herself—that is, she is capable of inventing her own plots, new plots. Just as Brookner is free to invoke the legacy of an earlier woman author, make use of it by leading her readers to expect a repetition of it, and then work her own radical variation upon it, so Edith is free to escape a Woolfian death. *Hotel du Lac* concludes as she buys her ticket for London and sends a telegram, one in which she determines her own fate through an act of revision and writing:

'Simmonds, Chiltern Street, London W1,' she wrote. 'Coming home.' But, after a moment, she thought that this was not entirely accurate and, crossing out the words 'Coming home,' wrote simply, 'Returning.' (184)

The reader's pleasure comes not merely from seeing Edith survive, but from the element of surprise, from discovering that she is not precisely Virginia Woolf or even Rachel Vinrace after all.

Brookner has returned to the paradigm of *The Voyage Out* in a more recent work, *A Friend from England,* where the Rachel/Helen pairing of Woolf's novel clearly has inspired the Rachel/Heather doubling in Brookner's—though with Rachel, this time, as the older, not the younger, of the two. As in *Hotel du Lac,* Brookner draws on Woolf's structure of a voyage to foreign parts that will parallel a more dangerous act of mental traveling into the individual psyche. Once again, too, the internal landscape that Brookner's heroine discovers proves to be a fluid, amorphous, and water-filled one, offering both the threat of drowning and the promise of ecstasy through the surrender of consciousness (a far more problematic source of experience than the wholly positive, "regenerative"[41] realm of water that Gayle Greene claims to find in Margaret Drabble's and other women's fictions):

I cannot look at weeping skies or raindrops pattering on windows, or, least of all, at the falling rain itself without getting up to wander nervously from room to room, wringing my hands, and wondering if I can last out until it stops. And if I am out, of course, it is a hundred times worse. With every splash of water on my face or my leg I have to suppress an involuntary cry. . . . If I am at home, I try not to look at the windows, but I find I am drawn to them, as if made to watch, repelled yet fascinated by the falling sheet of water, wondering what it would be like to stand in it and let my head fall back and my mouth and eyes fill. But this, of course, is to be resisted, as is any kind of relaxation of my vigilance. The temptation is both horrifying and enduring, and can never be resolved.[42]

And, as she does in *Hotel du Lac,* Brookner refuses to take the Woolfian course of decreeing a resolution. Her Rachel makes the journey to Venice, the city that lies "low in the water . . . under the weight of stone it had imposed on itself . . . apparently sinking,"[43] but does not die. She comes back to England, presumably to face over and over again both the peril and the lure of letting oneself "sink." To the reader who knows Woolf's oeuvre, Rachel's willingness—like Edith Hope's in *Hotel du Lac*—to make that daily effort must seem doubly brave, especially when set against Rachel Vinrace's quite different decision to go under at once. Thus, in both *A Friend from England* and *Hotel du Lac* in particular, Brookner shows her awareness of how valuable a complex "mother" and "daughter" relationship can be between two women's texts—an awareness that points once again toward her basically feminist aesthetic.

*   *   *

Men, in Anita Brookner's fiction, are distinguished chiefly by their absence, as they flit through the novels like unpossessable butterflies. Always irresponsible, they can only be counted upon to disappear when they are most desired or to reappear—as does the erring husband in *A Misalliance*—when it is too late. Every Brookner heroine begins her narrative in a mood of "questing unconsciously for that man, that alien, that stranger, that appointed one, who will deliver her, the sleepwalker, from her sleep"[44]; and each heroine is, at the end, still waiting, despite having realized that she does so in vain. But though hopeless waiting becomes the normal condition, life can be saved from emptiness, from the state of "lack" (on which Brookner puns in the title *Hotel du Lac*), by art. The female characters who are best equipped to carry on after their inevitable disappointments in love are, by no coincidence, the professional writers. Although Brookner raises over and over again "the question of what behaviour most becomes a woman,"[45] the answer she comes up with is usually the same: writing—if not original fiction, then at least the sort of academic writing *about* fiction in which Dr. Ruth Weiss of *A Start in Life* or Kitty Maule of *Providence* engages. And, for her heroines, literary creation proves possible only with the support, encouragement, example, and applause of other women, who are always reassuringly present long after the coveted men have vanished.

Brookner's narratives are—to borrow a term from Rosalind Coward's 1980 essay, "Are Women's Novels Feminist Novels?"—indisputably "women-centered." For female readers, moreover, they assist in what Bettina Aptheker describes in *Tapestries of Life* as the task of "putting women at the center of our thinking" by "start[ing] with women's experience and form[ing] the patterns from it."[46] Whether, on the other hand, they are wholly "feminist" or not seems more open to question. In the view of a critic such as Coward, for whom "feminism must always be the alignment of women in a political movement with particular political aims and objectives,"[47] they probably would not be. Indeed, as I said at the outset, Brookner herself would be the first to agree that these novels have nothing to do with feminism. But *if* one can define the championing of literature written by and to women, the valuing of aesthetic or emotional bonds between women artists and their female mentors and audiences, and the focusing of attention upon the woman writer as a character worthy of occupying the foreground of a novel, as literary acts that promote the general good, then Brookner and her artist heroines may stand up after all and receive their feminist honors. Such honors might be accepted reluctantly— might perhaps even be courteously refused—but they would, nonetheless, be well deserved.

Notes

1. Anita Brookner, *Hotel du Lac* (London: Jonathan Cape, 1984), p. 27.
2. *Hotel*, p. 26.
3. *Hotel*, p. 28.
4. Anita Brookner, *A Misalliance* (London: Jonathan Cape, 1986), p. 187.
5. *Hotel*, p. 88.
6. John Haffenden, "Anita Brookner," in *Novelists in Interview* (London: Methuen, 1985), p. 71.
7. Sheila Hale, "Self Reflecting," *Saturday Review* (May/June 1985), 37.
8. Haffenden, p. 70.
9. Anita Brookner, *Look at Me* (New York: Pantheon, 1983), p. 12.
10. *Hotel*, p. 100.
11. Haffenden, p. 70.
12. Anita Brookner, *A Friend from England* (London: Jonathan Cape, 1987), p. 175.
13. Evelyn Fox Keller and Helene Moglen, "Competition and Feminism: Conflicts for Academic Women," *Signs: Journal of Women in Culture and Society* 2.3 (1987), 509.
14. Keller and Moglen, p. 509.
15. Haffenden, p. 67.

16. Haffenden, p. 71.

17. *Friend,* p. 158.

18. Haffenden, p. 65.

19. Haffenden, p. 61.

20. *Friend,* p. 170.

21. *Friend,* p. 170.

22. *Friend,* pp. 170–71.

23. *Friend,* p. 171.

24. *Friend,* p. 172.

25. Haffenden, pp. 62–63.

26. Haffenden, p. 64.

27. Haffenden, p. 66.

28. Haffenden, p. 68.

29. Haffenden, p. 70.

30. Virginia Woolf, *A Room of One's Own* (1929; rpt. San Diego and New York: Harcourt Brace Jovanovich, 1989), p. 76.

31. *Hotel,* p. 104.

32. Anita Brookner, *Latecomers* (London: Jonathan Cape, 1988), p. 97.

33. Alison Booth, "Incomplete Stories: Womanhood and Artistic Ambition in *Daniel Deronda* and *Between the Acts,*" in this volume.

34. Josephine Donovan, "The Pattern of Birds and Beasts: Willa Cather and Women's Art," in this volume.

35. Hale, p. 36.

36. Haffenden, p. 71.

37. *Hotel,* p. 40.

38. Haffenden, p. 75.

39. Hale, p. 38.

40. Haffenden, p. 74.

41. Gayle Greene, "Margaret Drabble's *The Waterfall:* New System, New Morality," in this volume.

42. *Friend,* p. 177.

43. *Friend,* p. 189.

44. Anita Brookner, *Family and Friends* (New York: Pantheon, 1985), p. 69.

45. *Hotel,* p. 40.

46. Bettina Aptheker, *Tapestries of Life: Women's Work, Women's Consciousness, and the Meaning of Daily Experience* (Amherst: University of Massachusetts Press, 1989), pp. 7 and 11.

47. Rosalind Coward, "Are Women's Novels Feminist Novels?" in *The New Feminist Criticism: Essays on Women, Literature, and Theory,* ed. Elaine Showalter (New York: Pantheon Books, 1985), p. 238.

Chapter 6
Incomplete Stories: Womanhood and Artistic Ambition in *Daniel Deronda* and *Between the Acts*

Alison Booth

If Virginia Woolf had set out to nourish her daughters in feminist literary criticism, she could hardly have offered a richer source than *A Room of One's Own,* now piously invoked by feminists of every school. She not only fosters a female literary tradition but also offers a less adversarial mode of succession than that of the male-dominated tradition. "For we think back through our mothers if we are women," Woolf mildly declares in *A Room of One's Own.*[1] If elsewhere she warns that the woman writer must slay the motherly Angel in the House, she seems eager to rescue rather than to slay precursors more overshadowed than overshadowing.[2] Woolf's response to George Eliot, however, seems to betray some of the anxiety of the overshadowed successor. Not only in her criticism of Eliot but also in her revisionary treatment of the female artist in her novels, Woolf thinks back through Eliot as she rethinks the conflicting imperatives of womanhood and of art.

Not accidentally, Woolf most often chose to think back through predecessors whose motherhood was purely literary: the four great women novelists of the nineteenth century, Jane Austen, Charlotte and Emily Brontë, and George Eliot, none of whom were legally married or bore children during their active writing careers.[3] Important as each of these writers was for Woolf, I believe Eliot was the one she had most immediately to contend with, as the one who belonged to her parents' day, and moreover the one who illustrated just how divorced the public persona of a great woman of letters might have to be from the traditional feminine role. Eliot was the female precursor Woolf was most compelled to think back through, impossible as it was to call her "mother." The ambiguous idea of Eliot, exercising manly artistic authority yet ordering the martyrdom of such heroines as Maggie Tulliver in *The Mill on the Floss* and Dorothea Brooke in *Middlemarch*, haunted Woolf's own efforts to reconceive women's creativity beyond motherhood and self-sacrifice.[4]

Woolf led the way for feminist critics of Eliot by mapping the distance between the talents of Eliot's heroines and their achievements; the heroines remain "the incomplete version of the story of George Eliot herself."[5] This distance may be measured most accurately for my purposes here by identifying two conflicting unresolved plots in the heroines' stories: the plot of ambition, of a calling for public life; and the erotic plot that leads to the private life of marriage and potential motherhood (I adapt Nancy Miller's use of Freud's distinction in "The Relation of the Poet to Daydreaming").[6] As the narrator of *Middlemarch* laments, "Here and there a cygnet is reared uneasily among the ducklings in the brown pond, and never finds the living stream"; women generally do not go down in history as great originators because they seem destined to obscure, cyclical life as daughters, wives, and mothers.[7] Though Woolf like other twentieth-century women writers was able to imagine a reconciliation of ambition and erotic plots for some of her heroines, she too tends to conceive female narratives as incomplete stories, tales of unrecognized swans or arrested ducklings.[8] Even in thinking back through literary mothers or "aunts" like George Eliot, Woolf retells the "tragedy, or [melancholy] compromise" of the woman who finds that "the burden and the complexity of womanhood were not enough." That is, rejecting the mere erotic plot, Eliot or her heroine tries—and inevitably to some extent fails—to fulfill the ambition plot: "she must reach beyond the sanctuary and pluck for herself the strange bright fruits of art and knowledge" (*GE* [1919] 160). Woolf's way of "writing the woman artist" George Eliot offers a key, I believe, to the portraits of female artists in both authors' novels, particularly the open-ended final novels, *Daniel Deronda* and *Between the Acts*. In both cases, the heroines fail to complete the authors' stories, ambition and womanhood figuring as incompatible plots. In this essay I will interpret the female characters in the two last novels, with their varying theatrical talents, as suppressed figures not only for the authors' autobiographies but also for the "ancient consciousness" of feminine suffering in history. But first I want to elaborate on Woolf's "thinking back through" the great Victorian woman of letters as a paradigm for autobiographical portraits of the woman artist. A woman author's predecessors, like her own heroines, must somehow fail where she succeeds.

Woolf's version of the story of George Eliot is decidedly the in complete version of the story of Woolf herself. Eliot remains an ugly duckling to Woolf's swan.[9] Woolf's thinking back through her female predecessors, as well as her depiction of ambitious heroines, follows the tradition that female ambition plots must be incomplete and that women writers' heroines are especially autobiographical. Writing the woman artist, she almost invariably follows a pattern of sympathy for a martyr and criticism of a personality hampered by womanhood (as well as by social standing and appearance). Woolf readily acknowledged Eliot's greatness, especially her departure from the woman's sphere of the novel of manners: "She was one of the first English novelists to discover that men and women think as well as feel."[10] But the presumed autobiography in Eliot's works embarrasses her successor: Eliot's heroines "make her self-conscious, didactic, and occasionally vulgar" (*GE* [1919] 157), qualities proscribed in Woolf's own writings. The precursor's personality is also drastically handicapped by both femininity and manliness. According to Woolf, Eliot's experience—and hence, art—was narrowed by the enforced seclusion, in the Victorian period, of a woman living with a married man (*RO* 73–74). More disturbingly, Eliot lacked beauty and charm: "Her big nose, her little eyes, her heavy, horsey head loom from behind the printed page and make a critic of the other sex [or same sex?] uneasy."[11] Furthermore, Eliot was not a true lady ("she was the grand-daughter of a carpenter," *GE* [1919] 152); in contrast, Woolf was assured of her upper-class, clearly gendered heritage of Pattle beauty and Stephen intellect. Most importantly, Woolf believed she had overcome some of the handicaps Eliot had faced as an author: the modern novelist wrote undisguised by masculine pseudonym or style, and she openly championed women's place in the cultural tradition. In this capacity, she figures herself as the rescuer of the misunderstood literary aunt: "no one else has ever known her as I know her. . . . I think she is highly feminine . . . and I only wish she had lived nowadays, and so been saved all that nonsense. . . . It was an unfortunate thing to be the first woman of the age."[12] Virginia Woolf set out to be the first woman of her own age without the nonsense of Victorian piety, making a virtue rather than a handicap out of femininity.

Woolf may well seem justified in thinking back through Eliot with admiration, sympathy, and a degree of censure. Why, we may ask with Woolf, are there no full-fledged women artists in Eliot's oeuvre? Shouldn't Eliot have had the courage to let her heroines escape the sanctuary of womanhood to build their own workshops? Perhaps, but if so, we must also question Woolf's own attachment to that same sanctuary. Many of Woolf's female characters, strangely enough, still pace about in the empty structures of woman's "ancient . . . suffering and sensibility," though the author, like Eliot, had escaped into utterance (*GE* [1919] 159–60).

Certainly the modern author has loosened the grip of the story that consigns women to silent obscurity, in part, no doubt, because Woolf inherited more precedents of women's achievement and of feminist defense of women's rights. Woolf creates independent artists like Orlando and Lily Briscoe in *To the Lighthouse* who far outreach such characters as Maggie Tulliver, who refuses to emulate the performing heroine, Corinne, or Dorothea Brooke, who plays the "tragedy queen" all unawares.[13] As Susan Gubar observes, the female artist-characters invented by feminist-modernists benefit from a new valuation of domestic arts (consider Mrs. Ramsay's *boeuf en daube* in *To the Lighthouse*), and a new articulation of a silenced "women's language." Yet Woolf and her contemporaries still curtailed their female characters' careers because, Gubar argues, their own self-assertion had been an inadmissible rejection of their mothers and the "natural and distinct sphere" of womanhood.[14] I would add that Woolf came closer to creating an autobiographical portrait of the artist not only because of a new outlook on female creativity, but also because of the modern fashion for self-referential art. Moreover, Woolf could draw on a tradition that was only beginning in Eliot's day—fictional autobiographies of the woman writer, from Browning's *Aurora Leigh* to Dorothy Richardson's *Pilgrimage*. The fact remains that Woolf as much as Eliot confirms Carolyn Heilbrun's observation that "women writers do not imagine women characters with even the autonomy they themselves have achieved."[15]

Woolf's own depiction of Eliot, as I have been suggesting, provides a model for both novelists' views of the obstacles confronting a woman artist's development; in both these views, ambition and erotic plots are presumed to be incompatible for women.[16] I believe there are several reasons for this recurring pattern of failed ambition for the heroines of successful women authors. There is of course the conservative force of generic convention, as Nancy Miller and others have suggested. In Eliot's and Woolf's works I detect as well an even more powerful desire to preserve feminine difference in *spite* of convention. If women were to succeed in patriarchal terms, how would we be able to tell them apart from the patriarchs? An additional motive for Eliot and Woolf, I suspect, was to challenge the expectation that women's writings will be especially personal: autobiographical, unmediated utterances from the private sphere. Perhaps completion of the heroine's story would have seemed to bind them too closely to the plausibly limited destinies of their female characters and to their own constrained womanhood. Eliot and Woolf, who made the most successful bids for "greatness" of any English women writers, claimed the right to disguise in fiction their own ambition plots, much as they assumed the right to adopt the point of view of male characters and masculine or androgynous narrators. At the same time, instead of recreating woman in man's image, Eliot's and Woolf's novels record women's efforts to make an image or art out of themselves in the service of a collective, "selfless," human progress. In *Daniel Deronda* and *Between the Acts,* the suppressed feminine collectivity resurfaces as a threat to patriarchal civilization as well as a force for the common good; an array of frustrated female performers struggles against the restrictions the authors themselves had faced to win the crown of the realm of culture, while the conventional measures of success are subverted.

If the final novels of Eliot and Woolf, with their redundant examples of suffering theatrical women, are indeed to be read as rousing the "ancient consciousness of woman," a collective counterhistory of difference, we should consider for a moment longer the question of these authors' depiction of a feminine vocation of selflessness—a kind of *failing on purpose.* Obviously, this was not *their* vocation, famous, ambitious writers that they were. Perhaps they exempted themselves from the female erotic plot as though they were simply men of letters. We know, however, that each writer to some extent adhered, in her expressed views on women and in her portraits of female characters, to the traditional sexual differences that she sought to obliterate in her own authorship.

In spite of Eliot's and Woolf's explicit advocacy of a wider choice of vocations for women, both to a degree shared Elizabeth Gaskell's belief in the unchosen vocation of womanhood itself; as Gaskell puts it in *The Life of Charlotte Brontë,* "a woman's principal work in life is hardly left to her own choice; nor can she drop the domestic charges devolving on her . . . for the exercise of the most splendid talents that were ever bestowed."[17] Like their associates in contemporary feminist movements, Eliot and Woolf sought to demonstrate the historical conditioning of gender, yet they resorted nevertheless to an ideal of essential feminine selflessness as an antidote to masculine forms of power. Both would undoubtedly have concurred with John Stuart Mill when he noted in *The Subjection of Women,* "unnatural generally means only uncustomary," yet their works cling to the "moralities . . . and . . . sentimentalities" that tell women "it is their nature, to live for others."[18] Woolf shared her predecessor's belief that women more readily abjure egotism than men; for Eliot, women learn fellow-feeling by living for others, whereas for Woolf, women see through the boundaries of the self and mock the phallic "I" (*RO* 103). More the outspoken feminist, Woolf too cherished a feminine "function of love" or "possible maternity," in Eliot's terms, when she honored female precursors or heroines who live by nurturing others rather than inventing themselves. These women novelists, whatever their beliefs, invented themselves as partly exempt from the feminine duty to foreclose the ambition plot. They evaded the erotic plot as well, with their unconventional marriages, their childlessness, and their wide public acclaim.

Eliot and Woolf revert to the autobiographical problem of female talent and narrow opportunity again and again in their works. Eliot, however restlessly, tends to offer Jane Austen's solution for the exceptional heroine: the woman gives up vocation, as Dinah Morris gives up preaching in *Adam Bede,* to marry a mentor-hero.[19] Most often, Eliot's provincial martyrs are not even allowed the semblance of a public career. While Maggie Tulliver, her most autobiographical heroine, is endowed with some of Mary Anne Evans's intellectual advantages as well as a heroine's bonus of beauty, she finds fulfillment neither in her two forbidden liaisons with men nor in her frustrated attempts to earn a living. Her final sacrifice in drowning does punish the men who have tried to master her, but it also serves to exorcise the author's ambivalence toward women's desire and ambition: as Woolf observes, Eliot seems dismayed to find "a full-grown woman on her hands" (*GE* [1919] 158). Dorothea Brooke, though balked in her plans for architectural and social reform, is at least allowed to grow up: her mentor dies and she marries her lover, ultimately enjoying the compensations of "influence" as wife and mother. Earlier, Eliot had experimented with letting Romola preside over a kind of protofeminist sanctuary for women and children, having given up her ambition to be a scholar. Generally, however, Eliot submits female talent and passion to male guidance.

Less prescriptive and less given to full biographical history in the Victorian style, Woolf nevertheless retells the heroine's story much as Eliot would have done. At the outset, Rachel Vinrace in *The Voyage Out,* with her genuine talent as a pianist, might be another Maggie Tulliver dying of the full awakening of her sexuality. In *Night and Day,* Katharine Hilbery, caught between her cousin the romantic heroine and her friend the feminist spinster, "was a member of a very great profession. . . . She lived at home."[20] In the end (like Eliot and Woolf) she is rewarded with a companionable union, but not with a new profession. Some of Woolf's dominant female figures, such as Mrs. Dalloway or Mrs. Ramsay, seem to be middle-aged Dorothea Brookes, artists of the party, subscribing to the religion of influence. Yet Woolf also offers many versions of Romola, childless spinsters or widows who pursue their obscure vocations and redefine the whole world as their sanctuary.[21] Eleanor Pargiter in *The Years,* for instance, has succeeded where Dorothea failed in housing the poor, and attains happiness as an old spinster. Not one of Woolf's heroines is famous or even openly ambitious, whereas Eliot presents several beautiful self-promoters and one dark star, the Alcharisi.

Though more consistent than Eliot in aligning femininity and self-lessness, Woolf does offer the notable figures who devote themselves to art, Lily Briscoe and Orlando—but are they quite feminine? These two portraits convey little hope of women's success in both erotic and ambitious callings. Though Lily is not a writer, her artistry may be taken as a kind of serious visual parody of Woolf's innovative prose, whereas Orlando produces one derivative epic poem in the manner of Vita Sackville-West.[22] Yet it is Orlando who enjoys everything a heroic plot could desire, from manly adventure to womanly romance, whereas Lily, the more serious artist, lives in uneasy solitude and artistic obscurity, considering herself a failure as a woman. Neither of these portraits, I am suggesting, combines the artistic success, public acclaim, and loving domestic life that Eliot and Woolf achieved.

Each of the central female characters in *Daniel Deronda* and *Between the Acts* makes a living and an art of sorts out of her talent for self-invention within the limited medium of womanliness. For each of these women, being an object on view affords an opportunity and a burden; to make a spectacle of oneself is to risk failure, and success is won by controlled self-effacement. In *Daniel Deronda,* miniature Mirah, a gifted professional singer and actress, is the only important female character in either novel to fulfill the traditional romantic plot; with her feminine abhorrence of the public life, she is only too grateful to vanish in her husband Daniel's shadow. Gwendolen is Mirah's opposite, an ambitious amateur; she hopes to go on the stage but learns that her person will only bring a profit on the marriage market. The most frankly egotistical of Eliot's heroines is thus blocked in both ambition and romance plots, since wedlock proves a living nightmare. In addition to these young performers, Eliot represents for the first time in fiction the figure of a professional woman artist, the Alcharisi, a famous diva who combines Mirah's womanly gifts and Gwendolen's will to power.[23] Her public career founders (as Eliot's certainly did not) when Leonora, thinking she is losing her talent, flees into the refuge of marriage and motherhood.[24] Like Gwendolen and Mirah, she must capitulate to Daniel as an incarnation of Jewish patriarchy; she must painfully assume the domestic roles that she had sought to obliterate in her invented persona. Private life in each of these cases triumphs over the artistic career, but not without unresolved tensions.

In *Between the Acts,* Woolf creates a similar array of frustrated female talent, this time consisting not only of the powers of performance but also the powers of literary creation. The Victorian Lucy disguises herself as a typical old widow, yet stage-manages the rites at

Pointz Hall like a high priestess, defying her rationalist brother. Mrs. Manresa, a kind of amateur diva, plays Giles Oliver's fantasy of the earth mother without ever yielding to the role of victim like the Alcharisi or Grandcourt's mistress. Giles's wife Isa performs the parts of mother, jealous wife and potential adulteress with equal lack of conviction; unlike Gwendolen, she has a genuine if minor (and secret) talent as a poet. Finally, Miss La Trobe not only combines the talent and the "masculine" professionalism of Lily Briscoe but is also a writer who reshapes the English tradition more radically than Orlando does. Instead of performing before men's eyes, Miss La Trobe creates roles for the audience and villagers to perform, yet Woolf still withholds from her some of the powers she herself enjoyed. The pageant may be a refreshing departure from high modernist art, but it is after all an abortive, provincial performance by an unknown. Though in these war years Woolf expressed a sense that she had lost her public,[25] she was fully aware of her role as famous novelist, a role Miss La Trobe seems unfit to play. The playwright moreover lacks her creator's social standing and lifelong helpmeet: she lives in lonely poverty, deserted by her actress-lover. As an outsider, this female artist avoids the capitulation to men and to heterosexuality of each of the other talented women in these novels. Still, she remains an essentially private, obscure figure in keeping with Woolf's ideal of womanhood.

With varying degrees of talent and ambition, then, the primary female characters in these final novels fail to integrate the art and the life. Although it is unlikely that Woolf had *Daniel Deronda* in view as a specific precedent among Eliot's novels—she scarcely referred to this novel except as evidence of Eliot's final decline (*GE* [1921])—in effect *Between the Acts* extends and develops *Daniel Deronda,* above all in its creation of multiple images of women struggling with public and private performance and disrupting the masquerade of civilization. These authors paradoxically escaped the same old story of the talented woman's tragedy by retelling that story—their own artistic success bought at the price of their heroines' failure.

This failure may not, however, be quite what it seems, if one reconceives the terms of success. As I have suggested, the final novels offer women an alternative cultural role to that of power and domination patterned after great men. Here the authors come closer than ever before to articulating what Woolf describes as the "ancient consciousness of woman, charged with suffering and sensibility, and for so many ages dumb" (*GE* [1919] 159). Instead of defining women's tragedy and compromise in terms of traditional values, these novels peel away the veneer of contemporary civilization to expose a feminine counterhistory. Both novels set the ominously narrow circles of English upper-class society against a background of contemporary war (the Franco-Prussian and American Civil wars or World War *II*) and of anomie and sexual violence, while they uncover sources that still fuel civilization: the unconscious, ancient belief and ritual (Judaism or Egyptian myth and folk drama), and the secret sufferings of woman. For the authors themselves and for their created societies, theater challenges genre and convention by dissolving the marriage plot of the novel of manners and enacting a communal ritual apparently coextensive with the history of a people.[26] Elaborate textures of allusion and typology in both novels seem to assert, "We all . . . are savages still" (*BA* 199), particularly by conflating courtship and hunting, imperialism and sexual domination, and English customs and primitive totem worship.[27]

If in these novels the "ancient consciousness" of woman appears to lend itself to a regenerative influence—through a healthy recognition of racial, cultural, and sexual differences suppressed in a Eurocentric, phallocentric order—such collective consciousness is also shown to be doomed to suffer in silence or to suffer perhaps worse torments as it violates that silence. "[H]urrying desires" or "evil enchantments" haunt Gwendolen and Daniel's mother (*DD* 32, 693), while Lucy holds a vision of "the mammoth . . . from whom . . . we descend" and Isa murmurs "the burden of the past . . . crooned by singing women; what we must remember; what we would forget" (*BA* 8–9, 155). In Eliot's novel only the priestly men, Daniel and Mordecai, may tap ancient origins with the sense that they are sanctioned by tradition to rescue a dying race, whereas in Woolf's novel this function extends to women and certain outcast men. Miss La Trobe plumbs the mud for artistic regeneration without any of the guilty horror that possesses Giles or venturesome women in *Daniel Deronda* when confronted with their own savagery. That Woolf's text should greet the return of the repressed less warily than Eliot's, and that it should appeal to a matriarchal rather than a patriarchal succession to channel that return, fits our expectations for a feminist-modernist cultural perspective. Nevertheless, both novels align the repressed with the feminine, following the classic dualism that assigns emotion, the body, and the cycles of private life to women, and action, the mind, and public, progressive history to men.

Both Gwendolen and the Alcharisi, magnificent egotists, refuse to accept the feminine short end of the stick. They "have not felt exactly what other women feel, or say they feel" (*DD* 691), and instead they have tried to fulfill progressive ambition plots. Yet in the end they are ensnared in the perpetual emotions of womanhood; Eliot tries to recast their ultimate humiliation as in itself a mission (stagnation for the individual translates into a slow communal progression). Hence, the famous outburst on the significance of women (young heroines especially) in history: "What in the midst of that mighty drama are girls and their blind visions? They are the Yea or Nay of that good for which men are enduring and fighting. In these delicate vessels is borne onward through the ages the treasure of human affections" (*DD* 160). In reference to Gwendolen (and indirectly, to Daniel's mother), this is an extremely utopian vision of influence, however. The heroine's upbringing has failed to educe the "natural" feminine subservience; she is rather the vessel of an irrepressible female drive for preeminence—a darker image, perhaps, of Eliot's own ambition.

While Woolf seems to accept the sexual division of labor that Eliot outlines—men will fight a people's causes and women will remain vessels of human emotion—she too unsettles this scheme with the resurgence of uncivilized ambitions in women, but with less dread of the consequences. She figures this resurgence, as Eliot does, in terms that appear to attribute gender to nature; hence, both authors resort to a favorite Victorian metaphor for women's captivity, the hothouse, in which naturally flowerlike women are artificially cultivated. One of Woolf's accounts of her predecessor illustrates the function of this horticultural imagery: while Victorian men could explore exotic origins, Victorian women were constrained, in Woolf's words, merely to "dream of seeing 'the bread fruit tree, the fan-palm, and the papyrus,'" or to view specimens in botanical gardens; Eliot instead ventured out into "'the historical life of the world.'"[28] Eliot effectively dramatizes this same conceit of explorers and conservatory plants; at a crisis early in their courtship, Gwendolen tells the cosmopolitan hunter, Grandcourt:

We women can't go in search of adventures—to find out the North-West Passage or the source of the Nile, or to hunt tigers in the East. We must stay where we grow, or where the gardeners like to transplant us. . . . That is my notion about the plants: they are often bored, and that is the reason why some of them have got poisonous.

At this moment, Gwendolen believes she is merely performing her romantic part—believes, indeed, that she is a powerful huntress—but Grandcourt is turning her into a "statue" gripping "the handle of her whip" (171). She can only try to escape by pretending to drop this vain symbol of mastery.

A strikingly similar tableau of women's hapless urge for a wider sphere is staged in *Between the Acts*. Isa Oliver shares Gwendolen's desire to go "to the North Pole" rather than to "do as other women do" (*DD* 101), but she does not share Gwendolen's phobia of her own desires. Isa escapes in poetry: "To what dark antre of the unvisited earth, or wind-brushed forest, shall we go now? Or spin from star to star" (*BA* 51). But Isa too must play her static part in an English scene; as though replicating Gwendolen as statue with whip, Isa stands "like a statu[e] in a greenhouse" among plants undoubtedly poisonous, holding a knife as she continues the play: "And from her bosom's snowy antre drew the gleaming blade. 'Plunge blade!' she said. And struck. 'Faithless!' she cried. Knife too. It broke. So too my heart, she said" (*BA* 113). These heroines cannot act out their own violent wishes except in self-destructive repetition of old romantic plots. Their husbands lust for empire or war as they lust for women, by a double standard that forbids any answering lust in the oppressed. But these women prove that they can be as venomous as men, while their vitality surpasses that of Grandcourt the lizard or Giles the snake-slayer.

In spite of Eliot's and Woolf's leaning toward an ideal of natural femininity, then, they illustrate the distortions of its artificial cultivation. Marriages between warlike explorers and hothouse dreamers become fights to the death in both novels, while motherhood, the vocation offered to most women, has mysteriously lost its natural appeal.[29] *Between the Acts*, for the first time in either Eliot's or Woolf's novels, represents a young heroine, Isa, as a mother. More typically, motherhood is what happens after the heroine's story is over, as in the Finale of *Middlemarch*. In the background of *Daniel Deronda* and *Between the Acts*, the dead mothers of Mirah and Mordecai and of Lucy and Bart become "objects of universal veneration" like Mrs. Ramsay in *To the Lighthouse*, their ambitions long since submerged in the labor of creating *others'* selves.[30] Living mothers, apart from Mrs. Meyrick, are naturally more flawed, from Mrs. Davilow, who lives too vicariously through her "Spoiled Child," to the Alcharisi, who openly resents motherhood as a poor substitute for her career. The most daring figures in *Between the Acts* evade motherhood without being punished for it. Mrs. Swithin, mother of two, has outlived that stage to indulge in the liberties of a spinster aunt, whereas Mrs. Manresa remains childless and licentious. The hothouse captives lack the maternal feelings required for their unchosen vocation, Gwendolen dreading motherhood and Isa escaping the nursery in her imagination.

Marriage and motherhood, as these novels present it, are far from all-sufficient or inevitable vocations for women. Creative ambitions, channeled most often into theater, threaten to undermine the sexual hierarchy that seems so firmly based. Theater itself characterizes the ambiguities of women's position, as it can be used to reaffirm community and gender difference or to play up the shallowness of the sexual masquerade. The drawing-room theatricals of a traditional novel of manners reappear in Gwendolen's *tableaux vivants*, but the heroine rejects her "narrow theatre" (*DD* 94), much as the author herself expands the novel to encompass the scenes of Jewish life. The pageant in *Between the Acts* seems to unite the stratified rural community, while it parodies the sexual conventions of English literature through the ages, for instance in a pastiche of the Victorian novel that might be called wooing in the missionary position.[31] At the same time the interjections from the audience reveal a much less tidy social and sexual hierarchy that can only collapse into the dogfight of man and woman in Miss La Trobe's primitively new drama at the end.

Theater seems to focus the genteel woman's captivity—she must act her part—as well as her secret freedom to act any part. Even the frailest woman embodies an untapped power, as Cleopatra lurks "unacted" in both doll-like Mirah and "Old Flimsy," Lucy Swithin (*DD* 801, *BA* 153). On a practical level, theater may be one of the few dignified (if not wholly respectable) vocations open to women; the alternatives of teaching or ladylike handiwork would humiliate Gwendolen. Significantly, Eliot does not allow any professional lady novelists in her novel, though the wealthy, "ridiculous" Mrs. Arrowpoint has "literary tendencies" (Gwendolen makes fun of her: "Home-made books must be so nice" [74–75]). Eliot allots professional talent only to exotic Jewesses, Daniel's mother and wife-to-be (as outsiders they may sidestep the commandment of ladylike self-effacement), and then only as performers, not authors in their own right. The fame of the performer, like the beauty which itself was the prime factor in an actress's fame, was only temporary, as Eliot noted.[32] Like the woman in courtship, the actress may seem to rule supreme, but she generally cannot control the form of her career, which ends, like the bride's power, prematurely. The woman novelist may appear to gain respect for her achievements quite apart from any perceived shortcomings as a woman.

Woolf coincides with Eliot in permitting only a circumscribed artistic success to certain outsiders while implying that all women must be actresses. Isa, as an upper-class English young lady like Gwendolen, has been constrained to choose marriage, the only profession for which she is qualified. Whereas Gwendolen is a somewhat unsteady actress, betraying her feelings at times, Isa never loses her concentration in the role of "Sir Richard's daughter" (16) and loving wife of "The father of my children" (14). Gwendolen courts homage, while Isa improvises her poetry in private, yet both amateurs may be said to be collaborators in creating the novels in which they figure. As Gwendolen serves as a vessel of emotion in an otherwise dry novel, so Isa infuses intimacy in Miss La Trobe's pageant and Woolf's novel. Isa's own sentiment seems to blend with the rain that restores the illusion of the pageant: "blots of rain . . . trickled down her cheeks as if they were her own tears. But they were all people's tears, weeping for all people" (180–81). Isa, then, does not need to undergo Gwendolen's painful schooling in fellow-feeling; she is instinctively a vessel of human affections, the more so because she cannot freely express them (her rival Mrs. Manresa suspects her of having secretly written the pageant [61]). Thus, the authors forestall these women's self-fulfillment for the sake of their influence, for the kind of melancholy mission Gwendolen serves in teaching Daniel to resist her sinister sexuality.

What then of the stronger women who cannot be harnessed for unrewarded service to "human affections"? Like their authors, the divas Alcharisi and Manresa have spurned a regular private life in order to gain public life, but they gain no lasting fame or artistic success; they remain defined by their relation to men. What eminence they do gain is largely granted because they are somehow beyond the pale—like Eliot, great favorites with the gentlemen but not quite suitable company for the ladies. Leonora Charisi is endowed with beauty and rank, talent, ambition, and even public acclaim, in some ways exceeding her own author's fortune. Mrs. Manresa resembles her in being a queenly performer ("she acted her own emotions"), with the power to sway men and live "a myriad lives in one" (*DD* 691, 689). She too is an exotic (born in Tasmania), and like Woolf she is allied with the Jews by marriage (*BA* 39–40); cheerful where Leonora is bitter, she advertises her self-indulgence: "I do what I like" (55). The sexual suggestiveness in the portrait of the Alcharisi, particularly in the general assumption that Daniel is Sir Hugo's illegitimate son, has become explicit in Woolf's novel. Mrs. Manresa is able to keep her rich husband in the wings while she entertains male admirers unchecked. Yet Woolf's portrait of the patriarchal goddess is, if anything, more damning than Eliot's, as Mrs. Manresa (man-raiser) is thoroughly unoriginal, a hedonistic "barbarian" (176). Whereas Leonora's "nature gave [her] a charter"—"the voice and the genius matched the face" (*DD* 728), Mrs. Manresa has no pretensions to beauty or culture. It may have become easier for women to escape the sanctuary or hothouse in the world of Woolf's fiction, but somehow the more accessible "strange bright fruits" lose the flavor of desire. Only in the pageant can the fruit of the male tradition be appropriated by a community of common people led by a woman.

Perhaps we should view Miss La Trobe rather than Mrs. Manresa as Woolf's version of Eliot's self-chartered woman: an angry playwright almost entirely dissociated from men. Like the Alcharisi, La Trobe's foreign name with its definite article seems to announce her essential difference from the common woman: "Nature had somehow set her apart from her kind" (*BA* 211). Unlike the beautiful and esteemed

"Princess," however, Miss La Trobe lacks all the traditional signs of excellence in woman: she is "swarthy, sturdy and thick set," not "altogether a lady" (57–58); she resembles the "squat," "harsh" literary lady, Mrs. Arrowpoint (*DD* 74). Both the opera singer and the playwright fail to command their own lives, but La Trobe is granted far more power over the narrative as a whole. Daniel's mother is dying, her career long since dead, when she belatedly enters the stage of the novel; her problematic motherhood, not her artistic career, brings her before the reader's eyes. Miss La Trobe, while behind the scenes and excluded from the inner circle of Pointz Hall, is the most nearly omnipresent character in the book and governs the actions of most of the players; her rough artistry is both the core of the book, the pageant, and its frame, the new play at the end. Yet she is utterly alone with her misunderstood and fragmentary art; love for women must be sublimated into a "passion for getting things up" (58).

Among a variety of images of women's trammeled talent, these two belated artist figures verge more closely than ever before on the authors' autobiographies, while they are firmly placed outside the authors' circumstances. The Alcharisi seems to confess to Eliot's own defiance of her father's religion and of patriarchal law in her union with Lewes, and perhaps more importantly to her ambition and love of success. Yet the great opera singer, a beautiful Jewess with "masculine" ruthlessness, is not to be mistaken for George Eliot. Miss La Trobe bespeaks Woolf's dedicated struggle with her medium and her audience, her sense of isolation as well as her lesbianism. But no one surely would mistake the plain village bohemian for the beautiful lady of Bloomsbury, still less for a great woman of letters. It is tempting, however, to imagine Miss La Trobe as in some sense Woolf's reincarnation of Eliot. In her published writings on Eliot, Woolf dwelt on her manliness and ugliness, her lower-class background, her scandalous private life and her seclusion. Naturally, this incarnation is the incomplete story of the Grand Old Woman of Letters. La Trobe is an "outcast" yet "the slave of [her] audience" (*BA* 211), as indeed both Eliot and Woolf perceived themselves to be in spite of their artistic success. All women artists in these oeuvres are doomed to failure, however magnificent has been their demand for art and knowledge beyond a captive woman's reach.

I have suggested that the incompleteness of the heroine's stories registers more than the authors' nostalgia for an inviolate woman's sphere; in addition it affirms their escape from that sphere as consummate women of letters. At the same time, these portraits of thwarted female vocation emphasize the richly expressive and regenerative qualities of "ancient suffering and sensibility," while calling into question conventional measures of creative success.[33] Woolf more than Eliot could dispute the interdependence of artistry, authority, and masculine identity. The later woman author could reach, but she would not unquestioningly grasp. She would debunk the ideal of the Grand Old Woman of English Letters even as she paid tribute to her predecessor. Yet as Woolf, like Eliot's heroines, "uttered [her] demand for something . . . that is perhaps incompatible with the facts of human existence" (*GE* [1919] 159), in a sense she strove to complete, as her heroines were unable to do, the story of George Eliot herself.

Notes

1. *A Room of One's Own* (New York: Harcourt Brace Jovanovich, 1929), p. 79; this work will be parenthetically cited as *RO*. Margaret Stetz, in this volume, shows that Woolf's model of "thinking back through our mothers" can be applied to women writers who, like Anita Brookner and George Eliot, do not consciously affiliate themselves with a female or feminist tradition.

2. *A Room of One's Own*, p. 79; "Professions for Women," in *Virginia Woolf, Women and Writing*, ed. Michèle Barrett (New York: Harcourt Brace Jovanovich, 1979), p. 59. Sandra M. Gilbert and Susan Gubar draw on Woolf's concepts of "Milton's bogey" and "the Angel in the House" in reconstructing a female tradition, but Woolf's depiction of the literary landscape is far less bloody than *The Madwoman in the Attic: The Woman Writer and the Nineteenth-Century Literary Imagination* (New Haven, Conn.: Yale University Press, 1979), pp. 187–88, 17. See Gilbert and Gubar's "'Forward into the Past': The Complex Female Affiliation Complex": "in the twentieth century . . . Freud-derived Bloomian paradigms like . . . our own 'anxiety of authorship' must give way to a paradigm of ambivalent affiliation." Modern writers like Woolf base their creative enterprise on mother-daughter as well as father-daughter relations. Gilbert and Gubar compare Woolf's women artists with the failed women artists in Eliot's and other nineteenth-century women's writings (*No Man's Land: The Place of the Woman Writer in the Twentieth Century* [New Haven, Conn.: Yale University Press, 1988], vol. 1, pp. 192–93), but I believe they overemphasize the historical shift. Eliot can be seen in terms of "ambivalent affiliation," and Woolf's female artists are also incomplete stories, as I show here.

3. Woolf wrote essays reviving many lesser-known women writers, including some (for example, Elizabeth Gaskell) who integrated women's roles and professional writing. See *Women and Writing*, ed. Barrett. Yet it seems that one of Woolf's criteria for greatness is the exemption from the usual womanly life. Nevertheless, Woolf like Eliot and most nineteenth-century women writers respected the imperative "to embrace motherhood as a vocation—or, at the very least, to define any other vocation in terms of motherhood," in Margaret Homans's words (*Bearing the Word* [Chicago: University of Chicago Press, 1986], p. 153).

4. Woolf once announced to the novelist Rose Macaulay, "I think I shall prepare to be the Grand Old Woman of English letters" (Macaulay, "Virginia Woolf: II," *Horizon* 3 (1941), 316–18), humorously belittling the struggle for literary laurels that she dramatizes in essays on Eliot and others; she knew that an eminent woman forfeits feminine charm. I account for Woolf's debt to Eliot

as a "great" woman of letters in a forthcoming book, "Great Women of Letters: George Eliot, Virginia Woolf, and the Feminine in History."

5. Virginia Woolf, "George Eliot," *Women and Writing*, ed. Barrett, p. 160. This essay will be cited parenthetically as *GE* (1919) with page number.

6. Nancy K. Miller, "Emphasis Added: Plots and Plausibilities in Women's Fiction," in *The New Feminist Criticism: Essays on Women, Literature and Theory*, ed. Elaine Showalter (New York: Pantheon Books, 1985), pp. 345–46. Carolyn G. Heilbrun similarly outlines the divisions in women's biographical narratives: "the public and private lives cannot be linked, as in male narratives" (*Writing a Woman's Life* [New York: Ballantine, 1988], p. 25).

7. "Prelude," *Middlemarch* (Boston: Houghton Mifflin, 1956), p. 4.

8. A notable version of female genius destroyed by feminine fate is Judith Shakespeare, whose ambition plot, we might say, is cut short by her erotic plot. Her attempt at a theatrical career leads to sexual downfall and suicide (*RO* 48–50)—a danger that lurks in *Daniel Deronda* and *Between the Acts*.

9. Mary Jacobus aptly reads the centenary essay (1919) as Woolf's "elegy" for Eliot. As Jacobus explains, "Our mothers were killed by the burden and the complexity of womanhood; or like George Eliot, died in giving birth to their writing (as Dorothea rests in an unvisited tomb in order that 'George Eliot' may write her epitaph)" (Mary Jacobus, "The Difference of View," in *Reading Woman: Essays in Feminist Criticism* [New York: Columbia University Press, 1986], pp. 28–29).

10. Virginia Woolf, "George Eliot (1819–1880)," *London Daily Herald*, March 9, 1921, p. 7—henceforth cited as *GE* (1921).

11. "Indiscretions," *Women and Writing*, ed. Barrett, p. 72. In this same essay Woolf determines that Eliot is "an Aunt": "So treated she drops the apparatus of masculinity . . . and pours forth . . . the greatness and profundity of her soul" (75). Woolf here regards Eliot as neither the inhibiting mother-saint like Julia Stephen nor the sibyl with the male pseudonym, but an aunt-novelist (like Woolf's own aunt, Anne Thackeray Ritchie, who was a friend of George Eliot). Although Woolf criticized the masculine pseudonym, she understood its function in freeing the woman writer from criticism based on sex.

12. *The Letters of Virginia Woolf*, ed. Nigel Nicolson and Joanne Trautmann (New York: Harcourt Brace Jovanovich, 1976), vol. 2, pp. 321–22.

13. Ellen Moers, *Literary Women* (New York: Oxford University Press, 1985), pp. 173–75; *Middlemarch*, p. 91.

14. Susan Gubar, "The Birth of the Artist as Heroine: (Re)production, the *Künstlerroman* Tradition, and the Fiction of Katherine Mansfield," in *The Representation of Women in Fiction*, ed. Carolyn G. Heilbrun and Margaret R. Higonnet (Baltimore: Johns Hopkins University Press, 1983), pp. 39, 49–50. Josephine Donovan in this volume notes the attempt of "the art of the sophisticated daughter" to approach the art "integrated with its environment" created by ordinary women in the home.

15. Carolyn G. Heilbrun, *Reinventing Womanhood* (New York: Norton, 1979), p. 71.

16. Elizabeth Barrett Browning's Aurora Leigh postpones the erotic plot till she has become an eminent poet, at which time she concedes: "No perfect artist is developed here / From any imperfect woman. . . . / Art is much, but love is more" (*Aurora Leigh* [Chicago: Academy Chicago, 1979], Book 9, p. 341). This pioneering English female *Künstlerroman* offered an important precedent for both Eliot and Woolf, particularly in *Romola* and *Orlando*.

17. *The Life of Charlotte Brontë* (Harmondsworth, England: Penguin, 1975), vol. 2, p. 334. Eliot wished education to raise women to men's level while preserving feminine difference, the "function of love" based on "possible maternity" that teaches women domestic and social service (*The George Eliot Letters*, ed. Gordon S. Haight [New Haven, Conn.: Yale University Press, 1955], vol. 4, p. 468). Woolf more openly challenged the historical oppression of women, but she asked, "Ought not education to bring out and fortify the differences rather than the similarities" between the sexes? (*RO* 91). Although she theoretically repudiated the Victorian ideology of influence, she celebrated, in *A Room of One's Own, Three Guineas,* and elsewhere, qualities that had marginalized women.

18. *The Subjection of Women* (New York: Appleton, 1870), pp. 22, 27.

19. Esther Lyon, with talent only for a romantic plot, might be an Emma Woodhouse taught to pass up the lord of the manor for the yeoman, in this case Felix Holt.

20. Virginia Woolf, *Night and Day* (New York: Harcourt Brace Jovanovich, 1948), pp. 44–45.

21. Jane Marcus, "Liberty, Sorority, Misogyny," in *Virginia Woolf and the Languages of Patriarchy* (Bloomington: Indiana University Press, 1987), pp. 76–77.

22. Woolf claimed that Vita Sackville-West wrote with "a pen of brass," but according to Nigel Nicolson, Woolf did show "a certain admiration for Vita's writing," and admired her well-rounded life, including, as Woolf wrote in her diary, "her motherhood . . . her being, in short (what I have never been) a real woman" (Introduction, *The Letters of Virginia Woolf,* ed. Nigel Nicolson and Joanne Trautmann [New York: Harcourt Brace Jovanovich, 1977], vol. 3, p. xx).

23. Deborah Heller, "George Eliot's Jewish Feminist," *Atlantis* 8 (1983), 38. *Armgart* (1871), a dramatic poem about a great opera singer losing her voice, anticipates the Alcharisi's story.

24. Eliot did fear a loss of command over her public after *Middlemarch* (*The George Eliot Letters,* ed. Haight, vol. 6, pp. 301–2), and did, after *Daniel Deronda* (and George Henry Lewes's death), belatedly marry. We can only speculate whether she would have completed the novel she had begun at the time of her death.

25. *The Diary of Virginia Woolf,* ed. Anne Olivier Bell and Andrew McNeillie (New York: Harcourt Brace Jovanovich, 1984), vol. 5, p. 229.

26. See Daniel's discussion of the "National Tragedy" of the Jews (*Daniel Deronda* [Harmondsworth: Penguin Books, 1967], p. 575, henceforth parenthetically cited as *DD*), and Gordon S. Haight, *George Eliot: A Biography* (New York: Oxford University Press, 1968), pp. 406, 471. "And what about the Jews?" asks a member of the audience at Pointz Hall. "People like ourselves, beginning life again" (*Between the Acts* [New York: Harcourt Brace Jovanovich, 1969], p. 121, henceforth cited as *BA*). See Quentin Bell, *Virginia Woolf: A Biography* (New York: Harcourt Brace Jovanovich, 1972), vol. 2, p. 189, and *The Diary of Virginia Woolf,* vol. 5, pp. 139, 159, 193, 200.

27. The use of pagan mythology and Judeo-Christian typology is the most important feature of the cultural revision in these novels, too pervasive to reconstruct here. It is particularly evident in characters' (especially women's) overdetermined roles. For example, Gwendolen is Lamia and Persephone; Isa is Isis; Lucy is St. Lucy and St. Swithin.

28. "George Eliot," *The Nation and Athenaeum* 40 (30 October 1926), 149.

29. Nina Auerbach detects, particularly in the portrait of the Alcharisi, Eliot's own ambivalence about the Victorian cult of motherhood and her eventual repudiation of the maternal role she at times willingly played ("Artists and Mothers: A False Alliance," *Women and Literature* 6 [1978], 14).

30. *To the Lighthouse* (New York: Harcourt Brace Jovanovich, 1927), p. 81.

31. In the pageant, Eleanor Hardcastle accepts Edgar Thorold's proposal to share "a lifetime in the African desert among the heathens" (*BA* 166), whereas Jane Eyre and Aurora Leigh each decline a similar proposal from a zealous cousin.

32. See "Liszt, Wagner, and Weimar," in *Essays of George Eliot*, ed. Thomas Pinney (London: Routledge & Kegan Paul, 1963), pp. 98–99. As Mirah prepares for a career singing in English drawing rooms, there is much anxiety about her professional name and dress (like an authorial pseudonym). She has faith in her sincerity as a Jewess: "It is all real, you know . . . even if it seemed theatrical," whereas those helping her consider authenticity, and more importantly, the dangers of her commodification as female exotic (546).

33. See Pamela Caughie's chapter in this volume.

Part III
Confronting the Dilemma of
Role and Vocation

Chapter 7
When Privilege Is No Protection: The Woman Artist in *Quicksand* and *The House of Mirth*

Linda Dittmar

In memory of Joan Lidoff

> For feminism to succeed, it must integrate a radical position against class, race, and gender privilege together.
> —Nelly McKay

> Exploration not in the service of reconciling self to world, but creating a new world for a new self.
> —Rachel Blau DuPlessis

Narratives of artistic emergence often turn out to be narratives of transgression. At work here is the belief that artists free their authentic voices and give form to their unique perceptions only as they soar above society's stale values and stifling habits. On its face, this view would suggest a gender-free reading of the *Künstlerroman,* for the social conservativism and conceptual stagnation it identifies as blocking creativity afflict men and women alike. In practice, however, women's emergence as artists is by no means gender-free. While definitions of art, attitudes toward artists, and theories of artistic production have changed over time, patriarchal resistance to including women in the arts has been constant. Within patriarchy, women artists must transgress gender role expectations on top of everything else. True, the shift from Romanticism's glorification of the inspired lone genius—generally male, white, and sustained by middle-class consumers—toward a more flexibly democratic view of the artist, has been friendly to women, minorities, and others working at the margins of the "fine" (or "high") arts. Yet for all that, the fact remains that even today, let alone earlier in this century, masculinist constructions of gender continue to resist women's entry into full and equal participation in the arts.[1]

Such thinking may concede to women the more "feminine," imperma-
nent, and often unpaid or underpaid spheres of artistic production—
notably the ornamental, domestic, and performing arts—but it still
withholds welcome into such prestigious strongholds of "high" art as
sculpting, painting, and sometimes even writing, let alone composing,
directing, and conducting.

Within such territorialization, women cannot but experience ability and gender as interrelated. Their struggles to emerge as artists
come up against an ideology of gender that defines them as congeni-
tally—naturally and permanently—incapable of artistic creation. In
the context of this volume's focus on women artists, the disabling
effects of this ideology on women hardly need elaboration. What may
be less readily obvious is the fact that our society's use of essentialist
theories of competence to restrict access to the arts extends beyond
gender to include race, class, ethnicity, and more. In this respect art has
not differed from other modes of production and profit that justify
exclusionary practices by spurious theories of congenital ability. For
women, together with all marginalized groups, the first line of battle
concerns the fact that ideology thrives on the consent of those it op-
presses. That is, their emergence as artists must hinge on a reclaiming
of the self from the disabilities ascribed to it by those in power. In this
respect, *Künstlerromane* by women are narratives of decolonization as
well as of emergence. As the following discussion will show, such reclaiming and decolonizing are not easy to come by. Both the personal
struggle to reclaim the self and the political one to reclaim one's group
occur within ideologies designed to block them.

The difficulty of withstanding social constructions that deny the
woman artist access to her gifts is the subject of this essay. Using Edith
Wharton's *The House of Mirth* (1905) and Nella Larsen's *Quicksand*
(1928) as specific examples, I will focus on consent and resistance as
pivotal to emergence. While a comparative reading of these novels is
broadly useful as a study in women's collusion with patriarchal ideology, this pairing is especially illuminating because it highlights ways
beliefs concerning personal worth and birthrights get played out variously as considerations of class and race intersect with those of gender.
Here women's collusion with their social construction as nonartists by
gender gets modified and rearticulated through their social construction by race and class. Obviously, then, the problem of gender central
to women's *Künstlerromane* gets compounded by additional considerations—not only of race and class, but also of age, familial circumstances, sexual orientation, nationality, and ethnicity. Attention to this
fact reminds us that women, though united by gender, differ in myriad
ways, as other essays in this collection show.[2] Still, given the complexity

of such interrelations, it is helpful to study the whole in terms of its parts. Attention to gender as a separate category allows us to identify certain effects of ideology as an entry point into a more complex understanding of women's *Künstlerromane*.

Seen in these terms, the fact that this body of literature rarely shows empowerment to be as available to women as it is to their male counterparts, is especially noteworthy.[3] Over and again, the barrier these novels depict is the artist's construction as Woman—in her own eyes as well as in others'. Virginia Woolf keeps returning to this issue in *To the Lighthouse* (1927) with her use of the leitmotif of "Women can't paint, women can't write." She attributes these words to the particularly "odious" Mr. Tansley, but the important point about her use of this patriarchal prohibition is that she repeatedly situates its reception and recall in her female artist character, Lily Briscoe. Over the novel's duration, Briscoe's work keeps getting blocked by recollections of Tansley's words:

> Then why did she mind what he said? Women can't write, women can't paint—what did it matter coming from him. . . ? Why did her whole being bow, like corn under a wind, and erect itself again from this abasement only with a great and rather painful effort?[4]

It is the effect of Tansley's words on Briscoe, more than their origin in him, that concerns Woolf. For her the issue is not only men's hostility to women's creativity, but women's position within this hostility. For the women's *Künstlerroman*, the primary question is not whether women can paint or write but whether their art can flourish despite the injunction against their pursuing it.

To the Lighthouse has no clear answer to this question. Women, it suggests, collude in their relegation to the "feminine" sphere. While this collusion is profoundly conflicted even for Mrs. Ramsay, let alone Lily, it nonetheless reveals the role of ideology in gender relations as it affects women's access to art. It is not merely the public masculine censure Woolf locates in Tansley that threatens Lily, but the private feminine censure she locates in Mrs. Ramsay and in Lily herself. Ultimately, Lily withstands the call of the domestic sphere, but not without coming close to being engulfed by it through Mrs. Ramsay's mediation. As "the Angel in the House" Mrs. Ramsay establishes a model of feminine responsiveness that endangers the very integrity of the female self (her own included), let alone that self's capacity to transmute the restless flow of life into aesthetic articulation. Though Woolf associates Mrs. Ramsay with poetry and grants her the gift of art (for example, the dinner party), and though she casts her in the role of a maternal enabler whose fecund spirit nurtures Briscoe in her struggle to complete her painting,[5] Woolf does so with considerable ambivalence. She also has Mrs. Ramsay engineer Minta's unfortunate marriage, she makes the dinner party hover precariously between triumph and disaster, and on several occasions she has Mrs. Ramsay pressure Briscoe to accommodate men at a cost to her integrity. Mrs. Ramsay is not, then, a muse or a creator in the full sense. Rather, she embodies possibility—beckoning yet receding, felt but evanescent.[6]

It is not the biological fact of femaleness that ultimately keeps Woolf's women from art, but their conflicted collaboration in a construction of femininity that serves patriarchal interests. Women's non-domestic creativity can occur, it seems, only when gender is made irrelevant to the project at hand. In short, Woolf has to kill Rachel in *The Voyage Out* (1915) or resort to androgyny in *Orlando* (1928). In *To the Lighthouse* she develops the point more complexly when she shows Briscoe unable to create art from a position of gender awareness. To think of one's self as Woman, Woolf suggests, it to struggle with self-doubt and surrender repeatedly to the claims others make on one's time and energy. Only when Briscoe subordinates her identity as Woman to a gender-neutral state, can she assume a painterly relationship to her work:

She took up once more her old painting position with the dim eyes and the absent-minded manner, subduing all her impressions as a woman to something much more general; becoming once more under the power of that vision which she had seen clearly once. . . . It was a question, she remembered, of how to connect this mass on the right hand with that on the left. (*TTL* 82–83)

But such moments are rare in *To the Lighthouse*. More often, the clarity made possible by dimness and the creativity that gets released through the repression of gender give way to the social constraints that confound one's ability "to connect this mass on the right hand with that on the left." Indeed, more often Woolf at once suppresses Briscoe's capacity for beauty and erotic vitality outside of art, and withholds from her public recognition as a serious artist. She has her "worsted" (*TTL* 236) both as a woman and as an artist. During the dinner party she thwarts Briscoe's desire to revenge herself on Tansley; she delays completion of Briscoe's painting for some ten years; and even then she lets Briscoe expect no better than that it be forgotten in some attic. Indeed, ten years after that damaging encounter with Tansley, at the mature age of forty-four, Woolf still has Briscoe experience "blasts of doubt" (*TTL* 237) when she recalls his words.

That Woolf mediates this ambivalent presentation of Briscoe's art through an embattled, self-referential narrative, inscribes in the materiality of language what realistic novels like *Quicksand* and *House of*

Mirth tend to keep out of sight—namely, that the artist's difficulties are the author's too. At issue are not just the contradictory claims of patriarchal domesticity and autonomous articulation which Woolf situates in Briscoe, Mrs. Ramsay, and other women but also the epistemological disarray that Woolf inscribes in *To the Lighthouse*'s narrative procedures. While Guiget is certainly right to see the heterogeneity of this novel as "brimming with inward life and lyricism,"[7] Woolf's resorting to a discourse that depends on recurring shifts in subject position is profoundly conflicted. Above all, her writing articulates a groping for self-definition outside socially acceptable ideology. Woolf may be "deconstructive" in the Derridean sense of endlessly deferring meanings, as Toril Moi suggests, but what is important about her "ceaseless interplay of linguistic deferral and difference" is its application—in this case, that it suggests ambivalence about women's access to art.[8] Woolf's lyricism rests on a narrative process that repeatedly truncates, disperses, and represses meanings. Its inspirational side is that it valorizes process, as Pamela L. Caughie suggests, thus empowering readers to engage in social transformation. Its painful side is that it doubts attainment and foregrounds dispersal. Its dynamic anticanonic stance liberates creativity, but it also prevents one from escaping the uncertainties and contradictions endemic to social transformation.

In all this, Woolf's novel is a sobering reminder of the power of ideology. That even a writer as committed to women's empowerment as she was ended up tangled in the prohibition against women's entry into the arts is a useful stepping stone to such narratives of thoroughly failed emergence as *The House of Mirth* and *Quicksand*. Once we think of these two novels in relation to *To the Lighthouse* on the one hand and such works as Kate Chopin's *The Awakening* (1898) and Charlotte Perkins Gilman's "The Yellow Wallpaper" (1899) on the other, we can detect a pattern of ambivalence and frustration concerning women's emergence as artists that points to a social malaise. As all the essays in this section of *Writing the Woman Artist* suggest, at issue is not just women's exclusion from the arts but the difficulty both authors and characters experience resisting an essentialist construction of femininity which posits that such exclusion is appropriate. Seen together, the effects of the domestic ethos Jane Atteridge Rose uncovers in the fiction of Rebecca Harding Davis, the phases Katherine Kearns delineates in Lee Smith's work, the definition of artist that Mara Witzling sees Judy Chicago's struggling with the doubts, the disavowals Linda Hunt shows to affect Cora Sandel's binary view of gender, and the unresolved contradictions Renate Voris analyzes in Christa Wolf's work, are all anchored in a problematic epistemology of selfhood that confounds biology, social function, and art. Indeed, this short list opens up to a much longer one, one that includes the silences, defeats, and close calls from Harriette Simpson Arnow's *The Dollmaker* (1954) and Sylvia Plath's *The Bell Jar* (1962) to Toni Morrison's *The Bluest Eye* (1970), *Sula* (1973), and *Beloved* (1987), Maxine Hong Kingston's *The Woman Warrior* (1975), Nadine Gordimer's *Burger's Daughter* (1979), Alice Walker's *The Color Purple* (1982), Linda Ty-Casper's *Awaiting Trespass* (1985), and more. Taken in aggregate, these novels suggest that the proper subject of the women's *Künstlerromane* is women's intervention in gender ideology as a means to artistic emergence.

Though hardly exhaustive, the list above yields several important observations. For one thing, the "beautiful soul" scenario which Marianne Hirsch identifies as blocking women's artistic emergence in the nineteenth century carries over into the twentieth.[9] Moreover, differences among these novels reveal that social and historical differences bear directly on women's access to art. Hirsch's model applies most directly to white middle-class women, not all women. Arnow's treatment of transgression and disability differs from Hong Kingston's, and both differ from Wharton's on the one hand and from Morrison's on the other. As the following discussion of *Quicksand* and *The House of Mirth* shows in some detail, these differences register each writer's specific political as well as personal circumstances. Certainly the growing body of retrieved noncanonic women's writing demonstrates that barriers to women's emergence as artists involve more than gender ideology. Put differently, gender gets recast in relation to other ideologies of hegemony as it comes in contact with them. Thus, the aggregate emphasis on gender signaled by the above list and by this volume as a whole must be inflected through considerations of difference—economic, racial, national, and more. To all this Linda Alcoff's discussion of "positionality" is especially pertinent. Focusing on ways "woman gets defined and valued in terms of women's social position," she at once highlights the dangers of essentialism and the potentials for social transformation inherent in women's ability to reclaim their identity. Either way, her analysis is extendable to all value-laden social markings (for example, "black," "gay," and "ethnic"). Thus, read with an eye to difference, narratives of the woman artist show that women's experiences of blockage vary in kind and in degree depending on their "positionality."[10]

In this respect, *The House of Mirth* and *Quicksand* make for a useful comparison precisely because their juxtaposition serves to caution against an undifferentiated application of gender theory. For despite these two novels' shared orientation toward the "beautiful soul" version of thwarted artist narratives, it is their radically differing construction of each protagonist's identity as it responds to her race and social class that accounts for each plot's unfolding. On the one hand, both novels concern gifted young women who head for inexorable destruction despite considerable privilege each enjoys by birth and rearing. Wharton's Lily Bart and Larsen's Helga Crane are both single, intelligent, attractive, and resourceful. Though orphaned by their mothers and abandoned by their fathers (Helga literally, Lily figuratively), each has some family backing and affluent social connections. At the start of their respective novels, each seems equipped for comfortable survival: Lily is about to ensnare a rich husband, while Helga is teaching at a prestigious school and engaged to marry a socially prominent colleague. Yet for all these advantages, Lily sabotages her chances at prosperous marriages, alienates the aunt about to will her her wealth, and dies destitute having taken an overdose of a sleeping draught. And Helga, too, backs off from advantageous marriages, rejects the economic comforts offered by family and friends, and by the novel's end finds herself at death's door. Significantly, both Wharton and Larsen present their calamitous resolutions as inevitable. The stages of defeat to which each subjects her protagonist follow one another relentlessly, and in each case these stages are linked to a barely articulated resistance to gender construction (compare Chopin, Gilman, and Woolf).

Still, in certain other respects, the plots of these novels differ markedly. Helga marries and has children, while Lily does not. Both are barred from sexuality (Lily through celibacy, Helga by marrying a distasteful man and suffering difficult pregnancies), but the formulas for this repression are tellingly different: the upper-class white woman is kept on a pedestal, the middle-class black woman is allowed her sexuality but punished for it. Occupationally, the differences are also telling: Helga trains and supports herself with dignity as a salaried teacher, editor, and secretary, while Lily mainly lives off others in return for work assiduously disguised as friendship. (That Helga gets money from her American uncle and for a short time allows herself to be supported by her Danish relatives mirrors only fleetingly Lily's lifelong experience of compromised autonomy.) Indeed, Helga's access to middle-class comforts, let alone luxury, proves much more tenuous than Lily's; she is almost reduced to supporting herself as a maid, while the worst Lily need do is trim hats in a top millinery establishment.

As the above suggests, what separates *The House of Mirth* and *Quicksand* most pronouncedly are race and class considerations, though not in equal proportions. Ultimately, Larsen treats Helga's tenuous hold on class privilege as racially determined. As she presents it, it is Helga's origin that prevents her from claiming as a birthright what Lily takes for granted. At issue here is a tainted lineage that hangs over Helga like a curse. Thus, while Larsen links Helga to the uppercrust of conservative black education at Naxos, to Harlem's glamorous "renaissance" period, and to Copenhagen's affluent bourgeoisie, she has the entire narrative devolve on the fact that Helga was born to an interracial marriage, and an unstable one at that. It is as an educated black woman, not as an educated woman, that Helga cannot find appropriate work when she quits her teaching position; it is as a woman without "people" that she must carve out for herself a position among middle-class blacks; and it is as a black in Copenhagen and as a mulatta in the United States that she is appropriated into the racial fantasies others harbor on her behalf.

In all this, Larsen elides the issue of class. Her focus is, rather, on the anguish of devalued race. As she argues in the course of *Quicksand*'s unfolding (compare *Passing* too, 1929), our society's construction of race makes a minor genetic variant determine one's access to well-being in the broadest material and spiritual sense. That thoughts about race never enter Lily's consciousness is a measure of the assured self-acceptance that can come with being white. Though Lily is acutely aware of the finest nuances and slightest fluctuations of wealth, class, and ethnic privilege, the racially advantageous position she occupies is so secure that she never gives it a thought. For Helga such blindness would be unthinkable. It is her struggle to define for herself a racial identity within the contradictory social and political valuation of her blackness and whiteness that gives her life its particular direction. For her, even the absence of "people"—the family taint she cannot bear to reveal—is racially inflected. In *Quicksand* it is above all the nuances of color, and the histories and mythologies signified by these nuances, that set the terms on which one might consider the question of gendered self-definition.

In short, a comparative reading of *The House of Mirth* and *Quicksand* as *Künstlerromane* must take into account issues of racial difference and class position as these interact with the effects of gender inscription on artistic emergence. Especially given this volume's focus on women artists as a gender category, it is important to guard against over-generalizations that mask the fact that even the thwarting of woman's art involves other hegemonies besides gender. Still, before moving ahead with this line of thought, we need to backtrack briefly to address the prior question of whether *The House of Mirth* and *Quicksand* concern women artists at all. For the two are not explicit narratives of thwarted art along the lines of *The Awakening* or "The Yellow Wallpaper" or any of the other novels mentioned above. Lily and Helga do not partake even in the abortive emergence these novels describe, let alone in the fuller articulation *To the Lighthouse* allows Briscoe. Rather, Lily's and Helga's art functions only as a barely articulated subtext. Partly suppressed and partly made to serve the congruent needs of racism, capitalism, and patriarchy, their art gets compromised almost beyond recognition—almost, but not quite.

On its face, Lily and Helga neither produce art nor dream of doing so—whether by "art" we mean the "fine" arts or artisanal production. Neither can boast even such productivity as Alice Walker finds in her mother's garden, let alone in Phillis Wheatley's poems. Yet for all this lack of tangible products, Lily's and Helga's lives register an aesthetic sensibility and practice that nonetheless situate them within the *Künstlerroman* tradition. Above all, their art is ornamental and performing, and the fact that it occurs in the ordinary course of living does not make it any less of an art. For them, bodies, clothes, possessions, and even chance locale are the raw materials of fantasy; their sense of color, texture, and line yields arrangements that make those who view them (and their own self-viewing) resonate to implied narratives of pleasure and transcendence. Encoding themselves through dress, motion, prose, and set, they turn life itself into a heightened aesthetic production, with all the symbolic and sensory resonance associated with such performance. They are indeed artists—active participants in the production of cultural scripts. Their bodies may be "the blank page" Susan Gubar sees as suffering cultural inscription, but it is as active agents that they put themselves to this use.[11] This sense of agency is double-edged. Affirming women's will, it makes that will serve interests that thwart women's autonomy. Registering women's capacity for empowerment, it channels that very capacity toward social practices that will appropriate and neutralize it. As Wharton and Larsen present it, women's very potential for self-definition ends up betraying them as they allow their art to be absorbed into patriarchal agendas that valorize material consumption and an aesthetic of rareness.

Wharton alerts us to this danger at the very opening of *The House of Mirth*. Allowing us our first glimpse of Lily when Selden, Lily's ambivalent friend and would-be lover, spies her at Grand Central Station, her very language mingles notions of agency (that is, Lily's self-definition) and appropriation (that is, Selden's interpretation of Lily's appearance). Narrated from a third-person position that slides imperceptibly between Selden and a supposedly objective narrator, the novel's opening establishes a skeptically voyeuristic mode of reading from the outset, for the gaze that admires Lily also doubts her. It notes Lily's "radiance," her "vivid head," and "the girlish smoothness" of her skin, but it registers the purity of her "tint," not her color or complexion. It is Selden who commends the "modelling" of her ear and the "planting" of her lashes, and it is he who suspects her hair of being "ever so slightly brightened by art." Lily's very actions seem part of a "carefully elaborated plan." To him she is a "highly specialized" being, "fashioned" of the finest materials and covered with "a fine glaze of beauty and fastidiousness." Indeed, the preponderance of words suggesting artifice in these early pages accounts for Selden's distrust of Lily throughout the novel. As Wharton tells us at this early point, Selden always judges Lily in terms of the "argument from design," and during the Grand Central encounter it also occurs to him "that she must have cost a great deal to make, that a great many dull and ugly people must, in some mysterious way, have been sacrificed to produce her."[12]

Wharton lets this and similar remarks rest unexamined. She simply takes it for granted that beauty and art can only reside in the upper classes, and that they can only be attained at a cost to the lower ones. But while she accepts class privilege axiomatically, her novel is haunted by Selden's anxiety concerning "design." This paranoid attitude invokes religious preoccupations with "proofs" of God's existence ("proofs" based on scrutiny of the Purpose evident in Creation) by way of ascribing to the effects Lily produces a "design" in the sense of "plan" and even "scheming." Thus, while Selden wonders whether the Lily he knows is the "true" Lily or an impostor, his doubts about her authenticity raise for us the question of who has fashioned her in the first place, and to what end. Finally, at issue here is the extent to which the Lily visible to the world is or is not of her own making. If Alcoff is right (and I think she is) that "the identity of a woman is the product of her own interpretation and reconstruction of her history," then it is the use women make of their freedom to interpret and reconstruct their position that determines the extent of their autonomy.[13] If it is also true that the identity of women is the product of their inscription in history, then the use women might make of that freedom will most likely be inflected through their class and race position. In the case of Lily and her author, the important question is not, finally, whether Lily is or is not her own creation, but why Wharton does not grant her access to a more constructive use of her agency. Specifically, the question is why Wharton withholds from Lily awareness of her capacity to reconstitute her self-definition.

As it turns out, *The House of Mirth* never answers this question. Mingling Selden's point of view with a supposedly impartial authorial one and making Selden's apparent detachment pass for objectivity, Wharton at once credits and discredits his distrustful, paranoid gaze. Blending dramatized viewpoint and editorial commentary, she precludes definitive judgment. Just as Larsen elides the issue of class, burying it in considerations of race, Wharton elides the issue of choice. Among the consequences of this strategy, the most important for the current discussion of this novel as a *Künstlerroman* is the fact that

Wharton's evasiveness lets her suggest that Lily is both the product and the producer of art. She documents in detail the familial, social, and economic circumstances that fashioned her protagonist into an exquisite but doomed creature, but she also documents in equal detail Lily's willing collaboration and active share in her own fashioning.

In part, this double perspective reflects Wharton's position in regard to naturalism and realism, for her account attempts to balance personal free will and social determinism. In this respect, *The House of Mirth* articulates the preoccupation with psychology and social Darwinism lively at the time she was writing. However, seen from a feminist perspective, and especially in relation to women's art, this double perspective points to a different set of considerations. That Lily is at once artist and artifact, the willing and knowing producer of illusions but also the inert matter molded by others and the object that receives the gaze and fantasies of its spectators, makes her share the traditionally feminine dilemma of being torn between accommodation and self-determination. Cast in the role of the elusive object of desire, she would resemble Keats's archetypal nymph, captured in perpetual flight on his Grecian urn, were it not that she herself, knowingly, chooses and directs herself in the role. Repeatedly throughout the novel, she sets about producing narratives of Woman as a fetishized object of the desiring male gaze. Though she clearly relishes the aesthetic shaping of these narratives as a creative activity steeped in class privilege, the power she derives from such art rests on her willingness to collude with her own apparent objectification. Using herself as her own clay—assuming appropriate attitudes, at appropriate moments—to achieve dazzling effects, Lily the subject nonetheless resents this unproductive surplus. It is with considerable frustration that she protests, "I have to calculate and contrive, retreat and advance, as if I were going through an intricate dance, where one misstep would throw me hopelessly out of time" (*HOM* 45).

The shifting meaning of this sentence captures Lily's position throughout the novel. Starting off with a protest against contrivance, she stops short of refusing to engage in this dance and takes cover, instead, in anxiety about the high stakes that depend on such dancing. Like all women in her circle, she ends up refusing to violate the patriarchal prohibitions against women's open assertion of autonomy. (The two women Wharton allows such autonomy are the plain Gerty Farish, whose food smells of soapsuds, and the boring Lady Cressida, who "wears Indian jewelry and botanizes!") Women's creativity, Wharton suggests, can only emerge in mediated forms which comply with patriarchy's requirement that women's gifts serve men's erotic and economic interests. As a woman, Lily has no access to the "high" arts, and as a wealthy woman she has little access to any kind of productivity. Instead, she can only dream of eventually "doing over" this or that drawing room, and in the meantime she uses her laces and half-turned profile to cast her very person in the seductive role of spinning narratives of accommodation and inaccessibility.

Lily's wish to "do over" drawing rooms rests on a class privilege unavailable, say, to Alice Walker's mother, who took time off from her chores to coax flowers into bloom. Still, what is striking about Lily in this respect is not just the fact that her art presupposes wealth but that she is willing to mingle art and artifice, at a cost to integrity, for the sake of wealth. Selden first alerts us to this risk when he observes Lily making tea in his apartment. Admiring "her hand, polished as a bit of old ivory, with its slender pink nails and the sapphire bracelet slipping over her wrist," he is struck by the realization that "the links of her bracelet seemed like manacles chaining her to her fate" (*HOM* 5). One chapter later, when Lily sets about capturing Percy Gryce by repeating the tea ceremony on a lurching train, she deliberately makes her beautiful hands serve that fate. "Flitting above the table, looking miraculously free and slender" (*HOM* 17), they take part in a performance which, if successful, would mean her gaining a husband but losing her soul. That Lily ends up sabotaging her chances with Gryce does not quite redeem the situation. Ultimately, she cannot go along with the total obliteration of self which full compliance with patriarchal capitalism would entail, but over and over again she comes close to it. She may take unqualified pleasure in beauty for its own sake—as she does in the textures and tones of Selden's leather-bound books—but at least as often we find her presenting herself to the predatory gaze of others as a profit-making enterprise.

The treatment of Woman as at once the producer and the product of art, and of women's art as a repressed subtext, is evident in *Quicksand* too. Larsen also ascribes to her protagonist a fine-tuned aesthetic sensibility and a talent for studied self-presentation. Helga's appreciation of color and texture, of old laces and rare embroideries, is as keen as Lily's, and the two share a sophisticated pleasure in nuanced elegance and in the symbolic use of clothes and sets as elements within illusion-producing performance. In all these respects, Helga, too, fits in with the traditional feminine role of combining art and artifice to serve other agendas. It is over the particular agendas each protagonist serves that the two part ways. For while Lily's is primarily economic, Helga's centers on negotiating her double heritage as a black and a white within a racist society. Such differences are not to be overridden by the fact that the two are women. The race (and to a lesser extent class) differences that separate Lily and Helga are unbridgeable. Still, shared gender is relevant to our consideration of women's *Künstlerromane*, and it highlights the relation between art and politics in general.

Most importantly, a comparative reading of *Quicksand* and *The House of Mirth* illuminates ways women's art in particular gets appropriated to political ends, in that their plots concern the channeling of women's art toward serving patriarchal power relations within a capitalist and racist social organization. Encoding domestic, ornamental, and performing art as the proper sphere for women's creativity, these novels engage their protagonists in illusion-production that caters to male voyeurism and assures men of their power and worth. Ascribing Lily's and Helga's taste to caste privilege, they applaud refinement born of racial and economic advantage as a superior attainment that disdains, and thus subordinates, those lacking in privilege. It is not accidental that both Wharton and Larsen anchor their protagonists' collaboration with these agendas in narcissism—in elation at one's own desirability, triumph at one's power to inspire and control others' fantasies, and delight at one's exquisite rareness. Ironically, it is the very doubt on which such narcissism feeds—a patriarchally produced doubt about one's lovability, integrity, power, and access to pleasure—that leads Lily and Helga to consent to this appropriation of their talents.[14]

The narrative strategy Larsen uses to address the political appropriation of women's art differs markedly from Wharton's. As we have seen, Wharton's elaborate syntax and shifting system of barely attributable conjectures deflects judgment. It sets up an unstable, skeptical mode of reading that precludes clarity. In contrast, Larsen's syntax is direct, her narrative viewpoint is steady, and her presentation of Helga is free of the irony that colors Wharton's account. Larsen clearly guides our thinking about women's double position as artists and artifacts by letting events speak for themselves. The emphasis here is on factual information, not on diffuse conjecture. *Quicksand*'s chapters are short, and the breaks between them are pronounced. Its compressed laconic style is not coy. That it treats painful episodes sparingly mainly suggests held-back anger, as is evident when we compare Ralph Ellison's richly evocative treatment of Tuskegee (*Invisible Man*, 1952) with Larsen's Naxos. While Wharton has us question our capacity to see and judge, Larsen calls attention to her text's reluctance to utter. Combining factual reporting and stylistic repression, her writing signals a struggle to inhibit emotion.

At stake here is not a mere difference in style. Larsen's struggle is, above all, political. The holding back which pervades her text concerns the effect of her historically constituted "positionality" as a black woman, not just a woman, writing about racism from a position of personal ambivalence and within a social context that inhibits protest.

Lily's and Helga's investment in ornamental arts may be rooted in their shared need *as women* to side-step the prohibition against usurping male territory, and in their shared need and ability *as socially privileged* women to have their art collude with upper-class hegemony. But on top of that, the very narrative strategy each writer uses reminds us that the manner of presentation itself inscribes meanings—in this case, social and epistemological ambivalence on the part of Wharton, and racial ambivalence combined with political silencing on the part of Larsen.[15] While Wharton is at once dazzled and repelled by the world Lily inhabits, Larsen's difficulty is that on top of the gender and class blockages her female artist faces are racial prohibitions she hardly allows herself to name.

The opening strategy of each of these two novels captures this difference vividly. As we have seen, *The House of Mirth* situates Lily in Grand Central Station during rush hour in order to glamorize her at the expense of the rest of humanity. *Quicksand* is not so concerned with ascendance. Rather, its opening insists on our getting to know its protagonist outside her social construction.[16] Situating Helga in the near-void of a darkened room lit only by a single shaded light, it uses a chiaroscuro framing to spotlight her, making us appreciate her particular beauty all the more because of the seeming emptiness that envelops it. The emphasis here is on the "intensely personal taste" evident in the few objects the spotlight picks up—the blue Chinese carpet, oriental silk upholstery, some brightly-colored books among which the orientalist novel *Saïd the Fisherman* gets singled out, and a shining brass bowl crowded with many-colored nasturtiums. It would seem that love of color, shape, and texture is the only consideration here. Indeed, it is the abundance of such beauty, and Helga's luxuriance in it, that leads Ann Hostetler to ascribe to Helga's room "an exotic atmosphere of Beardsleyesque decadence."[17] But the scene deserves further scrutiny, given its function as the novel's opening tableau. While in the opening description of Lily in Grand Central Station Wharton places Selden (and by extension herself and us) in an ambivalent position of a desiring yet distrusting spectatorship, Larsen creates a spectatorial situation that edges towards voyeurism. Though she does so without the mediation of a gazing character, the scene's *chiaroscuro* elicits an effort to discern and interpret that foregrounds the thrill of constructing meaning, not luxury.

Larsen's treatment of Helga's head, framed in light but surrounded by a seeming void, builds on this spectatorial positioning of the reader: yellow satin skin, broad brows, soft and penetrating dark eyes, petulant but prettily sensuous lips, delicate ears, a good nose, and blue-black hair that is "plentiful and always straining in a little wayward, delightful way."[18] To the disinterested eye this is a person, a woman—attractive, lively, strong, and sensuous, but as yet abstracted from political inscription. What Larsen refrains from telling us in this opening passage is that Helga is black. Skin, lips, nose, and hair— Larsen's treatment has them elude (though never quite negate) racial coding, just as her description of Helga's taste for orientalist exoticism positions her outside of both Western and African aesthetics. Only at the end of the fourth paragraph does a character get identified by race (white), and that mention concerns a person who plays no part in the present plot and who gets noted fleetingly only, in a seemingly inconsequential adjective at the tail-end of a long sentence.[19] Indeed, even once the theme of racial conflict finally surfaces (the white man has just insulted a large black audience), Larsen does not elaborate on the incident. Here and throughout *Quicksand,* articulations of racial hurt and resentment come up against her resistance to straightforward racial coding. In contrast with the mulatta Audrey Denny—"the beautiful, calm, cool girl who had the assurance, the courage, so placidly to ignore racial barriers and give her attention to people" (*Q* 62)—Helga's kinship with "her people . . . these mysterious, these terrible, these fascinating, these lovable, dark hordes" (*Q* 95) is painfully ambivalent.

Larsen's linking of "lovable" and "dark hordes" captures the ambivalence that pervades *Quicksand* concerning the biological and cultural (and thus, ideological) valuation of racial difference. *Quicksand,* it turns out, can neither treat biological difference neutrally nor embrace race awareness without intense ambivalence. It at once registers an "inherent racial need for gorgeousness" and repudiates that gorgeousness as "savage." In particular, Larsen uses stylistic compression to slide almost imperceptibly between acceptance and repudiation. The two most sustained examples of such sliding occur during the cabaret and church episodes, where she has the traditional mainstays of black culture, secular and religious, function as catalysts for Helga's transformation. In the cabaret episode the music, motion, and variety of skin color project "a fantastic motley of ugliness and beauty, semi-barbaric, sophisticated, exotic." When the music of "the joyous, wild, murky orchestra" dies, "a shameful certainty that not only had she been in the jungle, but that she had enjoyed it," "taunts" Helga (*Q* 59). The "Bacchic vehemence" of the groaning, shouting, and writhing "like reptiles" which Larsen ascribes to the church service is not all that different. The scene at once exults and horrifies. It comes across as a "weird orgy" . . . "foul, vile, and terrible." It suggests a Jungian regression to "rites of a remote obscure origin" which have Helga "possessed by the same madness [as the rest of the congregation]; she too felt a brutal desire to sling herself about" (*Q* 113).

In all this, Larsen echoes Wharton's struggle with contradictory feelings which at once affirm and castigate the milieu she inhabits. Wharton's ambivalence centers especially on the operations of class privilege as these make women's art complicit with patriarchal capitalist interests; *The House of Mirth* forever oscillates between love of its subject matter and bitter recoil. Larsen's ambivalence includes Wharton's apposition of the free soul and social constraint (a characteristic *Künstlerroman* theme) as it relates to social privilege, but in *Quicksand* all this is permeated by intense racial anxiety. While Helga shares with Lily the condition of being apart, hers is defined racially. At the cabaret, "the inscrutability of the dozen or more brown faces, all cast from the same indefinite mold, and so like her own [presses] against her" (*Q* 54), making her keenly aware that "she didn't, in spite of her racial markings, belong to these dark segregated people. She was different" (*Q* 55).[20] Both writers recoil from prescriptive bourgeois complacency, especially as it affects women, yet neither can give up the attractions and benefits of class privilege. But Wharton articulates her ambivalence purely through considerations of class, in that she admires in Lily gifts which Lily can exercise only from a privileged class position. Lily's art presupposes wealth; even when destitute, tortoise-shell hairpins, gold-topped bottles, and a rose-colored pin-cushion define for Wharton Lily's artistic sensibility. Larsen also admires Helga for an artistic sensibility that presupposes economic well-being, except that her admiration mingles class privilege with racial ambivalence. That Helga recoils from both the studied respectability of Naxos's provincial elite and from Harlem's sophistication articulates racial as well as class agendas. As Mary Helen Washington puts it, Larsen's novels "are not about barriers to black social mobility and class privilege; they are about the chaos in the world of the black elite, the emptiness in the climb to bourgeois respectability. They are about the women in that world who are inhibited and stunted by cultural scripts that deny them any 'awakenings' and punish them for their defiance."[21] Significantly, that both Naxos and Harlem pressure black women to sustain the hegemony of a privileged male elite (represented by Vayle and Anderson), reflects anxiety about racial dignity as well as economic prosperity. Indeed, Larsen's black characters' insistent linking of propriety, good taste, and "uplift" to race awareness suggests that the specter of racial disenfranchisement always hovers at the edge of their well-being.

Within this tangle of interrelated modes of masculine hegemony, women's position is particularly difficult. Their problem is one of conflicting allegiances and contradictory definitions of self-interest.[22] Where class position urges alliance with men, gender requires revolt. Where racial oppression demands support of black institutions, gender—and sometimes class—stir antagonism. In this context, individuation is particularly hard for women artists. Denied a place in the masculine *Künstlerroman* tradition of solitary inspiration, excluded from the marketplace of artistic commerce, and expected to channel their gifts into the domestic and ornamental spheres of production where their art is usually unpaid, often discredited, and indeed rarely called "art"—women artists experience an overwhelming pressure to contain their creativity within socially approved bounds. *The House of Mirth* and *Quicksand* may situate this circumscribing of women's art in particular social configurations and at particular points in time, but overall, the dynamics of repression they uncover have not changed appreciably. Lily and Helga share with many the situation of being cast as ornaments and illusion-producers in ways that make their art a trap. For them, the medium for aesthetic articulation is also a questionable survival mechanism within a society that enlists their collusion as women with an ideology that thrives on race, class, and gender oppression.

It is no accident that both Wharton and Larsen examine this collusion by including in their respective novels episodes in which each protagonist literally casts herself as an artifact. Wharton has Lily participate in a *tableau vivant* entertainment, where Lily replicates Reynold's "Mrs. Lloyd" in a daringly unadorned self-presentation that flaunts her beauty. Larsen has Helga pose for a portrait in Denmark, where Helga projects a "barbaric" image through her attire. Both images are directed by men—the "society" portrait painter Paul Morpeth in New York, and his counterpart Axel Olsen in Denmark—and on both occasions self-presentation puts women in the disconcerting position of feeling at once used and empowered by the effects they produce through suggestive images. Lily, Wharton tells us, was "always inspirited by the prospect of showing her beauty in public. . . . Ah, it was good to be young, to be radiant, to glow with the sense of slenderness, strength, and elasticity of well-poised lines and happy tints; to feel one's self lifted to a height apart by that incommunicable grace which is the body's counterpart to genius" (*HOM* 113). And Helga, too, "began to feel a little excited, incited. . . . She was incited to make an impression, a voluptuous impression. She was incited to inflame attention and admiration. . . . And after a little while she gave herself up wholly to the fascinating business of being seen, gaped at, desired" (*Q* 74).

Significantly, Larsen's passage is more directly sensual than Wharton's. Both have their protagonists cast themselves—knowingly, deliberately, and not without pleasure—as objects of a desiring male gaze, except that Wharton invests class power in Lily's sense of being "lifted to a height apart" by her "incommunicable" grace, while Larsen invests erotic power in Helga's ability to "inflame" by using a "fantastic collection of garments" to project "a voluptuous impression." As Wharton treats it, the *tableau vivant* episode means that Lily's "vivid plastic sense, hitherto nurtured on no higher food than dressmaking and upholstery, found eager expression in the disposal of draperies, the study of attitudes, [and] the shifting of lights and shadows" (*HOM* 128). It is Lily's "artistic intelligence" (*HOM* 107) that attracts her author's admiration. In Helga's case the situation is different. Describing her as "bedecked in flaunting flashy things" and making her feel "like a veritable savage" (*Q* 69), Larsen recoils from the white gaze she has Helga attract in Denmark because that gaze treats Helga as "a curiosity, a stunt." It is this degrading white gaze that shames Helga into perceiving her own reflection in the monkey-like cavorting of two black vaudeville dancers she observes "pounding their thighs, slapping their hands together, twisting their legs, waving their abnormally long arms, [and] throwing their bodies about with a loose ease" (*Q* 82–83).[23]

This difference between the two renditions of women's self-presentation underscores the fact that each woman's participation in the production of art involves more than aesthetic considerations. This is especially obvious in Helga's case, whose self-presentation comes across to race-conscious eyes as indecently *outrée* in Naxos, as a tantalizing lure in Harlem, and as savagely voluptuous in Denmark. Seen in these terms, the orientalism Helga cultivates in Naxos is clearly defensive. Effacing racial specificity, it aims to forestall both the prurient "nativism" of the white gaze (Olsen et al.) and the constricting respectability of black "uplift." Taste, *Quicksand* suggests, is shaped by racial agendas. But even Lily, whose self-presentation seems to evoke abstract epistemological ruminations, ultimately encodes political ideology. Wharton's insistence on the evanescence of tableau art—on "the happy disposition of lights and the delusive interposition of layers of gauze" (*HOM* 130)—articulates a class-bound anxiety about authority and authenticity. While Helga's image mainly addresses the racial agendas of prosperous men, Lily's image addresses the ascendancy of the ruling class. In contrast with Larsen's anxiety that blackness—notably women's—may be inherently susceptible to degrading and even life-threatening sexual excess regardless of one's class position (Larsen suggests as much through her rendition of the trajectory of Helga's life and through her stylistic treatment of physicality in general), Wharton's anxiety is that art—notably women's, and specifically white upper-class women's art—may be vulnerable to a skepticism that endangers class hegemony. Seeing the tableau entertainment as a cross between "a superior kind of waxworks" and the "magic glimpses of the boundary world between fact and imagination" (*HOM* 130), she has this art hover at the edge of lower-class challenge to upper-class hegemony. Using Lily's self-presentation to raise questions about creative honesty and validity, she infuses this event with fin de siècle melancholy concerning the demise of clarity and the transience of class privilege.

Thus, Olsen's conviction that the lavishly exotic Helga he paints is, "the *true* Helga Crane" (*Q* 88, emphasis added), and Selden's belief that the Lily at whom he gazes in the tableau is "the *real* Lily Bart, divested of all the trivialities of her little world and catching for a moment a note of that eternal harmony of which her beauty was part" (*HOM* 131, emphasis added), are hardly disinterested, let alone accurate. These men's notions of "truth" and "reality" encode the social and political agendas that guide the gaze beyond considerations of line and color. Both the portrait and the tableau pose Woman as an inert and thus governable object of the male gaze; both are expensive to produce and assume wealthy consumers whose sense of economic as well as masculine power depends on their ability to subsidize luxury items; and both sustain white hegemony.[24] But within these shared agendas, the fact of racial difference in particular, and of class difference less explicitly, sends *Quicksand* and *The House of Mirth* hurtling in different directions. Larsen's text can never share Wharton's extreme privilege of color blindness. *Quicksand* is wrapped in a "shroud of color" (*Q* 75) while *The House of Mirth* is oblivious to it. Moreover, Larsen cannot indulge in Wharton's ambivalent melancholy concerning the passing of a social order that has privileged her. Such privilege as she allows her light-skinned middle-class mulatta to enjoy rests on poisonous self-denial. Larsen's struggle is with an ideology designed to oppress her by caste as well as by gender. As *Künstlerromane*, both novels clearly show the woman artist to be thwarted by a "social positionality" she feels powerless to change. But as racially distinct novels, both *Künstlerromane* show ways in which the effects of gender inscription on the artist get modified in relation to racial and economic considerations.

It is ultimately women's conflicting allegiances and contradictory self-definitions that account for the ways women collude with their own objectification.[25] At work here is not only a gendered inscription of spectatorship and voyeurism which current psychoanalytic theory tends to treat as a universal classless and raceless developmental issue. As this discussion of *Quicksand* and *The House of Mirth* suggests, at work are also specific political inscriptions of spectatorship and self-presentation. Once we recognize the nature of such inscription, it becomes clear that women, as well as men, can be invested in letting the female body serve as "the blank page" (Gubar) of gender, class, and race fantasies.

This is a problematic investment, of course. On the one hand, self-presentation involves will and mastery. As an art that taps narcissistic notions of self-sufficiency, it can empower its practitioners. At the same time, the self-presentation *Quicksand* and *The House of Mirth* contemplate clearly risks appropriation. It requires women to serve as fetish objects for male consumption and, on top of that, it tacitly normalizes a racist and classist ideology of dominance. Though the "happenings" and "performance art" of recent years show that self-presentation can be transgressive and even revolutionary, *Quicksand* and *The House of Mirth* do not head in that direction. Given the unresolved authorial ambivalence concerning privilege in these novels, their reluctant conformity to dominant values should come as no surprise. However, it is a conformity tinged with resistance. In this respect, both novels end up critiquing ideology. The resistance each offers may be oblique, contradictory, and unresolved, but it is precisely this hesitancy, inscribed across each writer's formal rendition of her plot, that invites scrutiny. As the preceding discussion suggests, once such scrutiny includes a comparative investigation of difference, it becomes clear that the lassitude and fatalism that affect each protagonist involve more than a latter-day "beautiful soul" syndrome (Hirsch), where the would-be woman artist gets punished for violating prohibitions against emergence. *Quicksand* and *The House of Mirth* show specific political influences at work, affecting the production or thwarting of woman's art. It is recognition of such specificity that frees women to understand their "positionality" and transcend the prohibitions they encounter.

Notes

1. For instance, the stridently masculine tenor of Carl Malmgren's " 'From Work to Text': The Modernist and Post-Modernist *Künstlerroman*," *Novel: A Forum on Fiction* 21.1 (1987), 5–28.

2. For further discussion of the relation between differences and commonality as a feminist issue, see Teresa de Lauretis, "Feminist Studies/Critical Studies: Issues, Terms, and Contexts," in *Feminist Studies, Critical Studies* (Bloomington: Indiana University Press, 1986), pp. 1–19.

3. This is not to deny Patricia Yaeger's caution that we should not assume that transgression is the best women can hope for. Her emphasis on "textual radiance" (in *Honey-Mad Women: Emancipatory Strategies in Women's Writing* [New York: Columbia University Press, 1988], p. 37) coheres with Alice Walker's gratitude to Phillis Wheatley for keeping alive the notion of the song (in *In Search of Our Mothers' Gardens: Womanist Prose* [New York: Harcourt, Brace Jovanovich, 1983], pp. 132–243).

4. Virginia Woolf, *To the Lighthouse* (New York: Harcourt Brace, 1927), p. 130. Further references are cited parenthetically as *TTL* with page numbers.

5. Virginia Woolf, "Professions for Women," in *Virginia Woolf: Women and Writing*, ed. Michèle Barrett (New York: Harcourt Brace Jovanovich, 1979), pp. 57–63.

6. Though this essay does not pursue the matrilineal bonding which empowers certain protagonists in women's _Künstlerromane_ (Wharton's, Larsen's, and Chopin's protagonists clearly suffer from maternal abandonment), Susan Gubar's "The Birth of the Artist" is an important supplement to my perspective. Compare Joan Lidoff, "Virginia Woolf's Feminine Sentence: The Mother-Daughter World of _To the Lighthouse_," _Literature and Psychology_ 32.3 (1986), 43–59.

7. Jean Guiget, _Virginia Woolf and Her Works_ (New York: Harvest, 1965), p. 260.

8. Toril Moi, _Sexual/Textual Politics: Feminist Literary Theory_ (New York: Methuen, 1985), p. 9.

9. Marianne Hirsch, "Spiritual _Bildung_: The Beautiful Soul as Paradigm," in _The Voyage In: Fictions of Female Development_, ed. Elizabeth Abel, Marianne Hirsch, and Elizabeth Langland (Hanover, N.H.: University of New England Press, 1983), pp. 23–48. According to this paradigm, "the story of the female spiritual _Bildung_ is the story of the potential artist who fails to make it," a woman whose inner development follows a circular path that precludes emergence.

10. Linda Alcoff, "Cultural Feminism Versus Poststructuralism: The Identity Crisis in Feminist Theory," _Signs: Journal of Women in Culture and Society_ 13.3 (1988), 405–36. Alcoff refers to the Combahee River Collective's "A Black Feminist Statement" and to their use of the phrase "identity politics" to signal a mode of political intervention and self-definition that refuses a passive surrender to "positionality" (431–32).

11. This view of the woman artist is more active, more participatory and even productive, than the description of women suffering cultural scripts to be inscribed on their bodies, as Gubar provides in " 'The Blank Page' and the Issue of Female Creativity," in _Writing and Sexual Difference_, ed. Elizabeth Abel (Chicago: University of Chicago Press, 1982), pp. 73–93.

12. Edith Wharton, _The House of Mirth_ (Boston: Houghton Mifflin, 1963), p. 3. Subsequent quotations from this book will be cited parenthetically as _HOM_.

13. Alcoff, "Cultural Feminism Versus Poststructuralism," p. 434. Note also Teresa de Lauretis, whose work serves Alcoff as an important point of departure. Alcoff's emphasis on " a conception of human subjectivity as an _emergent_ property of a historical experience" (431, emphasis added), opens up the possibility of "identity politics" as the route to social and personal change.

14. Compare Chopin's Edna Pontellier. Especially pertinent here is Joan Lidoff's "Another Sleeping Beauty: Narcissism in _The House of Mirth_," _American Quarterly_ 32.5 (1980), 519–39 (reprinted in _American Realism: New Essays_ [Baltimore: Johns Hopkins University Press, 1982]), which discusses the relation between narcissism and self-deprecation. While the personal underpinnings of narcissism are Lidoff's main concern, she includes attention to it as a consequence of constricting social arrangements. See also Voris's "The Hysteric and the Mimic," in this volume.

15. Raymond Hedin, "The Structuring of Emotion in Black American Fiction," _Novel: A Forum on Fiction_ 15.4 (1982), 35–43.

16. Larsen follows the same strategy in _Passing_, where she studiously introduces Irene and Clare as racially neutral. Her investment in this stance is at once personal and political. Her own social and creative decline is traceable to a corroding struggle to be accepted outside of social construction.

17. Ann E. Hostetler, "The Aesthetics of Race and Gender in Nella Larsen's *Quicksand*," *PMLA: Publications of the Modern Language Association of America* 105.1 (1990), 35–46.

18. Nella Larsen, *Quicksand* and *Passing* (New Brunswick, N.J.: Rutgers University Press, 1986), p. 2. Further references are cited parenthetically as *Q* with page numbers.

19. Compare detailed descriptions of similar incidents in Ralph Ellison's *Invisible Man* (New York: Random House, 1952) and Maya Angelou's *I Know Why the Caged Bird Sings* (New York: Random House, 1969).

20. For further discussion of "the tragic mulatta" theme and racial identification, see Cheryl A. Wall, "Passing for What? Aspects of Identity in Nella Larsen's Novels," *Black American Literature Forum* 20 (1986), 97–111; Barbara Christian, "The Rise and Fall of the Proper Mulatta," in *Black Women Novelists: The Development of a Tradition, 1892–1976* (Westport, Conn.: Greenwood Press, 1978); and Nathan I. Huggins, *Harlem Renaissance* (New York: Oxford University Press, 1971).

21. Mary Helen Washington, *Invented Lives: Narratives of Black Women, 1860–1960* (New York: Anchor, 1987), p. 160.

22. In this, Nancy Topping Bazin's discussion of socialization as it determines Lily's destruction applies to Helga, too. See "The Destruction of Lily Bart: Capitalism, Christianity, and Male Chauvinism," *The Denver Quarterly* 17.4 (1983), 97–108.

23. Ellison's treatment of Clifton's "Sambo" dolls in *Invisible Man* echoes Larsen's use of the vaudeville dancers.

24. For detailed analysis of the function of art within patriarchal capitalist exchange, see John Berger, *Ways of Seeing* (New York: Penguin, 1972).

25. See Judith Fetterly, "'The Temptation to be a Beautiful Object': Double Standard and Double Bind in *The House of Mirth*," *Studies in American Fiction* 5.2 (1977), 199–211, and Elaine Showalter, "The Death of the Lady (Novelist): Wharton's House of Mirth," in *Edith Wharton*, ed. Harold Bloom (New York: Chelsea House, 1986), pp. 139–154. As the above suggests, the general direction this work on Wharton takes is applicable to Larsen. That similar work on *Quicksand* is not as readily available reflects the neglect Larsen suffered for many years. In addition to Hostetler's *PMLA* essay, recent work on Larsen includes Hazel Carby's *Reconstructing Womanhood: The Emergence of the Afro-American Woman Novelist* (New York: Oxford University Press, 1987), and Thadious Davis's forthcoming biography of Nella Larsen.

Chapter 8
The Artist Manqué in the Fiction of Rebecca Harding Davis
Jane Atteridge Rose

The narrator of Rebecca Harding Davis's "Life in the Iron-Mills, or The Korl Woman "[1] concludes the tragic tale of Hugh Wolfe's artistic failure by contemplating the artist's unfinished creation: "Nothing remains to tell that the poor Welsh puddler once lived, but this figure of the mill-woman cut in korl." The "wan, woful face, through which the spirit of the dead korl-cutter looks out," haunts the narrator, "with its thwarted life, its mighty hunger, its unfinished work."[2]

It is not necessary to know this story of the redemptive death of Hugh Wolfe, the immigrant iron puddler who creates statues in odd moments at the mill, or of his devoted cousin Deb, to appreciate the presence of motifs central to feminist reading suggested by this passage. Wolfe emblemizes his own "reality of soul starvation, of living death" in his statue's "mad, half-despairing gesture of drowning" (23, 33). Like Hugh Wolfe's fictional life, the lives of nineteenth-century female writers are often revealed in their works. And often, like the statue of the korl woman, their texts delineate characters who are frustrated by their "thwarted life," who are unsuccessful in their "unfinished work," or who lack the fulfillment of their "mighty hunger."

"Life in the Iron-Mills," like much of Rebecca Harding Davis's work, illuminates the nineteenth-century female experience. Although the novella usually attracts attention as a landmark in proletarian fiction and in naturalistic realism,[3] this story, along with the rest of Davis's corpus, deserves more attention as a nineteenth-century woman's text.[4] Like a number of her stories, it is a *Künstlerroman* of an artist manqué.[5] Davis is here typical of nineteenth-century writing women, whose fictional female artists all experience various forms of failure.[6]

Because of the autobiographical relationship between the fictional artist and the female writer, the *Künstlerroman* of the artist manqué helps us to understand how female artists were affected by their ideological context.[7] Literary women of the last century were inextricably entangled in a web of beliefs that made their successful development as artists difficult, if not impossible.[8] Their fictions enact a conflict between an individual empowered with the potential for creative autonomy and the ideological restrictions undermining it. The winner in this contest, staged by female writers and waged by their fictive artist doubles, seems always to be domestic ideology. The individual artist fails, or surrenders, or turns traitor to her own cause.[9]

Rebecca Harding Davis's many *Künstlerromane*, written over a period of forty years, show that domestic ideology exerted its force at every stage of women's lives. When plotted chronologically beside her biography, variations in Davis's depiction of the artist and in the form of failure that each of her protagonists experiences reveal changes in her attitude toward her own role as a woman writer as her life progressed.[10] These changes, which mark three specific stages in her life, roughly coincide with the three defining elements of the artist manqué: the young artist, whose socially determined identity prohibits her free artistic expression, is frustrated; the mature artist, who attempts to reconcile her artistic identity with a domestic one in a society that defines the two as antithetical, is unsuccessful; and the older artist, who has long ago renounced art in order to realize a life as wife and mother, lacks fulfillment.

Though she sometimes defied or denied certain social expectations regarding her life and her work, Rebecca Harding Davis was a white, Protestant, middle-class woman of the nineteenth century. As such, she sincerely maintained many received domestic values concerning the role of women even though they conflicted with her artistic desire. Her fiction, like that of other female writers in this milieu, demonstrates that within domestic ideology the role of women was culturally invested with a number of values that determined self-perception.[11] For these women, the egoistic self-assertion necessary for an artist was antithetical to the passive, self-abnegating service that defined femininity. As a result, their texts, like Davis's, are often conflicted, especially when they treat artists striving to retain their integrity without disenfranchising themselves from society.

In her own life, Davis was constantly mediating the conflicting values that marked the nineteenth-century female writer and her texts. For instance, although, like other girls of her class, she returned to her parents' home after graduating as valedictorian from her three-year education at the Washington (Pennsylvania) Female Seminary, she not so typically lived a life of retirement there for the next twelve years—reading her brother's college books and writing, only rarely participating in the precourtship social life of her hometown, Wheeling, West Virginia. The facts of Davis's long life show that she continued, with remarkable success, to mediate between her equally strong antithetical desires to be a good writer and to be a good wife-mother.[12] However, her fictional enactments of this same conflict, which always delineate a failed artist, hint at her concern that in art, at least, compromise is a form of failure. Struggling against compromise leads only to frustration; acquiescing to it brings the pain of being unfulfilled.

Though men, her earliest artists of the 1860s, Hugh Wolfe of "Life in the Iron-Mills" (1861) and the Tom of "Blind Tom" (1862), articulate the frustration experienced by female artists.[13] Here, political issues that also pertain to gender are played out as problems of class. In both these stories, the protagonist's artistic freedom is prohibited by his socially prescribed role. The capitalists and slave owners, who define and limit, oppress the uneducated laborers and slaves, who have been limited by social definition. Domestic ideology also limited the potential of a class. Although Davis, like most nineteenth-century women, accepted her female definition as God-ordained, she maintained that society had erroneously limited that definition. This was particularly true early in her career when she suffered most from its restrictions.

Davis's Hugh Wolfe is frustrated in life by the inhumane economic forces that determine his inability to fulfill his creative desire, to finish his sculpture. His talent brings anguish, not joy because the korl woman fails to communicate Wolfe's inarticulate longing.[14] She is an insoluble puzzle to the mill officials who discover her—"some terrible problem lay in this woman's face, and troubled these men" (34). Worse, as expression stimulates greater comprehension, her full meaning remains outside her creator's ken also; all Wolfe can say is "She be hungry" (33). Like his statue of the korl woman, Hugh Wolfe fails to satisfy his hunger, to use his power, to find his voice; he kills himself. Davis's first protagonist, like the artist figure in the fiction of most female writers of this period, is both oppressed and repressed.

The anguish of frustrated creative desire voiced by her first artists, who, like Wolfe, cry that "all the world had gone wrong" (51), seems very close to Davis's own frustration as a young woman beginning her writing career. Never overtly defiant, Rebecca Harding—an anomaly in her time as a spinster apparently unconcerned about approaching thirty in the home of her parents, interested only in pursuing her unorthodox literary interests—surely knew frustration. She must have felt it as she exhausted her father's extensive library; as she mastered her brother's college curriculum; as she wrote, rewrote, and discarded innumerable manuscripts. Although at this time she had no name for her frustration, she would later repeatedly show her female protagonists rebelling against "decorative uselessness" and against the notion that purity requires innocence. Her frustrated desire to escape these restrictions at least temporarily is probably what first led her to develop her lifelong fondness for "vagabonding": hours-long walks with no predetermined destination.

Her vagabonding was itself a perhaps unconscious strategy for negotiating between illicit desire and propriety. Aimlessly, yet decorously, walking, she could escape the protective confines of her comfortable home in Wheeling and experience the nearby sights and sounds of its industrial riverfront, considered inappropriate for young ladies. She could know "the fog and mud and foul effluvia" of slums, where people passed "with drunken faces," going to the factories where "unsleeping engines groan and shriek" ("Iron-Mills" 14, 19).

Not surprisingly, Davis created her greatest number of male protagonists during this early period marked by frustration. Even as she wrote of artists whose freedom was restricted, her own artistic freedom was limited because she was a young woman; vagabonding could not take her everywhere. While her work was appearing in nearly every number of *Atlantic Monthly* and being praised by the Boston literati, family concern for propriety forced Davis to remain isolated at home.[15] In 1862, she lacked an escort and thus could not accept the repeated invitation of her *Atlantic* editor, James T. Fields, and his wife, Annie, to visit their home in Boston. In a letter to Annie Fields, she voiced her irritation over women's restrictions, complaining, "How good it must be to be a man when you want to travel."[16] In her fictive projections of frustrated artistic desire, Davis seems to have transcended her own specific gender oppression, transferring it to male protagonists and issues of class in "Iron-Mills" or race in "Blind Tom."

In these early stories, Davis created an antagonism between her protagonists and their society, which thwarts artistic development, silences expression, and inhibits self-comprehension. The conflicts of the early fictional artists suggest that anger at restricted artistic freedom composed at least one dimension of her own attitude toward society. Davis's ambivalence toward her frustrated creative desire and her guilt about being a woman with this desire are evident in every narrative strategy from her use of multiple anonymous identities to her ambivalent plots.[17] These strategies are nowhere more evident than in "Iron-Mills."

The conclusion to this story illustrates Davis's attempt to detach herself from her artist's tale. Here she amplifies the usual doubling of the *Künstlerroman* writer through her artist protagonist and creates a quadruple relationship between herself, the narrator, the protagonist, and the statue. Davis, the female author, has created a narrator whose sex is not designated and, therefore, particularly in 1861, would be assumed masculine. This fictive narrator—a writer, an artist, and a musician—sits in his library, amid such value-laden objects as "a broken figure of an angel pointing upward," a "dirty canary chirp[ing] desolately in a cage" (12), "a half-moulded child's head," and a rendering of Aphrodite (65). The narrator is pondering the mystery of a female statue, made of refuse korl, with "not one line of grace in it: a nude woman's form, muscular, grown coarse with labor, the powerful limbs instinct with some one poignant longing" (32). In this female image, the narrator comprehends the "spirit of the dead korl-cutter." He tells the story of its creator, Hugh Wolfe, the immigrant iron-foundry worker and repressed artist who committed suicide with his own sculpting knife rather than be confined in a jail, knowing only that "the world had gone all wrong" (51).

The narrator, the protagonist, and the statue are each a projection of spiritual longing. Davis projects her animus through her male narrative voice and her male artist protagonist and then, further, through them into their shared anima projection, the korl woman. It is this object that communicates "something pure and beautiful, which might have been and was not: a hope, a talent, a love, over which the soul mourns, like Esau deprived of his birthright" (64). The narrator ends the tale by looking on this image of desperate soul-starvation and saying simply, "I know" (64), uniting all the identities in sympathy with the repressed artist's "thwarted energy and unused power" (46).

Although Davis's cross-dressing of her protagonist as well as her narrator is extreme in "Iron-Mills," the autobiographical relationship between the artist-writer and her artist-creation asserted in this closing passage illuminates an anxiety of authorship that seems particularly female. The statue of the korl woman, to which the narrator has fallen heir, stands "in a corner of [the] library" in order to "keep it hid behind a curtain." But like any repressed desire, sometimes at night "the curtain is accidentally drawn back," and "its mighty hunger, its unfinished work" are painfully visible (64).

Davis's artists are also frustrated because they are anomalous in a worldview based on rigid gender distinction. In "Iron-Mills" Hugh Wolfe, the protagonist, is frustrated not just in his creative desire but also in his social relationships. A frail consumptive with a "meek, woman's face," he is known as one of the "girl-men" at the mill. Because of his atypical sensitivity, the other men call him "Molly Wolfe"

(24). Although it is more emphasized in her early works, Davis's artist protagonists are always androgynous, making them larger as artists but painfully less as social beings. This is true for most of the female artists of her later work also: Jane Derby, a professional writer in *Earthen Pitchers,* is typical in that she was aware of her unattractive "hard eyes; and that her lips were thin and her breast flat. 'Even Nature,' she said to herself, 'forgot that I was a woman.'"[18]

In "Blind Tom," published the year after "Iron-Mills," Davis grappled with another frustration for the creative spirit that was common to the experience of many women who, like herself, wanted to write stories unlike the sentimental romances considered appropriate for female authors. This story of an enslaved genius confronts the evil of sanctioned control over individual talent rather than the repression of it. It is basically a true account of a blind slave boy, who was owned by a south Georgia planter.[19] Tom was a musical prodigy of such unexplainable dimension that he was treated as an idiot savant, performing in packed concert halls throughout the slave states and even at the White House. Davis's account apparently results from her having seen his performance at one of these concerts. Although she had no insight into what Tom's soul longed to play, she was most pained by those moments in his concert when it became clear that he could not play what he wanted:

the moments when Tom was left to himself,—when a weary despair seemed to settle down on the distorted face, and the stubby little black fingers, wandering over the keys, spoke for Tom's own caged soul within. (585)

Davis, who in the writing of stories like "Blind Tom" was trying to break free of restrictions about appropriate subject matter and tone, keenly perceived that, like so many female writers of the period, the slave was not even free to use his gift as he chose. The music of Tom— like the statue of Hugh Wolfe, and the stories of their creator, a minimally educated young woman from West Virginia—proves that the divine spark of talent can appear in socially unacceptable, disenfranchised individuals. It also reminds us that, for the artist who must serve the two masters of self and society, creative desire can bring the gifted as much pain as it does joy.

The frustrated male artists of her early pieces, such as "Iron-Mills" and "Blind Tom," are also deformed. Though not physically impaired like Tom, Wolfe is considered by others to be deficient as a man. Also Deb Wolfe—who, though not an artist, shares the role of protagonist with her cousin—is a hunchbacked cripple. These protagonists all bear the physical mark of their anomalous, alienated condition. They suggest an anxiety felt by Davis, at this time a young woman in pursuit of art, that deformity was somehow concomitant with her vocation.

Rebecca Harding Davis's middle period is marked by her becoming a wife and mother. She married L. Clarke Davis and moved to his sister's Philadelphia home in March 1863. There Davis gave birth to her first son Richard on April 18, 1864, and she moved with husband and baby into the first home of her own in September of that year. Her third and last child was born in 1872. After her marriage at the age of thirty-one, Rebecca Harding Davis's personal life became more typical of that known by most wives in middle-class America, except that her domestic situation seems to have been happier than most. In her marriage to L. Clarke Davis, she enjoyed an experience rare in either the nineteenth or the twentieth century: she married a man who had first fallen in love with her mind through her writing. Clarke Davis always championed his wife's career; however, as a crusading journalist, his own literary taste for didactic fiction and the journals that specialized in it served to discourage her pursuit of objective realism. The work of Davis's middle period, primarily written in the late 1860s and 1870s, begins to take a view of the artist that differs from her earlier work. The change in her fiction parallels the great change in her life at this time from anomalous spinster and aspiring author to wife-mother and successful author.

While her earlier stories feature frustrated male artists whose creativity is stifled by their oppressive society, those written during this period, like "The Wife's Story" (1864) and "Marcia" (1876), feature female artists struggling with more internal conflicts. They also bear a greater resemblance to Davis in their ambivalence toward society and their prescribed role in it. These women must choose between feminine, maternal domesticity and egoistic, artistic ambition.[20] The *Künstlerromane*, written during this time when Davis was herself trying to integrate art with domesticity, reify the idea that the role of wife-mother and the role of artist are mutually exclusive.[21] The protagonists of these stories are unsuccessful because, either by external societal judgment or by their own, their pursuit of art causes them to fail as women or their need to accept their womanhood causes them to fail as artists.[22]

Interestingly, while Davis repeatedly enacted the failure of artistic-domestic resolution in her fiction, in her own life she was attaining it, though compromising quality to do so. Always writing at home, she never allowed pursuit of her art to take precedence over her role as wife-mother. Writing became, in these years, work of secondary importance. Fragments of a journal, written during this time, talk only about

Pet (Clarke), Hardy (Richard), Charlie, and Nolly (Nora); entries rarely mention the writing for publication that was occurring at the same time.[23] However, the constant reiteration of anxiety over failure in her fiction at this time suggests that Davis considered her recent move toward journalistic writing a sign of artistic failure.

The earliest of these tales, "The Wife's Story," marks a transition in Davis's attitude. This story reveals changes in her depiction of the artist and in her own narrative technique. This first appearance of a narrating protagonist is made doubly significant in that it is also one of her first stories in which the protagonist is a woman. Hetty, the wife, begins: "I will tell you the story of my life, since you ask it . . . though the meaning of the life of any woman of my character would be the same" (177). In this story—filled with the need to transfer, act out, and punish guilty desire—Davis's narrating protagonist, Hetty Manning, is an unhappy new wife-mother who longs to be a composer of opera. After she suffers humiliating failure in her one attempt to realize her dream, she renounces her artistic ambition for domesticity. Although the overt theme of this story is the necessary female renunciation of art, the story deconstructs itself with the voice of desire speaking more eloquently than the voice of guilt.[24] Suddenly, in the last pages, the reader is asked to disregard the protagonist's struggle against allowing "this power within me to rot and waste" (204), which has composed the entire story, as merely a hysterical dream. However, the dream has been so powerful that the reality is hard to accept.

Hetty, a New England woman who "had an unquiet brain and moderate power" (181), has been strongly influenced by Margaret Fuller. She is a recurring character type in Davis's fiction, suggestive of anxiety. A mature woman of developed sensibility who has married, rather late, a widower with several children, Hetty finds it impossible to acclimate herself to her new domestic role. She feels no kinship with her new family of exuberant but insensitive Westerners or even with her own new baby daughter, "a weazen-faced little mortal, crying night and day" (192). Having been raised on Fuller's motto, "The only object in life is to grow," she finds herself unable to abandon her dream:

There had been a time when I had dreams of attaining Margaret's stature, and as I thought of that, some old sublime flame stirred in me with a keen delight. New to me, almost; for, since my baby was born, my soul as well as my body had been weak and nauseated. (192)

In addition to Fuller's influence, the memory of Hetty's previous acquaintance with Rosa Bonheur haunts the fictional protagonist of this story. She remembers the Parisian artist saying of her art: "Any woman can be a wife or mother, but this is my work alone" (193). A new wife and mother, Hetty sits in the hearth glow of domestic peace, amid "the white bust of Psyche, and a chubby plaster angel" (185), and agonizes over her unrealized talent—her "gift," her "power"—asking, "was I to give it unused back to God? I could sing: not that only; I could compose music,—the highest soul-utterance" (193). She regrets her marriage, realizing, "If I remained with Doctor Manning, my role was outlined plain to the end: years of cooking, stitching, scraping together of cents" (194). Hetty's crime in this story is twofold: the rejection of her domestic role and the assertion of artistic egoism. "No poet or artist," she says, "was ever more sincere in the belief that the divine power spoke through him than I" (197).

Hetty does not leave her husband, though, and when events cause the family to move to Newport, Rhode Island, she eagerly goes too. There, Hetty meets an impresario from New York who is willing to produce her opera and to feature her in the leading role. One day, after long and troubled deliberation, she finally decides to do her opera. Her decision occurs during a solitary walk on the beach, in contemplation of the sea's affinity with her own soul: "It [the sea] was no work of God's praising Him continually: it was the eternal protest and outcry against Fate,—chained, helpless, unappealing" (200). When produced, her opera fails; the audience's rejection of her composition and of her performance is described in humiliating detail. This scene illuminates another dimension of the female artist's anxiety. In addition to fearing the consequences that will befall her rejection of the divinely ordained domestic role, there is the very real fear of independence. Independence is fantasized as a double-edged sword that is both attractive and frightening. Hetty leaves the theater penniless, homeless, hungry, ashamed, and beaten:

If the home I had desolated, the man and child I had abandoned, had chosen their revenge, they could not have asked that the woman's flesh and soul should rise in me with a hunger so mad as this, only to discover that [I would fail]. (213)

However, Davis has not yet punished her artist self-projection enough. Hetty soon discovers that her loving husband has been in the audience and has had a heart attack. Racked with grief and guilt, she wanders the Bowery, longing for death, until she awakes to find that the entire attempt at being an artist has all been a dream of her "brain-fever," which has hit her while out by the sea (217). Renouncing art as an enticing false value, she joyfully accepts her regained life as wife and mother.

The brain-fever, by which the dream-state rebellion of the new wife-mother in this story is both explained and excused, was a condition that Davis knew. "The Wife's Story" was written sometime during the first year of Davis's marriage when she was living with her husband's family in a strange city. She was also suffering a difficult pregnancy, which in its early stages was marked by a type of nervous breakdown, then called "brain-fever." Interestingly, her physician for this illness was probably S. Weir Mitchell, a family friend, who treated her, as he did Charlotte Perkins Gilman, author of "The Yellow Wallpaper," by restricting her reading and her writing.[25] Although Davis's story reflects a far less individuated response to the experience than Gilman's, it similarly illuminates the tragedy of a female writer's repressed, guilty desire.

Other tales of artistic-domestic conflict during this period—"Clement Moore's Vocation" (1870), *Earthen Pitchers* (1873–74), and "The Poetess of Clap City" (1875)—repeat variations on the theme of failure anxiety that appears in "A Wife's Story."[26] In each case the protagonist fails as an artist because she is internally or externally impelled to abandon art for womanhood. Sometimes she is tragically forced to surrender to social forces greater than herself, as in "Marcia," Davis's darkest, most realistic vision of the failed artist.

The story "Marcia," like "The Wife's Story," is typical of Davis's middle period in that it dramatizes an attempt to mediate the conflict between art and domesticity that ends in failure. Also like Hetty, Marcia Barr, the would-be writer from Yazoo, Mississippi, is a recurring female type in Davis's fiction who reflects another facet of Davis's self-image during this middle period. Marcia is courageous in her determination to break out of the oppressive rural culture that trapped her opium-addicted mother. Marcia describes her mother, a woman with "one of the finest minds in the world," more like a slave than a plantation mistress. She has never been "further than twenty miles from the plantation; she has read nothing, knows nothing" (925). Marcia herself is proud of her refusal to compromise her dream by accepting a protected life of marriage to a man who, like her father, "thinks women are like mares—only useful to bring forth children." But, according to the professional writer who narrates the story, she is tragically innocent:

The popular belief in the wings of genius, which can carry it over hard work and all such obstacles as ignorance of grammar or even the spelling-book, found in her a marked example. (926)

Although Marcia resembles Davis's young rebellious artists, her story, told from the perspective of the older narrator reveals a compromised vision that comes with age.

However, the narrator is moved by Marcia's valiant, if ingenuous, battle for independence. Marcia struggles to find work writing, suffering hunger and also frustration because she has "something to say, if people only would hear it" (927). After several years, when she has become a ragged, gaunt writer of social and commercial puffs for the papers, Zack Biron, her father's plantation overseer, comes to find her and take her home. He is "an ignorant, small-minded man" (926), but he is genuinely horrified by Marcia's straits and determined that she be cared for "like a lady" (928). In the narrator's description of the leave-taking of the new Marcia, "magnificent in plumes, the costliest that her owner's [husband's] money could buy," this story voices both sadness at Marcia's failure and horror at her victimization. Without question, defeat is total as Marcia hands the narrator her unpublished manu-scripts, asking, "Will you burn them for me? All: do not leave a line, a word" (928).

The voice of the author is totally conflicted in this story. The narrator, a writer and successful publisher whose own sex is fascinat-ingly indeterminate, voices attitudes that more closely resemble Davis's at this time than does the protagonist.[27] The narrator is ambivalent toward Marcia—admiring her grit and integrity, pitying her victimiza-tion, and blaming her innocence. Figures like Marcia, idealists who fail, reappear as admonitions in Davis's fiction and essays of this middle period and later. There is always much of Rebecca Harding, the young woman from West Virginia, in them. But in this story, Davis seems to have split herself into two; there is also much of her in the narrator, who constantly needs to validate the compromises she has made.

Most of Davis's middle-period artists are not as overtly victimized as Marcia Barr. More often, indoctrinated and defined by domestic ideology, their failure results from a subtler self-destruction. Usually, like Hetty Manning, the female artist voluntarily forsakes art in order to fulfill her redemptive role as wife-mother. This is the choice made by Maria Heald, the artist in "The Poetess of Clap City," and it is the true work discovered by the artist protagonist in "Clement Moore's Voca-tion." *Earthen Pitchers*, a serialized novel from Davis's middle period, enacts the title's implications: that the transcendent or autonomous motive of art is antithetical to the corporeal, serving nature of woman's domestic being. In this novel, Audry Swenson, a musician of promise, witnesses the atrophy of her unused talent; her complement, Jane Derby, a successful journalist, also renounces professional achievement for domesticity. The resolutions of all these stories are painfully ambig-uous regarding the tragedy or the wisdom of the protagonists' choices. They assert more than anything else a psyche in conflict. Like Maria in "The Poetess of Clap City," the two artists in *Earthen Pitchers* are forced to confront the facts that undeveloped power atrophies and wasted talent is irrevocably lost. Davis's fictional artists of this middle period fail in their attempts to deny their domestic role or to mediate it with their artistic aspirations. Their eventual success as wives and mothers is undermined by awareness of their failure as artists. Interestingly, Davis allows none of these artists the option of mediation through compromise that she herself chose.

These *Künstlerromane* were written by Davis at a time when she was enjoying the fulfilled life of a happily married mother of three children. But they are also the stories of a writer who, though always writing, was forsaking her talent, producing increasingly less of the intense, demanding fiction of which she was capable. Instead of submitting to the respected journals that continued to solicit her work, at this time she was more often submitting easy potboilers for popular children's and women's fashion magazines. These are what she had time and energy for, but the continued occasional appearance of her work in better journals demonstrates that she still knew and valued quality in her own writing. In her artists of this period, we see her ambivalence about the life she had chosen. Unlike the domestic contentment found in much of her fiction of this period, her stories of artists feature women who voice both anxiety about the compromising of their maternal, female role with their egoistic artistic desire and guilt about being unable to renounce that desire successfully.

The transition to the next period in Davis's fiction is marked by her development of an artist manqué in *A Law Unto Herself* (1877), written just a few years after *Earthen Pitchers*.[28] Cornelia Fleming, the female artist in this novel, is a minor character whose primary role is that of the other woman in a love triangle. However, she suggests a change in the nature of Davis's anxiety about her art from guilt to regret, which marks the older female artist. In the creation of this character's unfulfilled life, Davis seems again to be transferring attitudes to her characters; however, this instance seems motivated by the author's insecurity. Cornelia's inability to find fulfillment, which reinforces the idea that domestic desire cannot be repressed or mediated, hints at Davis's need for reassurance about the choice she herself had made. Even though Cornelia's failure at love has permitted her pursuit of art, she still finds herself unable to find satisfaction without domestic definition. In this case, Cornelia's singular pursuit of art results from, rather than causes, her inability to find completion in her womanhood. This scenario differs from those of Davis's previous period, in which the pursuit of art threatens success as a woman, and from those of her later period, in which the pursuit of domesticity causes her lack of fulfillment as an artist.

At the close of this story, Cornelia, who has lost the man of her dreams to the novel's protagonist, finally settles in Rome and brings to its artist colony all her frustrated domestic desire; "she makes her studio one of the pleasantest resorts for the young artists in Rome." There, with "her hair cut short" and "man's collar," she attempts to have both worlds—domestic centrality and artistic autonomy—but she fails to be successfully fulfilled by either. "A good fellow, Corny," the other artists say, "but what a pity that she is not a man" (731). Cornelia's ironic unfulfillment seems to reify Davis's fears about the impossibility of a woman's successful denial of her domestic urges: Cornelia is not only an artist manqué, she is also a male manqué.

When she wrote this story, Davis was the mother of three children, ranging in age from five to thirteen. She was also the wife of the editor of the *Philadelphia Inquirer*. Davis, who always practiced her belief that mothers should not work out of the home unless doing so was financially necessary, chose to subordinate her writing to her domestic commitments. Nevertheless, the prodigious output of her fifty-year career demonstrates that, while she was a wife and mother, Davis was also always a writer.[29] When her eldest son, Richard Harding Davis, was beginning his career, she once responded to a suggestion he had received that an unhappy writer should stop writing by saying, "God forbid. I would almost as soon say stop breathing, for it is the same thing."[30]

Davis's works of the late 1880s through the 1890s are the creations of a more mature woman with grown children, who as a writer was beginning to confront the consequences of her choices. In her treatment of the artist in stories like "Anne" (1889) and *Frances Waldeaux* (1897), artistic expression is linked with individualism more than with creativity.[31] While these stories are not marked with frustration or with anxiety about failure as thoroughly as the earlier artists' tales, they are tinged with regret and resignation at a lack of fulfillment.[32] Older women whose age and situation often closely resembles Davis's, these protagonists have either rejected the pursuit of art, seeing it as irreconcilable with domesticity, or like Davis, they have compromised their art in order to pursue it. In both cases they are unfulfilled.

The older artists of this period, like the title character of "Anne," mourn the loss of creative fulfillment but conclude eventually that its loss is the inevitable price of maturity. The creative impulse, seen in retrospect by the mature author and by her mature protagonist, is characterized by strength, beauty, and selfishness; these qualities seem to equate it with the shallowness of youth. In "Anne," the discovery of being unfulfilled as a woman is realized first as the discovery of being unfulfilled creatively, and both discoveries are revealed dramatically at a moment of middle-age crisis.

Davis's emphasis on the protagonist's interiority shows the ironic disparity between the female artist as expressive subject and the wife-mother as silenced object. Throughout there are two Anne's. The external Mrs. Anne Palmer, "a stout woman of fifty with grizzled hair and a big nose," tries to sing, but produces only a "discordant yawp." However, always "something within her" cries out, "I am here—Anne! I am beautiful and young. If this old throat were different my voice would ring through earth and heaven" (227).

Anne's mid-life crisis is the crushing discovery of being unfulfilled, common to the mature artist in Davis's later fiction. Anne, a "woman of masculine intellect" who has assumed management of the family peach farm since her husband's death and who, through shrewd stock investments has considerably improved the family estate, is bored with her life. Increasingly her mind wanders to her first love, George Forbes, now a famous author. Unknown to either of her two overly solicitous children, the Anne within is racked with discontent, crying out, "I should have had my true life" (232). This story of an artist whose situation—solicitous adult children, domestic comfort, and economic productivity—strongly resembles Davis's own is actually a rebellion fantasy by a woman who rarely in her own voice uttered discontent with her personal life.

In the story, the Anne within finally even convinces Mrs. Anne Palmer, the widow and mother of grown children, to run away:

She would go away. Why should she not go away? She had done her full duty to husband, children and property. Why should she not begin somewhere else, live out her own life? Why should she not have her chance for the few years left? Music and art and the companionship of thinkers and scholars, Mrs. Palmer's face grew pale as she named these things so long forbidden to her. (234)

She does run away, but eventually, like Hetty Manning and many other of Davis's rebellious women, she is led by events to realize that life is best and values are truest at home. Once again, though, Davis's commitment to her "it's-a-wonderful-life" theme is suspect. She first develops her comfortable conclusion in which Anne, who has been welcomed home, enjoys a "quiet, luxurious, happy life." But she adds a final reassertion of Anne's interiority that invites suspicion of the author's surface text:

Yet sometimes in the midst of all this comfort and sunshine a chance note of music or the sound of the restless wind will bring an expression into her eyes which her children do not understand, as if some creature unknown to them looked out of them.

At such times Mrs. Palmer will say to herself, "Poor Anne!" (242)

In her last novel, *Frances Waldeaux,* Davis again treats the elderly female artist, this time depicting her fictive double with satiric objectivity as an aging woman hack. This protagonist's discovery of unfulfillment is ironic. Well aware that she has injured her artistic potential in the name of motherhood, the protagonist discovers late in life that, in her attempt to live the domestic ideal of abnegation, she has actually annihilated any sense of herself as an individual.

Frances Waldeaux, widowed at a young age by a sweet but irresponsible wastrel, has made a successful career more like that of Davis's contemporary Fanny Fern than like Davis's. Frances is a successful writer of "comical squibs" that are "not vulgar but coarse and biting" (14). Like Fern, she also uses a pseudonym: "Quigg." Frances, however, maintains her anonymity for reasons slightly different from Fern's and from those that impelled Davis's frequent choice of anonymity. She hides her successful identity in order to delude her grown son into thinking that his support comes from his father's well-planned trust.

In this final treatment of the artist, Davis depicts her protagonist's failure to find fulfillment in her choices of self-abnegation as a writer and as a mother. In the character of Frances Waldeaux, Davis embodies the error of compromised choices and mediated desires, the choices that had directed Davis's own life. Frances's error originates in the sacrifice of her own identity. During an early conversation with her adored son, George, she reveals that she is unfulfilled to the point of hollowness:

I never think of you as my son, or a man, or anything outside of me—not at all. You are just me, doing the things I should have done if I had not been a woman. . . . when I was a girl it seemed as if there was something in me that I must say, so I tried to write poems. . . . I've been dumb, as you might say, for years. But when I read your article, George—do you know if I had written it I should have used just the phrases you did? . . . I am dumb, but you speak for me now. It is because we are just one. (9)

But they are not one; he leaves, and Frances is left alone. The novel's plot centers on Frances's gradual and troubled acceptance of George's right to an individual existence—his choice of career, his wife, and his home. It also deals with her discovery that domestic self-abnegation can be harmful. By turning to potboiling journalism, Frances has done what Maria Heald in "The Poetess of Clap City" refused to do: sold her "birthright"—her poems and her individual identity—"for a mess of pottage." Though more extreme, Frances's choice is essentially the one that Davis made. In earlier stories of anxiety the artists are frustrated by or fearful of unused talent. Even in later stories like "Anne," the artist regrets unused talent. In this last rendering, however, misuse of talent seems as disastrous as its disuse.

Frances Waldeaux is autobiographical in a number of ways, not the least of which is that the protagonist is a doting mother of a now-grown son in the support of whom she has silently, voluntarily sacrificed her integrity as a writer. This is a novel by a mother who took greater pride in the accomplishments of her son, Richard Harding Davis, than she ever did in her own work. However, this is also the final novel of an aging author who, looking back at her early work like "Life in the Iron-Mills" and remembering the indignant passion that had filled her with purpose, might have regretted the atrophy of that power. Finally, this is the work of a sixty-five-year-old widow, who for all her free-thinking individualism, was a product of her culture. No matter what special power she possessed, she also shared possession of her culture's dominant domestic ideology.

Rebecca Harding Davis, like her characters, an artist and a woman in the nineteenth century, was forced in every stage of her life to make choices that placed her in a dilemma, assuring failure—by being either frustrated, unsuccessful, or unfulfilled. She experienced the frustration of her artistic desires because they were incompatible with her role as wife-mother. She was unsuccessful in her attempts to mediate the role of artist with those that defined a woman, and she admitted failure in the necessary rejection of one of the conflicting roles. Finally, she recognized a lack of fulfillment within the narrow limitations of her selected identity; she even had to confront being unfulfilled by the compromises necessary to allow the female pursuit of art. Davis made choices that she knew were right for her as a woman, but choices that she also knew were wrong for her as an artist.

Like many other women writers, Davis often appeased the guilt and frustration inherent in the double-bind of being a female artist by becoming her own worst enemy, creating fictional projections of herself as artist and then negating their power, punishing them, or having them recant their unacceptable artistic desire. The paradigm of the artist manqué allowed women writers in the nineteenth century to exorcise their illicit desires by simultaneously asserting and denying them. It provided a way for a woman like Davis to fantasize her desire, to punish her guilt, to salve her pain, and still to be a writer.

Notes

1. "Life in the Iron-Mills," *Atlantic* 7 (1861), 430–51, did not appear with "The Korl Woman" as a subtitle, although Davis had submitted it as an alternative title to "Iron-Mills"; the reprint *Life in the Iron Mills and Other Stories*,

biographical interp. Tillie Olsen, rev. ed. (Old Westbury, N.Y.: Feminist Press, 1985), which is cited, prints the subtitle.

2. P. 64; korl is a pinkish-white, chalky substance left from the Bessemer steel smelting process.

3. This aspect of Davis's writing, which is indeed essential, is enriched, not refuted, by feminist reading. For various genre/tradition arguments, see James C. Austin, "Success and Failure of Rebecca Harding Davis," *Midcontinent American Studies Journal* 3 (1962), 44–49; Walter Hesford, "Literary Contexts of 'Life in the Iron-Mills,' " *American Literature* 49 (1977), 70–85; John Conran, "Assailant Landscapes and the Man of Feeling: Rebecca Harding Davis's *Life in the Iron Mills," Journal of American Culture* 3 (1980), 487–500; and Sharon M. Harris, "Rebecca Harding Davis: From Romanticism to Realism," *American Literary Realism* 21.2 (winter 1989), 4–20.

4. Tillie Olsen's insightful biographical interpretation of "Iron-Mills" gave Davis new literary life. But, while her Feminist Press editions (1972, 1985) have created a sizable readership, they have stimulated surprisingly little critical interest, compared with that in some other rediscovered woman writers. For discussion of Davis's fiction from a feminist perspective, see Margaret M. Culley, "Vain Dreams: The Dream Convention in Some Nineteenth-Century Women's Fiction," *Frontiers* 1.3 (1976), 94–104; Louise Duus, "Neither Saint nor Sinner: Women in Late Nineteenth-Century Fiction," *American Literary Realism* 7 (1974), 276–78; Charlotte Goodman, "Portraits of the *Artiste Manquée* by Three Women Novelists," *Frontiers* 5 (1981), 57–59; Jean Pfaelzer, "Rebecca Harding Davis: Domesticity, Social Order, and the Industrial Novel," *International Journal of Women's Studies* 4 (1981), 234–44, and the introduction to "Marcia," *Legacy* 4 (1987), 3–5; and Jane Atteridge Rose, "Reading 'Life in the Iron-Mills' Contextually: A Key to Rebecca Harding Davis' Fiction," in *Conversations: Contemporary Critical Theory and the Teaching of Literature,* ed. Charles Moran and Elizabeth Penfield (Urbana, Ill.: National Council of Teachers of English, 1990) 187–99. Also see brief references in Susan Gubar, "The Birth of the Artist as Heroine: (Re)production, the *Künstlerroman* Tradition, and the Fiction of Katherine Mansfield," in *The Representation of Women in Fiction,* ed. Carolyn G. Heilbrun and Margaret R. Higonnet (Baltimore: Johns Hopkins University Press, 1983), pp. 19–59; and Rachel Blau DuPlessis, "To 'bear my mother's name': *Künstlerromane* by Women Writers," in *Writing Beyond the Ending: Narrative Strategies of Twentieth-Century Women Writers* (Bloomington: Indiana University Press, 1985), pp. 84–104. For a concise overview, see Judith Fetterley, *Provisions* (Bloomington: Indiana University Press, 1985), pp. 306–14.

5. This French word *manqué* is critically appropriate as an umbrella term because it encompasses the various ways failure can occur: frustration, lack of success, lack of fulfillment.

6. For further discussion of this genre, see Linda Huf, *A Portrait of the Artist as a Young Woman: The Writer as Heroine in American Literature* (New York: Ungar, 1983); also see DuPlessis, Goodman, and Gubar.

7. This discussion is largely premised on two studies: the understanding of duplicity in nineteenth-century women's fiction, provided by Sandra M. Gilbert and Susan Gubar, *The Madwoman in the Attic: The Woman Writer and the Nineteenth-Century Literary Imagination* (New Haven, Conn.: Yale University Press, 1979); and the understanding of values implicitly operating in middle-class nineteenth-century America, provided by Jane Tompkins, *Sensational*

Designs (New York: Oxford University Press, 1985). It is also influenced by the understanding that women interpret and thereby reconstruct their particular position in history, provided by Linda Alcoff "Cultural Feminism Versus Post-Structuralism: The Identity Crisis in Feminist Theory," *Signs Journal of Women in Culture and Society* 13.3 (1988), 405–36.

8. For biographical reading of other women writers in consideration of ideological construction of female identity, see Mary Kelley, *Private Woman, Public Stage* (New York: Oxford University Press, 1984).

9. For further discussion of the artist manqué as evidence of women's collusion with patriarchal ideology continuing into the twentieth century, see Linda Dittmar, "When Privilege Is No Protection: The Woman Artist in *Quicksand* and *The House of Mirth*," in this volume. For a provocative alternative view of Elizabeth Barrett Browning's *Aurora Leigh*, often seen as the epitome of the nineteenth-century *Künstlerroman* of the artist manqué in its conclusion that "Art is much but Love is more," see Holly A. Laird, "*Aurora Leigh*: An Epical *Ars Poetica*," in this volume.

10. For biography of Davis, see Gerald Langford, *The Richard Harding Davis Years A Biography of a Mother and Son* (New York: Holt, Rinehart and Winston, 1961) and Sharon Harris, *Rebecca Harding Davis and American Realism* (Philadelphia: University of Pennsylvania Press, 1991).

11. For discussion of the socioeconomic aspects of domestic ideology, see Kirk Jeffrey, "The Family as Utopian Retreat from the City," *Soundings* 55 (1972), 22–41; Barbara Epstein, *The Politics of Domesticity* (Middletown, Conn.: Wesleyan University Press, 1981); and Susan Moller Okin, "The Woman and the Making of the Sentimental Family," *Philosophy and Public Affairs* 11 (1982), 65–88; for discussion of the religious aspects of domestic ideology, see Ann Douglas, *The Feminization of American Culture* (New York: Oxford University Press, 1985); and Tompkins, *Sensational Designs*.

12. In similar fashion, she dutifully moved to her husband's home in Philadelphia after her marriage, yet, once there, she spent more time in the library than she did keeping house. Later, when she had children, she always stayed home with them, but she spent the time writing.

13. "Blind Tom," *Atlantic* 10 (1862), 580–85; also as "Blind Black Tom," *All Year Round* 8 (1862), 126–29.

14. Many of Davis's protagonists suffer some form of "dumbness," her term for the silence that Tillie Olsen has shown to be the mark of women's texts in patriarchal culture (*Silences* [New York: Delacorte, 1978]). For another instance of silence, see Linda Hunt, "*The Alberta Trilogy*: Cora Sandel's Norwegian *Künstlerroman* and American Feminist Literary Discourse," in this volume.

15. The real dangers of life in a border state during the Civil War only exacerbated the status quo of double standards and dependency.

16. Rebecca Harding [Davis], letter to Annie Fields, May 27, 1862, Richard Harding Davis Collection (#6109), Manuscript Division, Special Collections Department, University of Virginia Library, Charlottesville.

17. Maintaining anonymity long after it had ceased as a convention, Davis established several identities through textual lineage, her two most used being "by the author of 'Margret Howth'" (realism) and "by the author of 'The Second Life'" (sensationalism). Sometimes she published very different stories simultaneously in the same journals.

18. *Earthen Pitchers*, in *Scribner's Monthly* 7 (1873–74), 73–81, 199–207, 274–81, 490–94, 595–600, 714–21.

19. The real enslaved musician was named Tom Cauthen and was the property of a plantation owner by that name in Columbus, Georgia.

20. "The Wife's Story," *Atlantic* 14 (1864), 1–19, rpt. Olsen, *Silences*, pp. 177–221; "Marcia," *Harper's* 53 (1876), 925–28, which is cited, has also been recently reprinted in *Legacy* 4 (1987), 6–10.

21. Although certainly less extreme, the perceived conflict between a life of art and a life of domesticity has not disappeared. Other essays in this volume demonstrate that the destructive power of this tension is not specific to one age or one culture. See Renate Voris, "The Hysteric and the Mimic: A Reading of Christa Wolf's *Quest for Christa T.*," Katherine Kearns, "From Shadow to Substance: The Empowerment of the Artist Figure in Lee Smith's Fiction," and Linda Hunt, "*The Alberta Trilogy*," all in this volume.

22. These stories, as a group, also show that this subject was an obsession of Davis's at this time of her life and not something tailored to appeal to a particular journal; her stories of failed artists appeared in *Atlantic*, *Harper's*, *Scribner's*, and *Peterson's* magazines, covering the total spectrum of fiction presses in the period after the Civil War.

23. Rebecca Harding Davis, Diary (1865–79), University of Virginia, Charlottesville.

24. Asserting that for nineteenth-century women dreams of artistic achievement were "not so much vain, as in vain," Culley argues that ambivalent dreams in fiction like "The Wife's Story" indicate that Davis and others "may have been unable to admit to themselves the full extent and meaning of their fantasies of the married woman in America" (102).

25. Rebecca Harding Davis, letter to Annie Fields (1866), University of Virginia, Charlottesville; on the occasion of Mitchell's first publication in *Atlantic*, Davis made reference to his care of her during her first, emotionally difficult pregnancy: "I owe much to him—life—and what is better than life." For fuller discussion, see Jane Atteridge Rose, "Images of Self: The Example of Rebecca Harding Davis and Charlotte Perkins Gilman," *English Language Notes* 29.1 (1991).

26. "Clement Moore's Vocation," *Peterson's* 57 (1870), 54–59; "The Poetess of Clap City," *Scribner's Monthly* 9 (1975), 612–15.

27. In her introduction to "Marcia," Pfaelzer defines the narrator as male, which the narrator's professional status would certainly indicate. However, comments like the narrator's statement that Biron did not have to be so quick declaring his business, because "any woman would soon have guessed" it, suggest the character is female. The most plausible explanation seems to be that Davis became so aligned with her male character that she let her persona slip.

28. *A Law Unto Herself*, in *Lippincott's* 2 (1877), 39–49, 167–82, 292–308, 464–78, 614–28, 719–31.

29. Davis wrote and published continuously from 1861 until three months before her death in January 1910. During this time she published well over five hundred stories and essays, in addition to twelve books. For bibliography, see Jane Atteridge Rose, "The Fiction and Non-Fiction of Rebecca Harding Davis," *American Literary Realism* 22.3 (spring 1990) pp. 67–86.

30. *The Adventures and Letters of Richard Harding Davis*, ed. Charles Belmont Davis (New York: Scribner's, 1917), pp. 34–35.

31. "Anne," *Harper's* 78 (1889), 744–50, rpt. in Olsen, *Silences,* 225–42; *Frances Waldeaux* (New York: Harper, 1897).

32. Kearns's reading of Lee Smith's fiction, in this volume, suggests an interesting contrast between nineteenth-century and twentieth-century projections of the woman artist. Davis's artists manqués, which reflect each stage of her life, never conquer or successfully reconcile the tension in their lives. Smith's sequence of artists, however, seem increasingly to have integrated their womanhood with their art.

Chapter 9
From Shadow to Substance: The Empowerment of the Artist Figure in Lee Smith's Fiction

Katherine Kearns

There is a steady progression in Lee Smith's novels from the female character as self-perceived artistic product to the female character as artist. Smith's seven novels together make an ongoing *Künstlerroman*, revealing her gradually less qualified acceptance of a female artist figure who, while remaining committed to a powerful maternal ethic, crafts an artistic product that is autonomous and permanent.[1] Smith's definition of the female artist and what she might legitimately produce may be seen to have progressed through three distinct phases. In the first, her characters' ambivalence and anxiety about a possible artistic vocation subvert both personal growth and artistic product. In this stage, which begins with *The Last Day the Dogbushes Bloomed* (1968), includes *Something in the Wind* (1971) and *Fancy Strut* (1973), and culminates in *Black Mountain Breakdown* (1980), the main female characters awkwardly seek to accommodate the heightened perceptions of the artist to their social surroundings. Anxious to be "normal"—to be beauty queens and majorettes and good wives—they move toward the immobilizing truth of *Black Mountain Breakdown:* that to be all things to all people is to be nothing, to risk becoming a mirror woman whose last refuge is the shroud of catatonia. Plagued by the sense that their only aesthetic ambition should be a traditionally defined "beautification" of the female self, they fail at both life and art; their own personas are so circumstantially defined that they can produce little of value. The second phase, which encompasses *Oral History* (1983) and *Family Linen* (1985), generates a body of powerful women antithetical to these impaired females. Highly intuitive and empathetic, they pour their generative and artistic capacities into the evanescent artistries of healing, nurturing, and oral storytelling. Smith's hard-won knowledge, purchased with the lessons accorded to the figures of her early phase, is channeled into figures of matriarchal power; these characters are not, however, self-defined artists, but artist/muses. Aesthetic icons of a higher order, they embody wisdom and goodness and transmute these qualities through the gifts they make to others. They are more enablers than artists themselves, so that only their daughters' names will be signed to the works we know.[2] If the first stage represents the artistic consciousness urging itself toward effacement, the second stage realizes powers willingly spent; the source is regenerative but the demands upon it everlasting. The last stage appears in *Fair and Tender Ladies* (1988), and here Smith's (partial) reconciliation of the artist's vocation to the imperatives of family and community life allows for the artistic product itself an intrinsic value as art. No longer oral history, the protagonist's own written language, opaque with significance, becomes testament to the perceived value of the artist/writer herself. Smith moves thus from the self-deprecatory implication that a woman's art provides license for ridicule and even for violation to a conviction that control over and production of an artifact that in some way documents oneself is both necessary and valuable.

Smith's third novel, the broadly allegorical comedy *Fancy Strut,* may be seen as a manifesto on self-conscious art and self-claimed artists; as such, it epitomizes Smith's early ambivalence about her own craft and about artistic pretensions generally.[3] A comic deflation of "art," it is also by extension an ironic deprecation of Smith's own role as creator, thus establishing in bold strokes the dualistic motives of her early artist figures. In *Fancy Strut* the scaffolding of the Speed Sesquicentennial stage set (= Art) goes up in flames and the bleachers (= Interpretation) fall inexplicably down into rubble. Hired by the town of Speed, Alabama, which plans to celebrate its founding with a pageant run by out-of-town professionals, the "Art Director" obfuscates rather than creates. He makes certain that each discrete element is practiced separately; the whole white population of Speed is fantastically costumed, just like characters in a novel, but kept from any idea of the pageant's purpose or meaning. The novel's climactic scene is the debacle of art, the collapse of pageantry; the stage and scaffolding catch on fire, the huge movie screen shrivels into cinders, and the townspeople begin rioting in the streets. The collapse of pretension is cathartic, and it is begun by a series of crudely symbolic acts in which it appears that Smith herself is burning down her own stage as a finale. When a hate-letter tied to a rock is tossed through the window, it is as if

Smith throws it herself, lampooning the mystery of the Word, of the Symbol, by giving it literal rock-hard weight and projectile force. The ending, a parodic "happily ever after" as subtle as a note on a rock, ties everything up neatly for everybody; significantly, the main woman character is reconciled to her husband and her domestic life and recognizes in an epiphanic moment that she wants to have a child. These people are, the author implies, only characters with names like Manly Neighbors and Buck Fire in a book called *Fancy Strut*. The display of pyrotechnics within is Smith's own fancy strut across the page.

Smith mocks herself as artist as she mocks the parodic "art" of the pageants and the majorette contests within *Fancy Strut*, a pattern she reifies within her fiction before *Fair and Tender Ladies* with her mockery of the artist figure and her scourging of the self-consciously artistic impulse. "Artists," from *Cakewalk* (1980), is a representative portrait of the artist who distorts the real for the sake of the symbolic. The artistic grandmother is a cautionary figure, proof to her granddaughter Jennifer that the subordination of life to art is a punishable offense. Jennifer documents a childhood summer when she was "all soul," "artistic," and "sensitive," and when she saw her grandmother, a devotee of correspondence school, as the epitome of culture and art. Her grandmother knows all about "Christianity. . . ; Greek mythology; English country houses; etiquette; Japanese flower arranging; . . . crewel embroidery; and the Romantic poets."[4] She paints wooden-looking birds and writes poetry and locks it away in a box. Jennifer herself experiments with art through painting, writing sonnets, and looking at art books. Like her grandmother's skewed vision, what Jennifer claims to see is divorced from what she looks at. When a friend accuses her of looking in an art book at "That naked guy," she responds, "That's not a naked guy, Scott. . . . That is Michelangelo's famous statue *David*. It's a work of Art, if you know anything about Art, which you don't, of course" (*Cakewalk* 112). Jennifer unsexes the naked figure into a "work of Art." But Jennifer's grandmother has literally rejected the real man, her husband, for what she calls Art. While she moves inexorably to senility, implicitly a direct product of her preference for the stasis of art over life, he makes love to a beautician, "a *fallen woman*," who loves him unselfishly (*Cakewalk* 117). In the end, the "artist" sits, senile, watching stockcar racing on TV and muttering, "Art, . . . I'm watching art, Jennifer" (*Cakewalk* 122).

As though to enforce an ironic inversion of the gradual generational emergence of the female artist,[5] Smith appropriates the name "Jennifer" for the ludicrously affected young writer who begins and ends *Oral History;* she is a youthful version of the grandmother of "Artists," as if the tendency to such foolishness is passed down and as if the artistic instinct is something that thwarts growth rather than encourages it. Bracketing the more serious narratives, Jennifer's language and demeanor is antithetical to the unpretentious artistry of other female characters within the novel. Raised in a middle-class suburb, Jennifer comes to visit her Appalachian relatives, who interest her solely because her professor of oral history is excited by their folkloric potential. Her journal is parodically artistic, peppered with the phrase, "resembling nothing so much as. . . ." The terrain "resembl[ed] nothing so much as a green-hued quilt." The house "resembled nothing so much as a house before someone moves in."[6] Jennifer's mannered prose underscores the necessarily exclusive nature of the visual metaphor, the breaking of a scene into fragments that lose their primary function to the thing they are said most to resemble. Dust becomes "an even lacy carpet on the floor," a metaphor that comically tacks the carpet to the floor with words, thus subverting all other properties of dust through concretization. Jennifer will make her own bogus artistic version of the past and present which depends entirely on her lack of knowing: she gets an A, marries her professor, and never sees her mountain relatives again.

Smith's artists manqués are simply not very good at using the tools of the trade, and the more formal education they endure, the more problematic their relationships both to formalized art and to traditionally defined female life become. Lacy of *Family Linen*, a middle-aged graduate student in English, gets mired in the intricate convolutions of "literary" language: thinking of irony, she meanders from Cape Canaveral to the house of Usher, relying herself, ironically enough, on the penile imagery of a rocket's penetration and on Poe's essentially misogynist vision. She feels her use of allusion and metaphor to be awkward, self-conscious; aware at some level that her language has been contaminated by canonical stereotypes, she feels as if pretension is reflexive. Exasperated, she reaches the conclusion that her head is "full of ridiculous things."[7] Lacy cannot quiet the yammering of metaphorical thinking: everything is like something else, but nothing in the traditional canon fits the meanings she senses to be appropriate to herself. Her intellectuality diffuses emotion and is felt as a kind of schizophrenia. Lacy feels that her head is filled with ridiculous things as if someone else has discarded them there, imposing upon her a habit of mind that makes her feel foolish; indeed, her conviction that her husband, now gone, "made her, fashioned her," and left her caught in his shell would tend to confirm her sense that she is "*Empty space*" (*FL* 70). Plagued always with the sense that she is laughable, Lacy is paralyzed into silence, entombed in the conviction that "she has nothing to say" (*FL* 131).

This is a profoundly ambivalent vision for a female artist: women—old, young, or middle-aged—who allow themselves the luxuries of introspection and artistic production are culpable. They forfeit love. Their distractedness makes them vulnerable, dangerous, and foolish. In *Family Linen*, Elizabeth Bird's journal, which reveals her to be self-consciously "literary," states the irreconcilable dichotomy between female life and art: "Alas! And let me quit that dreary house [her allegorical construct for memory], and abandon Symbol . . . the world has quite Enough, nay more than enough, of Pain to offer me" (*FL* 193). She marries for love, murders her husband with an ax, remarries, and resurrects an impenetrable construct of herself as "Lady." The first we hear of her is from Sybill, who says, "Well, my mother is a lady, I mean a *real* lady . . ." (*FL* 35). Not inconsequentially, Sybill also mentions in this context that her mother was, long ago, a once-published poet. Lacy attributes her own taste for poetry to her mother, who, she says ambiguously so that it includes both life and art, "could never tell good from bad" (*FL* 68). Elizabeth's pathology—her inability to tell good from bad, manifested in her writing, her choice of husband, and her murderous solution—seems inextricably linked to her interest in art. From childhood she is a "voracious" reader and a poet, predilections which, Smith implies, allow her literally to dismember her husband in the way the sonnet might "dismember" a woman by reducing her to Petrarchan components.

Smith underscores Elizabeth's function as the failed artist by making her journal comically overwritten and awkward. By making Elizabeth artistically overwrought, Smith undercuts the reader's sympathy for her, compromising what Josephine Donovan calls the gynocentric focus that would align readers with Elizabeth against her vicious husband, Jewel Rife.[8] Smith further deconstructs the text by making the journal itself, as her own artistic artifact, subject to self-conscious symbolic values. For example, the names she chooses for other characters are, as in *Fancy Strut*, intentionally unsubtle: *Ransom* McClain, who could have saved Elizabeth, *Grace* Harrison, who could have saved her father, *Lemuel* Bird, who like Lemuel Gulliver is a giant or a pygmy, depending on who is looking at him. Such signals echo Smith's essential ambivalence, as if Elizabeth's pretensions to seriousness not only lead her to violent madness but in some way suggest an unsavory weakness that predisposes her to it.

Elizabeth Bird's madness is atypically manifested in violence, but she acts for a body of other cautionary women in Smith's fiction whose intellectual and artistic needs lead to a dementia characterized more frequently by immobility and vertigo.[9] This madwoman figure reinforces Smith's subtext, which reveals the danger of losing one's footing in the step from role of "lady" to that of artist. In "Dear Phil Donahue" (*Cakewalk*) the dichotomy between "normalcy" and madness is literalized by a door separating domesticity from psychosis. The speaker walks from her kitchen into the garage, where she has been harboring a psychotic runaway boy. Filthy, he lies curled fetally in the darkness, and she lies down to join him there in a grotesque parody of the burdensome maternal/sexual role she plays in the house proper: performance art of the first order, the mad housewife sinking lethargically into excrement becomes both the fantasy and the fear of those who fail by omission or commission in the rites of femininity. Rebelling against domesticity, pretending toward the sensibilities of the artist, the "lady" invites her own dissolution: Elizabeth Bird is an extreme version of the inertly senile grandmother in "Artists"; Miss Iona, the hallucinatory journalist beset by vertigo in *Fancy Strut;* the near-schizophrenic fledgling artists, Susan Tobey of *The Last Day the Dogbushes Bloomed* and Brooke Kincaid of *Something in the Wind;* and the profoundly disturbed Crystal of *Black Mountain Breakdown*. Whether the artistic impulse is a symptom of madness or its cause remains ambiguous, but the warning is clear: the autonomous pleasure of artistic creation is profoundly dangerous.

Equally important, women with artistic and intellectual leanings so unsex themselves that they generate an antithesis, the freely sensual "fallen" woman. The Grandmother of "Artists," for example, is held against the redheaded "Jezebel" who provides sexual and maternal love. *Cakewalk* reiterates this dichotomy in "Between the Lines," "Artists," and "Cakewalk." In *Family Linen* Candy has been her sister's husband's lover for years, giving him what Myrtle, with all her marital theories, cannot, and Lacy has been abandoned for a younger woman in a "love nest." Where there is no one antithetically sensual woman, Smith provides a good-hearted prostitute, who succors all the men who must endure wives unsexed by intellect, or who are, themselves, plagued by intellect. Justine Poole, of *Oral History,* runs a brothel; a good cook and a good lover, she *likes* to make love. Geneva Hunt of *Fair and Tender Ladies* is the best cook and the most generous lover in town. There is always a female to fill the void between women distracted by their own minds and the men who are left to their own devices. The impossible reconciliation of the mother and the whore as she nurtures and satisfies every need, the figure of the happily sensual woman is Smith's wishful antidote to isolation.[10]

Women who pursue their artistic instincts are at great risk in Smith's fiction, not just for abandonment but for purposeful violation; the self-absorption necessary to artistic creation involves dropping one's guard, usually to disastrous effect. Just as a fixed artistic product invites the critic's anatomizing, so too does the still, inwardly turned female artist make herself vulnerable to those who interpret her aloneness as an invitation or as a challenge. *The Last Day the Dogbushes Bloomed, Something in the Wind,* and *Black Mountain Breakdown* document the catastrophic results of such vulnerability. Those who can sufficiently intellectualize their dilemmas may, like Lacy, guard themselves through a kind of self-preserving stasis. Those, like Jennifer, who are young and inexperienced enough to channel their energies through men, may temporarily forestall the consequences of their artistic instincts. But Smith's sense of danger is revealed within her texts by women whose artistic impulses are inextricably bound up with potential madness and with actual physical violation. She may be said in her early works to have performed a series of ritual sacrifices, a killing off of the artistic impulse, always with a resultant mutilation of the female subject who opens herself to the normalizing process.[11]

Nine-year-old Susan Tobey of *The Last Day the Dogbushes Bloomed* is, she announces, "a real good speller."[12] She can spell hard words like *hyacinth,* but her mother and sister seem to her to *be* flowers and the stuff of fairy tales. They are all romance, the queen and the princess, and Susan is the court historian, the namer of things. She is not, her gay sister Betty asserts, a "particularly gay" child; "she may even be somber," adds Susan's mother (*LDDB* 4). Thus Smith's earliest work articulates a female dilemma: whether to make oneself a work of art, as society seems to demand, or to be productive of art. *Dogbushes* is a first-person narrative. This is a point of view that disappears until *Fair and Tender Ladies* because by the end of this novel Susan has committed a cruelty (the uprooting of her neighbor's beloved rose garden), has been raped, and has appropriated a sinister male alter ego, the invisible "Little Arthur," who contaminates her vision and thus her voice. She looks from the back steps: "Little Arthur was under the dogbushes now and I was not surprised. I understood then that wherever I went, for maybe the whole rest of my life, Little Arthur would be somewhere close outside" (*LDDB* 180). Then Susan puts on her yellow dress, her red shoes without straps, and goes out to dinner with Daddy, transforming herself from artist to artistic product.

As Susan goes, so goes Brooke Kincaid of *Something in the Wind.* The novel begins with the death of Brooke's best friend, one who has helped her know what to think and say; his maleness has been her link to the world. Without him to translate for her, she is forced to confront her impotence. She carries *Ripley's Believe It Or Not* with her as a talisman against the conviction that she is becoming unmoored; its strange facts help to explain why the world is unfathomable to her. Brooke wants to be "normal": to go to college, but not to be too smart,

to have a boyfriend who is handsome and well attuned to social pro-
prieties. She wants the approval of her family but can attain it only by
making certain that her successes fall within the acceptable parameters. Her sister is providing the best of all examples, marrying well.
But Brooke knows that everything the world asks of her is against her
most fundamental nature, which is serious, intellectual, and creative.
She continues the pattern of Susan's disassociativeness as she splits
herself into Brooke and Brooke Proper and begins to refer to herself in
the third person: Her "life plan" involves imitation: "I would imitate
everybody until everything became second nature as the song says and
I wouldn't have to bother to imitate any more, I would simply *be*."[13] All
the energy that might have been directed into intellectual and artistic
accomplishment is translated into crafting an acceptable persona.

Art cannot accommodate itself to social normalcy, as Crystal Span-
gler of *Black Mountain Breakdown* finally proves; the tightly focused
third-person present-tense voice seems to pull Smith inexorably to the
eloquence of catatonia. Crystal's identities are all relative to her interpreters. Crystal is daddy's girl; he reads aloud to her in his darkened
room, spinning out stories into which she inserts herself. When her
father dies she translates herself into other texts: she is variously a good
girl-student-daughter, a bad girl, a religious girl, a college girl, a hippie
girl, a school-teacher girl, a well-married girl. This predilection is
literalized in her final obsession with Emma Turlington Field's diary,
and she moves toward silence and immobility in the preferred company of the text of a long-dead stranger, so distant a relative that no
one remembers her connection to the family. Field's "spidery" hand,
her writing "like bird tracks," represent the tenuous thread of continuity that holds Crystal in time and space.[14] When that journal is
burned, Crystal finds herself "out of the book," effaced (*BMB* 222).[15]
Her mystery, and men are intrigued to distraction by it, is that she is at
once a projection of their desires and a cipher. She sees herself as
nothing, and the meanings superimposed by her lovers only reinforce
her sense that she is forever metamorphic.

Crystal is Smith's extremity, a summing up of the damaged
women of her early novels into a wraith who feels herself to be so
transparent that she has to stand in front of something to appear to
have substance.[16] She is all contradiction. Appearing soft and infinitely malleable, blond with wide, doll-like blue eyes, she is also obdu-
rate. Often motionless and ultimately catatonic, she nonetheless frequently wrenches herself out of inertia into heated energy, so that even
in the end Agnes thinks, "Why, Crystal might jump right up from that
bed tomorrow and go off and get her Ph.D. or do something else
crazy. . . . Or she might stay right here and atrophy to death" (*BMB*

227–28).[17] Elisabeth Lenk sums up her type in her essay "The Self-reflecting Woman": "This woman was purely passive, an object only. She was loved, but she herself did not love; she was seen, but she herself did not see."[18] Crystal's catatonia is merely a logical conclusion to this state, the slightest extension from Catherine Clément's "indifferent hysteric" who "tries to signify eros through all the possible forms of anesthesia," who "defies stimulation," who "has put all her eroticizing into internal pain."[19] The many facets of her character are rearranged into art by each of her perceivers. She is the ultimate symbol, the missing half to every man's desires, to every woman's anxieties, and whatever she seems to become is through the infusion of others' meanings.[20] Crystal epitomizes the paradox of a femininity whose willfulness is employed in self-effacement, but all of Smith's female characters are born into a world which whispers that immobility is the only solution to its contradictory demands—to be everything and nothing, to be active and passive, to be sexual, virginal, maternal, and androgynous all at once. In Crystal she literalizes the female artist's dilemma—to speak and risk violation or to be mute in the asylum of immobility.[21]

Sybill Hess of *Family Linen* is Crystal's seeming opposite, but she is really the other side of the same counterfeit coin. Having refused the pyrrhic victory of passive resistance, she has excluded men from her life and sculpted herself. No fancy strutter, she is described as "a woman somehow almost military in the way she carries herself, the way her pretty graying hair is cut and waved so short, the way her gold clip-on earrings match the stickpin in the lapel of her navy blazer, and the way her clear red lipstick is so precisely applied" (*FL* 17). She has arranged a parodic construct of androgyny for herself, a refutation of the meticulously applied slash of red; she is a caricaturist, but she does paint her own mouth, from which carefully chosen language comes.[22] Sybill has the illusion of control that Crystal lacks until she is violated by her hidden knowledge of the past, and then she too becomes a medium, a vessel into which the sins of her father pour, from which the murmurings of the sibyl overflow through the mouth she had thought to control. She becomes, like Crystal, a hysteric, her body "transformed into a theater for forgotten scenes."[23]

In her second phase, Smith escapes from the diametrical and unsatisfactory resolutions implicit in Crystal and Sybill in a series of characters who neither surrender to masculinist demands nor waste their time in escaping them. These figures begin to appear first in the stories, like brief epiphanies, and emerge more fully realized in *Oral History* and *Family Linen,* where they are juxtaposed with damaged female characters to provide a balance of wholeness. These characters have in common what every failed artist in Smith's fiction lacks, from the utterly muted Crystal to the paradoxically sibylline Sybill: *they are in control of language.* Their words and stories are their own, and they speak or hold silence with authority and grace. But their artistry is dependent upon its integration into other, consciously acknowledged roles; they function first as mothers, wives, sisters, as cooks, hairdressers, and healers. They have retreated from any ambition toward documenting themselves through art, having reconciled the battle between the artist and the mother by contenting themselves with domestic artistries that are both beautiful and nurturing.

The prototypes for these women include Mrs. Darcy of "Mrs. Darcy Meets the Blue-eyed Stranger on the Beach" (*Cakewalk*), a healer whose hands translate her epiphany into healing warmth, and Florrie of "Cakewalk" whose artistry emerges in delicious, exquisitely decorated cakes which she then carelessly gives away; they embody the aesthetic of Smith's middle phase, but the third-person short story form does not give them their voices. The novels contain more fully realized characters. From *Oral History,* Granny Younger, who is a midwife, healer, and historian, and Sally, whose holistic sensuality emerges in storytelling, lovemaking, and cooking, both play substantial parts in the telling of Cantrell history, their narratives bracketing eighty years of family turmoil.[24] In *Family Linen,* Nettie and Candy use their voices sparingly, having learned that silence itself can speak clearly. When Lacy grabs Nettie, saying, "What do you think?" Nettie withholds the story she knows is better left untold, and thirty-nine pages of interior monologue document one wise moment of silence.

These women share the most fundamental requisite of the good artist: they are knowers. Having become acute observers, they have learned to see with remarkable insight what others can't even notice. Granny Younger, an herbalist who knows human nature as thoroughly as she knows mountain hollers, says, "I know what I know. I know moren most folks and that's a fact, you can ask anybody" (*OH* 27). Her insight into human behavior affords her a genuine foresight: "Sometimes I know the future in my breast. Sometimes I see the future coming out like a picture show, acrost the trail ahead" (*OH* 36). Candy correctly "thinks she was born knowing all about death" (*FL* 122). Nettie thinks, "Me, I've known more than I wanted to, all my life" (*FL* 213). These figures have learned to appropriate experience into wisdom without being irretrievably damaged. But, paradoxically, they choose a form of telling silence when they no longer hope to transcribe stories onto paper or when, as with Nettie and Candy, the real stories remain unspoken. They *know* through hard experience what Crystal implies: there may be no art that can reconcile a woman's voice to the world's. Oral history may be all there is to tell.[25]

Each of these characters has emerged from a troubled past to find a new sexual equilibrium. They have taken control of their lives and thus may control their narratives; no longer objects to be acted upon, they affect others with the potency of their earned freedom from coercion. Their sexuality no longer seems problematic to them. Not virginal, they choose, variously, to live celibately, to take lovers, to divorce and then marry men they love. Some kind of self-perceived sexual reconciliation is essential to narrative freedom in Smith's fiction, although the reader may find the implied alternatives problematic as they remain, inevitably, reactions grounded within the rules of hetero-sexual domesticity. Nettie, for example, thinks in self-definition, "What do I think? *Lord.* You're asking me? Me that has left one man and buried two?" (*OH* 213).[26] Her wisdom seems earned through hetero-sexual love and struggle but strengthened through celibacy, thus il-lustrating the difficult paradox that informs all of Smith's fiction—that loving, always defined maternally and heterosexually, is antithetical to autonomy. Yet sexual need thwarts narrative in Smith's fiction; it is not accidental that Lacy of *Family Linen* is accommodating her husband's abandonment of her at the same time she is stalled in her thesis. Smith's wise women have revolted from the more obvious coercions of sex. They refuse to see themselves as mere receptacles for anything—not for men or for knowledge—but instead they have a *conscious* wisdom that may, thus, be articulated.

Smith's middle-phase artist is what Rachel Blau DuPlessis calls the "maternal muse," one who "struggles with her condition to forge a work, usually one unique, unrepeatable work—an event, a gesture, an atmosphere—a work of synthesis and artistry that is consumed or used."[27] What these artist/muses make is at once both highly tangible and ineffable. Having struggled toward wholeness, they can provide for others, and with no defensive agenda, they are open to epiphany through the commonplace. What they make they offer up for con-sumption. They don't write bad poems or keep self-consciously artistic journals; in fact, they abnegate traditional art altogether. Smith repeat-edly reinforces in these transitional artist/muse figures an alternative vision to art as monument, for they are all like Florrie, whose mimesis is edible and freely given to be consumed. Paradoxically, the temporari-ness of their creations assures another kind of permanence than static, monumental art: their work is not only valuable in itself and within its context, but its value extends generationally as these women free their progeny to produce other forms of art.[28] As readers, we ourselves "write beyond the ending" of narratives in which the maternal muse is the dominant force, inspired to imagine an on-going narrative without the conventional closures explicitly set forth in a masculinist vision of female character.[29] Yet such art remains, in the context of Smith's work, essentially self-deprecating, as it represents, in a world where ambition is dangerous, a retreat from artistic ambition.

Candy, in her role as beautician, epitomizes the aesthetic of Smith's middle phase when she beautifies her mother for burial, an artistry antithetical to permanence. Candy's mother has spent her life ashamed of her daughter, but Candy, when called upon, goes willingly to prepare the body for burial. She sets and combs her hair, "thinking that hair is a funny thing—it's not like flesh. It doesn't change in death. . . . It's one of the great mysteries. Along with death. Candy has always been good with hair. And sometimes she thinks she was born knowing all about death, too, which might be why she's lived like she has" (*FL* 122). Candy perceives both her knowledge of death and her way with hair as something inborn. She would say, as she does of her happy, grown children, that "she can't take any credit. That's the way things are" (*FL* 113). She embodies what Sara Ruddick calls an "ethic of humility" which "accepts not only the facts of damage and death, but also the facts of the independent and uncontrollable, developing and increasingly separate existences of the lives it seeks to preserve."[30] She is a wise woman who would laugh to hear it, a minister in the most significant sense.

Just as Candy frees her children to become adults and makes her clients beautiful in their own eyes or as Granny Younger of *Oral History* moves her patients toward health, these muse figures give their work over to *become*. In *Oral History* the last extended narrative is Sally's, and she begins it by saying, "There's two things I like to do better than anything else in the world, even at my age—and one of them is talk. You all can guess what the other one is" (*OH* 233). Her ability to love, to make love, to fill up her husband with love as with food, is inextricably bound to her ability to fill him up with the regenerative energy of stories. He likes to listen to her, saying even during sex, "Talk to me." Telling him a story while he is home with a smashed leg, she reaches the end of her narrative while she fixes supper, and both the food and the narrative simmer into richness together. Her story satisfies the way her pot roast or her lovemaking would satisfy. It seems, in fact, because of Roy's broken leg, a substitution of one form of intimacy for another. The artist as healer/lover—one who succors, nourishes, satisfies, and temporarily mends in the perceiver what is fragmented and broken— is literalized by the intimate connection of the story she tells and the circumstances under which it is told.[31]

Smith's storytellers, because they talk with the sense that someone is listening, instinctively avoid literary devices that might constitute exclusion. They are seldom, for example, allusive, and their metaphors tend to be integrative and unobtrusive, taken from well-known surroundings. Granny Younger, whose narrative begins the body of *Oral History*, brings comfortable dead metaphors back to life in her storytelling: "mean as a snake," "without a pot to piss in." These storytellers reject the oversimplification implicit in purely linear narrative. Granny Younger is richly digressive; she punctuates her story with "I see I have forgot to mention Shelby Dick," or with the recipe to stop bleeding. At the end of *Oral History*, Sally retains Granny Younger's energetic immediacy. In an extended simile, she speaks of her family as being "like the kaleidoscope we got that year for Christmas that Lewis Ray took such a fit over, and wanted to hold all the time and not share, and got his way, of course, like he always did" (*OH* 238). Only after embedding the metaphor into history does Sally appropriate it for its symbolic value, making her mother the blue, unmoving center in kaleidoscopic family event. The simile is alive with meaning, the color blue as rife with associations to the Madonna and maternity as to the blues the characters sing; the mother is the spot of blue that keeps away the evil eye, and when she dies the geometrical wholeness of the family shatters. Dense with meaning, the kaleidoscope is nonetheless there because it is *there*.

Smith's artist/muse figures do not see themselves as autonomous, but as reciprocal. The fuller the life, the richer the narrative, filled with digressions that add layer upon layer to character, action, and context. Yet this immediacy, the very fullness of these characters who are so anchored in life, guarantees that they will all be oral historians, their art impromptu. Improvisational, their stories *must* rely completely on the goodness and the wisdom of the teller. This leaves no room for uncertainty or for the flaws inherent in most character, excluding all but the nearly magical seers from creativity while guaranteeing that the products of their creativity will be fleeting. Like food or medicine, the tangible manifestations of their productivity, their oral stories must be ingested and transmuted. The final product, whether it is curative energy or excrement, is dependent on the receiver, because in failing to make something immutable the artist yields control of the artifact. In the context of Smith's earlier novels, these muses seem another reaction posed within an essentially masculinist set of expectations.[32] Paradoxically, they imply a nearly impossible reconciliation of life and art, but it may be argued that they achieve this synthesis at the expense, finally, of themselves. Within Smith's fiction, which has worked so hard to discover how a woman may safely manifest her creativity, these muses hold forth, in direct contradiction to Smith's own vocation as novelist, an impossible model of egoless generosity.

Fair and Tender Ladies finally gives the protagonist her own voice translated by her own pen onto paper. Smith frees her character to articulate the dilemma of the artist torn between the need for autonomy and the demands of family and community. Ivy Rowe speaks over a sixty-one-year period from 1900 to 1961 through the naked form of personal letters, and she comes to seem utterly human in a way that the "good woman" muses of Smith's earlier novels, in their reconciliation to domesticity, never do. Ivy, like the muse figures, chooses domestic life over the necessarily more autonomous life of the self-defined artist, but she does so reluctantly and with full recognition of what she is forfeiting to her maternity. Smith makes the choice dramatically literal: Ivy finds at the moment she has decided to leave home for school in Boston that she is pregnant. Her illusion has been that she may make a choice between domesticity and intellectuality—between not becoming an artist and becoming one. Her pregnancy dispels the illusion of clarity, for while she resigns herself to poverty, a comparatively rural life, and a compromised education, she does not abandon her artistic impulses. In fact, she discovers that the very life she chooses, beginning with her unborn child and continuing through a long marriage and many more children and grandchildren, is the renewable source of her art. Even when she no longer believes that she will be "a writer," she continues to write because she must—her full life spills over onto the page, where she orders, clarifies, and makes real the discrete elements of her world.

Ivy announces in her first letter, "I want to be a writter, it is what I love the bestest in this world."[33] She doesn't just want to write, but to "be a famous writter" who "will write of love" (*FTL* 21). She plans to turn oral history into fiction: "And when I . . . become a writter, I will write of such a love and I will write of a man like my uncle Revel who can come like a storm in the night and knock a born lady off her feet" (*FTL* 80). Ivy has an ambition that no other character has dared to articulate and a potent artistic capacity which emerges with seeming inevitability in her daughter, who becomes the famous writer Ivy once hoped to be. Because writing—the act of signification—is a necessary step in her understanding of any event, Ivy confirms Smith's increasing conviction that to be an artist is to be a creator of self in its most essential sense. Ivy says again and again what she tells her daughter when she writes of Oakley's death: "Because I have written this letter to you, it is real now" (*FTL* 274). She recognizes the difference between memory and the translation of memory onto the immutable page, saying to Silvaney that she writes "to hold onto what is passing" (*FTL*

147). The very act of writing stirs the past into truth, turning memory into feeling.

When she stops writing for six years, she falls into a well of silence which she later describes as "a great soft darkness, a blackness so deep and soft that you can fall in there and get comfortable and never know you are falling in at all" (*FTL* 195). This silence is, for the writer, a loss of self: Ivy says, "But I have fallen down and down and down into this darkness, . . . and bits and pieces of me have rolled off and been lost along the way" (*FTL* 195). The state of "not-writing" is perceived by her to be a form of paralysis, as if she has been playing "statues" "and got flung down into darkness, frozen there" (*FTL* 196). Her character is not determined by others' expectations because through her writing she comes to know herself. Ivy can say, "you get so various as you get old! I have been so many people," because she has grown through the knowledge gained from her dialogue with the written word. Ivy finally confirms in Smith's fiction the value of art and of the female artist, as she proves with every word that the introspection of art affords an avenue to wisdom. As with the middle-phase muses, wisdom accompanies goodness. From such an artist, art can be as potent a curative for what is unwhole as Granny Younger's herbs or Sally's good food.

The epistolary form of *Fair and Tender Ladies* works at two levels to reinforce the validity of writing, for while Ivy's personal letters each presuppose a recipient, so that the letter has the same intimate immediacy as gifts of food or medicine, these epistles also are frequently directed to people who will never receive them—they instead are of intrinsic value to the writer herself. She writes first to the Dutch girl Hanneke, who never responds, saying finally, "I can't tell it to nobody else so I have writ it down for you cold Hanneke, Hanneke Queen, or for nobody, or may be it is for me" (*FTL* 39). She writes to her dead father because, she tells him, she has no one else to turn to; she is, in effect, turning to herself. She writes again and again to her lost sister, Silvaney, and when she discovers in 1918 that Silvaney has died, she continues to write to her, placing the letters in a trunk. The epistolary form reinforces the tenuous nature of communication, for even the people who receive the letters don't necessarily respond to them: Ivy's letters to her sister Beulah and to her grandfather are, for example, never answered. Smith implies, by providing a continuum of silence that runs from letters sent to the dead to letters sent to the unhearing, that art is always, at best, a communiqué that may be lost, misheard, or willfully mistaken. Like Celie in Walker's *The Color Purple*, Ivy writes to realize herself and her relations to others even when they cannot hear her words; for the artist, it is the writing that signifies.

Smith retains in *Fair and Tender Ladies* the crucial theme of madness by creating an intricate weave of linked character. Ivy is intertwined with her older sister, the mad wood nymph Silvaney. Ivy perceives Silvaney to be part of her: "it is like we are the same sometimes it is like we are one," she says, and "you are my soul, and my soul is as wild as ever" (*FTL* 17, 270). Silvaney is otherworldly, a fairy "all silverhaired like she was fotched up on the moon" (*FTL* 17). She is the lunatic in torment, with "a fire in her head shining through" that will, Ivy thinks, "burn her up" (*FTL* 65). Like Crystal, she has blue eyes "like lakes" but underneath "is flames, flames" (*FTL* 65). Smith splits the madness off from Ivy, sending Silvaney to the asylum; Silvaney is a conduit to carry away madness, the sacrificial figure who remains necessary for the female artist to survive. Thus exorcised, Ivy may accommodate the world without going mad; unlike her mother Maude, who finally is "gone from her eyes" to a place so deep that she becomes a version of Crystal, Ivy remains fiercely engaged.

Smith also creates a variation on the storytellers of her middle phase in Gaynelle and Virgie Cline, who become thoroughly magical, disassociated from everything mundane. Unlike Smith's other storytellers, who talk while they perform their domestic functions, Virgie and Gaynelle live by their art. Old maiden ladies who live in a tiny cabin on the mountainside, they raise only beans and flowers and have no cow, "but folks takes them food just to hear ther stories" (*FTL* 33). They are fairylike figures who themselves, Ivy thinks, do not need food because "they live on storys" (*FTL* 33). This is a graphic realization of storytelling as a form of nurture and a potent reflection of art's sustenative properties. Gaynelle and Virgie save Ivy from suicide; she feels "the only way I could keep from running back out in the snow was to hear a story" (*FTL* 33–34). The sisters cannot be heard unless they are telling a story, otherwise their voices sound "like fairy bells in the snow," and they "skitter like waterbugs over the snow" and disappear (*FTL* 38). Freed from all obligations, these magical sisters are artists who live, communicate, and heal through art. They are models of an unprecedented kind, and Ivy remembers even as she is dying how they "flew away across the snow" after storytelling (*FTL* 315).

Ivy's own language is a synthesis of her education, her constant reading, and her oral storytelling heritage. She is, like Granny Younger, digressive, pulling in contextual detail and then bringing one back with, "But I have gotten off the track as usual" (*FTL* 137). She does not hold with euphemisms; told that a woman is "indisposed" she writes, "It means her mama is laying in a hospital due to her nerves, while her father practices law" (*FTL* 53). In moments of immediacy she eases from past tense into present, echoing not only Granny Younger's voice but Smith's frequent use of the same device in her omniscient narrations (*FTL* 22). Her language has another layer, however, a conscious interweaving of allusions, metaphors, and similes. Byron, Shakespeare, Brontë, and the Bible are among a few of the texts she cites. Her metaphors are both natural—Silvaney's head during fever "was as hot as a skillet on the stove"—and allusive—the mountains "sparkle in the sun like a ladys dimond necklace." When she first calls her Dutch pen pal an "Ice Queen," her vision is clearly literary: "I feature your face as white as ice and your eyes so blue, like the Ice Queen but smiling with cherryred lips" (*FTL* 15–16). Later, when Hanneke fails to write to her, Ivy turns the Ice Queen metaphor to her own meaning, for coldness and ice are significant parts of her life which she may translate into the metaphor of cruel indifference.

Smith gives Ivy an unselfconsciously poetic voice, and her own voice has the grace of a confident artist; together they create the textural weave of a theme that begins, finally, to reconcile maternity and art. By intertwining Ivy's metaphorical language with a rich under-text of rebirth, Smith bespeaks her own growing confidence in the mutually regenerative powers of life and art. When her baby is born Ivy writes, "all the poems I ever knew raced through my head" (*FTL* 148). This a far cry from the deprecation of art as a "fancy strut," as maternal joy surges into poetic ecstasy. The birth motif is an integral part of the novel's setting and circumstance; it is seasonal, tied to natural cycles by Ivy's love for the land and by the voice of the father, saying "slow down now, Ivy. This is the taste of spring," and it is sexual as it emerges in birth and lovemaking. It is also classically allusive, as both Oakley, in the mine collapse, and Ivy herself descend into the underworld and emerge reborn. Ivy descends and is reborn many times, from when she knows she can't go to school and feels "like a big hot black cloud has come down on my sole," to her pregnancy, when she feels "I *was* that little baby caught inside of my own self and dying to escape," to her fall into darkness, to her cave-dwelling (*FTL* 61, 122). Smith seems to imply that the artistic process itself is a form of rebirth, each letter freeing some "little baby caught inside . . . and dying to escape" out into life.

The *Jane Eyre* allusions that run through the novel reinforce this weave of maternity and art, while the reference also signals the conflict between mother and artist that remains, for Smith, only partially re-solved.[34] Before Ivy has read *Jane Eyre* she says that she would "love so to have a gray dress with a white collar," thus invoking Jane's attire, with its symbolic values reinforced by the images of the nuns and school uniforms that give rise to Ivy's wish (*FTL* 61). Her first reference to the book says, "I am reading a grate book Jane Eyre, about a orphan. . . . Now Jane Eyre . . . is little and plane so far, she is like a elf

or a fairy. I wish it was me" (*FTL* 108). But Smith exploits the full power
of the allusion at the most crucial moment of Ivy's life: when she may
choose an abortion, with Doc Trout's and Geneva's encouragement, so
that she can go to Boston to study. Ivy has been, like Jane, orphaned,
her father dead and her mother far off in her remoteness. Jane's night
of doubt is ended by the metamorphosis of the moon into "a white
human form" who says, "My daughter, flee temptation!" Jane answers,
"Mother, I will."[35] Ivy's indecision is ended in the metamorphosis of a
figure as distant as the moon into her mother, who stands in the
doorway "in a long white gown with her long gray hair floating out
around her" and says, "*No you will not. . . . Ivy, you listen to me, . . . I am
your mother. . . .* We will keep this child" (*FTL* 123–24). This child
publishes the books that Ivy never had time to write.

   Fair and Tender Ladies strikes, thus, at the very heart of the dilemma
of the female artist as Smith sees it, and while, for Ivy, finally, maternity
and art are mutually generative, Smith's compromise remains as always
before in the direction of maternal selflessness; drawing ever closer to a
fully realized woman artist figure, Smith has not yet affected a completely equitable reconciliation between femaleness and art. Ivy says as
she is dying, "I thought then I would write of love (Ha!) but how little
we know, we spend our years as a tale that is told I have spent my years
so. I never became a writer atall. Instead I have loved, and loved, and
loved. I am fair wore out with it" (*FTL* 315). Smith cannot reconcile her
vision of what the artist is supposed to be with what a woman is
supposed to be, even now, for she cannot imagine an ordinary woman
on the Olympus of high intellect and seriousness where the "real"
artists reside. She introduces into this novel the unprecedented Miss
Torrington, a lesbian whose indifference to men, her intellectuality,
her northernness, and her passion for art put her at a great distance
from everyone around her; she is the Olympian figure who calls Ivy to
leave her family and home for Boston. Miss Torrington burns her
passionate belief in Ivy's ability into her with a kiss which Ivy remembers as she is dying as "her kiss like fire on the back of my neck yet
firstborn of all my kisses all my life" (*FTL* 315).[36] Paradoxically, it
brands her at once to both her loves, life and art, as it sends her in
panicked confusion into the arms of the man who makes her pregnant
with Joli. In choosing heterosexual love Ivy loses, by her definition of
art, the chance to become an artist; by implication, the only woman
who could reside in the marble halls of art would be one so centered in
her femaleness as to have achieved autonomy. To write books, Ivy's
daughter must divorce and send her son David to live with Ivy; Ivy, in
order sufficiently to love and nurture all of the brothers and sisters and
children and lovers and husbands that punctuate her life, must give up

seeing herself as an artist. Smith, so close, capitulates still to Barthes' ironic admonition in "Novels and Children": "Adapt the moral rule of your condition, but never compromise about the dogma on which it rests."[37]

For Smith, the genesis of the artist figure implies the increasing seriousness with which she perceives her own work and, by extension, the work of other women. Only one reconciled to her own artistic vocation may create female characters who think of themselves as worthy of self-documentation, without a concomitant self-ridicule or a fear of the ridicule of others. And only when the condition of "artist" is named and accepted can there be a self-acknowledged product—art— derived from it; until the artist herself claims a name for what she makes, the conferring of value by others remains a kind of condescension. The metamorphosis in Smith's fiction from anxiety and ambivalence to empowerment and from there to self-documentation, with its implicit valuation of its subject, reveals a partial portrait of the artist as woman. Smith takes us to the very crux of the matter, revealing the essential dilemmas of the artist as they impinge most particularly upon the imperatives of domesticity and maternity: autonomy and community, self-absorption and other-directedness, intellect and emotion remain in kaleidoscopic flux. Life, a beleaguered state, often mundane and irreconcilably contradictory, and always, for the mother-artist, participatory, hurtles itself against the niceties of art, and in the violence that ensues, both the artist and the artist figure are formed.

Notes

1. I will also refer to some of Smith's short stories, collected as *Cakewalk* (New York: G. P. Putnam's Sons, 1980). The term, "maternal ethic" is from Sara Ruddick, "Maternal Thinking," *Feminist Studies* 6 (summer 1980), 342–67.

2. Alice Walker, *In Search of Our Mothers' Gardens: Womanist Prose* (New York: Harcourt Brace Jovanovich, 1983), p. 243.

3. Lee Smith, *Fancy Strut* (New York: Harper & Row, 1973).

4. *Cakewalk,* p. 105. All further references to stories from *Cakewalk* are cited parenthetically.

5. See Alice Walker, and Rachel Blau DuPlessis, *Writing Beyond the Ending: Narrative Strategies of Twentieth-Century Women Writers* (Bloomington: Indiana University Press, 1985), pp. 93–94, for a discussion of the compensatory relationships between mothers and their artist daughters.

6. Lee Smith, *Oral History* (New York: G. P. Putnam's Sons, 1983), pp. 18– 19. Further references are cited parenthetically as *OH* with page numbers.

7. Lee Smith, *Family Linen* (New York: G. P. Putnam's Sons, 1985), p. 131. Further references are cited parenthetically as *FL* with page numbers.

8. Josephine Donovan, "Toward a Woman's Poetics," *Tulsa Studies in Women's Literature* 3 (winter 1984), 99–110.

9. See Gilles Deleuze and Felix Guattari, *Anti-Oedipus: Capitalism and*

Schizophrenia (Minneapolis: University of Minnesota Press, 1983), for the mobilizing efficacy of a "madness" that resists the collusion of systems. It is significant that Smith's madwomen reside on that part of the continuum nearest catatonia and furthest removed from action.

10. One should examine the figure of Fay in *Family Linen* as an alternative vision of the sensual woman, as she becomes the ultimate receptacle for all kinds of sexual, intellectual, and spiritual trash.

11. See Jane Atteridge Rose, "The Artist Manqué in the Fiction of Rebecca Harding Davis," in this volume for a discussion of the deformities Davis visits upon her artist figures as a result of her ambivalence about her own vocation as artist.

12. Lee Smith, *The Last Day the Dogbushes Bloomed* (New York: Harper & Row, 1968), p. 7. Further references are cited parenthetically as *LDDB* with page numbers.

13. Lee Smith, *Something in the Wind* (New York: Harper & Row, 1971), p. 25.

14. Lee Smith, *Black Mountain Breakdown* (New York: G. P. Putnam's Sons, 1980), pp. 192, 194. Further references are cited parenthetically as *BMB* with page numbers.

15. See Z. Nelly Martínez, "The Politics of the Woman Artist in Isabel Allende's *The House of the Spirits*," in this volume, for the implications of Alba's more affirmative use of an ancestral diary.

16. See Renate Voris, "The Hysteric and the Mimic: A Reading of Christa Wolf's *Quest for Christa T.*," in this volume, for a discussion of Christa T.'s "characterlessness," her "oscillating between creativity and procreativity, silence and speech, madness and mimicry."

17. See Linda Dittmar, "When Privilege Is No Protection: The Woman Artist in *Quicksand* and *The House of Mirth*," in this volume, for a discussion of the protagonists' simultaneous functions as artist and artifact. The role of artifact is literalized in both Larsen and Wharton in ways evocative of Crystal's catatonia, as the protagonists are transfixed variously through a portrait sitting and a *tableau vivant*. See too the precedents for this kind of figure discussed by Susan Gubar in "'The Blank Page' and the Issues of Female Creativity." About Gwendolen of Eliot's *Daniel Deronda*, Gubar says, "In the process of turning herself into an artistic object, she makes herself autistic." In *Writing and Sexual Difference*, ed. Elizabeth Abel (Chicago: University of Chicago Press, 1982), p. 80.

18. In *Feminist Aesthetics*, ed. Gisela Ecker, trans. Harriet Anderson (Boston: Beacon Press, 1985), pp. 56–57.

19. Catherine Clément, "The Guilty One," Hélène Cixous and Catherine Clément, *The Newly Born Woman*, trans. Betsy Wing, Theory and History of Literature, vol. 24 (Minneapolis: University of Minnesota Press, 1986), p. 39. Clément's descriptions of sorceress/hysteric figures and her discussion of the role of audience in their enactments provide provocative background for all of Smith's sexually damaged characters.

20. See Gadamer's discussion of the Greek word "symbol," which was originally a technical term for a token of remembrance; the *tessera hospitalis* was some object broken in two pieces, with half given to the guest, half kept. Throughout time, the fitting together of the halves acted as a kind of pass, "something in and through which we recognize someone already known to us." Hans-Georg Gadamer, *The Relevance of the Beautiful and Other Essays*, ed. Robert

Bernasconi, trans. Nicholas Walker (Cambridge: Cambridge University Press, 1986), p. 31.

21. Smith only added Crystal's rape after the novel was finished, at the suggestion of an editor who wanted Smith to give some clear reason for Crystal's breakdown. Unpublished interview with Katherine Kearns, 1982.

22. See Gubar, in *Writing and Sexual Difference*, p. 79, for further suggestions about the complexity of the painted mouth.

23. Cixous, *The Newly Born Woman*, p. 5.

24. I am omitting Red Emmy, whose status as a witch makes her, in the context of empowerment, an extremely complex and problematic character. For a discussion of the witch and the goddess see Martínez in this volume; her note 5 on the "wild zone" suggests one potential context for the Red Emmy figure.

25. See Josephine Donovan, "The Pattern of Birds and Beasts: Willa Cather and Women's Art," in this volume, for a discussion of Cather's conscious appropriation of an oral, word-of-mouth storytelling voice to represent herself more authentically as a woman.

26. See Voris's argument that the apparently radical text of *Christa T.* realizes its two protagonists, the narrator and Christa T., only within the *gynaeceum* and only through their relationships to men. See too Roland Barthes, *Mythologies*, trans. Annette Lavers (New York: Farrar, Straus & Giroux, 1972), pp. 50–52.

27. DuPlessis, *Writing Beyond the Ending*, p. 94.

28. Walker, *In Search of Our Mothers' Gardens*, p. 243.

29. See DuPlessis, "To 'bear my mother's name': *Künstlerromane* by Women Writers," in *Writing Beyond the Ending*.

30. Ruddick, p. 351.

31. See Martínez in this volume for a discussion of the artist as healer in the more politicized context of a totalitarian regime.

32. See Rose's discussion of Davis's lifelong battle to reconcile her domestic ideology to the necessarily more autonomous life of the artist.

33. Lee Smith, *Fair and Tender Ladies* (New York: G. P. Putnam's Sons, 1988), p. 15. Further references are cited parenthetically as *FTL* with page numbers.

34. Smith's choice of *Jane Eyre* as her most extended allusion powerfully underscores her ambivalent position about the woman artist in her roles as lover and wife.

35. Charlotte Brontë, *Jane Eyre* (New York: Holt, Rinehart and Winston, 1950), p. 368.

36. The manuscript has, stricken out, a first version that reads, "her kiss like fire on the back of my neck yet the mother of all my kisses all my life," reinforcing even here the maternal motif.

37. Barthes, *Mythologies*, p. 52.

Chapter 10
Through the Flower: Judy Chicago's Conflict Between a Woman-Centered Vision and the Male Artist Hero

Mara R. Witzling

Many women painters and sculptors of the past few centuries have used the written word as a means of validating their professional commitment.[1] Judy Chicago's *Through the Flower* is an excellent example of a work written by a visual artist to clarify and affirm her artistic vocation in a culture where as Chicago writes "simply by being a woman and an artist" one challenges assumptions of male dominance (43).[2] Chicago's autobiography is a clear and articulate discussion of the struggles involved in her development as a woman artist. It is, however, a paradoxical work. Although Chicago resolved her conflict between being a woman and being an artist by evolving a female-centered motif based on the metaphor of "moving through the flower," she continued to accept the post-Renaissance, patriarchal concept of the artist-hero who sacrifices all to his art. This essay will explore the tension between the traditional "male" model of artistic success and achievement that Chicago followed and the alternative "woman-centered" vision that she achieved in her art.

To claim her vocation as an artist takes a truly heroic stance on the part of a woman in a patriarchal culture that defines the active, creative woman as an anomaly.[3] The myth of the artist as a heroic figure, a genius of mythic proportions, is reinforced by such books as Vasari's *Lives of the Artists*. Over the years the image has evolved to include more problematic aspects, such as the concept of the artist as a lonely outsider.[4] However, the image of the artist in western culture is implicitly male, whether he is conceived as a reflection of God, the Ultimate Cre-

ator, or as a figure "born under saturn." Because there are few acceptable cultural examples for her to assume, the quest of the woman artist
is often cast in male terms. Concerning the process of self-actualization
Carol Gilligan has written that: "The sex differences depicted in the
fairy tales . . . indicate that active adventure is a male activity and that if
a woman is to embark on such adventures she must at least dress like a
man."[5]

In *Through the Flower,* Judy Chicago took a "male" script and wrote
herself into the role of protagonist, elevating her artistic development
to a heroic quest. As in many quest stories, where the (male) hero
makes numerous false starts and encounters many obstructions, but
through persistence, triumphs in the end, Chicago describes how she
challenged and surmounted the impediments in her way to finding her
own vision and the means of expressing it. The structure of *Through the
Flower* follows a conventional pattern that defines the artist as a heroic
outsider who creates because he is driven by inner necessity, and who
struggles against the world whose misunderstanding only serves to
make him more adamant in the pursuit of his unique vision.[6] Chicago
casts herself as the highly romanticized Michelangelo of *The Agony and
the Ecstasy* or the Van Gogh of *Lust for Life,* contemporary popularized
versions of Vasari's formulation of the trajectory of the artist's life.

Chicago's book bears a problematic relationship both to conventional *Bildungsroman* in which the young man is integrated into active
public life and to traditional feminine variations in which the young
woman is excluded from public success.[7] Chicago depicts her commitment to achievement in the public sphere as unwavering, which adheres more closely to the traditional male model than to the female
one. Rachel Blau DuPlessis has asserted that "the figure of a female
artist encodes the conflict between any empowered woman and the
barriers to her achievement" because it "dramatizes . . . the already
present contradiction in bourgeois ideology between the ideals of striving, improvement, and visible public works, and the feminine version
of that formula: passivity, 'accomplishments,' and invisible private
acts."[8] Although Chicago presents herself engaged in struggle against
society and the barriers it places in the way of her achievement, she is
never drawn into the nexus of the private sphere. While she feels
repressed by society's gender-based limitation of her artistic content,
she does not experience conflict between her artistic vocation and the
needs of her private life.[9] Early on, she conceptualized herself as an
artist, that is, an active, striving creator of public works. Unlike many
fictional *Künstlerromane* with female protagonists, Chicago's recounting of her life conforms to a plot in which the woman artist's success is
unmitigated.[10] She is proud of her "irrepressible self-confidence" (29)

that allowed her to shape her life into a coherent whole. In her auto-biography, Chicago relies on what Sidonie Smith has called "andro-centric fictions."[11] Although Smith finds that these myths were more frequently appropriated by women autobiographers prior to the twen-tieth century, they continue to persist in most autobiographies by twentieth-century women visual artists.[12] Perhaps one can conclude that the script recounting a woman visual artist's success has yet to be revised.

One important way in which Chicago's story does depart from the "male" norm is that the major obstacle she has to overcome is the tension she perceived between her artistic vocation and her gender. That she subtitled the book "my struggle as a woman artist" indicates how significantly she viewed her gender in the construction of her artistic persona. As discussed above, Chicago was not conflicted about identification with her artistic role.[13] Rather she felt that cultural as-sumptions about both art and artists prevented her from becoming attuned to her unique vision and finding the visual language with which to express it. The goal of her quest was to find a visual language that merged her identity as an artist with her identity as a woman.

Chicago's story is also informed by her gender in that she believed that her "femininity" necessitated a different kind of art. She prefaced the book with a quotation from Anaïs Nin's diary which strongly em-phasizes the "difference" of women's creativity: "I do not delude my-self, as Man does, that I create in proud isolation . . . Woman's creation, far from being like Man's must be exactly like her creation of children; that is, it must come out of her own blood, englobed by her womb, nourished with her own milk. It must be different from Man's abstrac-tions" (XIV).[14] Or as Chicago herself wrote: "I wanted to speak out of my femaleness" (203). Although she attempted to reckon with her "fe-maleness" only after achieving her artistic persona, her artistic break-through did not occur until she accepted what she characterized as her "femininity," both in terms of her method of working and in the formal elements of the work she produced.

Chicago's autobiography, then, is something of a hybrid in that she attempts to tell the story of a "feminine" creator through a "masculine" format in which she accepts the dominant culture's conception of artistic autonomy. Thus, it resembles other contemporary autobiogra-phies by women, which Smith characterizes as "negotiat[ing] stories of men and women," turning the female "self" and its story into "some amalgam, something neither conventionally male nor female, some energizing mutation played on autobiographical possibilities."[15] As the plot of *Through the Flower* unfolds, Chicago becomes increasingly aware of her special heritage as a woman artist. Yet, there is a level where the message of the book, and its vehicle, are in fundamental conflict.

Chicago adheres to convention by establishing the early experiences through which she became aware of her artistic calling at the beginning of her story.[16] Whereas most artists' biographies enumerate early incidents that reveal a heightened visual awareness, Chicago emphasizes her ability to achieve in the public sphere, despite societal restrictions on women.[17] "I had been able to overcome my conditioning," she writes, "because I had been brought up to believe that I could do what I wanted" (76). At the end of the first chapter she depicts herself as a romantic figure, standing on the beach, shattered by her first husband's accidental death, realizing that she must build her own identity based on her own needs, through her art. The remainder of the book is the story of her quest for artistic maturity, concluding in 1974, with "a major breakthrough" in her work. "I found a way to convey clearly the content that was still hidden in my earlier images," she wrote (206). Shortly after this discovery, she began preliminary work on *The Dinner Party,* her first mature piece of sculpture, created from the struggle she described in her book.

One indication of the dichotomy between Chicago's vision and her means of pursuing it is the tension between the importance of her mother and father to her process of individuation. On the surface, Chicago seems to credit her mother as a positive and active influence on her professional life. She writes that because her mother worked, "I suppose [that] gave me a sense that women 'did' something in the world" (1). The framing of that "I suppose," however, lends a somewhat grudging quality to her acknowledgment of her mother's influence. In the previous sentence Chicago reveals that her very first memory is of screaming in her crib as her mother, dressed for work in a business suit, is leaving her. In the following sentence she recounts that she was left with a "succession of housekeepers." The psychological implications of this feeling of maternal abandonment are fairly obvious, and in fact, it could be said that Chicago searched for her "mother" throughout her professional life both in her actual relationship with Miriam Schapiro and in her connections with her artistic and literary foremothers. The impact of this search on the achievement of her artistic maturity is crucial, and will be discussed in greater depth below. Her biological mother, however, is not a major figure in *Through the Flower.*

Although she credits her mother with nurturing her artistic abilities and with teaching her that women could achieve outside the domestic realm, Chicago describes her father as the major influence on her early years. Possibly his importance is enhanced because he died while she was still a teenager. In fact, she had one of her most serious arguments with him shortly before his death. However, it also should be pointed out that many of the women artists of the past centuries received their entrées into the art world through their fathers.[18] A father's support not only enabled access to the male-dominated academic tradition, but it allowed a daughter to internalize the power of hegemonic privilege. It is significant that although Chicago brought her artistic achievements to her mother, who had wanted to be a dancer, she felt that her father supported her intellectual triumphs, the "masculine" skills that enabled her to survive in the public sphere (2, 4). "I wanted to be a *person* like my father whom I loved and admired," she writes (3).

According to Chicago, her most difficult task in claiming intellectual power was to reconcile her desire to be an active agent in the world with her fear that her strength was destructive to men. She argued vehemently with her father and he died soon after. She kissed her Uncle Harry, and he died the next day (7, 21). She had a fight with her husband Jerry, and the next night he drove off a cliff and died. She began to feel that her "needs were threatening and [her] power devastating," (7), and she asked her therapist "did I kill everyone I loved?" Many achieving women within the patriarchy need to resolve this issue. If a woman cannot claim her own power because she is afraid of harming the men she cares about, her creativity will probably be thwarted. At the same time, the hidden beliefs of the patriarchy make it incredibly difficult for a woman to believe in her own strength. Because of the destructive models we are given, like Chicago, we are afraid of killing that which we love. Initially, Chicago felt that she would be punished for being strong (25). By the time she had finished writing *Through the Flower,* however, she understood that "women's power is seen . . . stereotypically" in predominantly male institutions. She realized that "male society makes women feel as if their power is not needed or valued, whereas in the female community, women's power is essential" (205). But before she could succeed in her struggle as a woman artist, Chicago had to learn to find strength in her creative power and to trust it.

At first Chicago attempted to gain artistic credibility by incorporating masculine traits, literally "dressing like a man" to internalize the power accorded her male colleagues. She encouraged them to consider her as one of the boys, a "serious artist," unlike other women who were "just chicks and cunts" (28). This attitude was expressed both in the media she pursued and the swagger she assumed. She describes how she "began to wear boots and smoke cigars" and "went to the motorcycle races and tried to act tough whenever [she] saw them" (her male classmates, 35). After finishing college she was "one woman among 250 men" when she graduated from auto-body school, where she went to prove something to the men (36). She writes, "I had begun to compensate for my situation as a woman by trying to continually prove that I was as tough as a man" (35). When a male mentor told her that she would have to "decide to be either a woman or an artist" (37), she opted for the latter and made sure that the art she made obliterated all traces of "femininity." In graduate school she had begun a series of paintings based on biomorphic forms such as phalluses and vaginas that expressed her feelings about the deaths of her father and husband Jerry. Her painting instructors were mortified and threatened to withdraw their support, and she "began to hide [her] subject matter" (33–34). The artistic style that dominated the art world while Chicago was in graduate school and during the following years was minimalism, characterized by its hard edges and cool surfaces. Exploration of personal content was deemed artistically "invalid." Chicago worked in the hard-edged style of the minimalists, producing works from hard materials with perfect finishes (43). In a work such as *Rainbow Picket* (1965), a series of brightly painted vertical slats, only the pastel colors express personal content. In spite of her attempts to conform, she writes that she was "continually made to feel by men in the art world that there was something 'wrong' with me" (39).

Until she realized that this state of being was tearing her apart, as well as stifling her art, she did not embark upon her real quest, which was her struggle to find and express her vision. In other words, she became determined to be accepted as both an artist *and* a woman, despite the contradictions between those terms as they are constructed in our society. Her decision in 1969 to change her name from Judy Gerowitz to Judy Chicago symbolized her determination, "an act of identifying [herself] as an independent woman" (63), possible only after she had begun to feel that she had "more permission to be [her]self" (62). This important moment marks the turning point of a woman artist's life in a *Künstlerroman*, for she "names herself"; that is, she attempts to define what she is to be, rather than accepting a patriarchically predetermined definition of her limitations.[19] From here on out, as Chicago rather than Gerowitz, she followed the lead of the mothers rather than that of the fathers. Her quest was to find an artistic vehicle for expressing the self that society denigrated which she perceived as her "femininity."

Chicago's quest for a means of reconciling the "woman" and "artist" aspects of her self led her to connect with several different mythic "mothers." The search for foremothers has been an important stage in the development of many contemporary creative women, both actual and fictional, who have experienced the need to "confront and incorporate matriarchal powers."[20] Her relationship with Miriam Schapiro was Chicago's first attempt at establishing such a connection. When she developed the women's art program at Fresno, she invited Schapiro to help her because she felt that she "needed an older woman, a mother" who could support her in the same way she was supporting her students" (82–83). This relationship ultimately proved unsuccessful. Just as the students related to Chicago and Schapiro as "parents against whose authority they would have to rebel" (108), the unspoken conflicts between Chicago and Schapiro led to the demise of their working relationship (110). Ultimately, Chicago felt that Schapiro had abandoned her, had "withdrawn her 'mothering'" (139), a feeling analogous to her sense of abandonment by her biological mother.

Chicago also searched for artistic foremothers in her encounters with the work of women artists, past and present, at that time completely omitted from the canon of art history. In addition, she tried to locate writings by and about historical and literary women. Familiarity with these women led her to recognize that heritage, and their legacy had an immediate impact on her work. Paintings such as the *Reincarnation Triptych* (1973) express her desire to create a reciprocal relationship with the foremothers she found in her search. Each panel in this tripartite work follows a similar format and is named for a noted female writer. A lush wavy pattern emanates from the center of each, and each is bordered by a scripted commentary about the writer represented. In addition, through variation of tone and hue, Chicago implies a transparent square form as overlapping the central area. The "overlay" with the past first explored in this early piece also informs her later, more mature, works.

Finally, work on *Womanhouse* during these same years exposed Chicago to one other aspect of her "female" heritage. In this large, environmental sculpture, on which she collaborated with her students and Schapiro, she first began to explore the artistic possibilities inherent to traditional women's culture, such as cooking, cleaning, and personal adornment. In its environmental, communal and performance orientations, *Womanhouse* also provided her with a model for future artistic endeavors.

The heart of Chicago's quest, however, was focused on her realization of the "big gap between [her] feelings as a woman and the visual language of the male culture," and her attempt to resolve it. As she had previously refused to be "an artist in a closet" she now refused to be "a woman in the closet" and, despite continual rejections, she continued to seek a vehicle that would visually express her "femininity."[21] By

1972, while working on the book *Through the Flower,* Chicago developed the female-centered motif and metaphor on which she based her mature style. "Moving 'through the flower' is a process that is available to all of us, a process that can lead us to a place where we can express our humanity and values as women through our work," she writes at the end of the book (206). The metaphor of moving through the flower, developed as she wrote the book, typifies the processes of blooming and passage. She writes that she used the flower "as the symbol of femininity" but "in my images the petals of the flower are parting to reveal an inviting but undefined space, the space beyond the confines of our own femininity. These works symbolized my longing for transcendence and personal growth. They were my first steps in being able to make clear, abstract images of my point of view as a woman."[22] Furthermore, she asserts that she and Schapiro had found the hidden content of many women's works to be "a frequent use of the central image, often a flower, or abstracted flower form, sometimes surrounded by folds or undulations, as in the structure of the vagina" (143).

The central image of the opening flower formed the basis of Chicago's next major works in which she deliberately stressed the sexual aspect of that motif. On the surface of *Female Rejection Drawing* (1974) she wrote, "In trying to peel back the structure I have used in my work because I felt I had to hide the real content, I found myself making a vaginal form. . . . Whenever I want to deal with the issue of vulnerability, emotional exposure or primitive feelings the only image I can think of is the vagina because . . . those aspects of human experience have been confined to the feminine and then deprecated." In other words, as she said elsewhere, "the woman artist, seeing herself as loathed, takes that very mark of her otherness and by asserting it as the hallmark of her iconography, establishes a vehicle by which to state the truth and beauty of her identity."[23] The visual structure of *Female Rejection Drawing* reinforces her theoretical stance. Here, a layer of radiating waves, progressing from cool blues at the outer edges to burning oranges and yellows in the center, seems to be "peeled back" in spiky points to reveal a pulsating, central yellow glow surrounded by spatially ambiguous folds. In its dynamic color and shifting planes, the image is overwhelmingly lush, sensual, and unabashedly sexual as well. Chicago speaks her message in a language that is no longer hidden. Furthermore, this structure, developed just before she finished writing *Through the Flower,* was used as the dominant form in the plates of *The Dinner Party* and the birthing women in *The Birth Project.* In these works women's sexuality, which had been reviled by patriarchal culture, is elevated to heroic proportions.

Thus, *Through the Flower* can be read as a story whose protagonist overcame life's obstacles and successfully achieved her quest. Chicago began as a girl who envied the power bestowed upon her father because he had a penis (3) but who was afraid that her own wielding of that power would prove destructive to men. She shows how she then passed through a stage where she attempted to gain that power herself by "dressing like a man," trying to be accepted as one of the boys, acquiring "macho" skills, and making art that suppressed any signs of "female weakness." She then tells of her pain at cutting herself off from her sexuality and her search for an idiom that would express it. Finally, she recounts her attempts to reconnect with a female community, her search for a mother in her relationships with Schapiro, Nin, and her literary and artistic foremothers, and how she herself was cast in the role of mother by the students she worked with. Ultimately, she depicts herself in encounters with equals, other women who also sought to establish a women's art community based on strength and self-acceptance. Chicago depicts herself as successful in her quest because by the conclusion of *Through the Flower* she has hit the stride of her artistic maturity. She has found a way of being both an artist and a woman in a society in which they are constructed as mutually exclusive.

Through the Flower communicates a contradictory message, however, one that is at odds with the allegedly "female" content that Chicago celebrates in her artwork, in that she has apparently internalized society's concept of "macho" as it relates to the production of art. That is, she sees art as an individual act, whose primacy forces the artist to sacrifice human relationships. It is no coincidence that her father appears to have had greater impact on her development than her mother. She characterizes herself as an exception, particularly in her ability to concentrate on work, which she believes is atypical of most women. In speaking of her experiences as a young art student in an environment where women were considered second-class citizens she says, "I had a tendency to pursue my own objectives regardless of the messages I received. This came partly from my irrepressible confidence that whatever I did was terrific, partly from my drive and determination, and partly as a result of my life experience with my father" (29). At the time she is "annoyed" that most of the other women students were passive and quiet in class but feels that she is "different" (30).

Although Chicago later repudiates the contempt for women embodied in this attitude, many of her comments throughout *Through the Flower* are informed by what can only be described as an intolerant and condescending attitude toward women.[24] She stresses the difference between her own drive to achieve and that of "most women she has encountered" in her discussion of her work with women students while establishing women's art programs. For example, she observes that, "one of the first things I discovered in working with the class was that asking the women if they wanted to be artists was not a reliable question because many of them did not have the assurance that they could actually become what they said they wanted to become. . . . wanting to be an artist . . . was, for some, only an idle fantasy, like wanting to go to the moon (71). She contrasts this attitude to her own "determination" and ability to stand up to conflict (71) and describes her "shock" at finding that she had "come through the society without being wiped out and that many other women had" (82). When she was sitting with her Fresno class at its first meeting, she discovered that she "didn't want to be identified with women like these chicks" and that their chitchat about boys, clothes, and food made her "bored as hell" (74). And it was clear to her that "one of the reasons that many of the women did not work consistently at their art (a common problem among female art students) was that their personal lives were very confused" (75). She takes a similar tone toward her *Birth Project* needleworkers, "so many of [whom] have no idea what the world is really like." They cause her to wonder "how women think they can do serious work while living a life that is so unfocused and fragmented,"[25] and to complain about how she "pulled out of the mire . . . these women . . . who allowed themselves to be distracted by their husbands' demands for donuts."[26]

Her frustration with the way in which society has crushed the wills of some women is understandable, as is her desire for change to allow the full potential of her students to flourish. So is her unwillingness to coddle women which in itself would be condescending and disrespectful of their potential as artists. One can agree that it is important to "make demands upon personalities who had usually been protected not pushed" (74), to insist on regular working hours for women who were used to a "self-indulgent world" and "did not usually have sufficient drive and ambition to keep them at a job when it becomes frustrating" (105–7), and to empower them by making them feel some responsibility for taking care of things in the world (80–81).

There is a real arrogance here, however, that negates her intent in finding and valuing traditionally defined "female" sensibility. The way a housewife and mother apportions her time and fulfills her tasks might be different from the way a male artist works in the studio, but it is inaccurate—and phallocentrically judgmental—to describe this approach as "self-indulgent." In fact, there are positive aspects to this traditionally "female" mode of structuring work, called by Kathryn Rabuzzi the "waiting mode," in which "letting go into possibilities prohibited by linear time" might very well enhance the process of artistic creation.[27] Likewise, "gossipy" interactions between women that focus on boyfriends, clothes, and food have a subtext of caring, an epistemological stance that Chicago completely ignores.[28] Furthermore Chicago does not connect her complaint that women art students do not talk about their art (85) with her own uneasiness during her student days with the pressure to swagger like "one of the boys." Although she prefaces her book with Nin's quotation repudiating "man's abstractions," she criticizes her women students for not adopting an abstract mode of interacting. Thus, she continues to accept the dominant culture's devaluation of "women's ways of knowing."[29] By negating the value of these modalities, Chicago dismisses an alternative way of being an artist, available to both women and men, that really could differ from the way the concept has been defined in the dominant discourse.

In *Through the Flower* Chicago reveals her bias that to be a serious artist one has to have one's life in order and live in a state of obsession. And the continuing story of her life bears this out. In her forward to the paperback edition she tells how she severed her ties with the Women's Building, a cooperative venture in Los Angeles, because she realized that she could not function in its collective structure but needed to have authority over her assistants (ix). In the Afterword to the revised and updated edition, Chicago describes how she had to sacrifice her marriage for her art. She writes that Anaïs Nin was wrong in saying that women could never completely "disconnect from the needs of others" because she found that indeed she could.[30]

In this way, the telling of Chicago's story ties into a fundamental cultural assumption concerning art and its production: that one must be a monomaniac to succeed as an artist. Donovan suggests that we need to consider whether the notion of masterpiece art is not reflective of a "masculine" psychology of autonomy rather than of a "feminine" psychology of emotional integration, according to the traditional definition of these behaviors.[31] The concept of the hero-artist needs to be subjected to a similar examination.

This is the dichotomy, then. On the one hand, Chicago has made great strides toward a woman-centered artistic vision in her work and in her method of pursuing it. Her central image grows from an unambiguous reference to female sexuality. She challenges patriarchal definitions of artistic acceptability in several ways, including her use of performance art, workshop production, embroidery, ceramics, and even the concept of a dinner party in itself. Her dismay at the tendency for some women to get derailed and distracted and to lead lives in which their creative potential is unfulfilled is also legitimate. Further-

more, much of the negative criticism she has received is a manifestation of our society's condemnation of female strength.[32] Society sanc-
tions the victimization of women and so many of us have internalized
it; we have difficulty putting our work first, and often allow the demands of external circumstances to sabotage it.[33] Like Avis in Phelps's
The Story of Avis we are always saying that we will get to our work after
the baby starts walking, after the chicken pox is over, after the company
has gone home.[34] And like Avis all that waiting unnerves us, saps our
creative energies till ultimately all we can do is wait until the next
generation.

Nonetheless, Chicago accepts the patriarchal assumption that to
be serious, the artist must be an autonomous, unconnected person,
whose personal relationships are sacrificed to the actualization of his or
her art. Although she prefaces her book with Nin's quotation, and although in the end she emphasizes how badly women's power is needed
in the female community and the importance of working within one,
Chicago has followed the single-minded, "male" path to artistic success. But the issue for so many creative women, and ultimately the
human issue, is whether this male model of vocation, of workaholism
that precludes the importance of anything else, is the only way of
becoming a serious artist. Need a woman, or a man for that matter, live
in a state of obsession in order to be successful as an artist?[35]

Might there not be another approach to the making of art, one
that is informed by ways of being in the world that have traditionally
been identified as "female"? Carol Gilligan, for example, argues that
often qualities that seem to make women victims are actually psychological strengths,[36] and Melody Graulich emphasizes that in the "initial
phases of feminist inquiry" when we attempt "to claim male territory as
our own," we fail to acknowledge women's achievements.[37] By demanding that her needleworkers put their needlework above accommodating their husbands' requests, Chicago neglects to understand
that one importance of the quilt is that it grew in piecework from the
mainstream of life within a family. The worry, of course, is that wom-
en's artistry will be subsumed by familial demands. However, at least
two of the "foremothers" cited by Chicago, Barbara Hepworth and
Käthe Kollwitz, describe how they were inspired rather than hindered
by their lives within a family. In each case, the impact was more than
simply being able to combine family and career. In her *Pictorial Autobiography,* Barbara Hepworth wrote, "A woman artist is not deprived by
cooking and having children"; rather, she felt that she was "nourished
by this rich life, provided one always does some work each day, even a
single half hour."[38] Chicago quotes her as saying "I rarely draw what I
see. I draw what I feel with my body" (142). Hepworth's work does

appear to have grown from her body, evocative of fruit, offspring, and female reproduction. Her vision of the earth, and her understanding of the visceral human connection with it, is truly biophilic.[39] Kollwitz too found her inspiration in daily life, writing that her works were all "extracts of my life. . . . Never have I done a work cold."[40] Passionately opposed to the destructiveness of war, she created images of mothers who were heroes rather than victims, whose concern transcended the personal sphere of their own biological children to that of protecting and nurturing the entire human species. Although Chicago praises Kollwitz and Hepworth for their innovative visions, she fails to recognize that the source of these visions might have been in their "connected" modes of living.[41]

Ultimately, we all, women and men, have to learn to reconcile the teachings of the fathers with those of the mothers. To become fully actualized human beings we all need to balance our nurturing tendencies with the intellectual power of logic and its concentrated use—and vice versa. In *Through the Flower* Chicago too readily accepts the idea that a healthy adult needs to subordinate relationships to the single-mindedness of work and expression of self. This approach is associated with "maleness" and is privileged in Western culture, while what Gilligan defines as "women's embeddedness in lives of relationship, their orientation to interdependence, their subordination of achievement to care, and their conflicts over competitive success" are perceived as developmental detriments.[42] Chicago seems too willing to see the ambiguity that stems from women's "different voice" as a problem, as a source of weakness rather than a potential strength. Although her vision has been enriched by an alternative interpretation of female sexuality, she still holds a denigrating view of traditionally "feminine" modes of being. The strengths inherent in caring, waiting, and connected knowing can also help humanity move through the flower, "to reach across the great gulf between masculine and feminine and gently, tenderly, but firmly heal it" (206) as Chicago desires. In regard to the making of art, as well as in human life in general, Carol Gilligan makes an important point when she writes that "a marriage between adult development as it is currently portrayed and women's development as it begins to be seen could lead to a changed understanding of human development and a more generative view."[43]

Through the Flower is an important book because the issues Chicago raises about the conflicts between the social constructions of "artist" and "woman" are not uniquely hers. Rather, documentary evidence shows that they have been experienced by many other women artists of the past few centuries.[44] Chicago takes us far in the process of writing the woman artist. But there is still much further to go.

Notes

1. See M. Witzling, *Voicing Our Visions: Writings by Nineteenth and Twentieth Century Women Artists* (forthcoming, Universe Books), for a discussion of how women who were visual artists have used the written word and a collection of their writings.

2. All quotations from *Through the Flower* are indicated parenthetically with page numbers. They are from the first paperback edition (Garden City, N.Y.: Anchor Books, 1977), unless otherwise noted.

3. Karen Elias-Button, "The Muse as Medusa," in *The Lost Tradition* (New York: F. Ungar Publishing Co., 1980), p. 201, quotes Sharon Barba and Laura Chester, *Rising Tides: Twentieth Century Women Poets* (New York: Washington Square Press, 1973), p. xxvi: "Women must learn the self-love, the self-idealizing, the self-mythologizing, that has made it possible for men to think of themselves as persons."

4. Giorgio Vasari, *Lives of the Artists* (1550). It must be mentioned that Vasari uses "feminine" epithets to describe the work of female artists, such as Properzia de' Rossi, whom he describes as being accomplished in household management and beautiful in body, as well a skilled carver (Parker and Pollock, *Old Mistresses* [New York: Pantheon Books, 1981], p. 9). See Maurice Beebe, *Ivory Towers and Sacred Founts* (New York: New York University Press, 1964), for a discussion of variations on the artist as hero theme and Rudolf and Margot Wittkower, *Born Under Saturn* (New York: Norton, 1969) for an analysis of the "mercurial" nature of the artist.

5. Carol Gilligan, *In a Different Voice* (Cambridge, Mass.: Harvard University Press, 1982), p. 13.

6. Use of the male pronoun here is deliberate. In light of the contrasts between the way Chicago tells her tale and the way it is usually told by and about women, I am convinced that the image that Chicago internalized and used as a model is the cultural stereotype of the dynamic, obsessed male artist, searching for the "torturous pinnacle mark."

7. See Renate Voris's essay in this volume, "The Hysteric and the Mimic: A Reading of Christa Wolf's *The Quest For Christa T.*," for a good discussion of the revision of the traditional *Bildungsroman* and its relationship to role and vocation as conceptualized by the woman artist.

8. Rachel Blau DuPlessis, "To 'bear my mother's name': *Künstlerromane* by Women Writers," in *Writing Beyond the Ending: Narrative Strategies of Twentieth-Century Women Writers* (Bloomington: Indiana University Press, 1985), p. 84.

9. Gilligan, *In a Different Voice*, identifies the "judgment of selfishness and morality of self-abnegation it implies" that "regularly appears at the fulcrum of novels of female adolescence, the turning point of the *Bildungsroman* that separates the invulnerability of childhood innocence from the responsibility of adult participation and choice" (p. 132). Elizabeth Stuart Phelps's *The Story of Avis* echoes this, for Avis becomes entangled in a web of commitments to others that ultimately paralyze her ability to actualize her artistic talents.

10. Grace Stewart, *A New Mythos: The Novel of the Artist as Heroine, 1877–1977* (St. Albans, Vt.: Eden Press, 1979), p. 100. She writes, "None of these novels depict a self-made, fully integrated human being, woman and artist."

11. Sidonie Smith, *A Poetics of Women's Autobiographies: Marginality and the Fictions of Self-Representation* (Bloomington: Indiana University Press, 1987), p. 174.

12. Smith, *Women's Autobiographies*, p. 174. It is interesting that Wendy Wassyng Roworth, in "Biography, Criticism, Art History: Angelica Kauffmann in Context" (in *Eighteenth-Century Women and the Arts,* ed. Frederick M. Keener and Susan E. Lovsch (New York: Greenwood Press, 1989) argues that Giovanni De Rossi's biography of Angelica Kauffmann deviated from the formula for discussing women artists, emulating instead Vasari's prototype for male artists. Two twentieth-century autobiographies by women artists that follow this prototype are Cecilia Beaux's *Background with Figures* (Boston: Houghton Mifflin, 1930), and Margaret Bourke-White's *Portrait of Myself* (New York: Simon and Schuster, 1963).

13. In this respect she is different from Lee Smith's artist figures, which Katherine Kearns analyzes in this volume.

14. The impact of female reproduction on women's creativity is discussed in Susan Gubar, "The Birth of the Artist as Heroine: (Re)production, the *Künstlerroman* tradition and the Fiction of Katherine Mansfield," in *The Representation of Women in Fiction,* ed. Carolyn G. Heilbrun and Margaret R. Higgonet (Baltimore: Johns Hopkins University Press, 1983).

15. Smith, *Women's Autobiography*, p. 175.

16. This is a standard device in biographies of artists, where the biographer looks for early signs of genius in the subject. Autobiographers do the same. Roy Pascal, *Design and Truth in Autobiography* (New York and London: Garland, 1985) (first published 1960), p. 135, says that artists' autobiographies are usually the story of a calling.

17. For example, Georgia O'Keeffe, in *Georgia O'Keeffe* (New York: Viking Press, rev. ed., 1977, unpaginated), writes: "My first memory is of the brightness of light—light all around." She then proceeds to describe in minute detail the quilt on which she was sitting when she saw this light. Cecilia Beaux, *Background with Figures,* first recalls a "delicate mist, shot with sunlight, a memory of sheer beauty" (p. 15). One could argue that these are self-conscious memories, deliberately chosen to convince the reader of the visual sensitivity of the author-artist. Nonetheless, it is significant that Chicago omits such recollections.

18. This theory was first advanced in Linda Nochlin's watershed article, "Why Have There Been No Great Women Artists?" *Art News* 69.9 (January 1971), 22ff. Lavinia Fontana, Artemisia Gentileschi, Caterina van Hemessen are some early women artists whose fathers were also painters. Of course, Kauffmann, herself, who worked alongside her father at only sixteen, also exemplifies this tendency.

19. Stewart, *A New Mythos*, p. 109. "To be conscious, to name, to identify, to be intelligent is to be masculine. To be the muse . . . is to be feminine. . . . The artist . . . must die as this mythic feminine woman in order to give birth to herself as an artist."

20. It is interesting that Chicago does not credit her biological mother with playing a role in her retrieval of her female roots. In 1928 Virginia Woolf wrote, "For we think back through her mothers if we are women." *A Room of One's Own* (Harmondsworth: Penguin Books, 1970), p. 96. Alice Walker, in her germinal essay "In Search of Our Mother's Gardens," in *In Search of Our Mother's Gardens: Womanist Prose* (New York: Harcourt Brace Jovanovich, 1983), pp. 231–44, considers the creative legacy of her biological mother and other black women of that generation and before. Stewart, "Demeter/Per-

sephone and the Artist as Heroine," pp. 40–106, deals extensively with the search for mothers in *Künstlerromane* by women authors. Elias-Button, "The Muse as Medusa," discusses the importance of "confrontation with and incorporation of . . . matriarchal powers" to the contemporary creative woman, p. 202. For her this force is represented as Medusa.

21. See *Through the Flower*, opposite p. 59, for a black-and-white reproduction of *Female Rejection Drawing*, the work on which the above thoughts are inscribed.

22. Page 141, referring to her first suite of lithographs on the theme, made during the summer of 1972 while working on "her book." Earlier she states, "Working on the book helped me to organize my thoughts and ideas and to examine the experiences I had been having. While I was writing it, I also began experimenting with overtly feminist visual images" (135); and "By the time Womanhouse closed, I had finished the first draft of my book . . . and in the process developed greater ease about expressing my own point of view" (137).

23. Page 144, quoting from Judy Chicago and Miriam Schapiro, "Female Imagery," *Womanspace Journal* 1.3 (summer 1973), 11–14. Some contemporary critics have responded negatively to what they perceive as the essentialist and reductive aspects of this interpretation. For example, see Karin Woodley, "The Inner Sanctum: The Dinner Party," in *Visibly Female*, ed. Hilary Robinson (London and New York: Universe Books and Camden Press, 1987), pp. 97–99.

24. Some contemporary readers, particularly students, who are exposed to *Through the Flower*, respond quite negatively to what they perceive as the condemnatory tone in Chicago's writing.

25. Judy Chicago, *The Birth Project* (Garden City, N.Y.: Doubleday, 1985), pp. 147–48.

26. Video tape by Vivian Kleiman, accompanying the traveling exhibition *The Birth Project*.

27. See Kathryn Allen Rabuzzi, *The Sacred and the Feminine: Toward a Theology of Housework* (New York: Seabury, 1982), on "Waiting," particularly pp. 150–53.

28. For a discussion of caring as a philosophical stance, see Nel Noddings, *Caring: A Feminist Approach to Ethics and Moral Education* (Berkeley: University of California Press, 1984). Patricia Meyers Spacks discusses the way "gossip penetrates to the truth of things" in her essay "In Praise of Gossip," *Hudson Review* 35 (1982), 25.

29. Mary Field Belenky, Blythe McVicker Clinchy, Nancy Rule Goldberger, and Jill Mattuck Tarule, *Women's Ways of Knowing* (New York: Basic Books, 1986). The authors argue that women tend to "know" in ways that are powerful, albeit less linear, logical, and abstract than men, and that these modalities have been denigrated by "the dominant intellectual ethos of our time" (p. ix).

30. See revised and updated edition (1982), p. 214.

31. See Josephine Donovan's essay in this volume, "The Pattern of Birds and Beasts: Willa Cather and Women's Art." See Belenky, Clinchy, Goldberger, and Tarule, *Women's Ways of Knowing*, for a discussion of how some women are at odds with the male model of knowing and how women are able to "find their voices" when they learn to enhance objective logic with more intuitive, "connected" ways of understanding the world.

32. Lisa Liebman's review of *The Birth Project* in *Vogue* ("Post-Partum

Oppression," August 1985) exemplifies this kind of cheap potshot. Liebman refers to Chicago as a "bully" and a "little Caesar."

33. Even without the responsibility of children, some women artists were kept from their art by the external pressures of life. The twentieth-century Canadian artist Emily Carr, who had fifteen unproductive years in her mid-life, is a case in point. Carr was involved in running a boarding house, an endeavor she had undertaken originally because she thought she could meld it with her art-making. See Doris Shadbolt, *The Art of Emily Carr* (Seattle and Toronto: University of Washington Press and Clarke, Irwin and Co., 1979).

34. The passage from *The Story of Avis:* "Women understand—only women altogether—what a dreary will-o-the-wisp is this old common, I had almost said commonplace, experience, 'When the fall sewing is done,' 'When the baby can walk,' 'When the housecleaning is over,' 'When we have got through with the whooping cough,' 'When I am a little stronger,' then I will write the poem, or learn the language, or study the great charity, or master the symphony; then I will act, dare, dream, become" (ed. Carol Farley Kessler [New Brunswick, N.J.: Rutgers University Press, 1985], p. 149). "Waiting," a performance piece by Faith Wilding from *Womanhouse*, makes the same point. Here, a monologue of waiting characterizes the life of a female, from infancy ("waiting for someone to pick me up") through adolescence ("waiting for my breasts to develop") and motherhood ("waiting for my baby to come," "Waiting for my baby to sleep through the night") to middle age ("waiting for fulfillment") and old age ("waiting for release"), pp. 213–17 in 1977 paperback edition of *Through the Flower*.

35. Even feminist writers make this assumption. For example, Stewart, *A New Mythos,* p. 14, quotes Mary Ellman, "Because our concept of creation is profoundly intellectual and self-directed, the procreative, other-directed, nourishing role of woman is antithetical to the role of artist." Carolyn Heilbrun, in her introduction to May Sarton's *Mrs. Stevens Hears the Mermaids Singing,* writes: "In seeing the artist as their own ideal, women have to a large extent betrayed themselves. They do not understand that . . . art cannot be achieved by those for whom anything else matters. Art is not a part-time occupation," p. xiv.

36. Gilligan, *In a Different Voice.* This is the book's central thesis, developed in depth in her last chapter, "Visions of Maturity." Melody Graulich, "Somebody Must Say These Things: An Essay for My Mother," *Women's Studies Quarterly* 13. 3–4 (1985), 6, in writing about Agnes Smedley's *Daughter of Earth* refers to Gilligan to demonstrate that "those qualities which Marie believes make women victims are actually psychological strengths, deriving from a young girl's feeling of attachment to her mother."

37. Graulich, "Somebody Must Say These Things," p. 6.

38. Barbara Hepworth, *A Pictorial Autobiography* (New York: Praegar, 1970), p. 20, also quoted in Witzling, *Voicing Our Visions.*

39. Mary Daly in *Pure Lust* (Boston: Beacon Press, 1984) posits the concept of "biophilic," a life-affirming consciousness, in opposition to phallocentric violence, annihilation and hatred of life. (See p. ix for introduction of concept.)

40. *The Diaries and Letters of Käthe Kollwitz* (Chicago: Henry Regnery, 1955), ed. Hans Kollwitz, trans. Richard and Clara Winston, p. 156 (April 16, 1917), also quoted in Witzling, *Voicing Our Visions.*

41. Belenky, Clinchy, Goldberger, and Tarule, *Women's Ways of Knowing.*

42. Gilligan, *In a Different Voice*, pp. 170–71.

43. Gilligan, *In a Different Voice*, p. 174.

44. See Witzling, *Voicing Our Visions*, for an analysis of the ways in which women artists have used the written word to negotiate the conflict between their gender and their vocation.

Chapter 11
The Alberta Trilogy: Cora Sandel's Norwegian *Künstlerroman* and American Feminist Literary Discourse

Linda Hunt

In recent years we have seen an increasing interest in how women writers have re-visioned artistic creativity and in how they have re-fashioned the *Künstlerroman*. These studies have prompted some very provocative theorizing, but the validity of such work would be enhanced if feminist scholars were to broaden their focus to include more literature not written in English. This essay explores Cora Sandel's *Alberta Trilogy*, three novels written in Norwegian which together constitute a *Künstlerroman* considered a modern classic throughout Scandinavia. Its purpose is to trace the protagonist's efforts to define and achieve an artistic identity, to reimagine the creative process within the context of a society mired in dualisms regarding gender, and to discuss how some American feminist literary thought is contradicted by or applies to Sandel's *Alberta and Jacob* (1926), *Alberta and Freedom* (1931), and *Alberta Alone* (1939) in the hope that these observations may help both to widen and direct the current discourse on the woman artist.

The *Alberta* books are autobiographical to some degree. The first novel traces the emotional development of the main character, Alberta, a lonely and repressed adolescent growing up in a Norwegian Arctic town at the turn of the century. Alberta suffers from an unhappy family life, from the constraints and devaluation women experience in a patriarchal world, and from her own apparent inability to conform to the roles society assigns. At times she finds relief in the fragments of poetry that appear to come unbidden from the depths of her being, mainly when she is at peace in the presence of nature.

In the second novel Alberta has escaped to the Bohemian fringe of Paris only to find that even there freedom is elusive for a woman. Making episodic, undisciplined, and almost furtive efforts to express herself in writing, she exists as a kind of impoverished "outlaw" (as her first lover calls her), not sure what she wants but only what she doesn't want, until she backs into a marriagelike relationship and motherhood. In the final volume, Alberta's need to write becomes more pressing as she gropes for a way out of a loveless relationship with the father of her child. Returning to Norway, she at last strikes out on her own, determined to achieve self-sufficiency and self-expression through a literary career.

The Alberta Trilogy ends ambiguously, but because the reader knows the books are in good measure autobiographical one can assume that Alberta Selmer succeeds in becoming a novelist. How does she overcome the obstacles that patriarchal society throws in the path of an aspiring female artist? Alberta must extricate herself from the binary oppositions of gender so central to patriarchal ideology, ideas that shackle her both externally and internally, the most damaging myth being the belief that men create while women only procreate.[1] To do this she must reconceptualize the idea of artistic productivity, thinking of it in terms of "an honest day's work," so that the artist becomes in her imagination not an exalted and isolated being set apart from routine activities and moral and social responsibilities,[2] but for the most part, an ordinary worker. As we will see, this reformulation of creative endeavor, which helps Alberta at last to channel her artistic gifts, departs significantly from the conceptual models that some contemporary American critics see modern feminist writers drawing on in their transformations of the artist novel genre.

Alberta must find ways to sustain her imagination—that is, to find muses that are distinct from those strategies adopted by the protagonists in *Künstlerromane* by and about men. While artist-heroes like James Joyce's Stephen Daedalus find inspiration in alterity—that is, in images of the "Other" against whom they can define themselves— Alberta creates herself as an artist by getting nourishment from other people in relationships characterized by commonality. Sandel thus redefines the *Künstlerroman* genre in such a way that her novels reflect differences between women and men regarding the relationship of self to other, differences most explicitly delineated in the work of object-relations psychologist Nancy Chodorow.[3] In tracing Alberta's development we will find that despite Sandel's affirmation of the importance to the aspiring woman artist of close relationships with other people, Sandel's vision of how a woman artist gives birth to herself is not entirely consistent: a few points of tension disrupt the narrative, revealing contradictions that keep her from imagining a future for Alberta which includes a nurturant female community.

The very title of the first volume—*Alberta and Jacob*—suggests contrast along gender lines, and Alberta Selmer's life and possibilities as a girl are shown to be, in many ways, the polar opposite of those of Jacob, her teenage brother. Most strikingly, Alberta appears destined for a life of entrapment within the domestic sphere, most likely as a wife and mother but possibly as a spinster pitied by the townspeople and obliged to care for aging, demanding parents. Jacob, on the other hand, has far more autonomy than his sister even while living at home, and before the novel's end, he has "turned his true face out to the world, a face full of undaunted confidence in his two strong arms."[4]

Numerous other gender-related contrasts between female confinement and male freedom are manifested throughout the novel, notably Jacob's sexual freedom—an aspect of a wider world of freedom, knowledge, and adventure available to him—as opposed to Alberta's restricted sexual development, reinforced by an awareness that female sexuality brings with it the imprisoning destiny of pregnancy and childbirth (illustrated most tellingly by Beda's forced marriage and symbolized by the ever-present figure of Nurse Jullum, the midwife). Her sense of confinement is further heightened by the contrast between the conversations of men which embrace "distant countries, world affairs, politics," as opposed to women's conversations which are preoccupied with domestic duties and gossip about pregnant neighbors (*AJ* 88); and the contrast between Jacob's freedom to reject the domestic sphere in pursuit of his own dreams as opposed to Alberta's obligation to stay on at home as a buffer between her warring parents.

In this first novel, Alberta's creative spark comes and goes of its own volition; perhaps this is one of the reasons she never regards her poetry as a possible corridor to a larger world. For the most part, especially in social situations, she is noted for her silence. Awkward and tongue-tied at a party on a summer night, she erupts with anger at a young man she has heard disparaging her father, but all she can do is throw back at him in a parodic manner the very words she overheard him use. Unable to find her own voice even in the throes of rage, she believes she will "die of muteness." Alberta's inability to express herself is one of the most powerful factors contributing to the reader's sense of her constriction.

If the primary binary opposition in *Alberta and Jacob* is between the narrowness of female options and the broadness of male opportunity (a dichotomy that continues throughout the last two novels), the most significant gendered polarities in *Alberta and Freedom* and *Alberta Alone* are related to artistic endeavor. The second novel opens with Alberta living among artists on the Left Bank of Paris, supporting herself by modeling and by pawning her meager belongings. Although many of her women friends and acquaintances paint, this is a world in which only male artists eventually win reputations and sell their work, while women artists simply grow old:

Trudging around Montparnasse . . . [t]hey . . . had wrinkles and untidy gray hair, and they dragged themselves around with large bags full of brushes over one arm. . . . They sat . . . and painted; fussing and wearisome, they filled the academies and life classes . . . they lived on nothing, making tea with egg water.[5]

Women's art is not taken seriously in this milieu, and as a result, the women find it difficult to take their own art seriously. Early on Alberta tells her closest friend, Liesel, that she "can't write." Not long after, we learn that she does still make occasional efforts. However, the passages devoted to her furtive writing read like a confession: she acknowledges that in her mind her writing is comparable with what "Eliel did with his clay" (*AF* 44), but she assuages her guilt for such hubris by insisting on the involuntariness of what she does. To even momentarily imagine her work as having the same conscious intent and significance as the work of Eliel, Liesel's sculptor lover, feels dangerously presumptuous. As a result, her writing comes to be described in her mind in such words or phrases as "this business with little scraps of paper," "untidy," "a muddle," "sore spot," and an "unhappy weakness" (*AF* 44–45), terms that reflect the traditional patriarchal equation of women with weakness, bodily functions, mental disorder, and chaos.

The gender ideology which has had such a negative effect on Alberta's attitude toward her writing is articulated explicitly by a male artist who is part of her circle. Drunk, he tells a woman painter:

'Frøken should go home to Norway and have *children* instead of hanging about here throwing Papa's money away learning to paint. For Frøken will never succeed. She should go home tomorrow and get herself a *child*. Then Frøken will be as *useful* as she could possibly be.' (*AF* 211)

That his view is no anomaly is shown by the critical and condescending way Sivert (later to be the father of Alberta's child) responds to a description of a painting Liesel is working on. Indeed, even female friends subvert Alberta's tenuous aspirations, citing the importance of heterosexual satisfaction over artistic fulfillment; " 'two arms around you at the end of the day' " (*AF* 71) are crucial, the other relatively insignificant.

Given this kind of "insidious propaganda," as Alberta calls it, it is not surprising that Alberta and her best friend succumb. Liesel, who, despite real talent, has always had a tendency to sabotage her best paintings, falls in love with Eliel. His work takes precedence over Liesel's, and both he and she define her primary role as that of hand-maid to the sacred flame of his talent. Given this world of gender polarities, one should not be surprised when Alberta recognizes that her friend has become, not a painter, but "a Muse" (*AF* 65).

Toward the close of *Alberta and Freedom* (the title's irony becomes increasingly apparent), Alberta becomes pregnant by Sivert. After years of writing only in the kind of guilty and undisciplined manner described above, it at last occurs to Alberta that she might become a serious artist only moments before she realizes she is with child. It is at this juncture that both Liesel (who has undergone an injurious abortion) and Alberta show that they have absorbed that most fundamental of patriarchal oppositions: the dichotomy between creation and pro-creation. Liesel speaks bitterly of what she clearly perceives as an inevitable cosmic irony: " 'That's precisely when it happens, when we think we're beginning to achieve something' " (*AF* 231).

Despite Sivert's urgings, Alberta refuses to place herself in the hands of an illegal abortionist. She does, however, take scalding hot baths—to no effect. Angry at her lover, tempted but afraid to tell him to get out of her life, Alberta's words, we are told, "died unborn." For the narrator, probing Alberta's consciousness, to use such a metaphor just at the point that Alberta has failed in an attempt to abort the child of her body, is evidence not only that, for her, self-expression and maternity are mutually exclusive, but that, in her mind, reproductive generativity has preempted the ability to articulate in language what she thinks and feels.

As the reader moves into the third novel, *Alberta Alone*, the pro-tagonist appears to have been defeated by the hegemony of categories that define men as free, women as bound, men as artists, women as helpmates and mothers. Alberta, Sivert, and their five-year-old boy are sharing a house on the coast of Brittany with Liesel (and Eliel when he deigns to visit) and a French couple and their child. Pierre, the French-man, is a respected novelist who has returned from World War I physically maimed and psychologically unable to take up his work. Alberta disparagingly compares herself to him: "He was a man, a breadwinner, a writer of repute into the bargain. . . . She was a woman and no more."[6] The "world at large," she believes, regards her "scrib-bling" (the word by which she and Sivert demean her artistic efforts) as "the last thing a wife and mother ought to undertake" and as "a burden that had to be borne" (*AA* 22). Concurrent with these beliefs is the awareness of her ineptitude as a wife and mother, brought into dramatic relief by the presence of Pierre's wife Jeanne, the model of domestic virtue.

Throughout this final novel the narrator, giving voice to Alberta's consciousness, describes women in terms of animal imagery, implying that they belong in the realm of biological immanence. Moreover, the characters are prone to make absolute statements and generalizations regarding the respective functions and natures of the two sexes. Even Alberta's small son is sure that he knows what mothers are supposed to do and what they like.

Liesel, depressed and defeated, has become an essentialist, quick to make statements that assume gender difference is innate: " 'We need so much tenderness, far more than men. How else should we commit ourselves to all that's so difficult? That's how nature has arranged things to get her own way' " (_AA_ 88). These remarks have to be understood in the light of the fact that infertility, the result of her long-ago abortion, has made Liesel insecure about her womanliness. She continually repeats her belief that women were meant to be mothers and that if only she had a child everything would be all right.

Alberta's progress toward penetrating her culture's myths of gender, uneven to the point of oscillation in the first two novels, is, even in this concluding book, a matter of stops and starts. While she never takes issue with Liesel's assumptions about men and women, one is not sure whether she is being tactful or whether she is inclined to agree. However, in the course of the narrative she begins to respond sharply to Sivert's maxims about women, sometimes with sarcasm and sometimes explosively. Lying in bed, he pontificates on what is natural to the relations between the sexes:

'You said, I love you first.'
'Did I? . . .'
'You did. And it's a mistake. It's the man who should say that sort of thing first.'
　Suddenly Alberta did not know whether to laugh or cry. 'You—you ninny!' she exclaimed in despair. (_AA_ 229)

Her ability to forcefully protest Sivert's absurd polarities of male and female in spite of being afraid of him is evidence of development on Alberta's part, and all of her articulate expressions of anger are steps toward the eventual completion of her manuscript at the book's conclusion. Alberta's achievement is possible only because she no longer sees men and women as opposites, and as a result she no longer sees "artist" and "woman" as contradictory terms. An examination of the means by which she is at last able to break through gendered oppositions is revealing.

An important step, as mentioned above, is the use of toil, in the sense of paid work, as a paradigm for the creative struggle. We are told in *Alberta Alone* that even during her pregnancy, in the very wake of her perception that creativity and procreativity are mutually exclusive for women, she had nonetheless resolved to try seriously to write once the baby was born in order "to earn her living and help to provide for their needs" (*AA* 110). The relentless demands of caring for a frail baby in impoverished and then wartime conditions make it impossible for her to act on that resolution, but what is important is Alberta's belief that her inhibitions might have collapsed in the face of economic need.

Another important step for Alberta is to redefine the prevailing notion of the figure of the artist. Certainly one can understand how the Romantic mystique of the artist which prevails in Montparnasse, problematic for any woman, would be particularly intimidating to someone like Alberta, who expects little from others, and certainly demands no prerogatives. Eliel is quite a contrast in that he persuades both himself and Liesel that everything must be sacrificed for his art; marriage is out of the question and Liesel's dangerous abortion essential because "Eliel must not be disturbed. He was so gifted. Someone was supposed to have used the word genius once" (*AF* 63–64). Throughout *Alberta and Freedom* and *Alberta Alone,* both Eliel and Sivert justify their ruthless egoism in terms of their duty to a higher purpose.

Odd Solumsmoen, Sandel's biographer, uses the Norwegian word *künstneregoisme* (the egoism of the artist) to justify Sivert's behavior, and Solumsmoen assumes that in leaving the child behind when she goes off to Oslo at the end of the trilogy Alberta is exhibiting the same selfishness that characterizes all of the male artists in the novel, selfishness that he views as an inevitable "part of the talent."[7] In fact, the Romantic myth that the artist must live for self and art alone *excludes* Alberta, who is not willing to put her own needs before those of her little boy. Even at the conclusion of the trilogy when she leaves the child behind with his father and grandparents, it is in the belief that their separation will be temporary and that only by leaving can she win back the boy's respect and affection. Because Alberta comes to view her art as work in the sense of a job that will pay money, it is possible for her to regard it as a path toward reconnection and reconciliation with her child in that caring for him includes being able to provide for him economically without compromising herself. In this way art and motherhood cease to be at odds.

In order for Alberta to redefine the vocation of the artist in terms of work and to imagine herself as capable of being such a worker, she must overcome another kind of mystification. As a child emotionally moved by her perception of her father's tired and brave but joyless perseverance as breadwinner (privileging it over her mother's domestic anxieties), Alberta has carried with her into adulthood an idealized image of man as "courageous wanderer through life," and "toiler" on "life's hard journey" (*AF* 99, 144, 198). This last phrase, used initially to describe Veigaard, Alberta's first lover, echoes throughout *Alberta and Freedom*. Used in reference to all the important men in Alberta's life, it underscores Alberta's initial susceptibility to being deeply stirred by masculine toil: a structure of belief that is altered as she comes to understand that meaningful work is not exclusively performed by men.

In *Alberta and Freedom*, Alberta's self-esteem (never strong) declines as her respect for work and her understanding of its psychological importance grows. When Jean, the man who removes the slop-bucket from her hotel room observes, "You are young, and you do nothing," she is stung by its truth (*AF* 81). Her aimless life as a bohemian observer of Paris's human drama increasingly loses its luster as she ponders "the feeling of human freedom that grows out of an honest day's work" (*AF* 94). After hearing of Veigaard's death, she realizes that toil can be a kind of safe harbor from the vicissitudes of personal life, but at this stage, the words, "long laborious journey," so similar to the wording she uses to evoke the work of men, can be applied only to her struggle to find love (*AF* 216).

The fact that the phrase, "life's hard journey," (180) is used only once in *Alberta Alone* (in reference to Pierre, Alberta's literary mentor) indicates that she gradually comes to demystify the work of men as she begins herself to claim the identity of artist/worker. While in *Alberta and Freedom* the sight of Sivert struggling over a painting prompts her to be "seized with a desire to be useful in her way, with carefully prepared meals" (*AF* 198), in the trilogy's final volume she gradually moves beyond the feeling that she is being "truant" from her real work— domestic chores—when she is writing. More and more she thinks of writing as a means to gain a livelihood, even if, for much of the novel, she continues to believe that her own talents are not up to the task. By the end she can explain to Sivert's mother, " 'I must start doing something, I must find a living, some people live by writing books. I've written a few trifles and got money by them. Now I'd like to try something a little bigger' " (*AA* 278).

Sivert's mother, a traditional Norwegian peasant woman, struggles to understand, at last giving Alberta what she needs, the recognition that her creative endeavors are a form of honest labor: "And so you're going out to work, Alberta? For I can imagine it's hard to write too" (*AA* 280). Fru Ness's support is important because Alberta has moved beyond the male identification of her girlhood self and now gains sustenance from a sense of solidarity with other women, especially other mothers. She sympathizes with their struggles while at the same time recognizing that domesticity will never be her arena.

It is interesting to compare Sandel's representations of domesticity with Susan Gubar's observations about the "revisionary domestic mythology" of Virginia Woolf, Dorothy Richardson, and Katherine Mansfield,[8] writers of *Künstlerromane* who shared both Sandel's feminism and her modernist interest in interiority, memory, and intense sensuous evocation of the moment.[9] Gubar points out that although Woolf, Richardson, and Mansfield show that they are aware of the negative aspects of woman's domestic role, they all insist on the analogy, even the unity, between women's generativity in the home as mothers, homemakers, and hostesses and their capacity to produce what is conventionally considered art; she quotes from Richardson's *Pilgrimage* in which the protagonist Miriam asserts, " 'whereas a few men here and there are creators, originators, artists . . . women are this all the time.' "[10] Gubar also discusses other writers, especially Anaïs Nin and Willa Cather, as participants in the feminist-modernist *Künstlerroman* tradition, but their place in it involves glorification of the creative womb or a sense of "a sustaining matrilinearity" linking them with women of the past instead of any positive evocation of domesticity.[11]

Sandel does not extol woman's ability to give birth nor her role in the domestic sphere. Far from valorizing traditional female culture, she provides only negative images of home and family life. Alberta's mother is hypercritical and miserable, and her house is a cold place both physically and emotionally. Pierre's wife, Jeanne, heightens her husband's sense of mental aridity by being a domestic paragon, and their daughter, by imitating her mother's matronly authority, compels Pierre to remark, " 'we might as well have the police in the house. We're under surveillance, Alberta' " (*AA* 11). The studio home in Paris that Alberta shares with Sivert and their child is a lonely place, and her domestic chores are presented as sheer drudgery. Moreover, while Alberta loves her son fiercely, her experience of maternity is joyless and is not celebrated as an aspect of her creative powers.

Although it is difficult to ascertain whether Sandel's refusal to paint an attractive picture of life within the domestic world and of woman's traditional role is typical of Scandinavian literature, two American scholars of Scandinavian literature state that in general Norwegian women authors, as well as women writers from other parts of Scandinavia, share Sandel's negativity toward domesticity; also, while frequently positive about motherhood, Scandinavian women writers generally do not mythologize women's reproductive capacities.[12] These attitudes certainly contrast with what Gubar says about the writers she examines and call into question some of her assumptions.

Gubar believes that women writing *Künstlerromane* in the first part of the twentieth century were able to redefine "women as paradigmatic creators" because new and positive scientific attitudes toward the female body and the development of reproductive technology gave women's ability to bear children a new prestige and freed them from compulsory maternity.[13] These developments did not have a comparable impact on Sandel's feelings about women's traditional role.

Another important distinction between Sandel and the writers Gubar examines is the fact that Sandel was a mother while the others were childless; the professional artist-heroines of Woolf, Richardson, and Cather are childless, as well. Significantly, despite contraceptive advances, Alberta and Liesel fall victim to lack of control over their reproductive powers. One cannot but feel strongly that further discussion of *Künstlerromane* by women must take the issue of motherhood on the part of both the writers and their characters into account. Sandel's ability to avoid undue valorization of Alberta's motherhood experience may very well be related to the fact that she herself had a child, although women who themselves are mothers are certainly capable of being overly romantic about maternity.

Also, Sandel would not be likely to make a claim for women's capacity for artistry on the basis of privileging uniquely female images of creativity—childbearing, domesticity, matrilinearity—as the aforementioned novelists do because the whole movement of *The Alberta Trilogy* is toward the collapse of binary oppositions of gender. The inapplicability of Gubar's generalizations about the feminist-modernist *Künstlerroman* tradition to Sandel, and, it seems, to other Scandinavian women writers, suggests that until American feminist literary scholars are more familiar with women's literature around the world we should be wary about the limitations of our knowledge.

Another indication that generalizations by American feminist critics about British and American artist novels do not have universal applicability is that Sandel's *Alberta Trilogy* differs from the *Künstlerromane* described in Rachel Blau DuPlessis's *Writing Beyond the Ending*. DuPlessis, who bases her discussion of the female artist novel on the work of Charlotte Perkins Gilman, Doris Lessing, Virginia Woolf, Tillie Olsen, and others, asserts, "the twentieth century female *Künstlerromane* solve the binary opposition between [artistic] work and domesticity by having the fictional artwork function as a labor of love, a continuation of the artisanal impulse of a thwarted parent, an emotional gift for family, child, self or others."[14] In other words, she sees the artwork produced in this literature as performing a kind of service that can be viewed as the equivalent, in a sense, of the giving behavior traditionally displayed by women in life and literature. In contrast, Alberta's precious manuscript is not, as far as the reader knows, in any way intended to meet the needs of others in the sense that DuPlessis intends. Once again, then, we find British and American twentieth-century feminist writers concerned with maintaining continuity with women's domestic past in a way that Sandel is not.

In many ways *The Alberta Trilogy* resembles nineteenth-century female *Künstlerromane* by women more than it does its twentieth-century manifestation because of Sandel's emphasis on contradictions between production and reproduction and her representation of how familial responsibilities can be destructive to woman's creative genius. In Victorian female artist fiction—books such as Elizabeth Stuart Phelps's *The Story of Avis* (1877), Olive Schreiner's *The Story of an African Farm* (1883), Rebecca Harding Davis's *Earthen Pitchers* (1873–74), and Kate Chopin's *The Awakening* (1899)—the artist heroines fail;[15] yet unlike these novels, the conclusion of *Alberta Alone* implies that its protagonist will succeed. This brings us to the question of how Alberta nourishes her imagination so that her success becomes possible.

Mary DeShazer, in her book, *Inspiring Women: Reimagining the Muse*, points out that women writers cannot and would not want to turn for inspiration and support to "the male pattern of reliance on a classical female 'Other,'" the conventional figure in Western literature who provides the artist with an opposite against whom he can define himself. She says,

[W]omen have struggled to define their artistic identities, their sources and resources of inspiration, on their own terms. Rather than invoking that passive inspirer . . . modern women claim as muses . . . women through whom they can find voice. These inspirational figures may be . . . women from their own lives—mothers, lovers, one or many sisters; aspects of their own psyches.[16]

She goes on to assert that while it would seem logical that "a woman . . . would invoke a male muse," this is "rarely the case, especially in the twentieth century."[17]

Comparing Alberta's means of finding support for her need to get in touch with and in control of her own creativity with DeShazer's understanding of how this is done by women, we find many parallels and some differences. Like DeShazer's women poets, Alberta's imagination is nurtured not, as in the male tradition, by figures representing that which is not the self but by women from her own life with whom she has much in common.[18] The female friends who sustain her are Liesel, also an artist manqué,[19] a woman whose experience—up until a certain point—virtually mirrors Alberta's adult life, and Lina, an older farmwoman Alberta meets after her return to Norway, who lives in the close harmony with nature which Alberta has come to crave.[20] Moreover, Lina's function is to be the "Good Mother" Mrs. Selmer was incapable of being to Alberta, and in this sense, she is an aspect of Alberta's psyche, a figure who symbolizes the younger woman's readiness to be healed of the damage done by her disapproving and rejecting biological mother.[21] It is in the way that Alberta in the end becomes her own muse by turning inward to her own psychic resources that DeShazer's theorizing most directly applies.

However, Sandel departs from DeShazer's models in the fact that Pierre, a man, and one with whom Alberta falls in love, plays a central role in helping Alberta to acknowledge and fulfill her artistic aspirations. We should note, however, that the fact that he has been maimed in the war and is now thwarted artistically, gives him the ability to empathize with frustration and powerlessness and thus with the experience of being a woman.[22]

Having problems in common with Alberta he can understand and affirm her need to gain possession of her creative gift, and because of his own commercial success before the war as well as his new cynicism, he reiterates throughout *Alberta Alone* an approach to the production of literature which emphasizes that it is a way to earn a living. As we have seen, the conceptualization of art as paid work is beneficial to Alberta.

Pierre's use of metaphor is also tonic in its impact. Sandel puts in Pierre's mouth the childbirth metaphor, a way of yoking artistic and biological creativity, which has a long literary history. He says,

'Don't let yourself be paralyzed by the bad days, when nothing happens. . . . If you try to help you catch hold of an arm or a leg and everything is at a deadlock, like an embryo lying in the position. Yet you must go on tugging and pulling. . . . The day you feel yourself grasping the head, then delivery begins in earnest . . .' (*AA* 35).

Susan Stanford Friedman, in a recent article on gender difference and the childbirth metaphor, argues that when a male writer uses it, the reader is necessarily aware of "the biological impossibility of men birthing both books and babies," and so Western culture's divergent assignment of artistic creativity to men and procreativity to women is affirmed."[23] On the other hand, she believes, the metaphor in the work of a female author expresses rebellion against the idea that women can only produce babies, establishing "a matrix of creativities based on women's doublebirthing potential."[24]

Pierre is, of course, a male character in a novel written by a woman, and he is using the metaphor to describe the creative process of a female character. It is fascinating to wonder whether Pierre would use the same image to describe his own creative process. Awareness of its physiological incongruity for a male artist does heighten the sense of collision between the two parts of the comparison. At the same time, however, one remains keenly aware that Pierre is *Sandel's* creation, the invention of a woman who has given birth to a work of art, and feels strongly that Pierre's effort to describe Alberta's creative process is based on his conviction that he works in the same way. One could conclude, then, that in allowing Pierre to link creativity and procreativity in his imagery, Sandel deliberately *raises* the question of whether woman's biological immanence is antithetical to creative transcendence without completely resolving it. The reader is reminded that the validity of woman's claim to the artist role remains a vexed issue for society, but what is significant for the ultimate realization of Alberta's literary talent is that she feels supported, thinking, "Pierre was right to talk of embryos" (*AA* 36).

Alberta's friend Liesel also fosters Alberta's talent by providing affection and companionship, and by encouraging her to write, but she is most helpful in that Alberta learns from Liesel's experience what *not* to do. Having seen the damage done to her friend by an illegal abortion, Alberta goes through with her pregnancy, acknowledging that her main motive was fear of harming her healthy body. As mentioned above, Liesel's abortion and consequent infertility lead to an insecurity about femininity which expresses itself in a need to reify gender, an attitude which is also a consequence of her desire to explain the failure of her artistic and personal ambitions. Liesel's ideas about what is natural to women and men, together with the ill health which has plagued her ever since the abortion, finally impel her to give up on being a painter and go home to live conventionally with her family in Germany.

The distance between Liesel and Alberta by the end of the trilogy can be measured by the fact that just minutes before Alberta meets Lina, the mother-surrogate who plays such a crucial role in freeing her creative energies, she is reading a letter from Liesel, who comments, "The artistic, poverty-stricken life isn't much fun in the long run. The men can do it, but not us" (*AA* 257). The pronoun "us" is somewhat ambiguous—does it refer to women in general or to Liesel and Alberta? The answer is probably both, and hence, it reflects Liesel's acceptance of dualities of gender and also her characteristic inability to adequately distinguish her identity from that of her friend.

Unlike Liesel, Alberta eventually learns that she is a separate being from those she loves. As a girl in *Alberta and Jacob* she is unable to be happy because she is always aware that members of her family are miserable, an indication of the insufficiently individuated sense of self that Nancy Chodorow says women are more likely to suffer from than men.[25] In *Alberta Alone* her heightened consciousness of her son's deficiencies surely stems from overidentification with him. However, by the end of the final volume, Alberta, physically separated from Pierre and Liesel when she returns to Norway, has internalized the caretaking relationship she has had with them and even aspects of their identities (e.g., Pierre's workmanlike approach to writing and his commitment to telling the truth). Like the psychologically healthy person Chodorow describes, she is fully differentiated from others, an integrated but "relational self" who has the capacity to be alone if necessary, and an artist who is ready to be her own muse.[26]

However, before Alberta reaches that point she must undergo an extremely stressful period. Upon returning to Norway, long past any illusions that she and Sivert can build a life together, Alberta is desperately aware that she must find a way out of her economic dependency, yet she still has no confidence in her ability to finish her novel. It is also increasingly clear that Sivert has been successful in alienating their little boy, Tot, from her.

But the return to her native land releases psychic forces that express themselves first in a series of dreams and then in her relationship with Lina. Alberta's most significant dream is distinctly Jungian, involving being led up a ladder by a "young girlish figure" who guides her to a wall which seems impenetrable except for a small hole in one corner. " 'You have arrived,' " says her guide, and when Alberta howls in frustration, the voice says repeatedly, "You must break through" (*AA* 252). She awakes screaming, but when Sivert, who has come to quiet her, says, " 'Pull yourself together. Or you'll have to go somewhere else. Tot is happy,' " (*AA* 253), she fixates on what he has said about the boy until it merges with the command from her dream:

'Break through, Tot's happy, break through, Tot's happy.'
    Alberta felt her eyes widen. She raised her head slightly from the pillow. (*AA* 254)

This extraordinary moment of insight is possible not because of any change in Alberta's external situation but because Alberta is at last ready to draw on the inner experience that has been strengthening her, without a great deal of outward change, throughout the three volumes. She is now able to conceive of separation from the son who only a few pages earlier was described as a "part of her," capable of recognizing her departure would do him no harm, that it is her only way out of an impossible situation, and by no means least important, that it is her only route back to him. She inwardly makes a great psychological leap. She takes another such leap in her first visit to Lina's room where she immediately, "without thinking," puts "her folder down on the table. There it lay as if it had come home" (*AA* 261).

The farmwoman, whose description fits that of the "wise old woman" who is often an archetypal guide for the soul in women's novels,[27] allows Alberta to use this room to work on her manuscript, and in it, over the course of the summer, she completes her novel. Lina compels Alberta to work in a disciplined way by setting a deadline: she must vacate the room by the date summer tenants are due to arrive. In finding a spiritual mother who both nurtures her and yet encourages her separateness, Alberta becomes capable of saving herself by mastery of language, overcoming the "muteness" which was her biological mother's inadvertent legacy.

Alberta can progress to this new stage only through asocial moments of epiphany triggered by archetypal dreams and connection with an archetypal mother figure. Unlike male heroes who develop by achieving an adult social identity, female heroes often don't attain maturity through action in the social world, and Alberta is an example of this.[28] The changes in her consciousness come about through social interaction, but Alberta cannot actually alter her *life* and seize control of her artistic ability until her psyche is, in a sense, "ripe."

Sandel's use of archetypes commonly found in women's literature to resolve her protagonist's dilemma does not mean that she subscribes to notions about female and male essences any more than does her apparent understanding of the ways in which issues of separation and autonomy are different for women than for men. Alberta must cope in a specifically female way with gender-related psychic obstacles to the realization of her gift—obstacles that exist because of women's particular experience in culture. In severing herself from her son, even temporarily, she indeed manages to "break through" one of society's most deep-rooted beliefs about what is natural for a woman.

In the trilogy's last scene, when Alberta walks down the road carrying a suitcase that contains her completed manuscript, everything she sees—a young mother with her child, a mare and her foal—seem to rebuke her, but she continues on her way. These images betray some hesitation on her part, a lack of certainty, but that is not surprising, for she has by no means achieved a happy ending. Alberta, who has journeyed in search of warmth and emotional security since childhood, sees ahead only "cold . . . no arms around her anymore . . . not even that of a child . . . naked life as far ahead as she could see" (283). Surely Sandel is reminding the reader that reunion with the child will be a central goal for Alberta when she has the narrator tell us at this point, "Then she remembered Brede [Tot's real name]" (*AA* 283).

As mentioned in the introduction to this essay, the *Alberta Trilogy* contains certain contradictions that interfere with the coherence of Sandel's vision of a world in which the binary oppositions of gender are dispelled. One is the episode in *Alberta and Freedom* when a Polish woman who shares Alberta's hotel presses her attentions upon the protagonist and forces upon her an unwanted kiss. Sandel's use of a lesbian as an emblem for female loneliness in this scene creates a rupture in the text.[29] Another disjunction occurs when we meet Sivert's unmarried sister near the end of *Alberta Alone,* for she too is depicted as mentally unhealthy, her peculiarities explained, even by androgynous (but married) Lina, to be the consequence of her spinsterhood. It may seem that Sandel is merely falling back on literary conventions in these two instances, but the suggestion could be made that she does so because she is not able to free herself completely of the notion that a woman needs a man.

By privileging heterosexuality Sandel affirms gender itself as a necessary dualism, and such disruptions of her assault on oppositions of male and female undermine her sense of Alberta's possibilities when she extricates herself from family. A less anxiety-ridden attitude toward women without men might have permitted Sandel to imagine a future for Alberta that included a sustaining community of women. Instead, despite having her reject the figure of the romanticized artist, Sandel makes Alberta confront her new life utterly alone.

The Alberta Trilogy transforms the paradigmatic male *Künstlerroman* in ways that often resemble the changes that other twentieth-century women writers make in revising traditionally male genres, modifications that in large part appear to stem from the importance to women of connection with others. Nevertheless, Sandel's trilogy contrasts sharply with the work of British and American feminist-modernists and the writings of other women working in English in that Sandel refuses to connect the creative powers of her female artist figure with the outlets for self-expression that have served generations of ordinary women who do not define themselves as artists and, in fact, shuns any uniquely female metaphors of creativity.[30] This rejection should be a salutary reminder that American feminist literary critics need to know well the work of women writers around the world not only to understand what they share but to chart suggestive discrepancies for further scholarly examination. Moreover, the greater our understanding of what separates the work of women authors from one another, the less danger we are in of essentializing the difference of women's writing.

Notes

1. The process of collapsing binary oppositions—to embrace multiple possibilities and alternatives, to accept contradictions rather than adhering to an either-or structure of thought—is explored in Holly A. Laird's essay on Elizabeth Barrett Browning, *"Aurora Leigh:* An Epical *Ars Poetica,"* and in Pamela L. Caughie's "'I must not settle into a figure': The Woman Artist in Virginia Woolf's Writings," in this volume. Both essays shed light on the importance of this process to Alberta's (and Sandel's) artistic growth.

2. For a discussion of how traditional ideas about the artist are antithetical to definitions of womanhood, see Grace Stewart's *A New Mythos: The Novel of the Artist as Heroine, 1877–1977* (St. Albans, Vt.: Eden Press, 1979), p. 14.

3. Chodorow, of course, makes it clear in all her work that gender differences are a social construction, the result of the fact that women are nearly always the primary caretakers of infants and children.

4. Cora Sandel, *Alberta and Jacob,* trans. Elizabeth Rokkan (Athens: Ohio University Press, 1984), p. 234. Further references to this work are cited parenthetically as *AJ* with page number.

5. Cora Sandel, *Alberta and Freedom,* trans. Elizabeth Rokkan (Athens: Ohio University Press, 1984), p. 19. Further references to this work are cited parenthetically as *AF* with page number. Alberta and her friends lack the self-confidence, the money, and the freedom from heterosexuality that made it possible for some women to be successful artistically and to establish a woman-loving artistic culture in Paris in this period. As Shari Benstock says, in *Women of the Left Bank: Paris, 1900–1940* (Austin: University of Texas Press, 1986), "homosexual women writers . . . were far less marginalized than heterosexual women who were unable (even unwilling) to establish any firm power base within the masculine culture" (451–52).

6. Cora Sandel, *Alberta Alone,* trans. Elizabeth Rokkan (Athens: Ohio University Press, 1984), p. 8. Further references to this work are cited parenthetically as *AA* with page number.

7. Odd Solumsmoen, "Cora Sandel i Kvinneåret," *Samtiden* 84 (1975),348. Solumsmoen's article was translated for me by Kristen Jaeger, a Norwegian graduate student at Ohio University.

8. Susan Gubar, "The Birth of the Artist as Heroine: (Re)production, the *Künstlerroman* Tradition, and the Fiction of Katherine Mansfield," in *The Representation of Women in Fiction,* ed. Carolyn G. Heilbrun and Margaret R. Higonnet (Baltimore: Johns Hopkins University Press, 1983), p. 34. Gubar also discusses female-specific metaphors of creativity and the celebration of uniquely female creative powers in the work of women writing in English in her essay, "'The Blank Page' and the Issues of Female Creativity," in *The New Feminist Criticism: Essays on Women's Literature and Theory,* ed. Elaine Showalter (New York: Pantheon Books, 1985).

9. The work of Woolf, Richardson, and Mansfield is much more formally innovative than *The Alberta Trilogy;* Sandel is more experimental in her last two novels. Also, Gubar notes in this essay that while Katherine Mansfield never wrote fiction about a professional woman artist, her focus on the female creative process and on the creativity of women is such that she places her in the feminist-modernist *Künstlerroman* tradition anyway.

10. Gubar, "Artist as Heroine," p. 40.

11. Also in this volume, Josephine Donovan's examination of Willa Cath-

er's artistic development provides some interesting points for comparison/ contrast in regard to Sandel and the fictional Alberta. Donovan is concerned with issues similar to those I raise in relation to Sandel's work, notably the importance of a positive, supportive mother figure to the woman artist and the question of whether women's domestic pursuits can be seen as a form of art. Of course, an important part of my argument is that Sandel's work deviates insignificant ways from what American critics see as characteristic of *Künstlerromane* by women.

12. Letter from Dr. Virpi Zuck, Professor of Germanic Languages and Literatures at the University of Oregon, dated October 19, 1987, and letter from Dr. Rochelle Wright, Associate Professor of Scandinavian at the University of Illinois, dated March 8, 1988. To support the fact that she sees "congruence with Sandel's anti-domestic stand," Zuck mentions the following Scandinavian women writers: Fredrika Runeberg, Minna Canth, Camilla Collett, Amalie Skram, Nini Roll Anker, and Ann Charlotte Leffler.

13. Gubar, "Artist as Heroine," p. 25.

14. Rachel Blau DuPlessis, *Writing Beyond the Ending: Narrative Strategies of Twentieth-Century Women Writers* (Bloomington: Indiana University Press, 1985), p. 104. It is important to point out that my reading differs radically from that of Virpi Zuck, whose article, "Cora Sandel, A Norwegian Feminist," *Edda* 1 (1981), 23–33, provides an analysis of *The Alberta Trilogy* that fits in with-DuPlessis's assertion of how women writers resolve the conflict between role and vocation. Zuck sees Alberta as a sort of literary missionary, sending forth her novel about the experience of women so that real women, her readers, will take strength from its feminist message and learn better how to conduct their own lives. I have carefully reread *Alberta Alone*, but have been unable to find any support for Zuck's argument.

15. Gubar notes that *Künstlerromane* by women writing in the nineteenth century tend to be more pessimistic about the artist-protagonist's chances for success and focus more on the obstacles created by husband, children, and household responsibilities.

16. Mary DeShazer, *Inspiring Women: Reimagining the Muse* (New York: Pergamon Press, 1986), p. ix. DeShazer is speaking here, and for the most part throughout her book, about women poets. Fiction writers are rarely explicit about invoking their muses.

17. DeShazer, *Inspiring Women*, p. 3.

18. See Elizabeth Abel's "(E)Merging Identities: The Dynamics of Female Friendship in Contemporary Fiction by Women" *Signs* 6 (1981), 413–35, for a discussion of how, in serious women's fiction, female friendship is more likely to be characterized by commonality than by complementarity.

19. Various approaches to the study of the figure of the artist manqué are undertaken in this volume, notably Linda Dittmar's "When Privilege Is No Protection: The Woman Artist in *Quicksand* and *The House of Mirth*," and Jane Rose's "The Artist Manqué in the Fiction of Rebecca Harding Davis." Both essays examine issues pertinent to the characters of Alberta and Liesel.

20. Judith Kegan Gardiner, in "The (US)es of (I)dentity: A Response to Abel on '(E)Merging Identities,' " *Signs* 6 (1981), 438, points out that the five contemporary women's *Bildungsromane* she and Abel examine are all "portraits of the artist in which the artist is represented by aspects of a pair of women rather than a single individual:" Liesel and Alberta are such a pair, and further thinking on this aspect of *Alberta and Freedom* and *Alberta Alone* should be

fruitful. Also relevant to the idea of "pairing"—though from a radically different standpoint—is Renate Voris's "The Hysteric and the Mimic: A Reading of Christa Wolf's *The Quest for Christa T.*" in this volume, a psychological, sociological, and linguistic study of the German novelist's work.

21. For a discussion of the dichotomy between what the authors call the "Good Mother" and the "Captor Mother," and the importance for the heroine of reconciliation with a mother figure, see Carol Pearson and Katherine Pope,*The Female Hero in American and British Literature* (New York: Bowker Press, 1981), pp. 101–3.

22. Elaine Showalter, in *A Literature of Their Own: British Women Novelists from Brontë to Lessing* (Princeton, N.J.: Princeton University Press, 1977), p. 150, explains why male characters in British women's fiction are often blinded, maimed, or go through a period of serious illness: a period of having to live under limitations, "in short of womanhood—was a healthy and instructive one for a hero."

23. Susan Stanford Friedman, "Creativity and the Childbirth Metaphor: Gender Difference in Literary Discourse," *Feminist Studies* 13 (1987), 56.

24. Friedman, p. 58.

25. Nancy Chodorow, *Reproduction of Mothering: Psychoanalysis and the Sociology of Gender* (Berkeley: University of California Press, 1978), p. 212.

26. Nancy Chodorow, "Gender, Relation, and Difference in Psychoanalytic Perspective," in *The Future of Difference,* ed. Hester Eisenstein and Alice Jardine (Boston: G. K. Hall, 1980), pp. 9–11.

27. See Annis Pratt's *Archetypal Patterns in Women's Fiction* (Bloomington: Indiana University Press, 1981) for a discussion of the "wise old woman" archetype.

28. See Pratt's discussion of the importance of asocial moments of epiphany and the difference between the development of female and male heroes in the *Bildungsroman*, pp. 36, 169. For an entirely different discussion of how *Bildungsromane* by women inevitably diverge from those by men, and one which focuses on *The Alberta Trilogy* (the only article in English on the trilogy that I am aware of), see Virpi Zuck's article, "Cora Sandel, A Norwegian Feminist." Also, my analysis of Sandel's use of archetypes in her resolution of *The Alberta Trilogy* owes a great deal, even in terms of the language used, to my previous analysis in the afterword to the Ohio University Press's editions of *Alberta and Jacob, Alberta and Freedom,* and *Alberta Alone.*

29. Sandel's use of the lesbian as a symbol of female loneliness is particularly ironic in light of what Benstock has to say about the comparative situations of heterosexual and homosexual women on the Left Bank. See note 6 above.

30. In her 1945 novel, *Krane's Cafe,* trans. Elizabeth Rokkan (Athens: Ohio State University Press, 1985), Sandel uses a dressmaker as her artist figure. However, the protagonist's creativity is totally thwarted because she has to conform to the tastes of her customers, so we cannot see this as an example of Sandel recognizing women's traditional domestic arts as even a minimally satisfactory outlet for artistic impulses.

Chapter 12
The Hysteric and the Mimic: Reading Christa Wolf's *The Quest for Christa T.*

Renate Voris

For Myra Love

> But for this reason I fancy
> that I am seeing myself lying in the coffin,
> and my two selves stare at each other
> in wonderment.
> —Karoline von Günderode

> Man likes woman peaceful—
> but woman is essentially unpeaceful,
> like a cat,
> however well she may have trained herself to be
> peaceable.
> ——Friedrich Nietzsche

To compare woman to a cat is banal. Yet the comparison is found in numerous texts of Nietzsche and Freud and for the same reasons as in Christa Wolf: the cat is an independent animal, little concerned with man, essentially narcissistic and affirmative, like a child and as such both self-sufficient and dependent.[1] For example:

that black green-eyed cat (2½) which was delicate and graceful and in an unmistakably oriental manner seductive, yet inside, alas, impudent and arrogant and lusty [*gierig*], in short: a woman.[2]

her supple [*geschmeidigen*] movements. . . .[3]

Femininity and narcissism are key concepts around which Christa Wolf's works revolve, including *The Quest for Christa T.* They are linked to alienation, the sinister motive in modernism and the modernist text, and Wolf's aesthetics and art as well. The question that disturbs me is: why are nearly all her female figures[4] mothers? And what is the relation between motherhood, art, and aesthetics? Was there, is there for

Wolf, an alternative to alienation? Is it motherhood? Is it art? Is it female narcissism? Or is it a combination of all three?

Freud, who in his essays on female sexuality offers massive affirmation of the "natural sexual inferiority" or "deficiency" of women, tells a different story of woman's sexuality in his essay "On Narcissism: An Introduction" (1914).[5] There he does not take sexual identity to be an inborn, biological essence, but in fact sees it as an unstable subject position that is socially and culturally constructed in the process of the child's insertion into society. The passage I have in mind concerns the difference in the love life of men and women. Freud argues the following thesis: there are fundamental differences between the sexes in their relation to the type of object-choice. Male narcissism is characterized by object-love of the anaclitic type (*Anlehnungstypus*) which includes the nurturing woman and the protective man (89–90). It shows a striking sexual overvaluation of the love object. The overvaluation has its source, Freud explains, in the original narcissism of the child which subsequently is transferred onto the sexual object. *Verliebtheit*, love and passion, is hence a neurotic condition, since it originates in the libidinal impoverishment of the ego that accompanies the sexual overvaluation of the love object (88).

Woman's development in her relation to a type of object-choice is different. Female narcissism, Freud argues, is characterized by object-choice of the narcissistic type, which includes the love for: (a) what one oneself is, (b) what one oneself was, (c) what one oneself would like to be, and (d) the person who once was a part of one's own self (90). This type of love is most frequently found in women, not, however, because of some biological determinant, but rather because of the woman's place in culture and society. It seems that, at the onset of puberty, the formation of the female sexual organs intensifies the original narcissism, which is unfavorable to the development of a normal (*ordentlichen*) object-love with its accompanying sexual overvaluation. Especially if she develops beauty, a state of self-sufficiency (*Selbstgenügsamkeit*) settles in, which compensates the woman for society's unwillingness to allow her freedom of object-choice (*die ihm sozial verkümmerte Freiheit der Objektwahl*) (89). The woman's "wildness," her "unpeaceable nature," is domesticated by the norms and rules of (patriarchal) society in that her Otherness, heterogeneity, is tamed through narcissism. Strictly speaking, such women love only themselves, and they do so with the intensity with which a man loves them. Their need does not make them aspire to love, but instead *to be* loved, and they are pleased by the man who fulfills this condition. The importance of this type of woman for the love life of humankind (*Menschen*) is of immense value, Freud concludes, for such women exercise the greatest charm (*Reiz*) over men for two reasons: (1)

aesthetic, because they are beautiful, and (2) psychological, because a person's narcissism exerts a great attraction over those who have fully relinquished their own narcissism and are in quest of object-love. Analogously, the charm (*Reiz*) of a child rests to a large extent on his or her narcissism, her self-sufficiency (*Selbstgenügsamkeit*) and inaccessibility (*Unzugänglichkeit*). Hence, also the charm of certain animals who seem indifferent toward us, such as cats and large beasts of prey (89). Is a woman ever able to love according to the male model (and vice versa)? Yes, Freud says, since "male" and "female" do not refer to biological but instead to psychological and cultural phenomena, to "functions" (*Funktionen*) (89) within a cultural field or social practice (such as writing). And if this is so, the obvious question is what determines the model according to which a woman loves? In his answer, Freud draws on the psychology of repression and the mechanism of displacement. Repression, as we know from Freud, originates in the ego, from the ego's self-esteem (*Selbstachtung*). Its condition is an ideal, an ideal ego (*Idealich*) that one has either erected or not erected in oneself. It explains why the same impressions, experiences, impulses, or wishes, which one person allows in herself or at least consciously deals with, are rejected in another or suppressed (*erstickt*) before they can ever become conscious. In case of the latter, narcissism is substituted for this new ideal ego, that is, whatever she projects as her ideal is the substitution for the lost narcissism of her childhood in which she was her own ideal (93–94).

In light of this theory and in keeping with this volume's questioning of material (including linguistic) conditions of women and men writing, I will undertake a reading of Wolf's novel, which deals with woman as well as with narcissism or alienation, by studying the arrangement and function of the main signifying units used in the narrative message, in order to determine the way in which this text represents feminine creativity. Since the title gestures toward the subject of the novel, a woman's "quest" for (self-)knowledge and (self-)development, I will begin by reading it as a text that quotes two literary traditions. The first is the classical German *Bildungsroman* (written by men), whose paradigm contains the fantasy of an originally unified subject split asunder in the confrontation with civilization, society, reality, a conflict that is solved—in however melancholy a way—by the integration of the individual, the (male) artist, into practical, active life; Goethe's *Wilhelm Meister* (1795/96 and 1821) constituted that model. The second literary convention cited here is the feminine version of that model, the nineteenth-century woman writer's *Bildungsroman*, whose paradigm contains the same individualistic fantasy of an originally unified subject that in the feminine version, however, is split asunder *not* by a "universal" conflict between the individual or the "self" and civilization or society and so on, but instead by the conflict between the desire for art and knowledge and the complete negation of that desire by a society whose norms and conventions restrict the woman to one role only: that of the mother (and not that of the physician, for instance, like Wilhelm Meister). The conflict is therefore not solved by the integration of the woman into active public life, but by her *exclusion* from it, a plot that almost invariably results in the death of the artist as a young woman; Bettina von Arnim's *Günderode* (1840) constituted this model.

In quoting these two literary conventions, a different paradigm emerges in Wolf's *Bildungsroman*. The conflict between vocation and role (= the masculine model) as well as that between art and womanhood (= the feminine model) are both interiorized, and in that movement are both recuperated and revised to become a conflict between two *vocations:* art *and* womanhood! The *desire* to create and the *desire* to recreate—two different but equal "selves"—are presented as that which defines the whole and essential woman. The question that motivates *The Quest for Christa T.* is therefore: when and where and why did the two "selves" that originally formed a harmonious whole become alienated, "staring" at each in wonderment or even enmity?[6] When and where and why did the alternatives that define the figure Christa T. collapse, and how did she experience that?

For Christa T. appears without a center. She resists coherence and structure by oscillating between creativity and procreativity, silence and speech, madness and mimicry, as well as "female" sexuality and "male" morality, childish play and parental control. Her "characterlessness" is contained in the novel's dominant rhetorical figure, repetition. In repetition, identity is split, since every repetition occurs in a different context. Meaning then appears to flicker between identity and nonidentity, sameness and difference, reconstruction and deconstruction. The novel's double-edged codeword, *Nachdenken,* supports the tension,[7] and so does the syntax that coordinates the transitive and the intransitive, in that the unconnected members of the essentially paratactic structure are connected by the use of anaphora.[8] On the semantic level, this text then plays out at once what Julia Kristeva has called the two fates of woman in Western culture: that of the classic hysteric who is denied her place in language, yet represents in that negativity a sort of disturbance of the symbolic order, of power and domination, *and* that of the mimic who takes her place in language and represents in that positivity a submission to the symbolic order, to masculine power and authority. In other words, the speaking subject occupies a position that alternates between feminine heritage and masculine heritage; the question that concerns me here is which of these two moments wins out in the end.

In any case, I read Wolf's novel as one that performs the rift experienced by women writers in bourgeois as well as socialist society, where the use of language itself may reinscribe the very structure by which the woman is oppressed.[9] I shall argue that this is indeed the story here, that *The Quest for Christa T.* is a most paradoxical text in that it challenges authority and patriarchy in a most authoritarian and patriarchal manner. My final question will be whether this paradox is offered to us for adherence or for criticism.

* * *

Wolf's novel, one of the most thoroughly discussed in scholarship on contemporary German literature,[10] appeared in 1968 in her home country, the (then) German Democratic Republic, amidst a debate among writers, literary scholars and critics, philosophers, and politicians about the question of the relation between subjectivity and history, the individual and (socialist) society, language and ethics. The debate centered on the familiar question of Western metaphysics that also moves the classical German *Bildungsroman:* how, if at all, and under what circumstances can one realize oneself in a work of art, a question the novel quotes (95) and varies by providing the socialist version of it: how, if at all, and under what circumstances is it possible for the artist within a planned (and rigidly organized) society to realize herself and be productive as an active member of that society (102)? The question for Wolf, the theorist, is the classical version, paraphrased from the first to the last sentence of the novel: *"the attempt to be oneself"* / "When, if not now?" The question of what role gender plays in the production and reception of art was not an issue, had never been an issue in the GDR, not for literary theorists or literary historians or Christa Wolf, as her essay of the same year, "The Reader and the Writer" (1968), as well as all subsequent writing on poetics and politics, show.[11] It remains a curious contradiction in her theory of literature that she subscribes to a materialist conception of art—with time and place as her major categories—but ignores entirely the materiality of language—that is, the discursivity of sex (or race, ethnicity, or even class)—and consequently overlooks the boundaries of a person's existence (just as did Georg Lukács, the most powerful and influential literary theorist in the cultural politics of the GDR during the first twenty years of "reconstruction"—Wolf's immediate social, biographical, and literary context). The question of women and fiction—as Virginia Woolf pondered it in 1928, for example, in the meaning of "women and what they are like," or "women and the fiction that they write," or "women and the fiction that is written about them," or "somehow all three"[12]—is a question that Wolf prefers not think aloud. In her silence she is a figure of her country, reproducing the vision (or delusion) that structures political, social, and cultural discourses: that with the coming of socialism and the abolition of class structure, workers as well as women will have been freed from oppression. That the system of patriarchy survived the transition from capitalism to socialism is only marginally contemplated, even by Wolf, thus revealing her and her society's blind spot: the repressive tendency in questions of sexual ideology.[13]

Yet it is precisely that relation—between language, body, and society—that is discreetly articulated in her textual practice, beginning with her first tale, *The Moscow Novella* (1961). A curious struggle then structures her works, a struggle that is represented in the *Quest for Christa T.*: between the reader-philosopher-theorist, who ponders the problematic epistemology of selfhood in terms of universals, and the writer-artist-practitioner, who *performs* it in terms of specifics.

*   *   *

The novel's plot revolves around death and birth. Its protagonist is ostensibly a woman who wanted to be a poet and became a mother instead. How that came about is told in twenty chapters whose main signifying units are childhood, adulthood and motherhood, and death by leukemia at the age of thirty-five. They are ordered chronologically from the present point of view by another woman, or mother, the narrator, who begins her tale with a eulogy, a sermon beyond the grave, circling around memory and forgetting. The dead woman has left behind a husband, three children, and the narrator, a friend since childhood. Besides the family and the friend, the dead woman has also left behind a large oeuvre—diaries, notebooks, sketches, and a thesis on the writer Theodor Storm, as well as short stories, poems, dialogues, and letters, all in no discernible order, mixing all sorts of discourses at times—autobiographical, theoretical, philological, poetic, polemical—written in part in the margins of books, even cookbooks, or on scraps of paper taken from her husband's desk. Why this woman—immensely privileged, it seems, for she is well educated, financially secure, artistically talented, with a love for words and the time to reflect upon them ("*To think that I can only cope with things by writing!*" 34, 96)—why this woman of letters and mother of three children has no paper, let alone a room of her own, is a mystery indeed, one the narrator wants to solve in her investigation into the "mess" (147). For it is she who, upon the death of the other, is charged by the husband with ordering the details of the wife's domestic and intellectual life; she is called upon in her capacity as witness (as a mother to a mother) and as examining magistrate, whose task is to inquire into the truth behind Christa's demise. "What do I reproach her for?" the narrator quotes a mutual friend. "For dying, for really dying. She always did everything as if it was for fun, as an experiment" (49–50). With the central opposition in place—play versus control—the narrator sets out on her own experiment in writing and living, gathers the fragments of the alien chaos and begins by thinking out the enigma of Christa T. on the model of the hysteric who holds a secret of which she herself is unaware and which she hides to herself ("a person with prospects, latent [*geheimen*] possibilities," 136). The narrator's goal is then the *solution* to the enigma, motivated both by death as a fact of life—Christa T.'s death and her own ("Not a person or thing in the world can make her dark fuzzy hair go gray as mine will," 4)—and by death as a subject of meditation and conquest:

So there she was, walking along in front, stalking head-in-air along the curb, and suddenly she put a rolled newspaper to her mouth and let go with her shout: HOOOHAAHOOO—something like that. . . . For me, unlike the others, it wasn't the first scene of this kind. I tried to recall a previous occasion when she could have walked on ahead of me, yet found there wasn't one. I'd simply known it. . . . suddenly I felt, with a sense of terror, that you'll come to a bad end if you suppress [*erstickt*] all the shouts prematurely; I had no time to lose. I wanted to share in a life that produced such shouts as her *hooohaahooo*, about which she must have knowledge. (9–11)

The word *terror* contains at its roots both the awesome and the fearful. It introduces the theme of repression and points to the accompanying mechanism of displacement, both condensed in the metaphor of suffocation (*erstickt*), which in turn echoes the metaphor Freud uses in his essay on narcissism. This then is the other tale told here, the narrator's tale. Its protagonist is a woman who became a mother *first* and is now *also* becoming a writer. It is the reversal of Christa T.'s tale.

But it is of course one and the same story, as the passage suggests, a story of a (self-)conscious quest for love. What kind of love? A scene that punctures the narrative three times, each time in a slightly different form, presents the meaning—an ideal meaning of love. The first time—and, not by chance, in the eulogy—the narrator resurrects the dead in the image of Woman-as-Child:

Effortlessly she walks before me, yes, that's her long stride, her shambling walk, and there too, proof enough, is the big red and white ball she's chasing on the beach. (4)

The second time she inserts the frame into the narrative is at about midpoint and at a time when she is concerned with Christa's bohemian lifestyle as a university student (chapter 8). What had seemed a child in the picture turns out to be a Woman-as-Mother:

How she runs, Christa T., after the huge white and red ball that the wind is driving across the beach, how she reaches it, laughs aloud, grabs it, brings it back to her small daughter, under our gaze, which she feels and to which she responds with a side glance, in no doubt as to our admiration. Justus, her husband, walks up to her, runs his hand through her hair, pulls her head back, hi Krischan! She laughs and shakes herself. And all the people along the beach can see her practicing How to Take Big Strides with her little Anna, using as background, brown and slim as she is, the whole sea which is foaming slightly and the pale sky overhead. Hi, Justus! she shouts. (74)

The third and last version—inserted toward the end of the novel when Christa's (fantasized) romance with her husband's hunting buddy is the context (chapter 17)—projects Woman-as-Wife:

I really must come back to the day we spent on the Baltic coast. To the gigantic white and red ball which the wind was driving along. To her supple [*geschmeidigen*] movements and to Justus's admiring looks and the way she tossed her head. To her laughter, which I can certainly never describe, but also never forget. She had a dark tan and I said: This has been *your* summer, she laughed, white teeth and tanned face. Justus took her by the hair, which she wore short, and kissed her on the mouth in front of all the people. She took it all seriously, laughing all along. I can still see the look in her eyes. (150)[14]

Reading the images vertically, and separately from the narrative context, our perception or sensibility is split between two conventionally conflicting figures. At the center stands the image of Woman, defined in the sequence first as Child, then as Mother, then as Wife. In the repetition and its variation, the figure seems interminable, unstable in its meaning, being both playful, indifferent, and self-sufficient, as well as controlled, object-oriented, and dependent. What controls her are the two empirical eyes that watch her, parental eyes ("under our gaze"), behind which appears a somewhat "gigantic" or godly third eye that peeps at the world out there as a stage ("in front of all the people"). It is a voyeuristic eye—Nietzsche called it the "Theatre-Eye"—the eye of the spectator/narrator amusing herself by watching the figure(s) on the beach/stage act out a morality play, the family plot. It is the eye that watches her (us?) or that she herself (we ourselves?) imagine watching her (us?) whenever she (we?) acts as a moral subject and views the world in terms of morality. The moral world needs a spectator, Nietzsche said, and he admonishes us to open up this gigantic third eye which looks at the world through the other two. The fact, though, that the subject has access to this godly, transcendental eye implies a paradox: it elevates it to the level of a god at the price that it is reduced to nothing.[15]

Identity or feminine sameness—mother and daughter having the same body—is the essential/essentialist presupposition structuring the vertical. Yet it *serves* also an image, authoritative and central, of man. This authoritativeness is present on the level of language, in the break in the logic of the third version ("She had a dark tan and I said: This has been *your* summer"), and on the level of structure, in the metonymic displacement of the metaphoric system. For if we read the three versions of the image within their temporal context, heterogeneity collapses into homogeneity, the unstable image into the stable sign "womanhood" with all its familiar connotations—the hearth, the home, the womb, the tomb. What seems unstable in the image becomes stable in the narrative, connecting form to meaning, word to substance. Moreover, an explicit dualism is established—female/male, exhibitionism/voyeurism, passivity/aggressivity, inside/outside, emotion/intellect, belly/head—with the first pole of the opposition as the positive to the negative: female-exhibitionism-passivity-inside-emotion-belly. Woman, the narrative's syntagmatic units and paradigmatic variations argue, does indeed have two desires. And yet she should not live them, should not "be" both child and adult, narcissus and nurturer, beast and mother. Woman must make a choice. And since it is she who by virtue of her anatomy, the womb, embodies, literally, nurture, the choice is clear: motherhood *first* (like the narrator), and only then a little bohemianism, a little individuality, a little romance. Thus, whether dead or alive, past or present, whether silent because she is physically dead, whether restless because she refuses conformity, whether creative because she resists domesticity, Christa T. is within this narrative always already confined to the statute of womanhood.[16]

Hence, woman in this text functions as a moral spectacle for the purpose of enlightening and educating its viewer (reader). It explains why the eye, exteriorized in the "big" and "huge" and "gigantic" (eye-)ball of the beach scene, is the privileged organ in the text, linking the kind of showing and telling here to a philosophical tradition, the Age of Enlightenment, whose most privileged emblem was the sun (the sky in Wolf's system) and whose most privileged organ the eye, wanting above all, as Foucault has argued, to see and oversee.[17]

Yet it may also mean the repetition of an all too familiar paradigm: that the female subject[18] is considered insufficient to occupy the position of the speaking subject, that she is, so to speak, spoken for, which might be one reason for the peculiar discourse. It appropriates Christa T.'s verses and cadences and uncanny babble ("HOOOHAAHOOO") by combining them with the narrator's showing and telling and chatter, evoking in that combination at once unreliability *and* discipline. Yet specular and linguistic authority rest with the reader-writer (= narrator), who legitimizes her posture by the "compulsion," she says, "to make her stand and be recognized" (5). This telos points to the hidden problem: a need for a looking glass that reflects that which is not: a whole and intact and powerful (female) figure. The genesis of a writer is plotted whose condition is the death of the Other. In the process, a series of genealogical connections is established—author/text, text/ meaning, reader/interpretation—underneath which lurks the imagery of succession, authority, and maternity: "to think her further" (*weiterzudenken*) (5). The discourse of power?

It functions as a compensation for psychological and social injuries:

The voice I hear isn't the voice of a ghost: no doubt about it, it's her voice, it is Christa T. Invoking her, lulling my suspicions, I even name her name, and now I'm quite certain of her. But all the time I know that it's a film of shadows being run off the reel, a film that was once projected in the real light of cities, landscapes, living rooms. Suspicions, suspicions: what is this fear doing to me? (4)

The phantom produces fear and fascination, expressed in the moving snapshot and described in the scene from girlhood recording Christa's enigmatic babble. The emotions are the same that one feels before a double or a ghost, before the abrupt reappearance of what one thought was forever overcome or lost, and what now exercises the greatest charm over the spectator/narrator and that for two reasons: aesthetic, because Christa T. is beautiful, and that is the first reason for the charm she exerts over her, and indifference, indifference *and* silence ("Not a word about this to me," 11), except for her laughter which, compared to language, is unstructured and more like singing, a sound rising from the body. This apparently monstrous laughter echoes the onomatopoeic babble from childhood, a terrifying, inaccessible sound around which the narrative curls itself[19] as if it wanted to contain it, in the dual sense: preserve and restrain it. The ambivalence unites the aesthetic and psychological (and social) and points again to the narrator's project, which defines itself in terms of finding an adequate language for the essence of that sound, that body, that alien Other ("To her laughter, which I can certainly never describe, but also never forget," 150).

This Otherness, heterogeneity, is present in the figure of narcissus or the child ("Effortlessly she walks before me," 4) or the cat ("her supple movements," 150), figures with whom the narrator is in love, passionately (fetishistically?), from the legs up ("How she runs," 74). As a Girl-Woman-Wife, Christa T.'s charm rests on her playfulness ("She always did everything as if it was for fun," 50) and her inaccessibility, aspiring not to love, but to be loved, a need the narrator condenses first in the figure of the Pan Piper seducing all by her mysterious howl, then in the figure of the tomcat roaming the city (*umherstreunen*)[20] as if in search of prey (49), and finally in the figure of the bourgeois or socialist housewife attracting guests and preventing strife by the sheer virtue of her presence (164). As a sexed (female) body, she seems painfully self-sufficient, indifferent, and theatrical, whether young ("The truth was: she didn't need us," 8), or adolescent ("She hardly ever talked about love. She kept herself to herself," 36), or mature ("our gaze, which she feels and to which she responds with a side glance, in no doubt as to our admiration," 74). No matter what time or what place therefore—in the schoolyard, on the beach, in the house—she exerts great charm over both women and men, while granting nothing in return, taking pleasure only in herself with an acute awareness of her own force ("about which she must have knowledge," 9–11).

Even as a writer, she seems indifferent to conventional fetishes, such as the work of art, reviews, praise, and critique, does not publish her works, scribbles wherever she can find a blank page, a scrap of paper, an empty margin, has no room of her own and does not seem to mind it, sits instead at her husband's desk during the early morning hours and writes about "The Big Hope, or The Difficulty of Saying 'I,'" only to toss away the sheet of paper on which it is written ("I saw the sheet of paper there . . . , but now it has disappeared," 169).

Yet it is during puberty that her narcissism appears most intense, as she assumes the role of the Pan Piper before a crowd of spectators. The exhibition expresses the social dimension of woman's narcissism and is a sign of her place in patriarchal culture and society, a society that denies her freedom of object-choice, as Freud formulates it. And the narrator enacts it, not, however, in a tableau, but in her figures of speech, as she traces the development of the female child from "girl" (*Mädchen*) to the (neuter) "miss" (*Fräulein*) to, abruptly, "the mother who cooks the soup" (21–22, 159), while the father roams the village archives in search of history (17) or the husband travels across the countryside in pursuit of (sick) cows (147).

The opposition movement/containment defines the law that governs the relation between the sexes, past and present, in bourgeois as well as socialist society. Accordingly, the little girl stands *inside* the fence, watching the boy leave the village ("He's free to do as he pleases," 22, 57); the adolescent maiden stays *inside* the fence, tempting the young man outside with a cherry (37, 91–92), like Eve with an apple inside a different yard; the adult women (Christa T. and the narrator) move *inside* the homely sanctuary, gazing out the window or over the balcony, while the men are, god only knows where (136, 143). Or the lonely lover hovers wretchedly *behind* the window, looking for the beloved to pass below (155–56). And, to end it all, the wife designs a house, lying down and dying in it.

Woman is present as a spectacle indeed, playing out the old bourgeois tragedy of sacrifice and sexuality, reminiscent of those nearly forgotten (historical/fictional) figures, Karoline von Günderode, the artist in Bettine von Arnim's novel, or Makarie, the eternal feminine in Goethe's novel. Both roles belong to the same repertoire, with von Arnim fantasizing the woman's essence to be art, fantasy, imagination, feeling (as opposed to the drudgery of motherhood and housewifery), and Goethe imagining woman's essence to be beauty, silence, selflessness, feeling (as opposed to the drudgery of fatherhood and public roles). What links them is the narcissistic woman, which is a type of woman men (and women) have fantasized as being the very essence of her, the eternal feminine. They have done so because this type corresponds best to the desires of men, since she represents the lost part of their narcissism,[21] which is the function, of course, that the figure of Christa T. has for the narrator. And she serves that function despite or, more exactly, *because* of the incongruity she exhibits.

For Christa T. appears to occupy the position *consciously;* she plays at one moment Dostoevsky's great criminal roaming the city in secrecy and with great cunning (49, 54), the next moment Sophie La Roche's Fräulein von Sternheim indulging in a feminine orgy of charity (118, 137–38), and then Flaubert's Madame Bovary searching for eternal love and passion (156). In her impersonations, she seems closer to the figure of Wilhelm Meister than to Karoline von Günderode, since Christa T. has the power, the narrator tells us, of *choosing* her role ("Christa T. couldn't say that she hadn't chosen her own role, and she didn't say it," 137).

In her art, however, she resembles Günderode, a broken voice with her slight lisp (6), a (symbolic) speech impediment, uttering here a sound, there a laugh; here a sentence, there a story; here a strophe, there a poem; here a letter, there a dialogue: unreliable, fragmented speech, as with Günderode who published her works under the pseudonym Tian. The masquerade is contained in the image of the woman of letters sitting at the husband's desk during the early morning hours, writing in secret, it seems, about "The Difficulty of Saying 'I,'" for fear perhaps of offending someone, including, significantly, her own sex— the narrator, who watches her undercover (168–69). It is a gesture in which a whole social situation can be read, showing not only how the political is inscribed in the relationship between men and women and the way these are institutionalized in marriage—with woman as both victim and perpetrator of her confinement to the sphere of domestic isolation and narrow social experience—but revealing moreover the social and cultural situation of the female artist as represented in German literature, past, present, and future: the female artist in the past (Makarie, for instance) as the bearer of silence; the female artist in the present as the breaker of silence (Günderode and Christa T. who write clandestinely); and the female artist in the future (the narrator) as the bearer *and* breaker of silence, realizing Christa T.'s "vision of herself" (117), of totality, in her desire to create, to be a poet, *and* her desire to recreate, to be a mother. In the imperfect, however, which is Christa T.'s time, voice and body are "still" dismembered, a vision expressed in the present in the interstices of the inserted fragments of poetry and chatter. The Other is absent, silent, figuring in that silence the classic hysteric who breaks out of a fixed and stable structure of identity by refusing to take her place in language: "Krischan, why don't you write?" (33, 171).

So the narrator does it for her, speaks both for and "as a woman," more precisely, as a *mother* who rigorously inserts the unreliable, the verses and cadences of the poet, into a whole and unified story about the effects of alienation in woman, in art, in aesthetics, a story with a beginning, a middle, and an end, disciplining the fragments into closure of representation. For it is in the rupture, rather: in the *purposeful* submission to the voice of that alien body as well as in the explicit indifference to interruption, that the feminine heritage is enacted here, revealing the cat that the narrator is: the domesticated cat! It is she who is narcissus, projecting onto paper the image of woman, with whose (imagined) intactness she is in love: in love with the mother that she is, in love with the child that she was, in love with the writer she is becoming, and in love with the person who once was part of her own self, her "brain child," Christa T., who is a wholesome form indeed, offered to "us" for love. The language of feeling begs it—pathos: "When should one live, if not in the time that's given to one?" . . . "When, if not now?" (70, 185) Her domestication then is the issue here, domestication that she aims to revise through, paradoxically, mimeticism.

Hence, the "wild" discourse as "an attempt to be oneself," juxtaposing quotation (the strange, the impersonal "one") and commentary (the familiar, the personal "self") in an often abrupt and disorienting manner, intending to formalize the effect of alienation in speaking. But speaking as what? "As a woman"? In the most erotic scene of the text, female desire does indeed "speak." There they are, two women, laughing, giggling, touching, woman in love with woman's body, woman feeling her way to her body, woman getting in touch with her sex (27).[22]

Bliss, momentary in-sight, displaced instantly by the sight that controls the narrative thread: here they are, two women, huddled against the wall under a glaring spotlight (the empirical and fantasized paternal/ maternal stare), divided, silent, mourning ("losing one another and ourselves," 14). It reveals the affect that moves the imagery—fear of feminine self-sufficiency—and the myth that moves the narrative— woman as victim—with the wall functioning as synecdoche to signal the whole, the house, the container, in which the female artist was once entrapped and in which the female artist is now contained *and* protected.

Therefore, the *gynaeceum* as the setting of the novel. It is the (dream-)house that contains *and* protects the nurturing women and that offers the difference of view. What the male artist once perceived (and perhaps till today) to be his conflict, that between vocation and role, and what the female artist once perceived (and perhaps till today) to be hers, that between art and motherhood, is here united to mirror the whole of woman's interior, her two *vocations*, that is, to create poetry (present in the verses and cadences of the other) *and* to recreate humankind by bearing "our" children and loving them (present in the narrator's chatter). This wholeness is evoked aesthetically in the closed form, pragmatically in the various versions of the snapshot, and thematically in the figural constellation of two women who share the "joys and burden of creation," literally, in the moment of motherhood, figuratively, in the moment of writing. The men are nearly always absent or just marginally present, like Justus. On the one hand, this exclusion signals woman's attempt to be "one self," to sound a voice that is in its duplicity distinct and separate from the voice of the male artist, like Wilhelm Meister who cannot speak literally, from the body, and perceives it therefore always as Other.

On the other hand and nevertheless, the exclusion magnifies what is *within*—repression, alienation, and amputation. Fear functions as agent, fear, significantly, of physical violence:

She wakes up in the night, the farmer and his wife are still there . . . the phonograph is playing. I'll dance with you into the skies above. . . . A screech. The farmer's wife has stepped on the tomcat, our good black tomcat, he's gentle and old, but he's hissing at the farmer's wife now . . . silence . . . then the farmer comes out with the tomcat, has grabbed him, cursing and swearing, as he flings him against the stable wall. Now you know how it sounds when bones crack, when something alive a moment ago drops to the ground. (20–21)

The wall and the dead cat again, this time as empirical event. The trauma haunts the narrative; its symptom is the paradoxical structure. Here, in the play with pronouns (she/I/you), the paradox expresses itself directly, for in it gender boundaries are at once transgressed and cemented, experience generalized and specified, history equated with biology: the death of the cat and the death of the child (22) and the death of the baby birds (31) and the death of the toad (109) show acts of absurd and "irrational" cruelty, directed against those who cannot defend themselves, namely women, children, animals, by those who can, namely men. Men, the text argues in the repetition of "male" violence outside a circle of nurturing women, men are strong, active, and violent while women are weak, passive, and nonviolent.[23] Thus, whereas the opposition movement/containment that structures the narcissistic system is presented as a cultural phenomenon, the opposition violence/nonviolence is grounded in sexual metaphysics.

This "lapse" represents next to the revolutionary moment—in the figure of narcissus or the hysteric—the *reactionary* instance of this text and supports my thesis that *The Quest for Christa T.* is a project that defines itself not in terms of undermining the notion of essence or ontology, but in terms of finding an adequate language for woman's Otherness, defined however in a most conventional way. "Female love" (as opposed to desire) is fantasized as the essence of woman, projected as originating in anatomy and, within that logic, as an alternative to "male aggressivity." It means that the problematic epistemology of selfhood, which the philosopher-theorist-reader poses in terms of universals ("how, if at all, and under what circumstances, can one realize oneself in a work of art," 95), is revised by the female artist-practitioner-writer not in terms of woman's difference but in terms of woman's anatomy. Consequently, in affirming the opposition masculine/feminine as a biological phenomenon, her question becomes how she can talk about herself as a woman and say "I" if the "I" secures the father's heritage (violence) and displaces the mother's (love). "She, with whom she associated herself, whom she was careful not to name, for what name could she have given her?" (170)

The name given to her is "Christa T.," abbreviating the father's name and thereby questioning the name as an index of sexual and social identity. "She" is then placed into a *gynaeceum*, a place full of harmony, free of domination and reification. It is the place from which the "one" speaks, in the form of quotation, and from which the "self" speaks, in the form of commentary. It is an "I" then that contains not only the paradigmatic (masculinist) fantasy of a unified subject, but also its negation, enacted in the play with pronouns of the third and first person. What holds the "she" and the "I" together is the conventional figure of Woman-as-Nurturer. It is present as a literal sign, referring to the physical process of lying spread-legged and supine, exposing the locus of the child's generation, the womb. It is present also as a metaphorical sign, identifying the creative act with bearing "brain children": "Feeling pain, longing, something like a second birth. And saying, finally, 'I': I am different" (57, 22). The first birth? The real child:

Her first child was born during this time, and the delivery was difficult. The child was in a bad position. For hours she strained uselessly. Of course it weakened her, but she didn't retreat into the feeling that the pains were an injustice being done to her. She had no sentimentality to spare and couldn't forget that she wanted to have the child and that the strict rhythm of rending strain and relaxation was necessary to produce it. (134)

This description serves well—and is meant to serve, especially in view of the genealogical connection established in the "preface" ("to think her further")—as an index of the narrative's rhythm of quotation and commentary, poetry and chatter, giving birth to the female artist from the spirit of Christa T.

Thus, just as in "male" fiction of past and present centuries, woman's brain is still connected to the womb. The metonymy signifies the recuperation of sexual metaphysics, sub-jecting the artist to the philistine ("She sees the advantage of being a woman," 123) and the hysteric to the mimic (the scenario of the eternal feminine) who lets the other speak only in order to subordinate her speech to the (sexist) narrative of procreation. So the text is dominated by the other figure of consciousness, one that has assumed her place in language and submitted to power and authority because, as Kristeva writes, she identifies with it and wants to take its place ("to think her further").[24] While it can be argued that the centrality of childbearing here aims to revise the convention of the male artist who has used the birth metaphor to legitimize his "brain children" and ascribe female creativity to the womb,[25] it can also be argued that it affirms the paternal metaphor because it links the woman of letters to the mother of children. The female artist writes from the body, so argues the text in its metaphors and metonymies, from the rifts and pains of childbearing (in the dual sense). It is her (metaphysical, not social) "fate" as an artist, in fact the origin of her speech, which is "female" precisely because of its (tragic) division between biological and intellectual energies, a no-win situation: "She wanted to unite that which cannot be united: to be loved by a man and to produce a work that can be measured against absolute standards," writes Christa Wolf about the woman artist Karoline von Günderode.[26]

And how does Christa T. experience the collapse of her alternatives? As a collapse of her vital system, literally. Symptomatic is her illness, leukemia, a disease of the blood where an overproduction of white (light = reason) blood cells kills the red (dark = vitality) blood cells. In the final analysis then, being a female artist is shown once again as self-sacrifice to woman, a plot that repeats what is (or ought to be) familiar not only from fiction written by men, but particularly by women, harking back to the literary convention of the nineteenth-century woman writer's *Bildungsroman* and forward to popular culture of the twentieth century, "women's magazines," for instance, where female artists are nearly uniformly represented with a book under one arm and a child under the other.[27] The strife between the two "selves"—or between sexuality and morality—is resolved by the mimic in favor of womanhood, of "life" (185, 69–77), of motherhood. The novel rewrites therefore the auto/biography of a female artist in the name of a certain ethic, with the narrator functioning as some sort of archaic mother, one yet with fatherly attributes, wanting to lead "her self" (and analogously her reader) down the redemptive path of object-love: the path of pregnancy. The nursery functions as a room of her own, which represents the vision (or delusion) of a society without contradictions, the feminine world, the *gynaeceum,* with women as nurturers and men as (hidden) protectors.[28]

This wishful vision explains why the female figure is erected as an object of the paternal/maternal gaze, as an organizing spectacle, an absence that structures the symbolic order here and sustains "our glances." Aesthetics is subjected to ethics, the erotic to morality, breaking the "spell of subjectivism" that the official propaganda of her country commands (67). But the motive is not just historical. It is also psychological, in that Christa T., the narrator's double, defines the other figure of consciousness, the "real," that "character" that has fully relinquished narcissism and is in quest of object-love. The "female model of love" (Freud), narcissistic "immoral" love, is displaced onto the "parental model" which is, as Freud reminds us, the most moral love of all. For it sacrifices the desire to be loved for the need to love, placing in the (absent) center *"His Majesty the Baby"* (Freud), a figure that functions as a substitution for the fantasy long lost. The child, therefore, is to become what the father is not, a "great man and a hero," or what the mother is not, a princess to a "prince." It serves as a substitution for the unfulfilled wishes and dreams of the parents. "Parental [childish] love," Freud concludes, "is nothing but the parents' narcissism born again, which, transformed into object-love, unmistakably reveals its former nature."[29]

A "Majestic Baby" is this (brain) child, Christa T., indeed. "She was all there," the narrator jubilates (174), lived "according to the laws of her own being" (170), produced, pell-mell, children and art, which, put together in the present, make her intact, unique, perfect, "most valiant"

(73), without "sentimentality to spare" (134), a woman of genius, without deficiencies, including "childish sexuality," to use Freud's phrase (*kindliche Sexualität*). Considered in this context, narcissism appears a perversion indeed.

Conversely, misery is idealized: "But how does one cut oneself away from oneself?" (27). Through *will,* sheer will: "Now she would have to answer the question: what are you going to be? She would have to say: I want [*Ich will*] to get up early every morning, first to look after the child and then see to breakfast for Justus and me" (137). This is life in the subjunctive, but "life" nevertheless. Its opposite, death, is caused by blindness to the needs of the other—the death of the cat(s): "That's what happens when you're not being attentive" (21). This somewhat Jesuitic morality reveals the mimic's blind spot, that is, history and (internalized) structures of power. Accordingly, narcissism is substituted by an ideal ego erected in herself and enabling her to reject the shadow, her own double, "as if possessed, plays out the shadow figures and *overcomes* to some extent what has brought him to the brink of destruction or self-destruction in the 'real' world."[30] Major uncertainties are thereby explained away, particularly woman's essentially unpeaceful nature, which is domesticated over again in the representation of femininity through motherhood.

Left for us to view is the image of the "Great Mother"—*protective* ("Worst of all, the fly circling the lamp every morning when you awake. Your mother can chase it away. To forget," 135), *creative* ("She cut blue fishes and yellow flowers out of colored paper and pasted them like an ornamental frame around the margins of the white paper; she painted big clear letters," 140), *sacrificing* ("as any mother would she quells the child's sense of strangeness by hugging Anna; but she doesn't have the illusion that she's hugging a part of herself. She lets the child go, and lets herself be looked at," 145), and *nurturing* ("She only cried when the doctor placed the child on her breast, when she called it by name: Anna," 134).[31]

But why link motherhood to biology? Why insist on a semantic identity between form and content, woman and tenderness ("Does one remember tenderness? Is it tenderness the child still knows today when it hears the words 'your mother'?" 134)? Why link it to anatomy, to a substance, rather than to a function that men can perform as well? And is the multiplicity not really a singularity since it is absurd to identify female sexuality with woman's reproductive function?

One reason for the reduction is psychological. The world has to have a center, since a centerless world is unthinkable, impossible to live. But the "old" center, the Father whose substance is violence, needs to be substituted by the Mother whose substance is love. "She" now stands high in the center and provides the single principle of coherence, one that controls the play with forms (child, artist, mother, wife, lover, etc.). Its opposite, plurality of meaning and plurality of the subject, caused by the absence of that transcendental signified (Love, in the sense of the Christian *Agape*), leads to chaos, violence, the apocalypse. Longing for presence—or "the inability to tolerate chaos," as Nietzsche would say—motivates the act of mastering heterogeneity, the uncanny, of collapsing instability into stability. The enigma of Christa T., that violent "wild" subject-in-process, flickering between pronouns, between the veils and cadences of the other and the showing and telling of the "self," is cemented into a Monument-of-the-Ideal-Woman, the Great Mother, whose condition is repression and whose mechanism is displacement. "Writing means making things large" (168). Indeed, but at the price of reducing the subject to nothing.

The other reason is historical. It is significant that narrated time begins under fascism (chapters 1 and 2) where the social, political, and cultural discourses aim at reducing woman to her sexual and reproductive function, conceiving her as nurturer (of man) and man as her protector and exaggerating thereby the division between the sexes. It leads/led, paradoxically, to belligerence and militarism.[32] Narrated time ends, equally significant, under socialism where political, social, and cultural discourses aim at securing woman's public function—as worker, writer, theorist, politician—while simultaneously assigning to her once again the essential quality of the nurturer of children and men.

The mimic repeats and affirms that ideology by adapting and obeying the moral rule of her condition without compromising about the dogma on which it rests.[33] That "gigantic" third eye is indeed present then, seeing the eye that watches her (us) whenever she (we) acts as moral subject and views the world in terms of morality. But does this mean that the little morality play staged in the *gynaeceum* is offered to us for criticism?

No, it is offered to us for adherence. The novel's structure serves as evidence, as does Christa Wolf's entire oeuvre in which female figures are if not already mothers, then at least always already married. Women in Wolf's works are shown without exception in their relationship to men, including in this novel, where the men are practically nowhere and therefore everywhere, like the sky, an authority that at once determines and limits the woman's condition, outside as well as inside.[34]

The novel's point of view also serves as evidence, as it is characterized by a propensity toward caricature, beginning with the moving snapshot of the lady on the beach and the meaning it takes on in the various contexts. Woman is presented there and here as almost eternally pregnant, literally, as being with child, and figuratively, as being with brain child. In the centrality of childbearing, which orders the images and sustains the narrative thread, woman's distinctive feature, the womb, is exaggerated to the point of being ridiculous. Perhaps that is the "real" significance of the red and white ball that in the three versions of the beach scene grows steadily from "big" to "huge" to "gigantic," pointing to the mother's womb as seen from below. The propensity toward caricature signifies what Elisabeth Lenk has called "pariah consciousness," that is, woman perceiving herself as an inferior being to man.[35]

Like the mimic here, a batlike soul, rather than a great cat, as her uncanny double, a soul yet waking to the consciousness of itself, but in darkness and secrecy and loneliness, tarrying a while, loveless and sinless.

Notes

1. For the comparison of woman to cat, see Friedrich Nietzsche, *Beyond Good and Evil*, trans. W. Kaufmann (New York: Random House, 1966), pp. 87 and 169, and *Nachgelassene Fragmente 1, Werke,* ed. G. Colli and M. Montinari, pt. 7, vol. 1 (Berlin: Walter de Gruyter, 1977) sec. 1[30], p. 12; also Sigmund Freud, "On Narcissism: An Introduction," *The Standard Edition of the Complete Psychological Works of Sigmund Freud,* trans. J. Strachey (London: Hogarth Press, 1957), vol. 14, pp. 73–102. Compare the German original "Zur Einführung des Narzissmus," *Freud–Studienausgabe* (Frankfurt am Main: Fischer, 1975), vol. 3, pp. 37–68. Subsequent references are to the English translation, cited parenthetically in the text; the translations have been modified in places where the English text reduces, in my view, the complexity of Freud's text. The following discussion of Freud's essay is indebted to Sarah Kofman, "The Narcissistic Woman: Freud and Girard," *diacritics* (September 1980), 36–45. See also Sarah Kofman, *Autobiogriffures: Du chat Murr d'Hoffmann* (Paris: Christian Bourgeois, 1976), pp. 36–37.

2. Christa Wolf, "Neue Lebensansichten eines Katers," *Gesammelte Erzählungen* (Darmstadt/Neuwied: Luchterhand, 1981), p. 98 (my translation). I am aware that Wolf's tale aims to satirize from a contemporary perspective her (socialist) society's philistinism in its view of the artist, just as E. T. A. Hoffmann did in the figure of the cat Murr and its view of the (Romantic) artist Kreisler in *Lebensansichten des Katers Murr* (1820/1822), a novel to which Wolf explicitly alludes. What escapes her is the philistinism in the cat's view of woman, as I shall argue in the following.

3. Christa Wolf, *The Quest for Christa T.,* trans. Christopher Middleton (New York: Farrar, Straus & Giroux, 1970), p. 150, originally in German *Nachdenken über Christa T.* (Halle: Mitteldeutscher Verlag, 1968). Subsequent references are to the English translation, cited parenthetically in the text. I have altered Middleton's punctuation and retained the original, since it captures Wolf's peculiar habit of constructing what we call run-on sentences which function for Wolf as an approximation of written speech to oral communication. Important for my argument is Wolf's use of the adjective *geschmeidig*

which in German applies to people's bodily movements only in reference to women: "Sie ist geschmeidig wie eine Katze" (see Duden's and Grimm's dictionaries).

4. A note on terminology: "female figure" and "female artist" refer only to the fictional characters; "woman writer" refers to the person who invented the narrative.

5. Freud (see note 1). Kofman sees a connection between Freud's story of woman's sexuality in society and culture here (1914) and his being "particularly taken" at the time with Lou Andreas-Salomé (Kofman 36). For a most exhaustive interpretation of the Freud-Salomé relationship see Biddy Martin, *Representing Woman: The (Life)Styles of Lou Andreas-Salomé* (Ithaca, N.Y.: Cornell University Press, 1991), pp. 267–320.

6. See my headnote which quotes Wolf's headnote to her novel about the poet(s) von Günderode (and Heinrich von Kleist), *No Place on Earth,* trans. Jan van Heurck (New York: Farrar, Straus & Giroux, 1982), originally in German *Kein Ort. Nirgends* (Berlin/Weimar: Aufbau, 1979).

7. English, *to reflect,* a verb that unites sight and reflection, (historical) object and (critical) subject, spatiality and temporality, as well as the limit and the infinite, since it means both to ponder something, someone, in order to know and understand, and to reflect, from the Latin *reflectere,* to bend back, to become mirrored. Compare the myth of Narcissus where we are confronted with a love for an object which is a mirage (Ovid, *Metamorphoses, III*). Useful for my discussion of the function of the myth in Wolf's novel is Jacques Lacan's "The Mirror Stage as Formative of the Function of the I," in *Écrits,* trans. Alan Sheridan (New York: Norton, 1977), pp. 1–7, and more important Julia Kristeva's "Narcissus: The New Insanity," where she points out that "Narcissus after all is guilty of being unaware of himself as source of the reflection" because "he, in fact, does not know who he is"; in *Tales of Love,* trans. Leon S. Roudiez (New York: Columbia University Press, 1987), pp. 103–21. Similarly, the narrator in Wolf's novel, who turns sight into origin without her knowing it.

8. For example: "Da mag sie schon monatelang in unserer Klasse gewesen sein. Da kannte ich ihre langen Glieder," and so on. See also Inta Ezergailis, *Women Writers: The Divided Self* (Bonn: Bouvier, 1982), pp. 66–67, 93–116, who reads this syntax as a refusal to superimpose an air of certainty or closure on the unfinished and uncertain life of her friend (67). I agree only partly with Ezergailis and fully instead with Adorno who argues that parataxis functions to express relations of power which include, by definition, both the role of the adversary and the aid (see my argument about the narrator's double role of hysteric and mimic); Theodor W. Adorno, "Parataxis," *Noten zur Literatur III* (Frankfurt am Main: Suhrkamp, 1973), pp. 156–209.

9. About this paradox of women's writing, see especially Mary Jacobus, "The Difference of View," *Reading Woman* (Ithaca, N.Y.: Cornell University Press, 1986), pp. 27–40. Regarding the coupling hysteric-mimic, see Julia Kristeva, "Die Produktivität der Frau," *Alternative* 19 (1976), 166–72; also "Narcissus" where Kristeva argues that the "feminine facet of [ideal] love is perhaps the most subtle sublimation of the secret, psychotic ground of hysteria" (*Tales* 112–13); also relevant is Kristeva's essay "Woman's Time," trans. Alice Jardine and Harry Blake, *Signs* 7.1 (1981), 5–35.

10. I consider the following the most incisive treatments of the novel— from a historicist perspective, Heinrich Mohr, "Produktive Sehnsucht. Struktur, Thematik und politische Relevanz von Christa Wolfs *Nachdenken über*

Christa T.," Basis 2 (1971), 191–233; Christa Thomassen, *Der lange Weg zu uns selbst. Christa Wolfs Roman "Nachdenken über Christa T." als Erfahrungs– und Handlungsmuster* (Kronberg: Scriptor, 1977). From a philosophical perspective, Andreas Huyssen, "Auf den Spuren Ernst Blochs. *Nachdenken über Christa Wolf," Basis* 5 (1975), 100–16; Ortrud Gutjahr, "'Erinnerte Zukunft'—Gedächtniskonstruktion und Subjektkonstitution im Werk Christa Wolfs," *Erinnerte Zukunft,* ed. Wolfram Mauser (Würzburg: Königshausen & Neumann, 1985), pp. 53–80; Wolfram Mauser, "'Gezeichnet zeichnend'—Tod und Verwandlung im Werk Christa Wolfs," *Erinnerte Zukunft,* pp. 181–205. From a psychoanalytic perspective, Bernhard Greiner, "Die Schwierigheit, 'ich' zu sagen: Christa Wolfs psychologische Orientierung des Erzählens," *Deutsche Vierteljahrsschrift* 55.2 (1981), 323–42; Sylvia Schmitz-Burgard, "Psychoanalyse eines Mythos: *Nachdenken über Christa T.," Monatshefte* 79.4 (1987), 463–77. From a poetological perspective, Wolfram and Helmtrud Mauser, *Christa Wolf: Nachdenken über Christa T.* (Munich: Fink, 1987); Ester Kleinbord Labovitz, *The Myth of the Heroine: The Female* Bildungsroman *in the Twentieth Century* (New York: Peter Lang, 1986), pp. 201–43. From a feminist (cultural theory and social history) perspective, Jeanette Clausen, "The Difficulty of Saying 'I' as Theme and Narrative Technique in the Works of Christa Wolf," *Amsterdamer Beiträge zur Neueren Germanistik* 10 (1979), 319–33; Elizabeth Abel, "(E)Merging Identities: The Dynamics of Female Friendship in Contemporary Fiction by Women," *Signs* 6.3 (1981), 413–35; Inta Ezergailis (see note 8); Sara Lennox, "'Der Versuch, man selbst zu sein': Christa Wolf und der Feminismus," in *Die Frau als Heldin und Autorin: Neue kritische Ansätze zur deutschen Literatur,* ed. Wolfgang Paulsen (Bern: Francke, 1979), pp. 217–22; Anna K. Kuhn, *Christa Wolf's Utopian Vision: From Marxism to Feminism* (New York and London: Cambridge University Press, 1988); Anne Herrmann, "The Elegiac Novel," in *The Dialogic and Difference* (New York: Columbia University Press, 1989), pp. 62–89. For a good selection of essays in English on Wolf, see *Responses to Christa Wolf,* ed. Marilyn Sibley Fries (Detroit: Wayne State University Press, 1989). The study that I find the most provocative and therefore the most influential on my work is Myra Love, "Christa Wolf and Feminism: Breaking the Patriarchal Connection," *New German Critique* 16 (1979), 31–53. Yet while I agree with Love that Wolf's novel breaks down the "patriarchal system" of dichotomous and mutually exclusive opposites, with the male as center over and against a female other, I disagree that that scenario contains the whole story and argue instead that besides the deconstructive the novel contains a *reconstructive* moment, with the female as center over and against a male other, which is of course a farce. Love ignores the process of signification, of ideological trickery, that is, the narrator as the bearer of accepted opinion. Moreover, to postulate that "female subjectivity" (Love's key category) is defined by intersubjectivity and non-reification and "male subjectivity" by self-reflection and reification repeats in its reference to biology ("female"/"male") the kind of dichotomous thinking Love aims to revise.

11. I do not mean to say that Wolf is not reflecting upon patriarchy, indeed she uses the term ten years later in her introduction to Maxie Wander's *Guten Morgen, du Schöne* (1975), a collection of interviews with women in the GDR, and again, still more polemically, in her lectures on poetics at the University of Frankfurt in 1982, which appeared in English under the title "Conditions of a Narrative: Cassandra" and were appended to Wolf's novel *Cassandra,* trans. Jan van Heurck (New York: Farrar, Straus & Giroux, 1984), pp. 141–305. But Wolf

never concerns herself with the question of the relation between gender and writing or, more precisely, with the question of what language actually *is*, how it functions in constituting subjectivity, and, moreover, what the relationship is between subjectivity (including "female") and power. (And power as a *discursive*—and not just as an economic—phenomenon was already a category in postwar German culture, West as well as East, not in Lukács's writing, to be sure, but indeed in Brecht's, for instance, whose works are, as Wolf herself tells it in her essay on Brecht, part of the literary canon in schools and universities.) Thus, in the name of—ironically—the bourgeois liberal notion of a split but harmonized unitary subject ("das Subjektwerden des Menschen—von Mann und Frau," see Wolf's essay to Wander), Wolf evades the consequences of her earlier theoretical (and radical) argument that "I without books am not I" in "The Reader and the Writer" (1968), *The Reader and the Writer: Essays, Sketches, Memories*, trans. Joan Becker (Berlin/GDR: Seven Seas Publishers, 1977), pp. 177–212. See also her essays on Karoline von Günderode and Bettine von Arnim which reveal the same blind spot(s), in Wolf, *Die Dimension des Autors* (Darmstadt/Neuwied: Luchterhand, 1987), pp. 511–610, as well as the series of interviews published as "Documentation: Christa Wolf," *German Quarterly* 57.1 (1984), 91–115. A good essay (in English) on the status of feminist discourse in the East-German academy and society is Chris Weedon's "Introduction" to her anthology *Die Frau in der DDR* (Oxford and New York: Basil Blackwell, 1988).

12. Virginia Woolf, *A Room of One's Own* (New York and London: Harcourt, Brace & World, 1957), p. 3.

13. Terry Eagleton writes that much of classical Marxist thought "was clearly incapable of explaining the particular conditions of women as an oppressed social group, or of contributing significantly to their transformation" because of its narrowly economic focus or the concomitant ignorance vis-à-vis the question of "sexual ideology, of the ways men and women image themselves and each other in male-dominated society, of perceptions and behaviour which range from the brutally explicit to the deeply unconscious." *Literary Theory: An Introduction* (Minneapolis: University of Minnesota Press, 1983), pp. 148–49). Is that Wolf's legacy, especially since she insists throughout her writing on equating patriarchy with capitalism ("Klassengesellschaft, das Patriarchat," see the essay on Maxie Wander and the lectures on poetics, as well as "Documentation," note 11)? It certainly is the legacy of her critics (see note 10) in East- as well as West-Germany (and the United States) whose writing on Wolf can be linked by the refusal to pose the question of the *effect* of sexual ideology in works by *women*, in this case, works by Wolf. (The question is usually reserved for writing by men).

14. I have altered slightly Middleton's translation and replaced "smile" by "laughter" since the original reads *Lachen* (and not *Lächeln*), a sound rising from the body, while "smile" refers to soundless "laughter," which makes no sense considering the narrator's fascination with that (apparently) uncanny sound.

15. See Friedrich Nietzsche's Aphorism 509 of *Morgenröte* and *Zur Genealogie der Moral*. I am indebted for this discussion to Rainer Nägele's lecture "Theatrical Speculation on Marat/Sade," MLA Convention, Chicago, December 28, 1985.

16. Not only does the narrator's "preface" invoke the birth metaphor, but within the total narrative the female figure is instantly associated with mother-

hood (and death, of course), as in the opening pages: "Then she began to blow, or to shout, there's no proper word for it. It was this I reminded her of, or wanted to, in my last letter, but she wasn't reading any more letters, she was dying. She was always tall, and thin, until the last years, after she'd had the children. So there she was, walking along in front, stalking head-in-air along the curb" (9).

17. Michel Foucault, *Discipline and Punish*, trans. Alan Sheridan (New York: Pantheon Books, 1977). Useful in this context is Wolf's essay of the same year as the novel, "The Reader and the Writer" (1968), which subscribes to a "poetics of the eye," that is, to the classical doctrine of art as mimesis; also in her lectures on poetics, especially pp. 272–305.

18. What I do *not* mean by the term is the *woman* author or some sort of "female" or "feminine" essence, or a "split subject" or a centered, unified subject as such, traditionally fantasized as "male," recently as "female." What I do mean by the term is a peculiar place of a thinking, acting, or writing subject, one that *refuses* a "human" or "female" nature by weaving together heterogeneity and contradiction, without wanting to dissolve them; that is, by a speaking subject (of a text) that repeatedly shifts its position vis-à-vis (gendered) experience and (gendered) discourse. Its object is *not* an identifiable object—neither the "total woman" nor the "total man"—but representation itself, fantasy, a psychic space, at once structured *and* heterogeneous. A (potential) example is Christa T.'s fragmented writing, organized around the *moment*, it seems, and, as one body, radically theatrical as well as perspectivist, reflecting perhaps the heterogeneity of subjectivity—prior, of course, to the intervention of the narrator and the obsession with truth and identity, with ordering, administering, classifying, categorizing, interpreting, and so on.

19. See pp. 4, 5, 6, 26, 117, and 169.

20. German *umherstreunen* refers to roaming animals, particularly to cats and dogs.

21. See Kofman, "The Narcissistic Woman," p. 39, and Freud, "On Narcissism," pp. 89–91.

22. On the demystification of female homosexuality, see Luce Irigaray, "This Sex Which Is Not One" (1977), in *This Sex Which Is Not One*, trans. Catherine Porter (Ithaca, N.Y.: Cornell University Press, 1983). Relevant to the image of giggling women in opposition to belligerent men is Jean-François Lyotard's "Something at Stake in the Women's Struggle," *sub-stance* 20 (1977), 9–17. Important in this connection is Wolf's brief "Interview with Myself" (1966), *The Reader and the Writer*, trans. Joan Becker (Berlin: Seven Seas Publishers, 1977), pp. 76–80.

23. See Wolf's lectures on poetics (note 11) where she consistently identifies aggressivity with "maleness" (e.g., pp. 153, 159, and 173); the double equation structures most of her work, up to her latest piece *Accident/A Day's News*, trans. Heike Schwarzbauer and Rick Takvorian (New York: Farrar, Straus & Giroux, 1989), originally in German, *Störfall. Nachrichten eines Tages* (Berlin and Weimar: Aufbau-Verlag, 1987).

24. Kristeva, "Produktivität," p. 168; compare Kristeva's discussion of "*love* and the exclusion of the impure" (*Tales* 109–113). See also Kofman who writes that if Freud "can in the course of his inquiry transform woman into a hysteric by rejecting all speculation and by appealing, as he says, only to the observed facts, it is because most women, throughout the course of history, have in fact been the accomplices of men. Do most mothers not seek above all

to turn their sons into heroes and great men and to be parties to their crimes, even at the risk of death?" (Kofman, "The Narcissistic Woman," 45). For a critique of (Wolf's) Hegelian speculative dialectic, see Jacques Derrida and Christie V. McDonald, "Choreographies" (Interview), *diacritics* 12 (1982), 66–76.

25. See Susan Gubar, "The Birth of the Artist as Heroine: (Re)production, the *Künstlerroman* Tradition, and the Fiction of Katherine Mansfield," in *The Representation of Women in Fiction*, ed. Carolyn G. Heilbrun and Margaret R. Higonnet (Baltimore: Johns Hopkins University Press, 1983), pp. 19–59. For a different view on nineteenth- and early twentieth-century women novelists and on the metonymy brain-womb, see Ann Ardis's essay in this volume, "'Retreat with Honour.'"

26. Christa Wolf, "Der Schatten eines Traumes. Karoline von Günderode—ein Entwurf" (1978); my translation. *Lesen und Schreiben. Neue Sammlung* (Darmstadt/Neuwied: Luchterhand, 1980), p. 242.

27. See Rachel Blau DuPlessis, "To 'bear my mother's name': *Künstlerromane* by Women Writers," in *Writing Beyond the Ending: Narrative Strategies of Twentieth-Century Women Writers* (Bloomington: Indiana University Press, 1985), pp. 84–104. Regarding popular culture, see especially the East-German "women's magazine" *Für Dich* and the West-German feminist magazine *Emma*. Relevant to this discussion is Irene Dölling's study, "Continuity and Change in the Media Image of Women: A Look at Illustrations in GDR Periodicals," *Studies in GDR Culture and Society 9* (Lanham and London: University Press of America, 1989), pp. 131–43. Compare Roland Barthes' incisive analysis of the French weekly *Elle* in *Mythologies* (New York: Hill and Wang, 1972), pp. 50–52.

28. Wolf's Büchner-Prize Acceptance Speech (1980) and its discussion of Georg Büchner's female figures (Rosetta, Marie, Marion, Julie, Lucile, and Lena) is relevant here, since Wolf refers to them exclusively in terms of their status as victims, ignoring the difference in social class that *also* characterizes them—"Unprotected on the perimeter," yet "unprotected" from what? ("'Shall I Garnish a Metaphor with an Almond Blossom?'" *New German Critique* 23 [1981], 6). For an (implicit) critique of the discourse of homologization, see Virginia Woolf, "Professions for Women" (1931), *Women and Writing*, ed. Michele Barrett (New York: Harcourt Brace Jovanovich, 1979), pp. 57–63. Also Mary Jacobus, "Review of *The Madwoman in the Attic*," *Signs* 6.3 (1981), 517–23.

29. Freud, "On Narcissism," p. 91.

30. *The Reader and the Writer*, p. 206 (my translation and emphasis); woven into this view are the cultural politics of the GDR—of Western industrial nations in general?—which emphasize not only the *perverse* aspect of the Narcissus myth, but its *morbidity* (which conflicts with the privileging of such values as normalcy, health, and sanity).

31. I have altered Middleton's translation slightly to conform to the original in its explicit reference to woman's body (*ihr das Kind auf die Brust legte*).

32. See Virginia Woolf, *Three Guineas* (1938), and Klaus Theweleit, *Male Fantasies*, trans. Stephen Convay (Minneapolis: University of Minnesota Press, 1987), a fascinating study of the misogynist attitudes of a group of military men, the German *Freikorps*. Compare to that Wolf's epistolary essay "Come! Into the Open, Friend!," trans. Maria Gilarden and Myra Love, *Connexions: An International Women's Quarterly* 13 (summer 1984), 12–14.

33. See Barthes, *Mythologies*, pp. 50–52.

34. The exceptions are Rita Seidel, the central figure of Wolf's novel *The Divided Heaven,* who leaves her lover in West-Berlin to return home and to work with her (surrogate) father, Metanagel, and Karoline von Günderode, the female artist figure in *No Place on Earth,* who is also a historical person, the poet of German romanticism, who committed suicide, because of an unhappy love affair—or so we are told by literary historians and, significantly, by Wolf herself in her essay on Günderode in *Lesen und Schreiben.*

35. Elisabeth Lenk, "Indiscretions of the Literary Beast: Pariah Consciousness of Women Writers Since Romanticism" (1981), trans. Maureen Krause, *New German Critique* 27 (1982), 101–14.

Part IV
Rethinking the Politics of Art

Chapter 13
"Sisters in Arms": The Warrior Construct in Writings by Contemporary U.S. Women of Color

Mary K. DeShazer

Introduction: Loosing Words of Fire

> The women say they have learned to rely on their own strength. They say they are aware of the force of their unity. They say, let those who call for a new language first learn violence. They say, let those who want to change the world first seize all the rifles. They say that they are starting from zero. They say that a new world is beginning.
>
> Monique Wittig, *Les Guérillères*

> We are Black people living in a time when the consciousness of our intended slaughter is all around us. People of Color are increasingly expendable, our government's policy both here and abroad. We are functioning under a government ready to repeat in El Salvador and Nicaragua the tragedy of Vietnam, a government which stands on the wrong side of every single battle for liberation taking place upon this globe. . . . Can anyone here still afford to believe that efforts to reclaim the future can be private or individual? Can anyone here still afford to believe that the pursuit of liberation can be the sole and particular province of any one particular race, or sex, or age, or religion, or sexuality, or class?
>
> Audre Lorde, *Sister Outsider*[1]

Although Wittig's epic celebration of women warriors eradicating male oppressors differs generically from Lorde's impassioned speech to the Black American left, the two writers share certain radical themes and goals. Both address the politics of oppression, decrying injustice and urging strong, immediate action in global battles for freedom. Both believe in unity as the guiding spirit of such action, in communal resistance as the strongest force and greatest resource for making fundamental change. And both dare to imagine, in feminist terms, the raw, exciting possibility of a truly liberated world.

Their intended audiences, liberatory tactics, and rhetorical strategies differ significantly, however. Wittig creates a woman-centered utopia of rebellion and revenge, a fantastical landscape populated by "the women"—raging furies fully armed, handily eliminating patriarchal adversaries. Her warriors resort to conventional military language and methods: they learn violence, seize all the guns, start from zero. Rhetorically, Wittig uses repetition aggressively to dramatize the authoritative power of women's voices raised collectively: "the women say . . . they say . . . they say . . . they say." Lorde, in contrast, writes to and for people of color—women and children in particular, but men as well—though certainly her final question raises the hope that individuals of all colors, classes, and so on will work together to combat oppression. Further, she decries militarization (as reflected in the U.S. government's imperialistic policies) rather than embracing it, for "the Master's tools will never dismantle the master's house."[2] Like Wittig she relies on repetition to strengthen her audience's resolve, but her repetition reverberates as a troubling rhetorical question: "can anyone here still afford to believe . . . ?" For Wittig, a white radical feminist, and her idealized revolutionaries, the tough decisions have apparently been made: violence is being met with violence, women are destroying men. For Lorde as a woman of color and for the real-life revolutionaries she addresses, the painful question of who unites with whom to wage what kind of battle is still very much in process.

The passage from Wittig illustrates what Teresa de Lauretis labels a "rhetoric of violence": it posits as utopian feminist strategy a totalizing patriarchal model for attacking and defeating "the women's" enemies, presumably men of any and all colors and classes. Lorde's statement critiques violent patriarchal rhetoric and practice and confronts that "othering" which deLauretis describes as "the violence of rhetoric," here depicted by the U.S. government's purposeful acts of erasure against those whose race, gender, sexuality, or class make them marginal and therefore disposable.[3] Lorde's rhetoric calls for collective resistance against the state rather than violence against "the men"; her political consciousness "stems from an awareness that the public is *personally* political." Chicana feminist theorist Aída Hurtado further clarifies strategic differences in political praxis of white women and women of color: "The political skills of feminists of color are neither the conventional political skills of white liberal feminists nor the free-spirited approaches of white radical feminists. Instead, feminists of color train to be urban guerrillas by doing battle every day with the apparatus of the state."[4] For Wittig's fictionalized women, rebellion takes an apocalyptic form; for Lorde's people of color, resistance occurs as sustained acts of daily confrontation, part of what Black sociologist Patricia Hill Collins has called "a self-defined standpoint on their own oppression."[5]

White political theorist Jean Bethke Elshtain has critiqued Wittig (along with Mary Daly, Susan Griffin, and other "hard-line feminist realists") for creating a "Manichean narrative" of oppressor/oppressed that "reiterates rather than deconstructs a patriarchal model of armed civic virtue"—a model that reinforces the "congealed typifications" she finds prevalent in both feminist and antifeminist writing about women, men, and war.[6] Although I do not completely agree with her argument, Elshtain's assessment of the dangers feminists may encounter in writing on women and violence raises some thorny questions. How can/should feminists claim a warrior identity if/when our goal is to eliminate oppression, injustice, and ultimately war itself? If we do claim such an identity, how can we avoid essentializing (men = Evil Enemies, women = Just Warriors) and instead problematize this construct, thereby increasing its accuracy and effectiveness? And might women of color, in particular, offer a distinctive re-vision of warriors and warring—of the rhetoric of violence and the violence of rhetoric—from which white feminists can/should learn?

In examining the warrior construct in writings by U.S. women of color, I am aware of the importance of identifying the place(s) from which I speak. I speak as a white southern academic feminist from a working-class background, a positionality that necessarily problematizes the lens through which I conduct my examination. I am reminded of de Lauretis's ironic act of quadruple dialectical displacement in which she offers a complex, subversive, and strategic reading of Spivak reading Derrida reading Nietzsche.[7] My own theoretical position and process are not subversive but feel to me equally complicated, as I struggle as a white U.S. feminist to understand and articulate, for example, Black feminist Audre Lorde's reading of her South African sister's reading of her daughter's violent death and the South African government's treachery. Such an effort demands of me a vigilant attention to the limitations, privileges, and constant shiftings of the place(s) from which I speak.

The dilemmas about essentialism, dichotomous thinking, and

complex positionalities suggested by Elshtain's critique and my questions and comments are further illustrated by Mary Daly's treatment of warriors in her *Wickedary,* purportedly a radical feminist "metadictionary." Here she defines *necrophilia* as "the most fundamental characteristic and first principle of patriarchy: hatred for and envy of Life." The Necrophilic State, she argues, is upheld by rape, genocide, and war, "the logical expression of phallocentric power." In contrast to these violent manifestations of phallic lust, she presents a woman-centered *biophilia:* "the original Lust for Life that is at the core of all Elemental E-motion; Pure Lust, which is the Nemesis of patriarchy."[8] Although Daly presumably means to include all radical women in her croneological vision of Hags and Witches weaving a new language on the boundaries of patriarchal space, she sometimes oversimplifies and/or essentializes: dystopian patriarchal terrain is countered by utopian, Amazonian borderlands. While most feminists would acknowledge that patriarchal space is malignant, we might not agree on whether some or all men inhabit it. Elizabeth V. Spelman criticizes Daly for "white solipsism" in relying on an "additive analysis" that argues that sexism is the root and paradigm of other forms of oppression, while racism is "a deformity within patriarchy." Since women of color experience racism and sexism simultaneously, Spelman concludes, Daly implicitly asks women of color to compartmentalize their struggles.[9] Furthermore, women-controlled borderlands are more ambiguous territories than Daly suggests. As Gloria Anzaldúa explains, for Chicana/*tejana* feminists, borderlands are places of contradiction where "keeping intact one's shifting and multiple identity and integrity is like trying to swim in a new element, an 'alien' element."[10] Since Daly does not identify explicitly what kinds of Crones inhabit her boundaries— that is, she does not acknowledge fully the importance of differences among women—we must wonder: where in her borderspace do women of color live? Doubly displaced by institutionalized racism as well as sexism, women of color have traditionally been marginalized, whether on the boundaries of the borderlands or in the institutions of the heartlands. There they have often had to fight not only white patriarchs but some white women and men of color as well—to proclaim their centrality in any struggle for liberation, indeed to assert their very presence. There they have become warriors, raging against their own invisibility.

Nowhere in the *Wickedary* does Daly gloss the word *warrior,* however, perhaps because she recognizes its complexity. At first glance it seems necrophilic, an "anti-biotic" metaphor identified with self-justifying patriarchal rhetoric. Some men love war, Vietnam veteran William Broyles informs readers of *Esquire,* because it allows them to intuit the intimate connection between "sex and destruction, beauty and horror, love and death."[11] Given this sort of masculinist reasoning, many feminists have viewed with ambivalence or rejected outright the term *warrior*—as creative identity and/or theoretical construct. Furthermore, many Third-World women realistically fear that naming themselves warriors will make them more vulnerable to dictators and torturers in their countries. Hence, the editor's disclaimer in a recent "Woman as Warrior" issue of *woman of power:*

Throughout this issue, the word warrior is used as a metaphor. It is not intended to mean that the women profiled or pictured are involved in military activity of any kind, or in the bearing or transporting of arms, or in armed resistance, insurrection or attempts to overthrow any government. This material should not be understood to mean such things or used against these women for purposes of persecution, interrogation, incarceration or further oppression.[12]

Yet many women of color do claim a warrior identity, especially in their poetry—an identity re-visioned not as a necrophilic zest for destruction but as an ongoing commitment to radical change. Toni Cade Bambara, for example, calls herself and other writers of color "creative combatants." Cherríe Moraga wars with her words, "to clarify my resistance to the literate." June Jordan declares herself "a woman searching for my savagery / even if it's doomed." Nellie Wong wants to "approach enemy lines, link arms with my people, to guard our dead." And Marjorie Agosin describes Third-World women as silence-breakers, storytellers, global warriors for change:

Our own history obliges us to speak, to loose words of fire. Thus we come out of the silence and darkness to show ourselves as we are: free women, warrior women. We are washers of clothes, teachers, lawyers, journalists, poets. We are mothers, sisters, wives, daughters. . . . We wage our war every day in the country called Chile or Guatemala or the United States. We are new women with new stories to tell.[13]

My examination of poetry and essays by contemporary U.S. women of color reveals three main ways in which they use the warrior construct. Some poets identify themselves explicitly as warriors, as in Audre Lorde's claim to be a "Black lesbian feminist warrior poet."[14] Others name themselves war correspondents, narrators from the front rather than active combatants, as in Ntozake Shange's assertion that "the front lines aren't always what you think they are."[15] A third group of poets invoke a warrior muse: a bellicose mother, historical foremother, goddess, or mythic hero who inspires the writer's art—as in Maxine Hong Kingston's invocation of the Chinese warrior Fa Mu Lan.[16] In the sections that follow I will examine each of these constructs and analyze why and how the warrior represents for many women of color a powerful force for global transformation.

The Poet as Warrior: Audre Lorde and Gloria Anzaldúa

> On worn kitchen stools and tables
> we are piecing our weapons together
> scraps of a different history . . .
>
> Audre Lorde, "Call"

> Now among the alien gods with weapons of magic I am.
> Navaho protection song cited by Gloria Anzaldúa[17]

The struggle to claim her racial, sexual, feminist, and warrior identities forms the core of Audre Lorde's poetics and politics. As she explains in an interview with Claudia Tate, her creative energy comes from being outspoken about these diverse parts of herself:

With respect to myself specifically, I feel that not to be open about any of the different "people" within my identity, particularly the "mes" who are challenged by a status quo, is to invite myself and other women, by my example, to live a lie. In other words, I would be giving in to a myth of sameness which I think can destroy us.[18]

Women must acknowledge our multiple identities and our differences, Lorde believes, if we are to remain strong.

Many of Lorde's early poems contain images of women as warriors: "warrior queens" ("Harriet"); "like a warrior woman" ("Chorus"); "like my warrior sisters" ("125th Street and Abomey"); "Assata my sister warrior" ("For Assata").[19] At times the epithet *warrior* becomes an emblem of hope for future generations: "I bless your child with the mother she has / with a future of warriors and growing fire" ("Dear Toni instead of a Letter").[20] For Lorde, the term *warrior* evokes centuries of history of African women's resistance to white authorities and other forces of suppression. Foremost among such warrior women were the legendary Amazons of Dahomey, about whom Lorde writes in "The Women of Dan." Here she enacts a strong revisionist impulse, for she insists that women's warring be not stealthy but open, visible.

> I come as a woman
> I do not come like a secret warrior
> with an unsheathed sword in my mouth hidden behind my
>   tongue
> slicing my throat to ribbons.

Dangerous to others but not to herself, the poet names her new weapons, erotic heat and poetic words, a combination vital for continued growth and vision.[21]

> I come like a woman
> who I am
> spreading out through the nights
> laughter and promise
> and dark heat
> warming whatever I touch
> that is living
> consuming
> only
> what is already dead.[22]

Like Mawulisa, a peace-loving Dahomean goddess about whom she often writes, Lorde resists war as a deceptive, vindictive enterprise. She refuses to be silenced or to destroy unnecessarily. Instead, she openly warns contemporary oppressors of her watchful presence and embraces her warrior identity through a passionate, ritualistic celebration with her sisters of Dan.

Lorde does not reject retribution altogether, however, nor is her presentation of women as warriors always ritualized or celebratory. Her latest volume of poetry, *Our Dead Behind Us*, is rife with horrific war imagery: arms, guns, battles, massacres, limpet mines, flames, explosions, blood, corpses, mournings for the dead. If unjust wars against indigenous peoples continue to be waged around the world by the U.S. and other imperialistic governments, Lorde believes radical women must spearhead the resistance; "this is the way in which the philosopher queen, the poet-warrior leads." Lorde is especially determined to speak of and for the voiceless, for "all those feisty, incorrigible black women who insist on standing up and saying 'I am and you cannot wipe me out, no matter how irritating I am, how much you fear what I might represent.'"[23] Many recent poems, therefore, support women and children engaged in global struggles for liberation—in South Africa, Grenada, Chile, and the U.S.S.R., to name only a few.

"Sisters in Arms" illustrates well the complexity of Lorde's most recent use of the warrior construct; in fact, it interweaves related images of the poet-warrior, the war correspondent, and the warrior muse. Sexuality and political struggle intersect, as Lorde describes sharing her bed and her arms (in both senses of the word) with a South African woman who learns that her fifteen-year-old daughter has just been brutally murdered near Durban, her body "hanging / gut-sprung on police wheels." The poet feels agony and helplessness:

> I could not return with you to bury the body
> reconstruct your nightly cardboards
> against the seeping Transvaal cold
> I could not plant the other limpet mine
> against a wall at the railroad station.

So Lorde does what she can—buys her lover a ticket to Durban (ironically, on her American Express card) and comforts her physically before her departure.

Written retrospectively, the poem reveals Lorde's fury at both the South African government's continuing atrocities against its Black people and the *New York Times's* scant coverage of what it euphemistically deems the "unrest" there. As a war correspondent, she reports graphically the horrors the *Times* chooses to hide: "Black children massacred at Sebokeng, / six-year olds imprisoned for threatening the state . . . / Thabo Sibeko, first grader, in his own blood / on his grandmother's parlor floor." The newspaper's evasions and these terrible truths haunt Lorde as she gardens haphazardly and recalls moments of intimacy and pain with her South African sister:

> we were two Black women touching our flame
> and we left our dead behind us
> I hovered you rose the last ritual of healing
> "It is spring" you whispered
> "I sold the ticket for guns and sulfa"
> and wherever I touch you
> I lick cold from my fingers
> taste rage

Lorde knows that the sisters who lay in one another's arms may also bear arms together one day, stronger for having shared erotic experience: "someday you will come to my country / and we will fight side by side?" Since she cannot go to South Africa, Lorde invokes in her stead the African warrior queen Mmanthatisi, who led the Sotho people during the *mfecane*, an earlier Black South African uprising. As this warrior muse "dresses again for battle, / knowing the men will follow," the poet chronicles her preparations, dreaming of Durban and the possibility of revolutionary change.[24]

Lorde shares the energy and fatigue of battle not only with her South African sister but also with the white woman from Mississippi with whom she lived for many years. In "Outlines" Lorde explores those complex internal wars that divide women against ourselves and each other, that raise not only our enemies' hands against us. Despite their private conflicts, however, the two women fight together against the forces of racism and homophobia:

> We rise to dogshit   dumped on our front porch
> the brass windchimes   from Sundance   stolen
> despair offerings of the 8 a.m. news
> reminding us we are still at war
> and not with each other.

As the Klan burns a cross ten blocks away, one woman exchanges concern with their neighbors while the speaker registers a shotgun, searching for courage. The poem's concluding lines present both women as warriors in an ongoing battle—for their survival as lesbians, as interracial lovers; and for the survival of women and the planet.

> we have chosen each other
> and the edge of each other's battles
> the war is the same
> if we lose
> someday women's blood will congeal
> upon a dead planet
> if we win
> there is no telling.[25]

Radical women must begin to imagine what is possible, Lorde reminds us, when we piece our weapons together and assemble a different history.

Sometimes conflicts between women are not soluble, however. Lorde points out in "Equal Opportunity" that not all women, not all women of color, are sisters in arms. "The american deputy assistant secretary of defense / for Equal Opportunity / and safety, is a home girl. / Blindness slashes our tapestry to shreds." The deputy is blind to her own tokenism and, most appallingly, to the terrible irony of her complicity in her department's invasion of Grenada. Against the deputy's naïveté and self-interest Lorde juxtaposes the victimization and quiet resistance of Imelda, a young Grenadian woman whose sister has been missing for ten days, whose hut has been destroyed by "armed men in moss-green jumpsuits / searching for weapons." Along with M-16s and rapacious soldiers, Imelda fears her child's death from malnutrition and dehydration, yet her prior experience with nervous armed soldiers has taught her how to talk to invaders, how to remain calm and dissemble: "no guns, man, no guns here. we glad you come.

you carry water?" Back in the United States, the deputy flexes her newly acquired muscle ("when I stand up to speak in uniform / you can believe everyone takes notice!"), extols her department's fine record of equal opportunity hiring for women, and Lorde concludes searingly, "swims toward safety / through a lake of her own blood."[26] This sister's violation of justice obviously pains the poet, as does her own obligation to present and condemn this home girl as a tool of the U.S. military machine. For Lorde, however, irresponsible actions against Third-World people by coopted women are surely indefensible.

The importance of personal accountability for the warrior poet, an issue raised by Lorde in this poem and throughout her work, is one of several characteristics that Patricia Hill Collins considers central to an alternative Black women's epistemology drawn from both feminist and Afrocentric standpoints. The other traits she enumerates—concrete experience as a source of knowledge and wisdom, dialogue as crucial to any struggle, and an ethic of caring grounded in empathy—characterize Lorde's poetic practice and theory as well. Lorde's aesthetic and political goals parallel those that Collins ascribes to Black feminist scholars who move among multiple epistemologies in complex acts of political translation, affirming alternate truths. Such writers and scholars "rearticulate a preexisting Black women's standpoint and recenter the language of existing discourse to accommodate these knowledge claims."[27]

The knowledge that Gloria Anzaldúa advances in her poetry and prose also emerges from a self-articulated standpoint of her oppression as a Chicana/*tejana* lesbian and her culturally specific forms and *historias* (history and stories) of rebellion. Anzaldúa's self-conceptualization as warrior poet differs from Lorde's in several ways. For Lorde and other African-American women, a root source of oppression is slavery, whether manifested in the nineteenth-century U.S. system or in South Africa's apartheid laws. For Anzaldúa and other Chicanas, historical conquests of their homelands and thefts of their native tongue are the foremost offenses. "Who is to say that robbing a people of its language is less violent than war?" Like hundreds of women before her, Anzaldúa refuses for her "wild tongue" to be tamed.[28] "My Chicana identity is grounded in the Indian woman's history of resistance," she explains. For centuries the *mestiza* has been silenced, threatened, imprisoned in abusive marriages, bludgeoned by the system; "for years she hid her flame but stoked and tended it." Today, Anzaldúa asserts, this brown-skinned warrior is coming into her own. "The spirit of the fire spurs her to fight for her own skin and a piece of the ground to stand on."[29]

For Anzaldúa as for many contemporary women of color, ground to stand on, a place to claim safely as home, constitutes a complex piece of racial and feminist identity invention. "There is nothing more important to me than home," Barbara Smith states in her introduction to *Home Girls;* and many of Anzaldúa's poems and essays imply a similar valuing of her ethnic milieu.[30] But a fierce ambivalence permeates her politics of location, because her homeland is neither clearly delineated nor completely safe. She was raised in the borderlands, that physical and psychical terrain "wherever two or more cultures edge each other, where people of different races occupy the same territory, where under, lower, middle and upper classes touch."[31] Anzaldúa's particular home is the Texas/Mexican border with its heavy Indian influence, its constant state of transition, its sense of itself as a separate country. Living in the interfaces between worlds, the Chicana must discover and use her *mestiza* consciousness.

Anzaldúa's war is both internal and external: to understand her multiple identities despite enormous insecurities and obstacles; to combat racism, sexism, heterosexism, and elitism in their many forms. Constantly juggling multiple cultures, "*la mestiza* undergoes a struggle for flesh, a struggle of borders, an inner war." On the one hand, Anzaldúa argues, this psychic unrest helps poets create; on the other, any cultural collision takes its toll. Attacks on indigenous peoples and their values demand a counterstance, yet as Anzaldúa notes, any counterstance risks replicating the polarized models of binary opposition she and other *mestizas* wish to reject. "A counterstance locks one into a duel of oppressor and oppressed; locked in mortal combat, like the cop and the criminal, both are reduced to a common denominator of violence."[32] Yet a self-defined stance of resistance can also represent proud defiance, a necessary step toward liberation.

In her poem "To live in the Borderlands means you," Anzaldúa explores this multifaceted Chicana identity and its warrior context. *En la frontera,* she finds it difficult to speak or be spoken to; "the wind steals your voice"; parts of her feel betrayed by other parts. Her racial identity is uncertain: "you are neither *hispaña india negra española / ni gabacha, eres mestiza, mulata,* half-breed / caught in the crossfire between camps." Likewise, she struggles with an ambiguous gender identity as the "forerunner of a new race, / half and half—both woman and man, neither— / a new gender." The poet must be a crossroads, both a victim of war and its soldier.

> In the borderlands
>   you are the battleground
>   where enemies are kin to each other;
>   you are at home, a stranger,
>   the border disputes have been settled

the volley of shots have shattered the truce
you are wounded, lost in action
dead, fighting back.[33]

In this milieu, survival is a key issue; the poet thus imagines herself fighting back even from death to ensure a future for her selves and her people.

One characteristic of Anzaldúa's warrior poetry that distinguishes it from Lorde's is its hybrid style: "Poetry, description, essay—we cross genres, cross the borders. It's a new poetics. It's a new aesthetics. And I don't even know if it's new. It's probably not new. . . . What's new is bringing it to the forefront and giving it a name. And making it part of the dialogue." Code-switching is a means of honoring her native tongue, Spanish, though she recognizes that it too has been historically the "oppressor's language." Still, she points out that "ethnic identity is twin skin to linguistic identity—I am my language"; to be denied it evokes both anger and shame. Poverty and classism further contribute to her feelings of internalized exile. For Lorde, Black warrior writing requires "the transformation of silence into language and action." For Anzaldúa, this endeavor is further problematized by her desire to use politically and aesthetically her Spanish, Indian, and English voices, her "serpent's tongue."[34]

Because of the risks inherent in resistance, both Lorde and Anzaldúa have claimed, women of color must work collaboratively to combat their multiple oppressions; in community lies power. Change "requires both the alchemist and the welder, the magician and the laborer, the witch and the warrior, the myth-smasher and the myth-maker." As warrior-poets, Lorde and Anzaldúa are committed to this collective defiance. "Hand in Hand we brew and forge a revolution."[35]

The Poet as War Correspondent: Ntozake Shange and June Jordan

Here, supposedly, we do not have "dissident" poets and writers—unless they are well rewarded runaways from the Soviet Union. Here we know about the poets and writers that major media eagerly allow us to see and consume. And then we do not hear about the other ones. But I am one of them. I am a dissident American poet and writer completely uninterested to run away from my country, my home.

June Jordan, *On Call*

I am a war correspondent . . . in a war of cultural and esthetic aggression.

Ntozake Shange, 1985 interview[36]

All feminist writers grapple with issues of censorship, external and internal. How much can we say, and how angrily, and still be published by university or commercial presses? How strongly should we defend freedom of the press when pornography and sexist exploitation of women are at issue? How rigorously should we conceal or reveal our most intimate truths when we write autobiographically? But as June Jordan points out, for the North American writer who is Black, female, and dissident, censorship requires daily confrontation. In her introduction to *On Call,* her stunning collection of political essays, Jordan addresses directly her own rejection by mainstream media:

If political writing by a Black woman did not strike so many editors as presumptuous or simply bizarre, then, perhaps, this book would not be needed. Instead, I might regularly appear, on a weekly or monthly schedule, as a national columnist. But if you will count the number of Black women with regular and national forums for their political ideas, and the ideas of their constituency, you will comprehend the politics of our exclusion: I cannot come up with the name of one Black woman in that position.[37]

Jordan goes on to assert that in the United States, Black people are systematically silenced, as evidenced by the *New York Times*'s failure to cite on its op-ed page, frequently and regularly, any African-American writer on the topic of South Africa. Such "whitelistings" necessitate the writer's taking matters into her own hands, addressing her constituency through radical or alternative presses, asserting her right to honest, informed reportage on global struggles for liberation.

As a political poet and essayist, Jordan has focused particularly on Third-World sites of turmoil and transformation: South Africa, Lebanon, Palestine, Guatemala, Nicaragua. She has traveled to these war-torn countries and has brought back eloquent, angry reports from the front. At times she struggles with her confusion over whether or how to become an actual combatant. "I must become a menace to my enemies," Jordan proclaims in a poem dedicated to Agostinho Neho, poet and former president of Angola; "I must become the action of my fate." The time for silence, passivity, fear is past, she warns her oppressors:

Be afraid . . .
I plan to blossom bloody on an afternoon
surrounded by my comrades singing
terrible revenge in merciless
accelerating
rhythms.[38]

The poet asserts here the bellicose power of her poetic meters and words, as she does again in "Poem for Guatemala": "I am learning new syllables / of revolution."[39] Despite efforts to censor her, Jordan insists on documenting her political efforts and views in a rhetoric and a poetics of anger, insight, and compassion.

Her writings on South Africa illustrate Jordan's role as an embattled war reporter attempting, in Charlotte Bunch's words, to "bring the global home."[40] For Jordan, "South Africa was how I came to understand that I am not against war. I am against losing the war. But war means that you fight. Who is fighting South Africa here, in my house? . . . I know my life depends on making this fight my own." In a sense, Jordan is a correspondent rather than a participant by default; she wants to be more active in South African liberation struggles from her U.S. vantage point but is uncertain how best to do so in an apathetic environment. "What can I join? Where are the streets side-to-side jammed with Americans who will not be moved, who will shout until the windows shatter from the walls? Is there a picket line that blocks the South African Embassy? Do the merchants dealing diamonds and gold loudly deny the blood on the counter? . . . No and no and no. . . . What is the difficulty? Has nobody heard the news?" Jordan's furious questions accumulate relentlessly, hammering readers of conscience with the awareness that concerned U.S. citizens have been derelict in not protesting more rigorously our government's complicity in apartheid. She speaks to and for many of us when she confesses her horror at the Reagan and Bush administrations' policies and acknowledges her own uncertainties: "I yet look for the dignity of an effective, defiant response."[41]

Jordan's commitment to struggling with this complex political issue is also apparent in her poetry. Here too she uses rhetorical questions and fierce irony to expose the political absurdities and atrocities of our times. "How many of my brothers and my sisters / will they kill / before I teach myself / retaliation?" she wonders in one poem.

> Shall we pick a number?
> South Africa for instance:
> do we agree that more than ten thousand
> in less than a year but than less than
> five thousand slaughtered in more than six
> months will
> WHAT IS THE MATTER WITH ME?
>
> I must become a menace to my enemies[42]

Elsewhere Jordan speaks of and for African women engaged in militant efforts toward liberation. Working for freedom in Mozambique or Angola "lifts / the head of the young girl / formerly burdened by laundry / and yams," she asserts; collective action brings dignity and hope. Paradoxically, killing is sometimes the only means of preserving life. Jordan refuses to present maternal nurture and possession of weapons as contradictions. "She / straps the baby to her back / and / she carries her rifle / like she means / means to kill / for the love / for the life / of us all."[43] The war correspondent's task, Jordan believes, is to foreground such complexities on behalf of women of color worldwide. Thus, her work documents both global movements for self-determination and the poet's own political struggles.

Like Jordan, Ntozake Shange has traveled in the Third World and chronicled the efforts toward liberation she has witnessed. But more explicitly than Jordan she embraces her role as a war correspondent, something she wanted to be from childhood on. At first her goal was romantic and frivolous, she explains, an idea she got from watching *It Happened One Night* with Clark Gable and Claudette Colbert. When her father dissuaded her from pursuing this occupation (because girls didn't do it), Shange turned to writing as a logical alternative. As a feminist poet and playwright with strong leftist political convictions, Shange has recognized that her current vocation and her fantasy one have merged. "I figured out that I am a war correspondent after all because I'm involved in a war of cultural and esthetic aggression. The front lines aren't always what you think they are."[44]

Shange's lyrical reportage and idealistic vision are evident in "Bocas: A Daughter's Geography." Her lyricism contrasts sharply with Jordan's pained, raw questionings, her uncertainty as to the appropriate reportorial stance for the feminist war correspondent. Shange's speaker is embattled, but she asserts herself as powerful and victorious. A mother, she embraces an identity global in its parameters:

i have a daughter/mozambique
i have a son/angola
our twins
salvador & johannesburg/cannot speak
the same language
but we fight the same old men/in the new world.

Her litany of places in which poor people are rising up continues, haunting and incantatory: Habana, Guyana, Santiago, Managua. The patriarchs who dominate the world's peoples are tunnel-visioned, "unaware of . . . all the dark urchins / rounding out the globe / primitively whispering / the earth is not flat old men." The poet juxtaposes ironically the men's flatness, their one-dimensionality, with the round, wholesome humanity of the embattled daughters and sons. People of color have power in both their numbers and the justice of their causes, Shange implies; if they but persevere, "the same men who thought the earth was flat"—who lack empathy and vision—will "go on over the edge." This victory will make possible mass and massive revolutionary nurture, "feeding our children the sun."[45]

Aída Hurtado's assessment of women of color's resistance strategies helps us understand both the particularities of Jordan's and Shange's rhetorical stances and the common concerns that may distinguish their poetry and praxis as Black women from those of white feminists. According to Hurtado, women of color have more and earlier experience in developing effective ways of using anger to promote sociocultural change than middle-class white feminists, who are often protected by classism and racism. As a consequence, many white women do not acquire their political consciousnesses until they become adults. Because their childhoods were "safer," white women may have less anger (or be less strategic in expressing and using the anger they feel) at gender-related and other oppressions. White feminists and feminists of color today may experience differently, for example, the rampant loss of children in our culture to poverty, police brutality, and drugs. Hurtado quotes Audre Lorde's address to white feminists: "Some problems we share as women, some we do not. You fear your children will grow up to join the patriarchy and testify against you, we fear our children will be dragged from a car and shot down in the street and you will turn your backs upon the reasons they are dying."[46]

Hurtado claims that women of color are often more effective than white feminists in expressing their rage—in Jordan's and Shange's cases, in political poetry and essays. Even so, their expressions of fury may take different forms according to their particular experience of racism, classism, and gender oppression. The slaughter of innocent children drives a pessimistic Jordan most often toward the prosaic, it seems to me; the horrors she witnesses are too stark to be rendered metaphorically. With Pablo Neruda, she would claim that "the blood of the children / flowed out onto the streets / like . . . like the blood of the children."[47] An angry optimism, in contrast, underlies Shange's lyric intensity and rich metaphors; for her, "dark urchins" are the hope of the revolution as well as its casualties. Shange also seems to believe in an "essential" women's inclination toward peace and nurture, a viewpoint I see no evidence of Jordan's sharing. Patriarchal forces do not understand, Shange asserts, that women "see the world in a way that allows us to care more about people than about military power. The power we see is the power to feed, the power to nourish and to educate. But these kinds of powers are not respected, and so it's part of our responsibility as writers to make these things important."[48] As Adrienne Rich has said, even common words must be reconsidered, laid aside, recast with new meanings.[49] At the head of this list of re-visioned words, for Shange as for Rich, is power.

With other writers who identify themselves as warriors or war correspondents, Jordan and Shange support the last-resort strategies of countermilitancy that women are evincing throughout the Third World. (Or the First World, for as Jordan notes, "Third World" is a gross misnomer when applied to indigenous peoples.) Specifically, women of color honor their sister combatants in their dedications, prefaces, and introductions. Shange, for example, dedicates *See No Evil,* her collection of revolutionary essays, to "the 30 million african women / in the NEW WORLD OF WHOM I AM A PROUD SURVIVOR" and to the armed women of Nicaragua, Guatemala, El Salvador, Mozambique, Angola, Namibia, and South Africa. Jordan describes with admiration seeing all the Nicaraguan people armed, "nine year olds, Black women, elderly men . . . people forming volunteer militia to defend the revolution they had made." Combating cultural aggression requires global consciousness-raising, these two poets believe, and it is the writer's responsibility to instill this awareness through her art. *"When will we seize the world around us with our freedom?"*[50]

The Warrior as Muse for Women of Color

My mother taught me the song of the warrior woman, Fa Mu Lan. I would have to grow up a woman warrior.
Maxine Hong Kingston, *The Woman Warrior*

Find the muse within you. The voice that lies buried under you, dig it up. Do not fake it, try to sell it for a handclap or your name in print.
Gloria Anzaldúa, *This Bridge Called My Back*[51]

White male poets have traditionally imagined the quintessential source of poetry as a female muse, an inspirer whom they have invoked through the ages and by whose aid they claim to create. This figure has been described as the male poet's inspiring anima who influences him in her roles as shamaness, sibyl, priestess; as the power that kindles his vision. Whether wise woman or human lover, the muse has existed for man as a series of opposites: he is subject, she is object; he is lover, she is beloved; he is begetter, she is begotten upon. As divine inspirer and a sexual and creative stimulus, the muse has been a central symbolic aspect of the male literary imagination.

In many respects the concept of the muse has been a luxury of race and gender privilege, a metaphor of colonization. Yet a surprising number of women poets today are reimagining the muse in non-hierarchical ways, rejecting the passive, objectified version of men poets and revisioning her instead as an active source of inspiration, a force born of their own artistic energy and will. Feminist poets often name as muses women from their lives—mothers, sisters, lovers, and friends. Some women invoke goddesses and mythic women, especially in poems about creative process: Ishtar, Isis, and Astarte from Eastern myths; Demeter, Artemis, and Eurydice from ancient Greece; Seboulisa and Mawulisa from African lore. A striking number of women focus on figures traditionally viewed as evil or dangerous to men: Kali, Circe, Medusa, Helen of Troy, the Furies, the Amazons. Unable or unwilling to idealize their inspirational sources as passive Others, many women poets employ powerful muses as extensions of their own imaginations and partners in their creative endeavors.[52]

For U.S. women of color, the muse is often depicted as a warrior or a goddess of war who guides the poet in her cultural as well as creative battles. The reasons for choosing such a muse seem obvious when we consider the ravagings women of color throughout the world have undergone from poverty, starvation, war, and dislocation. Many U.S. writers recognize that they write from a position of relative security, a recognition that fuels not complacency but empathy with and rage on behalf of their sisters. To invoke a militant muse is therefore to add their voices—angry, impassioned—to others speaking out against oppression. Yet the muses of women of color differ according to a given poet's particular material and cultural circumstances. Contemporary African-American poets like Audre Lorde and Ntozake Shange honor powerful goddess mothers from African oral traditions, legendary figures who pass on an Afrocentric spiritual legacy. Chinese-American writers like Maxine Hong Kingston and Nellie Wong pay tribute to their biological warrior mothers whose particular immigrant experiences on "Gold Mountain" forced them to resist with strength they did not know they had.[53]

In "Call," for example, Audre Lorde invokes as muse the African mother goddess Seboulisa, said to ride through the world on the back of the Rainbow Serpent Aido Hwedo. This goddess sustains not only Lorde but also her African sisters in struggle. "I am a Black woman turning / mouthing your name as a password / through seductions self-slaughter," Lorde claims in her address to the goddess.

> . . . I believe in the holy ghost
> mother

in your flames beyond our vision
blown light through the fingers of women
enduring warring
sometimes outside your name
we do not choose all our rituals
Thandi Modise winged girl of Soweto
brought fire back home in the snout of a mortar
and passes the word from her prison cell whispering
Aido Hwedo is coming[54]

Although Seboulisa is a peace-loving goddess, she does not shrink from warring when there is no alternative. Here the poet suggests that the goddess's spirit is being served in her own art and in countermilitant "crimes" by South African rebels like Thandi Modise, herself now a legendary figure. By invoking a muse who supports war, Lorde can mourn "our dead behind us" and affirm their revolutionary zeal.

For Chinese-American writers Maxine Hong Kingston and Nellie Wong the warrior-muse is connected not to African history but to the marginalization experienced by their immigrant families. In *The Woman Warrior* Kingston names her mother shaman and revels in her subversive wisdom, though she also suffers from the "talk stories" her mother forces upon her: "My mother has given me pictures to dream. . . . I push the deformed into my dreams, which are in Chinese, the language of impossible stories." From her mother's endless tales come Kingston's inspiration and creative ambition but also an internalized sense of shame and loss. "When we Chinese girls listened to the adults talk-story, we learned that we failed if we grew up to be but wives or slaves. We could be heroines, swordswomen." Her mother's chant of Fa Mu Lan, the Chinese swordswoman who, according to legend, replaced her father in battle, was especially compelling to the young Kingston. "She taught me the song of the warrior woman. . . . I would have to grow up a woman warrior." Yet the same woman who taught her daughter such songs confessed to her, "You have no idea how I have fallen coming to America." As an adult Kingston finds she "hates armies" and prefers instead to use words as weapons. Like Shange and Jordan, she will challenge racist and classist oppressors via her reportage. "The swordswoman and I are not so dissimilar. What we have in common are the words at our backs. The idioms for revenge are 'report a crime' and 'report to five families.' The reporting is the vengeance—not the beheading, not the gutting, but the words. And I have so many words—'chink' words and 'gook' words too—that they do not fit on my skin."[55]

Nellie Wong's "From a Heart of Rice Straw" also pays homage to her mother as warrior muse, and like Kingston, she reveals both shame and inspiration at the heart of her homage. Ostensibly this poem chronicles two combat stories, a family quarrel in which Wong's father was accused of theft and assaulted by his angry brother and a San Francisco newspaper's condescending account of this unfortunate incident as just "another Tong war" in Oakland Chinatown. But Wong recognizes that the main warrior in this saga, her mother, has been silenced and made invisible, due in part to the stereotype of the Asian-American woman as the "ideal minority."[56] Thus, she retells this family story, reclaiming her mother as muse and as mouthpiece.

When her father was stabbed, Wong's mother chased the offender through the streets of Oakland Chinatown, oblivious to her own danger, finally to capture him. "The cops said you were brave. The neighbors said / you were brave. The relatives shook their heads, / the bravery of a Gold Mountain woman unknown / in the old home village." But this courage was soon forgotten by everyone except Wong's mother. As a younger woman the poet had tired of her mother's tale of vengeance: "Ma, you've told this story one hundred times." As a feminist thinking back through her mother, however, the poet honors the rebellious and self-naming mother whose inspiration she once denied:

Well, I'm not ashamed of you anymore, Momma.
My heart, once bent and cracked, once
ashamed of your China ways.
Ma, hear me now, tell me your story
again and again.[57]

Chinese-American women turn not only to biological mothers as muses but also to revolutionary activists from their country of origin. One warrior Wong honors is the Chinese writer Ding Ling, whom she discovered during the 1970s and reveres as an artist and a fighting woman imprisoned during the Cultural Revolution for her radical beliefs. Wong's epigraph to *The Death of Long Steam Lady* quotes Ding Ling: "Our joy is a battle within a storm and not playing the harp under the moon or reciting poetry in front of a flower." Poetry is subversive and defiant, Wong claims, and to brave any battle feminist writers must learn how our literary mothers have survived. Ding Ling provides such inspiration: "Ding Ling, imprisoned for expressing her anguish, her love and compassion for China's women, for recording the conditions of their lives. . . . Now there is information trickling out that she is writing again, silenced for so many years. Now you want to search for more of her work . . . jewels you want to hold in your hand. Now you want . . . to find the grandmothers you wish to adopt."[58]

Naming their own muses, adopting bellicose grandmothers, empowers U.S. women of color to chart new courses of battle. Fear of reprisal when they break silence, the ambivalence that accompanies marginalization, inchoate rage at the forces of oppression—all can be debilitating emotions unless they speak as individual and collective resisters, artistic as well as political transformers. "Put your shit on paper," Gloria Anzaldúa exhorts her sisters. "We are not reconciled to the oppressors who whet their howl on our grief. We are not reconciled."[59]

Conclusion: The Place from Which We Speak

> This is the profound paradox of the feminist speaking in our contemporary culture: she proceeds from a belief in a world from which . . . Truth has disappeared. This paradox, it seems to me, can lead to (at least) three possible scenarios: a renewed silence, a form of religion (from mysticism to political orthodoxy), or a continual attention—historical, ideological, and affective—to the place from which we speak.
>
> Alice A. Jardine, *Gynesis*

> Not knowing
> what deaths you saw today
> I've got to take you
> as you come, battle-bruised
> refusing our enemy, fear.
>
> Cherríe Moraga, *Loving in the War Years*[60]

We can return now to the questions I posed earlier in this essay. Why is the warrior construct so prevalent among women of color? Do they simply reverse the patriarchal paradigm of the Just Warrior versus the Monolithic Enemy, thereby replicating the dominant discourse's binary oppositions, or do they reconceptualize warriors and warring from a multiconscious feminist perspective that acknowledges the political and creative complexities of such metaphors and identities?

Recent feminist theorists, both white women and women of color, suggest that in reconsidering the construct *woman*, a necessary departure point for any feminist politics or poetics, we pay closer attention to the place(s) from which we speak. Alice Jardine rejects silence, mysticism, and political orthodoxy as essentialist stances antithetical to a dynamic feminist enterprise and stresses instead a constant reassessment of our historical and ideological contexts. Similarly, Linda Alcoff critiques both cultural feminists (whose stances imply an innate female essence) and post-structuralist feminists (whose nominalist views theorize women out of existence) as providing retrogressive models of gender analysis and feminist praxis. As an alternative to these self-defeating theoretical and political positions, Alcoff posits the concept of identity politics as defined and practiced by U.S. women of color. Identity here is acknowledged as a sociocultural construct but serves also as a necessary political point of departure: one's particular experience of the intersections of gender/race/class/sexuality informs a position from which to act and speak. For Alcoff, identity politics thus avoids the pitfalls of cultural or post-structural feminist theory: "the position that women find themselves in can be actively utilized (rather than transcended) as a location for the construction of meaning."[61]

Through identity politics women of color problematize such feminist concepts as *sexism* and *enemy*. Alcoff cites Chicana feminist Cherríe Moraga as a writer who recognizes the simultaneity of oppressions and thus resists essentialist formulations. "When you start to talk about sexism," Moraga asserts, "the world becomes increasingly complex. The power no longer breaks down into neat little hierarchical categories, but becomes a series of starts and detours. Since the categories are not easy to arrive at, the enemy is not easy to name. It is all so difficult to unravel."[62] As maleness cannot be wholly Other for women of color, neither can the enemy be wholly Other.

Instead, diverse and multiple sources of oppression contribute to the appropriation of the warrior construct by women of color: internal "enemies" such as guilt over their own perceived inactions or inadequacies, alienation from some members of their racial or ethnic group or from white liberal feminists, fear of military reprisals against them; and external "enemies" as embodied in white patriarchs and imperialists, women who deny their white skin privilege, men of color who perpetuate sexist ideologies in their movement work. As warriors using words to combat simultaneous oppressions, women writers of color do not claim to be always redemptive, ever just, always clear about the source(s) of a particular oppressive act or the "rightness" of a decision at hand. Certainly the warrior aspect of their identities remains, in Moraga's phrase, "difficult to unravel." Yet women of color *are* clear that resistance is essential—that, as Alcoff argues, "their position within the network lacks power and mobility and requires radical change."[63] Operating from complex and particular historical contexts, they use the warrior construct both to articulate an impassioned feminist politics and to inspire them to undertake its attendant sociocultural transformations.

Examined from this vantage point, Cherríe Moraga's assertion that "I love women to the point of killing for us all" is neither hyperbolic nor malevolent; it reflects instead the historical, ideological, and affective locus from which she speaks.[64] Moraga and her lover have had to learn to love in the war years, to receive each other battle-bruised, to combat a racist and sexist death machine "out there" and an internal enemy, fear, at home. Women warriors' rage and retribution are facets of their identity politics—in Moraga's case, part of her class-related and culturally specific distrust of the formal English language, her "resistance to the literate" (Moraga claims that "words are a war to me").[65] Similarly, Lorde's assertion "I am a bleak heroism of words / that refuse / to be buried alive / with the liars" constitutes an aesthetic as well as a political stance of defiance.[66] Finally, the warrior construct offers a metaphor and an identity by which white feminists, especially those who have experienced ethnic, religious, or heterosexist margin-alization, can delineate a position of cameraderie and affiliation with their sisters of color. "There must be those among whom we can sit down and weep, and still be counted as warriors," Adrienne Rich proclaims in *Sources,* where she explores for the first time the intersec-tion of her lesbian feminism and her once-denied Jewish identity.[67] For women of color and for many of their white sisters, the warrior con-struct resonates, multifaceted.

Notes

I would like to thank Sallie Bingham and the Kentucky Foundation for Women for grant support while I was writing this article.
    1. Monique Wittig, *Les Guérillères,* trans. David LeVay (New York: Viking Press, 1969), p. 85; Audre Lorde, "Learning from the 60s," *Sister Outsider: Essays and Speeches by Audre Lorde* (Trumansburg, N.Y.: Crossing Press, 1984), p. 140. I use the term "women of color" in the sense that Sri Lankan feminist Asoka Bandarage explains and advocates it: "Recently, *women of color* has become a popular term among Asian, African, Latin and Native American women living in the West. It is especially popular among those who are femi-nists but who have fundamental disagreements with the white middle-class women's movement. For women who are oppressed by both patriarchy and white supremacy, women of color—mujeres de color—provides a unifying conceptual formula and a direction for political organizing." Bandarage fur-ther notes that Black nationalists George Padmore and Marcus Garvey were among the first to use the term "people of color" to promote political mobiliza-tion and positive self-definition. See Bandarage, "Women of Color: Toward a Celebration of Power," *woman of power* 4 (fall 1986), 8–14, 82–83.
    2. Audre Lorde, "The Master's Tools Will Never Dismantle the Master's House," in *Sister Outsider,* pp. 110–13.
    3. Teresa de Lauretis, *Technologies of Gender: Essays on Theory, Film, and Fiction* (Bloomington: Indiana University Press, 1987), pp. 31–50.
    4. Aída Hurtado, "Relating to Privilege: Seduction and Rejection in the Subordination of White Women and Women of Color," *Signs: Journal of Women in Culture and Society* 14.4 (summer 1989), 849–54.
    5. Patricia Hill Collins, "The Social Construction of Black Feminist Thought," *Signs* 14.4 (summer 1989), 747.
    6. Jean Bethke Elshtain, *Women and War* (New York: Basic Books, 1987),

pp. 237–41. Elshtain fails to mention that all of the feminist writers she critiques for creating "Manichean narratives" are white. My contention is that women of color are less likely to essentialize "the enemy" in such terms.

7. de Lauretis, *Technologies*, pp. 44–48.

8. Mary Daly, with Jane Caputi, *Webster's First New Intergalactic Wickedary of the English Language* (Boston: Beacon Press, 1987). "Necrophilia" is defined on pp. 83–84, "biophilia" on p. 67, crones and "crone-ology" on pp. 114–16.

9. Elizabeth V. Spelman, *Inessential Woman: Problems of Exclusion in Feminist Thought* (Boston: Beacon Press, 1988), pp. 123–25.

10. Gloria Anzaldúa, *Borderlands/La Frontera: The New Mestiza* (San Francisco: Spinsters/aunt lute, 1987), preface.

11. William Broyles, Jr., "Why Men Love War," *Esquire* (December 1984), 61–62. Again, it is worth noting that when Broyles says "men," he actually describes a certain group of white men who are perhaps more likely to love war because it is more often their choice to participate in it. He does not acknowledge that men of color have not traditionally been among the military elite who declare war nor the economically secure who can buy their way out of it—that in fact, men of color have been drafted in disproportionate numbers and typically serve at lower ranks than their white counterparts. Nor does he note that many men of color identify strongly with "the enemy," most likely people of color. On these and related points, see Spelman, *Inessential Woman*, pp. 114–15.

12. Judith Beckett, "Searching for Amazons," *woman of power* 3 (winter–spring 1986), 5.

13. Toni Cade Bambara, foreword to *This Bridge Called My Back: Writings by Radical Women of Color,* ed. Cherríe Moraga and Gloria Anzaldúa (Watertown, Mass.: Persephone Press, 1981; rpt. New York: Kitchen Table Women of Color Press, 1983), xvii; Cherríe Moraga, "It's the Poverty," cited in Gloria Anzaldúa, "Speaking in Tongues: A Letter to Third World Women Writers," in *This Bridge*, p. 166; June Jordan, "Poem for Nana," in *Passion* (Boston: Beacon Press, 1980), p. 2; Nellie Wong, "How to Guard Our Dead?" in *The Death of Long Steam Lady* (Los Angeles: West End Press, 1984), p. 44; Marjorie Agosin, "Needle and Thread Warriors: Women of Chile," *woman of power* 3, 35.

14. Lorde interview in Claudia Tate, *Black Women Writers at Work* (New York: Continuum Press, 1983), p. 102.

15. Stella Dong, "Interview with Ntozake Shange," *Publishers Weekly* (May 3, 1985), 74–75.

16. Maxine Hong Kingston, *The Woman Warrior: Memoirs of a Girlhood Among Ghosts* (New York: Random House, 1975), p. 24.

17. Audre Lorde, "Call," in *Our Dead Behind Us* (New York: Norton, 1986), p. 73; song cited by Gloria Anzaldúa, *Borderlands* p. 11.

18. Tate, *Black Women Writers*, p. 102.

19. Audre Lorde, *The Black Unicorn: Poems* (New York: Norton, 1978), pp. 21, 44, 12–13.

20. Audre Lorde, *Chosen Poems, Old and New* (New York: Norton, 1982), p. 58.

21. In *Inessential Woman* Elizabeth Spelman discusses "somatophobia," fear and disdain of the body, as a racist as well as a misogynistic attitude. To understand oppression fully, she argues, feminists must recognize that women are differently embodied and consider the particular meanings assigned culturally to these various embodiments (126–29). For Lorde, to be a warrior is to

recognize the body as a source and site of resistance and empowerment. See her essay "Uses of the Erotic: The Erotic as Power," *Sister Outsider*, pp. 53–54.

22. Lorde, "The Women of Dan," *Black Unicorn*, pp. 14–15.

23. Tate, *Black Women Writers*, p. 104.

24. Lorde, "Sisters in Arms," *Our Dead*, pp. 3–5.

25. Lorde, "Outlines," *Our Dead*, pp. 8–13.

26. Lorde, "Equal Opportunity," *Our Dead*, pp. 16–18.

27. Collins, "Black Feminist Thought," p. 772.

28. The quotation is from Ray Gwyn Smith's unpublished book *Moorland in Cold Country*, cited in Anzaldúa, *Borderlands*, p. 54. Anzaldúa's chapter is entitled "How to Tame a Wild Tongue."

29. Anzaldúa, *Borderlands*, pp. 21–23.

30. Barbara Smith, ed., *Home Girls: A Black Feminist Anthology* (New York: Kitchen Table Women of Color Press, 1983).

31. Anzaldúa, *Borderlands*, preface.

32. Anzaldúa, *Borderlands*, p. 78.

33. Anzaldúa, *Borderlands*, pp. 194–95.

34. Anzaldúa, "Border Crossings," *Trivia: A Journal of Ideas* 14 (1989), 49–50. Anzaldúa notes here that Chicanas are not the only feminist writers of color who use hybrid language. She cites Ginny Lem, who writes in Chinese and English, and Janice Mirikitani, who writes in Japanese and English, as sisters in this regard.

35. Moraga and Anzaldúa, *This Bridge*, p. 196.

36. June Jordan, introduction to *On Call: Political Essays* (Boston: South End Press, 1985), p. 2; Shange, Dong interview, pp. 74–75.

37. Jordan, introduction, *On Call*, p. 1.

38. June Jordan, "I Must Become a Menace to My Enemies," in *Things That I Do in the Dark* (Boston: Beacon Press, 1981), p. 145.

39. June Jordan, "Poem for Guatemala," in *Living Room* (Boston: Beacon Press, 1985).

40. Charlotte Bunch, "Bringing the Global Home," in *Passionate Politics: Feminist Theory in Action* (New York: St. Martin's Press, 1987), pp. 328–45.

41. Jordan, "South Africa: Bringing It All Back Home," *On Call*, pp. 17–18.

42. Jordan, "I Must Become a Menace to my Enemies," *Things That I Do*, p. 146.

43. Jordan, "From *The Talking Back of Miss Valentine Jones*," *Things That I Do*, p. 154.

44. Shange, Dong interview, pp. 74–75.

45. Ntozake Shange, *A Daughter's Geography* (New York: St. Martin's Press, 1983), pp. 22–23.

46. Hurtado, "Relating to Privilege," pp. 853–54. Lorde's statement is from *Sister Outsider*, pp. 131–32.

47. Neruda is quoted by Carolyn Forché, "El Salvador: An Aide Memoire," *American Poetry Review* (July–August 1981), 3–8, in a discussion of her experiences as a reporter and poet in El Salvador in 1980.

48. Tate, *Black Women Writers*, p. 157.

49. Adrienne Rich, "Power and Danger: Works of a Common Woman," in *On Lies, Secrets, and Silences: Selected Prose, 1966–1978* (New York: Norton, 1979), p. 247.

50. Ntozake Shange, preface to *See No Evil: Prefaces, Essays and Accounts,*

1976–83 (San Francisco: Momo's Press, 1984); Jordan, "Nicaragua: Why I Had to Go There," in *On Call,* pp. 70–75.

51. Kingston, *Woman Warrior,* p. 24; Anzaldúa, "Speaking in Tongues," *This Bridge,* p. 173.

52. For a discussion of men and women poets' female muses, see Mary K. DeShazer, *Inspiring Women: Reimagining the Muse* (Oxford and New York: Pergamon Press, 1986); for an analysis of women poets' "revisionist mythologies," see Alicia Suskin Ostriker, *Stealing the Language: The Emergence of Women's Poetry in America* (Boston: Beacon Press, 1986).

53. Although Kingston's *Woman Warrior* is generally considered autobiographical fiction or memoir rather than poetry, its many lyrical passages and lush images seem to me to justify considering it as prose poetry or, to use Anzaldúa's term, hybrid writing.

54. Lorde, "Call," *Our Dead,* p. 74.

55. Kingston, *Woman Warrior.* Quotes are taken from pp. 101–02, 23, 24, and 62–63.

56. On this point, see Mitsuye Yamada, "Invisibility Is an Unnatural Disaster," in *This Bridge,* pp. 35–40; and Hurtado, "Relating to Privilege," p. 835, n. 6.

57. Nellie Wong, *Dreams in Harrison Railroad Park* (Berkeley, Calif.: Kelsey St. Press, 1977), pp. 40–41. The phrase "think back through our mothers" is taken from Virginia Woolf, *A Room of One's Own* (New York: Harcourt Brace and World, 1929).

58. Nellie Wong, "In Search of the Self as Hero: Confetti of Voices on a New Year's Night, A Letter to Myself," *This Bridge,* p. 178.

59. Anzaldúa, "Speaking in Tongues," *This Bridge,* p. 173.

60. Alice A. Jardine, *Gynesis: Configurations of Woman and Modernity* (Ithaca: Cornell University Press, 1985), p. 434; Cherríe Moraga, *Loving in the War Years* (Boston: South End Press, 1983), p. 30.

61. Linda Alcoff, "Cultural Feminism Versus Post-structuralism: The Identity Crisis in Feminist Theory," *Signs: Journal of Women in Culture and Society* 13 (spring 1988), pp. 405–36.

62. Cherríe Moraga, "From a Long Line of Vendidas: Chicanas and Feminism," in *Feminist Studies, Critical Studies,* ed. Teresa de Lauretis (Bloomington: Indiana University Press, 1986), p. 180.

63. Alcoff, "Cultural Feminism," p. 434.

64. Cherríe Moraga, *Loving in the War Years,* p. 117.

65. Moraga, "It's the Poverty," cited in *This Bridge,* p. 166.

66. Lorde, "Learning to Write," *Our Dead,* p. 53.

67. Adrienne Rich, "Sources XXII," in *Your Native Land, Your Life: Poems* (New York: Norton, 1986), p. 25.

Chapter 14
The Politics of the Woman Artist in Isabel Allende's
The House of the Spirits

Z. Nelly Martínez

Isabel Allende's celebrated novel *The House of the Spirits*[1] presents the reader with a special view of the woman writer. Its narrator, Alba Trueba, is not a born writer but rather is made into one by circumstances. Imprisoned for political reasons, kept in solitary confinement, and repeatedly raped and tortured, she must write to denounce the regime that has so victimized her, but first she must survive the horror.

To be sure, Alba's experience in a prison cell recalls that of a number of imprisoned women and men in "real" life who, although not professional writers, are moved to record their ordeal from within the confines of a cell, and from the experience of a violated mind and body. This marginal literature, aptly labeled "subterranean poetry,"[2] reveals life experiences that echo Alba's: in a good number of cases these ordeals lead to the release of creative and thus liberating energies, which symbolically demolish the prison walls and heal both the body and the mind. One "subterranean" poem reads:

> . . . geography has been reduced to a few meters
> only with our eyes we can go far
> not with our feet
> But, inside of us, there grows another geography
> open
> boundless.[3]

The insight of a "boundless" intimate space is echoed in another poem, where it is presented as enfolding the life-giving and enlightening power of the spirit:

> They left behind
> only that which they thought useless.
> They took away everything
> except the Spirit,
> which they were incapable of seeing.
> From it life was reborn,
> a new path was opened up
> and the darkness
> became Light for me.[4]

Similarly, in Allende's fictional world this inner realm is interpreted in terms of the liberating power of the spirit. As such, this power infuses the death and rebirth experience Alba undergoes while in solitary confinement. It also manifests itself, although in an altogether different light, in the host of playful spirits that forever haunt Alba's ancestral home and render it magical. The power of the spirit then, which I will also interpret here in terms of the erotic, reveals ever-creative energies which are in fact expressions of the lifeforce.

Allende's novel can thus be read as subscribing to the idea, upheld by many nowadays, that the patriarchal order is built upon the repression of primal energies, traditionally identified with the lifeforce.[5] To the extent that these primal energies represent aspects of reality that can never be appropriated by the established order, they are seen as overflowing boundaries and as constituting a perennial threat to this order's stability. Alba's victory over male violence and over death, which is the climax of her descent into the hell of solitary confinement, attests to the liberation of these primordial forces and links this liberation with the emergence of woman in today's world, and of what has been traditionally associated with the feminine.

The truth is that, regardless if the protagonist of a tale of horror such as Alba's is female or male, the descent into the dictatorial hell is potentially empowering. A dictatorship, which is unquestionably the most extreme and most cruel manifestation of patriarchal might, sends people underground, literally and symbolically. And it is in the "underground" of their innermost being that people are able to empower themselves by their spontaneous contact with the creative, life-giving source—a source from which they have traditionally been alienated. The liberation of this inner power, which I identify with the archetypal Mother and associate with the archetypal figures of the goddess and

the witch, ultimately suggests the possibility of a world healed of patriarchal excesses—a world made holy, whole.[6]

*   *   *

Why witches? *Because witches are alive.* Because they are in direct
contact with the life of their own bodies and bodies of others, with the
life force itself.

Xavière Gauthier[7]

The wholeness which we have been discussing in these pages is a
wholeness based on a multidimensional vision of the world, rather
than on a single vision which has dominated Western culture and
most theological thought.

Sheila D. Collins[8]

The House of the Spirits chronicles the vicissitudes of four generations of the patrician Trueba family, headed by Esteban, a wealthy
landlord and mine owner. Although never fully acknowledged by the
narrative voice, the action of the novel takes place in a setting unmistakably Chilean. Also unmistakably, it reaches its highest point with the
military coup that overthrew the freely elected government of Salvador Allende in 1973 and instituted a reign of terror such as Chile had
never known before. That this fictional family enfolds historical events
in its story is vital to an understanding of the novelist's aim.

As well as telling the story of those who hold power, the novel
recounts the drama of the underdogs—the *inquilinos* who labor in the
hacienda owned by Esteban Trueba. With the advent of the socialist
regime, the *inquilinos* are pitted against the powerful overlord, but end
up defeated and banished from the *hacienda* at the time of the military
takeover. The quintessential patriarch, Esteban Trueba repeatedly imposes his will on others and infringes upon their rights, thus enacting
the violation of human integrity which has been identified with patriarchy and which here inevitably results in the cruel excesses of the
totalitarian regime. The "divide and conquer" syndrome, which lies at
the basis of the patriarchal order, finds an adequate metaphor in the
act of violation, a constant in the novel.[9] Typically, Trueba can also be
seen as the archetypal father: he is responsible for the great number of
"illegitimate" children born to the females of the *hacienda* who are
helpless under his dominion.

Although *The House of the Spirits* returns often to look at the imposing Trueba, it focuses primarily on three women: Trueba's wife Clara,
his daughter Blanca, and his granddaughter Alba. The latter disappears and is subsequently raped and tortured by the military, shortly
after the coup. At the close of the novel, these events bring the non-
agenarian Trueba to the painful awareness of the evils inherent in the

oppressive social order he has helped perpetuate. To symbolize this redemptive awareness, Allende makes him assist in the telling of the story, done by the main narrator, Alba, who most adequately fulfills the role of the artist in the novel.

A collection of letters exchanged betwen Alba's mother and grandmother prior to her birth, and a diary that Clara has kept since early childhood, serve as the basis for the novel Alba composes. Articulated primarily by a female voice which echoes the voices of all the women in the family, the novel subtly defies the established order while vehemently denouncing its excesses. Alba's narrative role also draws attention to the plight of the woman artist in countries devastated by a dictatorial regime. In addition to exposing the evils of patriarchy, she must denounce the horrors of a tyrannical rule that, as experience has proven in the everyday world and as the novel rightly suggests, brutally silences opposition through both the official discourse and the murderous security forces.

By attempting to break the cloak of silence with her novel, Allende herself joins ranks with a number of female writers in Latin America— Luisa Valenzuela and Marta Traba, among others—who similarly have struggled to subvert patriarchal and dictatorial discourse by the power of writing.[10] However, unlike Valenzuela and Traba, who regard the uprooting of repressive rule in Latin America as highly problematic, Allende suggests the possibility of change: in her darkest hour in prison, Alba discovers an inner source of power, a font of love and inspiration, which is immune to dictatorial horror. This inner source symbolizes the power of the spirit—an all-pervading, although largely repressed potency which I interpret here as endlessly seeking to heal and transform the world.[11]

Clearly, the central point of my work is that in Allende's *The House of the Spirits* the role of the woman artist involves both politics and spirituality. In this context, the term "spirit" disregards its traditional conventions and hints instead at an intimate source of power. Spirit is power because it re-creates human experience, re-writes history, if you like, drawing its inspiration from the innermost depths of being rather than relying on an external deity. Allende suggests that patriarchy, based largely on such an external (masculine) deity, represses this creative (feminine) force. Because of this repression, it is demonstrably death-oriented, a fact that comes across powerfully in Allende's text: the totalitarian regime represents the ultimate aberration of Western man's secular ambition to divide and conquer, to arrest change and exercise control over the spirit, the lifeforce.

Similarly, Alba's rape by her captors (a crime which is but one of the diabolical rituals of torture and death the novel denounces) not only represents the consummation of man's attempts to control women's bodies and appropriate their sexuality but also symbolizes the patriarchal desire to rule over the spirit, the fundamental ground of being. It is in this regard that the spirit in Allende's novel may be said to symbolize the erotic: while Western man has quite successfully attempted to appropriate human sexuality by making it an instrument of his power, he has proved himself incapable of also appropriating the erotic. In fact Eros, a force of such fundamental dynamism as to escape all human control, represents sexuality delivered from the patriarchal order.

Useful here is Jacques Lacan's conception of "desire," which is reminiscent of the Platonic Eros and relates to my interpretation of the erotic. Aptly described in terms of "a fundamental movement which leads man on without his being able to master it"[12] and which is potentially empowering, desire, like Eros, suggests the intimate source of power Allende exalts. This leads us to Audre Lorde, the American writer who also understands the erotic in terms of power. Not surprisingly, for Lorde this power, which she regards as rising "from our deepest and nonrational knowledge"[13] and as ever-creative, is ultimately "an assertion of the lifeforce in women."[14] Also useful here is Michel Foucault's opposition between *ars erotica* and *scientia sexualis*, an opposition that brings attention to the repressive power of Western sexuality and to the liberating power of Eros.[15] Thus Foucault equates (Western) knowledge with (patriarchal) might and sees art as expressive of Eros and hence as a liberating force. Free and creative, Eros is evidently subversive and hence demonic in the Western imagination. As it infuses Alba's experience and filters through her writing, Eros poses a threat to the stability of the system.

For, indeed, Alba's novel, in particular the passages that attest to her victory over rape, torture, and death, may be interpreted as a release of the erotic (more about this point later), and hence, as a demonic, subversive act. The writing of the novel, as well as its many potential readings, aims at symbolically subverting the dictatorial death machine by a celebration of Eros. This celebration is ultimately intended to heal the fragmented realm of the fathers and to render the world alive and whole. Thus, the role of the woman artist in Allende's novel is fundamentally that of a healer. Significantly, the image of the healer brings to mind those of the old wise woman and of the witch of medieval times. Since these images fit all the Trueba women, I shall focus on them briefly.

Regarded by many as a remnant of the immemorial matriarchal cultures and the repository of wisdom and of arcane power, the medieval matron posed a serious threat to the masculine church and its claim to intellectual supremacy. Thus, the patriarchal mind turned the wise old woman into a terrifying witch, who was literally "seen" by the religious zealots consorting with the devil "to overthrow God's kingdom by black magic."[16] As the noted feminist Barbara G. Walker has pointed out, the witch-hunt craze unleashed all over Europe and the resultant massacre of innocent women served as a model for the persecution of alleged subversives, similarly accused of consorting with "evil" forces, throughout the centuries.[17] Allende's novel faithfully reproduces this persecution while exposing the Chilean massacre.

To the extent that she resorts to "black magic" (the spirit, the erotic), thus undermining the realm of the fathers, Alba embodies the witch. To the extent that the Trueba women are nonsubmissive, wildly imaginative and dangerously eccentric, and thus shake the very foundations of patriarchy, all of them equally stand for the witch. Characteristically, Alba's great-grandmother, Nivea, a feminist *avant la lettre* and a dedicated suffragist, challenges tradition by viewing herself in particular, and other women in general, as potentially autonomous human beings endowed with the power to take charge of their own lives. For their part, Alba and her mother Blanca are genuine renegades who defy the social hierarchy by falling for men far below their station. Alba herself is an underground agent earnestly helping those who are hounded by the military. Finally Alba's grandmother Clara, who distinctly embodies the witch with her heretical comments and her divinatory and psychokinetic power, also represents the primal goddess, the lifeforce itself.

To be sure, there is a link between the witch and the goddess since the former, in the guise of the crone, symbolizes the dark, destructive aspects of the latter. Unlike the patriarchal god, who is conceived solely as the supreme creator (destruction being the devil's and the witches' department), the goddess (like Eros) embodies destruction as well as creation and thereby suggests unremitting re-creation. Appropriately, this process of unceasing re-creation is implicit in the three phases of the goddess: the maiden, the mother and the crone, that is, the creator, the preserver and the destroyer.[18] In *The House of the Spirits* the bond established between mother, daughter and granddaughter, which suggests a subtle matrilinearity or, better yet, a subtle "matricircularity," is evocative of the ever-creative goddess. In truth, the cyclical interpretation of the world involved in goddess worship finds a most adequate symbol in the circle—the "yonic" *circle* (from Sanskrit, vulva, womb), which Walker sees as counteracting the traditional "phallic" *line*.[19]

In effect, the re-creative worldview implicit in Allende's novel undermines the patriarchal linear interpretation. I shall return to this point, so let me only suggest now that whereas patrilinearity exalts the power of the past to perpetuate itself by rigorously shaping the future, matricircularity brings attention to the infinite potential for change contained in the present. If the phallic line projects humans back into an idealized beginning and forward into a dreaded, apocalyptic ending, the yonic circle unremittingly returns them to the present and projects them into the depths of their being—the realm of darkness and death but also the possible source of a rebirth and a transformation. As I shall attempt to demonstrate, Alba's experience in solitary confinement, where she confronts death but where she also contacts her inner power, may be seen as a descent into chaos and as a death followed by a rebirth.

Clearly, the cyclical understanding of reality implicit both in the matricircular view and in Allende's novel suggests the integration of this terrifying realm into the totality of experience—this integration being the precondition for the transformation and healing the novel exalts. The patriarchal order, which has systematically struggled to subdue chaos by the forceful imposition of repressive patterns, has ended by projecting it on undesirable and expendable "others" (witches, heretics, subversives, the devil), and/or on an otherworld of never-ending horror—a hell where the sinful atone eternally for their alleged transgressions.[20] The circular view, on the other hand, devalues the traditional conceptions of hell as well as that of heaven: there is neither hell nor heaven, but eternal transformation, in a universe that exalts the ever-changing goddess and dethrones the never-changing god. Thus, Allende, while devaluing the traditional notion of a male divinity, also devalues the idea of punishment and of hell. This is a crucial point, since dictatorial power aims at punishing and/or disposing of the "sinful" by confining them in the worst of hells: the torture chamber.

The devaluing of the patriarchal god and the exaltation of the goddess is particularly relevant within a Latin American context. In a social milieu where military rulers assume a truly godlike role, this mighty female figure is wonderfully empowering for dissenting women. Expressly called upon by the institutionalized powers to "redeem" the world from evil and bring order out of chaos by stamping out all subversive action, the military tyrant may be seen as reenacting the role of the vengeful Judeo-Christian god while acting out his inquisitorial powers. Moreover, as he administers "justice" with an iron hand, the tyrant in Allende's novel condemns the "guilty" to clandestine detention centers which make real the Judeo-Christian hell: the terrible ordeal Alba and a multitude of women and men must endure in the torture chambers erected by the oppressors, graphically portrays this hell.

Not accidentally, the description of divine punishment presented by a local priest, Father Restrepo, in the initial chapter of the novel, corresponds almost verbatim to the description of the horror inflicted upon Alba and her prison-mates in the last chapters of the work:

The faithful followed him from parish to parish, sweating as he described the torments of the damned in hell, the bodies ripped apart by various ingenious torture apparatuses, the eternal flames, the hooks that pierced the male member, the disgusting reptiles that crept up female orifices, and the myriad other sufferings that he wove into his sermons to strike the fear of God into the hearts of his parishioners. (3)[21]

Ironically, the uneasy silence that follows the priest's sermon is finally broken by the innocently defiant remarks from Clara, who is only a child at the time: "Psst! Father Restrepo! If that story about hell is a lie, we're all fucked, aren't we . . ." (7). However innocent the source, these words are truly heretical in their context, and not surprisingly, the priest's condemnation of Clara, "Possessed . . . She's possessed by the devil!" (7) is tantamount to an accusation of witchcraft.

It is doubly ironic that future events within the family, as well as within the country, prove the priest's assessment of Clara right—an assessment which, unbeknownst to father Restrepo, equally applies to the other females of the Trueba household. For in these women, most particularly in Clara, who writes the family diary, and in Alba, who turns the diary into the novel we read, Allende has expressed the subversive power of the witch as well as the re-creative power of the goddess. It is a power that momentarily silences the all-pervading word of god the father and allows for insight—an in-depth vision that delivers both language and consciousness from the patriarchal prison and asserts the potency of the spirit to re-name and thus to re-create the world.

Clearly, this re-creative process is inherent in the near-death experience Alba undergoes while in solitary confinement—an experience of expanded consciousness that allows her to perceive new meanings with which to defy the patriarchal order, denounce the dictatorship and reinterpret the world. Embodying the goddess, her long-dead grandmother appears to Alba in her solitary confinement and urges her to rise and write, to celebrate life unyieldingly in the midst of death and despair: "her grandmother Clara, whom she had invoked so many times to help her die, appeared with the novel idea that the point was not to die, since death came anyway, but to survive, which would be a miracle" (414).

By heeding her grandmother's plea, Alba heals the split between her outer self, which seeks to perish, and her innermost self, which urges her to live. Thus, she is reborn to an awareness of herself as whole and to a sense of mission which moves her to assume her task courageously. The writing of the novel, which is aimed at telling the world "about the terrible secret she is living" (414), is a genuine political act—a political act grounded in an experience of wholeness, of contact with a divine source, of a revelation. In the long run, Alba's experience of wholeness culminates in her awareness of the world as whole: as a dynamic and self-transforming interrelatedness of which she herself, her grandmother, and all others are integral parts.

It is evident, then, that Alba's role as a woman artist in the novel is to be interpreted in conjunction with the role played by Clara, who has led Alba to transformation. In fact, the world Clara inhabits is a metaphor for the integrative, life-affirming universe Alba has envisioned during her solitary confinement. This world, which in the novel implies the spirit released, is presented as magical: not only does Clara possess divinatory and psychokinetic power, but the house itself is inhabited by mischievous spirits forever ridiculing Trueba's control.

A metaphorical "wild zone"[22] presided over by a witch, Clara's world is captured on a canvas which shows

a middle-aged woman dressed in white, with silvery hair and the sweet gaze of a trapeze artist, resting in a rocking chair that hangs suspended just above the floor, floating amidst flowered curtains, a vase flying upside down, and a fat black cat that observes the scene like an important gentleman. (267)

This picture reveals a period in the Trueba household "when divine good humor and the hidden forces of human nature acted with impunity to provoke a state of emergency and upheaval in the laws of physics and logics" (267). Playful and irreverent, these forces subvert the kingdom of the fathers and render the world bewitched. This magic world is also symbolized by the additions Clara had made to the rear section of the Trueba mansion. Designed along purely classical lines, Esteban Trueba's house attests to patriarchal wealth and power, as well as to patriarchy's eternal ideal of "order and peace, beauty and civilization" (13). Trueba could hardly have anticipated that

the solemn, cubic, dense, pompous house, which sat like a hat amid its green and geometric surroundings, would end up full of protuberances and incrustations, of twisted staircases that led to empty space, of turrets . . . doors hanging in midair . . . all of which were Clara's inspiration. (93)

In the long run, the mansion is transformed into an "enchanted labyrinth" (93), a "magic universe" (281), which plays havoc in the orderly and civilized patriarchal realm.

After Clara's death, however, this magical universe vanishes, and a long period of decline sets in at the Trueba mansion. It behooves Alba, years later, not only to restore the magic but also to project it to the world. While Clara's experience has remained within the confines of the home, Alba's transcends the home and encompasses her ravaged country through the performance of the ultimate artistic act: healing.

In contrast to Clara's magic, which may be viewed in more traditional terms, Alba's may be regarded as "modern."[23] Hers is a magic that not only plays havoc with the patriarchal order but also aims at incarnating the witch and the goddess in the world, on the stage of history. Thus, Alba's text not only raises the voices of dissent, but it also incites further dissent by urging all women to use their largely untapped source of power, their innermost spirit, and to participate in the task of drastically transforming, healing, the world.

Alba's belief in the need to transcend her individual self and to share with others in the liberation of the spirit is validated by her experience with a number of women she meets in the detention center. Although they have been humiliated, tortured and raped, and one of them has even been made to abort, these women have bonded together to confront their torturers by defiantly singing the joy of life: "And they sang even stronger but the guards did not come in, for they had learned that there is no way to avoid the unavoidable" (427). Just as does Alba's novel, their Ode to Joy, which the women spontaneously compose and sing, expresses the indomitable desire to celebrate the spirit, to turn off the dictatorial death-machine and create a life-giving wholeness. Thus, "modern magic," which both the novel and this Ode to Joy represent, may be described as Heide Göttner-Abendroth suggests as a set of symbolic practices based "on an ethos of totality" and intended "to influence psychosocial reality"[24] by drawing others into the celebration of the spirit. Not surprisingly, this novel reaches inward and calls on two of its own characters, Alba and Esteban, to "write" the book. At the same time it reaches outward to seize the reader, drawing her or him into one of the most symbolic practices: the act of reading.

The idea of totality, which returns us to Alba's experience of the world as a transformative wholeness, ultimately leads to a conception of time which, as I suggested earlier, is crucial to Allende's interpretation of the woman artist. Inasmuch as the experience of wholeness implies a purposeful alignment with the never-ending flow of life, a flow which is forever taking place now, Alba's new awareness establishes her firmly in the present—the "now" experience which, as she begins to suspect, contains all time. This intuition subverts her up-to-now linear view of time which comprehends the dynamics of history largely in terms of predetermination, of an unremitting repetition of archetypal acts regarded as belonging to the "natural" order. From Alba's new integrative perspective, the past, existing only as memory and hence open to transformation, loses its grip over the present as well as its power to effectively predetermine the future. In the final analysis, Alba's integrative perception challenges the patriarchal "reading" of history in linear terms as well as the patriarchal linear "making" of history by endlessly repeated violent acts. Of these violent acts, literal and symbolic, man's rape of woman is the archetypal model.

While in prison, Alba is raped by her blood relative, Colonel García, a man whose grandmother is the first female among the *inquilinos* to fall prey to Alba's grandfather's lust. Alba's rape allegorizes this archetypal enactment:

The day my [Alba's] grandfather tumbled his [Colonel García's] grandmother, Pancha García, among the rushes of the river bank, he added another link to the chain of events that had to complete itself. Afterwards the grandson of the woman who was raped repeats the gesture with the granddaughter of the rapist, and perhaps forty years from now my grandson will knock García's granddaughter down among the rushes, and so on down through the centuries in an unending tale of sorrow, blood, and love. (431–32)

Thus, Alba understands that the rape suffered by that obscure woman has set in motion a seemingly inexorable chain of violations, which she may choose to perpetuate by seeking revenge or to upset by drawing upon her experience of the inner source. Asserting that her task has to do with life rather than with death, the heroine of Allende's novel chooses not to avenge herself for the myriad humiliations she has suffered: "my revenge would be just another part of the same inexorable rite. I have to break that terrible chain" (414).

For indeed Alba's subversion of the "inexorable rite" challenges the patriarchal linear view of time and decisively installs her in the ever-creative present: "we believe in the fiction of the past, present, and future, but it may also be true that everything happens simultaneously—as the three Mora sisters said, who could see the spirits of all eras mingled in the space" (432). Allende evidently suggests that it is from within the present—the only temporality that may lead human beings inward to an awareness of their intrinsic power—that the world may be endlessly transformed. Alba's awareness of the ever-present source shakes the foundation of patriarchy, which has been obsessed with perpetuating itself by perpetuating the past. Thus, her avowed intention to write the novel in order to "reclaim the past" (1, 433) may be viewed here as her resolve to reinterpret history from the vantage point of an enlightened present. Ultimately, this reinterpretation recalls the matricircular view of reality I suggested earlier and its defiance of the phallic line.

Shortly after her ordeal, Alba begins to suspect that the deeper significance of the tumultuous history that has ravished her country and victimized her, lies not in examining the occurrences from a linear, that is, patriarchal perspective, but rather in integrating them into a dynamic whole. By doing so, Alba seeks to elucidate other possible relations between past and present occurrences, and ultimately to unveil other possible meanings:

When I was in the doghouse, I felt as if I were assembling a jigsaw puzzle in which each piece had a specific place. Before I put the puzzle together, it all seemed incomprehensible to me, but I was sure that if I ever managed to complete it, the separate parts would each have meaning and the whole would be harmonious. Each piece has a reason for being the way it is, *even Colonel García.* (432, emphasis added)

Alba's suspicion that the linear view of time is indeed a "fiction" and that everything does "happen simultaneously" discloses her newly acquired awareness that the past is not to be regarded as an external power that tyranically controls the present. Enfolded as memory, the past is *dynamically* contained in Alba's experience of the present, and through the awareness of her innermost power, the past may be subverted. The productive coexistence of the present and the past is symbolized in the novel by the fact that Alba detects her grandmother's voice filtering through her own while she is composing the novel:

At times I felt as if I had lived all this before and that I have already written these very words, but I know it was not I: it was another woman who kept her notebooks so that one day I could use them. I write, she wrote, that memory is fragile and the space of a single life is brief, passing so quickly that we never get a chance to see the relationship between events. (432)

Through Alba, her alter ego, Allende persuasively argues that a revolutionary re-reading of the past not only transforms the present but may also subvert a seemingly unavoidable (patriarchal) future.

It is evident, then, that Alba has begun to "read" new and, in fact, revolutionary meanings into the text of her country's and family's histories and into the text of the world. As an integral part of the totality, on the other hand, she may not only read it differently but may equally participate, through writing, in the unfolding of new meanings. It is clear that by their defiance of the security forces, the women in the detention center have also begun to "read" and unfold revolutionary meanings in the text of their repressive culture. Women's courage to defy the dictatorial rule and assert their power is further symbolized by the humble female who assists Alba after she is released and left in an isolated area by her captors:

I told her she had run an enormous risk, rescuing me, and she smiled. It was then I understood that the days of Colonel García and all those like him are numbered, because they have not been able to destroy the spirit of these women. (492)

Bonded together by the same earnest desire to affirm life, Alba and the women she encounters have released a hitherto largely untapped source of power, which promises to significantly alter and eventually transform the patriarchal order. Identified with Eros, this power may be viewed as healing not only the mind but the whole being.

*   *   *

Let's not repress something as simple as wanting to live life itself. Oral drive, anal drive, vocal drive, all drives are good forces, and among them the gestational drive—just like wanting to write: a desire to live oneself within, wanting the belly, the tongue, the blood.

Hélène Cixous[25]

when we begin to live from within outward, in touch with the power of the erotic within ourselves, and allowing that power to inform and illuminate our actions upon the world around us, then we begin to be responsible to ourselves in the deepest sense.

Audre Lorde[26]

At this point, I would like to return to my interpretation of the spirit in terms of the erotic and relate it to a figure that has also captured the imagination of numerous contemporary feminists. I refer to the archetypal Mother who, in her divine and demonic aspects, recalls the goddess and the witch, and thereby the process of endless re-creation they embody. It is no accident that Audre Lorde has referred to a source of power within herself, which she identifies with the Black Mother in all women. She relates the Mother to the erotic which, as previously stated, she insightfully interprets as "an assertion of the lifeforce in women."

Transcending traditional sexuality which centers on parts of the body and is repressive, the erotic involves the entire body, the spirit, and the mind and is liberating and creative, producing mental creations as well as new life. (Thus, in Allende's novel motherhood is presented not as passive regenerativeness but rather as lucid and liberating creativity.) Unlike patriarchal sexuality which aims at domination and is "deadly serious," as it may climax in torture and sadistic pleasure, the erotic points to an abundance of life and thereby to playfulness and joy, as well as a demythifying humor traditionally curtailed by Western culture. Unlike traditional sexuality which reaffirms the law of the father, the erotic undermines this law while expressing the subversive power of the Mother. Clara's magical kingdom in the Trueba mansion is an embodiment of the erotic, and she herself represents the Mother.

Clearly, the mighty female figure both Allende and Lorde evoke in their writings relates to the pre-Oedipal Mother, with whom the child intimately identifies prior to its entry into the symbolic order, the realm of the father.[27] Forever latent in the depths of our being, the pre-Oedipal Mother embodies the creative urge which relates the unconscious mind to the body and thus suggests a common ground for both the gestational and the artistic drives. It is in this context that she has become the primordial source of insight and inspiration to some noted feminists such as the French Hélène Cixous.[28] When Cixous interprets women's writing as expressive of "a desire to live oneself within" and as a manifestation of the body as well as of the mind, she is in fact alluding to the pre-Oedipal Mother and to the all-encompassing creative force she represents. And although the Mother, "The Voice . . . [that] sings from a time before law,"[29] as Cixous has described her, also relates to darkness and chaos and hence to death, she is primarily an expression of the continuity of life, of its ongoing victory over death. Thus, she may be conceived, to quote Lorde once again, as "the *yes* within ourselves,"[30] a "yes to life" which, as manifestation of the erotic, heals the entire being, the body as well as the mind.[31]

I would like to suggest now that the surrender to the creative urge embodied in the Mother, a surrender which describes Alba's encounter with Clara in the doghouse and results in her determination to survive and write about her experience, be interpreted in terms of Eros as bliss. Paradoxically, it is a bliss born out of intense sorrow, which involves her whole being and devalues the limited patriarchal conception of pleasure. Consequently, the Mother, an expression of "the Voice before the law," may likewise be regarded as an expression of "the body before the law." To put it differently, the Mother represents the body before patriarchal attempts to subdue Eros by "sexualizing" it, that is, by inscribing on the body the patriarchal "truth" of sex. As is well known, this sexualization of the body is founded upon the primacy of the phallus and upon the phallic view of pleasure as possession and control.

This point is crucial in the novel, since Allende unabashedly focuses on the ultimate sexual pleasure in the patriarchal world—that of possession and control by torturing and rape, by maiming unto death. Indeed, the spirit of the Marquis de Sade is alive and well in Allende's fictional universe: in just a few pages of her novel the author manages to expose almost every method of torture practiced in the world today. As is to be expected, among these methods, the rape of women and the desecration of their bodies figure prominently. Not accidentally, Alba's urgency in composing the novel results in the healing of both her violated mind and her violated body—an all-embracing healing that may be viewed as a celebration of Eros.

As manifestation of the erotic, the Mother may be said to "desexualize" the body, that is, to exorcise from it the evils of the patriarchal view of sexuality *while eroticizing the entire being*. For Eros, manifesting the spirit, ultimately reveals an indomitable human desire to conquer death and destruction by affirming life and creativity. Thus, at one level, Alba's surrender to Eros in the doghouse is presented as a symbolic cleansing of her body of the multiple violations it has endured—a cleansing that heals the body and results in the conception of a child. At another level, her surrender to the erotic is presented as a symbolic rising from the dead into the chaos before creation. The multitude of characters flooding the doghouse and demanding a participatory role in the telling of the story embody this overpowering chaos. Born out of despair, Alba's experience is rapturous, nonetheless, because it bears witness to her blissful contact with the Mother:

Alba tried to obey her grandmother, but as soon as she began to take notes with her mind, the doghouse filled with all the characters of her story, who rushed in, shoved each other out of the way to wrap her in their anecdotes, their vices, and their virtues, trampled on her intentions to compose a documentary, and threw her testimony to the floor. (414)

Subsequently, Alba finds a way to bring order out of chaos and to emerge victorious from this overwhelming creative outburst:

But she invented a code for recalling things in order, and then she was able to bury herself so deeply in her story that she stopped eating, scratching herself, smelling herself, and complaining, and overcame all her varied agonies. (414)

(Alba's "code for recalling things in order" relates, of course, to her insight that she must examine the family events not from a linear, but from an integrative holistic perspective.)

If, as Cixous suggests, and Allende appears to confirm, writing as a form of creativity involves the body in an essential way, in Alba's case it involves a body that has been tortured, maimed, and left to die. Both her writing and her pregnancy in the end, a pregnancy that may well be the outcome of the rapes she has endured, represent the ultimate challenge to tyranny and its horrors. Thus, it comes as no surprise that, after her release from prison, Alba is immune to her tormentor's cruelty: "They took her back to Colonel García, whose hatred had returned during these days, but she did not recognize him. *She was beyond his power*" (415, emphasis added).

The last scene in the novel, which shows an expectant Alba setting out to write her text, is especially significant in that it points to the all-embracing healing the novel proclaims and returns the reader to the three-faceted goddess. Here Alba represents both the maiden and the mother and also the witch, since her writing is aimed at subverting the established order. Furthermore, the matricircularity herein implied and also suggested by the fact that the novel begins and ends with an identical phrase, once again brings attention to the present: in this case, however, the present refers to the time of Alba's actual writing and of the reader's endless "re-writing" of the text. By thus symbolically affirming the present and its infinite potential for the production of meaning, Allende invites us to draw upon the ever-creative source we all share and to participate in the never-ending reading and "rewriting" of her novel.

The writing of the novel, with which Alba is entrusted and which engages the reader, is intended ultimately as a call to all women and men to awaken the long-dormant and internal source of power and to participate in its unfolding. Allende suggests that it is only by aligning themselves with "spirit," "magic," or Eros that human beings may recover their wholeness and thereby recover the wholeness which *is*, in fact, the world—an interrelatedness that celebrates cooperation rather than competition, and deliverance rather than repression; a place where women and what has traditionally been understood as the feminine principle play integral roles. Unlike the patriarchal god who stands for immutability and permanence and focuses on a male figure, the goddess allegorizes a process of constant change that involves both sexes equally, as symbolized by Esteban's eventual participation as narrator of the story.

In *The House of the Spirits*, politics and spirituality are wed: if "the personal is political," it may likewise be deeply spiritual. For Allende, evidently, a social revolution must be grounded in a revolution of consciousness. It is a revolution that not only delivers us from false consciousness but that also reveals the enfolded goddess, that is, the creative energies traditionally alienated in the male god. Interestingly, a character in the novel is made to comment that "Marxism doesn't stand a chance in Latin America . . . [because] it doesn't allow for the magical side of things" (306–7). Allende's revolutionary insight allows for that magic but, unlike a number of Latin American male novelists, who perceive it only "out there" in the world, she sees the magic primarily in the innermost depths of being: in the recondite regions where the Mother reigns supreme and which contain the disturbing voice of the witch and the life-giving power of the goddess.

In summary, *The House of the Spirits* presents the artist as healer, as the celebrant of the forces of life and as the lucid participant in the struggle to transform society and ultimately to sacralize the world—to render it holy, whole. Allende is indeed implying that unless women assume the role history is demanding of them, the Chilean holocaust, which has paralleled countless others, may become the world's.

Notes

1. Isabel Allende, *The House of the Spirits,* trans. Magda Bogin (New York: Bantam Books, 1985). Allende has published two other novels: *Of Love and Shadows* (New York: Alfred A. Knopf, 1987) and *Eva Luna* (New York: Alfred A. Knopf, 1988).

2. See, for instance, Bruno Serrano, ed., *Poesía prisionera: Escritura de cinco mujeres encarceladas* (Santiago de Chile: Bruno Serrano, 1988), p. 8. Another text bearing witness to writing done in prison is the collection *Escritos en la cárcel: La expresión poética de los presos políticos* (Montevideo: Impresora Pelacayo, 1886). There is also a record by political prisoners produced in Argentina in 1984, shortly after the end of the recent military dictatorship: *Desde la cárcel: Canciones de detenidos y desaparecidos argentinos 76/80* (Buenos Aires: Todas las voces). These collections have not been translated into English. Their respective titles in English are: *Poets in Prison: Writing by Five Imprisoned Women, Writing from Jail: The Poetic Expression of Political Prisoners,* and *From Prison: Songs of Argentinian Detainees and Disappeared.*

3. Lucía Fabri, "Caña," in the above-mentioned *Escritos en la cárcel,* p. 31.

4. Julia Esquivel, "Parable," in *You Can't Drown the Fire: Latin American Women Writing in Exile,* ed. Alicia Partnoy (Pittsburgh and San Francisco: Cleis Press, 1988), p. 197. Partnoy's efforts at compiling writings by women who have been imprisoned or were otherwise forced to exile themselves from their native countries, is highly commendable. Partnoy was herself a detainee and a "disappeared" in her native Argentina. After moving to the United States, she published her "memoirs" of prison life. See *The Little School: Tales of Disappearance and Survival in Argentina* (Pittsburgh and San Francisco: Cleis Press, 1986).

5. See, among the numerous recent texts on the subject, David Bohm, *Wholeness and the Implicate Order* (London: Routledge and Kegan Paul, 1980). A professor of theoretical physics in London, Bohm is the author of several well-known works, such as *Causality and Chance in Modern Physics* (London: Routledge & Kegan Paul, 1957), *Quantum Theory* (Englewood Cliffs, N.J.: Prentice-Hall, 1951), and *The Special Theory of Relativity* (New York: W. A. Benjamin, 1965). The "implicate" or enfolded order Bohm proposes, which is the counterpart of the "explicate" or unfolded order of everyday experience, points to the primal energies which I interpret in terms of the lifeforce.

6. In keeping with the nonhierarchical worldview which I detect in Allende's novel, I shall not capitalize such terms as goddess, god, father, or witch. I shall capitalize, however, the term Mother in an attempt to honor the all-embracing creative powers she represents.

7. Xavière Gauthier, "Why Witches?" ed. Elaine Marks and Isabelle de Courtivon, *New French Feminisms: An Anthology,* trans. Erica M. Eisinger (New York: Schocken Books, 1981), p. 200.

8. Sheila D. Collins, *A Different Heaven and Earth* (Valley Forge, Pa.: Judson Press, 1983), p. 183.

9. Bent on control, Western man has consistently fragmented and di-

chotomized the world: the first term of the dichotomy, which is viewed as wielding power over the other, represents the many faces of the father.

10. Luisa Valenzuela, *The Lizard's Tail,* trans. Gregory Rabassa (New York: Farrar, Straus and Giroux, 1983); *Strange Things Happen Here: 26 Short Stories and a Novel,* trans. Helen Lane (New York: Harcourt Brace Jovanovich, 1979); and *Other Weapons,* trans. Deborah Bonner (Hanover, N.H.: Ediciones del Norte, 1985). Also, Marta Traba, *Mothers and Shadows* (London: Readers International, 1986).

11. As presented in Allende's text, the unfolding of the spirit mirrors the release of feminine power in the world today, a power open to both females and males. In the view of a number of contemporary feminists engaged in what may be termed "postpatriarchal spirituality," feminine power emerges from within the depths of human experience thus opposing male power traditionally exerted from without. See Charlene Spretnak, ed., *The Politics of Women's Spirituality: Essays on the Rise of Spiritual Power Within the Feminist Movement* (Garden City, N.Y.: Anchor Books, 1982).

12. See Antoine Vergote, "From Freud's 'Other Scene' to Lacan's 'Other'," in *Interpreting Lacan,* ed. Joseph H. Smith and William Kerrigan (New Haven, Conn., and London: Yale University Press, 1983), p. 213. Author's emphasis. Evidently, Lacanian "desire" implies an enlargement of the Freudian understanding of sexuality. In this context, the unconscious drives and wishes that Freud examined are viewed as expressions or manifestations of that fundamental dynamic.

To be sure, the erotic also relates to Herbert Marcuse's Freudian interpretation of Eros, which he defines as "the great unifying force that preserves all life." See his *Eros and Civilization: A Philosophical Inquiry into Freud* (Boston: Beacon Press, 1966), p. 27. Finally, my understanding of the erotic has affinities with Mary Daly's conception of female "Pure Lust," which she developed in her work *Pure Lust: Elemental Feminist Philosophy* (Boston: Beacon Press, 1984). Rejecting traditional male lust, which she views as "a fusion of obsession and aggression," an aggression that "rapes, dismembers, and kills women and all living things within its reach" (p. 1), Daly defines Pure Lust as, "pure Passion: unadulterated, absolute, simple sheer striving for *abundance of be-ing*" (p. 3, emphasis added).

13. Audre Lorde, "Uses of the Erotic: The Erotic as Power," *Sister Outsider: Essays and Speeches* (Trumansburg, N.Y.: The Crossing Press Feminist Series), p. 53. Lorde's work is also examined elsewhere in this volume. See, for example, Estella Lauter's "Re-visioning creativity: Audre Lorde's Refiguration of Eros and the Black Mother Poet Within."

14. Lorde, "Uses of the Erotic," p. 55.

15. See *"Scientia Sexualis,"* in Michel Foucault, *The History of Sexuality, Volume I: An Introduction,* trans. Robert Hurley (New York: Vintage Books, 1980), p. 57.

16. Barbara G. Walker, *The Crone: Women of Age, Wisdom and Power* (San Francisco: Harper and Row, 1985), p. 125. In addition to being repositories of traditional wisdom, the medieval matrons were generally self-supporting and independent, that is, free of male control. Clearly, this freedom and independence, as well as the fact that they adhered to "pagan" customs, made them most undesirable characters in the eyes of the patriarchal masters.

17. As described by Walker, the methods of torture employed by the European inquisitors show an uncanny resemblance to those utilized at pres-

ent in countries ruled by state terrorism. The same opinion is shared by Ximena Bunster-Burotto in "Surviving Beyond Fear: Women and Torture in Latin America," in *Women and Change in Latin America*, ed. June Nash and Helen Safa (Mass.: Bergin and Garvey Publishers, 1986), p. 323.

18. Interestingly, the maiden and the mother aspects of the goddess were merged into the Christian symbol of the virgin mother and hence deprived of divine status. The crone aspect, because it stood for destruction and death, was sent underground by the patriarchal church. Patriarchy is indeed founded on the violent repression of the dark aspects of reality.

19. "Hence the typical masculine notion of life as linear, not cyclic, ending not in reabsorption but in eternal stasis, in either heaven or hell," writes Walker. "The patriarchs' choice between 'good' and 'evil' is irrelevant. . . . The real choice is between the (phallic) line and the (yonic) circle; between death as a mere passage in time to a mysterious imagined world that can never change, and death as a real dissolution according to the law of nature, where change is the only constant," *The Crone*, pp. 32–33.

20. See Walker, *The Crone*.

21. The reference to "the disgusting reptiles that crept up female orifices" alludes to that diabolical combination of rape and torture, widely practiced at present, whereby live rats are introduced into women's vaginas.

22. The concept of the "wild zone" was proposed some years ago by the British anthropologist Edward Ardener. See his "Belief and the Problem of Women" and "The 'Problem' Revisited," in *Perceiving Women*, ed. Shirley Ardener (London: J. M. Dent and Sons, 1981). Originating with Ardener's observation of the women's world among the Bakweri people of western Cameroon—their rites of passage and fertility rites—, the "wild zone" designates the territorial world that falls outside the boundaries of patriarchal organization. "Where society is defined by men," argues the author, "some features of women do not fit that definition" (23). Thus, the "wild," the untamed, points to the second term of the dichotomy Self/not-Self when the dichotomy, in Ardener's words, has been raised "to the level of society's own self-definition" (23).

Ardener's concept is versatile and bears further elaboration. Elaine Showalter, for one, has applied the notion to the realm of women's culture in general. In her view, the "wild zone" designates a female space which may be interpreted not only in experiential and spatial terms but in metaphysical terms as well, as "a projection of the unconscious." See her "Feminist Criticism in the Wilderness," in *The New Feminist Criticism: Essays on Women, Literature and Theory*, ed. Elaine Showalter (New York: Pantheon Books, 1985), p. 262. Enfolding a perennial desire for transformation and renewal, the wild zone ultimately discloses a purposeful alignment and a full enjoyment of the spirit, the life force. Clearly, the witch and the goddess inhabit this subversive realm.

23. I refer to Heide Göttner-Abendroth. In her article "Nine Principles of a Matriarchal Aesthetic," this critic touches on magic, which she sees both in traditional and modern terms. While the former aims at influencing natural reality by means of such rituals as dancing, the latter seeks to influence psychosocial reality by means of such symbolic practices as literature. In the author's view, the release of the magical presupposes a world delivered from patriarchal constraints, a dynamic and integrative realm where "the goddess can dance again." In *Feminist Aesthetics*, ed. Harriet Anderson, trans. Gisela Ecker (London: The Women's Press, 1985), p. 84.

24. Göttner-Abendroth, "Nine Principles," p. 86.

25. Hélène Cixous, "Sorties: Out And Out: Attacks/Ways Out/Forays," in *The Newly Born Woman*, ed. Hélène Cixous and Catherine Clément, trans. Betsy Wing, Theory and History of Literature, Vol. 24 (Minneapolis: University of Minnesota Press, 1986), p. 99.

26. Lorde, "Uses of the Erotic," p. 58.

27. "Symbolic" here discloses Jacques Lacan's usage of the term. In Lacanian theory, the order of the symbolic, to which the child accedes at the time of the Oedipal crisis, represents the patriarchal order. The term alludes to the fact that the child's entry into the symbolic order involves its access to language and thereby to the law of the Father, which is inscribed in language.

28. For Cixous, the Mother is the embodiment of an inner voice that can be heard only by those who "live themselves within." The author associates the Mother, who "resides" in the depths of people's being, with the natural mother, whose voice is silenced by the discourse of the father.

29. Cixous, "Sorties," p. 93.

30. Lorde, "Uses of the Erotic," p. 57 (emphasis added).

31. In this context, let us recall Lacan's suggestion, made on the basis of the fact that the French nouns *nom* and *non* have identical pronunciations, that the "name" of the Father (*le nom du Père*) is an echo of his "no" (*le non du Père*).

Chapter 15
Margaret Drabble's *The Waterfall*: New System, New Morality

Gayle Greene

> I tried for so long to . . . find a style that would express it, to find
> a system that would excuse me, to construct a new medium . . .
> so what can I make that will admit me and encompass me?
>
> I must make an effort to comprehend it. I will take it all to
> pieces, I will resolve it to its parts, and then I will put it together
> again. I will reconstitute it in a form that I can accept, a fictitious
> form. If I need a morality, I will create one.
>
> —*The Waterfall*[1]

"How any feminist could appreciate *The Waterfall* will remain a mystery," says Lynn Veach Sadler in a recent study of Margaret Drabble.[2] Drabble herself calls it "a very neurotic book,"[3] a "wicked book"—"I've been attacked really very seriously and I can only respect the attack by people who say that you should not put into peoples' heads the idea that one can be saved from fairly pathological conditions by loving a man."[4] Jane Gray, abandoned by her husband as she is on the verge of delivering a baby, withdraws to her bed in near catatonia, frozen into an "ice age of inactivity" (7), "empty, solitary, neglected, cold" (8). What is born in the opening pages is not only a child but a passion—for James, her cousin Lucy's husband. "Submit[ting] . . . helplessly to the current" (39), Jane is saved by love, Sleeping Beauty awakened; as she "delivers" a child, she is herself "delivered" (10, 159). No wonder that the novel reminded Bernard Bergonzi of "women's magazine fiction"[5] and that those who have read *The Waterfall*—in the way critics often approach Drabble's fiction—as social realism significant for what it reveals "about life,"[6] are disappointed.

But this account of events leaves out what is most important in *The Waterfall*—the reworking of tradition. For Jane is not only a woman abandoned by one man and saved by another: she is also a woman writer—a poet and novelist—who uses "the power of the pen"[7] to repudiate "the old novels" in which "the price of love was death" (256) and define a new relation to the myth of romantic salvation. As a first-person narrator who is writing a novel about Jane in the third person, she not only enlists romantic precedence to justify her behavior but also interrogates her stylized, romantic fictionalization by means of an analytical first-person critique; and from this processive re-vision of "I" by "she" and "she" by "I," she forges a new "system" and "morality" (47, 53). *The Waterfall* is Drabble's most self-consciously intertextual work, a metafiction that draws attention to problems of finding a style and making an ending, a writerly text that invites the reader to participate in the production of meaning and challenges the ideological complicity of realism. Its dialogic structure opposes generic modes, perspectives, and views of language in what Julia Kristeva terms (in her essay on M.M. Bakhtin) a "polyphonic" text that transgresses "linguistic, logical, and social codes."[8]

Drabble has referred to Doris Lessing as "both mother and seer"[9]; nowhere is her indebtedness more apparent than in *The Waterfall*. As in *The Golden Notebook*, it is the protagonist's dissolution of self, her breakdown into a lover, that enables her to make connections with others and to forge an identity that is both connected and separate, relational and autonomous. In the same way that Anna Wulf writes "The Shadow of the Third" in order to understand her feelings for Michael, so too does Jane write to "comprehend" her experience with James;[10] and just as the conventional novel Anna writes demonstrates Lessing's sense of the limits of conventional form, so too does Jane's novel, the "story of she," provide Drabble's commentary on narrative form. But Drabble's interrogation of convention goes farther than Lessing's, extending beyond narrative to an investigation of language itself. Whereas the various notebooks and novels with which Anna tries to "cage the *truth*"[11] differ in genre and form, they do not differ in style, for though she may question language, Anna assumes it as a means of representation. But Jane's first- and third-person narratives test out modes of representation which rest on different assumptions about the relationship of language to reality and explore various potentials of language. Moreover, Jane creates her new "system" from a verbal medium reconstituted by re-combinations of words according to principles that subvert conventional relations between subject and object, by means of which she shakes words free from their usual meanings and liberates them from their customary positions in a discourse inscribing hierarchy and possession. Taking her metaphors where Jane finds her salvation, Drabble makes her protagonist's newly-discovered sexuality the source of an alternative discourse with the revolutionary implications of "*l'écriture féminine*," "writing the female body." *The Waterfall* is—in Cixous's terms from "The Laugh of the Medusa"—"a new insurgent writing" that "wrecks partitions, classes, rhetorics, regulations and codes" and "change[s] the rules of the old game."[12]

Old-Fashioned, Unforgiving Stories

When Jane turns to literary tradition for understanding of her passion—"love is nothing new" (161)—she is appalled at the effect literature has had on her life, its power to "move" her disastrously (92). So keen is her sense of its influence that she "blames the poets" for her marriage to Malcolm: "Love at first sight: I have heard of it, and like a doomed romantic I looked for it" (91). When Jane "falls" for her cousin Lucy's husband, she finds precedents in the heroines of nineteenth-century novels, especially Maggie Tulliver, who was also in love with her cousin Lucy's "man"—"Perhaps I'll go mad with guilt, like Sue Bridehead, or drown myself in an effort to reclaim lost renunciations, like Maggie Tulliver. Those fictitious heroines, how they haunt me." But Maggie "drifted off down the river, abandoning herself to the water . . . and then, like a woman of another age, she refrained" (161–62), so *The Mill on the Floss* does not help Jane to understand her situation any more than the other "old novels" she considers—*Jane Eyre, Jude the Obscure, Thérèse Raquin, Nana.* Like Lessing's Anna Wulf and Martha Quest, Godwin's Jane Clifford, Jong's Isadore Wing, Atwood's Lady Oracle, and Laurence's Morag Gunn, Jane finds the fictions of the past irrelevant to her experience in the present: "In this age [since Freud], what is to be done? We drown in the first chapter" (162).

Drabble evokes *The Mill on the Floss* as representative of the tradition Jane must define herself against. Maggie's ending, her renunciation of her cousin Lucy's man and her return to an unforgiving family ("all that superego gathered together in a last effort to prove that she loved the brother more than the man" [162]), is—as Tony Tanner describes it—a "return to the past and its binding patterns," a "reinsert[ion of] herself into a social discourse that will deny her any social identity . . . [and] that effectively prescribes her own annihilation." Maggie is (in Tanner's terms) "cramped up in the room of an old language," unable to reformulate the patterns of the past or to generate new meanings, for there is "no conceivable possibility of her renaming [her brother] and the whole male-dominated society he represents." Her drowning represents a surrender to psychological and social forces more powerful than she is; Tanner describes it as "thalassic" and "regressive," noting that this type of water imagery is frequent in the novel of adultery.[13] Thus as unconventional as George Eliot was in her life, she condemned Maggie to the "current" she herself escaped; and Jane also cites Zola, who, notwithstanding the strict sexual morality of his fiction, could be seen enjoying the company of his mistress and babes in the Tuileries, "more charitable to the flesh in his life than in his art" (138). Besides Thérèse Raquin and Maggie Tulliver, one might mention—as Gail Godwin's Jane does—Emma Bovary, Anna Karenina, Hetty Sorel, Lily Bart: "literature's graveyard positively choked with women who . . . commit adultery, have sex without marriage . . . and thus, according to the literary convention of the time, must die."[14]

But Jane's passion for her cousin Lucy's husband, far from incurring the punishment that it did in the "old-fashioned," "unforgiving" (138) novels, "releases [her] from enclosure" (169), liberates her from isolation and "delivers" her to a new life. Unlike "a woman of another age," Jane plunges in, "drowns in a willing sea" (29), "drowns in the first chapter" (162), to discover in passion "salvation" rather than damnation. The birth of passion is vividly recounted in the opening section, along with the birth of a child; Jane's discovery of sexuality is linked to maternity in an experience of what Julia Kristeva calls "la mère qui jouit," the mother who has "jouissance,"[15] with the connection between the two emphasized by the pun on "deliverance" (10, 159). Born in a bed still wet with blood and other aftermath of birth, Jane's passion for James is also "like death" ("like death, like birth," 158), but though the old pun on "die" is nearly literalized when James almost dies in the car accident, it is finally like "rebirth" (159), as James recovers, their love continues, and Jane finds new energy in all areas of her life. her life.

Drabble's repudiation of "an old-fashioned," "unforgiving" (138) discourse indicates her awareness of the ideological complicity of narrative form. Roland Barthes and others explain the inherently conservative tendencies of "realist" narrative: though realism offers itself as a neutral or "innocent" reflection of a preexistent reality, it produces meaning by evoking and combining cultural codes that are the received ideas of the culture. Achieving its "realism" by drawing on familiar systems, it seems realistic because it reaffirms the familiar; it thus "does the work of ideology" by smoothing over contradictions and containing tendencies toward change.[16] Nancy K. Miller discusses the laws of probability and possibility that govern realist fiction as a kind of "contract" between writer and reader; Roland Barthes refers to "the constraints of the discourse."[17] One of the most constraining of these conventions is the ending, which Catherine Belsey describes as an imperative to closure which is also an "imperative to disclosure," a tendency toward the reestablishment of an initial order and the revelation of a single, univocal truth—which Stephen Heath describes as a tendency toward "containment" or "homogeneity" that masks contradictions and neutralizes the potential for change.[18] The romance plot, which centers on love and concludes with the woman's marriage or death, reinforces particularly conservative assumptions about woman, the "happy ending" signifying her integration into society, the unhappy ending signifying her failure to negotiate the teleological love relation.[19]

Moreover, since each invocation of a code is also its reinforcement or reinscription, literature does more than encode or transmit ideology; it actually creates it, structures our sense of the world, so that to invoke conventional resolutions such as marriage or death is in some sense to necessitate them, to perpetuate them as the myths of our culture. No wonder that Jane protests against a tradition that so narrowly defines her and that Lessing's major novel, *The Golden Notebook*, expresses what she calls her "sense of despair about writing a conventional novel."[20] The radically innovative form of *The Golden Notebook* is Lessing's attempt to create "something new" against "the nightmare repetition" of history and the past, an effort that informs all her fiction[21] and that leads her (and other feminist writers) to science fiction.

The Waterfall offers a "new system" less spectacularly pyrotechnical than *The Golden Notebook*, though it has implications as revolutionary. As in Lessing's novel, the protagonists' means of reconstituting tradition is "the power of the pen": Drabble assumes a view of "authorship" like Cixous's, as the site of resistance or change.[22] Jane's task is no less than the creation of "a system that would excuse [her]" (47) and "a morality that condones her" (53–54).

Though the "convention" she is "reconstituting"—adulterous yet redemptive passion—is "conventional" to the point of cliché, it also raises bewildering moral and philosophical problems that make her task difficult. For one thing, it brings social and ethical systems into conflict with emotional and sexual imperatives—conflicts which, as Jane suggests, are not easily resolved:

I have often thought . . . that the ways of regarding an event, so different, don't add up to a whole; they are mutually exclusive: the social view, the sexual view, the circumstantial view, the moral view, these visions contradict one another, they destroy one another. They cannot co-exist. (47)

For another thing, it creates epistemological and linguistic problems, for whereas the old Jane modeled her life on the virtues of "abnegation," "denial," and "renunciation," the new Jane now names these virtues vices (53). Thus, though "delivering" her, this passion has called into question "the true end of life," and with that, "the qualities" on which the end "depends" (52)—and with those, language itself:

The names of the qualities are interchangeable—vice, virtue; redemption, corruption; courage, weakness—and hence the confusion of abstraction, the proliferation of aphorism and paradox. In the human world, perhaps there are merely likenesses. (52)

In fact, Drabble shows "transgression" as having effects like those which it had in "the old novels," the dissolution of categories and meanings. As Tanner explains, adultery, like "adulteration," introduces an "irresolvable category—confusion," an "unassimilable conflation of what society insists should be separate categories and functions."[23]

But Drabble sees such dissolution as cause for celebration rather than mourning, as allowing a breaking of boundaries, of containments and confines, and a dissolution of oppositions that releases new possibilities; for her, as for Lessing, break-through requires break-down. "Drowning," in the numerous "seas," "currents," "floods," and "waterfalls" of this novel, is regenerative rather than regressive—or rather, it is regenerative *because* it is regressive, signifying a therapeutic journey back to beginnings, to an experience of sexuality and maternity that becomes the basis of a new discourse. Still, since language is Jane's means of reconstituting experience, her sense of the "interchangeability" of names and the "confusion of abstraction" cannot help but trouble her.

Jane longs for clarity—"I see no virtue in confusion, I see true virtue in clarity, in consistency, in communication, in honesty"—but despairs of achieving it: "so here I am, resorting to that old broken medium" (47). She imagines some lost state of innocence where words corresponded to things, and expresses this nostalgia in her response to that song of Malcolm's that so disastrously seduced her—"I wanted to find the source of that sound . . . I wanted to believe that what I heard was true" (95–96)—and in her desire for a "name" amidst the disturbing phenomena of the racetrack James takes her to:

She could smell the curious dangerous sulfurous burning smell from the track, and wondered what it was, what name it had: she thought she would ask James, and find if the name corresponded to the hot cinders and petrol and rubber. Perhaps it would be a word she would never again be able to dispense with, an important word, that she still now at that instant lacked. (81)

She will need to relinquish this longing for a Word and resign herself to a struggle with words, to a medium that is "broken and fragmented" (47), "merely a likeness" (52).

Dialogic Process: Working It Through

Jane's division of her narrative into "I" and "she" enables her to express the complexities of her experience, to voice both surrender to and scepticism of the passion that grips her. But it is also a means of exploring two discourses, two ways of "comprehending" her experience, the "she" testing an "artistic" mode and the "I," an analytic mode. This dialogizing enables her to explore not only the potentials but also the limits of each discourse, for, as in *The Golden Notebook*, each version qualifies and is qualified by the other, the analytical "I" sections implicitly and explicitly commenting on the limitations of the literary "she," and the "she" sections doing the same for the analytical mode.[24]

The third-person sections are stylized and conventional, "structured and orchestrated" (249), and enlist poetic figures—metaphor, analogy, simile—and allusions to literature, legend, myth. By conventional means, these sections express conventional attitudes toward a conventional subject—romantic abandon to an irresistible and (as Jane imagines) doomed passion. In the first section, a striking rendering in the third person of the birth of Jane's child and her love for James, Jane draws on an array of literary associations to tell an archetypal tale of bereavement and deliverance. She evokes a stylized and ritualized image of a woman weeping, waiting—"like a victim she waited: meek like a sacrifice." The conventions of this mode require passivity of the woman, submission and surrender, and prescribe the complementary role of rescuer or savior for the man—a role James cheerfully accepts:

"I'll wait for you," she said: long dead through all her bandages, ripped and defeated, she committed herself to waiting . . .
. . . .
"And in the end, then, will you rescue me?"
"Oh yes, when it's time, I'll rescue you." (38)

That Jane's "abandon" is born of "abandonment" points to the association of "passion" with "suffering" that is practically a defining characteristic of love in the Western world, especially for a woman.[25] James states his attraction to Jane's pain in terms that emphasize his role as possessor—"and when I saw your tears I knew that I would have you, I knew that you were mine" (39); though his terms also draw attention to the sinister potentials of their postures.

The novel Jane is writing, the highly stylized, conventionalized "story of she," is an old tale which is crafted from the discourses of the past in a way that calls attention to the pastiche. By means of its "romantic accoutrements" (245) and its compelling imagery of drowning ("waterfall," "currents," "floods"), Jane justifies surrender: "waters closed over their heads . . . lost" (37). Though she blames the "lying poets" for "disguising," "excusing," "purifying," "dignifying" truths that are ugly and cruel (93), she is quite capable of enlisting their devices to shield herself from aspects of her situation too harsh to face:

abandonment, abandon, adultery, betrayal, faithlessness. But as art-fully and elegantly as Jane portrays the lovers in these sections, Drab-ble suggests that such stylization masks patterns of domination and subordination, patterns encoded in the custom, law, and literature of our culture—"conventions." Moreover, Drabble's metafiction shows Jane's reliance on convention making her "conventional," making her the subject of another's discourse, a "she" instead of an "I."[26]

But that literary convention may encompass more complex atti-tudes is suggested by Jane's evocation of the paradox and hyperbole of Petrarchan and metaphysical Renaissance love poetry:

the ways in which they knew and did not know each other, seemed to her to possess a significance that she could hardly bear: such hesitant distance in so small a space, such lengthy knowledge and such ignorance. (36)

These lines contain allusions to Donne ("one small room an every-where") and to Marlowe ("infinite riches in a little room"). The di-alogue that follows James's claim that he'd "have died" if Jane had refused him—" 'it can't be true,' 'of course it's true,' he said, lying there on his back" (36)—recalls the "true and not true" of Shakespeare's *Troilus and Cressida,* with its self-conscious, self-parodic Petrarchanism. Probably James would not have died if Jane had refused him—that he is "lying there" suggests more than a physical posture—and Jane herself "lies" in this opening section when she tells him she no longer writes, though she also says this lie "might have been true" (25)—and indeed, it *is* true to the convention she has evoked, which requires her helplessness. Jane's choice of the name "Bianca" for her baby, signifi-cant for one who sees her own name (Jane Gray the martyr) as symbol of her fate, is also involved with a lie, for she tells her mother "Malcolm chose it" (42); and it is a "lie" in another sense, in that "Bianca," together with "Gray," is a contradiction in terms, an oxymoron—"a good pun" (42). Though Jane's first choice, "Viola," which she associ-ates with violation (17), would have been truer to her sense of herself as a victim, "Bianca Gray" comes from a part of her that recognizes the need of a more complex and playful mode, a mode which, moreover, "transgresses" the limits of logical discourse. Oxymoron, pun, and hyperbole are, as Tanner suggests, characteristic "language of adul-tery" in that they "bypass the orthodox rules governing communica-tion and relationships" and "bring together entities (meanings/people) that have 'conventionally' been differentiated and kept apart" (23). They are also, traditionally, the language of love and faith because, though illogical and literally "untrue," they speak to a truth beyond reason. Such figures become appropriate to Jane's sense of the com-plexity of their relationship, a relationship that encompasses faith and faithlessness, grace and betrayal, sacred and profane, and look forward to the wit and playfulness she later attains.

But at this point Jane is incapable of accepting the consolations of convention for very long. Her impulse to another kind of truth, to the "whole truth," causes her to repudiate the very illusions she has created and to plunge furiously into self-scrutiny and self-accusation, using the first-person pronoun and a language of analytical-psychoanalytical investigation. Her repudiation, in the first sentence of the second section, is startling—"It won't, of course, do"—for, swept along by the compelling style of the first section as we have been, we are now asked to withdraw our assent—"Because it's obvious that I haven't told the truth"—

And yet I haven't lied. I've merely omitted: merely, professionally, edited . . . I have lied, but only by omission. Of the truth, I haven't told enough. (47)

Repudiating the "artistic" mode of the first section, Jane launches into the analytical mode of the second section, an investigation, in the first-person pronoun, of family and social backgrounds, James's and her own. Here she tries to "explain" (70) their love in terms of what she calls "the Freudian family nexus" (137), her relationships, past and present, with her parents and her cousin Lucy. No elegant, artistic ambiguities are tolerated here: this mode insists, rather, that "lies" and "truth" must be clearly differentiated and that language is adequate to the task.

But this mode does not "do" either, for such counting of cost, reckoning of cause, quantifying of quality, are no more adequate to love than they are to grace, for both love and grace are miraculous non sequiturs, effects disproportionate to cause: "do not let me find myself reasons . . . What I deserved was . . . pain. What I received was grace" (51). And besides, the "end" here—"drowned" (70)—is identical to that of the other mode: "it ends in the same place. . . . And since there is no other way, I will go back to that other story, to that other woman, who lived a life too pure, too lovely, to be mine" (70). The submersion in one attitude produces a swing to its opposite and the analytical mode is repudiated for the artistic in the seesaw pattern of self-revision which continues until nearly the end. Each section qualifies, retracts, and adds to the preceding sections, as Jane tries to comprehend the whole.

In the next section of the story of "she," Jane again invokes stylized, conventional images of male-female behavior. Playing the role of "his woman" (71), she "submits herself" to James's "addiction" for cars: "She had thought that she would judge and condemn, but there was no judgment left in her. She wanted to be what he wanted, to do what he said" (71–72). At the race track with James, she delights in feeling that "nothing, nothing at all is expected of me: I am merely a woman, merely an attendant woman . . . a proper woman, at last" (80). While James is racing his car around the track, she enjoys playing the "proper woman" in another way, gathering children to her at a nearby playground. Though "usually she hated the cold muddy park, the grimy squares, the dead end of her freedom, the walled, railed plots and enclosures"—and in this she differs from Margaret of Roiphe's *Up the Sandbox*—her transfigured state has released her from enclosure: "This place looked different: it was high and open" (81), "absolved and beautified" (86).

But the conventional roles also have other potentials, as suggested by James's rather alarming "then let me kill you" (77), which is, on one level, a sexual invitation, but, on another level, reveals the sadomasochistic possibilities implicit in their stances.[27] Yet the pun also introduces an element of verbal play into their dialogue; again, the "artistic" mode can accommodate complex and multiple perspectives in a way that the "narrative explanation," with its insistence on "fact," cannot:

"I love you, I love you," he said to her . . . and she believed him; she believed . . . even when she thought that she knew that he was lying. I lie to you because I lie with you—the loveliest of ambiguities, though sadly restricted to one language: untranslatable, and lacking therefore the absolute truth that seemed to inform it. (71)

Jane evokes Shakespeare's Sonnet 138—"When my love swears that she is made of truth / I do believe her, though I know she lies"—to express her sense of the ambiguity that now seems the "truth" of her experience. Still, her desire that "lie" have an "absolute truth" indicates that she has not yet relinquished her belief in an absolute beyond the "broken and fragmented" (47), human and fallible, medium of language.

But the equanimity achieved here, the acceptance of "lies" as a condition of life, is dashed by the first line of the next section—"lies, lies, it's all lies. A pack of lies" (89)—in the seesaw movement which is by this time familiar. Jane now accuses herself of using "analogies" to "deceive" and to "misrepresent," condemning these lies as active "commissions" and all verbal representations as "misrepresentations" that have made their love "unreal" (89). Jane's notion of "truth" now requires a connection with "reality," with "the outside world . . . the breath of coarser air . . . the real air"; and she resolves to give love "a quotidian reality" (90) by telling the stories of Malcolm and Lucy. But the "facts" of her life with Malcolm turn out to be more complicated than she had imagined, for having concluded her apparently straightforward account of the marriage with Malcolm's violent departure, she

cannot resist quoting one of his letters from an earlier, happier time—
a letter filled with "endearments," "solicitude," "affection," "tenderness" (119) that calls into question her entire interpretation. The point
made—that her knowledge of the end of the marriage has determined
the pattern remembered and the story told—recalls the realization
Anna Wulf comes to, after attempting to record "the truth" of a single
day in her relationship with Michael, that a written record can be no
more than "analysis after the event" (*The Golden Notebook*, 228–29,
331–68). Jane realizes that even her straightforward account has "betray[ed] the texture of a life" (119)—that her "facts" are as fictitious as
her fictions.

Besides, this investigation of family relationships only brings her
back to "the narrative explanation"—"I wanted James because he was
[Lucy's], because I wanted to be her" (137)—a mode that she cannot
sustain even through the end of this section. Two pages before the end
she complains, "I am getting tired of all this Freudian family nexus, I
want to get back to that schizoid third-person dialogue" (137). Before
she can leave it, though, she feels compelled to relate "one or two more
sordid conditions": "Firstly . . . I don't think I could have slept with
James if the house I did it in hadn't been technically mine." But she
cannot sustain this rationalization for the time required to complete
it—"What a liar I am. I'd have slept with James anywhere"—and she
rejects, not only the claim, but the very terms of the claim, "mine" and
"thine," as false to her sense of herself as "receiver of free gifts" (137–
38). Her inability to complete this thought—"I began the last paragraph with the word 'firstly,' so I must have been intending to begin this
with 'secondly,' but I can't remember"—testifies to her exhaustion of
the analytical mode: "Anyway I'm tired of all this. It has a certain kind
of truth, but it isn't the truth I care for (Ah, ambiguity)" (138).

Thus Jane again retreats to the mode that allows "ambiguity,"
evoking conventional representations of a woman waiting at a window
("helpless, ill with longing"), enlisting Shakespeare and Tennyson
("Mariana at the moated grange" p. 141):

As she sat there, waiting for him . . . She wondered if other people had ever
suffered so . . . She vainly believed . . . that she was the only woman who had
waited as she waited. (139)

The stylization is so extreme as to make her feel that "she [is] taking
part in some elaborate delicate ritual" (140), and in fact, her interactions with James in these sections do follow the rules of an "old game,"
of conventional codes that conventionalize them both. More complex
potentials are evoked in her paradoxical sense that "it could not last.
But it did not seem to end" (139); " 'he will not come,' she said, but he

did come, he continued to come, he continued to put an end to those hours of waiting" (141). The paradoxical truth suggested here—of an end that is continual and renewing—is that implied by the pun on "die," a logical impossibility that can be accommodated by the literary, but not the analytical, mode.

But Jane is incapable of sustaining the literary mode either, and the shifts follow one another more rapidly as a "protesting" voice makes itself heard almost immediately:

At times something in her would attempt to defy this entire subjugation; she would hear within her a mute and reasonable voice, another woman's voice, raised in protestation, asking him what he thought he was doing, where was Lucy, did Lucy know what he was up to, why on earth wasn't he at work like everyone else. (141)

And this voice asserts itself beyond the internal monologue that comprises most of the novel, intruding into the dialogue, as, "stepping dangerously out on to the unmarked squares of real life, of the outer world" (141), she asks James why he never works. The two answers he gives—"So that I can be with you"; and "It's because of the boredom, you know. Because really, I've got nothing else to do" (141–42)—come from the two discourses of the novel: the first is from the literary and conventional ("the courteous answer of the role that he had for some reason chosen to play"), and the second, from the prosaic and mundane. Though this latter is not "courteous," this is the language the lovers need to learn in order to make their concerns real to each other, to give love "a quotidian reality":

As the weeks drew on they had learned what questions to ask each other: they had asked each other these things at first out of a merely hopeful faith in the communication value of words, any words, though their hearts were on quite other subjects, inarticulate, inexpressible. But already she was beginning to understand his answers, they were more to her now than representations of speech and symbols uttered as in another language. . . . These things, that had seemed at first beyond the grasp of her imagination, were becoming familiar to her: thin papery structures that they had built between them, faint shadows and airy bridges, would one day perhaps bear the weight of quite ordinary feet. This, in her better moments, was what she hoped. It seemed almost to promise a kind of future. (150–51)

The discussion of stale bread that follows—which James assures her "matters"—is a humble beginning. And such banalities do seem to create the condition that enables each of them to take further risks: James risks the card trick called the "waterfall" and Jane risks orgasm which she associates metaphorically with a waterfall.

Throughout most of the novel Jane needs to keep the literary and analytical discourses separate, relegating them to different pronouns and sections. Only near the end does she risk "some kind of unity" (220), "coming together" (109) when she shifts, for the first time in midsection (242), from "she" into "I," and remaining in "I" for the rest of the novel—putting all of herself into one pronoun as Anna Wulf puts "all of [her]self into one notebook."[28] It is not only her passion for James that enables her to attain this new unity, but also the near-fatal accident that forces her to develop new strengths in coping with the situation as she awaits his recovery. But previous to James, it was having a baby that indicated her potential for "coming together" and even made her question the conventional mind/body terms of the dichotomy, since "the bodily level was in many ways more profound, more human, more myself" (108–9). As she shifts into "I," she quotes a fragment of poetry, perhaps her own—"Jane Gray / Head on the block" (242)—which is her only explicit reference to the historical personage whose name she bears, symbol of the martyrdom she has always seen as her fate. Her new strengths enable her to dissociate herself from the doom implied by this name, to acknowledge that her presentation of herself "as a woman on the verge of collapse" was "a plea for acquittal" (243); absolving herself of innocence, she can absolve herself of guilt.

Unforgiving and Unpunished—Illimitable Circles

Jane may not approve of the open-ended quality of her story—"It's odd that there should be no ending" (249)—but Drabble's refusal of the end is a repudiation of the *telos* of romance and of "closure which is also a disclosure" and a containment of contradiction and change. Though Jane seeks a conclusion in the conventions of the past and considers killing James or herself or maiming him so badly that she "could keep" him—"I search now for a conclusion, for an elegant vague figure that would wipe out all the conflicts, all the bitterness, all the compromise that is yet to be endured" (247)—"the truth" conforms to neither of these, and she must resign herself to the ongoing and inconclusive quality of her experience:

There isn't any conclusion. A death would have been the answer, but nobody died. . . .
A feminine ending?
Or, I could have maimed James so badly, in this narrative, that I would have been allowed to have him, as Jane Eyre had her blinded Rochester. But I hadn't the heart to do it, I loved him too much, and anyway it wouldn't have been the truth because the truth is that he recovered. (248)

Still, Jane's sense of the world has been so structured by literary conventions and "fictitious heroines" that her own experience seems "inartistic," "immoral," "unserious," by contrast:

But it's hardly a tragic ending, to so potentially tragic a tale. In fact, I am rather ashamed of the amount of amusement that my present life affords me, and of how much I seem to have gained by it. One shouldn't get away with such things. In a way it makes the whole business seem . . . less serious.
. . . .
We should have died, I suppose . . . It isn't artistic to linger on like this. It isn't moral either . . . It's odd that there should be no ending. (249)

Jane concludes "gratuitously," "irrelevantly," "immorally," with a description of her trip with James to the Goredale Scar: "and it must be irrelevant because the only moral of it could be that one can get away with anything. . . . I write about it simply . . . because it is so lovely" (252). But unable to rest with this "sublimely" beautiful scene, she goes on to recount their "ridiculous" gagging on the mixture of scotch and talcum powder in the hotel room later that night, which she calls "a fitting conclusion to the sublimities of nature" (255)—though it is "fitting" only in that it is so absurdly unfitting, so lacking in the conventional attributes of closure. But she cannot rest there, either, for she cannot resist adding a postscript "formulating that final, indelicate irony . . . if we hadn't had that accident I would quite possibly have died myself of thrombosis" (265). This postscript resists "final formulation" (as Rose says); but more, it suggests that "final formulations" are never possible, for since the accident which seemed to fulfill Jane's prognosis of doom actually became the means of averting doom (by making her stop taking the birth control pills that were giving her thrombosis), "the pattern" can never be known, and "perhaps" even now, as Jane suggests, "the pattern is not completed" (249).[29]

Drabble resists imposing a pattern on the events of the novel and allows for the muddle and process still to be lived through. She leaves us with a number of unanswered questions: What does the future hold? Will Jane stay married to Malcolm? What does it mean that James stays with Lucy? What does Lucy think? They seem to be "a resilient couple" (250), but it is nevertheless difficult for James to spend much time with Jane, for they have managed only this one trip together, to the Goredale Scar. Jane never knows Lucy's view of things— "I did not know how she saw it. . . . I have often wondered" (234)—but she does not inquire too deeply: "I do not understand it. I do not understand it at all" (249).

Jane offers a term for her conclusion—"a feminine ending" (211, 248). In its most specific sense, a "feminine ending" is an unaccented syllable at the end of a life of poetry, a variation that "gives a sense of movement and an irregularity to the meter."[30] But in the context of the novel, it assumes rich extraliterary—"generic" as well as generic— associations. The ending of *The Waterfall* may be seen as "feminine" in that it lacks resolution or closure; in that it is "open"—to interpretation and to process; in that it is unpunishing, "irregular," "immoral." In not limiting or closing, it is like the "illimitable, circular, inexhaustible sea" (221); or like the *texte féminine* which Cixous describes as "always endless, without ending: there's no closure, it doesn't stop."[31] Drabble associates Jane's liberation with "fluidity, diffusion, duration . . . a giving, expending, dispensing of pleasure without concern about ends or closure,"[32] with a "feminine form" that refuses end or closure.

Still, the novel progresses in certain linear ways, and Jane makes progress in all areas of her life. From her initial state of passivity and isolation, she develops the capacity to act and reach out to others. She sets her house in order, embarks on a successful literary career, saves her children from the worst effects of her nature, makes new friends, and even manages to continue her passionate relationship with James:

I had found, in James, reciprocation: I had found a fitting, unrejecting object for desire. One is not saved from neurosis, one is not released from the fated pattern . . . but sometimes, by accident or endeavor (I do not know which, in writing this I try to decide which), one may find a way of walking that predestined path more willingly. In company, even: one might find a way of being less alone, and thus confining the dangerous outward spreading of emotion, the dark contaminating stain, which when undirected and unaccepted kills and destroys. My need for James had not saved me from myself, but it had perhaps saved others from me. (169–70)

In a way, Jane gets everything, love, work, children—the "all" which women today are insisting is their right—though she does not get it "all together": the children are Malcolm's, and James remains married to her cousin and sceptical of her new strengths, personal and professional. But though her "unity" derives from such strangely disjointed circumstances, her good luck is sufficient to make her revise her sense of herself as a victim: "It is all so different from what I had expected. It is all so much more cheerful" (251).

Jane finds "deliverance" in the most traditional places, in love and motherhood, but Drabble has re-evaluated female sexuality and maternity in a way that challenges traditional hierarchies. In this she is more hopeful and also more radical than the early Lessing. Whereas sexuality traps Martha Quest in the "cycle of birth" and "cycle of procreation,"[33] symbolized by the ferris wheel that turns ominously outside her window, and Martha is sickened by her ride on this wheel, Jane "had always liked movement; as a child had been intoxicated by fairground roundabouts . . . wouldn't have minded going around that fatal track with James" (82–83). Whereas Martha naively believes she can "cut the cycle" and "free" her child from the nightmare of determined behavior merely by giving her away, Jane, strengthened by those same sexual and maternal instincts that Lessing sees as impediments, actually does "break the fatal hereditary chain" (145, 170).[34] Drabble sees sexuality as enhancing rather than diminishing—the roundabout and the "illimitable, circular inexhaustible sea" are exhilarating and liberatory.

Impossible Possession

In its refusal of closure or enclosure, the "feminine ending" of *The Waterfall* is an instance of its "writing the female body." A more profound instance of *"l'écriture féminine"* is in the punning that extends throughout the novel. Jane's wordplay liberates words such as "do," "make," and "have" from syntax and word order in which they denote possession and product, something one person does to another, and makes them not only describe but also reflect processes of reciprocity and mutuality. Jane describes orgasm as resulting from reciprocity of desire: "he had been as desperate to make her as she to be made. And he had done it: he had made her, in his own image"; "She was his, but by having her he had made himself hers" (159). The circular structure of the sentences mirrors a process of mutual possession and mutual deliverance: "She was his offspring, as he, lying there between her legs, had been hers" (159). Sexual punning has figured in their conversation just previous to this, which concerned card tricks, sex, poetry, the purpose of each, and the relation of expertise to practice. James deprecates his skill at cards—"the things I do aren't worth doing" (154)—and in the ensuing dialogue, the referent to "it" slips from skill at cards to skill at sex: "If one's going to do it . . . one has to learn to do it well" (155). Jane then compares the symmetry of the waterfall to the rhyme of her verse, claiming that poetry is as "pointless" as card tricks:

It's no good, you know, rhymes in verse are a trivial matter, as trivial as playing cards, as pointless as fast cars. It's no good, any of it. It doesn't do any good. I try to justify it, but there isn't any justification, there isn't any meaning. It can't be important, poetry. (155)

Poetry, like card tricks, doesn't "do" any good; neither makes anything or makes anything happen; both are without "end" or "justification." These terms recall Jane's earlier anxieties about unfulfilled goals, when as a child, she had been asked the purpose of her marbles: "Do you *do* anything with them?"—a question that filled her with unease—"for what, after all, did one do with things when one had got them" (124):

I always felt myself, with those marbles, to be on the edge of some discovery, some activity too delightful to bear, and yet I could never quite reach it: it always eluded me and whatever I did . . . never quite fulfilled the glorious expectation of having them. I felt there was always something left undone, some final joyful possession of them, some way to have my having of them more completely . . . but the moment never happened, it would fade and drop away from us . . . leading us nowhere, each time bypassing its rightful end. (125)

"Some joyful possession," some "glorious expectation of having," "some way to have," has always eluded her—was always "left undone," "its rightful end" "bypassed." This cluster of words ("do," "have," "possess," "ends") describes the failure of Jane's efforts—her "doing" and "having"—to achieve "ends," a failure she relates explicitly to sex—"And so it was with sex" (125). It is this failure that James sets right:

And how could I refuse James, who gave me that moment, who gave to me this impossible arrival, condemning me, by that gift, to an endless ritual of desire, to an endless repetition of phrases and gestures, all redeemed, all beautified to me by impossible, impossible possession? (125)

In these terms, what James has given Jane is a way of "doing" which is its own "justification," which is without goal, without "ends"—that is, "endless." In this context, Jane's description of their reciprocity—"she was his, but by having her he had made himself hers"—suggests an "impossible possession" by subverting customary subject-verb order and transforming "have" from something one person does to another to something two people do with each other, mirroring, in the circularity of its construction, a process that is endless. Her wordplay transforms enclosures to openings, limits to limitlessness, endings to endlessness and thereby transcends the confines of "an old language."[35] This discourse mirrors the life-giving, transformative exchange Cixous describes as resulting from "*jouissance*"—"an 'economy' that can no longer be put in economic terms," a giving without "measure" or "assurance" that one will "get back," in order "that there may be life, thought, transformation"; and it represents a challenge to the phallocentric "opposition, hierarchizing exchange, the struggle for mastery which can end only in at least one death."[36]

Also significant is the figure of speech Jane evokes to confront the most desolate of possibilities—at the end of the long, sleepless night she spends in the hotel waiting for James's recovery—that her passion, born of "need and weakness," was only a "miraged oasis" (221). That "I" uses metaphor is in itself evidence of Jane's "coming together," since metaphor has always been more characteristic of "she"; and that Jane works through her doubts by developing the metaphor is an affirmation of faith, not only in love, but in poetry:

We were starving when we met . . . and we saw love as the miraged oasis. . . .
Like deluded travelers, we had carefully approached, hardly able to trust the
image's persistence. . . . But when we got there . . . When I got there, the image
remained, it sustained my possession of it, and the water was not sour. . . . Nor
were the leaves green merely through the glamor of distance . . . they remained green to the touch, dense endless foresting boughs, an undiscovered
country . . . miles of verdure, rivers, rushes, colored birds, miles with no sign of
an ending, and perhaps, beyond them all, no ending but the illimitable, circular, inexhaustible sea. (221)

Standing behind the first-person pronoun, Jane recombines and redefines the cluster of words relating to limits, boundaries, possession,
in an evocation of undiscovered country with "no sign of an ending"
beyond which is the illimitable, inexhaustible sea—an image which,
she asserts, "sustains possession." The passage rings changes on the
novel's water imagery, transforming the waterfall, forceful and compelling though it is, to the more impressive, encompassing sea—endless and illimitable. The "illimitable, circular, inexhaustible sea" re-
verses the traditional meaning of water in the "novel of adultery" from
a symbol of "thalassic," regressive surrender to a symbol of liberating
jouissance. This is the same ocean Cixous associates with female libido to
suggest energies not confined by "boundaries" or "limits," the sexuality
inscribed within the *texte féminine.*[37]

But "feminine ending" refers to literary convention as well as to
female anatomy, and Drabble's use of this term in some sense reinstates
the value of the literary mode she has so scrutinized. In fact, though
the "poetic" is exposed as "lying" and limiting, it turns out to be more
adequate in the end than the analytic—as, in moments of crisis, Jane
turns to figures to express "what cannot be explained":

There is one thing that I can find no way to explain, and that I must recount in
amazement, in gratitude . . . he made the new earth grow, he made it blossom. . . . He changed me forever and I am now what he made. I doubt, at
times, I panic, I lose faith; but doubt, as they say, is not accessible to un-
believers. (245–46)

Her final summation of their experience enlists metaphor and bawdy
pun ("made") in expression of what there is "no way to explain."

But the "truth" is not contained in either "poetic" or "analytic"
discourse. By juxtaposing the two discourses without privileging either, Drabble exposes the inadequacies of literary convention but also
demonstrates that a factual account is no more "objective" or free of
distortions. The "truth" is in a mode that has elements of both but is
different from either, encompassing multiple perspectives, heterogeneous rather than homogeneous—and it is in the exploratory and

revisionary processes that go into making this mode. Evidence of Jane's "coming together" in the final sections is her attainment of a complex, ironical, equivocal tone, a tone that combines irreverence and play with a sense of the solemnity of events. When, for example, James protests at being made the object of literary exploitation, she "persuades" him "by a little casuistry" that the "very good sequence of poems" she wrote while he was in hospital was "an act of affirmation . . . like his reunion with his car, and he accepted the analogy, though I daresay it would not bear inspection" (250–51). Jane's humoring of James, this gentle recognition of his limits, this wit on the deadliest of subjects, is evidence of her new lightness and play—in fact, of the same sort of "mixture of wit and common sense" that she attributes to the adulterous Galsworthy cousins, who rejoiced at the coincidence of their common surname which proved such a convenience in their adulterous affair (252). That "what's in a name" turns out not to be doom but a cheerful convenience suggests a view of life and of language in which "analogy," metaphor, pun, and even "casuistry" are not "lies," but enabling constructions.[38]

Jane had once wished to write "a poem as round and hard as a stone," but she realized that such a poem "would say nothing" (69). Rather than a story which is closed, completed, contained, Drabble offers an unfinished tale of unpunished passion, elusive of final formulations, subject to uncertainties and contradictions—"an event seen from angles" (47) simultaneously serious and open to play; which—as Barthes describes the writerly text—"is ourselves writing before the infinite play of the world . . . is traversed, stopped, plasticized by some singular system . . . "[39] Jane never does find "the source" of Malcolm's "note," the referent or real thing to which words refer; she experiences no "final vision" or "final revelation" (196), "no sudden light" (233). She finds her "truth," rather, in an equivocal medium, "broken and fragmented" (47), "merely a likeness," open to "confusion" and "paradox" (52), and above all—in the process of her struggle with that medium.[40] But the release from the absolute is also a release from "the end" she anticipated—from the *telos* her story was tending to, the conclusion that would have doomed her. This release from the fixed and the final is liberating, for, as Barthes suggests, to refuse "to assign . . . an ultimate meaning to the text (and to the world as text) liberates what may be called an anti-theological activity, an activity that is truly revolutionary, since to refuse to fix meaning is, in the end, to refuse God and his hypostases—reason, science, law."[41] In its cheerful subversion of the tradition that has defined women so problematically, *The Waterfall* transforms "an old story" to "something new."

How any feminist could appreciate this novel—and nearly every feminist I know does—is no mystery. Our tradition-bound hearts persist in the illusion that a passionate love can release us from isolation, sweep us away to a sea of love; our modern minds know better. In articulating a female space that realizes the revolutionary potentials of *jouissance, The Waterfall* holds out the possibility that love need not bind and destroy—the possibility of an "impossible possession" that allows us possession of another, by another, while also granting us possession of ourselves.

Notes

1. Margaret Drabble, *The Waterfall* (New York: Fawcett Popular Library, 1977), pp. 47, 53. All further references are cited parenthetically with page numbers to this edition.

2. Lynn Veach Sadler, *Margaret Drabble* (Boston: Twayne, 1986), p. 131.

3. Joanne V. Creighton, "An Interview with Margaret Drabble," Hampstead, September 4, 1979, in *Margaret Drabble: Golden Realms,* ed. Dorey Schmidt (Edinburg, Tex.: Pan American University School of Humanities, 1982), Living Author Series No. 4, pp. 18–31, p. 18.

4. Nancy S. Hardin, interview with Margaret Drabble, Hampstead, October 1972, in *Interviews with Contemporary Writers,* ed. L. S. Dembo (Madison: University of Wisconsin Press, 1983), pp. 89–111 (here, 109). "It's a very peculiar book. . . . I can see why feminists don't like it—because it's about a passionate heterosexual love affair which disturbs everything. It disturbs all one's preconceptions about what's important in life. I think passionate heterosexual love affairs are extremely important. . . . When I wrote that book there was no feminist criticism around . . . and so I was not in any way conscious of any reaction. I don't suppose I would have cared if I had been"; interview by Gillian Parker and Janet Todd, *Women Writers Talking,* ed. Janet Todd (New York: Holmes and Meier, 1983), pp. 161–95 (here, 166).

5. Bernard Bergonzi, *Contemporary Novelists,* ed. James Vinson (New York: St. Martin's Press, 1976), pp. 373–74.

6. In the lead essay in Schmidt's *Margaret Drabble* anthology, "Margaret Drabble's Golden Vision," Nora Stovel describes Drabble as "a social realist [who] has held the mirror up to contemporary society" (14). Ellen Z. Lambert describes Drabble's work as generally "praised for its fine criticism of contemporary English society and . . . sympathetic portrayal of domestic life—love, marriage, and the bearing of children" ("Margaret Drabble and the Sense of Possibility," *University of Toronto Quarterly* 49 [spring 1980], 228–51, [here, 228]). Even with a novel so obviously self-referential as *The Waterfall,* critics have concentrated on such questions as character and development of the protagonist. Virginia K. Beards, "Margaret Drabble: Novels of a Cautious Feminist," *Critique: Studies in Modern Fiction* 15.2 (1973), sees the novel's focus as "exclusively sexual"—as concerning "a female destroyed by her physiology and culture" (43). Marion Vlastos Libby focuses on the novel's "stultifying determinism" ("Fate and Feminism in the Novels of Margaret Drabble," *Contemporary Literature* 16.2 [spring 1975], 186, 175–76). Roberta Rubenstein is concerned with questions of style, in her discussion of Drabble's "evocative use of myths and allegories of sacred and profane love" ("*The Waterfall:* The Myth

of Psyche, Romantic Tradition, and the Female Quest," in Schmidt, *Margaret Drabble,* p. 139), but she does not address the novel's striking structural features. Joan Manheimer usefully describes the alternating pronouns as "imply[ing] that the development of identity . . . is function of a dialectic between the self as object and the self as subject" ("Margaret Drabble and the Journey to the Self," *Studies in the Literary Imagination* 11.2 [fall 1978], 139), but she does not investigate the literary/aesthetic implications of the division. Even Joanne V. Creighton, who discusses the novel as "a nontraditional work" that invites consideration "as a fictional construction," is concerned to defend the "realism" of the protagonist, "the 'real' character Jane" ("Reading Margaret Drabble's *The Waterfall,*" in *Critical Essays on Margaret Drabble,* ed. Ellen Cronan Rose [Boston: G. K. Hall, 1985], pp. 106, 116–17). Those critics who address the novel's self-reflexiveness (Eleanor Honig Skoller, Ellen Cronan Rose, Jean Wyatt, and Joanne S. Frye) are discussed below.

7. This is Sandra M. Gilbert and Susan Gubar's term in *The Madwoman in the Attic: The Woman Writer and the Nineteenth-Century Literary Imagination* (New Haven, Conn.: Yale University Press, 1979), chapters 1 and 2.

8. Julia Kristeva, "Word, Dialogue, and Novel," in *Desire in Language: A Semiotic Approach to Literature and Art,* ed. Leon S. Roudiez, trans. T. Gora, A. Jardine, and L. S. Roudiez (New York: Columbia University Press, 1980), pp. 71, 86. In "Discourse in the Novel" (*The Dialogic Imagination: Four Essays,* ed. Michael Holquist, trans. Caryl Emerson and Michael Holquist [Austin: University of Texas Press, 1981], pp. 259–422), M. M. Bakhtin distinguishes between those texts which unify the heterogeneous stylistic elements or "heteroglossia" into a single system and those that do not.

9. Review of Lessing's *Stories* in the *Saturday Review,* May 27, 1978; cited in Ellen Cronan Rose, "Twenty Questions," *Doris Lessing Newsletter* 4.2 (winter 1980), 5.

10. Jane uses the word "comprehend" to mean both "understand" and "include" (53, 90).

11. Doris Lessing, *The Golden Notebook* (New York: Ballantine, 1973), p. 660. All further references are cited parenthetically with page numbers to this edition.

12. Hélène Cixous, "The Laugh of the Medusa," *Signs* 1.4 (summer 1976), rpt. *New French Feminisms: An Anthology,* ed. Elaine Marks and Isabelle de Courtivron (Amherst: University of Massachusetts Press, 1980), pp. 245–64, here p. 256. In this manifesto of *l'écriture féminine,* Cixous describes the radical implications of "writing the female body" in terms of a polymorphous female sexuality that subverts hierarchies based on a "reigning phallus." Luce Irigaray similarly sees woman's experience of *jouissance* ("pleasure," but more specifically the physical pleasures of sexuality which have been repressed by phallogocentric culture) as revolutionary; *This Sex Which Is Not One* (Ithaca, N.Y.: Cornell University Press, 1985). Julia Kristeva sees both men and women as having access to a prelinguistic *jouissance* which she calls the "semiotic"; *Revolution in Poetic Language* (New York: Columbia University Press, 1984). For differences in their positions, see Ann Rosalind Jones, "Inscribing Femininity: French Theories of the Feminine," in *Making a Difference: Feminist Literary Criticism,* ed. Gayle Greene and Coppélia Kahn (London: Methuen, 1985), pp. 80–112.

13. Tony Tanner, *Adultery in the Novel: Contract and Transgression* (Baltimore: Johns Hopkins University Press, 1979), pp. 69–72.

14. Gail Godwin, *The Odd Woman* (New York: Warner Books, 1974), p. 320.

15. Kristeva describes *la mère qui jouit* as a challenge to phallocentrism in *About Chinese Women* (New York: Urigen Books, 1977), especially chapter 3, "The Virgin of the Word"; and *Desire in Language,* especially "Motherhood According to Giovanni Bellini," pp. 237–70; see also Marks and Courtivron, eds., *New French Feminisms,* p. 36.

16. Catherine Belsey, *Critical Practice* (London: Methuen, 1980), p. 72. In her discussion of the post-Saussurean position represented by Barthes, Belsey refers to realism as "the accomplice of ideology" (73): "It is intelligible as 'realist' precisely because it reproduces what we already seem to know" (47); "to this extent it is a predominantly conservative form" (51). See also pp. 46, 52.

17. Nancy K. Miller, "Emphasis Added: Plots and Plausibilities in Women's Fiction," *PMLA* 96.1 (January 1981), 36–48; Barthes, *S/Z* (New York: Hill and Wang, 1974), p. 135. See also Pierre Macherey, *A Theory of Literary Production,* trans. Geoffrey Wall (London: Routledge and Kegan Paul, 1978), pp. 48–49, 106–7.

18. The term "closure which is disclosure" is Belsey's, *Critical Practice,* p. 80. The terms "homogeneity" and "containment" are Stephen Heath's: "the point of the action, the goal of its advance, is the recovery of homogeneity"; realist narrative is "aimed at containment," *Touch of Evil, Screen* 16.2 (1975), 91, and 16.1, 49; in Rosalind Coward and John Ellis, *Language and Materialism: Developments in Semiology and the Theory of the Subject* (London: Routledge & Kegan Paul, 1977), p. 49. Fredric Jameson refers to narrative's "strategies of containment" in *The Political Unconscious: Narrative as a Socially Symbolic Act* (Ithaca, N.Y.: Cornell University Press, 1981), p. 53.

19. Rachel Blau DuPlessis discusses nineteenth-century fiction in these terms in *Writing Beyond the Ending: Narrative Strategies of Twentieth-Century Women Writers* (Bloomington: Indiana University Press, 1985), especially chapter 1, "Endings and Contradictions." DuPlessis argues that in nineteenth-century narrative, love is woman's quest and vocation, absorbing all possible *Bildung,* defining her success or failure and her transition to adulthood. The happy ending, marriage, symbolizes her successful integration into society, and the unhappy ending, death, her failure to negotiate entrance into the teleological love relation. Such conventions had their basis in social practices—and they in turn reinforced social practices—which assured women's dependence, so that "to change the story," as twentieth-century women writers do, signals a "dissent from social norms as well as narrative forms" (21). DuPlessis' description of the project of modern and contemporary women novelists as "writing beyond the ending," beyond the *telos* of romance and its regimen of resolutions, applies to *The Waterfall.*

20. Florence Howe, "A Conversation with Doris Lessing" (1966), in *Doris Lessing: Critical Essays,* ed. Annis Pratt and L. S. Dembo (Madison: University of Wisconsin Press, 1974), p. 11.

21. The term "something new" recurs throughout *The Golden Notebook* (61, 353, 472–73, 479) and throughout *The Children of Violence* (*Martha Quest,* 8–9, 53, 141, 216; *Landlocked,* 177) where it points to the quest—both Lessing's and her protagonist's—for an alternative to the "nightmare repetition" of history and the past (*A Proper Marriage,* 77, 95). References to the *Children of Violence* novels are to the New American Library editions.

22. "Laugh of the Medusa"; and Cixous and Catherine Clément, *The Newly-Born Woman,* trans. Betsy Wing, Theory and History of Literature, Vol. 24 (Minneapolis: University of Minnesota Press, 1986).

23. Tanner, *Adultery in the Novel*, p. 12. Tanner describes adultery as "an act of transgression, a violation of boundaries that leads to instability, asymmetry, disorder" (12) and "threatens the very existence of civilization . . . itself . . . threatening . . . all existing bonds that held together states, armies, families, lovers, friends" (24), for "if rules of marriage, economic rules, and linguistic rules are in some way systematically interdependent, then the breakdown of one implies the possible breakdown of all three" (85). He also goes so far as to call adultery "the generative form of Western literature as we know it" (12).

24. My reading of the alternating pronouns takes issue with Ellen Cronan Rose's, though it also owes much to her "Feminine Endings—and Beginnings: Margaret Drabble's *The Waterfall*," *Contemporary Literature* 21.1 (1980), 81–99. Rose argues that Jane "has divided herself into Jane, the woman (whose experience is liquid and formless), and Jane Gray, the artist (who gives form, order, and shapeliness to that experience)"—in search of a form that "amalgamates feminine fluidity and masculine shapeliness" (89, 90, 96). She describes Jane's division as representing a split between "the 'I' who meditates on the art of writing and the 'she' who has a love affair," with the "she" representing the "essentially passive sexuality" and "inchoate liquid 'femininity'" which Jane must bring together with the "rational, productive, 'masculine' aspect," the "Apollonian, 'male'" principle of artistic "shaping" expressed by the "I" (92; see also *The Novels of Margaret Drabble: Equivocal Figures* [Totowa, N.J.: Barnes and Noble, 1980], pp. 49–70). But I see the "she" sections as too carefully crafted and literarily self-conscious to represent the "inchoate" or "formless": in fact, it is *these* sections that explore the problem of artistic shaping, whereas the "I" sections dismiss the entire enterprise of artistic shaping as "lies" and are primarily concerned with analyzing the causes of passion. Jean Wyatt's description of the alternating pronouns as reflecting "the conflict between Jane's desire to live out the intensities of a romantic love story and her desire to understand the truth of her own experience" is closer to my sense of the novel; "Escaping Literary Designs: The Politics of Reading and Writing in Margaret Drabble's *The Waterfall*," *Perspectives on Contemporary Literature* 2 (1985), 38. So too is Mary Hurley Moran's description of the third-person sections as "consciously artistic" and "narrated in a heavily cadenced . . . style that draws attention to itself," as "highly stylized and self-consciously romantic," and her description of Jane's development toward connecting the refined, airtight world of the romance with "the 'coarser air' of ordinary reality"; *Margaret Drabble: Existing Within Structures* (Carbondale: Southern Illinois University Press, 1983), pp. 87–89. Joanne S. Frye describes the "she" as enacting "the cultural expectations of femininity" and the I as "claim[ing] narrative agency": "It is only as she increasingly withdraws from the 'she' narrative . . . that she begins to elude its teleological pull toward . . . 'drowning'" and "free[s] herself from entextualization"; *Living Stories, Telling Lives: Women and the Novel in Contemporary Experience* (Ann Arbor: University of Michigan Press, 1986), pp. 154, 155, 160, 163.

25. That "passion" is derived from *patior*, "I suffer", a deponent verb, whose grammatical form is the passive, suggests that the "passivity" of suffering is inscribed within language.

26. Jane's tale may be conventional but it also makes some startling twists on convention. When she describes herself and James as "separated by her condition more safely than by Tristram's sword" (40), the image provides a striking variant on the barrier that separated the lovers in medieval versions,

enforcing their waiting and intensifying their desire: Drabble replaces the barren, death-dealing metal of Tristram's sword, symbol of male law and boundary, with the condition of female openness and vulnerability after child-birth—which serves not simply as barrier, but as "a prolonged initiation, an ordeal more fitting than human ingenuity could have devised" (40) and which, like the childbirth that imposes it, is generative, has "issue."

27. Such potentials are suggested elsewhere, as in the lovers' dialogue just after James has returned from holiday:

> "I'd have liked to have locked you up in here . . . to put you under a stone, to make sure you'd stay where I wanted you."
> "Cruel, you are," she said, smiling.
> . . . .
> "You had to sit here and wait for me. You had to sit here and miss me. I hope you were sad enough . . . the sadder the better. . . ."
> [She was] amazed at his acceptance of her dreadful tribute.
> "I like it," he said, "it's what I want." (174–75)

28. Manheimer describes this shift as signifying "Jane's increasing maturity" (139); Rose notes that the shift "signals the unification of the divided self who is Jane Gray" ("Feminine Endings," 92); Rubenstein similarly suggests that it signals the end of "the inner division that has plagued Jane and forced her to split her story into two perspectives" (in Schmidt, *Margaret Drabble*, p. 152).

29. Rose, "Feminine Endings," p. 96; and *Equivocal Figures*, p. 66. Creighton describes the novel as "full of 'unresolved ambiguities'— . . . gaps or spaces, disharmonies or tensions" that do not fit "into traditional novelistic or psychic resolution and unity" and suggests that "remission from the heavily-orchestrated endings of women's stories, lives, and books is exactly what [Jane's] story is about" (in Rose, *Equivocal Figures*, pp. 117 and 115). Skoller observes that Drabble's "reconstitution" "is not resolution or synthesis but invention that renders the work and the world as incomplete" ("The Progress of a Letter: Truth, Feminism, and *The Waterfall*," in Rose, *Equivocal Figures*, p. 122). See also Lorna Irvine's excellent discussion of Drabble's avoidance of endings as an affirmation of life, futurity, and "personal and cultural continuity" ("No Sense of an Ending: Drabble's Continuous Fictions," in Rose, *Equivocal Figures*, pp. 73–86).

30. William Flint Thrall and Addison Hibbard, *A Handbook to Literature* (New York: The Odyssey Press, 1960), p. 200.

31. Hélène Cixous, "Castration or Decapitation," trans. Annette Kahn *Signs* 7.1 (summer 1981), 53. It is interesting that Drabble refers to *The Waterfall* as "the most female of all my books" ("Say a Good Word for the Curse," *Good Housekeeping* [English edition], February 1978, p. 51; in Rose, "Feminine Endings," p. 81).

32. Marks and Courtivron, *New French Feminisms*, pp. 36–37, n. 8.

33. *A Proper Marriage* (New York: New American Library, 1964), pp. 251, 152.

34. Drabble describes herself as "happier in a more traditional domestic life" than Lessing and therefore as "having more faith in ordinary structures and democratic processes than she does"; see Dee Preussner, "Talking with Margaret Drabble," *Modern Fiction Studies* 25.4 (1979–80), 569.

35. Probably such wordplay combines conscious and unconscious processes. Tanner cites Freud's discussion of "joke work" as exploiting "the doublesidedness and duplicity of speech"; *Jokes and Their Relation to the Unconscious, The Standard Edition of The Complete Psychological Works of Sigmund Freud,* ed. James Strachey, vol. 8 (London: Hogarth Press, 1960), pp. 169–72. Tanner calls literature "a complex kind of 'joke-work' . . . the profoundest kind of play work," both "basic responses on the part of man at finding himself irreversibly involved in language"; in both, "purposive intention and the processes of the unconscious meet" (334–35). Rosalind Coward and John Ellis, citing Kristeva's *Revolution in Poetic Language,* describe "the influx of unconscious processes" (149) as allowing for the expression of repressed material; Barthes describes "the text that discomforts . . . [and] unsettles the reader's historical, cultural, psychological assumptions," in *The Pleasure of the Text,* trans. Richard Miller (New York: Hill and Wang, 1975), p. 14.

36. "Laugh of the Medusa," p. 264. Cixous describes this "exchange" in paradoxical terms that similarly recall Drabble's: "The woman arriving over and over again does not stand still; she's everywhere, she exchanges, she is the desire-that-gives. . . . She comes in, comes-in-between herself me and you, between the other me where one is always infinitely more than one and more than me, without the fear of ever reaching a limit; she thrills in our becoming. And we'll keep on becoming!" (263–64).

37. Not "inscribed . . . within boundaries . . . without ever inscribing or discerning contours," female sexuality is like the sea: "we are ourselves sea, sand, coral, sea-weed, beaches, tides, swimmers, children, waves. . . . We know how to speak them all" ("Laugh of the Medusa," pp. 259–60). In *Diving Deep and Surfacing: Women Writers on Spiritual Quest* (Boston: Beacon, 1980), Carol Christ discusses the water imagery that recurs so frequently in contemporary women's fiction. Consider the sea in Lessing's *Landlocked* and *The Summer Before the Dark*; the lake in Atwood's *Surfacing* and *Lady Oracle*; the oceans, rivers, streams, and pools in Iris Murdoch's *The Nice and the Good, The Sea, The Sea, Nuns and Soldiers,* and *The Good Apprentice*; the lake, floods, and rain in Marilynne Robinson's *Housekeeping*—to name only a few.

38. Jane's fiction captures the multifacetedness of her experience, whereas her poetry expresses only one side—only the pain, never the joy. In her loneliness after Malcolm's departure, she "was writing [poetry] more copiously, more fluently, than . . . ever . . . before," and she uses an image for her writing uncannily like one of Cixous's—"the ink was pouring on to the sheets like blood" (115; compare "Laugh of the Medusa," p. 261). Once she starts loving James, she stops writing poetry because, as she says, "I did not know how to write about joy, I could find no words, no patterns for the damp and intimate secrets of love" (115), but when James is nearly killed, she writes "a very good sequence of poems" (250). Jane's fiction, however—and Drabble's—encompasses "misery" as well as "joy" (114–15), pleasure and pain, "finds words for" the "wetness" of love and wounds.

39. Roland Barthes, *S/Z,* trans. Richard Miller (New York: Hill and Wang, 1974), p. 5.

40. Wyatt suggests the revolutionary nature of this process when she describes Jane's "conflicting versions of her life" as allowing "Drabble to show all the effort, backsliding and uncertain progress of someone trying literally to change her mind" (44).

41. Roland Barthes, *Image-Music-Text,* trans. Stephen Heath (London:

Fontana, 1977), p. 147. Skoller arrives at conclusions similar to mine, though by a very different route. She sees *The Waterfall* as characterized by an "exercise of the play, the instability and uncertainty in/of language" which is a "feminization of writing" "open[ing] the way to a multiplicity of meanings . . . that cannot be exhausted by one essential meaning or truth" (in Rose, 1985, pp. 125–26). Citing Derrida, she suggests that "Drabble is presenting us with a notion of meaning that is produced in a relation of difference in which identity does not exist" (129).

Chapter 16
"Retreat with Honour": Mary Cholmondeley's Presentation of the New Woman Artist in *Red Pottage*

Ann L. Ardis

She was called "Novissima": the New Woman, the Odd Woman, the Wild Woman, and the Superfluous Woman in popular English novels of the 1880s and 1890s.[1] Caricatured in *Punch* for writing "she-notes," she was also considered a "socio-literary portent" of political, moral, and literary anarchy.[2] As the anonymous author of a *Westminster Review* article claimed in 1888: "the stirrings and rumblings now perceivable in the social and industrial world, the Bitter cries of the disinherited classes, the Social Wreckage which is becoming able to make itself unpleasantly prominent, the problem of the Great Cities, [and] the spread of Socialism and Nihilism" are all "intimately connected" with the New Woman's attempts to pursue nondomestic, nonmaternal activities in the public sphere. Having noted that social change, once instigated, cannot be revoked, this author ends his essay by reminding his readers of an ancient fable with a modern moral. When the Fisherman liberated the genie in Hans Christian Andersen's fairy tale, the genie "promptly rewarded him by proposing to annihilate him." As with the Fisherman, "so it will fare with the modern emancipators." Although the world has decided that "the Ego [of Woman] shall have the apple," the world "cannot forsee the changes which its liberality will bring about." "The Ego [of Woman] is a mighty Gen[ie], and the acrid smoke of its ascent may disintegrate many precious superorganic structures."[3]

In spite of such dire, apocalyptic predictions, Western culture survived the turn of the century. Moreover, even if certain "precious superorganic structures" like the novel changed utterly in the process, twentieth-century critics rarely credit the New Woman and the New Woman novel with having participated in this transformation. In other words, in contrast to the high-pitched polemic of the 1880s and 1890s, recent critics typically view the New Woman novel's contribution to literary history as a very local one. Most agree that the New Woman novel's sole legacy to the modern literary tradition is a new type of female character: a woman variously known as an "articulate heroine," a heroine of "the novel of liberal feminism," a "sexually aware but domestically inclined heroine," or a woman "terrified by childbirth and disgusted by sex."[4] In short, most recent critics isolate the novelty of the New Woman novel at the level of character, dismissing all other forms of experimentation in this fiction.

I want to challenge this consensus through a reading of Mary Cholmondeley's *Red Pottage* (1899). I choose this novel as my representative text because it is about the New Woman novel. That is, it is a novel about a New Woman, Hester Gresley, who writes two New Woman novels about the other important female character in *Red Pottage*, Rachel West. Many other New Woman novels present the New Woman as an artist.[5] Among these, *Red Pottage* deserves to be singled out because it explicitly addresses the problem of critical misrepresentation which has plagued the New Woman novel since the 1890s. The New Women in this novel are neither "sexually aware but domestically inclined" nor "terrified by childbirth and disgusted by sex." Furthermore, *Red Pottage* does not represent the New Woman novelist "retreat[ing] from revolt" to find "a higher female truth" in private fantasies.[6] Instead, the climax of *Red Pottage* suggests that the New Woman novelist's retreat was, if it must bear that name, a "retreat with honour": a retreat necessitated by the public's unwillingness to endorse the New Woman's agenda of radical social and literary change at the turn of the century.

I borrow the term "retreat with honour" from George Gissing's *The Odd Women*. In chapter 31 of Gissing's novel Rhoda Nunn realizes that Everard Barfoot was never entirely sincere about his interest in establishing a relationship with a woman who is not an "angel in the house." Such a relationship, Gissing implies, would leave room for a woman's commitment to work outside her father's or her husband's home. It would allow her expression of nonmaternal sexuality; it would be made and remade continually through dialogue, rather than forged in iron by civil law. In the chapter entitled "Retreat with Honour," Rhoda withdraws from her relationship with Barfoot when she realizes he cannot sustain this latter kind of dialogue in particular. She retreats—with honour. In her novel about the New Woman artist,

Cholmondeley depicts a very similar kind of retreat: a retreat that is an acknowledgment of external, rather than internal, impediments to the New Woman's "advance." While critics such as Elaine Showalter and Patricia Stubbs emphasize turn-of-the-century women writers' self-imposed limitations and self-destructiveness, my discussion of *Red Pottage* will call attention to the external checks on women's creativity in a patriarchal culture. My analysis differs from but also complements the work of other feminist critics insofar as I will highlight the factors influencing the woman writer's literary production over which she has no control, for example, the signification of her gender for her audience's reception of her text.[7]

The key scene in *Red Pottage* in this regard concerns the reading and the subsequent destruction of a New Woman novel. The fact that Hester Gresley's second novel is never published has nothing to do with Hester's being a feminist who "show[s] the limits of [her] world in [her] writing."[8] This novel was accepted for publication before Hester's brother took it upon himself to edit and then to destroy the text, claiming to do so "for [Hester's] sake, and for the sake of the innocent minds which might be perverted by it."[9] In other words, it is never published because a single reader deemed this New Woman novel "profane [and] wicked" (276). It never gains a wider audience because Hester's brother fails to value it as he would his own work, or the work of another man. Notably, when he asks his archbishop for advice about what to do with this, to him, highly offensive piece of writing, the Reverend Gresley refers to the novel as a "letter": a private, a personal, a *female* piece of writing.[10] Thus, misrepresenting Hester's work to his superior, he gains the requisite authorization for its destruction.

It is important to recognize the Reverend Gresley's response not as an idiosyncratic personal judgment but as an instance of the general critical response toward New Woman novels at the turn of the century.[11] The care with which Mary Cholmondeley details the reading of her protagonist's text invites us to read this scene in the context of the polemic written about fiction like Hester's in the 1880s and 1890s. Cholmondeley is not simply creating a fictional conflict between siblings, I think. She is reflecting upon what Barbara Herrnstein Smith calls the "cultural production of literary value." She is commenting upon the way New Woman novels were evaluated in the 1890s: calling attention to the way they were denied value as documents of universal, transhistorical "human" truth and marginalized instead as "women's fiction."[12]

Consider, for example, the following remarks, which typify the critical commentary on New Woman fiction at the turn of the century. In 1894 the anonymous author of an essay published in *All The Year*

Round entitled, "A Century of Feminine Fiction," prefaces a critique of New Woman novels by noting how women writers such as Fanny Burney and Jane Austen had "vindicated the right of [the female] sex to an equal share in a fair and noble province of letters" at the beginning of the nineteenth century.[13] "The novels which we owe to English ladies [e.g., Burney, Austen, Elizabeth Gaskell, Charlotte Brontë, George Eliot and Dinah Craik] form no small part of the literary glory of our country," he goes on to note. In contrast to these accomplishments, however, "the stories woven by feminine imaginations within the last decade have served but to reveal a passion for thinly-veiled pruriency" (538). And it "needs but a very superficial knowledge of too many of the most widely read novels of the day to see . . . how real the danger that threatens society from the flood of unwholesome and pestilential novels, poured forth . . . from the distorted minds of some of the most gifted women of our time" (539).

Writing in 1895, Hugh M. Stutfield echoes this author's concern about the "socio-literary" radicalism of this fiction in an essay for *Blackwood's* entitled, "Tommyrotics." "I do not wish to say anything unfair," he begins, "but I think it cannot be denied that women are chiefly responsible for the 'booming' of books that are 'close to life'— life, that is to say, as viewed through sex-maniacal glasses."[14] Applying Max Nordau's theory of cultural degeneration to current developments in English fiction, he then advises his readers to steer clear of fiction by George Egerton and Sarah Grand in particular: "some critics are trying to make us believe [their work] is high-class literature" (844).[15]

Unlike these critics, William Courtney does not comment upon the prurient content of New Woman novels. He does, however, blame women writers for the decline in the aesthetic quality of recent fiction. Indeed, this alleged decline prompts the publication of his study, *The Feminine Note in Fiction*, in 1904. The following passage is from his introduction, where he states in brief the argument he pursues subsequently through detailed discussion of specific texts.

Recently complaints have been heard that the novel as a work of art is disappearing and giving place to monographs on given subjects, or else individual studies of character. If the complaint be true, the reason is that more and more in our modern age novels are written by women for women. . . . It is the neutrality of the artistic mind which the female novelist seems to find it difficult to realize.[16]

Note the difference between the argument in "A Century of Feminine Fiction" and *The Feminine Note*. While the earlier critic focuses on ideological issues (specifically, the effect explicit representation of female sexuality will have both on readers and on narrative conventions), Courtney emphasizes aesthetics. Introducing a distinction between the novel "as a work of art" and novels "for" women, he makes art a male domain. He feminizes the New Woman novel so as to discredit its ideological experimentation. He feminizes it so that he can marginalize it, leave it out of the literary tradition he is defining by negation in his study.

The feminization of the literary marketplace in the nineteenth century has been discussed by a number of feminist critics. In *Desire and Domestic Fiction,* for example, Nancy Armstrong explains how women writers at the beginning of the nineteenth century turned their exclusion from the political world into an advantage by annexing the novel to the domestic sphere and claiming emotion as a "female domain of knowledge."[17] In *Thomas Hardy and Women: Sexual Ideology and Narrative Form,* Penny Boumelha considers male reactions to such female authority at the end of the century, noting male writers' anxieties about their female competitors. Not only were editors actively seeking novels written "from the Standpoint of Woman" in the 1890s; male writers such as Hardy and James feared they were encroaching on female space, and risking emasculation, by writing in this female genre, Boumelha argues.[18]

There is much to value in both of these arguments, but I find Gaye Tuchman and Nina Fortin's characterization of the nineteenth-century marketplace more helpful in trying to understand either Reverend Gresley's reaction to his sister's novel in *Red Pottage* or the comments included above from essays written about the New Woman novel in the 1890s. In "Edging Women Out: Some Suggestions About the Structure of Opportunities and the Victorian Novel," Tuchman and Fortin conclude from their statistical analyses of the Macmillan publishing house records that "The growing prestige of the novel in England in the Victorian period was one of the factors *limiting* the opportunities for women to have their work seriously considered" (emphasis added).[19] As the cultural status of the novel increased through the century, as more men wrote fiction, fewer women succeeded in getting their work published. Thus, Tuchman and Fortin propose that the Victorian novel displays what sociologists term the "empty field phenomenon": "when a field or occupation is not socially valued, women and other minorities will populate it heavily." "[A]s a field loses social value, when 'proletarianization' occurs, (white) men may decamp and leave the field to women (and other minorities)." Conversely, "If the field grows in prestige, (white) men may push women (and other minorities) out" (309).[20]

If Courtney's argument in *The Feminine Note in Fiction* might serve as an exemplary instance of the empty field phenomenon, it also suggests yet another way in which women were edged out of the literary marketplace at the turn of the century: through development of a "sexualized idiom" for literary evaluation.[21] As Barbara Herrnstein Smith has noted, we make a text a "timeless classic" by "transferring the locus of its interest [from ideology] to more formal or structural features." Conversely, we establish the noncanonical status of a text by highlighting what is "technically crude, philosophically naïve, or narrowly topical."[22] Significantly, the sexualized idiom that a critic such as Courtney deploys not only codes controversial ideological material as aesthetic irregularities; it also links such irregularities to female authorship. Thus, Courtney can proclaim that the novel as "a work of art" is disappearing because women writers lack "the neutrality of the artistic mind." He can refuse to recognize women's writing as art—and shuffle their work off into a female ghetto. "[D]eeply perturbed" by Hester's novel, Cholmondeley's Reverend Gresley settles his conscience by getting his archbishop's permission to burn her "letter." The parallel is clear: while Courtney does not literally burn women's writing, he accomplishes the metaphorical equivalent by using it as a topos of disvalue.

If I chose to accept the terms of Courtney's argument, his framing of the issues, I might perhaps want to defend the aesthetic value of *Red Pottage* at this point. I might want to argue that *Red Pottage* is as good a novel as, say *Tess of the D'Urbervilles* or *Jude the Obscure*—to name the only New Woman novels readers today would probably recognize by title. Instead, I want to highlight ideology, not aesthetics, as I try to pick up where critics such as Hugh Stutfield and the author of "A Century of Feminine Fiction" left off. I noted earlier that Hester's brother called her work "profane" and "wicked." Taking *Red Pottage* as a representative New Woman novel, I want now to enumerate the heresies of this fiction, which proved so offensive to the critical establishment in the 1890s.[23]

The New Woman novel's crime against Arnoldian culture and its rebellion against nineteenth-century novelistic conventions has to do with three things. First, its focus on women's relationships with women. Second, its interest in legitimizing women's assumption of nondomestic, nonmaternal responsibilities. (In Cholmondeley's case, this is more specifically an interest in the New Woman artist.) And finally, its interest in replacing a rigidly developmental model of literary "character" with a more fluid conceptualization of identity.[24] Each of these features of the New Woman novel is discussed below as they appear in *Red Pottage*.

In its most radical form, the New Woman novel derails the traditional marriage plot. It grants priority—prime time, prime narrative space—to the relationships between women that remain in the margins of most realist novels.[25] Thus, for example, mother-daughter relationships figure prominently in many New Woman novels.[26] Women's friendships are highlighted in others.[27] Often the latter are relationships that never would have been formed so long as the women involved made bonding with a man their chief concern. They are relationships, for example, between women who once perceived themselves as rivals for a man's attention; or they are relationships between women of different social classes.

Red Pottage focuses on a cross-class relationship. The novel's double-plot structure cements the friendship of childhood friends whose adult lives take them into very different social circles. But Cholmondeley adds a further dimension to Hester Gresley's friendship with Rachel West. Not only does she suggest that Hester's friendship sustains Rachel through a series of difficult relationships with men and a period of economic misfortune. Cholmondeley also presents Hester's love for Rachel as the primary motivation for her art. Rachel's love for Hester inspires Hester first to conceive of herself as an artist and then to write two New Woman novels about Rachel, the New Woman she loves in her "real" life. Rachel's love for Hester, in other words, sparks Hester's sudden insight into her artistic vocation. In an emotionally charged scene early in the novel, Hester's despair, her fear that she will always remain her aunt's dependent, gives way to a sense of her power to transform the world through art.

The two girls stood long together cheek against cheek.
And as Hester leaned against Rachel the yearning of her soul towards her suddenly lit up something which had long lain colossal but inapprehended in the depths of her mind. Her paroxysm of despair at her own powerlessness was followed by a lightning flash of self-revelation. She saw, as in a dream, terrible, beautiful, inaccessible, but distinct, where her power lay, of which restless bewildering hints had so often mocked her. She had but to touch the houses and they would fall down. She held her hands tightly together lest she should do it. The strength as of an infinite ocean swept in beneath her weakness, and bore it upon its surface like a leaf.
"You must go home," said Rachel gently, remembering Lady Susan's punctual habits.
Hester kissed her absently and went out into the new world which had been pressing upon her all her life, the gate of which Love had opened for her. For Love has many keys besides that of her own dwelling. Some who know her slightly affirm that she can only open her own cheap patent padlock with a secret word on it that everybody knows. But some who know her better hold that hers is the master-key which will one day turn all the locks in all the world. (37–38)

A short break follows this paragraph in the text, after which the narrator describes the "harvest of astonished indignation and admiration" reaped by the publication, a year later, of Hester's first book, *An Idyll of East London* (38). As a child, Hester had amused Rachel by telling her long involved stories about the lives of their favorite toys. As an adult, as one of those proverbial Victorian "daughters of educated men" Virginia Woolf writes about who are chronically underemployed serving tea in their parents' homes, Hester has never been encouraged to try her hand at any kind of writing, professional or personal. Now, however, she reveals an astonishing talent—a talent her acquaintances in Society have great difficulty in acknowledging, for they cannot understand "how she came to know so much of a life of which they decided she could know nothing" (38). Since they themselves know nothing about life in the East End, they assume Hester's experience is equally limited. They are charmed by the boldness of Hester's writing, but they refuse to take seriously her criticisms of the bourgeois social system.

In "The Untenable," the final dialogue in *The Newly Born Woman*, Hélène Cixous and Catherine Clément discuss whether Freud's Dora did anything more than introduce controllable dissension into her bourgeois family.[28] According to Cixous, Dora represents "a force that works to dismantle [patriarchal] structures" (156). Dora "broke something": she "ma[d]e the little circus [of the patriarchal family] not work anymore" (157). Clement disagrees, making a distinction between "those who nicely fulfill their function of challenging [the patriarchal system] with all possible violence" and those "who arrive at symbolic inscription" (157). Those who "cros[s] over to the symbolic act," she contends, write a defiance that is truly revolutionary. Such an act changes the symbolic order itself; it is not strictly individual and limited in the way that the hysteric's rebelliousness is (157).

Society's reaction to Hester's first novel suggests, I think, that Clement is perhaps too optimistic in her valorization of symbolic inscription. At least in the case of the New Woman novel, the process of aesthetic evaluation serves to contain or quarantine the revolutionary power of writing. Mary Cholmondeley's Hester Gresley wants to make "the houses . . . fall down" (37). She intends to unlock "all the locks in all the world" (38). She cannot, however, keep her readers from suppressing the temporality, the historical specificity, of her text, thereby turning it into an aesthetic object. Nor can she deflect her audience's scepticism about her authorship of this text.[29]

If Hester's first novel, *An Idyll of East London,* is vulnerable to misprision or misappropriation, her second is even more so. The scene in chapter 39 in which the Reverend Mr. Gresley reads *Husks* is the climax of *Red Pottage*. It is also the prime instance in this novel of Cholmondeley's sensitivity to the lack of fit or congruity between women's writing and the critical paradigms deployed by a masculinist reader.

To give Mr. Gresley full credit, he first sits down with Hester's manuscript intending simply to read it. Hester had helped him proof his theological treatise, he acknowledges; he will now return the favor. Soon, however, Gresley begins "correct[ing]" the "obvious little mistakes" in the manuscript (257). As the chapter progresses, as the excerpts from Hester's novel get longer, we see him commenting ever more freely on the text. And the following passage brings him up short.

When we look back and see in how many characters we have lived and loved and suffered and died before we reached the character that momentarily clothes us, and from which our soul is struggling out to clothe itself anew; when we feel how the sympathy even of those who love us best is always with out last expression, never with our present feeling, always with the last dead self on which our climbing feet are set—   (258)

We never know how Hester completed this meditation. For Gresley stops reading Hester's novel at this point in order to comment on his sister's "hope[less] confus[ion]" (258). Unable to understand what Hester is saying in this passage, Reverend Gresley assumes she has muddled the classic conceit regarding the seven stages of man's life in speaking of "dead selves" rather than of "rungs on the ladder" of life. In other words, he imposes a conventional meaning on her unconventional text—which in fact challenges essentialist notions of "character."[30] Cholmondeley's narrator leaves no possibility for confusion: Reverend Gresley misinterprets this passage. Refusing to acknowledge his own misreading, however, he sees this awkward handling of an allusion as one more reason to judge this "the worst book I have come across" (261). "Deeply perturbed," by the book, he consults with his archdeacon the very next day—and gains the latter's approval to burn this "letter" which, as he argues, would have brought the writer's family such shame (262).

When Hester arrives home from a short holiday and learns what her brother has done, she attempts, but fails utterly, to make him understand the terrible wrong he has done her. She even compares her love for the book with Gresley's love for his son: "When Regie was ill, . . . I did what I could," she reminds him. "I did not let your child die. Why have you killed mine?" When Gresley fails to respond, she leaves him to rescue "the mass of thin black films that had once been paper" from the still-smoldering "crater of grey ashes" in the back garden, burning her hands quite badly in the process (277).

I read this sequence of scenes (the book reading, the book burning, and the conversation between Hester and her brother afterward),
as an important moment in the history of the New Woman novel. In
this, the most self-reflexive chapter of a highly reflexive text, Cholmondeley reminds us of the hostility with which the New Woman artist's
work was received by critics at the turn of the century. But the Reverend Gresley's misreading of the novel-within-the-novel might also remind us of more recent misreadings of noncanonical works like *Red
Pottage*. In her pioneering study, *A Literature of Their Own*, Elaine Showalter, for one, describes the New Woman novelists as women "disgusted
by sex and terrified by childbirth," women who "withdr[e]w from the
world [to] find a higher female truth."[31] It seems to me that Cholmondeley shows us a woman who loves her nephew enough to have decided
to spend the entire proceeds of her second novel (had it been published, that is) on his education. Hester is, moreover, a New Woman
who describes her book as her child in a desperate, unsuccessful,
attempt to make her brother understand its value to her. In other
words, she describes her work in terms of conventional Victorian notions of a woman's "natural" capacity to mother a child because she
seeks to make her work accessible to her brother's highly conventional
understanding of "womanly" behavior. Her novel is her child because
she has invested time and energy into it in excess of what she gave in
nursing her nephew. It is her child because, when published, it would
have gained a life of its own, an adult independence now impossible,
thanks to Mr. Gresley's intervention.

This aspect of *Red Pottage* is best illuminated not by studies of
Cholmondeley's novel in particular or of New Woman novels in general but by Margaret Homans's work in *Bearing the Word: Language and
Female Experience in Nineteenth-Century Women's Writing*.[32] Homans describes Victorian women writers' attempts to come to terms with a
culturally imposed opposition between biological and literary creativity, maternal "duty" and writerly "egotism." Cholmondeley's characterization of Hester Gresley deserves recognition as yet another instance
of this struggle. By characterizing writing as mothering, Hester seems
to be trying to make her fiction writing acceptable to her very conventional brother. Hester denies the conventional opposition between
writing and mothering as she figures the former in terms of the latter:
"I did not let your child die. Why have you killed mine?" But her
brother cannot grasp this reformulation of Victorian sexual ideology.
By misreading the long passage from her second novel quoted above,
he proves resistant to such literalism. Indeed, his imposition of a
classical rhetorical trope on Hester's text exemplifies the privileging of
figurative over literal language that Homans identifies as the preferred

form of meaning in a patriarchal, phallogocentric culture. Notably, Gresley does not want to read literally. He would prefer to burn what he does not want to see introduced into the symbolic order: a conceptualization of identity that does not assume the psyche is a closed energy system; a conceptualization of identity that might almost be called postmodern in its sensitivity to the construction of the subject through language. *Red Pottage* ends on a particularly painful note. Hester Gresley lives out her life as a spinster. Her second book is never published, and the end of *Red Pottage* finds her still mourning that loss. Her hands heal, but Cholmondeley's narrator does not promise us that she will write, let alone publish, again. In other words, Hester has failed both as a woman and as a writer in her own culture's terms—even though, in characterizing authorship as parenting and in making her art an expression of her love for Rachel, she has reconceived the relation of art to life and legitimized her writing. In this last regard, to borrow Gissing's phrase once again, her "retreat," necessitated by the destruction of several years' worth of work, can only be described as a "retreat with honour."

And yet, we need not take this as the end point in the New Woman artist's brief career. In closing, let me suggest how the heresies of a novel like *Red Pottage* might fuel a modernist's efforts to renegotiate the woman artist's relationship to her culture.

It might be argued that a New Woman novelist like Mary Cholmondeley's meditation on identity in her novel-within-the-novel anticipates modernist experiments with both the conceptualization and the representation of subjectivity. In "Gendered Doubleness and the 'Origins' of Modernist Form," Marianne DeKoven claims that Kate Chopin and Charlotte Perkins Gilman are "as responsible for 'originating' modernism" as more customarily accredited male modernists and protomodernists such as Joyce, Conrad, and James.[33] We might want to extend Dekoven's argument, to build on it by moving beyond newly canonized feminist works such as *The Awakening* and "The Yellow Wallpaper" and focusing instead on turn-of-the-century women writers who continue to be hidden from history: writers such as Emma Francis Brooke, Mary Cholmondeley, Gertrude Dix, Ella Hepworth Dixon, "George Egerton" (Mary Chavelita Bright), Sarah Grand, Annie Holdsworth, Edith Johnstone, Arabella Kenealy, Dorothy Leighton, Netta Syrett, and "George Paston" (Emily Morse Symonds) (to name only the authors whose works are footnoted in this study).

But even without considering more than a single text, *Red Pottage*, we might also realize that some of these turn-of-the-century women writers' concerns remain incompatible with the tenets of high modernism. For one, Cholmondeley's insistence that art is an act of political engagement stands at odds with the supposedly apolitical formalism of the modernists.[34] Moreover, her characterization of Hester Gresley's deep love for Rachel West, her friend and her artistic subject, is to be contrasted with, for example, Joyce's oft-quoted characterization of the artist's godlike remove from his work in *Portrait of the Artist as a Young Man.*[35] Alone among critics writing on the New Woman novel in recent years, Linda Dowling recognizes both the New Woman and the Decadent as "harbingers" of the "disenchantment of culture with culture" that would become known as modernism.[36] Even as we recognize the links between these figures from the 1890s and later developments in the early twentieth-century literary "scene" in England, we also need to acknowledge an important difference in their respective situations. Unlike T. S. Eliot, Wyndham Lewis, Ezra Pound, and other modernists, neither the Decadent nor the New Woman criticized bourgeois culture from the relatively secure vantage point of membership in a recognized, socially as well as ideologically cohesive avant-garde. Neither, in other words, was protected in any way from the bourgeois public's understandably hostile reactions to their attacks on its values. Thus, Oscar Wilde was convicted for his homosexuality—not for his refutation of the reflection theory of art. As Cholmondeley suggests in the book-burning scene in *Red Pottage,* the New Woman and the New Woman novel were also tried and convicted for their refusal to respect literary and social conventions regarding sex, gender, and class distinctions. In this respect, it would seem that the modernist "blasts" of a Pound or a Wyndham Lewis were safer than the heresies of the New Woman novel. Ironically enough, the former could be accommodated fairly easily by the bourgeois culture it challenged; the latter, on the other hand, is too radical on too many counts to become culturally stabilized in the same manner. The latter is, moreover, "female"— whether or not it was in fact written by a woman—at a point in time when femaleness was perceived as a very real threat to the "virility" of Western culture.[37]

And yet, having said this, we need only think of Virginia Woolf's *To the Lighthouse* to recognize how a twentieth-century writer might once again "advance" the figure of the New Woman artist in the cause of her modernism. Cholmondeley's Hester Gresley is undeniably a prototype of Lily Briscoe: a New Woman who battles against an internalized adage that "women can't paint, women can't write"; a New Woman whose art is an expression of her love for another woman; a New Woman who acknowledges both the complexity of art's interaction with life and the fiction of artistic objectivity.

Significantly, Lily Briscoe is no more "terrified by childbirth and disgusted by sex" than Hester Gresley. We might keep Woolf's deeply sympathetic presentation of the New Woman artist in mind, together with the book-burning scene in *Red Pottage*, as we remember one of the most damning recent criticisms of the New Woman novelists. "It is a pity," Elaine Showalter writes in *A Literature of Their Own*, "that the feminists, showing the limits of their world in their writing, also elevated their restricted view into a sacred vision."[38] In fact, it is a pity that recent critics have responded so negatively to the works of these little-known turn-of-the-century writers. These novels are an important part of what might be called a prehistory of modernism. To paraphrase the *Speaker* review quoted at the outset of this essay, they are "socio-literary portents" not of "anarchy" but of modernism. Of course, they offer us values different from those we associate with the "virile" manifestos, the "hard" poetry, and the antihumanist, "geometric" fiction of T. E. Hulme, Ezra Pound, and Wyndham Lewis. But that is no reason to dismiss them outright as minor works by minor women writers. Instead, we might value them for what they reveal about the cultural and sexual politics occluded by the modernist rhetoric of impersonality and apolitical objectivity.

*   *   *

I would like to thank both the American Association of University Women's Education Foundation, for its support the year I began work on the book-length study of New Woman novels from which this essay derives, and Suzanne Jones, for all of her editorial suggestions along the way.

Notes

1. See respectively [H. S. Scott and E. B. Hall], "Character Note. The New Woman," *Cornhill* 23 (1894), 365–68; George Gissing, *The Odd Woman* (London: W. Heinemann, 1893); Elizabeth Lynn Linton, "The Wild Women as Politicians," *Nineteenth Century* 30 (1891), 79–88, "The Wild Women as Social Insurgents," *Nineteenth Century* 30 (1891), 596–605, and "Partisans of Wild Women," *Nineteenth Century* 31 (1892), 455–64; and Emma Frances Brooke, *A Superfluous Woman* (New York: Cassell, 1894).

2. "Borgia Smudgiton," "She-Notes," *Punch* 106 (1894), 109, 129; "Socio-Literary Portents," *Speaker* (December 22, 1894), 283–85.

3. "The Apple and the Ego of Woman," *Westminster Review* 131 (1889), 376–82.

4. See, respectively, Lloyd Fernando, *The "New Woman" in the Late Victorian Novel* (State College: Pennsylvania State University Press, 1977), p. 131; Penny Boumelha, *Thomas Hardy and Women: Sexual Ideology and Narrative Form* (Totowa, N.J.: Barnes and Noble, 1982), pp. 74–85; Gail Cunningham, *The New*

Woman and the Victorian Novel (London: Macmillan, 1978), p. 210; and Elaine Showalter, *A Literature of Their Own: British Women Novelists from Brontë to Lessing* (Princeton, N.J.: Princeton University Press, 1977), p. 190. Other studies of this fiction include: Gerd Björhovde, *Rebellious Structures: Women Writers and the Crisis of the Novel, 1880–1900* (Oxford: Norwegian University Press, 1987); A. R. Cunningham, "The 'New Woman Fiction' of the 1890s," *Victorian Studies* 17 (1973), 177–86; Linda Dowling, "The Decadent and the New Woman in the 1890s," *Nineteenth-Century Fiction* 33 (1979), 434–54; Lloyd Fernando, "The Radical Ideology of the 'New Woman,'" *Southern Review* 2 (1967), 206–22; Susan Gorsky, "Old Maids and New Women: Alternatives to Marriage in the English Woman's Novel," *Journal of Popular Culture* 7 (1973), 68–85; Sandra Gilbert and Susan Gubar, "Home Rule: The Colonies of the New Woman," in *No Man's Land 2. Sexchanges* (New Haven, Conn., and London: Yale University Press, 1989), pp. 47–82; Wendell Harris, "George Egerton: Forgotten Realist," *Victorian Newsletter* 33 (1968), 31–35; Margaret Stetz, "Odd Woman, Half Woman, Superfluous Woman: What Was the New Woman?" *Iris* 11 (1984), 20–21; and Patricia Stubbs, *Feminism and the Novel: Women and Fiction, 1880–1920* (Totowa, N.J.: Barnes and Noble, 1979). Interestingly enough, with the exception of Björhovde's recent study, the most negative judgments of this fiction are made in the book-length studies; essays in journals have done nothing to dislodge those judgments.

5. See Mona Caird, *The Daughters of Danaeus* (London: Bliss, Sands & Foster, 1894); Gertrude Dix, *The Image-Breakers* (London: W. Heinemann, 1900); "Sarah Grand" [Frances McFall], *The Beth-Book* (London: W. Heinemann, 1897; rpt. Penguin, 1979); W. S. Holnut, *Olympia's Journal* (London: George Bell, 1897); Edith Johnstone, *A Sunless Heart* (London: Ward, Lock & Bowden, 1894); and "George Paston" (Emily Morse Symonds), *A Writer of Books* (New York: D. Appleton, 1899).

6. Showalter, *A Literature of Their Own*, p. 215.

7. This reading is informed by the work of both Monique Wittig and Susan Lanser; see, respectively, "The Mark of Gender," in *The Poetics of Gender*, ed. Nancy Miller (New York: Columbia University Press, 1986), pp. 63–73, and "Toward a Feminist Narratology," *Style* 20 (1986), 341–63.

8. Showalter, *A Literature of Their Own*, p. 215.

9. Mary Cholmondeley, *Red Pottage* (London: Edward Arnold, 1899; rpt. Penguin, 1985). Further references are cited parenthetically in the text with page numbers.

10. As Jane Gallop, among others, has noted, "women write letters—personal, intimate, in relation; men write books—universal, public, in general circulation" ("Annie Leclerc Writing a Letter, with Vermeer," in Miller, *The Poetics of Gender*, p. 139).

11. For an interesting discussion of the literary representation of the reading public's reactions to experimental fiction in the 1890s, see Margaret Diane Stetz, "Life's 'Half-Profits': Writers and Their Readers in Fiction of the 1890s," in *Nineteenth-Century Lives*, ed. Laurence Lockridge, John Maynard, and Donald Stone (Cambridge: Cambridge University Press, 1989), pp. 169–87.

12. Barbara Herrnstein Smith, "Contingencies of Value," *Critical Inquiry* 10 (1983), 1–35.

13. "A Century of Feminine Fiction," *All The Year Round* (8 December, 1894), 537–40.

14. Hugh Stutfield, "Tommyrotics," *Blackwood's Magazine* 157 (1895), 833–45.

15. Max Nordau, *Degeneration* (London: W. Heinemann, 1895). For similar arguments about the New Woman novel's "erotomania," see Thomas Bradfield, "A Dominant Note in Some Recent Fiction," *Westminster Review* 142 (1894), 543; B. A. Crackanthorpe, "Sex in Modern Fiction," *Nineteenth Century* 218 (1895), 607–16; Hubert Crackanthorpe, "Reticence in Literature: Some Roundabout Remarks," *Yellow Book* 2 (1894), 259–69; D. F. Hannigan, "Sex in Fiction," *Westminster Review* 143 (1895), 616–25; Janet Hogarth, "Literary Degenerates," *Fortnightly Review* 63 (1895), 586–92; James Ashcroft Noble, "The Fiction of Sexuality," *Contemporary Review* 67 (1895), 490–98; Margaret Oliphant, "The Anti-Marriage League," *Blackwood's Magazine* 159 (1896), 135–49; and Arthur Waugh, "Reticence in Literature," *Yellow Book* 1 (1894), 201–19.

16. William Courtney, *The Feminine Note in Fiction* (London: Chapman & Hall, 1904), p. xii.

17. Nancy Armstrong, *Desire and Domestic Fiction: A Political History of the Novel* (Oxford: Oxford University Press, 1987), pp. 28–58.

18. Boumelha, *Thomas Hardy and Women*, pp. 63–65.

19. Gaye Tuchman and Nina Fortin, "Edging Women Out: Some Suggestions about the Structure of Opportunities and the Victorian Novel," *Signs* 6 (1980), 308–25. See also the book by the same title they have published since then (New Haven and London: Yale University Press, 1989).

20. For turn-of-the-century accounts of the novel's rise in prestige—and the threat posed to this prestige by women's writing—see, for example, Edmund Gosse, *Questions at Issue* (London: Heinemann, 1893); Mrs. Lynn Linton, "Literature: Then and Now," *Fortnightly Review* 56 (1890), 517–31; Percy Russell, *The Literary Manual: A Complete Guide to Authorship* (London: London Literary Society, 1886), pp. 32–33, 47–49. The argumentative strategy common to such works: a canon of "recognized" masterpieces is offered as a substitute for the women's fiction which was proving so popular with turn-of-the-century readers. An *Athenaeum* reviewer puts it best in a discussion of George Egerton's *Discords* in 1895: "there are not wanting signs that the present outburst of sexual hysterics (for which, to their disgrace, women have been chiefly responsible) has spent its fury, and will give place before long to the recognized masters of English fiction" (March 23, 1895, p. 375). In this context, Heinemann's 1895 advertisement for its new fiction series is worth noting as well. Having made a small fortune off of novels like Sarah Grand's *The Heavenly Twins* in 1893 and 1894, Heinemann's dissociated itself from "erotomania" in 1895 and promoted a new image for itself as a more conservative publishing house. The 1895 *Athenaeum* advertisement for a new fiction series begins with the following: "a recent tendency in literary criticism" has "obscur[ed] the central features of literature, and the beauty of the greatest writing . . . by an exaggerated attention to points which are rather scientific than literary." In contrast, Heinemann's new fiction series, under the editorship of Edmund Gosse, proposes a return to Arnoldian principles; in this series, "[l]iterature will be interpreted as the most perfect utterance of the ripest thought by the finest minds, and to the classics of each country rather than its oddities and . . . its obsolete features will particular attention be directed" (July 27, 1895). It goes almost without saying that, having published a significant number of works by women in the "Pioneer Series" of the early 1890s, Heinemann's roster of authors in this new series will be predominantly male.

21. The term is Sandra Gilbert and Susan Gubar's, as used in "Sexual Linguistics: Women's Sentence, Man's Sentencing," *No Man's Land 1: The Place of the Woman Writer in the Twentieth Century* (New Haven, Conn. and London: Yale University Press, 1988), pp. 227–71. I am not suggesting that this kind of sexualized idiom is entirely new at the turn of the century—George Eliot's infamous essay, "Silly Women Novelists," comes to mind immediately as an earlier instance of a gendered scale of literary value. What I am suggesting is that critics used this idiom at the turn of the century in order to curtail the novel's association with popular culture, since the latter as Andreas Huyssen argues, is the feminine "other" to high art in the twentieth century; see "Mass Culture as Woman: 'Modernism's Other,'" in *After the Great Divide* (Bloomington: Indiana University Press, 1986), pp. 44–64.

22. Herrnstein Smith, "Contingencies of Value," p. 28.

23. See Lynda Bundtzen's discussion of Adrienne Rich's notion of women writers' heretical disloyalty to civilization in this volume; while Rich's meaning of cultural heresy pertains here, Reverend Gresley is also responding quite specifically to Hester's satiric characterizations of church clergy who abuse their role as intercessor between God and the individual believer.

24. The argument I outline in brief here is developed more fully in my book *New Women, New Novels: Feminism and Early Modernism* (New Brunswick, N.J.: Rutgers University Press, 1990).

25. I am, of course, generalizing excessively here so as not to get bogged down in fine distinctions. For more detailed discussions of the "muted" female subculture in nineteenth-century novels and women writers' reworkings of the classic marriage plot, see both Nina Auerbach's *Communities of Women* (Cambridge: Harvard University Press, 1978) and Rachel Blau DuPlessis's *Writing Beyond the Ending: Narrative Strategies of Twentieth-Century Women Writers* (Bloomington: Indiana University Press, 1985).

26. See Emma Frances Brooke, *A Superfluous Woman* (New York: Cassell, 1894); Mona Caird, *The Wing of Azrael* (London: Trubner & Co., 1889) and *The Daughters of Danaus* (London: Bliss, Sands & Foster, 1894); Arabella Kenealy, *Dr. Janet of Harley Street* (London: Digby, Long & Co., 1893); Elizabeth Linton, *The Rebel of the Family* (London: Chatto & Windus, 1880); and Netta Syrett, *Nobody's Fault* (London: John Lane, 1896) and *Roseanne* (London: Hurst & Blackett, 1902).

27. See William Barry, *The Two Standards* (London: T. Fisher Unwin, 1898); Rhoda Broughton, *Dear Faustina* (London: Richard Bentley & Son, 1897); Gertrude Dix, *The Image-Breakers;* Menie Muriel Dowie, *Gallia* (London: Methuen & Co., 1895); George Gissing, *The Odd Woman* (London: W. Heinemann, 1893); Thomas Hardy, *Jude the Obscure* (London: Osgood, McIlvaine & Co., 1896); Annie Holdsworth, *Joanna Trail, Spinster* (London: W. Heinemann, 1894); and Dorothy Leighton, *Disillusion* (London: Henry & Co., 1894) and *As a Man Is Able: A Study in Human Relationships* (London: W. Heinemann, 1893).

28. Hélène Cixous and Catherine Clément, *The Newly Born Woman*, Theory and History of Literature, Vol. 24 (Minneapolis: University of Minnesota Press, 1986), pp. 147–60. In this volume see Gayle Greene's use of Cixous's argument in reading Margaret Drabble's *The Waterfall*.

29. For an important discussion of the function of authorship, see Michel Foucault, "What Is an Author," in *Textual Strategies: Perspectives in Post-Structuralist Criticism*, ed. Josue Harari (Ithaca, N.Y.: Cornell University Press, 1979),

pp. 141–60. Significantly, Hester's public is as eager to appropriate her writing as it is reluctant to grant her status as an author.

30. In this passage Hester is offering her readers a model of identity very different from that which is assumed in more conventional Victorian novels. Rather than conceiving of "the self" as unified, rather than assuming that identity is sustained over time, she describes the self as discontinuous over both time and space. The child is not father to the man; nor is the individual the same person in all of his or her relationships with other individuals. Instead, Hester seems to be posing questions about the individual's sense of self-in-relation to other individuals. This passage speaks directly to the chief conflict between two characters in the main plot of *Red Pottage*. Hugh Morgan is in love with Rachel West, Hester's best friend. But he is also trying to extricate himself rather ignominiously from an affair with another woman. He thinks of that affair as something that the "child" Hugh did and that the adult, the "real" Hugh, cannot be held responsible for. Rachel feels otherwise—wanting him to understand the ethical implications of his sexual promiscuity. Hester offers them a third way to think about their conflict in this passage. To conceive of identity nondevelopmentally would mean that Hugh need not be punished for his past actions; it would also require him to commit himself to a new kind of dialogue with Rachel. In other words, Hester is radically revising the Victorian notion of *Bildung*—of progress or development in either a character or a novel. See Mara R. Witzling's "*Through the Flower*: Judy Chicago's Conflict Between a Woman-Centered Vision and the Male Artist Hero" in this volume for a more traditional use of this term.

31. Showalter, *A Literature of Their Own*, p. 215.

32. Margaret Homans, *Bearing the Word: Language and Female Experience in Nineteenth-Century Women's Writing* (Chicago and London: University of Chicago Press, 1986). For readings of *Red Pottage*, see Vineta Colby, "'Devoted Amateur': Mary Cholmondeley and *Red Pottage*," *Essays in Criticism* 20 (1970), 213–28; Elaine Showalter's introduction to the Penguin reprint; and Gilbert and Gubar, *No Man's Land*, pp. 166–67. For other interpretations of the relation between writing and mothering, see Nina Auerbach, "Artists and Mothers: A False Alliance," *Women and Literature* 6 (spring 1978), 1–17; and Susan Rubin Suleiman, "Writing and Motherhood," in *The (M)other Tongue: Essays in Feminist Psychoanalytic Interpretation*, ed. Shirley Nelson Garner, Claire Kahane, and Madelon Sprengnether (Ithaca, N.Y.: Cornell University Press, 1985), pp. 352–77.

33. Marianne DeKoven, "Gendered Doubleness and the 'Origins' of Modernist Form," *Tulsa Studies in Women's Literature* 8 (1989), 19–42.

34. Both Michael Levenson, in *A Genealogy of Modernism: English Literary Doctrine, 1909–1922* (Cambridge and New York: Cambridge University Press, 1984), and Marjorie Perloff, in *The Futurist Moment: Avant-Garde, Avant-Guerre, and the Rupture of Language* (Chicago: University of Chicago Press, 1986), describe the way in which high modernism turned away from its roots in what Levenson calls "civic realism," a prewar commitment to political as well as literary radicalism. The New Woman novel's agenda seems to be more compatible with the earlier "phase" in modernism than with the later one.

35. See Susan Stanford Friedman's essay in this volume, "Portrait of the Artist as a Young Woman: H.D.'s Rescriptions of Joyce, Lawrence, and Pound," for a very similar characterization of writing as love, as identification not distance.

36. Dowling, "The Decadent and the New Woman in the 1890s," p. 434.

37. See Alice Jardine's argument about the "woman in effect" in *Gynesis: Configurations of Woman and Modernity* (Ithaca, N.Y.: Cornell University Press, 1985), pp. 31–49; Andreas Huyssen on the feminization of mass culture by high modernism, "Mass Culture as Woman: 'Modernism's Other,'" in *After the Great Divide*, pp. 44–64; and the first two volumes of *No Man's Land*.

38. Showalter, *A Literature of Their Own*, p. 215.

Part V
Reconceiving Feminist Aesthetics

Chapter 17
Aurora Leigh: An Epical *Ars Poetica*
Holly A. Laird

Ellen Moers called the Victorian period the "epic age" of women's writing (a phrase she picked up from Virginia Woolf)—that historic period when a new nation of literature by women received its foundations. Yet Moers wrote also that Elizabeth Barrett Browning's Aurora Leigh "may always be a heroine of limited appeal: the literary woman's heroine," in spite of her prior claim that the pen and printing press were the first means widely available to women to make themselves heard, to change their world, or to live a life of heroic "action."[1] It is always worrisome to find this kind of contradiction in claims made for women, and this is an especially thorny one: why is it not "appealingly" heroic to achieve stature as a writer? Moers probably felt that a contemplative heroine—more specifically, a woman of letters—could not be popular among women readers of the twentieth century. If not, this is our loss, and if there is anything the feminist critic can do to recover it, she should try. But as Janice Radway has shown, women readers even of Harlequin Romances read to satisfy a thirst for heroines— heroines who are often writers—and these readers admire Harlequin authors, frequently aspiring to follow them to authorship.[2] Moers's casual dismissal of the literary heroine, still more worrisomely, calls to mind the masculinist assumption that heroism belongs to traditionally virile efforts, which writing ceased to be when invaded by women. As it happens, one of the most influential writers of the Victorian age, Carlyle, believed that one could achieve modern heroism only through the pen, a belief whose most obvious descendant in the twentieth century is Marshall McLuhan's claim for the cultural primacy of modern media. To discard Barrett Browning's heroism is thus to discard the distinctive vision nineteenth-century thinkers had of themselves, a vision to which we remain indebted in our own information-happy age.

It is certainly no mistake that a woman writer appears at the center of Browning's epic, and Aurora Leigh is as convincingly courageous a heroine as has ever been created. As remarkable as its heroine, more-over, is the poetics she articulates: a poetics in which the central con-cern is with her "epic" age and the "heroic" artist. Ellen Moers could well have grounded her own theories about women's writing in Brown-ing's earlier effort. It is odd that—popular as this work was in its own time, crucial as it remains in reconstructing the history of women's writing—its contribution to literary criticism has been so thoroughly overlooked by contemporary feminist theorists.[3] Again, I suspect this has something to do with twentieth-century attitudes to Victorian thought, about which the twentieth-century reader has frequently been ambivalent.[4] The poetics of Aurora Leigh belongs on any syllabus that already includes Wollstonecraft and Woolf. It belongs in any an-thology of "The History of Criticism: Plato to the Present" (as long as we go on having such anthologies), even though it might never quite fit an anthology and excerpts would not do it justice.[5] Although I do not want to claim—as Lawrence Lipking has appeared to do for Madame de Staël—that Browning is the first or best claimant to the title of Aristotle's sister,[6] I do want to indicate the trenchancy, range, and relevance of the poetics contained in Aurora Leigh, to sketch in the place Browning should all along have held as a theorist among her famous male compatriots, both Romantic and Victorian. I will argue that, in the context of Carlylian thought, Browning devised what she called a "twofold" vision of heroism in art and in life, an unironic vision of differences well suited to a feminist aesthetic. She created not merely a powerful philosophy for epic poetry, a poetics, but an epical enactment of that philosophy, an embodied ars.

Browning developed something quite different from the Roman-ticist poetics for which Lipking argued by way of de Staël, herself an important and acknowledged precursor to Browning. Lipking's aim was to decipher a model for a "woman's poetics" not by turning to a field outside English studies—philosophy, psychoanalysis, or history—but rather by adopting terms from an Aristotelian tradition, a poetics logically induced from literature. The classic defenses of poetry are not in fact autonomous, not without philosophical, psychological, and his-torical assumptions; nonetheless, the Aristotelian tradition offers a convenient place to begin evaluation of Aurora Leigh because Browning herself spoke this language. In addition, since Lipking's Romanticist views are familiar to today's critics and still attractive, and since Lipking's model represents an important strand in feminist thought—arguing for an alternative poetics grounded in women's experience and in recognition of their "abandonment" by men—a brief review of his conclusions provides a useful foil for Browning's.[7]

Through reading de Staël (and a number of men writing on women), Lipking reached three important conclusions, all of which often crop up in feminist defenses of women's literature: first, that a poetics of women's literature would take as the chief purpose of literature "expression" not "imitation," hence, its central feature would be "speech" and "discourse" rather than plot; second, following from the first, that poetry is personal and passionate rather than impersonal or disinterested, and to speak confers privilege and power, interests and rights, which have not historically been neutrally allocated; and finally, that literature is written within and for communities rather than by and for a sequence of heroic individuals, that traditions of writing are and should be linked by "affiliation" not only by "authority" (something made possible, according to Lipking, by the advent of the printing press and the democratization of writing). A poetics that includes these three criteria provides both a description of what men's literature reveals about women and a reformative vision of what literature can do for disenfranchised women. But summarized in this way, Lipking's claims look more universal than they are—and than they have appeared to feminist readers of his essay.[8] The effect of his argument is to recolonize women, to allow them personal expression rather than heroic authority, to hear them speaking as agonized sufferers but not as proud suffragists, and to discover no other Aristotelian voice among them than that of de Staël.

But the literary woman was a triumphant figure in the nineteenth century; such women had risen above the norm, could speak their minds, and win the respect of all. Neither the heroine nor the author of *Aurora Leigh* was an abandoned woman speaking of her private woes to a small community. She seemed to speak for her age. She also spoke for a poetics distinct from and in some ways more comprehensive than that of Wordsworth, of Lipking's de Staël, or even of Carlyle, though it is Carlyle alone of these three whom Aurora explicitly mentions in her discourse on poetry in Book V of *Aurora Leigh*. The debt to Carlyle is obviously profound: what one finds in Browning's heroine is a revised version of Carlyle's theory, widely held by others of this period, of the modern hero as a man of letters.[9] His or her compelling desire is to challenge formulaic positions, whether the conservative ideas of an old aristocracy or the new socialism of Charles Kingsley, to struggle against systemized thought of any kind for the sake of a lived philosophy (for

Carlyle, a transcendentalist vitalism, for Browning, a Christian human-
ism). To be heroic is to struggle through the written word: to write
one's life and to write it as heroic struggle.

Browning confronted the same challenges faced later by Arnold,
as he tried to cope with the differences he perceived between Classics
and Romantics: how to balance social duty with aesthetic interest, how
to restore ancient epic actions to a contemporary literature absorbed in
self-expression, how to move from a failure of belief to renewed belief
or from the failure of previous systems of thought to a workable
philosophy, how to reconcile the heritage of the past with the changes
of the present, how to ground subjective perceptions in a persuasively
disinterested stance. To these conflicts Browning responded quite differently from either Carlyle or Arnold, though she resembles Carlyle
more than Arnold in her response since, like Carlyle, she avoided both
Arnold's reactive neoclassicism and Pater's radical aestheticism, choosing instead to view these conflicting demands as compatible—choosing
a dualistic vision. Browning follows Carlyle's precedent in an especially
important respect, in moving from a worry about either/or choices (the
Carlylian opposites of chaos and order, belief and unbelief, usefulness
and pleasure, past and present) to the risky acceptance of both/and
(the Carlylian vision of the coexistence of antagonistic possibilities).
And, of course, she added to this list of conflicts the struggle between
man and woman.

She wrote—as she believed her husband Robert also wrote—
straddling Arnold's two worlds: in early correspondence with Robert,
she praised him in terms that she would clearly have liked to hear
applied to herself, "you have in your vision two worlds—or to use the
language of the schools of the day, you are both subjective and objective in the habits of your mind. You can deal both with abstract thought
and with human passion in the most passionate sense."[10] But she
differs even from her husband in this vision, first, as Meredith Raymond explains, by insisting on the "poet's unique role" and "individuality" in "gathering" inspiration rather than on the primal, Platonic
source alone,[11] and second, as Dolores Rosenblum argues, by adhering
to *uni*ronic vision:

> Robert Browning, then, with his ironic distance and shifting realities, would
> seem to be the more "modern" poet, less in the grip of Romantic projections.
> But as much as she, too, is committed to the deconstruction of Romantic
> projections, Barrett Browning is equally committed to the epiphanic vision
> which would empower the oppressed—whether the Italian people or all
> women. . . . Because she, too, wants access to power, the female poet looks
> through appearances to the visionary distances; because she cannot forget
> female powerlessness, however, she keeps looking steadfastly at the close-up
> view, the swarthiest face of things.[12]

Paradoxically, it would seem that Elizabeth Barrett Browning differs from Robert both in her greater concern with the knotty problems of the present and in her greater investment in visionary transcendence. She differs from Robert Browning, Arnold, and Carlyle in her greater capacity for reconciling discordant viewpoints.

Yet the philosophy gradually articulated by Aurora Leigh and the poetics she unfolds at the center of the poem in Book V are not only revisions of Carlylian thought.[13] Her point of departure is a series of conflicts that include Carlyle's ideas as one side of an intellectual debate. In *Aurora Leigh,* Browning's central *aesthetic* choice and worry appears to be between the Wordsworthian advocacy of a solitary songster inspired by the deep urgings of nature [14] and the Carlylian demand for a didactic writer with urban concerns that he records through rhetorical narratives. Of course, Wordsworth and Carlyle actually developed somewhat more complex scenarios than this, such that, paradoxically, we see Wordsworth finding solace both in the visions that come when he is alone and in the prospect of extending this vision to a larger community; while Carlyle's outspoken hero is often depicted as a wandering and visionary outcast who acquires stature and influence in the present age only through the written word. But neither Wordsworth nor Carlyle was able to urge this particular set of opposed possibilities with equal fervor. Browning confronts the choice quite directly, and she comes up with a poem and a poetics to embrace both.

Her poetic hero is a Carlylian character with the power to teach, persuade, and prophesy,

> poets should
> Exert a double vision; should have eyes
> To see near things as comprehensively
> As if afar they took their point of sight,
> And distant things as intimately deep
> As if they touched them   (V:183–87)

yet is also soulful, vulnerable, sensitive, and capable of a long, gradual growth of the mind: "And take for a worthier stage the soul itself" (V:340). Her hero-poet lives both in country and city, indulges in both ethical discussion and ecstatic inspiration, is keen both to aesthetic beauty and to social truth, and is both personally interested in events around her and cautious to see them from more than one side. Her story takes form both as a mimetic narrative and an expressive poem (Browning called it a "novel-poem"[15] as well as "unscrupulously epic" [V:214]). Later in the poem, Aurora summarizes its character as both an "imitation" of nature and "archetypal" in its symbolism (VII:835–

43). In short, this is a poetics that gives equal weight to action and character, to mimesis and expressive form, to the double aim to teach and to delight. Why and how the poem achieved aesthetic success in having it both ways it not something I have space to explore in this essay except to note that it was addressed to an audience happily alive to the appeal of large, baggy, multipurposed poems; many readers in *Aurora Leigh*'s Victorian audience responded to the formal aspects of the poem, to its richly imagistic lyricism and large-spirited narrative, with great enthusiasm.[16]

While this concern with a double vision deeply informs Aurora's professed poetics and is, as I will further argue below, its most distinctive feature, the discourse on poetry in Book V officially begins, like previous classic defenses of poetry, with a more specific issue likely to concern all writers of her time: the question whether she was living in an age in which heroical epic poetry could be written. She addresses the problem convincingly and wittily, first by cutting the classics down to the size of the present:

> The critics say that epics have died out
> With Agamemnon and the goat-nursed gods;
> I'll not believe it. I could never deem,
> As Payne Knight did . . .
> . . . .
> That Homer's heroes measured twelve feet high.
> They were but men:—his Helen's hair turned grey
> Like any plain Miss Smith's who wears a front;
> And Hector's infant whimpered at a plume
> As yours last Friday at a turkey-cock.   (V:139–50)

Second, she appeals to the possibility for heroism in any age and time:

> All actual heroes are essential men,
> And all men possible heroes: every age,
> Heroic in proportions, double-faced,
> Looks backward and before, expects a morn
> And claims an epos.
>   Ay, but every age
> Appears to souls who live in't (ask Carlyle)
> Most unheroic. Ours, for instance, ours: (V:151–57)

Finally, she places the responsibility for recognizing heroism squarely with the poet: "the poets abound / Who scorn to touch [the age] with a finger-tip" (V:158–59). Browning joins another common debate of her age in arguing that the poet's subject should be the present rather than Carlyle's fabled past, and she argues that this is a noble subject against his tendency to see the present primarily as an object for satire. The task of seeing the age in this way remains with the poet: whether the age is great or not depends on whether or not its poets can see from two perspectives at once, see the world small and see it large.

In the course of this general argument, Aurora also indicates, indirectly, where to find epic battlegrounds in the present. The great battles of the age are waged, as Aurora's must be waged, in verbal debate:

> Nay, if there's room for poets in this world
> A little overgrown (I think there is),
> Their sole work is to represent the age,
> Their age, not Charlemagne's,—this live, throbbing age,
> That brawls, cheats, maddens, calculates, aspires,
> And spends more passion, more heroic heat,
> Betwixt the mirrors of its drawing-rooms,
> Than Roland with his knights at Roncesvalles.
> . . . .
> . . . King Arthur's self
> Was commonplace to Lady Guenever;
> And Camelot to minstrels seemed as flat
> As Fleet Street to our poets.   (V:200–13)

Browning is humorously, yet correctly, specific about where epic debates predominantly occurred: in the social arena of women's drawing rooms and in the bookshops of Fleet Street. Although she does not reiterate them here, the rest of her poem is devoted to the social issues most debated: between the classes, between the sexes, between poetry and social science, between belief and agnosticism. These, in addition to her aesthetic choices, are the proper subject of her poem.

Nonetheless, her avowed aim is not finally to dramatize or announce the victory of any one side of these various issues over the other. Her key terms—as resonant for her as Arnold's "disinterestedness," Wordsworth's "feeling," or Aristotle's "mythos"—are the "twofold," "double vision," and "double-faced."[17] Her use of these terms anticipates the obsession of twentieth-century criticism with the terminology of irony, double perspective, binary opposition, *différance*. In contrast to New Critical irony and structuralist binarism, whose self-cancellations enable the critic to achieve a transcendent detachment, and in contrast to Derridean *différance* with its endlessly radicalizing erosions, Browning's terminology enacts embrasure, enfolding possibilities, multiplying choices, permitting alternatives. Browning's usage in particular of "twofold" and "double vision" anticipates a number of contemporary feminist theorists, who have adopted the vocabulary of "doubleness" to call for a similarly syncretic criticism. A notable difference here is that contemporary feminists tend to use such terms to indicate the difficult dilemmas in which they find themselves, to indicate, for example, the necessity for women to see as men but also as women, to see as women but also as different women—as African-Americans, lesbians, Third-World women—to see as women but also beyond gender, or to see from within an experience but also from without. Browning adopts yet another term, expressive of difficulty, but she again translates it into a word for conciliated opposites. More provocative than "twofold" is the conventionally duplicitous "double-faced," which Browning transforms by continually placing the term in contexts in which it is redefined and revalued as an expression for empathetic vision. For Browning, to see with a "double vision" does not, however, occur without struggle: it is to be able, in another of her formulations, to stand "face to face" with the world, confronting and accepting, opening oneself to and recognizing all that is other to oneself.[18]

Browning's terms receive very various applications in Aurora Leigh's hands. The age is "double-faced" in the citation above, in that, while inhering in the present moment, it looks into both the past and the future. More important, Browning believed that to lead others to a larger vision, she must meet "face to face & without mask the Humanity of the age"[19] and "exert a double vision" (V:184) by seeing both near and far. The artist must strive for a "twofold" life ("O sorrowful great gift / Conferred on poets, of a twofold life, / When one life has been fond enough for pain!" V:380–82); that is, she must both be and see, to "stand up straight as demigods" (V:384). Rearticulating these premises in Book VII, Aurora Leigh sums up in an impressive monologue:

> a twofold world
> Must go to a perfect cosmos. Natural things
> And spiritual,—who separates those two
> In art, in morals, or the social drift,
> Tears up the bond of nature and brings death
> . . . .
>   We divide
> This apple of life, and cut it through the pips:
> The perfect round which fitted Venus' hand
> Has perished as utterly as if we ate

Both halves. Without the spiritual, observe,
The natural's impossible—no form,
No motion: without sensuous, spiritual
Is inappreciable,—no beauty or power:
And in this twofold sphere the twofold man
(For still the artist is intensely a man)
Holds firmly by the natural, to reach
The spiritual beyond it,—fixes still
. . . man, the twofold creature, apprehends
The twofold manner, in and outwardly,
And nothing in the world comes single to him,
A mere itself,—cup, column, or candlestick   (VII:762–805)

Even in her twofold nature, then, the poet does not in fact transcend her fellow creatures, but remains "man, the twofold creature." To be fully "twofold" may be extraordinary, but it can be achieved by anyone with enough will and aspiration; thus, at the end of the poem, even Aurora's hitherto antivisionary cousin Romney, who has devoted his life to everyday problems and practical reforms, can—though as blind as Milton—see with a poet's vision the New Jerusalem.

But the thorniest dialectic of all in this poem is the twofold *gender* of "man." Without the intense, personal experience of writing always in relation to men—in conflict with Romney's desire for a wife, in the shadow of his prejudices about women poets, and in competition with the great male poets of past and present—Aurora's (and Browning's) "twofold" philosophy might never have emerged. Aurora's struggle and ambition as a female animates all the other issues in the poem, most obviously in what she sees as possible "near" and "far" for herself and other women. The poem's feminism clearly has fueled the controversy surrounding it—Browning's gender carried much of the blame for flaws perceived by critics of her day[20]—and most feminist scholars consider the gender issue to be the most distinctive feature of Aurora/Browning's aesthetics. A woman artist is the subject of this poem, and her gender is her major obstacle in setting out on a career. Aurora's speculations about gender literally surround the poetics of Book V, constituting its narrative frame: her thoughts are most directly focused on gender when she is struggling with the fact of being female in her world, but being female is also her most recurrent worry when trying to write.

Even so, whether as a personal, sociological, or aesthetic problem, femaleness is seen by Aurora as a provisional, man-made obstacle that can be overcome. Aurora dedicates herself unhesitatingly to writing as well as any male ever wrote:

> Measure not the work
> Until the day's out and the labor done,
> . . . .
> And, in that we have nobly striven at least,
> Deal with us nobly, women though we be,
> And honor us with truth if not with praise.   (V:77–83)

Every artist has a gender (since the artist is "intensely a man"), but writes both in and beyond gender. Aurora does not see herself (and neither, of course, did Browning) as writing exclusively for or about women. She writes as a literate and thoughtful woman for and about both men and women. Speaking in anger to Romney, she makes her position clear,

> 'You misconceive the question like a man,
> Who sees a woman as the complement
> Of his sex merely. You forget too much
> That every creature, female as the male,
> Stands single in responsible act and thought
> As also in birth and death. Whoever says
> To a loyal woman, "Love and work with me,"
> Will get fair answers if the work and love,
> Being good themselves, are good for her—
> . . . .
> But *me* your work
> Is not the best for,—nor your love the best,
> Nor able to commend the kind of work
> For love's sake merely. . . .
> For me,
> Perhaps I am not worthy, as you say,
> Of work like this: perhaps a woman's soul
> Aspires, and not creates: yet we aspire,
> And yet I'll try out your perhapses, sir,
> And if I fail . . . why, burn me up my straw
> Like other false works—I'll not ask for grace;
> Your scorn is better, cousin Romney. I
> Who love my art, would never wish it lower
> To suit my stature.'   (II:434–94)

Her poetics could not, then, be seen as an "alternative" poetics exclusively for women: it is a poetics for everyone, feminist in that it sees everyone as gendered, and everyone as in need of re-education about women's capacities.

The poem thus to some extent provides its own theoretical context for its celebrated imagery of childbearing women—imagery that forces us literally to see Aurora's ambitions for the female artist, and to see physical femaleness as twofold, sometimes grotesque, sometimes ennobled, and capable of the most diverse symbolism.[21] At the climax of her speech about the possibility for a contemporary epic, she depicts the age itself as female:

> Never flinch,
> But still, unscrupulously epic, catch
> Upon the burning lava of a song
> The full-veined, heaving, double-breasted Age:
> That, when the next shall come, the men of that
> May touch the impress with reverent hand, and say
> "Behold,—behold the paps we all have sucked!
> This bosom seems to beat still, or at least
> It sets ours beating. This is living art,
> Which thus presents and thus records true life."   (V:213–22)

Aurora does not argue for a gender-free art but for an art that is great with life, and women may represent (flesh out) that life quite literally.

Aurora's epic poetics would not slip easily, however, into a standard anthology of "The History of Criticism" because, of course, it is embedded in a narrative context. *Aurora Leigh* is an extensive *ars poetica*, and although its poetics appears to emerge primarily from a (male) Aristotelian tradition, its *ars* emerges from the modern (woman's) novel.[22] Aurora's theory of art and the artist in Book V takes place while she is writing her books, philosophizing about them, trying to make a living, and suffering from solitude. A nonwriter reading the entire poem could glean from it an accurate description of a successful writer's life, of a lengthy career struggle, of writer's blocks, of post-writing depression, and of a writing woman's solitude, courage, self-doubt, and lucky chances. It is precisely through this contextualization that Browning's poetics works for and, in my view, reaches her most far-flung goals. Browning places her theory in action; she refuses to divorce philosophical rationalization from practical contexts; hers is meant to be a "living" word.

The poetics of Book V is placed at the center of the poem (complete with an invocation to the Muse). Structurally, this gives Aurora's poetics prominence and tends to lift it out of context. Book V is the "visionary" book of the epic. But it is as carefully located in a narrative context as any other section of the poem—more precisely, it is placed at the high point in Aurora's career. When Book V opens, Aurora has been in London for several years,[23] struggling for a living, and she has reached the point where she is nearly ready to write an epic. After calling for new inspiration and reiterating her desire to write as well as any man has ever written, she reviews her career up to this point, her ballads, her sonnets, her descriptive poems, and her pastorals; and she concludes that she will have failed in her ambitions if she does not go on to attempt the highest form, the form in which she must recreate her world in its entirety, an epic. From this humbling recognition she moves immediately to a justification of the epic form itself. When 200 lines later, she returns to herself, to her personal struggles and long working days, and announces to us and to herself "Behold, at last, a book" (V:352), we see in retrospect that her poetics has served a double purpose. While we have been listening to her apology for epic poetry, she has been conceiving her poem—writing her *Aurora Leigh*. Her poetics is a way of thinking out loud as she talks herself into writing this poem, justifying it not only to us but to herself. She then returns to meditating on the poem and the artist for another seventy lines or so, until again she returns to her personal life; and it appears in retrospect that she has meanwhile been revising, putting the final touches not only on her theory, but on her epic poem. In *Aurora Leigh*, philosophy and poetry go literally hand in hand.

This deft interlacing of Aurora's thoughts with her actions means that when she turns almost immediately in the fifth book from writing her poem to mourning the failures of her personal life as a woman, the transition is less abrupt, less contradictory than it might seem in a simple plot summary. Nothing now is left to Aurora to achieve in her career, and she remains a lonely woman, lonelier still with her great work complete; she is ripe for a postpartum depression. Aurora herself explains the shift in terms familiar to us from her previous theorizing about art: "To have our books / Appraised by love, associated with love, / While *we* sit loveless!" (V:474–76). Since she had meant, like most nineteenth-century poets, to produce an art embedded in life and life-giving, her own dismal life must undercut the success of her book. In perfecting one at the expense of the other, she has risked injuring both. True to her insistence on a Johnsonian appeal from art to nature, her ideas are subjected to skeptical questioning and proof by her subsequent experiences of solitude and eventual reunion with Romney.

Unlike Rasselas's, both her theories and her poetic creations survive their long test and receive fresh application when she comes face to face with Romney. The ending has provoked as much controversy as any other element in the book, for Aurora's new eagerness to serve Romney who all along has stood as her opposite (earthy while she is ethereal, a leader of men while she is a mere woman, a social activist while she insists on poetry), for the symbolic castration of the blinded

Romney, and for the fact that both of these contribute to the striking but unacknowledged resemblance to the ending of *Jane Eyre* (which Browning appears to have forgotten when she echoed it here). The issues are perhaps too complex to explore thoroughly in this essay, but the ending may at least be reevaluated in light of Aurora's own poetics. While as acute a critic as Rachel Blau DuPlessis believes that because Aurora seeks to serve a "castrated" Romney in the end, this work "did not change the nineteenth-century convention of representation that saw the price of artistic ambition as the loss of femininity,"[24] what is most striking about this ending—when read in the context of Aurora's ideas—is her triumph in having it all: she has fame *and* Romney, Romney's love *and* respect, a new reason for working *and* a companion for her work (she will now work to embody the visions of them both). In the clear symbolism of this ending, Romney has learned to respect the visionary poet, while Aurora (without ceasing to write) can have a nitty-gritty life of her own. The difficulty of achieving all this is almost as great in our own time as it was in Browning's, though many more women are now trying. I suspect that, whatever other reasons readers have had for doubting this ending, its overflowing optimism has amazed them and, in some minds, marked it "female." But this was Aurora's vision, a vision that Browning herself realized, and the possibility for its triumph is one which the feminist reader should surely wish to grasp as her own.

Whatever our judgments of the way *Aurora Leigh* ends, the "twofold," "double-faced" character of Aurora's reasoning—of speculation wrestling with her own experimental life—remains one of the most compelling, though elusive, aesthetic features of this poem; it may also be the most useful feature to any feminist interested in binding *theoria* to *praxis*. A poetics emerges from its context in the poem in such a way as to resist being abstracted from its practical consequences. Moreover, while the poetics I have detailed belongs to the fictional Aurora, we are urged to believe with the first readers of the poem that Aurora was a portrait of the artist, and not to flinch from looking with a double vision at the artist in her art. We owe it as much to ourselves as to Browning to reconstruct this epical encounter of a woman's mind with *herstory*. Aurora is witness to the fact that Browning, at least, knew her achievement for what it was even as she wrote it: an unscrupulous epic by a woman poet.

Notes

1. Ellen Moers, *Literary Women* (Garden City, N.Y.: Doubleday, 1977; rpt. New York: Oxford University Press, 1985), pp. 14–15, 41.

2. Janice Radway, *Reading the Romance: Women, Patriarchy, and Popular Literature* (Chapel Hill: University of North Carolina Press, 1984). While professors of English are carefully training their students to appreciate Wordsworth, it is appalling to see a modern critic discard *Aurora Leigh* even for the educated reader, as did Virginia Radley: "the poet is to be commended for her effort, and for the sporadic but brilliant results that effort yielded. There is no question, however, that the total work is unwieldy, shapeless, amorphous, and philosophically untenable. While it will continue to be of interest to literary historians, it will never have much appeal for the general reading public (although an educated one) or, for that matter, for the mass of graduate students in English who seek a thesis topic with the urgent specter of 'Time's winged chariot' behind them," *Elizabeth Barrett Browning* (New York: Twayne, 1972), p. 125.

3. Although among feminist scholars and Victorianists there is resurgent interest in Browning's poetics, there are no accounts of *Aurora Leigh* as a comprehensive *ars poetica,* and I know of no contemporary outline for, or overview of, a feminist aesthetic that taps Browning's ideas or mentions her precedent.

4. Virginia Woolf may have initiated such a response in the case of *Aurora Leigh* when she gave a mixed review of the poem's success, overlooking and thus undermining Browning's own defense. But *Aurora Leigh* anticipates many of the issues that worry Woolf in *A Room of One's Own,* including most prominently the basic needs for a room of one's own and (in Aurora Leigh's day) £300: "You're richer than you fancy. The will says, / *Three hundred pounds, and any other sum / Of which the said testatrix dies possessed*" (emphasis in text). (ll. 300–302). See Virginia Woolf, *"Aurora Leigh,"* in *The Second Common Reader* (New York: Harcourt, Brace, & World, 1960), pp. 182–92; Elizabeth Barrett Browning, *Aurora Leigh,* II:987–89, in *The Complete Works of Elizabeth Barrett Browning,* ed. Charlotte Porter and Helen A. Clarke, vols. 4 and 5 (1900; rpt. New York: AMS Press, 1973). Subsequent citations of *Aurora Leigh* refer to this edition and appear parenthetically in the text.

5. Standard classroom anthologies by male editors cannot be counted on to contain representative selections of women's theories: Walter Jackson Bate includes a single text, Woolf's "Modern Fiction" in his *Criticism: The Major Texts* (New York: Harcourt Brace Jovanovich, 1970); no women theorists are included in Hazard Adams, *Critical Theory since Plato* (New York: Harcourt Brace Jovanovich, 1971). For a more representative selection of women critics (not, however, including Browning), see *Literary Criticism and Theory: The Greeks to the Present,* ed. Robert Con Davis and Laurie Finke (New York: Longman, 1989).

6. Lawrence Lipking, "Aristotle's Sister: A Poetics of Abandonment," *Critical Inquiry* 10 (September 1983), 61–81. Lipking has incorporated this essay in an expanded form into his *Abandoned Women and Poetic Tradition* (Chicago: University of Chicago Press, 1988).

7. As Josephine Donovan points out, Lipking's discussion replicates the efforts of women theorists—including Susan S. Lanser, Evelyn Torton Beck, Michele Barrett, and Elaine Showalter—to establish, in Showalter's terminology, a "gynocriticism." Donovan criticizes Lipking for extracting this poetics, somewhat contradictorily, from men's writing about women and from the European sentimentalist tradition, in which young heroines are typically seduced and abandoned. (Donovan follows Nancy K. Miller in this last description of the "heroine's text.") Donovan argues that a poetics should be grounded

wholly in works by women and that it should be a "women's" not a "woman's" poetics, reflecting women's diverse experiences. Even so, Lipking's emphasis on women's suffering and solitude, the constriction of their lives to the private sphere, their understanding of and insistence on the importance of their personal lives when they finally do speak, and their yearning for community are often cited prominently in feminist discussions of women's experiences. See Josephine Donovan's "Toward a Women's Poetics," in *Feminist Issues in Literary Scholarship*, ed. Shari Benstock (Bloomington: Indiana University Press, 1987), pp. 98–109.

8. See, for example, Joan DeJean, "Fictions of Sappho," *Critical Inquiry* 13.4 (1987), 787–805; Donovan, "Toward a Women's Poetics," pp. 99–100, 105–7; and Jane Marcus, "Still Practice, A/Wrested Alphabet: Toward a Feminist Aesthetic," in Benstock, *Feminist Issues in Literary Scholarship*, pp. 81–84.

9. Carlyle's ideas about heroism appear throughout his works, but most comprehensively in *On Heroes, Hero-Worship, and the Heroic in History* (1841; rpt. New York: AMS Press, 1969). While several critics have noted the influence both of a Carlylian work ethic and of his attack on materialism in Aurora Leigh's philosophy, none have recognized the relevance of the Carlylian (Wo)Man of Letters to this poetics. See Helen Cooper, *Elizabeth Barrett Browning, Woman and Artist* (Chapel Hill: University of North Carolina Press, 1988), p. 162; Deirdre David, "'Art's a Service': Social Wound, Sexual Politics, and *Aurora Leigh*," *Browning Institute Studies* 13 (1985), 133–34; Alethea Hayter, *Mrs. Browning: A Poet's Work and Its Setting* (London: Faber & Faber, 1962), p. 159; and Dorothy Mermin, *Elizabeth Barrett Browning: The Origins of a New Poetry* (Chicago: University of Chicago Press, 1989), p. 202.

In constructing her "epic," Browning was by no means indebted to male writers alone. A number of critics argue that the unique shape of her "novel-poem" arises from her combination of aspects of women's novels and of men's poems; I will argue something similar below. For discussions of sources for the narrative of *Aurora Leigh* in works by both men and women writers, see especially Kathleen Blake, "Elizabeth Barrett Browning and Wordsworth: The Romantic Poet as a Woman," *Victorian Poetry* 24 (winter 1986), 387–98; Hayter, *Mrs. Browning*, pp. 159–62; Julia Bolton Holloway, "*Aurora Leigh* and *Jane Eyre*," *The Brontë Society* 17.2 (1977), 126–32; Cora Kaplan, *Aurora Leigh and Other Poems* (London: The Women's Press Ltd., 1978), pp. 5–36; Mermin, *Elizabeth Barrett Browning*, pp. 183–224; Dolores Rosenblum, "Face to Face: Elizabeth Barrett Browning's *Aurora Leigh* and Nineteenth-Century Poetry," *Victorian Studies* 26 (spring 1983), 321–38, and "*Casa Guidi Windows* and *Aurora Leigh*: The Genesis of Elizabeth Barrett Browning's Visionary Aesthetic," *Tulsa Studies in Women's Literature* 4.1 (1985), 61–68; and Marjorie Stone, "Genre Subversion and Gender Inversion: *The Princess* and *Aurora Leigh*," *Victorian Poetry* 25 (summer 1987), 101–27.

10. *The Letters of Robert Browning and Elizabeth Barrett Browning 1845–1846*, ed. Elvan Kintner (Cambridge: Harvard University Press, 1969), vol. 1, p. 9.

11. Meredith Raymond, "Elizabeth Barrett Browning's Poetics 1845–1846: 'The Ascending Gyre,'" *Browning Society Notes* 11 (1981), 2.

12. Dolores Rosenblum, "*Casa Guidi*," pp. 66–67. Nina Auerbach conducts a provocative analysis of the literary "marriage" of the Brownings, in which Robert's irony operates at the expense of Elizabeth, in "Robert Browning's Last Word," *Victorian Poetry* 22.2 (1984), 161–73.

13. Lipking extols the prospect for a woman's poetics to "repair the balance of theory," but he believes this means that a feminist aesthetic must be necessarily reactive and that this is not entirely satisfactory: "Insofar as [a poetics of 'abandonment'] accurately represents the strategies of female authors within and against the dominant culture, it stands for a history of subordination and reaction that many women oppose more strenuously than they do the patriarchs themselves" (p. 78). Like Lipking's poetics, Browning's is reformative rather than anarchic or revolutionary, but it is not the plight of women alone to find themselves "reacting" at the moment of attempted "origination"; male critics are as burdened in this way as women.

14. Kathleen Blake demonstrates important parallels between Browning and Wordsworth, but I must disagree with her that Browning refutes Victorian objectivity in favor of Romanticist subjectivism: Victorian authors (notably, Arnold, Carlyle, Tennyson, and Robert Browning) viewed the claims of objectivity and subjectivity as in conflict and believed that a reconciliation should be achieved; Browning was as deeply invested in this problem as any of her peers. Blake's essay reflects the persistent critical tendency to privilege Wordsworth's aesthetics over any other in the nineteenth century. See Blake, "Elizabeth Barrett Browning and Wordsworth," pp. 387–98. The allusion to Wordsworth's "Immortality Ode" in the opening lines of the poem has been widely recognized by critics, but following on its heels is Byronic satire (as Alethea Hayter points out, *Mrs. Browning,* p. 162), a kind of satire in which Carlyle also specialized. Aurora refers reverently to Keats in Book I, ll. 1003–15, but later she chooses epic poetry over the Keatsian lyricism with which her career began.

15. *Letters,* vol. 1, p. 31.

16. Amply documented by critics is the immediate and enormous popularity of the work; the enthusiasm of progressive writers, such as D. G. Rossetti, Swinburne, Landor, and others; and the anxiety expressed by the major quarterlies over its strong views and strong language. As Cora Kaplan reminds us, "everybody in polite society read it, even the Queen, and Barrett Browning was delighted by reports that it had corrupted women of sixty and been banned by horrified parents" (p. 12). But, as mentioned above, praise for the poem has often been mixed. As Radley notes, the reviews "affixed to the Porter-Clarke edition of the works, contain such diametrically opposed critical opinions as to make the reader wonder if the reviewers could possibly be discussing the same work " (*Elizabeth Barrett Browning,* p. 124). Both Virginia Woolf and Moers, for example, enjoyed reading *Aurora Leigh,* for its "speed and energy, forthrightness and complete self-confidence," *"Aurora Leigh,"* p. 184; quoted in Moers, *Literary Women,* p. 59. Woolf, however, also thought *Aurora Leigh* would have made a first-rate novel without the poetry; while Moers decided it would be first-rate poetry if it were less of a novel: "we need to slow down, to stop running against conventions" and "retreat into solitude, silence, decorum, and rhymed obscurity with Emily Dickinson" (p. 60). Although complex circumstances must have affected such discrepant evaluations, the most compelling discussions I know of Browning's challenge to genre boundaries in this poem are those of Susan Stanford Friedman, "Gender and Genre Anxiety: Elizabeth Barrett Browning and H.D. as Epic Poets," *Tulsa Studies in Women's Literature* 5.2 (1986), 203–28; Dorothy Mermin, "Gender and Genre in *Aurora Leigh,"* *The Victorian Newsletter* 69 (spring 1986), 7–11; and Stone, "Genre Subversion and Gender Inversion," pp. 101–27.

17. Rosenblum argues that Barrett Browning's "double vision" affects

even her technique and "requires constant shifts in focus" from near to far and back again ("*Casa Guidi*," p. 65). In addition to recognizing the importance of the "twofold" in Browning's poetics, Raymond points to a lesser "three-fold division" of "the poetic power" among "the senses, the intellect, and the soul," which in the fully successful poet may be united (p. 1), but this latter set of distinctions sinks from view in *Aurora Leigh*.

18. In a discussion of Eliza Haywood's literary criticism, Kristina Straub employs the vocabulary of doubleness (of "double vision," seeing "double," "double position" as woman and critic, doubled "perspective," "double writing," and "double reading"), not directly from Haywood, but by inference, and she cites parallel instances in the theories of Joan Kelly, Naomi Schor, and Bonnie Zimmerman. The notion of "doubleness" is pervasive in current feminist criticism. Browning's idea of the "double-faced" should similarly be contrasted with a necessary "duplicity" discussed by Straub, Schor, and Jonathan Culler, among others. See Kristina Straub, "Women, Gender, and Criticism," in *Literary Criticism and Theory: The Greeks to the Present*, pp. 859–66, 871–76. Also see Jonathan Culler, "Reading as a Woman," *On Deconstruction: Theory and Criticism after Structuralism* (Ithaca, N.Y.: Cornell University Press, 1982), pp. 43–64; Joan Kelly, "The Doubled Vision of Feminist Theory," in *Sex and Class in Women's History*, ed. Judith L. Newton, Mary P. Ryan, and Judith Walkowitz (London: Routledge & Kegan Paul, 1983), pp. 259–70; Naomi Schor, "Reading Double: Sand's Difference," in *The Poetics of Gender*, ed. Nancy K. Miller (New York: Columbia University Press, 1986), pp. 248–69; and Bonnie Zimmerman, "What Has Never Been: An Overview of Lesbian Feminist Criticism," in *The New Feminist Criticism: Essays on Women, Literature, and Theory*, ed. Elaine Showalter (New York: Pantheon Books, 1985), pp. 200–24.

19. *Letters*, vol. 1, p. 31.

20. Browning's contemporary Sydney Dobell wrote, for example, that *Aurora Leigh* "contains some of the finest poetry written in the century; poetry such as Shakespeare's sister might have written if he had had a twin. . . . But it is no poem. No woman can write a poem"; quoted in Jerome Buckley, *The Victorian Temper* (Cambridge: Cambridge University Press, 1981), p. 63.

21. On the imagery of motherhood and manhood in this poem, see, for example, Sandra Donaldson, "'Motherhood's Advent in Power': Elizabeth Barrett Browning's Poems about Motherhood," *Victorian Poetry* 18 (spring 1980), 51–60; and Virginia Steinmetz, "Beyond the Sun: Patriarchal Images in *Aurora Leigh*," *Studies in Browning and His Circle* 9 (winter 1981), 18–41, and "Images of 'Mother-Want' in Elizabeth Barrett Browning's *Aurora Leigh*," *Victorian Poetry* 21 (winter 1983), 351–67.

22. For accounts of other aspects of the structure of this poem—which has otherwise received little attention—see C. Castan, "Structural Problems and the Poetry of *Aurora Leigh*," *Browning Society Notes* 7.3 (1977), 73–81; and Cooper, *Elizabeth Barrett Browning*, pp. 153–55. Two particularly interesting discussions of character changes in Aurora may be found in Barbara Gelpi, "*Aurora Leigh*: The Vocation of the Woman Poet," *Victorian Poetry* 19 (spring 1981), 35–48; and Sandra Gilbert, "From Patria to Matria: Elizabeth Barrett Browning's Risorgimento," *PMLA* 99.2 (1984), 194–211.

23. The precise number of years is uncertain. Castan and Cooper both believe that the narrating Aurora is 27 years old from the opening of the poem through Book V, until in ll. 1171–76 the narrated Aurora catches up with the narrator and they remain together to the end of the poem. But the poem

moves back and forth between past and present when narrating the writing of Aurora's epic in Book V, from, for example, "Alas, I still see something to be done, / . . . / Behold, at last, a book" to "I laboured on alone" (V:344–52, 421), suggesting the "journalistic" style that Cooper describes in Books VIII and IX, pp. 153, 201, n. 17.

24. Rachel Blau DuPlessis, *Writing Beyond the Ending: Narrative Strategies of Twentieth-Century Women Writers* (Bloomington: Indiana University Press, 1985), p. 87.

Chapter 18
"I must not settle into a figure": The Woman Artist in Virginia Woolf's Writings

Pamela L. Caughie

> A woman's writing is always feminine; it cannot help being feminine: the only difficulty lies in defining what we mean by feminine.
> —Virginia Woolf, "Women Novelists"[1]

So many of Virginia Woolf's novels and essays portray an artist: Terence Hewet (*The Voyage Out*), Ralph Denham and William Rodney (*Night and Day*), Lily Briscoe and Augustus Carmichael (*To the Lighthouse*), Orlando in that eponymous novel, Mary Carmichael (*A Room of One's Own*), Bernard and Neville (*The Waves*), Elizabeth Barrett Browning (*Flush*), and Miss La Trobe (*Between the Acts*). Even those characters who are not ostensibly creative artists function as artist figures in their works: Rhoda (*The Waves*), Sara (*The Years*), and Isa (*Between the Acts*) turn mundane events and commonplace remarks into private poetry, and Mrs. Dalloway and Mrs. Ramsay create transient works of art out of social occasions and personal relationships. Often Woolf's artist figures comment directly on their difficulties in narrating the work we are reading, for example, the biographers of *Jacob's Room* and *Orlando* and the narrators of "An Unwritten Novel" and "Mr. Bennett and Mrs. Brown." Most of these artist figures are women, and even many of the male artists, such as Terence Hewet and especially Bernard, are described as having the "sensibility" of a woman. What are all these portraits of the artist about if not the continual investigation of the creative process itself and, in particular, the quest for a female aesthetics?

And yet, a curious pattern emerges in these portraits. With the exception of Orlando and Augustus Carmichael, who eventually receive recognition for their poetry, and Mrs. Dalloway and Mrs. Ramsay, whose parties finally come off, none of Woolf's fictional artists is confident, skillful, successful, or even very productive. Although Lily may have her vision and La Trobe may produce her play, each artist questions the achievement of her art, and so do many readers. If in these works on the artist figure Woolf investigates art itself and if she seeks a female aesthetic tradition, why then do so few of these artists create a consummate work of art or articulate a consistent theory of art? In other words, why all these failed artists?[2]

Of course, the question so often asked by Woolf's critics is a loaded one. For this question rests on two assumptions: one, that Woolf is investigating the *nature* of women's art, in terms of the relation between art and life, and seeking "the appropriate female form"; and two, that frustration, doubt, and inconclusiveness express the *failure* of art.[3] Both assumptions are bound up with a modernist aesthetics, one that informs much of our critical terminology and one that Woolf seems to question every bit as much as she does an aesthetics of realism. I want to begin this essay by calling into question certain assumptions about art that inform much criticism of Woolf's novels on the artist figure. In addition, I want to suggest an alternative approach to these novels that can enable us to see how Woolf herself questions these assumptions that we often take for granted: in particular, the assumptions that the artist is a *special* and *self-sufficient* individual, that the artwork is *original* and *autonomous,* that art represents life or reveals *truth,* and that to investigate women's creative process is to seek *the defining traits* of a female aesthetics. Questioning such assumptions led Woolf to posit a different conception of the artist and a different model for narrative discourse so that our usual ways of measuring success and failure no longer pertain. The point of Woolf's many portraits of the woman artist is not to find the distinctive conventions of a female aesthetics, but to resist the rigid systematizing of conventions, the tendency to turn certain narrative forms into abiding formulas. For if Woolf valued anything in the artist it was her freedom to change.

To trace Woolf's changing notions, I want to focus on the works that directly and self-consciously explore the female creative process—*To the Lighthouse* (1927), *Orlando* (1928), *A Room of One's Own* (1929), and *Between the Acts* (1941).[4] Most critical commentaries see Woolf's artists as engaging in the *same* artistic quest—the quest for aesthetic harmony, unity, or autonomy (Leaska, Naremore, DiBattista); the quest for the right relation between art and life (Friedman, Fussell); the quest for the essence beneath or the truth beyond all surface manifestations and conventional forms (Hafley, Richter)—motivated by the desire to make something lasting and permanent (Transue, Guiguet).[5] Whether critics see Woolf's artist figures as exemplars of the modernist artist or the woman artist, they assume the artist's desire is for freedom, originality, and authenticity. In doing so, these critics confuse Woolf's and her artists' continual and *changing* investigations of the creative process with the quest for the appropriate (modernist or female) artistic form. It is this confusion as well that leads some critics to conclude that Woolf finally despairs of ever fulfilling her quest (for example, DiBattista and Zwerdling on *Between the Acts*).

Such readings accept authenticity, autonomy, permanence, and uniqueness as their aesthetic standards and assume that the correspondence of art to life is *the defining* relation of the novel. Such standards are not wrong, but they are not always appropriate. Indeed, they can obscure other kinds of relations (such as the relation between the artwork and its audience) and other ways of valuing art. Woolf's concern in her novels on the artist figure is with the *production* of women's art, certainly, and her experiments with narrative form create new modes for women's writing. But are we able to, and do we want to, isolate the features of some characteristic female form and to present this as a norm for women's writing? What Woolf defies in her novels and essays, I argue, is any attempt to *define* fiction by standards to which it conforms or from which it deviates. That is, we can argue that women's art diverges from patriarchal art only to the extent that we accept those conventions that have been codified by patriarchal theorists. Once we expose those conventions as arbitrary constructs, as a universalizing of provisional and provincial concepts of art, as so much feminist criticism has successfully done, then we have made the concept of *any* appropriate form suspect. Woolf was more apt to affirm the tenuous and provisional status of literary forms than to replace one highly valued form with another. And it is this affirmation of art as disposable not lapidary that enables Woolf to stress the difference women's art makes without the need to specify that difference in terms of a definitive distinction between men's and women's art. In other words, the features we either valorize or lament in women's art (for example, inconclusiveness, contradictions, ambivalence) are not the *property* of women writers; rather, they are the *effects* of a different way of conceiving art, one that calls into question the values of permanency, authenticity, and uniqueness—modernist values on which many feminist aesthetics seem to rest. If Woolf's works on the artist are inconclusive, fragmentary, and nonauthoritative, it is not because Woolf writes essentially as a woman but because she changes continually as a writer, testing out different conceptions of art.

To say that each of these novels, then, is about Woolf's own art or women's art in general is not yet to say what *kinds* of aesthetic relations each explores. Painting a picture (*To the Lighthouse*), writing a poem (*Orlando*), preparing a lecture (*A Room of One's Own*), and producing a play (*Between the Acts*) are analogous activities only in the most general sense. To subsume them under one category (for example, texts about women's writing) is to posit a similarity of structure and purpose where there is a diversity of functions and motives. An alternative, then, to discussing Woolf's novels on the artist in terms of the *nature* of women's art is to consider them in terms of the various *functions* of the artworks themselves. That is, rather than reading these works in the same way, as separate attempts to paint a portrait of the woman artist, we can read them differently, as changing strategies and motives that resist any consistent or consummate portrait of the artist. From Lily's private vision to La Trobe's public performance, Woolf enacts various aesthetic theories and exposes the partial and artificial nature of *any* literary form. As she tests out a variety of possibilities for women's writing, Woolf explores art's potential functions and changes our expectations of what art is or does.

My argument, then, is that we need not read these works by Woolf as the attempt to codify a female aesthetics or to portray a woman artist who successfully integrates her art and her life; for the desire to create an authentic art form is a desire bound up with a particular conception of art, and there are many and varying relations between art and life, not merely two options of integration or alienation.[6] In offering an alternative way of looking at Woolf's artists, I want to argue that the continual process of adaptation may be far more successful than any appropriate, authentic, or lapidary achievement. Thus, if Woolf does refuse to complete the story of the woman artist's development, as Alison Booth says of Woolf's last novel, it may be because she desires to keep that story open, and thus open to change.

*   *   *

With Lily Briscoe in *To the Lighthouse*, Woolf creates her first artist figure to tell the story of her own artwork as well as the story in which her artwork figures, and it is this narrative function of the artist that leads Woolf to question some of the modernist assumptions with which she began this work.[7] The structure of Woolf's novel is the progression of Lily's painting: its inception in Lily's desire to paint Mrs. Ramsay (Part I); its dissolution following the death of Mrs. Ramsay (Part II); its renewal ten years later when Lily returns to the Ramsays' summer home (Part III); and, its completion as the exhausted artist lays down her brush, declaring in the last line of the novel: "I have had my vision." As Patricia Waugh notes, *To the Lighthouse* is one of the earliest novels to stress "a sense of fictitiousness," both the fictitious status of what it represents ("life itself") and the fictitious status of its own representations (the text itself).[8] The involuted structure of this as well as other novels on the artist suggests the way the subject matter of the novel (Lily's painting) turns in on and reflects its form (Woolf's experimental narrative). That is, the subject (in this case, a woman's creative process) is a *function* of the novel's particular discourse. If *To the Lighthouse* is in quest of its status as art, then in generalizing on this work we must remember that a *particular kind* of painting, and a *particular kind* of discourse, are at issue here. As Lily explains to William Bankes in Part I, her painting makes "no attempt at likeness . . . the picture was not of them [Mrs. Ramsay and James]."[9] The painting, she continues, is a matter of *relations,* and it is these relations I want to consider.

Throughout the novel, Woolf presents Lily's art as a matter of relating two things: the mass on the right of her canvas and the mass on the left; Mrs. Ramsay in the window and Mr. Ramsay in the boat; the shore on which she stands and the sea to which she looks. Early in the novel, this relation is one of connection: "It was a question, [Lily] remembered, how to connect this mass on the right hand with that on the left. She might do it by bringing the line of the branch across so . . ." (*TTL* 82–83). Most critics accept this connection between two things as the essence not only of this novel, but of Woolf's art in general. "Throughout Mrs. Woolf's work," writes James Naremore, "the chief problem for her and for her characters is to overcome the space between things, to attain an absolute unity with the world."[10] Certainly this line across the canvas that presages Lily's final brush stroke endorses such a reading. However, this is only one moment of Woolf's novel. By the time Lily completes her painting, the relation she seeks has changed, from connecting two things to maintaining a balance between forces (*TTL* 287). As Lily nears the completion of her painting, she thinks:

One wanted . . . to be on a level with ordinary experience, to feel simply that's a chair, that's a table, and yet at the same time, It's a miracle, it's an ecstasy. The problem [of relations] might be solved after all. (*TTL* 299–300)

The problem *is* solved but not by synthesizing two things or by choosing between them. The problem is solved, or rather, removed, by a change in Lily's concerns: the distinction to be made is no longer between two things but *between different ways of relating things.* And what effects this change is Lily's function as narrator in Part III.

While Lily paints her picture in sections 3 to 13 of Part III, she moves back and forth between a loss of consciousness of outer things as she "tunnels" into the past, and a return to consciousness of external things as she looks out to sea. This oscillating movement between the memories Lily re-creates from the first part of the novel and the events she observes in this third part has two functions. First, it involves the reader in the artist's production. Lily's memories (unlike, say, Proust's) are not private but shared in that they activate the reader's memories.

For example, when Lily hears a voice saying "women can't paint, women can't write," we have identified that voice long before Lily dips into her memory far enough to pull out the name Charles Tansley. Such involvement of the reader is a common strategy of Woolf's works on the artist figure. In the last chapter of *A Room of One's Own* we encounter repetitions of events and phrases from the chapters before, and in the last section of *The Waves* we share with Bernard memories of earlier scenes and images. A related experience is our remembering enough of English drama to catch parodies of Elizabethan, Restoration, and Victorian plays in La Trobe's pageant in *Between the Acts*. This reworking of earlier scenes implicates the reader in the narrative process, merging our memories with the artist's.

Second, this losing consciousness of outer things and returning to it suggests that balance between fact and vision that Lily desires. But the language of these boat scenes indicates that what Lily looks at is also narrated, not merely observed. At the end of Section 3, Lily walks across the lawn and looks at the boats going out to sea:

there was one rather apart from the others. The sail was even now being hoisted. She *decided* that there in that very distant and entirely silent little boat Mr. Ramsay was sitting with Cam and James. Now they had got the sail up; now after a little flagging and hesitation the sails filled and, shrouded in profound silence, she watched the boat take its way with deliberation past the other boats out to sea. (*TTL* 241–42; emphasis added)

Lily *selects* one boat and *decides* that this is the Ramsays'. The boat, the whole scene, is "shrouded in profound silence" until someone, here, the artist, gives it shape by giving it some sequence (*now* they had got the sail up; *now* the sails filled). It is as if Lily narrates the boat scene given to us in the next section. Earlier that morning Lily had wondered how to make sense of the chaos of emotions, actions, and voices that filled the house after that ten-year passage of time: "If only she could put them together, she felt, write them out in some sentence, then she would have got at the truth of things" (*TTL* 219). Mr. Ramsay's trip to the lighthouse seems to be that sequence.

Throughout this next section, Section 4, Woolf employs the conditional verb *would be,* at times suggesting the children's thoughts—"He would be impatient in a moment, James thought"—but at others suggesting someone imagining the scene:

Now they would sail on for hours like this, and Mr. Ramsay would ask old Macalister a question—about the great storm last winter probably—and old Macalister would answer it, and they would puff their pipes together, and Macalister would take a tarry rope in his fingers, tying or untying some knot, and the boy would fish, and never say a word to any one. (*TTL* 244)

If we are in the minds of the children in such passages, the verbs would suggest their knowledge of their father's behavior on such boat trips, yet this is supposedly their first trip to the lighthouse. *Would* calls attention to the *telling* of the boat scene; we are not watching *what* happens but *how* what happens could be narrated. Someone is creating all this, while we watch, and that someone seems to be Lily, who stands on shore watching the little boat: "Yes, the breeze was freshening." *Yes* evokes the presence of a perceiver, someone creating and confirming this vision, and links the various sections: "Yes, that is their boat, Lily Briscoe decided." The words *now, would,* and *yes* evoke Lily's function as narrator. The return to Lily on the shore in Section 5 reminds us of the unreality of the life in that boat, shrouded in silence, compared with her actions on shore.

By means of Lily's function as narrator, Woolf stresses the reciprocal relation between life and art. She reveals how the creative process actualizes the daily life. By calling attention to Lily's *stories*—of Mrs. Ramsay, of Paul and Minta, of Mr. Ramsay and the children—Woolf reveals that the nature of the relation between fact and vision, art and life, has changed. We are no longer concerned with *the* connection or *the* correspondence between two realms, but with the connections we posit among a variety of elements selected from a range of possibilities. That is, we are no longer concerned with *formal* relations but with *narrative* relations. Acknowledging this change in relations, we can better explain Lily's remark about the status of her artwork. Asking again the recurring question of this last part ("What does it mean?") Lily thinks of how Mr. Carmichael would presumably have answered: "nothing stays; all changes; but not words, not paint" (*TTL* 267). One can see why this attitude has brought Mr. Carmichael fame as a poet following World War I. This attitude validates the artist's activity in terms of its product, the thing that endures. When Lily thinks of her painting, however, she qualifies this view:

Yet it would be hung in the attics, she thought; it would be rolled up and flung under a sofa; yet even so, even of a picture like that, it was true. One might say, even of this scrawl, not of that actual picture, perhaps, but of what it attempted, that it "remained for ever." (*TTL* 267)[11]

Lily judges her art not in terms of what it produces (order, truth, vision), but in terms of what it attempts; that is, in terms of its commitment to a form of behavior, not its devotion to a type of painting.

Woolf reiterates this point in *A Room of One's Own* when her narrator remarks that "good writers are good human beings" and that their writing is what matters, "and whether it matters for ages or only for hours, nobody can say."[12] Whether or not Lily's painting will be hung in an attic, whether or not women's writings will be canonized, and whether or not La Trobe's play will be remembered matters less, Woolf implies, than the fact that these women artists are creating. Their art is consumable, or disposable, not enduring. Failing to note the change in relations that occurs in these texts, however, most critics accept these remarks at face value.[13] But a particular conception of art is at issue here, not a distinction between two types of art. What makes Woolf's assertions more modest than the wholesale endorsement of any artistic activity by women is a change in motive, from the desire to connect two things and to make a lasting product, to the desire to maintain a multiple perspective and to participate in an ongoing activity. It is not old and new or male and female literature that Woolf distinguishes between, but different motives for writing. Since literature is "attached ever so lightly perhaps, but still attached to life at all four corners" (*ROO* 43), and since life is constantly changing, literature must change continually as well. And since life is an effect of the artistic relations that shape it, new forms of painting (and narrating) can help to bring about new forms of life.

Woolf expresses this relation in the wave-like rhythm of Lily's painting. Lily feels urged forward and held back simultaneously. Her pauses and strokes form one process, so that the moments when the artist is not painting are just as essential as the strokes themselves. In this last section, Woolf explores the oscillating relations between the thing and the process that produces the thing. The aesthetic object consists not just of the marks on a canvas, or the words on a page, but of the pauses or spaces between them, not just of the continuous narrative but of the breaks in the narrative as well. This wavelike movement also characterizes other works on the artist figure: in the pattern of digression and return that structures *A Room of One's Own*, in the oscillation between dark and light in the cab scene of *Orlando*, in the catchwords of *Between the Acts*, "unity" and "dispersal." Even the rhythm of repeated phrases in one novel recurs in the phrases of another: "Which is happiness . . . which pain" in *The Waves* echoes "Which was truth and which was illusion" in *A Room of One's Own*, and the narrator's continual action of "looking out of the window" in *A Room of One's Own* mimics Lily's looking out to sea. The similar patterning implies likeness while the words stress difference. This rhythmic variation implies both continuity and change. It is what keeps our fictions from hardening into some permanent form. Even those moments when all seems to come together into a unified whole, as when Mrs. Ramsay says, "Life stand still here," even those moments disintegrate as we grasp them: the dinner scene breaks up and becomes the past as we look at it, Lily's vision becomes the past as she has it, and La Trobe's audience disperses just as it has converged. Even as Lily, in her intense desire to touch that empty center, cries out, "Mrs. Ramsay, Mrs. Ramsay," for one moment stepping into the "waters of annihilation," even then Lily must return to external things.[14] But we have seen through Lily's dual function as artist and narrator, as the one who observes and the one who organizes those boat scenes, that these external things are not the reality against which the artwork must be measured. The reality is itself a construct, a plurality of stories others have created.

And so the final brush stroke signifies the artist's commitment to a certain behavior, not the answer to a general question, "What does it mean?" The dramatic gesture with which Lily completes her painting recalls the initial brush stroke. Earlier Woolf had stressed the inception of the work, the courage of the artist to commit herself to the project before her. For the first strokes of the artist, like the first words of the novelist, eliminate other possibilities and both inscribe and fill in the space to be enclosed. After that gap of ten years, Lily, early in Part III, stands empty and blank before her canvas:

Where to begin?—that was the question at what point to make the first mark? One line placed on the canvas committed her to innumerable risks, to frequent and irrevocable decisions. . . . Still the risk must be run; the mark made. (*TTL* 235)

Similarly, the last stroke of the painting claims attention:

With a sudden intensity, as if she saw it clear for a second, she drew a line there, in the centre. It was done; it was finished. Yes, she thought, laying down her brush in extreme fatigue, I have had my vision. (*TTL* 310)

Already, with the last stroke of the brush, with the last words of the novel, the vision is past, recedes as the harmony of the dinner scene recedes, as the wave recedes; for the vision must be perpetually re-made, the relations must be forever reestablished. This line is not the integration of two kinds of experience (art and life), but the affirmation of one form of activity. That gesture implies not so much the completion of the act as its exhaustion, the crossing out of the current enterprise and the crossing over to a new one.[15]

*   *   *

The implications of this change in aesthetic motives, from connecting two things to exploring different relations, can best be seen in Woolf's next two, and closely related, works on the artist figure: *Orlando* and *A Room of One's Own*. Both works trace the historical emergence of the woman writer; both present a theory of androgyny; both detail the sexual and textual relations between women; and both convey their arguments in the very rhetoric and structure of the texts themselves.

A Room of One's Own is written in the form of a lecture, or rather, the story of how the lecturer came to the opinion she holds on the topic, women and fiction: "a woman must have money and a room of her own if she is to write fiction; and that, as you will see, leaves the great problem of the true nature of woman and the true nature of fiction unsolved" (*ROO* 4). In this sentence Woolf has already disappointed our expectations, that she will tell us something *about* women and *about* fiction, yet most readers continue to seek out conclusions about the nature of these things. The problem of the "true nature," like the problem of the relation of art to life, remains unsolved because Woolf's essay, as we will see, investigates ever-shifting relations. As in *Orlando,* Woolf makes her method of constructing this story self-conscious. She exaggerates her diction ("On the further bank the willows wept in perpetual lamentation, their hair about their shoulders"); she employs metafictional comments ("As I have said already that it was an October day, I dare not forfeit your respect and imperil the fair name of fiction by changing the season"); and, she tells stories within her stories (the story of Mary Seton's mother; the story of William Shakespeare's sister). However, of most importance for our concerns here is her use of the fluctuating narrative persona and the changing interrogative approaches. For both strategies illuminate her conception of the artist and the artwork and demonstrate the *point* of her essay, which she states in the first paragraph:

—one cannot hope to tell the truth. One can only show how one came to hold whatever opinion one does hold. One can only give one's audience the chance of drawing their own conclusions as they observe the limitations, the prejudices, the idiosyncrasies of the speaker. Fiction here is likely to contain more truth than fact. (*ROO* 4)

The truth to be "found out or made up," as Woolf says, is an *effect* of the narrative strategies. From the beginning, then, Woolf undercuts our expectations for lectures, and literature: that is, that the speaker will tell the truth, will base her argument on facts, will come to some sort of conclusion, will take a firm position and will maintain a stable identity.

Truth through fiction, truth through lies—the avowed intentions of this essay would seem disturbing, and indeed they are for many modernist writers and for many Woolf critics. In "How It Strikes a Contemporary," Woolf says of modernist writers: "They cannot tell stories because they do not believe the stories are true."[16] Fiction lies because it is no longer grounded in a common belief that informed, so they believe, literature of the past. For the moderns, this lack of belief in their stories leads to despair of something lost. For Woolf, and the women writers of *A Room,* this lack of belief leads to affirmation of something gained. Theirs is not the *loss* of a common ground to our stories, but the realization that the common ground is shifting, unstable, slippery. And what contributes to this realization is Woolf's own story of the woman writer in history, a story not known to most modernist male writers. The male modernists respond to the perceived loss of a common ground by turning inward to their own experiences (as Woolf argues in "The Leaning Tower") or by forging a new order, some metaphysical or mythical system that can ground belief. Woolf responds by adopting her aesthetic model, making it more flexible and responsive to change.

As the narrating "I" tries to explain how she came to her conclusion about the money and the room and to discover the conditions "most propitious to the act of creation" (*ROO* 52), she undertakes various approaches: introspection (Chapter 1), theory (Chapter 2), historical reconstruction (Chapter 3), literary history (Chapter 4), and textual analysis (Chapter 5). In each chapter, the narrator draws various contrasts between women and men: men are prosperous and women are poor (Chapter 1); men draw conclusions and women draw pictures (Chapter 2); men desire fame and women desire anonymity (Chapter 3); the values of women are not the values of men (Chapter 4); a woman's sentence is not a man's (Chapter 5). After so many such contrasts, the "I" writes in Chapter 6 what will be the opening sentence of her lecture: "it is fatal for anyone who writes to think of their sex" (*ROO* 108). Yet it seems as if the narrator has thought of little else! We come to an apparent contradiction. Accepting this assertion at face value, Elaine Showalter concludes, quoting from Woolf's review of American fiction, that for Woolf, "consciousness of self, of race, of sex, of civilization . . . [has] nothing to do with art."[17] But surely Woolf was conscious of her sex when she wrote *Orlando* and *A Room of One's Own.* Surely she was conscious of British civilization when she wrote *Between the Acts.* Sex matters to Woolf, history matters, facts matter—the problem is our tendency to see these things in terms of stable oppositions (male/female, past/present, fact/fiction) and to fix labels on things. When the narrator considers the "comparative values" of women and men, charwoman and barrister, she cannot draw a conclusion because the measuring rods, as she calls them, change, just as they change in this essay. As the "I" remarks, "it is notoriously difficult to fix labels of merit in such a way that they do not come off" (*ROO* 110). Sexual differences have everything to do with art; it is just that sexual differences in writing are provisional, variable, and contingent. What Woolf opposes is not gender distinctions but a certain way of thinking about gender distinctions: "this pitting of sex against sex, of quality against quality" (*ROO* 110), this thinking in terms of "two parties" and "opposing faction[s]" (*ROO* 62). The way out of these oppositions has been demonstrated in Woolf's essay: to consider the text in terms of the task it undertakes as well as the truth it reveals; to adopt various methods, not to codify the right one; and, to see the artist as a composite figure, not an empirical being or self-sufficient individual.

For this reason, Woolf begins the essay by insisting that the "I" who narrates this work "is only a convenient term for somebody who has no real being" (*ROO* 4). As the "I" tells us this story, it fluctuates; in an aside, the narrator says, "call me Mary Beton, Mary Seton, Mary Carmichael or by any name you please—it is not a matter of any importance" (*ROO* 5).[18] It is not the individual writer that matters, but the *female storyteller* in general, one who must be "found out or made up." In this text, the female narrator is an *effect* of her narration. Like Lily, the "I" is both narrator and character in this text. "I" is as much a fiction as is its text; for it is constructed in relation to its own stories.[19] If "I" were an empirical being with a name, then contradictions would be legion in this work. Since the "I" changes, however, and since there is no common ground to these stories (on the contrary, "truth is only to be had by laying together many varieties of error"), what appear to be contradictions may well indicate a change in mind, or at least, in method. Thus, the argument is an effect of its discourse, not a "nugget of pure truth [wrapped] up between the pages" (*ROO* 3). Just as Mr. A's argument for the self-sufficient individual is an effect of his barlike narrative "I" that casts its shadow over all he writes (*ROO* 103), just as Professor Von X's conclusion about the inferiority of women is achieved by isolating certain pieces of information about women from their historical and social contexts (*ROO* 31–32), so the narrator of *A Room* makes her argument against categorical distinctions by means of her fluctuating "I" and her changing method that keep our distinctions context-bound and task-specific. The composite "I" undercuts the sanctity, the authority and the self-identity of the one who speaks.[20]

Thus, what Showalter, Patricia Meyer Spacks, Diane Filby Gillespie, and other critics see as *interfering* with Woolf's argument actually *makes* it. Woolf's continually experimenting form that Gillespie regrets, her evasiveness that Spacks laments, and her "elusive" strategies, which deny "any earnest or subversive intention," that Showalter dismisses must be seen in relation to the point of the essay and the consequence of the aesthetics Woolf is demonstrating.[21] If truth lay outside of or existed prior to the story, then the method would indeed be distracting. If the world and the writer were stable and self-contained, then such a playful and elusive argument would be suspect. Yet paying attention to her narrative, not reading through it as Showalter suggests, we soon see that Woolf's argument is not, as these critics would have it, for distinguishing between male and female writing, for establishing a countertradition in literature, or for determining the right relation between women's writing and man's world. The changeable "I" and flexible approach suggest that the truth we seek is not single but multiple, not subjective but intersubjective. What is "honest" about Woolf's method is its very self-consciousness; what is "feminist" is its very flexibility. What the woman artist needs is not just freedom from a male tradition, but the freedom to change our very concept of tradition, whether matriarchal or patriarchal.

Of course, Woolf's emphasis on the writer as a component of tradition ("the experience of the mass is behind the single voice") recalls Eliot's "Tradition and the Individual Talent." Woolf and Eliot agree that "books are the outcome of many years of thinking in common" (*ROO* 68). However, a metaphorical contrast can help us to see the difference. Where Eliot's tradition is a restricted club, to which new members are admitted by meeting certain criteria and thereby affirming the club's values and assuring its integrity, Woolf's tradition is a cab, a public conveyance that can transport all kinds of occupants and follow all kinds of routes.[22] But more important, that cab, that tradition, is a *fiction* created by Woolf in the course of this very essay. That is, Eliot's tradition can be traced, Woolf's must be *constructed;* and in that fact, in its very *fictitiousness,* lies its power. Put another way, the telling difference between Eliot's and Woolf's traditions is simply this: Woolf tells a different story of tradition by rewriting our familiar history. For if Woolf believes in the necessity of fictions, those sustaining illusions of our lives, if she recognizes that fiction works in and out of our daily lives (*ROO* 4), if she sees that how we write is tied up with how we live (*ROO* 48) and how we live with what we read (*ROO* 80), then whose stories get told makes all the difference.[23] For this reason, we must recover women's stories of the past, but whether these are "found out or made up" (*ROO* 64), whether they are based in fact or in fiction, is not a matter of any importance. What matters is the *effect* of the stories we tell. And to paraphrase Woolf's comment on the Manx cat, which lacks a tail, it's amazing what a difference a tale can make (*ROO* 13).

We have trouble reaching a conclusion about this essay, then, if we see Woolf's goal either as creating a countertradition of female works or as adding women's works to the established tradition. Woolf is doing neither. Rather, the point of the essay is to introduce into the concept of tradition the concept of change. It is thinking of the literary tradition as homogeneous and authoritarian that leads the modernist writers discussed in "How It Strikes a Contemporary" and some women writers discussed in *A Room* to assert their *difference* from the past and to adopt the language of liberation, transcendence, and novelty. If modernist or women writers break out of traditional forms, what matters, Woolf's narrator says, is the point and the situation of such change:

> Mary [Carmichael] is tampering with the expected sequence. First she broke the sentence; now she has broken the sequence. Very well, she has every right to do both these things if she does them not for the sake of breaking, but for the sake of creating. Which of the two it is I cannot be sure until she has faced herself with a situation. (*ROO* 85)

As the narrator has done, and as La Trobe will do, the woman writer must break the sequence as a way of effecting change; however, she must also expose the sequence as a way of measuring and evaluating change. Too much emphasis on difference fosters the illusion that the artist is transcending obstacles and achieving freedom. Too much emphasis on sameness neglects the multiplicity and instability of any age, or either sex, and fosters the acceptance of the prevailing opinion, or a common belief.

In arguing for continuity in women's literature without specifying a common core of shared features or beliefs, Woolf enacts various theories of women's writing rather than defining the relation between their writing and their lives. In doing so, Woolf calls into question two common beliefs. The first is a mimetic theory of representation. By means of her wordplay and role-playing and her changing investigative methods, Woolf reinforces Bernard's comment in *The Waves:* "Life is not susceptible perhaps to the treatment we give it when we try to tell it."[24] Life is not *like* the stories we tell. There is always something left out of our arbitrary designs, as Bernard says. To compare lives with stories, as Woolf does in this work and in *Orlando,* and yet to constantly remind us that life is not a fiction, is not to say there is something beyond our fictions that cannot be captured in words. Rather, it is to call into question the correspondence of art to life, and a correspondence theory of truth.[25]

The second belief Woolf undercuts is the belief in empirical stability. Woolf demonstrates this lack of empirical stability, which prevents us from drawing definitive distinctions between two things, through her narrator and her double perspective, which recalls Lily's: one needs "to think poetically and prosaically at one and the same moment, thus keeping in touch with fact . . . but not losing sight of fiction either" (*ROO* 46). The one is no more true than the other, and in this text at least, there is no point to distinguishing finally between them. It is the way of relating things that matters, and the writer's function is to differentiate the undifferentiated mass of common life by making some sequence, telling some story. Looking out the window, the "I" creates another scene:

> At this moment, as so often happens in London, there was a complete lull and suspension of traffic. Nothing came down the street; nobody passed. A single leaf detached itself from the plane tree at the end of the street, and in that pause and suspension fell. Somehow it was like a signal falling, a signal pointing to a force in things which one had overlooked. It seemed to point to a river, which flowed past, invisibly, round the corner, down the street, and took people and eddied them along, as the stream at Oxbridge had taken the undergraduate in his boat and the dead leaves. Now it was bringing from one side of the street to the other diagonally a girl in patent leather boots, and then a young man in a maroon overcoat; it was also bringing a taxi-cab; and it brought all three together at a point directly beneath my window; where the taxi stopped; and the girl and the young man stopped; and they got into the taxi; and then the cab glided off as if it were swept on by the current elsewhere.
>
> The sight was ordinary enough; what was strange was the rhythmical order with which my imagination had invested it. (*ROO* 100)

This is not the mind of the individual artist, as the nonempirical "I" makes clear. Nor is it the mind of Eliot's tradition, as the three Marys make clear. Rather, this is the cohesive principle in literature; it is the creation of a writer who thinks back through her ancestors, mothers as well as fathers (*ROO* 107). It is not the personal or the impersonal element but the interpersonal relation, a relation brought out in Woolf's related work on the artist figure. Both continuity and change in literature are figured in the poet Orlando.

*   *   *

Orlando is a biographical novel about a poet who lives and loves for over three centuries (and who is likely to live and love three more), changing from a man to a woman halfway through the work. The androgynous Orlando is often seen to be the quintessential artist, just as *Orlando,* written by a feminist for a bisexual (Vita Sackville-West) about a transsexual, would seem to be the quintessential woman's text. Yet it is such conclusions that the method of *Orlando* resists. The appropriate identity and writing is not androgynous; rather, androgyny defies an appropriate identity and writing. In Carolyn Heilbrun's words, androgyny frees the writer "from the confines of the appropriate."[26] Androgyny in *Orlando,* like equivocation in *A Room of One's Own,* is for Woolf a stance against "the desire to prevail."[27]

With its eponymous protagonist who changes from a man to a woman halfway through the novel, with its capricious narrator who at times speaks in the character of Orlando's male biographer and at others sounds suspiciously like *Orlando's* female author, this novel reveals the difficulty of making clear-cut distinctions about sexual identity in writing. Woolf brings out the arbitrariness of sexual identity, and the arbitrariness of literary language, through Orlando's switching from one sex to the other, one century to another, and one poetic language to another, as well as through the shifting of her own rhetoric and metaphors in this novel.[28] *Orlando,* then, is a novel about writing, about constructing lives, identities, fictions. As such, it shows us the positive consequences of accepting these things as variable constructions, not as stable forms. What *Orlando* shows us is that the distinction between two things—between the traditional and the innovative, the conventional and the authentic, the normative and the deviant—changes, like Orlando's sex, with time and circumstance.[29]

Sexual identity and literary language are closely related in this novel. In fact, the text of *Orlando* is as unstable as the sex of Orlando. Just as the androgynous Orlando brings the question of sexual identity to the fore, the obtrusive narrator brings the textual language to the fore by intruding to discuss his own art (*O* 65), to mock his own method (*O* 266), and to characterize his own readers (*O* 73). Just as Orlando's identity swings from the extreme of conventionality (Orlando as a boy slicing at the swinging Moor's head) to the extreme of eccentricity (Orlando as a woman discovering that she has three sons by another woman), so the language shifts from the transparent conventionality of clichés (to put it in a nutshell, by the skin of his teeth) to the opaque originality of Orlando and Shel's cypher language (Rattigan Glumphoboo). Just as the bombastic masque of the three Sisters hyperbolizes Orlando's sex change, so the exaggerated lyricisms, the hackneyed expressions, the strings of metaphors and the self-conscious diction exaggerate the language of this text. And just as sexual differences are put into confusion ("You're a woman, Shel!" she cried. "You're a man, Orlando!" he cried), so are the extremes of rhetoric. For as Woolf reveals in her mocking reference to her own "Time Passes" section of *To the Lighthouse,* what is highly original in one context can, in another, be a tedious, grandiloquent way of saying simply "time passed" (*O* 97–98).

In this way, Woolf shows us that sexual identity is as flexible as literary language, literary language as fluctuant as sexual identity. This novel expresses the difficulty of reaching conclusions about what sexual identity is or what literary language should be. For both are based on making distinctions which cannot be fixed by reference to something stable beyond. Thus, to speak directly and with certainty on any matter is beyond the novelist Woolf as it is the poet Orlando.

So then he tried saying the grass is green and the sky is blue and so to propitiate the austere spirit of poetry. . . . "The sky is blue," he said, "the grass is green." Looking up, he saw that, on the contrary, the sky is like the veils which a thousand Madonnas have let fall from their hair; and the grass fleets and darkens like a flight of girls fleeing the embraces of hairy satyrs from enchanted woods. "Upon my word," he said, . . . "I don't see that one's more true than another. Both are utterly false." (*O* 101–2)

As Orlando discovers, poetry and nature, language and identity, must be learned together.[30] Thus, the traits of a female aesthetics must not be sought in the intrinsic features of women's lives but in the changing relations between lives and literature. A female aesthetics is determined as much by our assumptions about art—the questions we ask of it, the uses we make of it—as by our assumptions and knowledge about women.[31]

What we need in order to read *Orlando,* then, is a model for literary discourse that enables us to conceive art not in terms of its relation to something beyond (for example, life itself), but in terms of its various purposes and effects. Such a conceptual change encourages us to look at the multiple relations among various signifying systems, such as language, fashion, gender, and genre.[32] This is the point of the vacillating rhetoric and the epicene protagonist of Woolf's novel. Orlando's identity, like her poem, is "compounded of many humours," composed of "odds and ends," a "meeting-place of dissemblables" (*O* 73, 176). Orlando continually wavers between beliefs, changes or disguises her sex, moves in harmony with and at odds with the times. So too Woolf's novel offers support for differing positions without arguing for any one.[33] It is in the midst of all these contrarieties, in the midst of such violent shifts in viewpoint, that Woolf offers her famous statement of androgyny, not as a metaphysical or feminist theory, not as a resolution to or synthesis of contrarieties, but as a way to remain suspended between opposed beliefs:

For here again, we come to a dilemma. Different though the sexes are, they intermix. In every human being a vacillation from one sex to the other takes place, and often it is only the clothes that keep the male or female likeness, while underneath the sex is the very opposite of what it is above. (*O* 189)

Androgyny embodies this oscillation between positions. It figures a basic ambiguity, not only a sexual ambiguity but a textual one as well. Androgyny is a refusal to choose, or to even accept the terms of such a choice. The shifting and blurring of sexual identities, like the shifting and blurring of literary genres, periods, and styles, undermines any two-termed choice, and disrupts meaning brought about by fixed polarities, by defined standards, by rigid categories.

Thus, Woolf does not define the appropriate identity or writing in this novel, for any identity assumed finally, definitively, essentially will be constraining, and any writing deemed authentic, appropriate, or natural will be illusory. Neither Woolf nor Orlando rejects past aesthetic conventions or prescribes new more suitable ones. Instead, they both take from the past what is useful to them, use up conventions, dispose of them, and thus expose them as provisional and changeable, disclose their dependence on certain contexts. *Enacting* a type of discourse rather than codifying one, as Woolf does in this novel as well as in *A Room*, exposes the supposed universality of aesthetic standards of value without offering a new totalizing aesthetics. In fact, Woolf's novel challenges the very assumptions about self and art on which the concept of an appropriate aesthetics rests. Thus, *Orlando* must be accounted for in terms of a different conception of self and art: in terms of a dramatic self not an authentic one, in terms of a disposable art not an appropriate one. Orlando's androgyny and diuturnity are not a testament to some essential and enduring creative imagination, but an affirmation of adaptation and change, and of the life-sustaining impulse to create fictions.

If art fails, then, it cannot be because it is inadequate to its essential task of representing the true self or the real world. If it fails, it can only be because, as Woolf implies here, no one responds to it. No sooner has Orlando finished her poem than it clamors to be read. For what is the text, "the thing itself" as Orlando calls it, but "a voice answering a voice" (*O* 325)? The private art of Lily or the young Orlando soon palls; we need the dramatic voice of a Bernard or La Trobe. Increasingly in Woolf's later works on the artist we see an emphasis on the public and interpersonal status of the artwork. It is in the use of art by its audience, Woolf implies, that we must locate its significance and value. Yet the critical preoccupation with the relation between art and life neglects this relation between art and its users. In her final novel on the artist figure, the posthumous *Between the Acts*, the fictional audience as well as the reading audience plays an active role in the artist's production.

*   *   *

Woolf's last novel, not surprisingly, is often read as the "final stage" in her "eternal quest" for that right relation between opposed things (Guiguet 323), and often as her despair of ever finding that relation. Although Lily doubts her painting and Bernard doubts his stories, here the artist's doubt seems to pervade the very texture of Woolf's novel. As Naremore writes, in defending the novel against charges of formlessness:

In other words, what Leavis and Friedman have taken to be the absence of structure is in fact a conscious faulting of structure, a questioning of the power of 'significant form' that runs far deeper than Lily Briscoe's feeling that her vision is past or Bernard's criticism of words and compacted shapes—deeper because the criticism is embodied in the very form of the work, as in no other novel by Virginia Woolf. (*The World Without a Self* 236)

How we read this structure depends, of course, on what we compare it to and on what we see as Woolf's point in the novel. What others see as a despair of art and a faulting of structure, I see as a testing out of the aesthetic assumptions we have been tracing in her works on the artist figure. Looked at from the perspective of the *function* of art, this structure suggests not the failure of art, but a means of assuring its survival.[34]

La Trobe's play, a review of English literary history, cannot be evaluated apart from both the texts and contexts it evokes and recon-structs. Those contexts are not always delimitable, though. In one scene, for example, we watch a play within La Trobe's play as the actors represent the audience of the Globe Theatre and watch the parody of an Elizabethan play. As we read, we are reminded of our situation in relation to this novel: Virginia Woolf creates characters who play char-acters created by La Trobe, who is recreating characters from earlier dramas (Congreve's, for instance) who are themselves parodies of his-torical figures, and these figures are characters in another text, the text of English history. There seems to be no end to this chain of creations, unless it is in the prehistoric mud that covered England before human life appeared, the fertile mud from which La Trobe creates anew at the end.[35] While the fragmented conversations, the interrupted scenes, and the abrupt endings of both the play and the novel suggest an uneasiness about the future and the efficacy of literature, the con-tinuity provided by the chorus and the music, by the familiar scenes and sayings, by the landscape of Pointz Hall, and by the annual occur-rence of this pageant assure us that this creative process has been functioning for a long long time, and will continue to function into the postwar era.

Here, on the brink of war, the consequences of Woolf's concern with making art responsive to change and with seeing it in relation to others are tested out in La Trobe's collaborative and heteronomous production. In no other work of Woolf's artists does the audience play such an important part. Its members provide the stage, the props, and the money. They provide the stimulus and the occasion. And they provide the final scene of the play as they are caught in the mirrors of the actors. Of course, this relation between the artist and the audience is far from serene. The audience is caught by the artist's noose (*BA* 122, 180). And the artist must give way to the demands of her audience:

Writing this skimble-skamble stuff in her cottage, she had agreed to cut the play here; a slave to her audience—to Mrs. Sands' grumble—about tea; about dinner—she had gashed the scene here. (BA 94)

More than any other artwork we have considered, La Trobe's play reveals the extent to which art depends on its audience as well as on various contingencies, such as bad weather, teatime, limited budgets, and world war.

Between the Acts, even in its title, does not just account for such contingencies and interruptions, which so enrage La Trobe, it gives them preference. Those numerous breaks that many critics see as a sign of discontinuity and a faulting of structure actually enable the acts to be continually renewed. If the purpose of the artwork were to produce harmony and unity among its elements and its audience, then certainly such breaks would be disturbing. But Woolf's humor and exaggeration in presenting such an attitude in this work undermine such readings. For example, in response to the interruption for tea cited above, La Trobe behaves rather extremely: "Curse! Blast! Damn 'em! Miss La Trobe in her rage stubbed her toe against a root" (BA 94). Even in her writing itself, Woolf calls into question such harmony by calling attention to her transitions:

Then suddenly, as the illusion petered out, the cows took up the burden. . . . The cows annihilated the gap; bridged the distance; filled the emptiness and continued the emotion. (BA 140–41)

If Woolf took her text quite seriously, we would read such intrusions of nature as evidence of the pattern behind "the cotton-wool of daily life."[36] Such transitions, however, are not only contrived, they are contrived to look contrived.

The problem of interpretation, then, does not lie in the discontinuity or the exaggeration of the text, but in the responses of its readers. What frustrates the audience of La Trobe's play is not the interruptions (for those are there in response to the audience's demands for some intermissions) or the exaggerations (for the audience is willing to observe the conventions and to consider the artist's means). What frustrates them is their desire "to leave a theatre knowing exactly what was meant" (BA 164) in a play where nothing is concluded and no one takes responsibility. The futility of such a response is brought out in Mr. Streatfield's hesitant and trite exegesis (BA 191–92). The only definite conclusion he can reach is the amount the pageant has grossed. If we try to summarize what Woolf's novel is about, we are likely to be about as articulate and illuminating as he is. For the point of the novel is not to make some statement about the present condition of art or its future fate. To see this June day in 1939, poised on the brink of war, as offering impoverished material to the artist is to give preference to certain kinds of material and certain kinds of criteria. But if we can't predict the future, it might be best not to limit the artist's means. The significance of both La Trobe's play and Woolf's novel is to be found in their *effects* on their audiences. The point of each production is to change our responses to art. Their art does not tell us what the world is or should be like; it changes our behavior in the world by changing our relations to the various discourses that construct it. These texts make us self-conscious of the different ways we use literature, whether for the sake of profits, for the sake of pleasure, or for the sake of tradition. Their art, like La Trobe's final scene, brings us back to ourselves.

In the last scene, the audience must confront themselves not only in the mirrors held up to them by the actors, but in La Trobe's "ten mins. of present time" as well. This is an uncomfortable moment for the audience, for the empty stage makes us painfully aware of our own reactions. And by their very absence, the conventions we rely on in these productions are brought to the fore. At this point, a voice from the bushes, "a megaphonic, anonymous, loud-speaking affirmation," enjoins the audience to *"break the rhythm and forget the rhyme. And calmly consider ourselves. Ourselves"* (BA 187). This voice, like the play itself, is the great leveler, linking universal events (a pilot dropping a bomb) with the local (a new bungalow spoiling a view) and implicating us all in the perpetuation of literature and culture. At the end, the artist refuses to come out of the bushes, leaving the audience unsure of whom to thank and whom to make responsible, but also leaving them with a sense of the commonality of the artist and the complicity of the audience.

If we see women's art in particular as disposable or provisional, as many feminists want to do, we run the risk of concluding that, in *Between the Acts,* it is the woman artist (or the lesbian or the foreigner, since La Trobe is all three) who is unable to unify this society on the brink of destruction, or that it is the woman artist who has the responsibility of saving us (as Woolf's male interlocutor in *Three Guineas* suggests that women like Woolf are responsible for maintaining peace). But while it is significant that La Trobe is a woman, a foreigner, and a lesbian, the very structure of her play, and of Woolf's novel, conveys a different point: that recognizing such differences requires a new way of conceiving social, aesthetic, and personal relations. If, however, we accept *all* art forms as arbitrary, disposable and contingent, then the mood of Woolf's last novel is not one of despair, but one of affirmation. What many critics interpret as doubt and disillusionment is merely the text's refusal to be lured by its own voice, to harden into "significant form," or to take itself too seriously. A refusal to take oneself too seriously may be a kind of defense when facing the threat of an ending or of an impending war, but it can also be a way to avoid setting up oneself or one's art as an authority or model. The intervals between the acts of La Trobe's play—like the numerous breaks in Woolf's novel, the "Time Passes" section of *To the Lighthouse* and the interchapters of *The Waves*—may disrupt the narrative, but such interruptions also ensure its continual renewal, its beginning again and its beginning anew. This process is most clearly evident in La Trobe's art: she cuts and rearranges her script to suit the desires and the needs of an audience both familiar and new, *familiar* in that they gather for this pageant every year, *new* in that "they" are never the same.

*   *   *

To answer my opening questions, then, I would argue that Woolf creates no ultimate portrait of the woman artist because no one portrait will suffice. She creates no successful woman artist because the standards for success change. As she writes in her review of Brimley Johnson's *The Women Novelists,* from which my headnote is taken: "He shows his wisdom not only by advancing a great many suggestions [about what women's writing is], but also by accepting the fact, upsetting though it is, that women are apt to differ" (*WW* 70). In her writings on the artist figure, Woolf is clearly concerned with how to write as a woman, yet for her, this concern meant not prescribing an aesthetics for women artists, but learning how to adapt and survive as a woman writer.

Notes

This essay is adapted from chapters 1 and 2 of my book, *Virginia Woolf and Postmodernism: Literature in Quest and Question of Itself* (Urbana: University of Illinois Press, 1991).

1. Virginia Woolf, "Women Novelists," in *Virginia Woolf: Women and Writing,* ed. Michèle Barrett (New York and London: Harcourt Brace Jovanovich, 1979), p. 70; hereafter cited as *WW.* My title quotation is taken from Woolf's diary for March 1932. See *The Diary of Virginia Woolf,* vol. 4, ed. Anne Olivier Bell (New York and London: Harcourt Brace Jovanovich, 1982), p. 85.

2. This question is similar to the one Alison Booth imagines Woolf asking of Eliot's oeuvre in this volume. While Booth, drawing on Carolyn Heilbrun, offers one explanation in terms of the *obstacles* to women's writing, I offer another in terms of Woolf's investigation of the *possibilities* of women's writing. In contrast to Booth, I look not at the link between Woolf's art and her life, but at the ways in which her experiments with writing changed her concept of the relation between art and life.

3. These assumptions inform much of Woolf criticism. For instance, Jane Marcus, in her introduction to *New Feminist Essays on Virginia Woolf* (Lincoln: University of Nebraska Press, 1981), claims Woolf gave other women writers "the feminine sentence" and "the appropriate female form" (xiv). And many readers of Woolf's last novel, *Between the Acts,* interpret La Trobe's inconclusive production as a failed attempt to communicate with her audience and attribute this failure to Woolf's despair of art in the face of World War II. See, for example, Alex Zwerdling's *Virginia Woolf and the Real World* (Berkeley: University of California Press, 1986) and Maria DiBattista's *Virginia Woolf's Major Novels: The Fables of Anon* (New Haven, Conn.: Yale University Press, 1980).

4. It is my focus on self-conscious art that leads me to single out these particular artist figures in Woolf's canon. For a different discussion of women and art in Woolf's writings, see Barbara Hill Rigney's essay on Clarissa Dalloway, Mrs. Ramsay, and Jinny (*The Waves*) in "Objects of Vision: Women as Art in the Novels of Virginia Woolf," in *Critical Essays on Virginia Woolf,* ed. Morris Beja (Boston: G. K. Hall, 1985), pp. 239–248; Elizabeth Abel's " 'Cam the Wicked': Woolf's Portrait of the Artist as her Father's Daughter," *Virginia Woolf and Bloomsbury: A Centenary Celebration,* ed. Jane Marcus (Bloomington: Indiana University Press, 1987) pp. 170–194; Marianne Hirsch, *The Mother/Daughter Plot: Narrative, Psychoanalysis, Feminism* (Bloomington: Indiana University Press, 1989), chapter 3; and Sandra Gilbert and Susan Gubar's *No Man's Land: The Place of the Woman Writer in the Twentieth Century* (New Haven, Conn.: Yale University Press, 1988), chapter 4.

5. Maria DiBattista, *Virginia Woolf's Major Novels: The Fables of Anon* (New Haven, Conn.: Yale University Press, 1980); Norman Friedman, "The Waters of Annihilation: Double Vision in *To the Lighthouse,*" *ELH* 22 (1955), 61–79; B. H. Fussell, "Woolf's Peculiar Comic World: *Between the Acts,*" in *Virginia Woolf: Revaluation and Continuity* ed. Ralph Freedman (Berkeley: University of California Press, 1980); Jean Guiguet, *Virginia Woolf and Her Works,* trans. Jean Stewart (New York: Harcourt, Brace and World, 1966); James Hafley, *The Glass Roof: Virginia Woolf as Novelist* (Berkeley: University of California Press, 1954); Mitchell Leaska, *Virginia Woolf's Lighthouse: A Study in Critical Method* (New York: Columbia University Press, 1970); James Naremore, *The World Without a Self: Virginia Woolf and the Novel* (New Haven, Conn.: Yale University Press, 1973); Harvena Richter, *Virginia Woolf: The Inward Voyage* (Princeton, N.J.: Princeton University Press, 1970); and Pamela Transue, *Virginia Woolf and the Politics of Style* (New York: State University of New York Press, 1986).

6. What Barbara Herrnstein Smith refers to as "surfacing from the deep" in the last chapter of *On the Margins of Discourse*—that is, a conceptual model for narrative discourse that recognizes dynamic and multiple relations rather than relying on some correspondence between surface and depth—is similar to the distinction I'm making here. Smith conceives literature not in terms of categorical distinctions but in terms of the multiple and shifting relations among a variety of engendering motives and conditions. *On the Margins of Discourse: The Relation of Literature to Language* (Chicago: University of Chicago Press, 1978).

7. In "Unmaking and Making in *To the Lighthouse,*" Gayatri Spivack notes Lily's narrative function as the time-keeper of the novel (*Woman and Language in Literature and Society,* ed. Sally McConnell-Ginet, Ruth Borker and Nelly Furman [New York: Praeger, 1980], p. 315).

8. Patricia Waugh, *Metafiction: The Theory and Practice of Self-Conscious Fiction* (New York: Methuen, 1984), p. 6

9. Virginia Woolf, *To the Lighthouse* (New York and London: Harcourt Brace and World, 1927; rpt. 1955), p. 81. Additional references are cited parenthetically as *TTL* with page numbers.

10. James Naremore, *The World Without a Self: Virginia Woolf and the Novel*, (New Haven, Conn.: Yale University Press, 1973), p. 242.

11. Patricia Waugh draws the same contrast between Mr. Carmichael's modernist conception of art and Lily's more provisional conception in *Feminine Fictions: Revisiting the Postmodern* (London: Routledge and Kegan Paul, 1989), p. 99.

12. Virginia Woolf, *A Room of One's Own* (New York and London: Harcourt Brace and World, 1929; rpt. 1957), p. 110. Additional references are cited parenthetically as *ROO* with page numbers.

13. For instance, Josephine Donovan, in her essay in this collection, implies that *women's* art is rooted in the everyday world and valued as consumable not as a commodity to be exchanged. Jane Marcus, in *Virginia Woolf and the Languages of Patriarchy* (Bloomington: Indiana University Press, 1987), says that opposed to male discourse, *women's* writing is unbounded, fluid, non-authoritative, an aesthetics of process not finished products. And Lawrence Lipking, in "Aristotle's Sister," *Critical Inquiry* 10 (September 1983), 61–81 suggests that *women's* art in particular is disposable in that it has no name, no authority, no effect on the real world. That is, many critics acccept as the *properties* of women's art what are actually the *effects* of a different way of conceiving art in general. For a more detailed critique of Lipking's essay, see Holly Laird's contribution to this collection.

14. Virginia Woolf dramatizes such disruption in section 6. At the moment of greatest intensity, when Lily steps into the waters of annihilation in her frantic desire to bring back the dead Mrs. Ramsay, at that moment Woolf breaks the spell with this scene: "[Macalister's boy took one of the fish and cut a square out of its side to bait his hook with. The mutilated body (it was alive still) was thrown back into the sea.]" (*TTL* 268). This is life, "startling, unexpected, sunknown." The brackets, conventionally used to indicate an interruption, remind us of the reports of external events placed in brackets in "Time Passes" and presage the scenes where nature intrudes in the play of *Between the Acts*. Who tells us this scene? The very ambiguity of the perceiver and reporter of this scene, the startling break from Lily's consciousness, and the indifferent cruelty of the action make us feel the shock of life intruding on our illusion. This section does not just function thematically but structurally. It keeps us from wading into the waters of annihilation by manifesting the structure of the text and by checking the consoling power of art. It reminds us that there *is* something beyond the text, but that something cannot be assimilated until it is made part of a sequence. In the placement of this section, Woolf makes us conscious of the process she has been investigating through Lily's painting, the moving back and forth from outer world to inner and of the virtual boundary between the two. See also Marianne Hirsch's discussion of this scene in terms of the reader's response in *The Mother/Daughter Plot* (115).

15. One might compare my reading of *To the Lighthouse* with Marianne Hirsch's in *The Mother/Daughter Plot*. Hirsch argues, as I do, that "Lily's solution to what art should be and her completion of the painting" depend on her rejection of the aesthetic criteria of harmony, balance, order, and permanence (112–13). Thus, the end of the novel does not resolve the tensions between two forces, says Hirsch, but maintains them, and Lily's line can be said to connect

the masses on the right and left of her canvas as well as to acknowledge their disconnection (114). Yet where Hirsch, like Rachel Blau DuPlessis in *Writing Beyond the Ending: Narrative Strategies of Twentieth-Century Women Writers* (Bloomington: Indiana University Press, 1985), discusses such writing by women in terms of the "aesthetic of 'both/and'" (115), I argue for a pragmatic reading based on multiple and changing relations, not *two* relations. See also Christine Froula's explanation of Woolf's continual experimentation and Lily's disposable art in "Rewriting Genesis: Gender and Culture in Twentieth-Century Texts," *Tulsa Studies in Women's Literature* 7.2 (fall 1988), 216.

16. Virginia Woolf, "How It Strikes a Contemporary," in *The Common Reader* (New York and London: Harcourt Brace and World, 1925; rpt. 1953), 244.

17. Elaine Showalter, *A Literature of Their Own* (Princeton, N.J.: Princeton University Press, 1977), p. 289.

18. For an informed discussion of Woolf's use of the three Marys as well as her subversive strategies in this essay, see Jane Marcus's "Sapphistry: Narration as Lesbian Seduction in *A Room of One's Own*," in her *Virginia Woolf and the Languages of Patriarchy*, pp. 163–87.

19. As Peggy Kamuf puts it, the author occupies "only a relative position in a discursive or textual network," not the primary or central one. See "Penelope at Work: Interruptions in *A Room of One's Own*," *Novel* 16 (fall 1982), 12.

20. I mean "authority" here both in the sense of a consistent and conclusive position supported by factual evidence, and in the sense of an individual who is appealed to as one who knows, more than others, what she's talking about. Barbara Johnson, in an essay on Zora Neale Hurston, argues that the concept of an authentic voice or discourse must be redefined as the ability to "articulate the incompatible forces" which divide the self, not as the integration of two roles. "The sign of an authentic voice," Johnson writes, "is thus not self-identity but self-difference" (*A World of Difference* [Baltimore: Johns Hopkins University Press, 1987], p. 164). Again, I refer my readers to Peggy Kamuf's excellent essay on *A Room of One's Own*, "Penelope at Work." Kamuf reads this essay as "turning away from the historical preoccupation with the subject, closing the book on the 'I'" (11).

21. Diane Filby Gillespie, "Political Aesthetics: Virginia Woolf and Dorothy Richardson," in Marcus's *Virginia Woolf: A Feminist Slant* (Lincoln: University of Nebraska Press, 1983), pp. 132–151; Patricia Meyer Spacks, *The Female Imagination* (New York: Knopf, 1975), p. 14; Showalter, *A Literature of Their Own*, p. 283.

22. Compare Terry Eagleton's similar metaphor for Eliot's tradition in *Literary Theory: An Introduction* (Minneapolis: University of Minnesota Press, 1983), 39.

23. Jane Tompkins, in her introduction to *Reader-Response Criticism: From Formalism to Post-Structuralism* (Baltimore: Johns Hopkins University Press, 1980) writes: "When discourse is responsible for reality and not merely a reflection of it, then whose discourse prevails makes all the difference" (xxv). In her essay, "Reading Ourselves: Toward a Feminist Theory of Reading," Patrocinio Schweickart makes an observation similar to Woolf's point in *A Room*: "For feminists, the question of *how* we read is inextricably linked with the question of *what* we read" (*Gender and Reading: Essays on Readers, Texts, and Contexts*, ed. Elizabeth Flynn and Patrocinio Schweickart [Baltimore: Johns Hopkins University Press, 1986], p. 40).

24. Virginia Woolf, *"Jacob's Room" and "The Waves": The Complete Novels* (New York: Harcourt Brace and World, 1923, 1931; rpt. 1959), p. 362.

25. On the correspondence theory of truth, see, for example, Barbara Herrnstein Smith's works cited in this essay.

26. Carolyn Heilbrun, *Toward A Recognition of Androgyny* (New York: Knopf, 1973), p. x.

27. Virginia Woolf, *Orlando* (New York and London: Harcourt Brace Jovanovich, 1928, rpt. 1956), p. 149. Additional references are cited parenthetically as *O* with page numbers. My discussion of *Orlando* is drawn from an earlier essay entitled "Virginia Woolf's Double Discourse," in Marleen Barr and Richard Feldstein, eds., *Discontented Discourses: Feminism/Textual Intervention/Psychoanalysis* (Urbana: University of Illinois Press, 1989), pp. 41–53.

28. Most commentators fail to note that Woolf employs three metaphors for sexual identity in this novel: androgyny, transvestism, and transsexualism. Certainly the three are closely related, as Sandra Gilbert says, but to treat them as essentially the same is to ignore their telling differences. It is to equate nature (androgyny), costume (transvestism), and action (transsexualism). That is, it is like saying nouns, modifiers, and verbs perform essentially the same functions. See Gilbert's "Costumes of the Mind: Transvestism as Metaphor in Modern Literature," *Critical Inquiry* 7 (winter 1980), 391–417.

29. Sherron E. Knopp claims Woolf "annihilates such categories" as normal and abnormal sexuality, and thus "puts a strain on conventional language." See "Sapphism and the Subversiveness of Virginia Woolf's *Orlando*," *PMLA* 19 (January 1988), 30.

30. Thomas Kuhn writes that "nature and words are learned together" (*The Structure of Scientific Revolutions*, 2nd ed. [Chicago: University of Chicago Press, 1970], p. 191).

31. The fact that as feminist critics we discover certain patterns in women's writing, certain shared features or strategies, does not necessarily mean that these are grounded in women's unique experiences; rather, it may reveal that as women readers we have learned a set of conventions that enables us to produce similar patterns in women's texts. As Barbara Herrnstein Smith remarks, general patterns are not *abstracted* from works of art but *constructed* by someone on some occasion for some purpose and in accord with some set of principles. Thus, the aesthetic standards we praise in women's writings are no more natural and enduring than those (masculinist) standards they displace, which is not to say they are not useful and valuable. See Smith's "Narrative Versions, Narrative Theories," *Critical Inquiry* 7 (autumn 1980), 218, and *On the Margins of Discourse*, p. 184.

32. In *Reading Woman: Essays in Feminist Criticism* (New York: Columbia University Press, 1986), Mary Jacobus discusses *Orlando* in terms of language and clothing. And Shoshana Felman discusses sexual identity as "conditioned by the functioning of language" in "Rereading Femininity," *Yale French Studies* 62 (1981), 29.

33. For example, Woolf writes: "Society is the most powerful concoction in the world and society has no existence whatsoever" (194); there is not much difference between the sexes, for Orlando remains "practically the same" throughout, and the difference is "one of great profundity" (138, 188); "clothes are but a symbol of something hid deep beneath," and clothes "wear us," changing "our view of the world and the world's view of us" (187–88).

34. See Alison Booth's essay in this volume for a different assessment of

Woolf's last novel from my own. My argument here might usefully be compared with Estella Lauter's in the last section of her essay, "Re-visioning Creativity" in this volume. Lauter counters the dominant concept of creativity as something "fragile," requiring the artist to withdraw in order to "cultivate" her art, with the concept of art as "multifaceted," necessitating its dissemination among the populace. Only in this way, suggests Lauter, can the female artist participate in "the creative enterprise of cultural change."

35. Virginia Woolf, *Between the Acts* (New York and London: Harcourt Brace Jovanovich, 1941; rpt. 1969), p. 212. Additional references are cited parenthetically as *BA* with page numbers.

36. Virginia Woolf, *Moments of Being,* ed. Jeanne Schulkind (Frogmore, St. Albans: Triad/Panther Books, 1978), p. 83.

Chapter 19
Re-visioning Creativity: Audre Lorde's Refiguration of Eros as the Black Mother Within

Estella Lauter

In her essays collected in *Sister Outsider*, Audre Lorde performs a complex act of cultural re-visioning wherein she reappropriates the ground of creativity for women of all kinds. She does so by envisioning a figure of "the Black mother who is the poet . . . in every one of us,"[1] and linking her with an "erotic" lifeforce that she finds necessary to creative work. The figure revises well-known Greek myths that represent the erotic either in terms of the male god Eros, whose passions are sexual, or of Aphrodite whose activities are seductive. It also revises the Jungian tendency to associate women with Eros, understood as psychological relatedness in opposition to Logos, the principle of abstract thought supposedly embodied by men. Neither exclusively physical in orientation nor wholly concerned with relationship, Lorde's female figure of the erotic potential that lies within both women and men is a deep-seated capacity for joy and excellence that she hopes women will realize in order to effect social change.

The essays are compelling, but for every reader who loves them, there is another who wonders if Lorde's vision would trap women again in a stereotypical identification with motherhood and feeling. Why does Lorde identify creativity with the "erotic"—at its worst, another tool of women's oppression? Who is the Black mother within? Is "she" Lorde's muse, or an archetype, or a woman-made symbol? How can the figure be female and still exist in all of us? Wouldn't it be experienced differently by Black and white people? In the present anti-Romantic climate of thought, where all such figures seem suspect, what value does Lorde's vision have in our ongoing effort to understand creativity?

I can only suggest answers to these far-reaching questions in the space of one essay; nonetheless, I have chosen to map out an approach to the above set of questions by viewing Lorde's figure of creativity in several contexts: her essays, her poems and biography, the Western mythology she revises, works by other women, and the theory of creativity.

The Erotic as Black Mother

Lorde's exploration of the erotic as Black mother begins in "Poetry Is Not a Luxury" (1977), where she imagines a "dark place" within "each of us as women," and explains that such places are dark because they are "ancient and hidden" (SO 36). Within them, each woman holds "an incredible reserve of creativity and power, of unexamined and unrecorded emotion and feeling" (SO 37) which, when subjected to "honest exploration," become

sanctuaries and spawning grounds for the most radical and daring of ideas. They become a safe-house for that difference so necessary to change and the conceptualization of any meaningful action. (SO 37)

Poetry, she argues, is the best vehicle of exploration, and it is particularly important to women because it allows us to express our hidden source of power in a culture that otherwise devalues feeling:

The white fathers told us: I think, therefore I am. The Black mother within each of us—the poet—whispers in our dreams: I feel, therefore I can be free. Poetry coins the language to express and charter this revolutionary demand, the implementation of that freedom. (SO 38)

In this essay, Lorde's personal discovery of a hidden bond between her own mother's spirit and herself (in her poem "Black Mother Woman," CP 52–53) becomes a hypothesis about a "place" of power in all women (previously unexplored feeling) and a source of power (the Black mother poet) that lies beyond all the separate places.

Perhaps because the figure of the Black mother seemed too problematic or exclusive, Lorde renamed this source of power and information "the erotic" in "Uses of the Erotic: The Erotic as Power" (1978) while continuing to identify it as female: born of Chaos, it "lies in a deeply female and spiritual plane" (SO 53); it is "an assertion of the lifeforce of women" (SO 55); it is the "nurturer or nursemaid of all our deepest knowledge" (SO 56). "The *yes* within ourselves" (SO 57), the erotic is a "lifeforce" or drive toward satisfaction and completion, toward excellence, which informs our physical, emotional, psychic, and intellectual experience as we become responsible to ourselves (*SO* 53–54). It is at once a capacity for self-connection (the intuition of one's deepest desires) and for sharing with others. When we release it from the patriarchal prison of genital (hetero)sexuality where it has been an instrument of women's subjugation for centuries, it operates in all of our activities: not only in our lovemaking but in our artmaking, in our work as well as in our play. It involves the capacity to act in accord with the full measure of joy we are able to feel. The acts Lorde mentions to exemplify creative joy include "dancing, building a bookcase, writing a poem, examining an idea" (*SO* 57). The sharing of joy may be "physical, emotional, psychic, or intellectual" (*SO* 56).

As if the formulation were not already complex enough, Lorde also gives us several metaphors for the erotic in this essay. (Emphasis throughout this paragraph has been added.) It is a "*well* of replenishing and provocative force to the woman who does not fear its revelation, nor succumb to the belief that sensation is enough" (*SO* 54). Within its framework, Lorde can conceive of work as "a longed-for *bed* which I enter gratefully and from which I rise up empowered" (*SO* 55). Sensual rather than exclusively sexual, the erotic forms a *bridge* between the spiritual and the political (*SO* 56), and because it encourages sharing, it also creates bridges between people who are otherwise threatened by their differences from each other (*SO* 56). Erotic knowledge serves as a *lens* through which we may scrutinize experience in terms of its capacity to bring us joy (*SO* 57). Or it acts as a *pellet of color* (like the coloring used for margarine in the United States during the 1940s) that need only be released from its packet to energize, heighten, and strengthen one's experience (*SO* 57). Finally, it is an *electrical charge* that can give us the energy to pursue change (*SO* 59).

Well, bed, bridge, lens, pellet, electrical charge—all these powerful images are drawn into association with the Black mother poet when Lorde repersonifies the erotic in "An Interview: Audre Lorde and Adrienne Rich" (1979). Here she identifies the figure as the source not only of poetry but of all creativity. Affirming that it is a resource available to men and to whites as well as to Black women, she associates it again with chaos, saying that if we (humankind) do not learn its lessons, we run the risk of commiting the same cultural mistakes all over again. The primary lesson Lorde gives is that

we must never close our eyes to the terror, to the chaos which is Black which is creative which is female which is dark which is rejected which is messy which is . . . . Sinister, smelly, erotic, confused, upsetting. (*SO* 101)

Lorde appropriates the term for sexual pleasure, then, to indicate the intensity of the joy she intends to associate with creative action in all its phases. She denies the idea of absolute difference by asserting the erotic as a potential that is available to anyone—regardless of gender or color or sexual identification—but particularly open to women. She also challenges other binary oppositions between emotion and thought, poetry and action, love and power.

The Erotic in Lorde's Life and Works

The benefits to Lorde of her erotic conceptualization of creativity are clear. As she reappropriated it, the erotic became a center of energy and authority from which she could break open the constraints imposed by patriarchal society and believe in a new future. One can hear the strength it brought to her voice—surely one of the strongest female voices in the history of poetry—in any reading of her work. By following Lorde's own discoveries, recorded in her poems, her biomythography and her published journals, we may see how her vision empowered her.

In the mid-1950s, Lorde began her process of re-visioning with images from Western mythology. In "The Maiden," for example, Lorde assumed the persona of an immortal being like Aphrodite who becomes mortal in the process of fleeing from her male pursuers toward an ever-receding and so "dried out bed / of my mother sea" (*CP* 8). The prognosis for this figure, who stands at the end of the poem "mouthing the ocean names of night," is not good.[2]

By the time she wrote "Coal" in 1962, however, Lorde had begun to envision herself in a different, far more positive way:

> I
> is the total black, being spoken
> from the earth's inside.   (*C* 6)

Here she identified with the creative force that she would later name the "Black mother within," placing it deep inside the earth—diamond, created simultaneously with earth itself. Not created by the Word, as in the Bible, the earth is itself the source of sounds that become words in the throats of her children. Thus, the speaker's selfhood, associated as it is with words, comes from this "total black" that both expresses and extends her racial heritage. One of the words she speaks is "Love," a word that opens like a diamond when it is struck by sunlight, and she asks us to take her word "for jewel in the open light."

In "The Winds of Orisha" (*CP* 48–49) from 1970, Lorde took a critical step toward her vision of the erotic through African mythology. The speaker here imagines herself as born from "Mother Yemanja," making her the sister of Oya, one of the many Orisha (whom Lorde explains in *The Black Unicorn*, p. 120, are divine but not omnipotent beings of the Yoruba and the Dan or Dahomey in western Nigeria). She imagines that she and Oya will work together to quicken the roots of grass that have been deprived of rain. Oya will come out of the mouths of the daughters and sons of the "wheat men" against their patriarchal conception of power, while the poet-speaker will replace the promises of rain in their daily papers and almanacs with "the dark cloud / meaning something entire / and different" (*CP* 49). The "dark cloud" that will bring another kind of rain than the wheat men expect is, of course, poetry born of the Black mother.

A year later in 1971, Lorde could take on the difficult task in "Black Mother Woman" (*CP* 52–53) of clarifying the difference between the figure she had acknowledged as her creative wellspring (Mother Yemanja, mother of all the Orisha and the goddess of oceans to whom Lorde had been trying to return since the 1950s in her poetry) and the actual woman who mothered her. Here, she remembers her own mother's "heavy love," "deceitful longings," "furies," "long suffering eyes" and "denials" (*CP* 52–53). Lorde's real mother, we learn later in *Zami: A New Spelling of My Name* (1982), was indeed "buried in myths of little worth" as this poem says; her heavy-handedness with her daughter came from her own "nightmare of weakness." But the daughter has been able to "peel away" her anger "down to the core of love" (*CP* 53). At this core, the spirit of the mother rises in the daughter, who serves as a temple to preserve it. The daughter's energy does not run completely free; her own eyes still conceal "conflicting rebellions." But she has learned from her mother's denials to define herself. The "tough chestnut," the "stanchion" against weakness she finds in her mother and herself, is love—the "place" of power within each of us that she identifies in "Poetry Is Not a Luxury" (*SO* 36–37).

In "Love Poem," also dated 1971, Lorde clearly identified the sexual dimension in her growing sense of power. She had celebrated lesbian love before, most memorably in "On a Night of the Full Moon" (1968, *CP* 20–21), but that love had not had the restorative effect she imagines here in her imagery of spreading honey on the earth. Here she remembers feeling like the wind (a version of Oya!), "howling into" her lover's "entrances," releasing honey from her hips over the valley "carved out by the mouth of rain" (*CP* 77). Painful in its intensity, the experience nonetheless liberates her as a greedy gull is free to "swing out over the earth / over and over / again" (*CP* 77). Although the poem could not be published in *From a Land Where Other People Live* because of its lesbian content, it marked a turning point in Lorde's understanding of her power—that it lay in her willingness to speak out of the feelings that made her most vulnerable (*SO* 99) in both her own and the dominant culture.

In the title poem of *The Black Unicorn* (published at about the same time Lorde delivered her talk "Uses of the Erotic" at the Berkshire Conference on the History of Women but written before the essay), Lorde records another key experience of empowerment: her discovery in her African sources that the unicorn, a widespread mythic symbol of imagination, was Black. The poem is an important link in her thinking about female creativity, because in her iconography, the figure stands not for latent, spiritualized sexuality as creative impetus, as interpreters of the white unicorn would have it, but for the greed, impatience, restlessness, and unrelenting energy of sexual fertilization—of the gull she had discovered in herself in love. The horn of the unicorn rests not on the maiden's lap, but "deep in her moonpit / growing" (*BU* 3). Mistaken for a shadow (in Jungian terms, the recessive, negative, or even evil capacities of humankind), the unicorn was

> taken
>
> . . . .
> through a cold country
> where mist painted mockeries
> of my fury.   (*BU* 3)

The blackness and the erotic basis of creativity have been ignored and deprecated. The Black unicorn "is not / free," (*BU* 3) nor is the creativity that Lorde envisions free in our culture.

In "A Woman Speaks" (*BU* 4), Lorde reasserted the femaleness of the erotic, which may have been obscured by the tendency to see the unicorn as phallic. If we want to know the magic woman who speaks, we must

> look into the entrails of Uranus
> where the restless oceans pound.   (*BU* 4)

Merging Greek and African mythologies (the magic woman is also sister to witches in Dahomey), she refers here to Aphrodite's birth. Although Lorde does not specifically mention the Black mother, the speaker clearly has the erotic characteristics the poet envisioned in her interview with Rich (*SO* 101):

> I am treacherous with old magic
> and the noon's new fury
> with all your wide futures
> promised   (*BU* 5)

Like the Dahomean god/dess Mawulisa, the woman partakes of both moon and sun, is beyond propitiation, unrelenting, permanent, treacherous and Black; the sea takes its shape from her—as does the reader's future. Always seeking, she is proud, capable of love without pity, hate without scorn. Like the ancient women of Dan whom Lorde commemorates throughout *The Black Unicorn,* who may have served as the basis for Greek myths of Amazons, this figure is a warrior. If the Black unicorn has not already done so, she should serve to rid us of any lingering sentimental fantasies we may retain about creativity or love.

The prose books that followed Lorde's essay "Uses of the Erotic," *The Cancer Journals* (1980) and *Zami* (1982), give us a unique opportunity to see the material effect of her vision on her life. One of the forms the erotic takes in *The Cancer Journals* is decidedly sexual. In the days immediately after her mastectomy, masturbation brought back a flicker of love's fire (*CJ* 25). Another is communal. In the second week after surgery, when she awoke in the night feeling "I'd give anything to have done it differently," she quickly realized that she would *not* have given the people or poetry she loved for her right breast (*CJ* 76). Ultimately, she says, it was the "love of women" that healed her, even the love of unknown women that poured in during her convalescence:

support will always have a special and vividly erotic set of image/meanings for me now, one of which is floating upon a sea within a ring of women like warm bubbles keeping me afloat upon the surface of that sea. I can feel the texture of inviting water just beneath their eyes, and do not fear it. It is the sweet smell of their breath and laughter and voices calling my name that gives me volition, helps me remember I want to turn away from looking down. These images flow quickly, the tangible floods of energy rolling off these women toward me that I converted into power to heal myself. (*CJ* 39)

Still another form of the erotic is spiritual. Lorde is anxious to distinguish her experience of self-affirmation from the "false spirituality" of some goddess worship (*CJ* 39) and from "the superficial farce of 'looking on the bright side of things'" (*CJ* 74). Whereas such approaches may bypass the harsh realities of our civilization, the love Lorde espouses awakens her to the present more fully. Her own prayer to the goddess Seboulisa, another Orisha, in "October" (1980) asks for help to attend to the tasks at hand "with passion," and to name "this tree / under which I am lying" (*CP* 108)—not to die a stranger in her own land. Far from being protected in a cocoon of nostalgia for a mythical past, she is a "wild bridge / swaying in place" (*CP* 108).

Sexual, communal, and spiritual at once, *Zami* is a tribute to the many women who participated in Lorde's process of growth, including the mythological figures of Mawulisa (identified as "the great mother of us all") and "Afrekete, her youngest daughter, the mischievous linguist, trickster, best-beloved, whom we must all become" (Z 255). The book is identified as a "biomythography," I believe, not because the incidents reported are untrue (many are verifiable in other sources), but because it reaches beyond autobiography toward myth.

The mythic dimension of Lorde's story is most apparent in her account of her relationship with Afrekete, embodied in Kitty, a woman who entered Lorde's life unexpectedly when she was mourning the loss of a lover, and then disappeared abruptly, leaving her print "with the resonance and power of an emotional tattoo":

We had come together like elements erupting into an electric storm, exchanging energy, sharing charge, brief and drenching. Then we parted, passed, reformed, reshaping ourselves the better for the exchange. (Z 253)

Both maternal in her role as guide (Z 249), and tricksterlike in her capacity to transform Audre (Z 246, 247), Afrekete is credited (Z 2, 3, 5) as the power behind Lorde's voice that enables her to address both sisters and strangers (Z 252) and to discover herself as "*Zami. A Carriacou name for women who work together as friends and lovers*" (Z 255).

On one level, then, *Zami* is a tribute to the real women who taught Lorde to express the full range of her being in lesbian relationships; on another, it is a tribute to the enduring female presence she had earlier identified as the Black mother, the erotic, and the Orisha at various moments. Here she even thinks of her body as

a living representation of other life older longer wiser. The mountains and valleys, trees, rocks. Sand and flowers and water and stone. Made in earth. (Z 7)

Lorde's latest book of poems, *Our Dead Behind Us* (1986), is full of the violence of the world's current wars interspersed with rituals of love and healing, such as the lovemaking of the two Black women in "Sisters in Arms" who "left our dead behind us" for a few moments (*ODBU* 4; see Mary DeShazer's reading of the poem in this volume). The penultimate poem, however, introduces a "net of possible" into the "storm-flung" landscapes she has described (*ODBU* 71–72). The Black mother poet is behind this poem as a source of transformation, "seizing us in her arms like a warrior lover" (*ODBU* 71).

The book's final poem, "Call," affirms Lorde's hope for the future in a chant announcing that "Aido Hwedo is coming" (*ODBU* 73). Speaking to the "fire-tongued" mothers who represent Aido Hwedo, the goddesses (Orisha) Oya, Seboulisa, Mawu, and Afrekete, whom Lorde acknowledges as "given" (*ODBU* 75), the poet cries,

Mother   loosen my tongue
or adorn me

> with a lighter burden
> Aido Hwedo is coming.   (*ODBU* 75)

Aido Hwedo is the Rainbow Serpent, but also names all the ancient, forgotten deities "who must be worshipped" (*ODBU* 75). So the poet's "call" is at once to the Black mother (addressed here as "Holy ghost woman") for help, and to the reader to join all those mentioned in the poem (including the woman "who scrubs the capitol toilets, members of the poet's family, the girl who brought fire to Soweto, Rosa Parks, Fannie Lou Hamer, and Winnie Mandela) who worship the ancient forces of life—for which the poet's "whole life has been an altar" (*ODBU* 74). In the final stanza, Aido Hwedo is said to be calling too, calling forth the words from the poet's throat. "We" are said to be among those daughters who "are learning by heart / what has never been taught" (*ODBU* 75).

We are asked here to join Lorde, not so much in worship of the specific goddesses whom she serves, but in her belief that our unnamed deities embody the creative energies we abandoned in building a culture. We need them (and we can find them in our own unnamed and unrecognized feelings) in order to realize our creative potential. As I read them, the poems and the essays that figure the Black mother within and the erotic energy of creation (identified with the Orisha of Nigerian origin), are deeply mythological in the best sense of the word. They represent a belief in the power of women to create a better life for ourselves and others—a belief forged in the crucible of Lorde's own experience of growing up Black in a cultural desert that affected her most deeply by destroying her mother's capacity to love herself and therefore to accept her daughter. That belief allowed Lorde to make "a burst of light" out of her struggle with liver cancer from 1984 on, a burst of energy for and insight into survival in a racist world (*BL* 132–33).

The Context of Myth

In order to understand and appreciate the magnitude of Lorde's achievement,[3] we need to remind ourselves of the governing stories behind the code we (regardless of gender, race, or sexual preference) have learned, albeit differently, as participants in Western cultures.

"The very word *erotic* comes from the Greek word *eros*," Lorde says, "the personification of love in all its aspects—born of chaos, and personifying creative power and harmony" (*SO* 55). Lorde's re-vision of the erotic amounts to changing the meaning of a key word in the symbolic code of the West. Such an act is not accomplished easily, as

Alice's resistance to the Cheshire cat in Lewis Carroll's famous tale attests.[4] Especially when the word has come accompanied by powerful figures and stories, change occurs reluctantly. Lorde's brilliance lies in her poetic formulation of an alternative to the figure of Eros.

The Eros we know best in the twentieth century is the Greek divinity who "expresses the outgoing aggressive libido, striving desirousness, and the insistent urge to join and to penetrate."[5] As described in the tale of Cupid and Psyche by the second century CE Latin writer Apuleius,[6] Eros was the charming but spoiled son of Aphrodite, whom the human Psyche nearly forfeited her life to win back. If it was ever intended as a tale about the source of women's creative ability to overcome obstacles and achieve her goals, this story locates such power in Psyche's desire for Eros's love and in her receptivity to aid from others; it names her goal as procreation. As punishment for her transgressions against Aphrodite and Eros, she bears a daughter rather than a son; as reward for her perseverance, she is made immortal. Clearly, this is not what Lorde has in mind.

Lorde refers instead to much older stories, more closely related to the one Hesiod told in his *Theogony* (c. 730–700 BCE), to which she alludes in her poem "A Woman Speaks" (*BU* 4), where Eros is one of four primary deities, along with Chaos, Gaea, and Tartarus.[7] In still another (Orphic) version, Eros hatched from an egg laid by Black-winged Night and fertilized by Wind. Golden-winged, with four heads to represent the four seasons, she/he lived in a cave with Night and created earth, sky, sun, and moon.[8] Other sources give Chaos as parent, as does Lorde. In pre-Hellenic thought, despite differing accounts of "his" parentage or generation, Eros was a "semi-abstract personification of a cosmic force," a force that acted to coordinate the elements, bring harmony to chaos, and permit life to develop.[9] By the time of Pericles and Plato, Joseph Campbell says, the abstract principle of Eros was recognized as "the informing god of all things":

For no one achieves excellence in his life task without love for it, in himself without love for himself, or in his family without love for his home. Love brings everything to flower, each in terms of its own potential, and so is the true pedagogue of the open free society.[10]

The most complete expression of this ideal is, of course, Plato's *Symposium*.

Lorde draws on all these sources—even the later more patriarchal ones in her concept of excellence—for her idea of the erotic, in keeping with her belief that "there are no new ideas. There are only new ways of making them felt" (*SO* 39). But she revises all of them. Judging from her 1979 interview with Rich where she associated her figure with "the chaos" which is Black, creative, female, dark, rejected, messy, sinister, smelly, erotic, confused, and upsetting" (*SO* 101), her primary inspiration was the earlier stratum of stories where Eros was the sibling or offspring of Chaos (which was interpreted as Nothingness in Greek thought). In Lorde's language, we move back into the cave with Night, before the creation of Uranos (sky) and the so-called order of the Olympian gods (patriarchy), but with key differences. The erotic figure she creates is female. It is not a void, but a creative ground of being. And it does not need to be overcome by reason, although it arises in feeling; it is not antithetical to reason and works in conjunction with thought.

This last point separates Lorde's formulation from Jung's designation of Eros as the feminine tendency to relatedness as opposed to Logos, or "the creative and ordering intelligence" supposedly embodied most frequently in men.[11] Lorde's idea would not restrict women's creativity in any way—not to "relatedness" or procreativity and its many surrogates, nor to any realm of action.

Why did Lorde not simply appropriate Aphrodite, the female figure for the erotic as she is known through Hesiod, Homer, and especially Sappho?[12] The first answer must be that she was not Black. The second is that she was not adequate. Not only was her power seductive rather than active, she was cut off from the dimensions of intellectual creativity and mothering that Lorde embodies in her figure.

If we searched the evidence of Aphrodite's precursors (Phoenician Astarte, early Greek *aos,* Minoan "Dove Goddess," Semitic Ishtar, Sumerian Inanna, Egyptian Hathor or Isis, Old European "Bird Goddess," proto-Indo-European *awsos*[13]), we would probably find the maternal characteristics Lorde has in mind. Paul Friedrich suggests that these sources eventually reconnect sexuality with mothering.[14] By merging Aphrodite with Ereshkigal and Medusa, we might also recover the greedy and terrible dimensions of Lorde's figure.[15]

Still, none of these figures is obviously Black. We might push back even further, as Lorde urged Mary Daly to do (*SO* 67–68), to reconnect these European deities with African goddesses who probably preceded them (just as Black human beings probably preceded whites). Even in the modern versions of Nigerian goddesses such as Oya, Lorde found embodiments of energy (of storms and womanness) not yet restrained by sociological and patriarchal concerns.[16] But where would we find the intellectual dimension of creativity in women that Lorde envisions? Lorde has joined many mythologized aspects of human creativity into one figure so that we may understand them as belonging to women. Subtly but firmly, she seeks to change patriarchal symbolic codes at the level of myth. The power to create belongs to women as well as to men.

Lorde extends the word "erotic" well beyond its sexual connotations to mean a much larger kind of longing for life. She asks us to believe that the human species can evolve by claiming its recessive elements:

The possible shapes of what has not been before exist only in that back place, where we keep those unnamed, untamed longings for something different and beyond what is now called possible, and to which our understanding can only build roads. . . . (*SO* 101)

By embodying these untamed longings in the figure of the Black mother, Lorde opens creativity to everyone at the same time she claims it for women. Since the figure refers to the energies that patriarchal cultures have repressed or distorted as feminine, they are properly represented now in female form—a judgment that Z. Nelly Martínez confirms in this volume in her essay on Isabel Allende. But Lorde's use of the African god/dess Aido Hwedo to represent all the repressed, female, Black energies of our culture (*ODBU* 75) also indicates that the figure she has in mind is not exclusively female!

Lorde's figure of the Black mother is certainly far more than a personal source of inspiration. It is different from a model of the woman artist, because it is really not a model at all and it has no precise human correlative. It is an archetype in the feminist sense of representing women's repeated experiences of repressed energy, but it is not a transcendent form.[17] It is, instead, an embodiment of energy to draw upon—an embodiment with a history. The figure had to be maternal to convey Lorde's sense of its generativity, and what version of the mother is more repressed (oppressed) in its history, yet more symbolically generative, than the Black mother? Lorde's vision differs from the well-known Jungian notion of coming to terms with the "Shadow," because that strategy leaves intact the evaluation of repressed experience as negative. Lorde reveals instead that Blackness was positive in prehistory and wrongly repressed. What she calls upon us to negotiate, then, is not our relationship with Blackness but our relationship with thousands of years of conscious repression. By reuniting all people with her African sources through the crucible of her imagination, Lorde allows Blacks and whites, women and men, to reconceive this erotic energy in terms that allow for social action.

Lorde's purpose, we must remember, is to encourage change. To those who ask why one would work toward this end through poetry and myth, Lorde might reply, as I would, that significant change takes place on many levels, and that without changing our myths, we are unlikely to be able to change our lives. The process of re-mythologizing is deeply embedded in Afro-American culture, which brilliantly reconceived the story of Moses to enable those in bondage to envision themselves as free.[18] When Lorde encourages us all to hear the Black mother poet whisper, "I feel, therefore I can be free" (*SO* 38), she seeks to renew the spirit of rebellion in the dominant culture.

Other Works, Other Lives

If Lorde's figure of the erotic as Black mother is to be useful to bring about change in other lives, however, it must be shared. Thus, it is important to ask whether or not it resonates in the works of other women and how broadly it is shared. Can such a figure serve women who no longer "believe in" either Greek or African myths? Is it useful only to women of color? Does it speak outside the "world" of poetry? The task I propose here could take years to complete; I offer only enough examples to show what I would accept as evidence of a shared mythic frame of reference. I have not looked for duplications of Lorde's Black mother so much as for a shared story or set of images and intuitions that link women's creativity with erotic feeling. Works by two Black poets, Ntozake Shange and June Jordan, came to mind immediately, as did works by two white women, Denise Levertov and Georgia O'Keeffe. If these examples are at all indicative of the beliefs women artists hold about their own creativity, Lorde's formulation may indeed have struck a mythic chord.

I thought first of the brilliant ending of Ntozake Shange's choreopoem *for colored girls who have considered suicide/when the rainbow is enuf* (1977).[19] All six women named for colors come together in this scene to reveal what has saved them from suicide—a justifiable response to the anguish recorded in previous scenes. Each had felt she was "missin somethin" that neither a man nor a mama could give her, and each experienced a "layin on of hands," which the lady in purple describes as "the holiness of myself released" (*fcg* 62). The lady in red describes her blessing as an erotic embrace from nature; as a result, she says,

> i found god in myself
> & i loved her
> i loved her fiercely   (*fcg* 63)

These lines, repeated softly by all the others, become a song of joy to end this moving collage of Black women's lives. No less maternal or sensual than the Black mother or Afrekete, this internal caretaker brings tears that weave "garments for the moon" to the eyes of the speaker.

Shange's own corresponding experience of empowerment involved, not a specific conversion to goddess worship, but a growing belief that she "waz worth loving" (*ne* 26), which required a decision to write out of her own experience as a woman, instead of being "just like a man" (*ne* 17). As a result, Shange "waz left with an arena of her own" (*ne* 17)—an arena which soon included music, poetry, and dance together in a distinctive way, both avant-garde and ancient. And in this arena, she conceived of song as a generative, female, erotic force that keeps life moving. Using some of the same images as Lorde, she invites:

> so come with me to this place
> i know where music expects me
> & when she finds me
> > i am bathed in the ocean's breath
> > > & the soft glory of my laughter   (*ne* 144)

Song is personified as female and oceanic, the world in ourselves to which we can "come" to be "our own children." It is the ancient but internal lifegiving force Lorde identified as erotic.

Not a god, this force nonetheless reveals to us our need for another kind of god. I quote "We Need a God Who Bleeds Now" in its entirety not only because of its resonance with Lorde's imagery but also because of its extraordinary re-visionary depth:

> we need a god who bleeds now
> a god whose wounds are not
> some small male vengeance
> some pitiful concession to humility
> a desert swept with dryin marrow in honor of the lord
>
> we need a god who bleeds
> spreads her lunar vulva & showers us in shades of scarlet
> thick and warm like the breath of her
> our mothers tearing   to let us   in
> this place breaks open
> like our mothers bleeding
> the planet is heaving   mourning our ignorance
> the moon tugs the seas
> to hold her/ to hold her
> embrace swelling hills/ i am
> not wounded i am bleeding to life
>
> we need a god who bleeds now
> whose wounds are not the end of anything   (*ADG* 51)

The act of imagining such a god helps to revalue the physical vulnerability of women, allowing the speaker to see how she is "bleeding to life." Creativity need not be the result of woundedness and sacrifice; it can also be the result of natural processes coming to fruition. The "passion" of Christ, which denies the body in favor of transcendence, is not the only viable model of creative transformation.

Passion is the title of a volume of poems by June Jordan,[20] whose bent is less religious than Lorde's or Shange's, but whose poetry comes from an equally "dark" place within her, which she simply calls "love":

> These poems
> they are things that I do
> in the dark
> reaching for you
> whoever you are
>
> . . . .
> These skeletal lines
> they are desperate arms for my longing and love.   (*TIDD* ix)

She casts herself here as "a stranger learning to worship the strangers / around me / whoever you are" (*TIDD* ix). Jordan's "love" is perhaps less joyful than Lorde's or Shange's, but she shares with both a communal desire. She is also throughout much of her poetry "a woman searching for her savagery" (*P* 2), and her presence is often scrappy, as was Lorde's warrior goddess (*BU* 4–5); she calls her autobiography *Civil Wars*. But in an essay delivered at about the same time that Lorde wrote "Uses of the Erotic," she asserted unequivocally that "it is always the love that will carry action into positive new places" (*CW* 142).

Jordan means by love something rather different from the norms of romantic love and maternal love, parallel to Lorde's concept, although it is stated in other terms:

I am a feminist, and what that means to me is . . . that I must undertake to love myself and respect myself. . . . It means that I must everlastingly seek to cleanse myself of the hatred and contempt that surrounds and permeates my identity, as a woman, and as a Black human being. . . . It means that the achievement of self-love and self-respect will require inordinate, hourly vigilance, and that I am entering my soul into a struggle that will most certainly transform the experience of all the peoples of the earth. (*CW* 142)

The task Jordan sets herself in the essay and in her poetry is to love women who are unlike herself in status, class, race, and culture and to love men who are able to respect and love her, until she can embrace the "whole world, without fear, and also without self-sacrifice" (*CW*

143–44). Careful to separate her idea from maternal self-sacrifice, she also differentiates it from sexual love, whether lesbian, bisexual, or heterosexual, saying that she has in mind a "steady-state deep caring and respect for every other human being" (*CW* 144) derived from self-love.[21]

Jordan comes closer to Lorde's way of speaking about the erotic in *Living Room,* a book that demands a more livable world. There, in a long reflection on order and disorder, natural and unnatural states of being, having said that the times are not good for women, Blacks, gays, young people, or old people, she turns her poem inside out and claims: "this is the only time to come together / Fractious / Kicking / Spilling / Burly / Whirling / Raucous / Messy / Free / Exploding like the seeds of a natural disorder" (*LR* 20). Like Lorde's vision of the erotic, this natural disorder is fertile with energy that will "carry action into positive new places" (*CW* 142).

I have no doubt that similarly enriching connections exist between Lorde's figure and the work of other Black women. But what about women who are not Black? Have they also felt Lorde's challenge to acknowledge the erotic wellspring within? Have they figured creative energy as black in some sense? I think the answer will be "yes," and I refer to Paula Bennett's recent summary of the way Medusa (recall my point above about Medusa's relationship to Aphrodite) has functioned to liberate the creative energies of poets of several colors and persuasions.[22] On another tack, Denise Levertov's poem "Song for Ishtar" comes to mind as a poetic credo that might well embody exactly the process of discovery Lorde recommends. Too well known to need quoting here, the poem expresses Levertov's joy at finding the "black of desire" in herself[23] as she rocks and grunts and shines in the erotic embrace of Ishtar, another of the goddesses in Aphrodite's ancestry. The poem came at the beginning of a book that enfranchised Levertov by establishing her voice and a style that has already influenced two generations in the creation of a more inclusive, politically concerned poetry. Elsewhere in this volume Susan Stanford Friedman discusses H.D.'s equation "love is writing"—another possibility for comparison with Lorde.

Finally (for the moment), I think Lorde's re-vision of the erotic may explain, better than any other theory, Georgia O'Keeffe's famous discovery in 1915 that she had things in her head no one else had seen. A wild energy is present both in her letters to Anita Pollitzer and in the drawings on paper from 1915–16 when she allowed herself only charcoal (compare with Lorde's "Coal") to discover her own distinctive imaginative stance and began to see natural forms in terms of her own feelings.[24] The drawings express the sense of joy (and terror) she

found in her life and work. Later, when she was preparing the drawings for publication, she said they were the best she had ever done
because in them she had been most free.

Lorde's vision may indeed function differently for Black women
than it does for white women or men. The act of revaluing Blackness is
material *and* symbolic for Blacks, but only symbolic for whites. Difference, as Barbara Christian has pointed out, is vitally important to
Lorde; nonetheless, she presents her vision to Blacks and whites as a
tool to negotiate differences so that they can become "a source of
creative dialogue rather than a threat."[25] Shange and Jordan also
intend to speak across the lines of race and ethnicity, and they do. Why
shouldn't they? A poet's separate cultural identity need not prevent her
vision from affecting the dominant culture. Nor need the fear of
"essentialism" send us skittering away from the power to be gained
from shared visions. Presumably, each person would tap into her own
repressed feeling differently to discover its particular generative force.
But if a central task of female development in patriarchy is to overcome—materially and symbolically—the image of the negative mother
learned from watching all our mothers' relative helplessness in the
dominant culture and from receiving projections of that image onto
ourselves,[26] then Lorde's revaluation of erotic energy in the name of
the Black mother has much to offer women despite all our differences.

The Context of Theory

What credibility does Lorde's formulation have in late capitalist Western cultures? In a time of deep reservation about all Platonic theories
that claim some reality beyond what we can observe, what relevance
can Lorde's vision of a mythic figure underlying women's creativity
possibly have? Paradoxically, it may turn out to be more workable than
other feminist theories that identify specific psychological motivations
for creativity (for example, anger or substitution for procreation) or
which focus on traits of "the creative personality" (androgyny).

Perhaps we can best measure Lorde's achievement by looking at it
in the light of the most anti-Platonic book available on the subject of
creativity. In *The Mind's Best Work,* David Perkins systematically disposes
of a number of old saws about creativity, the most important of which is
that "it" is an entity—a gift, a unique process, an identifiable ability—
of any kind.[27] Perkins presents creativity as a "set" (I prefer the term
"web"), in which abilities, talents, attitudes, beliefs, values, and purpose
exist in varying proportions in relationship to opportunities. The abilities are not mysterious; they are capacities for remembering, noticing,
making analogies, having insights, and so on. Talents may extend those

abilities into less common modes of expression. A key attitude is receptivity to the notion that a single problem may admit many solutions. The key belief is in one's capacity to solve problems. Crucial values concern originality and excellence. And the sense of purpose which is essential in some measure may come from many sources. The creative person needs sufficient strength to be different. She or he needs sufficient psychological, social, and environmental support to find the opportunities to match her abilities. If creativity is fragile, as our culture would like us to believe, this is not because it is rare or unstable but because the phenomenon is so multifaceted. Rather than spending our resources to "isolate" it so that we can "cultivate" it like an exotic plant, we should spend them in teaching people how to see its webs, to keep from destroying them.

From this perspective, the cultural value of Lorde's approach comes into clearer focus. Women have not lacked abilities and talents to create in a variety of fields, nor have they (we) lacked the attitude of receptivity that allows for multiple solutions to a single problem. Opportunities have not always been available but are becoming more so. Women remain underrepresented, however, in the endeavors marked as creative. Why? In part, of course, the answer lies in sexist attitudes, but the key to the power of these attitudes may be that potentially creative women share them. In *Female Authority,* Polly Young-Eisendrath and Florence Wiedemann document from clinical evidence the ways women internalize the culture's messages about female inferiority first by forming a "negative mother complex" and by giving up to males, in the depths of their imagination, the authority to decide for themselves what is true or good or beautiful.[28] From this position, it is difficult indeed to believe in one's own capacity to solve problems; to hold originality and excellence as key values; to feel a strong sense of purpose. Just here lies the brilliance of Lorde's formulation.

Lorde's figure of an erotic wellspring provides the basis for belief in female authority because it removes the necessity for certification of one's ideas by the dominant group. The creative impetus is in all of us in our capacity for feeling. Lorde speaks of creative process as a matter of tapping or honoring the "deep place" from which perception comes; rationality, she says, serves feeling and knowledge by building roads from one place to another, but "Perceptions precede analysis just as visions precede action or accomplishments" (*SO* 100, 105). The figure of the Black mother within allows us to stop questioning our perceptions before they have a chance to become poems.

Lorde's figure of the Black mother poet, then, symbolizes the belief in one's own authority to create, and her association of it with the erotic, with Eros in female form, is a potentially useful strategy for rethinking women's relationship with love, a concept that has often worked in Western culture to prevent women from realizing creative as opposed to procreative potential. Lorde's figure addresses the root problem of women's motivation for creative activity. If a woman believes that the source of creativity lies within her, perhaps she can more readily marshal her resources to combat the external conditions of her life. With the help of figures such as Lorde's (and also Virginia Woolf's, explored by Pamela Caughie in this volume)—figures that refuse to freeze and ration creative energies—perhaps women can not only survive as artists but also re-envision survival itself as a matter of reclaiming what has been repressed and nourishing the capacity to change.

In my view, then, Lorde has begun an invaluable process of re-envisioning Eros and of recovering the energy of love in all its dimensions for women to direct as they wish into the creative enterprise of cultural change.

Notes

This essay was completed at the Center for Twentieth Century Studies, University of Wisconsin-Milwaukee, where I was a Fellow in the Humanities in 1988–89, and where I benefitted from Cheryl Johnson's friendship. Research support from the Frankenthal Professorship at the University of Wisconsin–Green Bay has greatly facilitated my studies. Thanks to the members of the morning group on women's cultures at the 1988 meeting of the Society for Values in Higher Education for their encouragement in the early stages of this project.

1. In *Sister Outsider: Essays and Speeches by Audre Lorde* (Trumansburg, N.Y.: Crossing Press, 1984), p. 100. Additional references are cited parenthetically as *SO* with page numbers. Other works by Lorde are abbreviated as follows: *CP: Chosen Poems—Old and New* (New York: Norton, 1982); *C: Coal* (New York: Norton, 1976); *BU: The Black Unicorn* (New York: Norton, 1978); *CJ: The Cancer Journals* (San Francisco: Spinsters Ink, 1980); *Z: Zami: A New Spelling of My Name* (Trumansburg, N.Y.: The Crossing Press, 1982); *ODBU: Our Dead Behind Us* (New York: Norton, 1986); *BL: A Burst of Light* (Ithaca, N.Y.: Firebrand, 1988).

2. I think of Anne Sexton's longing for the maternal sea in her later poetry and feel thankful that Lorde continued her quest for a female source of power. See my *Women as Mythmakers* (Bloomington: Indiana University Press, 1984), pp. 34–42. I am indebted to Annis Pratt for identifying the figure in Lorde's poem as Aphrodite. The later stages of this essay emerged in dialogue about her book-length manuscript on the representation of goddesses in poetry.

3. Lorde's achievement may be even more substantial if, as I think, she has also revised African mythology. At the moment, I do not possess sufficient expertise to make this argument.

4. Lewis Carroll, *Alice's Adventures in Wonderland and Through the Looking*

Glass (New York: Clarkson N. Potter, 1960). See especially p. 89 where, once Alice grants the Cheshire Cat's apparently harmless premise that "a dog's not mad," the Cat's (il)logical analysis of madness prevails, no matter what Alice calls it.

5. Edward C. Whitmont, *The Return of the Goddess* (New York: Crossroad, 1982), p. 130.

6. See Erich Neumann, *Amor and Psyche,* trans. Ralph Mannheim (Princeton, N.J.: Princeton University Press, 1956), pp. 3–53.

7. Joseph Campbell, *The Masks of God: Occidental Mythology* (New York: Viking, 1964), p. 234.

8. Robert Graves, *The Greek Myths: I* (Middlesex, England: Penguin, 1956), pp. 30–31.

9. *New Larousse Encyclopedia of Mythology* (London: Hamlyn, 1977), p. 132.

10. Campbell, *Masks of God,* p. 227.

11. Whitmont, *Return of the Goddess,* p. 130. Whitmont also disputes the association of women with Eros and men with Logos, but his reformulation of women's essential nature seems unlikely to help women to conceptualize their ability to reshape culture. Those who think Lorde's position is essentialist should compare it carefully with Whitmont's account of women's relationship to Eros.

12. Paul Friedrich, *The Meaning of Aphrodite* (Chicago: University of Chicago Press, 1978), chapter 3, pp. 55–71.

13. Friedrich, *Meaning of Aphrodite,* p. 52. The terms in italics and quotation marks are linguistic and archaeological reconstructions rather than names of deities.

14. Friedrich, *Meaning of Aphrodite,* chapter 9, pp. 181–84.

15. Whitmont, *Return of the Goddess,* pp. 134–35.

16. Judith Gleason associates Oya with Inanna in *Oya: In Praise of the Goddess* (Boston: Shambhala, 1987), p. 11.

17. Estella Lauter and Carol Schreier Rupprecht, eds., *Feminist Archetypal Theory: Interdisciplinary Re-visions of Jungian Thought* (Knoxville: University of Tennessee Press, 1985), pp. 12–16.

18. Jane Campbell, *Mythic Black Fiction: The Transformation of History* (Knoxville: University of Tennessee Press, 1986), Introduction. Lorde is able, as Campbell notes earlier writers were not, to create a positive image.

19. Books by Ntozake Shange will be abbreviated in the text as follows: *fcg: for colored girls who have considered suicide / when the rainbow is enuf: a choreopoem* (New York: Macmillan, 1977); *ne: nappy edges* (New York: Bantam, 1978); *ADG: A Daughter's Geography* (New York: St. Martin's Press, 1983); *SNE: See No Evil: Prefaces, Essays and Accounts, 1976–1983* (San Francisco: Momo's Press, 1984).

20. June Jordan's books are abbreviated in the text as follows: *ND: New Days* (New York: Emerson Hall Publishers, 1974); *TIDD: Things That I Do in the Dark: Selected Poems* (New York: Random House, 1977); *P: Passion: New Poems, 1977–1980* (Boston: Beacon, 1980); *CW: Civil Wars* (Boston: Beacon, 1981); *LR: Living Room* (New York: Thunder's Mouth Press, 1985).

21. Compare Jordan's idea with the concept of "one-caring" in Nel Noddings, *Caring: A Feminine Approach to Ethics and Moral Education* (Berkeley: University of California Press, 1984), pp. 30–58.

22. Paula Bennett, *My Life a Loaded Gun: Female Creativity and Feminist Poetics* (Boston: Beacon, 1986), Conclusion. Also see my essay on visual art by

women in the late 1980s, "Women as Mythmakers Revisited," *Quadrant* 23.1 (Spring 1990), 35–52.

23. Denise Levertov, *O Taste and See* (New York: New Directions, 1964), p. 3.

24. Jack Cowart, Juan Hamilton, and Sarah Greenough, *Georgia O'Keeffe: Art and Letters* (Boston: Little Brown, 1988), pp. 141–158 and plates 4, 11, 14, 17, and 26.

25. Barbara Christian, "The Dynamics of Difference: Book Review of Audre Lorde's *Sister Outsider* (1984)," in *Black Feminist Criticism: Perspectives on Black Women Writers* (New York: Pergamon Press, 1985), p. 208.

26. Polly Young-Eisendrath and Florence Wiedemann, *Female Authority: Empowering Women Through Psychotherapy* (New York: Guilford Press, 1987), pp. 43–48.

27. David Perkins, *The Mind's Best Work* (Cambridge, Mass.: Harvard University Press, 1981).

28. Young-Eisendrath and Wiedemann, *Female Authority,* pp. 8–11.

Selected Bibliography

Abel, Elizabeth. "(E)Merging Identities: The Dynamics of Female Friendship in Contemporary Fiction by Women." *Signs* 6.3 (1981), 413–35.
———, ed. *Writing and Sexual Difference*. Chicago: University of Chicago Press, 1982.
Abel, Elizabeth, Marianne Hirsch, and Elizabeth Langland, eds. *The Voyage In: Fictions of Female Development*. Hanover, N.H.: New England University Press, 1983.
Adorno, Theodor W. Parataxis. *Noten zur Literatur III*. Frankfurt am Main: Suhrkamp, 1973.
Alcoff, Linda. "Cultural Feminism Versus Poststructuralism: The Identity Crisis in Feminist Theory." *Signs* 13.3 (spring 1988), 405–36.
Anzaldúa, Gloria. *Borderlands/La Frontera: The New Mestiza*. San Francisco: Spinsters/aunt lute, 1987.
Aptheker, Bettina. *Tapestries of Life: Women's Work, Women's Consciousness, and the Meaning of Daily Experience*. Amherst: University of Massachusetts Press, 1989.
Armstrong, Nancy. *Desire and Domestic Fiction: A Political History of the Novel*. Oxford: Oxford University Press, 1987.
Auerbach, Nina. *Communities of Women*. Cambridge, Mass.: Harvard University Press, 1978.
Bakhtin, M. M. *The Dialogic Imagination: Four Essays*. Ed. Michael Holquist. Trans. Caryl Emerson and Michael Holquist. Austin: University of Texas Press, 1981.
Bandarage, Asoka. "Women of Color: Toward a Celebration of Power." *woman of power* IV (fall 1986), 8–14, 82–83.
Barr, Marlene, and Richard Feldstein, eds. *Discontented Discourses: Feminism/Textual Intervention/Psychoanalysis*. Urbana and Chicago: University of Illinois Press, 1989.
Barrett, Michèle, ed. *Virginia Woolf: Women and Writing*. New York: Harcourt Brace Jovanovich, 1979.
Barthes, Roland. *Image-Music-Text*. Trans. Stephen Heath. London: Fontana, 1977.
———. *Mythologies*. Trans. Annette Lavers. New York: Farrar, Straus, Giroux, 1972.
———. *S/Z*. Trans. Richard Miller. New York: Hill and Wang, 1974.

————. *The Pleasure of the Text*. Trans. Richard Miller. New York: Hill and Wang, 1975.

Beebe, Maurice. *Ivory Towers and Sacred Founts: The Artist as Hero in Fiction from Goethe to Joyce*. New York: New York University Press, 1964.

Belenky, Mary Field, Blythe McVicker Clinchy, Nancy Rule Goldberger, and Jill Mattuck Tarule. *Women's Ways of Knowing*. New York: Basic Books, 1986.

Belsey, Catherine. *Critical Practice*. London: Methuen, 1980.

Bennett, Paula. *My Life a Loaded Gun: Female Creativity and Feminist Poetics*. Boston: Beacon Press, 1986.

Benstock, Shari. *Women of the Left Bank: Paris, 1900–1940*. Austin: University of Texas Press, 1986.

————, ed. *Feminist Issues in Literary Scholarship*. Bloomington: Indiana University Press, 1987.

Berger, John. *Ways of Seeing*. New York: Penguin, 1972.

Bergonzi, Bernard. *Contemporary Novelists*. Ed. James Vinson. New York: St. Martin's Press, 1976.

Bohm, David. *Wholeness and the Implicate Order*. London: Routledge and Kegan Paul, 1980.

Bunch, Charlotte. *Passionate Politics: Feminist Theory in Action*. New York: St. Martin's Press, 1987.

Campbell, Jane. *Mythic Black Fiction: The Transformation of History*. Knoxville: University of Tennessee Press, 1986.

Campbell, Joseph. *The Masks of God: Occidental Mythology*. New York: Viking, 1964.

Carby, Hazel. *Reconstructing Womanhood: The Emergence of the Afro-American Woman Novelist*. New York: Oxford University Press, 1987.

Chodorow, Nancy. *The Reproduction of Mothering: Psychoanalysis and the Sociology of Gender*. Berkeley: University of California Press, 1978.

Christ, Carol. *Diving Deep and Surfacing: Women Writers on Spiritual Quest*. Boston: Beacon Press, 1980.

Christian, Barbara. *Black Feminist Criticism: Perspectives on Black Women Writers*. New York: Pergamon Press, 1985.

————. *Black Women Novelists: The Development of a Tradition, 1892–1976*. Westport, Conn.: Greenwood Press, 1978.

Cixous, Hélène. "The Laugh of the Medusa." *Signs* 1.4 (1976), 875–93. Rpt. in *New French Feminisms: An Anthology*. Ed. Elaine Marks and Isabelle de Courtivron. Amherst: University of Massachusetts Press, 1980; rpt. New York: Schocken Books, 1981, pp. 245–64.

————. "Castration or Decapitation?" Trans. Annette Kuhn. *Signs* 7.1 (summer 1981), 36–55.

Cixous, Hélène, and Catherine Clement. *The Newly Born Woman*. Theory and History of Literature, Vol. 24. Trans. Betsy Wing. Minneapolis: University of Minnesota Press, 1986.

Clayton, Jay, and Eric Rothstein, eds. *Influence and Intertextuality*. Madison: University of Wisconsin Press, 1991.

Collins, Patricia Hill. "The Social Construction of Black Feminist Thought." *Signs* 14.4 (1989), 745–73.

Collins, Sheila D. *A Different Heaven and Earth*. Valley Forge, Pa.: Judson Press, 1983, p. 183.

Coward, Rosalind, and John Ellis. *Language and Materialism: Developments in Semiology and the Theory of the Subject*. London: Routledge and Kegan Paul, 1977.

Cunningham, A. R. "The 'New Woman Fiction' of the 1890s." *Victorian Studies* 17.2 (1973), 177–86.

Cunningham, Gail. *The New Woman and the Victorian Novel.* London: Macmillan, 1978.

Daims, Diva. "A Criticism of Their Own: Turn-of-the-Century Feminist Writers." *Turn-of-the-Century Women* 2.2 (1985), 22–31.

Daly, Mary. *Beyond God the Father: Toward a Philosophy of Women's Liberation.* Boston: Beacon Press, 1973.

———. *Gyn/Ecology: The Metaethics of Radical Feminism.* Boston: Beacon Press, 1978.

———. *Pure Lust: Elemental Feminist Philosophy.* Boston: Beacon Press, 1984.

———, with Jane Caputi. *Webster's First New Intergalactic Wickedary of the English Language.* Boston: Beacon Press, 1987.

DeJean, Joan. "Fictions of Sappho." *Critical Inquiry* 13.4 (1987), 787–805.

DeKoven, Marianne. "Gendered Doubleness and the 'Origins' of Modernist Form." *Tulsa Studies in Women's Literature* 8.2 (1989), 19–42.

de Lauretis, Teresa. *Alice Doesn't: Feminism, Semiotics, Cinema.* Bloomington: Indiana University Press, 1984.

———. *Technologies of Gender.* Bloomington: Indiana University Press, 1987.

———, ed. *Feminist Studies, Critical Studies.* Bloomington: Indiana University Press, 1986.

DeShazer, Mary K. *Inspiring Women: Reimagining the Muse.* New York: Pergamon Press, 1986.

Doane, Janice, and Devon Hodges. *Nostalgia and Sexual Difference: The Resistance to Contemporary Feminism.* New York: Methuen, 1987.

Donovan, Josephine. *After the Fall: The Demeter-Persephone Myth in Cather, Wharton, and Glasgow.* University Park: Pennsylvania State University Press, 1989.

———. *Feminist Theory: The Intellectual Traditions of American Feminism.* New York: Continuum, 1985.

Dowling, Linda. "The Decadent and the New Woman in the 1890s." *Nineteenth-Century Fiction* 33. 4 (1979), 434–54.

DuPlessis, Rachel Blau. *Writing Beyond the Ending: Narrative Strategies of Twentieth-Century Women Writers.* Bloomington: Indiana University Press, 1985.

Dworkin, Andrea. *Pornography: Men Possessing Women.* London: The Women's Press, 1988.

Eagleton, Terry. *Literary Theory: An Introduction.* Minneapolis: University of Minnesota Press, 1983.

Ecker, Gisela, ed. *Feminist Aesthetics.* Trans. Harriet Anderson. Boston: Beacon Press, 1985.

Eisenstein, Hester, and Alice Jardine, eds. *The Future of Difference.* Boston: G. K. Hall, 1980.

Eliade, Mircea. *The Sacred and the Profane.* 1957. Rpt. New York: Harper, 1961.

Elshtain, Jean Bethke. *Women and War.* New York: Basic Books, 1987.

Epstein, Barbara. *The Politics of Domesticity.* Middletown, Conn.: Wesleyan University Press, 1981.

Ezergailis, Inta. *Women Writers: The Divided Self.* Bonn: Bouvier, 1982.

Felman, Shoshana. "Rereading Femininity." *Yale French Studies* 62 (1981), 19–44.

Felski, Rita. *Beyond Feminist Aesthetics: Feminist Literature and Social Change.* Cambridge, Mass.: Harvard University Press, 1989.

Fernando, Lloyd. *The "New-Woman" in the Late Victorian Novel.* State College: Pennsylvania State University Press, 1977.

————. "The Radical Ideology of the 'New Woman.'" *Southern Review* 2 (1967), 206–22.

Fetterley, Judith. *Provisions*. Bloomington: Indiana University Press, 1985.

Fleischmann, Fritz, ed. *American Novelists Revisited: Essays in Feminist Criticism*. Boston: G. K. Hall, 1982.

Flynn, Elizabeth A., and Patrocinio Schweikart, eds. *Gender and Reading: Essays on Readers, Texts, and Contexts*. Baltimore: Johns Hopkins University Press, 1986.

Foucault, Michel. *The History of Sexuality, Volume I: An Introduction*. Trans. Robert Hurley. New York: Pantheon Books, 1978.

————. "What Is an Author?" *Textual Strategies: Perspectives in Post-Structuralist Criticism*. Ed. Josue Harari. Ithaca, N.Y.: Cornell University Press, 1979, pp. 147–60.

————. "Weavings: Intertextuality and the (Re)Birth of the Author." In *Influence and Intertextuality*. Ed. Jay Clayton and Eric Rothstein. Madison: University of Wisconsin Press, 1991

Freidman, Susan Stanford. "Creativity and the Childbirth Metaphor: Gender Difference in Literary Discourse." *Feminist Studies* 13.1 (1987), 49–82.

Freud, Sigmund. *The Standard Edition of the Complete Psychological Works of Sigmund Freud*. Trans. J. Strachey. London: Hogarth Press, 1957.

Froula, Christine. "Rewriting Genesis: Gender and Culture in Twentieth-Century Texts." *Tulsa Studies in Women's Literature* 7.2 (1988), 197–237.

Frye, Joanne S. *Living Stories, Telling Lives: Women and the Novel in Contemporary Experience*. Ann Arbor: University of Michigan Press, 1986.

Gadamer, Hans–Georg. *The Relevance of the Beautiful and Other Essays*. Trans. Nicholas Walker. Ed. Robert Bernasconi. Cambridge: Cambridge University Press, 1986.

Gallop, Jane. *The Daughter's Seduction: Feminism and Psychoanalysis*. Ithaca, N.Y.: Cornell University Press, 1982.

Gardiner, Judith Kegan. "The (US)es of (I)dentity: A Response to Abel on (E)merging Identities." *Signs* 6.3 (1981), 436–42.

Garner, Shirley Nelson, Claire Kahane, and Madelon Sprengnether, eds. *The (M)other Tongue: Essays in Feminist Psychoanalytic Interpretation*. Ithaca, N.Y.: Cornell University Press, 1985.

Gilbert, Sandra M. "Costumes of the Mind: Transvestism as Metaphor in Modern Literature." *Critical Inquiry* 7.2 (1980), 391–417.

Gilbert, Sandra M., and Susan Gubar. *The Madwoman in the Attic: The Woman Writer and the Nineteenth-Century Literary Imagination*. New Haven, Conn.: Yale University Press, 1979.

————. *No Man's Land: The Place of the Woman Writer in the Twentieth Century*, Vol. I, *The War of the Words*. New Haven, Conn.: Yale University Press, 1988.

————. *No Man's Land: The Place of the Woman Writer in the Twentieth Century*, Vol. II, *Sex Changes*. New Haven, Conn.: Yale University Press, 1989.

Gilligan, Carol. *In a Different Voice: Psychological Theory and Women's Development*. Cambridge, Mass.: Harvard University Press, 1982.

Gleason, Judith. *Oya: In Praise of the Goddess*. Boston: Shambala, 1987.

Greene, Gayle, and Coppélia Kahn, eds. *Making a Difference: Feminist Literary Criticism*. London: Methuen, 1985.

Griffin, Susan. *Pornography and Silence: Culture's Revenge Against Nature*. New York: Harper & Row, 1981.

Harding, Sandra, and Merrill B. Hintikka, eds. *Discovering Reality*. Dordrecht: Reidel, 1983.

Hartsock, Nancy C. M. *Money, Sex and Power: Toward a Feminist Historical Materialism*. New York: Longman, 1983.

Hedin, Raymond. "The Structuring of Emotion in Black American Fiction." *Novel: A Forum on Fiction* 15. 4 (1982), 35–43.

Heilbrun, Carolyn G. *Reinventing Womanhood*. New York: Norton, 1979.

———. *Toward a Recognition of Androgyny*. New York: Knopf, 1973.

———. *Writing a Woman's Life*. New York: Ballantine, 1988.

Heilbrun, Carolyn G., and Margaret R. Higonnet, eds. *The Representation of Women in Fiction*. Baltimore: Johns Hopkins University Press, 1983.

Hirsch, Marianne. *The Mother/Daughter Plot: Narrative, Psychoanalysis, Feminism*. Bloomington: Indiana University Press, 1989.

Homans, Margaret. *Bearing the Word: Language and Female Experience in Nineteenth-Century Women's Writing*. Chicago: University of Chicago Press, 1986.

———. *Women Writers and Poetic Identity: Dorothy Wordsworth, Emily Brontë, and Emily Dickinson*. Princeton, N.J.: Princeton University Press, 1980.

Huf, Linda. *A Portrait of the Artist as a Young Woman: The Writer as Heroine in American Literature*. New York: Frederick Ungar, 1983.

Huggins, Nathan I. *Harlem Renaissance*. New York: Oxford University Press, 1971.

Hurtado, Aída. "Relating to Privilege: Seduction and Rejection in the Subordination of White Women and Women of Color," *Signs* 14.4 (summer 1989), 833–55.

Huyssen, Andreas. *After the Great Divide: Modernism, Mass Culture, Postmodernism*. Bloomington: Indiana University Press, 1981.

Irigaray, Luce. *This Sex Which Is Not One*. Trans. Catherine Porter with Carolyn Burke. Ithaca, N.Y.: Cornell University Press, 1985.

Jacobus, Mary. "Review of *The Madwoman in the Attic*." *Signs* 6.3 (1981), 517–23.

———. *Reading Woman: Essays in Feminist Criticism*. New York: Columbia University Press, 1986.

Jameson, Fredric. *The Political Unconscious: Narrative as a Socially Symbolic Act*. Ithaca, N.Y.: Cornell University Press, 1981.

Jardine, Alice. *Gynesis: Configurations of Woman and Modernity*. Ithaca, N.Y.: Cornell University Press, 1985.

Johnson, Barbara. *A World of Difference*. Baltimore: Johns Hopkins University Press, 1987.

Keller, Evelyn Fox, and Helene Moglen. "Competition and Feminism: Conflicts for Academic Women." *Signs* 2.3 (1987), 493–511.

Kelley, Mary. *Private Woman, Public Stage*. New York: Oxford University Press, 1984.

Kofman, Sarah. "The Narcissistic Woman: Freud and Girard." *diacritics* 10.3 (1980), 36–45.

———. *Autobiogriffures. Du chat Murr d'Hoffmann*. Paris: Christian Bourgeois, 1976.

Kristeva, Julia. *About Chinese Women*. New York: Urigen Books, 1977.

———. *Desire in Language: A Semiotic Approach to Literature and Art*. Ed. Leon S. Roudiez. Trans. T. Gora, A. Jardine, and L. S. Roudiez. New York: Columbia University Press, 1980.

———. *Revolution in Poetic Language*. Trans. Margaret Waller. New York: Columbia University Press, 1984.

————. "Women's Time," trans. Alice Jardine and Harry Blake. *Signs* 7.1 (1981), 5–35.

Kuhn, Thomas. *The Structure of Scientific Revolutions.* Chicago: University of Chicago Press, 1970.

Labovitz, Ester Kleinbord. *The Myth of the Heroine: The Female Bildungsroman in the Twentieth Century.* New York: Peter Lang, 1986.

Lacan, Jacques. *Écrits: A Selection.* Trans. Alan Sheridan. New York: W. W. Norton, 1977.

Lanser, Susan. "Toward a Feminist Narratology." *Style* 20.3 (1986), 341–63.

Lauter, Estella. *Women as Mythmakers: Poetry and Visual Art by Twentieth-Century Women.* Bloomington: Indiana University Press, 1984.

Lauter, Estella, and Carol Schreier Rupprecht, eds. *Feminist Archetypal Theory: Interdisciplinary Re-visions of Jungian Thought.* Knoxville: University of Tennessee Press, 1985.

Levenson, Michael. *A Geneaology of Modernism: English Literary Doctrine, 1909– 1922.* Cambridge: Cambridge University Press, 1984.

Lipking, Lawrence. "Aristotle's Sister: A Poetics of Abandonment." *Critical Inquiry* 10.4 (1983), 61–81.

Lorde, Audre. *Sister Outsider: Essays and Speeches by Audre Lorde.* Trumansburg, N.Y.: Crossing Press, 1984.

————. *The Black Unicorn: Poems.* New York: W. W. Norton, 1978.

Lyotard, Jean-Francois. "Something at Stake in the Women's Struggle." *substance* 20 (1977), 9–17.

Macherey, Pierre. *A Theory of Literary Production.* Trans. Geoffrey Wall. London: Routledge and Kegan Paul, 1978.

Malmgren, Carl D. "'From Work to Text': The Modernist and Postmodernist *Künstlerroman.*" *Novel: A Forum on Fiction* 21.1 (1987), 5–28.

Marcus, Jane. *Virginia Woolf and the Languages of Patriarchy.* Bloomington: Indiana University Press, 1987.

Marks, Elaine, and Isabelle de Courtivron, eds. *New French Feminisms: An Anthology.* New York: Schocken Books, 1981.

McConnell–Ginet, Sally, Ruth Borker, and Nelly Furman, eds. *Woman and Language in Literature and Society.* New York: Praeger, 1980.

McDowell, Deborah E. "'The Changing Same': Generational Connections and Black Women Novelists." *New Literary History* 18.2 (1987), 281–302.

McKay, Nellie. "Response to 'The Philosophical Bases of Feminist Literary Criticisms.'" *New Literary History* 19. 1 (1987), 161–67.

Middlebrook, Diane, and Marilyn Yalom, eds. *Coming to Light: American Women Poets in the Twentieth Century.* Ann Arbor: University of Michigan Press, 1985.

Miller, Nancy K., ed. *The Poetics of Gender.* New York: Columbia University Press, 1986.

Mitchell, Juliet, and Jacqueline Rose, eds. *Jacques Lacan and the école freudienne.* Trans. Jacqueline Rose. New York: Norton, 1985.

Moers, Ellen. *Literary Women.* Garden City, N.Y.: Doubleday, 1977. Reprint New York: Oxford University Press, 1985.

Moi, Toril. *Sexual/Textual Politics: Feminist Literary Theory.* New York: Methuen, 1985.

Moraga, Cherríe, and Gloria Anzaldúa, eds. *This Bridge Called My Back: Writings by Radical Women of Color.* Watertown, Mass.: Persephone Press, 1981.

Nash, June, and Helen Safa, eds. *Women and Change in Latin America.* Massachusetts: Bergin and Garvey, 1986.

Nietzsche, Friedrich. *Beyond Good and Evil.* Trans. W. Kaufmann. New York: Random House, 1966.

Noddings, Nel. *Caring: A Feminine Approach to Ethics and Moral Education.* Berkeley: University of California Press, 1984.

Nochlin, Linda. "Why Have There Been No Great Women Artists?" *Art News* 69.9 (1971), 22–39, 67–71.

Olney, James, ed. *Autobiography: Essays Theoretical and Critical.* Princeton, N.J.: Princeton University Press, 1980.

Olsen, Tillie. *Silences.* New York: Delacorte Press, 1979.

Ostriker, Alicia. *Stealing the Language: The Emergence of Women's Poetry in America.* Boston: Beacon Press, 1986.

Parker, Rozsicka, and Griselda Pollock. *Old Mistresses.* New York: Pantheon Books, 1981.

Pearson, Carol, and Katherine Pope. *The Female Hero in British and American Literature.* New York: Bowker Press, 1981.

Perkins, David. *The Mind's Best Work.* Cambridge, Mass.: Harvard University Press, 1981.

Perloff, Marjorie. *The Futurist Moment: Avant-Garde, Avant Guerre, and the Language of Rupture.* Chicago: University of Chicago Press, 1986.

Phelan, James E., ed. *Reading Narrative: Form, Ethics, Ideology.* Columbus: Ohio State University Press, 1989.

Poovey, Mary. "Feminism and Deconstruction," *Feminist Studies* 14.1 (spring 1988), 51–65.

Pratt, Annis. *Archetypal Patterns in Women's Fiction.* Bloomington: Indiana University Press, 1981.

Rabuzzi, Kathryn Allen. *The Sacred and the Feminine: Toward a Theology of Housework.* New York: Seabury Press, 1982.

Radway, Janice. *Reading the Romance: Women, Patriarchy, and Popular Literature.* Chapel Hill: University of North Carolina Press, 1984.

Rich, Adrienne. *Blood, Bread, and Poetry: Selected Prose, 1979–1985.* New York: W. W. Norton, 1986.

———. *Of Woman Born: Motherhood as Experience and Institution.* New York: W. W. Norton, 1978.

———. *On Lies, Secrets and Silences: Selected Prose, 1966–1978.* New York: W. W. Norton, 1979.

Ruddick, Sara. "Maternal Thinking." *Feminist Studies* 6.2 (1980), 342–67.

Scarry, Elaine. *The Body in Pain: The Making and the Unmaking of the World.* New York: Oxford University Press, 1985.

Showalter, Elaine. *A Literature of Their Own: British Women Novelists from Brontë to Lessing.* Princeton, N.J.: Princeton University Press, 1977.

———, ed. *The New Feminist Criticism: Essays on Women, Literature and Theory.* New York: Pantheon Books, 1985.

Smith, Barbara Herrnstein. "Contingencies of Value." *Critical Inquiry* 10.1 (1983), 1–35.

———. "Narrative Versions, Narrative Theory." *Critical Inquiry* 7.1 (1980), 213–36.

———. *On the Margins of Discourse: The Relation of Literature to Language.* Chicago: University of Chicago Press, 1978.

Smith, Sidonie. *A Poetics of Women's Autobiography: Marginality and the Fictions of Self-Representation.* Bloomington: Indiana University Press, 1987.

Spacks, Patricia Meyer. *The Female Imagination.* New York: Knopf, 1975.

Spelman, Elizabeth V. *Inessential Woman: Problems of Exclusion in Feminist Thought.* Boston: Beacon Press, 1988.

Spretnak, Charlene, ed. *The Politics of Women's Spirituality: Essays on the Rise of Spiritual Power Within the Feminist Movement* Garden City, N.Y.: Anchor Books, 1982.

Stetz, Margaret Diane. "Life's 'Half Profits': Writers and Their Readers in Fiction of the 1890s." *Nineteenth-Century Lives.* Ed. Laurence Lockridge, John Maynard, and Donald Stone. Cambridge: Cambridge University Press, 1989, pp. 169–87.

———. "Odd Woman, Half Woman, Superfluous Woman: What Was the New Woman?" *Iris, a Journal about Women* 11 (1984), 20–21.

Stewart, Grace. *A New Mythos: The Novel of the Artist as Heroine, 1877–1977.* St. Alban's, Vt.: Eden Press, 1979.

Stubbs, Patricia. *Feminism and the Novel: Women and Fiction. 1880–1920.* Totowa, N.J.: Barnes & Noble, 1979.

Suleiman, Susan Rubin, ed. *The Female Body in Western Culture: Contemporary Perspectives.* Cambridge, Mass.: Harvard University Press, 1986.

Tanner, Tony. *Adultery in the Novel: Contract and Transgression.* Baltimore: Johns Hopkins University Press, 1979.

Tate, Claudia. *Black Women Writers at Work.* New York: Continuum Press, 1983.

Theweleit, Klaus. *Male Fantasies.* Trans. Stephen Conway. Minneapolis: University of Minnesota Press, 1987.

Todd, Janet. *Women Writers Talking.* New York: Holmes & Meier, 1983.

Todorov, Tzvetan. *The Poetics of Prose.* Trans. Richard Howard. Ithaca, N.Y.: Cornell University Press, 1977.

Tompkins, Jane. *Sensational Designs.* New York: Oxford University Press, 1985.

———, ed. *Reader-Response Criticism: From Formalism to Post-Structuralism.* Baltimore: Johns Hopkins University Press, 1980.

Tuchman, Gaye, and Nina Fortin. "Edging Women Out: The Structure of Opportunities and the Victorian Novel." *Signs* 6.2 (1980), 308–25.

Walker, Alice. *In Search of Our Mothers' Gardens.* New York: Harcourt Brace Jovanovich, 1983.

Walker, Barbara G. *The Crone: Women of Age, Wisdom and Power.* San Francisco: Harper & Row, 1985.

Warner, Marina. *Monuments and Maidens: The Allegory of the Female Form.* New York: Atheneum, 1985.

Washington, Mary Helen. *Invented Lives: Narratives of Black Women, 1860–1960.* New York: Anchor, 1987.

Waugh, Patricia. *Feminine Fictions: Revisiting the Postmodern.* New York: Routledge, 1989.

———. *Metafiction: The Theory and Practice of Self-Conscious Fiction.* New York: Methuen, 1984.

Weedon, Chris. *Feminist Practice and Poststructuralist Theory.* Oxford: Basil Blackwell, 1987.

Whitmont, Edward C. *The Return of the Goddess.* New York: Crossroad, 1982.

Woolf, Virginia. *A Room of One's Own.* 1929. Reprint New York: Harcourt Brace Jovanovich, 1989.

Yaeger, Patricia. *Honey-Mad Women: Emancipatory Strategies in Women's Writing.* New York: Columbia University Press, 1988.

Young-Eisendrath, Polly, and Florence Wiedemann. *Female Authority: Empowering Women Through Psychotherapy.* New York: Guilford Press, 1987.

Contributors

Ann L. Ardis is Assistant Professor of English at the University of Delaware. She has written articles on feminist criticism and Beatrice Webb, and she is the author of *New Woman, New Novels: Feminism and Early Modernism* (1991).

Alison Booth, Assistant Professor of English at the University of Virginia, has published articles on George Eliot, Charles Dickens, and Samuel Butler. Forthcoming works include *The Great Women of Letters: George Eliot, Virginia Woolf, and the Feminine in History* (1992) and an edited collection of essays, *Famous Last Words: Women Against Novelistic Endings* (1992). She is currently researching a project on women's travel narratives and cultural studies, from Anna Jameson to Ruth Benedict.

Kathleen Brogan is Assistant Professor of English at Wellesley College and is currently working on a book-length study of Elizabeth Bishop.

Lynda K. Bundtzen is Professor of English at Williams College and a former Chair of the Women's Studies Program. She is the author of *Plath's Incarnations: Women and the Creative Process,* which won the Alice and Edith Hamilton Prize awarded by the University of Michigan Press in 1980. She has also published several articles on film. Her current projects include a book on Adrienne Rich and a book on auteurs and their women (Antonioni, Bergman, Fellini, and Truffaut).

Pamela L. Caughie is Assistant Professor of English at Loyola University of Chicago. Her publications include articles on Virginia Woolf, feminist theory, and twentieth-century fiction and a book, *Virginia Woolf and Postmodernism: Literature in Quest and Question of Itself* (1991).

Mary K. DeShazer is Associate Professor of Women's Studies and English and Coordinator of the Women's Studies Program at Wake

Forest University. She is the author of a book on women poets and creative identity, *Inspiring Women: Reimagining the Muse* (1986). Her chapter in this volume is part of her book-in-progress, titled "Sister Warriors: Contemporary Women's Poetry of Political Protest."

Linda Dittmar is Professor of English at the University of Massachusetts–Boston, where she teaches courses in the novel, film, and women's studies. She has published essays on literature, film, and pedagogy, and she coedited *From Hanoi to Hollywood: The Vietnam War in Film* (1990) with Gene Michaud. She is currently working on a book-length study of the filmic representation of women speaking.

Josephine Donovan is Professor of English at the University of Maine. She is the author of numerous books and articles on women's literature and feminist literary criticism, most recently, *After the Fall: The Demeter-Persephone Myth in Wharton, Cather, and Glasgow* (1989).

Susan Stanford Friedman is Professor of English and Women's Studies at the University of Wisconsin–Madison. She is the author of *Psyche Reborn: The Emergence of H.D.* (1981), *Penelope's Web: Gender, Modernity, H.D.'s Fiction* (1990), and articles on narrative theory, psychoanalysis, women's poetry, childbirth metaphors, gender and genre, and women's studies. She is at work on "Portrait of an Analysis with Freud: The Letters of H.D., Bryher, and Their Friends, 1933–1934" and "Return of the Repressed in Modernist Narratives."

Gayle Greene has published articles on Shakespeare, contemporary women writers, and feminist literary theory. A Professor of English at Scripps College (Claremont, California), she coedited *The Woman's Part: Feminist Criticism of Shakespeare* (1980) and *Making a Difference: Feminist Literary Criticism* (1985). She is completing a book titled "Revisions: Contemporary Women Writers and the Tradition."

Linda Hunt is Associate Professor of English and Director of Women's Studies at Ohio University. She is the author of *A Woman's Portion: Ideology, Culture, and the British Female Novel Tradition* (1988), and she has also published a number of articles on women's fiction.

Suzanne W. Jones is Coordinator of Women's Studies and Assistant Professor of English at the University of Richmond. She has written articles on Kate Chopin, Alice Walker, Gail Godwin, Lee Smith, William Faulkner, and F. Scott Fitzgerald, and she is the editor of a collection of stories, *Growing Up in the South* (1991). Her current project is a study of race and gender in contemporary southern fiction.

Katherine Kearns teaches English at the Louisiana School for Math, Science, and the Arts in Natchitoches. She has written articles on Robert Frost, Lee Smith, Sylvia Wilkinson, and Kate Chopin. She is working on a book on Robert Frost and a collection of essays on Kate Chopin.

Holly A. Laird is Editor of *Tulsa Studies in Women's Literature* and Associate Professor of English at the University of Tulsa, and is at work on a book provisionally titled "Wordsworth's Sisters: Nineteenth-Century British Women Poets." She is the author of *Self and Sequence: The Poetry of D. H. Lawrence* (1988).

Estella Lauter is Frankenthal Professor of Humanistic Studies at the University of Wisconsin–Green Bay, where she teaches courses in women's studies, poetry, criticism, and American Indian studies. Her book, *Women as Mythmakers* (1984), won the Chicago Women in Publishing Award for Excellence in 1985. With Carol Schreier Rupprecht, she coauthored and coedited *Feminist Archetypal Theory: Interdisciplinary Re-Visions of Jungian Thought* (1985). She coedited with Jean-Pierre Barricelli and Joseph Gibaldi *Teaching Literature and Other Arts* (1990). She is currently at work on a book titled "Assuming Aesthetic Authority: Feminist Interventions in Aesthetics."

Z. Nelly Martínez is Associate Professor of Hispanic Studies at McGill University. Her work focuses mainly on Spanish-American twentieth-century fiction and deconstruction and feminist criticism. She has also done research on the philosophies emanating from contemporary physics and on the implications of these philosophies for feminist theory. She has edited a collection of the works of Argentinian author Ernesto Sabato, and she is completing a book on another Argentinian author, Luisa Valenzuela, which deals with women's writing within a patriarchal and dictatorial context.

Jane Atteridge Rose is Assistant Professor of English at Georgia College. Her research focuses on recovery and revision of nineteenth-century American women writers. Currently she is writing a book on Rebecca Harding Davis and editing a reprinting of regional fiction by Lillie Buffum Chance Wyman.

Margaret Diane Stetz, Founding Editor of the journal *Turn-of-the-Century Women,* teaches English and women's studies at Georgetown University. Among her numerous published articles on British literature are essays on Dickens, Thackeray, Gissing, Forster, Pym, Brookner, and West. She is co-author with Mark Samuels Lasner of *England in the 1880s: Old Guard and Avant-Garde* (1989) and *England in the 1890s: Literary Publishing at the Bodley Head* (1990).

Renate Voris is Associate Professor of German at the University of Virginia. Her research has focused on nineteenth- and twentieth-century German literature, Continental theory and aesthetics, including feminist, as well as semiotics of theater and cinema. She is the author of *Peter Handke* (1978 and 1984), *Adolf Muschg* (1984), and *"Was will das Weib?"—Theorien des Femininen* (1991). She is editing a collection of essays, "Hamletmachines: Melancholia and Literature," and writing a book, "Discourse and Counterdiscourse of Bertolt Brecht."

Mara R. Witzling teaches art history at the University of New Hampshire. She has published articles on medieval illuminated manuscripts and on women artists and their challenge to the canon of art history. Her book, *Voicing Our Visions: Writings by 19th and 20th Century Women Artists* (1991), examines the ways in which women artists have used the written word as a safe space to articulate their visions, and it includes a collection of their writings.

Index

ending, 311, 320–22, 328n.19, 330n.29, 365; closure, 310, 319–22, 328n.18; "feminine," 320, 322
Engels, Friedrich, 85
England, 26, 110, 130n.32, 389
epic, 354, 356, 358–59, 363–65, 367n.9, 368n.14
epistemology: as shaped by material practices, 85–86; black women's, 270; of caring, 206; of identity, 137; of self-hood, 247
Epstein, Barbara, 172n.11
Ereshkigal, 408
Eros, 17, 24, 48, 49, 291–92, 299–302, 304n.12, 398, 407–8, 415–16, 417n.11
erotic, 23, 288, 291–92, 299–301, 304n.12, 398–401, 403–10; as communal, 17, 404; as power, 149; as sexual, 17, 404, 409; as spiritual, 17, 404; desire to create, 17; energy, 414; knowledge, 400; lesbian, 25; lifeforce, 398–99, 409, 411; play, 58n.2; scene, 245. *See also* creativity
eroticism, 249; feminine, 40n.15
Esquivel, Julia, 303n.4; "Parable," 303n.4, 137
essentialism, 13, 117, 134, 137, 138, 211n.22, 219, 229, 241, 263, 281–82, 284n.6, 414, 417n.11. *See also* feminine essence
ethic, 249; Judeo-Christian, 96; maternal, 175, 193n.1; of caring, 206, 211n.28, 270; of humility, 186; of sanctity of life, 82; socialist, 237; work, 367n.9
ethnicity, 1, 41n.19, 134, 237, 414; Asian American, 280; Chicana, 264, 270–71; Chinese American, 279–80
eulogy, 238
Europe, 26, 292
Eurocentric, 121
Eurydice, 25, 278
Evans, Mary Anne, 118
exclusion, 76, 187
exile, 272
Ezergailis, Inta, 253n.8, 254n.10

Fa Mu Lan, 265, 279
Fabri, Lucia, 303; "Cāna," 303
fame, 46–47, 59n.18
family, 139, 162, 164; as inspiration for the artist, 207; as related to woman art-

ist's *Bildung*, 28–29; woman artist figure and the demands of, 176, 188, 226–27, 229; woman writer and the demands of, 9, 44
fantasy, 141, 151, 168
father, 208, 250, 304n.9; as artist, 210n.18; daughter's relationship with, 127n.2; discourse of, 306n.18; fictional, 139, 164, 169, 182, 216–17, 220, 243, 258n.34, 334, 337; law of the, 306n.27; male artist figure's repressed desire for, 28, 40n.18; woman artist figure's, 247; woman writer's relationship with, 44, 158, 199–210, 204, 280
Faust, 3
feeling, 399
Felman, Shoshana, 396n.32
Felski, Rita, 13
female: affiliation complex, 7, 127n.2; betrayal, 92; development, 77n.15; experience, 69; form, 393n.3; friends, 97, 98, 102, 217, 224, 231n.18, 278, 338–39; genius, 128n.8; imagination, 50; landscape, 88; multiplicity, 77n.15; nemesis, 97–98; poet, 72; relationship, 83; reproduction, 210; subculture, 348n.25. *See also* body; community; identity; self
feminine, 82, 203, 288, 409; duty, 118; essence, 117, 236, 244, 247,256n.18; eternal, 244, 248; exotic, 130n.32; fate, 128n.8; imagination, 226; mystique, 4; psychology of emotional integration, 206; ritual, 90; role, 113, 144; sentence, 393n.3; sphere, 89, 135; spirits, 89; subjectivity, 8; symbol, 88, 92; tradition, 92; ultra-, 99–100; utopia, 92
femininity, 30, 81, 115, 123, 136, 156, 180, 183, 198, 201–3, 226, 233, 250, 329n.24, 365; as selflessness, 119
feminism, 98–99, 111, 133, 222, 361; cultural, 18n.3; lesbian, 283; reluctant, 102
feminist: activism, 45, 57; American, critics, 214, 223–24, 229; British, critics, 224, 229; criticism, 1, 13, 16, 60, 83, 101, 113, 207, 212n.35, 214, 326n.4, 335, 337, 353, 355, 361, 365, 366n.3; East German, critics, 255n.11; literature, 99, 111; message, 231n.14; method, 383, 409; movement, 4, 98,

This book was set in Baskerville and Eras typefaces. Baskerville was designed by John Baskerville at his private press in Birmingham, England, in the eighteenth century. The first typeface to depart from oldstyle typeface design, Baskerville has more variation between thick and thin strokes. In an effort to insure that the thick and thin strokes of his typeface reproduced well on paper, John Baskerville developed the first wove paper, the surface of which was much smoother than the laid paper of the time. The development of wove paper was partly responsible for the introduction of typefaces classified as modern, which have even more contrast between thick and thin strokes.

Eras was designed in 1969 by Studio Hollenstein in Paris for the Wagner Typefoundry. A contemporary script-like version of a sans-serif typeface, the letters of Eras have a monotone stroke and are slightly inclined.

Printed on acid-free paper.